After Political Correctness

POLITICS & CULTURE

Avery Gordon and Michael Ryan, *editors*

Politics and Culture is a serial publication that will publish material from a diverse number of disciplinary perspectives, from literature to law, from anthropology to political science, from cultural studies to sociology. The serial is concerned with the political significance of cultural forms and practices as well as with the cultural character of social institutions and political formations.

2

POLITICS AND CULTURE

AFTER POLITICAL CORRECTNESS

The Humanities and
Society in the 1990s

edited by
CHRISTOPHER NEWFIELD
& RONALD STRICKLAND

WESTVIEW PRESS
Boulder • San Francisco • Oxford

Politics and Culture 2

Copyright © 1995 by Westview Press, Inc.

Published in 1995 in the United States of America by Westview Press, Inc., 5500 Central Avenue, Boulder, Colorado 80301-2877, and in the United Kingdom by Westview Press, 12 Hid's Copse Road, Cumnor Hill, Oxford OX2 9JJ

Library of Congress Cataloging-in-Publication Data
After political correctness : the humanities and society in the 1990s
    / edited by Christopher Newfield & Ronald Strickland.
      p.   cm. — (Politics and culture)
    ISBN 0-8133-2336-3 — ISBN 0-8133-2337-1 (pbk.)
    1. Humanities.   2. Humanities—Political aspects—United States.
3. Political correctness—United States.   4. Education, Higher—
Political aspects—United States.   I. Newfield, Christopher.
II. Strickland, Ronald.   III. Series.
AZ221.A38   1995
001.3—dc20   94-33692
                                                                              CIP

Printed and bound in the United States of America

The paper used in this publication meets the requirements
of the American National Standard for Permanence of Paper
for Printed Library Materials Z39.48-1984.

10   9   8   7   6   5   4   3   2   1

Contents

PART THREE
AFTER PC: REDESIGNING DISCIPLINES AND INSTITUTIONS

1

Introduction: Going Public

CHRISTOPHER NEWFIELD & RONALD STRICKLAND

AFTER POLITICAL CORRECTNESS DEVELOPED out of our belief that the attack on political correctness in the humanities was also the humanities' biggest opportunity in years. Though conservatives managed to taint entire academic disciplines, the aroused media attention marked an opening for the academic intellectual. Though university humanists went from irrelevant to dangerous overnight, the PC controversies rejuvenated debate over the purposes of higher education. Though hostile attention is rarely better than none, this time it signaled vulnerability in a conservative cultural order that, during the Reagan Restoration, had seemed relatively secure.

This volume is part of a new phase in the debate among different visions of the humanities. Following the early PC attacks in late 1990, the Center and Left spawned truth squads to refute, rebut, and reject the Right's evidence and conclusions, especially those based on a few anecdotes trapped in a widening circuit of media repetition. These rebuttals were remarkably effective: The news of another side moved the PC conflict from accusation to debate, and mainstream interest faded to the letters pages of book reviews. The next phase, now unevenly under way, involves a broad spectrum of progressive humanists moving beyond temporary self-defense toward a greatly expanded public presence.

The essays in this collection offer a number of perspectives on the debate about political correctness, but they are most concerned with developing prospects for a more public humanities. The writers assembled here believe that the present task is looking forward and detailing the ways and means of moving ahead.

The most urgent project involves redesigning and expanding the social and cultural role of the academic humanities. But this project will be most successful when it more clearly accounts for the meanings and effects of the PC debates. The forces shaping the debate have not gone away, and many of our contributors detail the long-range social changes and underlying cultural shifts that were often dimly rendered, and inaccurately described, by the immediate controversy. PC retained a visible public presence during the first year of Bill Clinton's administration, where it served as a one-size-fits-all brand name for a radicalism both dangerous and defunct. Thus PC played a key role in forcing Clinton to withdraw his nomination of law professor Lani Guinier to head the civil rights division of the Justice Department. A term once used to glamorize attacks on obscure progressives could now obligate a U.S. president to bow humiliatingly to a carefully fabricated ideological test unrelated to anticipated job performance. Clinton's retreat also suggested that, by 1993, the PC attacks had acquired as much influence over the political *center* as over its original sponsors on the right.

Episodes like this suggest that the issues of PC politics and culture first raised in connection with humanities scholarship cannot be turned back into academic questions. The continuing power of the attacks on PC reveals the urgency of a widespread, passionate, collaborative reimagining of the humanities *after* the PC debates.

We think that reimagining the humanities will require a major revitalization of relations between the university humanities and various U.S. publics. At the moment, these relations are instructional (within the university), haphazard (with nonstudents), or controlled by our counterparts in think tanks and the media. Our crucial task within the humanities is to take active control of our relations to the rest of the world.

As this more public phase unfolds, numerous academic humanists will become public intellectuals by making their research relevant and accessible to general concerns. Cultural scholarship will stop playing a supporting role to policy experts on social questions and establish culture's independence. The university community will redress its own outdated administrative hierarchies and compartments and make itself a model of self-guided, democratic adaptation to new possibilities. Researchers will gain more support for their long-range, difficult, indispensable work by more fully explaining it to the taxpayer. Professors will expand the social influence of the humanities by improving links with related institutions such as state humanities councils, local arts boards, high schools, and policy institutes. Humanists will renegotiate their share of university resources with the sciences, to the benefit of underfunded areas of cultural research. Scholarly productivity will be shown the friend of good teaching. A diverse Left will be admitted alongside the "mainstream" and Right as a constructive participant in cultural and social debates. The media will demand not merely wider circulation for important professors but new applications of scholarly rigor to current affairs. Thousands of supporters of Bruins and Fighting Illini football will shift their donations to courses in cultural analysis.

Well, one step at a time. But though these changes may seem utopian and impossible, many of them have long been under way, off camera, propelled by often obscure progressive labors undertaken by countless devoted educators, students, and staff over the course of many years. This volume seeks to build on these traditions while calling for the redevelopment of the humanities in the direction of public concerns.

Cultural Democracy: The Stakes of PC

First, some background. The anti-PC attacks led with an intertwining pair of complaints: PC was an agent of aggressive minority groups pressing excessive group demands, and PC said that everything was political. The humanities, to anti-PC writers, had become unable to withstand the intrusion of cultural conflict and social power into the fields that were thought to provide unifying acculturation. The attacks associated *racial difference* and *cultural dissent* with a menace to civil order. The passing of the Cold War and years of 1980s-style affluence had yielded social fragmentation even in a nominally victorious United States. Much of this ostensible fragmentation had cropped up in the cultural realm, for political opposition remained quite weak. The humanities, as expert discourse on cultural matters, were on the front lines of media-defined social conflict for the first time since the 1960s.[1]

Those alarmed at PC developments saw a conjuncture of race consciousness and populist energies emerging among university-based professional managers of culture. The control of racially differentiated democracy was at issue at a time when, to many conservatives, democratic excesses in the university seemed to reject enlightened hierarchy in favor of reopened questions about cultural autonomy and social equity for the dissident and the different. As Senator Alan Simpson (R–Wyoming) put the problem, "When you're hearing too much from groups who feel disenfranchised, then watch out for democracy."

It was particularly important that these stirrings occurred in cultural fields, whose everyday "realness" had coincided with an important governing role. Culture had long been a refuge for sanctioned supremacism: while most whites could concede that African Americans, Chicanos, and other racialized groups should have full political equality, they could simultaneously hold that these groups need not be granted cultural equality. Hence, many of the racial incidents on college campuses, such as the "black Beethoven" at Stanford, mocked *cultural* equality between races. In the traditional view, culture, when undistorted by "politics," was a sphere of color-blind merit. It was a realm where inequality was inevitable, even integral to judgment, where until kingdom come Chicano students—who most agreed should suffer no social discrimination—could legitimately be obliged to master Saul Bellow rather than Ana Castillo on the ground of his putatively greater artistic significance. Culture, in this context, was populist and anti-democratic at the same time, celebrating art's representations of everyday life while enforcing hierarchical discriminations (no matter how often the specific ranking might change).

The academic humanities, for all their intellectual brilliance and advancement, continued to bear the traces of this role. More than twenty years after the early development of feminist and ethnic studies in the university, the humanities remained largely segregated. In addition to being staffed by almost entirely Anglo personnel, fields like American Studies had little intellectual contact with "ethnic" studies, which housed the bulk of most of the humanities' faculty of color. Whereas the 1960s and after saw U.S. history experiencing a renaissance in the study of African American history, labor history, the histories of slavery and Reconstruction, the history of immigration, urban studies, and other forms of history "from below," explicitly *cultural* fields such as English and art history remained strongly Euro-American in both curricula and personnel. Reinforcing this segregation, these humanists almost entirely ignored the extent to which democratic power sharing seemed wrong and unnecessary in their institutional lives.

Much of the PC scare focused on academic places where cultural democracy seemed to be getting out of hand—students disagreeing with established scholars, university administrations restricting certain kinds of abusive speech at the request of its targets, "excessive sensitivity" to different racial positions, scholarly innovations not governed by tradition. Anti-PC writers often said they were only objecting to politics in cultural scholarship, but "politics" covered nearly any conceptual innovation, especially one that drew public interest. The assault on politics often carried over into attacks on the democratic production of knowledge, including its negotiation, testing, and give-and-take with a variety of groups and actual outcomes.

To PC warriors, democracy posed three particular problems. They generated responses that we schematize here.

1. *Difference.* The United States does not operate as "one nation" or a single "common culture" possessed of uniform standards. Descriptively speaking, the United States is multicultural and always has been; it is in fact multinational, having formed itself through the forced absorption of many sovereign native peoples. It possesses huge regional, ethnic, racial, religious, linguistic, political, and cultural variations.

PC Response: Increase awareness of cultural and other differences and see conflicts between different values, group behavior, and so on, as resolvable by *negotiation* rather than by the invocation of universal laws. For example, Lani Guinier was PC in describing racial division in voting patterns. She said things like "As a general rule, whites do not vote for blacks."

Anti-PC Response: Submit fundamental differences to a common standard. If possible, blame conflict on the messenger. Hence President Clinton, having won in part by moving Democratic reform agendas away from race, applied the label "divisive and polarizing" not to the white reluctance to vote for black candidates but to Guinier herself, whom he chided for failing to regard blacks and whites as interchangeable members of a "single society." Much of this response stigmatized difference and diversity as a threat to order and depicted common values and shared knowledge as the main thing standing between a free society and civil war.[2]

Most people may disagree with George Will's view that "the domestic forces" opposed to "common culture" are more dangerous than our military adversaries, but the Right and Center have successfully spread the idea that common culture "is the nation's social cement."[3]

The PC label continues to be used to stigmatize the assertion of difference. Two years after the first PC wave subsided, Sheldon Hackney, now director of the National Endowment for the Humanities, condemned PC at his confirmation hearings. Following the pattern noted above, he described it as "the notion that every thought is a political thought" and being "overly solicitous of minority groups and fashionable and trendy concerns."[4] Politics, "minority groups," and trendiness all represent the presence of social and intellectual differences within an apparently solid consensus, but these differences remain public liabilities no matter how much important progress they may inspire in a field. Hackney's confirmation hinged on his triple rejection, signaling the ideological muster that the PC wars instantly imposed on the Clinton years.

2. Dissent. Where difference and diversity go, dissent is sure to follow. By the late 1980s, ideas that had been suppressed or unheard in American political life appeared on a steady march through academic research.

PC Response: Dissent reflects novelty and negotiation and is the source not only of redress and emancipation but of most original research and creative intellectual change. Such change is as important to humanistic as it is to scientific knowledge. The transformations in humanities research in the past ten or twenty years—false moves and all—have made huge contributions to cultural knowledge and social possibilities. These should be proclaimed and developed.

Anti-PC Response: Most "innovation" in the humanities has amounted to an assault on our cultural legacy by special interests and unhappy radicals. Such dissent could exist as long as it had no influence; it could talk as long as nobody listened (at important schools).

Invoking Clinton's liberal anti-PC response once again, Guinier's scholarly articles were deemed reason to disqualify her for public office; her work suggested that she might bring unconventional ideas to a policy position. Throughout the PC wars, dissent posed a surprising danger, whether it appeared in the comments of students in a feminist studies class, an article by Robert Reich, the appearance of *I, Rigoberta Menchú* on a college reading list, an advertisement for a director of "multicultural affairs," or the presence of a couple of thousand progressives with job security in the college classrooms of a nation of 260 million.

3. Self-Determination. The idea that social, political, and cultural differences are real and legitimate and that the resulting dissent is inevitable and good led to the possibility that these ideas might be put into action. The question was how much authority and agency would be granted to different individuals and groups in a heterogeneous culture.

PC Response: Unity and harmony must not eliminate difference, cannot remedy injustice, and fail as descriptions of multicultural reality. Therefore, cultural analysis must acknowledge the desire for and the effects of cultural autonomy, which is often more valuable and practical than cultural unity. Cultural autonomy entails autonomy of cultural analysis. It requires the power to respond to a cultural system with real independence. Scholars and policymakers tacitly express solidarity with such positions when they support students attempting to control their exposure to racist pranks or when they suggest legal remedies for acknowledged inequities or when they promote the teaching of African history without subordination to European history in predominantly African American classrooms.

Anti-PC Response: Order requires consensus if not uniformity. Challenging such a consensus is "political"; done in the name of self-rule, it is the prologue to civil war.

From this perspective, even mainstream admissions procedures, when sensitive to racial difference, were subject to attack for rejecting meritocratic uniformity as a response to all differences in outcome. Anti-PC writers attacked those who challenged the authority of established general norms such as white-majority integrationism, "color-blind" free speech, or heterosexuality. Anti-PC rejected the idea that such norms should be modified where they run into opposition from those they primarily affected, as in hate-speech codes. Anti-PC deemed the needs or desires of various members of a diverse population less important than the sovereignty of a uniform standard. These positions did not accept the possibility that any group more worldly than the Amish might make its own rules.

On each of these counts the anti-PC position, whether liberal or conservative, opposed a democracy that seemed too spontaneous, popular, or inclusive of everyone. It suggested that multiracial democracy threatened the country's governability.

The problems with this view need ongoing critique, but critique is not enough. Progressives need to detail the value and viability of social difference, dissent, and self-determination. They also need to redevelop full-scale, entirely interactive, continuously modified models of democracy as alternatives to the compromise structures most of us find acceptable now.

We don't want to predict the forms these public efforts will take or imagine the changes they will require. But as PC anxiety continues to operate far from home, these three elements of a democratic approach to the humanities need a particular boost.

Around *diversity* or difference, the humanities could continue to develop modes of cultural negotiation and coexistence that do not require common culture but allow separatism, conflict, autonomy, and other aspects of our actually existing arrangements. *Dissent* needs a fuller narrative life as a creative force and a major source of progress and pleasure. Continuous dissent not only is a minimum criterion of a democratic society but prevents the intellectual frostbite that marked whole disciplines and institutions during the Cold War. The same goes for *self-determination*, which needs ongoing rearticulation as a right, as a positive good, and as the only solution to current social deadlock and decay.

Ten Opportunities for the Public Humanities

The newly public humanities of the coming decade, as they move closer to the center of national life, will have gotten themselves there not by demanding public respect but by better addressing public needs. Addressing these needs entails a confidence in progressive wares, a confidence in the public, and a confidence in the national value of humanities scholarship that we have not witnessed in our time in the university. The progressive humanities have ceded leadership on their own issues to activists, media producers, and policy intellectuals of every kind, and though they boast tireless crusaders like Noam Chomsky and Cornel West and others working wonderfully with less acclaim, such figures remain isolated in university culture. Progressive thinking about the university itself is seriously in arrears. How will this often distrustful and wounded group welcome the public into the university in all of its difficult combinations of radical and conservative, reactionary and advance guard? How will it learn from the public while still believing that its own knowledge has much to teach? How will it learn to take risks with discoveries as yet unauthorized? How will it come to believe that it is central to the unfolding of national history?

Events both favoring and opposing progressive academia have already outrun its self-analysis and even its fantasy life. We think that such action, such thinking, such scholarly insistence, such collaborative redirection must have established a couple of things. As we noted in the last section, progressives must confront the democratic stakes of the PC wars head-on. But they must cope more aggressively with the Left's continual fits of depression. As part of this work, we offer ten signs that progressive pessimism is simply one-sided.

In so doing we will try not to underplay the financial power, moral tenacity, and ideological predominance of conservatives. But the Left's narrative of decline has been selective, exaggerated, provincial, and often most relevant to the failures of humanists to influence other members of their own professional-managerial class (lodged in the sciences, public policy, the media, corporate management, and their own departments). The current situation is contradictorily good and bad for progressives. The clouds are most visible, so here we focus on the silver linings.

Free Publicity

The first of these opportunities involves inadvertent yet tremendous public exposure for progressives during the PC debates. Even during the early siege of PC bashing, we could say, if not exactly "There's no such thing as bad publicity," then at least "No publicity is bad for long." PC-bashing fundamentalists assumed the public importance of the university's research and teaching about cultural issues that most humanists rarely dream of demanding on their own. This was particularly true of the Left, too accustomed to feeling unpopular and always expecting, if it ventures onto the playground, to be beaten up. It would be too much to expect progressives to thank these vindictive conservatives for the sudden air time, but in any case the effect of the Right's public attacks was to overcome the humanities' code of modesty where the Left's own efforts had failed.

Humanities educators have long taken pride in what Joan Scott here calls "our most valuable—and pleasurable—activity: thinking hard about everything … and teaching others how to think that way." We teach rigorous reading skills, modes of expression, general habits of critical analysis, the history of literary achievement, and the subtler means of self-development. But these strengths have not generally allowed humanists to see themselves as providers of a legitimate form of public knowledge. We have been unable to attract broad attention to these activities as relevant to current affairs, even of the cultural kind. Such functions as arts reviewing, editing, taste making, and other less formal modes of ongoing popular discussion have become the province of journalists, and they frequently regard professors as pedants, antiquarians, and unprintably obscure stylists.

Humanities research is not organized or funded in the belief that it addresses public issues in any direct way. Ironically mirroring their right-wing watchdogs, humanists have most frequently associated policy or social interests with an undue "politicization" of literary issues. They have poorly explained the direct relevance of literary study to the vocations that the vast majority of literature majors will actually pursue. The community they address is a highly specialized and professional one, generally removed from these other vocations and from the market for culture that these vocations allow. It's hard to imagine how the humanities would have overcome these inhibiting traditions in order to address the public had they not been forced into the open by the demand that they defend themselves.

Public Interest in Culture

This public attention was not dominated by the Right's rejection and disdain. Though the early publicity was shaped by the PC bashers' views, it was sustained by a broader and very diverse public concern with the issues raised by the debate. The popular appeal of anti-multiculturalist arguments like those of Arthur Schlesinger Jr. can be seen as an ambivalent expression of this public concern. Schlesinger's views are appealing to many nonacademics in part because he is more available in mainstream venues than, say, Molefi Asante or one of Schlesinger's white leftist critics and because their knowledge about actual African American Studies programs and courses is largely secondhand. But those who find Schlesinger appealing in this context are not necessarily adopting his position so much as using ideas at hand—ones friendly to their current assumptions—to try to cope with serious social problems. A defense of someone like Schlesinger is often a defense of the debate's general principles or stakes. Schlesinger is important to such a reader less because he expresses the unuttered thoughts of the white masses about Afrocentricity's danger to domestic peace than because he is concerned with the issue of domestic peace. Furthermore, a sanctioned figure like Schlesinger is sometimes used simply to authorize discussing such a thorny problem in milieus where controversy is discouraged.

Nonacademics who are concerned about the issues Schlesinger raises are paying tribute more to the social importance of culture than to Schlesinger himself. Around the issue of multiculturalism, rather than siding with the Right many are trying to side with culture and to subordinate academic in-house conflicts to the kind of serious sociocultural discussion that the humanities supposedly sponsor. Nonacademics can of course see through oversimplified accounts of multiculturalism; substantial efforts must be made to disseminate more complex accounts such as those of George Yúdice, Grant Farred, A. R. Lategola, Rajeswari Mohan, and Jean Howard in this collection.

We see the temporary success of the Right as a symptom not simply of its general power, which goes without saying, but of the public potential of the humanities generally. The meanings of public debates are often concealed, contested, and emergent—they are an ongoing process rather than a fixed position. The Right's obvious control of much of the public debate should never be seen as control over a very heterogeneous public mind. Since many people are interested in cultural problems without being ultimately subservient to their packaging, progressives should do much more to respect various publics' multiple interests by conceptualizing stronger alternatives.

Anti-PC groups tried to redefine progressive thought as subversive. We tend to think that this conservative ploy has worked less well with most publics than with progressive intellectuals themselves, who have been tempted to approach various cultural and policy debates as stigmatized outsiders. The actual case may simply be that nonacademics do not consider progressive academics subversive but merely impractical and irrelevant. Mainstreaming and influence are often confused (as in Clintonism), but they should be rigorously distinguished. The appropriate response is not to appear more mainstream but to become more involved, more practical, and more specific.

Accountability Is Democratic

If bad publicity was good, so was the call for increased attention to university life. Intensified public scrutiny, although obviously harmful in many ways, also denoted movement toward a more democratic social position for the university. Put this way, the right-wing attack temporarily hijacked an impulse toward public sovereignty over major institutions. This attack succeeded for the moment in presenting itself as the champion of an academic glasnost bitterly resisted by the Left (see Vincent Pecora's essay below). The crackdown used a rhetoric of expanded democracy that should not be dismissed by a Left that has spent decades calling for exactly that. Progressives can hardly demand democracy in foreign policy while presuming that their universities need never explain their purposes and achievements to society. Too often, different publics see the university and its apparatus of selective admissions, endless judgment-passing, arcane learning, and complicated, secretive procedures as just another Kafkaesque bureaucracy.

We want to stress that the university must remain intellectually independent and self-governed, at least to the extent that it is now. It should exist in partnership with institutions such as the government and high-tech corporations without the latter's being able to dictate terms. Democratic accountability must remain decentralized and local: it must mean inclusive, open self-management—a government of peers—rather than a government of remote control. But progressives have too often felt that the whole question of governance is someone else's problem, and conservatives have therefore had too easy a time stepping into the breach. Rather than resenting or dodging the issue, progressives should speed up development of their own more open forms of publicly attentive democracy and implement these in their own institutions. The populist rhetoric of PC bashers gives the rest of us a golden opportunity to call their bluff.

Demographics Are Democratic

The United States continues to become less white, less upper-middle-class, less automatically served by the political "mainstream." These trends are particularly acute in large metropolitan areas. California, for example, will have a "minority majority" population early in the next century; Los Angeles County, by some counts, already does. Student demographics have changed rapidly: the University of California at Berkeley's white undergraduate population is now only about one-third of total enrollment. Changes at the faculty level are slower but steady. According to one report, "in 1991–92, 12.3 per cent of the nation's full-time professors were black, Hispanic, American Indian, or Asian American, up from 11.5 per cent two years earlier. Blacks made up 4.7 per cent of the professorate in 1991, compared with 4.5 per cent in 1989 and 4.1 per cent in 1985."[5] Another report notes, "In 1990, 76% of America's young black men had completed high school, up from 66% in 1980 and 55% in 1970. ... More young blacks are enrolled in college: 33% in 1990, up from 26% in 1970."[6] In 1992 women made up 51 percent of college instructors and 13 percent of full professors, up from 1974's 10 percent.[7] These changes are small, but, as conservative future shock, the future has already arrived.

Now, of course, none of these statistical shifts guarantee any kind of political or cultural change or ensure the opening of the university. Several of the contributors to this volume—including Paul Lauter, A. R. Lategola, and Thomas Wallace—note that changes in racial demographics have coincided with a persistent national squeeze on education at all levels. The private sector also dampens the effects of the educational gains of people of color. "While blacks have narrowed the academic gap, the racial wage gap has widened. In 1973, white high school graduates earned 10% more than black grads; by 1989, the gap was 17%. In 1973, white college graduates earned 4% more than blacks; by 1989, the gap was 16%."[8] The

United States certainly could manage demographic changes with poverty, as it has done in the past, but this does not change the fact that hitherto "minority" are increasingly "majority" concerns. These concerns have already achieved a political and cultural presence that progressives would be foolish to underestimate.

"Vocational" Skills Are Public Skills

One of the least auspicious trends in the university humanities harbors potential benefits. This is the tendency toward rendering the humanities as a service area where students acquire skills whose functions are divorced from cultural studies and subordinated to the logics of other fields. As funding shortages increase, English departments may be forced to devote more resources to entry-level composition and superficial canon surveys, while their students, rather than seeing literary study as an autonomous discipline, go on to major in business economics, environmental biology, or some other area. The budget crisis could, in other words, be used to reduce the humanities' intellectual sovereignty and place them under the control of the vocations.

But this trend can be met with a pair of responses. First, as Ron Strickland explains in his essay, composition study, too long the unwanted stepchild of English departments, has developed an array of strategies for transforming functionalist fields into sites where students learn analytical skills that can make them more independent. Rather than seeing humanities skills as swamped by the world of business or of other professions, we might see composition as empowering students who will go on to get "regular" jobs—developing attitudes of independence and powers of communication that could change the workplace. There is no reason to assume in advance that the vocational aspect of the humanities is a defeat; to the contrary, vocationalism is one of the major gateways to social influence.

Given the opportunity to influence business culture, literary study must rethink its relation to vocational fields. It has been so modest for so long about its vocational possibilities that it has made itself useless—even a burden—to its own more "applied" branches, which it tends to belittle. Scholarly and vocational humanists should work together in mapping the outcomes of humanistic study. They should engage in mutual assistance to increase their relevance to the working lives of our students, whom we now abandon on the threshold of their careers with little tracking, counseling, or outreach to potential employers. National and international business increasingly depends on communications skills, every kind of information processing and networking, and, above all, an accurate and sophisticated awareness of cultural life. If a more coordinated range of humanities fields develops and espouses its own perspectives on workplace practices and possibilities, the workplace's increasing dependence on humanities skills could offer the humanities expanded—and no less progressive—influence in business.

The Waning of Corporate Paternalism

High-tech capitalism produces increasing numbers of temporary workers. Although we deplore the personal and social costs of this development, we believe that some temporary workers could become a new and potentially powerful voice. Some recent work has correctly focused on the destructive power of flexible capitalism (see Richard Ohmann's analysis below). Flexibility seems to work entirely in the corporation's favor; it changes skills, people, communities, and continents to its own immediate advantage. Flexible capitalism has not only exported manufacturing jobs to lower-wage countries, continuing the downward pressure on wages (sliding 20 percent in the past twenty years) that began the early 1970s. It is starting to export service jobs and professional-managerial positions in their wake. When it is not exporting jobs it is destabilizing many of those that are left. "Flexcap," as Ohmann calls it, turns an increasing proportion of adult workers into "contingent" employees, losing hours, wage levels, benefits, and labor rights. Between 1982 and 1992 the number of temporary workers tripled. None of the precariousness of their situation can be explained by allegations of their personal inadequacy; to the contrary, they are often supercompetent, having to adjust to different projects, new equipment and skills, and changed work settings again and again and again. The temporary worker seems the disenfranchised worker, and the uncertainty and insecurity of this condition is temporarily efficient but often painful and unjust.

Nonetheless, a new phase in the temp economy may be around the corner. This new phase will be ushered in not by a change in temp ideology but by the continuing squeeze on the payoff of a temp's pliability. The "working smarter" strategy that President Clinton and Labor Secretary Robert Reich want to import to the United States from Germany is already failing there as German companies discover the benefits of getting others to work smart and cheap. In the past three decades, the West's economy has liquefied its own systems of production, its structures of ownership, the union movement, entire communities, and even the economically activist state. But it is now turning on itself, liquefying its own corporate skeleton in a restless quest for ever more perfect lubrication. As growing numbers of highly skilled and highly educated workers, especially those providing what Reich terms "symbolic-analytic services"—information managers with high-level communications and problem-solving skills—enter the temporary and freelance workforce, the power of corporate hierarchy over its employees will come under pressure.

The high-tech worker has advanced powers of information processing. The contingency of her work requires unprecedented powers of autonomous negotiation. It also eliminates the material foundation of much corporate sovereignty—the company's function as a long-term, benevolent caretaker. The contingency of work may force a new competency in democratic social skills. In a bad business climate, the temp worker could evolve from freelancer to free associator, matching flexible management with flexible organizing, the sort of provisional alliances so long envisioned by postmodern cultural theory. Although this kind of leverage is not generally available to routine production and service workers, the diminishing returns of hyperflexibility may press the temp's unusual combinations of skill, skepticism, and autonomy into organized service. These efforts could exploit the flexible corporation's dependence on high levels of cooperation and socialization and the declining rewards of hierarchical control. This corporation's liquid workforce may show increasing interest in reinvented systems of collective, democratic behavior.

These new systems should be more intensively researched and elaborated by cultural scholars. The relevant forms of complex group behavior have for years been regarded by corporations as "cultural" but have been described and shaped by a range of consultants and organizational analysts with little background in culture in the traditional sense. Humanists have a tremendous opportunity to link their expertise to problems in business governance that have never been more proximate to the cultural realm. Recognizing the interconnections between cultural and social issues, they could enter debates long ago forfeited to policy wonks.

The Worlding of the Humanities

This move outward has actually been in rehearsal since the 1970s. The Left, of course, usually reads this period as a narrative of its own decline. The political and economic condition of the country has declined steadily since 1973, but the same should not be so readily assumed about progressive thought. For example, this period has seen a remarkable proliferation of innovative methods and subjects in the academic humanities. Although these academic movements have been complicated and uneven (see Donald Lazere's essay as an example of the view that the rise of poststructural theory has had negligible consequences), a brief list of recovered, invented, or expanded fields defies many a progressive's pessimism: feminism, race studies, lesbian and gay studies, marxist literary and social theory, deconstruction and other forms of radical philosophy, new historicism, and many others. All of these have brought increased conceptual sophistication to broad trends of opening (canons, methods), unsettling (textual meaning, disciplinary boundaries), and reconstructing (cultural politics). These decades have marked not simply the turning inward of 1960s social energy or Althusser's struggle in theory but, with apologies to Edward Said, the worlding of the literary profession.

The contrary impression—of the Left's defeat—expresses an academic melancholia that has overlooked its own resources. This melancholia has involved a sense of the futility of one's academic pursuits; compulsive specialization is one means of this feeling's disavowal. The sense of futility refers to an inability to effect historical change; the melancholia arises from the felt loss of history. The (usually male) academic in mourning feels "no compelling historical design urg[ing him] to plunge into the next task."[9] It is, of course, impossible to be free of this feeling, since the 1960s prematurely promised many teachers and intellectuals that they were drawing closer to history's center stage. In this context, theoretical advances have often been read as symptoms of dissolution, as involving the sense that social movements are fragmented, texts are indeterminate, ideology is indissolvable, personal agency is unstable, resistance is contained, power is undecipherable, epistemic gaps are unbridgeable, and history is unavailable.

In fact, however, recent theory offers partial relief from the idea that the intellectual has been left behind by some coherent linear progress and from the related idea that history has been captured by the Right. The academic intellectual may still feel isolated, but even those theories that seem most cynical about society and history have eased the trauma by arguing that there is no nondiscursive, linear, determinate thing of history to be isolated from. Postmodernism and other alleged nihilisms have helped us not only to know but to live a history without guarantees. As the Right assumes, recent theory readily supports reconceived political and cultural agency.

The Relevance of 1960s Traditions

Other opportunities lie in the apparent defeat of 1960s prophecies. We see the failed actualization of some of these desires as owing in part to their internal inadequacies and to the Right's superior firepower but mostly to their advanced arrival on the scene. The Lincoln Brigade was accused of "premature antifascism" in fighting Franco in Spain before the United States entered World War II; many 1960s thinkers were guilty merely of "premature radicalism." Their ideas were not so much wrong as incomplete, not so much crushed as ahead of time. Conservatives have been right here as well: many of the ideas first popularized in 1960s academia *are* resurgent. A few examples:

- The sense that the rationale of literary study is in need of renovation. This idea builds on work begun over thirty years ago by groups like the Radical Caucus and advocates of Black Studies programs.
- An urgency about opening the university to traditionally underrepresented groups and the accompanying belief that this is a historic opportunity for academics to push for social equity and intellectual expansion.
- The trickle-up sense that academic women and people of color have much to teach that the university needs to learn more rapidly.
- Interest in the way in which the university's priorities are influenced by the state and in which its built-in political commitments prevent it from being one of society's leading institutions.

These are only some of the ideas that, though inadequate in various ways and relatively marginal to social or cultural developments like AIDS activism and hip-hop culture, were prescient and often effective. Ideas like these form a resource that the PC attacks have ironically brought back into the minds even of their initial targets.

The Budget Spotlight on Educational Institutions

The national budget crisis of the early 1990s is the fruit of a long-term conservative strategy to force the downsizing of social welfare systems in spite of their popularity. In this context, education has been redefined as a form of welfare, and, as

Paul Lauter shows below, it has lost disproportionate ground. It has formed a shrinking portion of most state budgets in a period in which officials from coast to coast have ostensibly decided that education is our best hope for economic survival. Higher education seems to be an institution in decline, but at the same moment its crises are encouraging its faculty to apply themselves anew to its resurrection.

Cultural scholars have offered analyses of the circulation of power and cultural capital in a variety of institutional frames and historical periods. But they have not paid sufficient attention to the movements of power and culture in our own. The educational budget crisis, starting in Massachusetts in the 1980s and then heading west and promising to linger there, could lead to better analysis and organization of the university itself.

Signs of this shift are beginning to appear. Mainstream publications such as *Atlantic Monthly* and *Business Week* have turned their attention from the university's harboring of intellectual subversives to the structural obstacles to containing educational costs, and academics should be at least as far down this road as the mainstream press.[10] Our activism within the university will have important consequences for legal relations, faculty solidarity, educational priorities, extra-university alliances, public outreach, overall political skills, and the promotion of a wider range of research. As with the other double-edged problems we've noted, attacks on education may produce educational progress.

The Success of the Public Intellectual

The passion of recent attacks on some public intellectuals suggests that the public intellectual is alive and well. This may not apply to the same degree to the academic intellectual, but the difference should be taken as a challenge rather than a prediction of defeat. Various kinds of public intellectual are doing just fine.

Media intellectuals are addressing pressing public issues with tremendous speed, if not always with critical rigor. We've mentioned some examples above. If people want to know more about why the Los Angeles Police Department beat Rodney King, they tune in to Phil Donahue's interview with Officer Theodore Bresinio three days after his federal trial concludes. If they want to know why Bill Clinton has become economically aligned with Alan Greenspan and the bankers at the Fed, they watch Ted Koppel on *Nightline*. If they worry about the effects of household toxins, they listen to the health researchers lined up for *Jenny Jones*. If they want to know what edition of *Ulysses* to give their kid in college or whether to see *Indecent Proposal,* they read the *New York Times*. If they've always wondered about sex in prison visiting rooms, they set their VCR to tape *Geraldo*. People want to know about these and a whole lot of other, broadly cultural things, and although there are good reasons that most academic knowledge wouldn't work in these exact venues, that doesn't diminish massive public interest in those who provide public knowledge.

Organic or oppositional intellectuals have never had the chance to be alienated from the public in the first place. Their academic efforts began outside the university, were mostly supported there, and have identified them as outsiders in the eyes of administrators and mainstream humanists. These figures include the feminists who legitimated linking academic work to gender issues that seemed purely political. They include the founders of Black Studies, Chicano Studies, Native American Studies, and Asian American Studies programs. Little intellectual progress in these areas was achieved without community pressure, whether in the form of student activism or business roundtables. The pattern has repeated itself with Lesbian and Gay Studies. Although the final academic movers of such initiatives may be tenured professors, most post-1960s disciplinary innovation, absent these public contacts, would not have occurred. Organic academic intellectuals offer rich examples of leadership.

Teaching intellectuals have been maintaining creative and highly valued links between the university and society for years but without the recognition that accrues to researchers. This is especially true of teachers of composition, who have long theorized intellectual issues from the perspective of dynamic social environments, starting with the classroom, and who have always felt compelled to respond to everyday issues.

Community intellectuals have drastically changed the conceptualization of cultural and social issues, often with local issues uppermost in mind. In his essay here, George Yúdice discusses some recent community-based achievements in building multiissue coalitions free of the usual limits of identity politics. An exclusive focus on important macro-level events—a Republican White House, the International Monetary Fund in Africa, women's health and child nutrition—can obscure a wealth of innovation largely unknown to professional-managerial intellectuals in academia and the media.

Artistic producers have taken university material and joined it to everyday life, forging combinations sometimes far ahead of the work of academics. Pop culture crosses over to academia with a great deal of ease, even if it doesn't want to live there.

We don't think that academics should abandon their own methods, their experimentalism, their sometimes peculiar and improbable agendas in a rush to engage the normalizing world. But the notion that the world simply normalizes is a bit of debilitating academic self-flattery belied by an obvious public interest in intellectuals who offer explanations and options about things that variously goad and pressure them.

Going Public: Ways and Means

The humanities have always been represented by small numbers of eminent public figures, but they have never sought or offered general and everyday contact between the body of academic humanists and their social worlds. This is what we hope will change. We see "going public" as a matter not of intensified media access for intellectual leaders but of changing the social positions and possibilities of humanists as a group. In using the term we have at least the following things in mind:

1. Going public esteems and promotes the already existing academic humanities and social sciences. Higher education boasts a number of resources that should be better known and more completely utilized.

- The university is relatively independent of the immediate needs of business and government (especially at its arts-and-humanities end).
- The university sponsors cultural knowledge at a level of sophistication, precision, and rigor rare in other institutions.
- The university generates knowledge that, although certainly opinionated and controversial, is less partisan—more long-term, more carefully thought and rethought, more comprehensive—than knowledge produced by government and commerce.
- Professional scholars are fully embedded in their social places and relations, conditioned by them, and responsive to them.
- University faculty answer to the highest standards of accuracy and enduring value of any institution in the United States.
- Through research and teaching, the university is already set up for public service.
- The university treats students of all levels as self-directed producers and creators rather than as consumers and takers of orders and engenders the skills of independence.

The university's function needs to be better understood and explained, for, as the above list suggests, it is complex. It is autonomous yet engaged, in partnership with the rest of society while necessarily retaining unique and separate functions. Even as the humanities become more relevant to the public, the university must remain a haven for knowledge not available through other media—for knowledge marked by inclusiveness, depth, accuracy, fairness, and enough fearless principle to push to its strongest conclusions.

2. Going public reconceptualizes the "public."

- "The public" does not exist. Instead there is a variety of different publics whose boundaries overlap and shift. The "public" conjured by the PC debates was the projection of the more specialized perspectives of the policy and media professionals who sponsored the debate.
- Communication and cooperation among and within these multiple publics is governed by negotiation rather than "common culture."
- These publics are not objects of address but partners in collaboration. Information and insight flow in both directions.

- These publics encourage being positive even as we stay critical. Rather than scaring people off with too much boldness and practical radicalism, humanists have often bored them with too little.
- Publics do not exist in stable units waiting to be addressed. They are constructed through unfolding interactions of attention and address. The general model here should be our own: not a scripted video or a press release but the collective self-authoring of successful seminars.
- Publics are often so different as to require translation between them. Going public will mean that academic humanists will find themselves in radically unfamiliar places, with groups to which they have never been useful before.
- One neglected public is our fellow professional culture managers in the media, policy institutions, and consulting and lobbying operations. They don't hear from us enough. Social scientists have been talking to them for a long time, and humanists might be able to learn more about doing it from them.

3. Going public involves reconceptualizing the university.

- The university should practice what it preaches and offer itself as an example of successful change rather than as a fountainhead of critical advice. This would mean demonstrating, and not just talking about, better gender relations through feminism, better knowledge through racial diversity, happier cooperation through muted management, or greater creativity through shared resources.
- Confronting their own traditions of managerial governance, university humanists should move the university away from top-down managerialism toward the sort of efficient, liberating democracy that political theorists and corporate strategies regard as utopian.
- Academic humanists should clarify their messages. This means not watering them down but making them more pointed. Nor does it mean sacrificing rigor; it means more immediacy, excitement, and connection to the everyday.
- Academic humanists should overhaul their medium. The humanist side of campus is in desperate need of better outside relationships. As Ellen Messer-Davidow details in her essay here, the Right's successes in the PC debates proved the effectiveness of developing complex connective tissue between the university and the other information organs of social life. This will require greatly improved collaborative infrastructures, broader fund-raising processes, more streamlined packaging of interpretive results for the media's use, enhanced horizontal links among humanists in different universities and departments, and what Messer-Davidow calls "vertical" links between universities and other cultural and policy institutions.
- We need something no less important to communication: to radiate the pleasure of academia's cultural work. If we stick with a more familiar sense

that the university humanities are on the sidelines of history, we will miss out on a new era for the powers of culture.

As we write, the university retains its unsettling aura for some of the original opponents of PC. In July 1993 George Will clinched his attack on soft immigration policies with this solution: "Here is an immigration policy: for every 10 immigrants, deport an unhappy tenured professor."[11] Professors really *are* the answer to major social issues.

It should by now be obvious that no degree of scholarly retreat or ostentatious self-policing will appease this kind of thinking. We shouldn't even try. Our disturbing aspects are our sources of value—the disorder of any construction zone, the confusing mistakes that mark new stages, and the unanticipated shocks and wild turns of all previously unthinkable breakthroughs. They are a sign that we are fulfilling knowledge's most basic purpose by creating new possibilities and making old dreams come to life. To disown the mess is to discredit the humanities as a serious form of knowledge. The only solution is to take pleasure again in our power of change and to make society as happy about it as we ourselves could be.

NOTES

1. For a discussion that links racial to democratic anxiety, see Christopher Newfield, "What Was 'Political Correctness'? Race, the Right, and Managerial Democracy in the Humanities," *Critical Inquiry* 19 (Winter 1993):308–336.

2. By 1991, Afrocentricity was routinely identified as a rejection of common standards of historical scholarship. Widely vilified antidiscrimination protests on college campuses often rested their analysis on cultural differences. Codes that attempted to penalize hate speech, for example, asserted a context-dependent difference in meaning between a white student's calling an African American woman a "water buffalo" (to cite a recent case at the University of Pennsylvania) and that student's applying the same term to another white person. Gay civil rights insisted that lesbians and gay men should have differences of sexuality protected by law, while state measures in Colorado and Oregon specifically tried to strip sexual difference of legal recognition by presuming heterosexuality as a common standard. The presence of "gays in the military" was similarly labeled by proponents of the ban on gays as a danger to "unit cohesion" and military discipline—again, to a common culture that provides social order.

3. George F. Will, "Literary Politics," *Newsweek* 22 (April 1991):72.

4. Adam Clymer, "Clinton Nominee Defends Himself," *New York Times,* 26 June 1993, A6.

5. Denise Magner, "Duke U. Struggles to Make Good on Pledge to Hire Black Professors," *Chronicle of Higher Education,* 24 March 1993, A13.

6. Richard Rothstein, "Employers, Not Schools, Fail Black Youth," *Los Angeles Times,* 18 April 1993, M5.

7. Editors, "Revolution and Reaction," *Women's Review of Books* 9:5 (February 1992):13.

8. Rothstein, "Employers," M5.

9. Louis Kampk, "Annals of Academic Life: An Exemplary Tale." In *Left Politics and the Literary Profession,* ed. Lennard J. Davis and M. Bella Mirabella, 311. New York: Columbia University Press, 1990.

10. Elliott Negin, "Why College Tuitions Are So High," *Atlantic Monthly* (March 1993):22–43; Christopher Farrell, "Time to Prune the Ivy," *Business Week* (24 May 1993):112–118.

11. George F. Will, "Assimilation Is Not a Dirty Word," *Los Angeles Times,* 29 July 1993, B7.

PART ONE

THE GENEALOGY OF THE ANTI-PC AGENDA

2

Managing the Anti-PC Industry

SARA DIAMOND

IN THE MIND-SET of right-wing strategists, academia is hotly contested terrain, and the stakes could not be higher. Who will decide what versions of reality young people will be exposed to? Who will become the officially recognized "experts" advising policymakers in government and influencing public opinion via the mass media? A large cohort of white men holding sway over academia since the 1950s is now retiring, and many of their seats are being filled by women and people of color. The more diverse the student body and faculty become, the more outmoded curricula inevitably—and justifiably—will be called into question.

It is precisely at this time that the Right has revived its long-standing concern with purported leftist domination of academia. The demise of "international communism" as an adversarial preoccupation leaves right-wing intellectuals with an obvious target of next resort: the liberals and radicals who have managed to hold some ground during the dark ages of the Reagan-Bush administrations' education budget cuts.

Case Study: University of Texas at Austin

The National Association of Scholars (NAS) is leading the drive to preserve academia's preferential option for all that is rich, white, macho, and ancient. It has been particularly active at the University of Texas at Austin (UT), site of a full-scale right-wing backlash. In the spring of 1990, the Texas chapter of the NAS emerged in reaction to proposed changes in a lower-division writing course. In a climate of

Portions of this essay were published in *Z* in February 1991 and July-August 1993 and are reprinted here with changes by permission.

increasing racial and sexual harassment at UT, the English professor Linda Brodkey proposed that E306 be revised to include readings about civil rights issues from a sociology textbook on race and gender. The idea was to give students provocative and socially relevant themes around which to construct their own written arguments. Among the English department faculty, opinion was divided, but before any compromise could be reached the campus Right took the proposal and ran with it. Two Texas NAS members, Alan Gribben from the English department and Daniel Bonevac from Philosophy, made wild allegations about leftist "indoctrination" plots. During a local PBS television debate, Bonevac charged that E306 should really be called "Marxism 306." The Heritage Foundation's syndicated columnist William Murchison was drafted to write biting columns for the *Dallas Morning News.* By summer's end the course revisions—intended to be in place for the fall semester—had been postponed for at least a year. In September the English department faculty voted to accept the revised course pending approval by the dean of the College of Liberal Arts and the university president. In its Fall 1990 newsletter the NAS claimed victory in "resisting a powerful attempt to distort and politicize the curriculum."

While embroiled in the English department fracas, the Texas Association of Scholars (TAS) held its first public event, in March 1990, a conference entitled "Ideologically Based Suppression of Research in Social Science." Exhibit A of the "suppressed" scholars was the TAS's chapter head Joseph Horn, a psychology professor who peddled theories on ethnic-group differences in intelligence. Horn was then also an assistant dean in the College of Liberal Arts and the faculty adviser to UT's Young Conservatives. Horn encouraged the student rightists to hold rallies and circulate petitions against a Black Student Association proposal to hire more tenured black faculty and to require all students to take three hours of African or African American studies. The Chicano student newspaper *Tejas* published an investigative report on Horn's political and academic career and an editorial calling for his resignation as dean. Horn's student group then launched a campaign to protest university funding of *Tejas.* The administration caved in and decided that state funding might be used to write, edit, and publish 50 copies of the paper—one for each class member and the journalism faculty—but not the total circulation of about 5,000 for the student body. The other three journalism-class publications received no such treatment.

The incidents at UT suggested that right-wing strategy for academia had moved from an early phase, in the 1980s, of funding like-minded professors and student projects and harassing progressive faculty to confrontations of a more profound and conceptual nature. Now the target was the very idea of using civil rights literature to teach writing skills or of a journalism course offering publishing experience for groups underrepresented in the corporate media. The Right consistently claims to oppose what it calls "the politicization of the academy." Translated, this means opposition to what the Left calls "diversity" and "multiculturalism."

Origin of the Species

The National Association of Scholars is the first concerted effort to organize right-wing faculty. It began in 1987, but its genealogy can be traced to the Institute for Educational Affairs (IEA), founded in 1978 by the neoconservative writer Irving Kristol and former Treasury Secretary William Simon. The IEA has since served as a conduit for corporate funding of selected academics. (In September 1990 IEA changed its name to the Madison Center for Educational Affairs.) It is bankrolled by corporate foundations, including Coors, Mobil, Smith Richardson, Earhart, Scaife, and Olin. IEA board members—some of whom are also trustees of the contributing foundations—dole out respectable sums to up-and-coming graduate students and junior faculty, according to the minutes of one IEA meeting, "in order to give their work impact and promote their careers."

From the start, IEA differed from an "Old Right" academic project, the Intercollegiate Studies Institute (ISI), started in 1952 by associates of William F. Buckley Jr. ISI continues to hold conferences and publish journals, but the articles are too philosophical and lackluster to attract much attention. The Madison Center is the force behind a crop of sixty provocative tabloids published on fifty-seven campuses. The most notorious, the *Dartmouth Review,* has repeatedly drawn fire for its bigoted invectives. In 1986, on Martin Luther King Jr.'s birthday, *Review* staffers tore down shanties built by the college's antiapartheid groups. In a stunt timed for the 1990 Yom Kippur holiday, the *Review* published a quotation from Hitler's *Mein Kampf* on its masthead. Dartmouth President James Freedman responded by denouncing the paper—and its outside agitators William F. Buckley Jr., Patrick Buchanan, George Gilder, and William Rusher—in a *New York Times* op-ed piece. But while the spotlight has been fixed on IEA's irritating student press, its intellectual authors have quietly laid the groundwork for more insidious means of putting liberal and progressive academics on the defensive.

Behind the Supply Lines

The immediate predecessor of the NAS was a group called the Campus Coalition for Democracy, headquartered, as was the NAS, in Princeton. The Coalition began in 1982 and was headed by Stephen H. Balch, a professor of government at the City University of New York.[1] (Balch later became president of the NAS.) In 1983 the Campus Coalition held a conference at Long Island University attended by about 120 people. The subject was Central America, and the list of speakers was impressive. Jeane Kirkpatrick gave the plenary address. Panel speakers included Assistant Secretary of State Elliott Abrams, Penn Kemble of the Institute on Religion and Democracy, Michael Ledeen of the Center for Strategic and International Studies, William Doherty of the American Institute for Free Labor Development, and Contra leader Arturo Cruz. The conference program acknowledged funding from the Long Island University John P. McGrath Fund and from the

Committee for the Free World (CFW). The CFW, headed by Elliott Abrams's mother-in-law Midge Decter, was at the time one of the most important assets in the Reagan administration's war against Nicaragua. Campus Coalition's president Balch solicited advice from the CFW's Steven Munson on getting money from the IEA.

By late 1984 the campus organizing plan was spelled out in a confidential memo, "The Report on the Universities," written by Roderic R. Richardson for the Smith Richardson Foundation.[2] (It is worth noting that this foundation has had a history of sponsoring CIA-linked media projects and leadership training programs for CIA and Defense Department personnel.)[3] The document proposed to distinguish two possible anti-Left strategies: "deterrence activism" and "highground articulation," also termed "idea marketing." Deterrence activism, wrote Richardson, "exists purely in response to the left-wing agenda. It is not very interesting, frankly, boring, and it is the kind of activism sponsored heretofore. At best it is a form of cheerleading that can focus some attention on stirring media events." Instead, Richardson advocated "highground activism" or "articulation," "the attempt to steal one or another highground away from the left, by both action, and articulation. As noted, it involves doing things like insisting on rigorous discussion and debates, setting up political unions, battling divestiture and other causes, not by calling their goals wrong, necessarily, but by proposing better ways of solving the problem. Student journalism is a highground approach." Richardson recommended that the Right "mimick left-wing organization" by forming what he called regional resource centers, starting with a faculty network "in one area of the country, say, New England or around New York. The aim of such a group is to set up a permanent network, to defuse the left, to grab the highground, to change the atmosphere on campuses, and perhaps, to help command a corner of the national agenda." He wrote that he already had support for his plan, but he warned that "the New Right, perceiving a vacuum, might well try to take over the student activist and journalism movements."

The Usual Suspects

Before the regional resource center plan could get off the ground, a faction farther right than Richardson and the IEA launched Accuracy in Academe (AIA). A spin-off of Reed Irvine's Accuracy in Media, AIA recruited classroom spies and began compiling a data base on professors it labeled "left-wing propagandists." AIA's first executive director, Les Csorba, was a twenty-two-year-old activist fresh from the University of California at Davis, where he had organized a harassment campaign against the visiting lecturer Saul Landau in 1985. Its president, John LeBoutillier, a former member of Congress, was then a leader in the World Anti-Communist League (WACL), as were three other members of its initial advisory board. Irvine himself had at one time been prominent in the WACL. At the time of AIA's founding in 1985, the WACL was one of the most important coordinating bodies for death squad activities in Central America and elsewhere.[4] Not because of these connections but because of its pit-bull tactics, AIA attracted media attention and earned a reputation as campus "thought police."

Among AIA's strongest detractors were fellow rightists, including Midge Decter of the CFW. In a December 1985 *New York Times* op-ed piece, Decter expressed agreement with Irvine's view of the professorate but charged AIA with mimicking 1960s radicals who had turned the universities into "a veritable hotbed of reckless, mindless anti-Americanism." Advocating the "highground" strategy of her colleagues at the Smith-Richardson Foundation, Decter wrote, "The only way to deal with words and ideas and teachings one deplores is to offer better words and ideas and teachings."[5] Decter projected herself as a true believer in "academic freedom" when in fact she and her ilk were motivated less by civil libertarianism than by the shrewd understanding that the most effective ideological warfare strategy is to sneak up on the enemy. AIA was such a crude and noisy operation that it might have discredited other right-wing strategies.

In 1986 Decter's *Commentary* published an important article, "The Tenured Left," by Stephen H. Balch and Herbert I. London. Balch was then associate professor of government at the John Jay College of Criminal Justice in New York. Herbert London was and is dean of the Gallatin Division of New York University and a fellow of the Pentagon-funded Hudson Institute in Indiana. Balch and London expressed their distaste for AIA by making a phony analogy between it and the campus antiapartheid movement. The only difference, as far as they could see, was that AIA's efforts, "unlike those of the divestiture campaign, have been wholly confined to the realm of public criticism, neither fomenting disruption, nor toying with the possibilities of violent confrontation, nor obliging university administrators or faculty members to adopt an institutional stand."[6]

Their argument continued: antiapartheid protesters were getting slaps on the wrists while AIA activists were being labeled troublemakers, and all because the academy was dominated by leftists. Among the "evidence" presented was that the *American Sociological Review* had given its lead article space to a real live marxist—who also happened to be an associate editor of the journal. The marxist in question was the University of California at Berkeley sociologist Michael Burawoy. Balch and London trashed Burawoy's field study of a Hungarian manufacturing plant because the work was done in collaboration with János Lukács of the Hungarian Academy of Sciences. The logic was that Burawoy's work could not be scientifically valid so long as his fellow sociologist was a citizen of a communist regime. (Presumably Balch and London would approve work by Burawoy and Lukács since Hungary's turn toward capitalism.)

The tactic remained red-baiting particular scholars. By 1987 the Right's antiprogressive argument was broadened with the publication of Allan Bloom's bestseller *The Closing of the American Mind*. With generous funding from the Earhart and Olin Foundations, Bloom's book constructed a case against the concept of "cultural relativism," propagated by leftist intellectuals but manifested throughout society in everything from too little Bible reading to too much rock 'n' roll. Bloom attributed the "dumbing-down" of the U.S. citizenry to a gradual erosion of ethnocentric prejudices. "Cultural relativism," he wrote, "succeeds in destroying the West's universal or intellectually imperialistic claims, leaving it to be just another culture."[7]

Enter the NAS

In late 1987 the NAS was formally inaugurated, with Herbert London named chair of the board and Stephen Balch president. Among the prominent board members were Leslie Lenkowsky, formerly research director of the Smith-Richardson Foundation, who was at one time acting director of the U.S. Information Agency. Lenkowsky directed the IEA–Madison Center until 1990, when he left to become president of the Hudson Institute. A preliminary survey of tax returns from some of the same right-wing foundations funding IEA–Madison Center shows the NAS with an annual budget well in excess of a half million dollars.[8]

The first few issues of the NAS's quarterly journal, *Academic Questions,* took aim at feminist scholarship, affirmative action, supposed leftist control of Latin American, African, and Asian Studies programs, and even student evaluations of professors. Subsequent articles were more broad-brush in approach. One six-page article lamented college students' use of highlighter pens. Beyond its surface absurdity, the point of the article was that students should not be so free to choose what *they* thought they needed to remember from any assigned reading. The argument underlying a Fall 1990 article on "the radical politicization of liberal education" relied on a patently false assertion; John Agresto, president of St. John's College in New Mexico, claimed that radicals deny the possibility of reading texts "nonpolitically" because they deny "transtemporal and universal truths or principles."[9]

The NAS has taken credit for the repeal of a University of Michigan (UM) speech code intended to reduce racist and sexist incidents on campus. With support from the NAS and the Michigan chapter of the American Civil Liberties Union (ACLU), Wesley Wynne, a graduate student in biological psychology, sued his alma mater and won. In 1989 a federal court ruled that UM's speech code was so broadly defined as to threaten the First Amendment.

According to a favorable article in the *Chronicle of Higher Education* in 1990, the NAS had fourteen hundred members, statewide affiliates in seventeen states, and campus chapters at the Universities of Minnesota at Twin Peaks, New Mexico at Albuquerque, and Texas at Austin and at Duke and Emory Universities, and it had concrete plans to expand its influence.[10] In early 1990 all NAS members received a thirty-eight-page questionnaire prepared by the affiliated Madison Center, founded in 1988 by Allan Bloom and then–Secretary of Education William Bennett. (In September 1990 the Center merged with the Institute for Educational Affairs and became known as the Madison Center for Educational Affairs.) The survey was an amazingly thorough intelligence-gathering tool. Respondents were asked to provide detailed answers to questions such as "How often does the administration play an active role in tenure decisions?" "What are the prevailing attitudes toward ROTC and CIA recruitment on campus?" "How conspicuous is the homosexual faculty presence on campus?" Some of these data were destined to become part of *The Common Sense Guide to American Colleges, 1991–1992*, which was intended, according to the Madison Center's vice president, Charles Horner (a former State Department, U.S. Information Agency, and RAND Corporation official), to focus on "how education and teaching has fared under the mixed influences of the last 15 or 20 years."

The NAS set up a research center in Princeton—consistent with the 1984 Richardson plan—to "accumulate information on the issues and trends of contemporary higher education." In its Fall 1990 newsletter it appealed to its members to send in course descriptions and proposals, departmental newsletters, and the like, for trend analysis to be conducted by its research director Glenn Ricketts. Its Faculty and Executive Search Service is a small-scale employment service provided free to members. Caucuses have been formed within the professional associations organized by various academic disciplines. Already, the NAS and the Intercollegiate Studies Institute (ISI) have formed antiliberal groupings within the Modern Language Association, the American Historical Association, and the American Philosophical Association, according to the ISI's national director, Chris Long.

A November 1990 mailing to the sociology-anthropology section of the NAS from Dan McMurry of Middle Tennessee State University spelled out an effort to "reform from within" the American Sociological Association (ASA). Hardly a hotbed of radicalism, the ASA exists to promote the careers of its members, who are mostly mild-mannered theorists more interested in studying the world than in changing it. The NAS planned to begin sponsoring special sessions at ASA meetings. This was convenient—the president of the ASA at the time was the University of Chicago professor James S. Coleman, a prominent member of the NAS. The "Dear Colleague" letter warned NAS members to "avoid being regarded as conservative. We hope to cast our nets widely."

Knowledge Is Power

The NAS will succeed if and only if progressives fail to do their homework. The first step is for people to learn the nature of the right-wing game plan on their own campuses. Who are the administrators and faculty seeking to block proposals and hirings that would improve university teaching and research? Which faculty are vulnerable to attack from the Right, and how might they be supported? Are their opponents motivated by misguided notions of what academic pluralism should mean, or are they part of an NAS chapter or something like it? In what ways are rightist faculty mobilizing students to do their bidding? The right-wing student groups that have harassed liberal professors are often the same ones involved in racist and sexist attacks on other students and in infiltration of the student Left.

An energetic analysis and discussion of the Right's intellectual arguments is as important as knowing the political lineup on campus. Just as the Smith-Richardson Foundation advocated "highground articulation," the Left should take the initiative in debates around important questions for which there are no easy answers. Should degree programs include a core curriculum, including specific sets of books that simply must be mastered by everyone within the discipline? Do punitive sanctions for users of "fighting words" on campus really reduce racist and sexist violence, or are such measures misguided infringements of free speech that may also have the effect of exacerbating conflict? The campus Left ought not to find itself taking knee-jerk positions that seem "politically correct" or expedient in a short-term sense. Rather, it should develop a deserved reputation as the group most open to rational, democratic decision making, even if that means taking positions—for principled reasons—that are also voiced by some conservatives. To do otherwise might mean surrendering education as one more institution committed to the preservation of the powers that be.

PC's Bottom Line

Political correctness was only one of the issues placed on the national agenda by the neoconservative and anticommunist movements during the twelve-year reign of Ronald Reagan and George Bush. Years before the NAS took form, right-wing intellectuals watched with disdain as a cohort of left-leaning baby boomers—many of them schooled in the movements of the sixties—became comfortably ensconced in academia. In reality, there were never as many "tenured radicals" as the Right imagined, but the intent of those allied with the NAS was transparent. The idea was through rhetoric and anecdote to tarnish a range of progressive trends in university curricula, hiring, and admissions policies.

As the crisis of ideological conformity intensified, so did the threat to universities' financial solvency. The end of the Cold War brought no hoped-for world peace and prosperity. In states like California—with economies buoyed for decades by the defense industry—military base closures and unyielding rates of unemployment began to spell big trouble for the state legislatures charged with balancing budgets. The NAS continued to vent its members' pet grievances: A job seeker was passed over in the name of "diversity"; someone else was insulted by students protesting a careless racist remark; a new disciplinary fashion deprived an older group of scholars of their former prominence. Had the controversy been confined to the realm of academic professionals, "political correctness" would not have become a major media watchword in the 1990s. Budget-conscious university administrators looked around and considered which of the humanities and social science programs they might cut with the greatest expediency. "Back to basics" was a welcome refrain. For reasons of their own, groups like the NAS raise the question, as in the title of their 1993 conference, "What Should a University Be?" We ought to have more than one answer to that question, but in these times of economic austerity, answers, too, are in short supply.

Fanning the Flames

In 1991 it was impossible to escape the daily barrage of op-ed page warnings about the scourge of "political correctness." From Ivy League to community colleges— so the storytellers claimed—leftists, radical feminists, and angry people of color had seized the wheels of higher education. The fate of Western civilization hung in the balance. Dinesh D'Souza became an overnight success with his *Illiberal Education,* a grab bag of anecdotes about campus zealotry. Leading the anti-PC charge was the NAS.

Progressive intellectuals began to fight back, mainly by exposing the PC hunters' decidedly political agenda and by grappling rationally with PC-related campus issues such as speech codes and multicultural curriculum requirements. Gerald Graff's Teachers for a Democratic Culture and Stanley Aronowitz's Union of Democratic Intellectuals sought to open lines of communication among people concerned with true academic freedom and the threat posed to it by the Right. It was only a matter of time before the PC scare stories had lost their power to interest—let alone alarm—the larger public and the editors of the mainstream press. The mass propaganda campaign against political correctness, like other moral panics of the Reagan-Bush era, filtered into the memory banks of what we call "conventional wisdom."

One by-product of the anti-PC campaign was the NAS's consolidation of a network of 3,000 faculty members organized into twenty-nine state affiliates. Gracing the NAS advisory board is an array of prominent neoconservative intellectuals including Jeane Kirkpatrick, Irving Kristol, Seymour Martin Lipset, and John Bunzel. The membership itself covers the spectrum from high-status private universities to small community colleges. It has cost the NAS a bundle in promotional work to recruit each member, and this would not have been possible without its bottomless pit of corporate foundation grants. But a handful of well-coordinated NAS members on any given campus can make a big difference during hiring and curriculum battles. Recently NAS members at the University of New Mexico came to the aid of a part-time instructor charged with using racist rhetoric. At the University of Minnesota, two NAS professors used the campus newspaper to "expose" a supposedly rough-handed sexual harassment training session required for liberal arts faculty.

Aware of the NAS's limited local successes and its polemicists' larger role in the anti-PC campaign, I signed up to attend its fourth national convention, held in April 1993 at San Francisco's Park Lane Parc Fifty-Five Hotel. The event offered no major surprises, but it was a good chance to hear NAS members' viewpoints. Naturally, I was one of only about two dozen women present among 250 registrants, virtually all of them middle-aged and white, except for two invited black speakers. (But, then, how "politically correct" of me to have noticed!)

NAS President Stephen Balch opened the conference with a call for members to recognize their accomplishments in making "political correctness" a household word. He urged them to prepare for a "protracted journey toward higher education reform" and to move from a critique of PC to "building institutions" and finding ways to wield political influence via conservative alumni and state legislators. The first panel was scheduled to take on one of the most important questions facing anyone concerned about an educated citizenry: "Can Higher Education Be Mass Education?" First up was Jeffrey Hart, professor of English at Dartmouth College and a former long-time editor of Buckley's *National Review.* Hart pulled no punches. Because inherent intelligence capabilities are distributed unevenly along a bell-shaped curve, what proportion of the population, he asked, can go on to universities without making a joke of the adjective "higher"? His crude elitism won over the NAS audience. He stressed the frivolity of gearing academic standards to people better off relegated to blue-collar destinies. "I'd just as soon the fellow fixing my auto brakes is not at the same time pondering *Finnegan's Wake,*" he chuckled.

Next to speak was Barry Munitz, chancellor of the twenty-campus California State University system, who thought it would be a dandy idea if his auto mechanic might also be thinking about great works of literature. His curriculum vitae had impressed the California legislators who had hired him two years before to make the financially strapped Cal State system function like a for-profit corporation. Munitz was vice chair of Pacific Lumber's parent corporation, Maxxam Inc., responsible for raiding parts of California's forests. Formerly chancellor of the University of Houston, he also sat on the board of one of Texas's failed savings and loans. As a bottom-line kind of a guy, Munitz emphasized the demographics of California's changing student population. Between 1970 and 2020, California's kindergarten-through-high-school population will have grown from 4.5 million to 10.5 million students. Among these, the percentage of Anglos will have dropped from 74 percent to 25 percent; the percentage of African Americans will have remained constant; Asians will have jumped from 2 to 19 percent of the total; and the percentage of Hispanic students will have grown from 15 to 48 percent. Munitz was later taken to task by NAS members for his mere acknowledgment of California's changing ethnic makeup, but his point was that, ethnicity aside, California's so-called master plan for higher education remained valid. The state had pledged several decades ago to make an affordable college education available to every California resident. The top eighth of high school students are supposed to be able to attend the University of California, the top third a California State University campus, and the top two-thirds a community college of their choice. Munitz offered no clue as to how the state could maintain such access when spiraling fees were driving students away, but he said that there were "life-and-death matters" at stake in California's current educational crisis. "What happens to the economy of California and the United States if we don't try to take a large number of young people and make them better?"

Munitz's speech was not exactly music to the NAS members' ears. After the first panel, they lined up one after another to blast Munitz and the last speaker, Robert Rosenzweig from the Association of American Universities, for not indicting fellow college administrators, particularly over affirmative action in hiring and admissions. Barry Gross, the NAS's treasurer, summed up the prevailing sentiment that vocational schools are the proper destination for working-class high school graduates. To send them into the universities is to lower the standards for those who *really* belong there. Jeffrey Hart said it best: "The broadening of the student body has led to a corruption of the curriculum."

This blatant elitism, of course, contradicted another theme prevalent throughout the NAS conference. People seemed to believe that leftist intellectuals constituted a "cultural elite" now in charge of most social science and humanities departments. After lunch the first day of the conference, the keynote speaker and University of California at Los Angeles public policy professor James Q. Wilson explained that today's "threat to academic freedom" comes from within the universities themselves. This is why the media and the general public hardly know that there's a problem. Academia has endured the dangers of marxism, Wilson said. "But at least marxists had a coherent theory. Marxism as a pseudoscience has not survived, but the marxist animus against bourgeois culture has endured, and like a vampire it can assume many forms." Masquerading, especially in the humanities, as postmodernism, deconstructionism, and other brands of esoterica, this new "vampire" makes old-fashioned marxism look like the Sunday choir. "The university has always had leftists, but never before like the ones we have now," Wilson warned. "These new leftists rebel against *reason,* not just against institutions."

In his nostalgic preference for old-fashioned marxists over their postmodern distant cousins, of course, Wilson conveniently glossed over the history of academic institutions, never a hospitable place for active leftists. The McCarthy era purges were welcomed by the neoconservatives' 1950s forerunners, most explicitly by Sidney Hook, in whose memory the National Association of Scholars grants an annual award. (The Sidney Hook Memorial Award for 1993 was accepted by the liberal Yale historian C. Vann Woodward.)

Gerald Early entertained the NAS crowd by reminding them that they should be thankful that a sympathetic scholar like himself now ran the African and Afro-American Studies department at Washington University in St. Louis. A few members of the NAS's sociology subsection balked when Early blamed the radical sociologists of the early 1960s for spawning what he considered dubious new fields such as women's and ethnic studies. (Scholars committed to "reason" and "truth" at least ought to get their facts straight.)

A Blast from the Past

In an effort to dispel its neoconservative reputation, the NAS balanced its panels with a politically correct number of token liberals. The University of California at Berkeley sociology professor Todd Gitlin joined a panel entitled "The Mission of the University: Intellectual Discovery or Social Transformation?" For this scene Gitlin was cast as the kind of leftist an NAS member could agree to disagree with. But Gitlin's presence proved too much for fellow sixties veteran David Horowitz, who rose from the crowd to attack him as an unrepentant "apologist" for the Left. Gitlin denied the charge and called Horowitz a few choice names while Balch tried to restore gentlemanly decorum.

Unofficially, some NAS members object to Horowitz's militant theatrics and the yellow journalism of the new tabloid he and Peter Collier mass-produce, *Heterodoxy*. In a recent letter to the editor, NAS member Alan Kors of the University of Pennsylvania took *Heterodoxy* to task for the "anti-intellectualism" of its "obsession with gay and lesbian issues." In lockstep with the rest of the Right, Horowitz and Collier have taken to queer-baiting in almost every issue. They answered Kors's letter to the effect that they don't object to garden-variety gays and lesbians. "Our issue," they write, "is with the homosexual Left, often self-identified as the Queer Left, which has an agenda that is socially destructive and intellectually fascistic."[11] To drive home the gay-red connection, a *Heterodoxy* cover story on "Queer Studies" dressed a cartoon of Karl Marx in a steel mesh bra, garter belt, stockings, and high heels, with a vibrator in one hand and a whip in the other—pretty sophisticated stuff.

But no one can argue with *Heterodoxy* as an attention grabber. Publicity hounds Horowitz and Collier were featured in a recent promotional article for *Heterodoxy* in the *San Francisco Chronicle*. The supposedly respectable *Chronicle of Higher Education* did its own puff piece on the latest venture of the "two disillusioned radicals" and solicited comments from friends and detractors. Stephen Balch praised *Heterodoxy* for its "rock-em, sock-em commentary" and "investigative journalism." Horowitz and Collier call their work a "samizdat publication inside the gulag of the PC university." *Heterodoxy* is really the latest meal ticket for Horowitz and Collier to feed from the same corporate foundation troughs that sustain NAS and a host of right-wing think tanks. Through his Los Angeles–based Center for the Study of Popular Culture—funded by the Olin, Bradley, Scaife, and other foundations to the tune of about $700,000 a year—Horowitz has purchased mailing lists to mail as many as 80,000 free copies of each issue of *Heterodoxy*. With only about 8,000 paid subscribers, *Heterodoxy* depends on the same right-wing funders who in the mid-1980s launched Horowitz and Collier on a series of "Second Thoughts" conferences, where the two "former radicals" rehearsed their political conversion stories like a pair of missionaries sent from on high.

Heterodoxy is a forum for its editors to keep fighting old enemies from the sixties and to establish themselves as arbiters of the Right's current preoccupations. Under the title "Alien Nation: The Illegal Lobby," *Heterodoxy* contributor K.

L. Billingsley promotes anxiety about "illegal aliens" from Mexico. "Civic structures are rupturing under the load, school curricula are being changed, prisons and hospitals are becoming inadvertent Ellis Islands, and an ecosystem of crime has sprung up around these immigrants." Why can't the INS patrol the borders? Billingsley asks. "The short answer is that there is a powerful lobby for illegal immigration, a network of organizations that includes the Mexican American Legal Defense and Education Fund (MALDEF), the Latino Issues Forum, the National Council of La Raza, the Coalition for Immigrant and Refugee Rights and Services, etc."[12] What these organizations have to do with academic political correctness is anyone's guess.

But *Heterodoxy*'s obsession with "criminals" and sexual deviance suggests a method to the apparent madness of the hunt for political correctness. Neoconservative social scientists—including a few now at home within the NAS—have built careers explaining social movements they don't like as the domain of irrational paranoids who just won't play by the rules of "democracy." One of the neoconservatives' intellectual accomplishments was to build theories that obscured the rational motives driving social movements. These theories, first generated in application to the "radical Right" (an oxymoron), were later deployed against the New Left. The current neoconservative attack on feminists and multiculturalists works by perpetuating caricatures of slightly demented zealots hungry for power.

It might be tempting to see the PC hunters, likewise, as reacting in a thoroughly paranoid style against unreal threats to their high status in academia. But that would be to deny that the old guard really does have something to worry about. No longer can universities, if they so desire, deny access to women and people of color with impunity. Some academic trendiness is worthy of mockery. Plenty is now also up for debate, though fair debate may be impossible inside institutions never intended to be democratic. In defense of the status quo, right-wing intellectuals resort to the reliable tactic of stigmatizing potential contenders for power and scarce resources. Jobs, publishing venues, status within disciplinary pecking orders—these are like gold for the "politically correct" and "incorrect" alike.

Multicultural educators seek to level the playing field in part by reducing the stigma attached to social groups traditionally subordinate—if visible at all—in privileged places like universities. If the point of the PC hunters is to restigmatize emergent groups demanding a piece of the pie, it is at the same time to elevate the status of a threatened intellectual elite. The NAS represents a cohort of aging academics who see their colleagues' empty seats being filled by new categories of outsiders, and precisely at a time when the financial squeeze is on.

Fiddling While Rome Burns

What betrays the NAS's professed concern with academic "standards" more than anything else is the PC hunters' neglect of the universities' bottom-line crisis.

While our campuses are falling apart before our eyes, the organized defenders of Western civilization are busy counting how many deconstructionists can dance on the head of a pin. Conditions of fiscal austerity threaten university departments and faculty of various political stripes. One unintended consequence of the NAS's ceaseless carping about campus political correctness may be to discredit the whole enterprise of taxpayer-funded education—precisely at a time when state legislators may welcome excuses for budget cuts.

California, the nation's most populous state, can no longer afford to send all its qualified students to college at an affordable price. No doubt the situation is similar elsewhere. For the past few years the state legislature has steadily reduced funding and increased student fees for University of California and California State University campuses. Students faced with fee hikes as high as 30–40 percent a year find course offerings drastically reduced, entire departments eliminated.

At some California campuses, local corporations have volunteered to sponsor select courses. The dangers are obvious. As they routinely influence state legislators' priorities, corporations are never really out of the loop. But given a direct role within particular universities, they will fund only those programs deemed economically correct. That means little funding for the humanities and social sciences but plenty of resources for business schools, physical sciences, and other fields deemed eminently practical to the production of a technical workforce.

Opponents of diversity and multicultural education may get their way by default. Direct corporate funding may persuade politicians and taxpayers, too, that universities can survive without public money. The job of state legislators is to satisfy their campaign donors, balance budgets, and keep conflicting groups of citizens from voting them out of office. To the extent that universities appear as hotbeds of contentiousness, the politicians can more legitimately reduce their share of funding. Then higher education will surely not be for everyone.

NOTES

1. Historical data on the activities of the Campus Coalition for Democracy and its evolution into the National Association of Scholars can be found in the files of Midge Decter's Committee for the Free World, Hoover Institution Archives, Stanford University (see especially the detailed correspondence in Box 2, file Balch, Stephen, and box 40, file Balch). In a letter of 3 August 1987, Stephen Balch wrote to Midge Decter to inform her of the Coalition's intention to adopt a less "sharply political" name, the National Association of Scholars.

2. "Report on the Universities," dated 20 December 1984 and written by R. Randolph Richardson, is an internal Richardson Foundation memorandum in the files of the Committee for the Free World, Box 7, Hoover Institution Archives, Stanford University.

3. See John S. Friedman, "Public TV's CIA Show," *The Nation,* 19–26 July 1980, 73–77.

4. Scott Anderson and Jon Lee Anderson, *Inside the League* (New York: Dodd, Mead, 1986).

5. Midge Decter, "More Bullying on Campus," *New York Times,* 10 December 1985, A31.

6. Stephen H. Balch and Herbert I. London, "The Tenured Left," *Commentary*, October 1986, 41.

7. Allan Bloom, *The Closing of the American Mind* (New York: Simon and Schuster, 1987), 39.

8. See also Ellen Messer-Davidow, "Manufacturing the Attack on Liberalized Higher Education," *Social Text* 36 (Fall 1993), 60.

9. John Agresto, "The Politicization of Liberal Education," *Academic Questions,* Fall 1990, 71.

10. Carolyn J. Mooney, "Academic Group Fighting the 'Politically Correct Left' Gains Momentum," *Chronicle of Higher Education,* 12 December 1990, 1, 13.

11. [Letter], *Heterodoxy,* March 1993, 2.

12. K. L. Billingsley, "Alien Nation: The Illegal Lobby," *Heterodoxy,* March 1993, 4.

3

Manufacturing the Attack on Liberalized Higher Education

I. The PC Debate

So far as the general reading public knew, the PC debate burst suddenly onto the American scene toward the end of 1990. News-magazine readers learned about "political correctness" in the academy from feature stories in *Newsweek* and *Time*,[1] while higher-brow readers encountered it somewhat earlier in 1990, perusing Richard Bernstein's "The Rising Hegemony of the Politically Correct" in the *New York Times*, John Searle's "The Storm over the University" in the *New York Review of Books*, and a forum in the *New York Times* on "Opening Academia without Closing It Down."[2] Business readers of the *Wall Street Journal* may have noticed early warnings of PC sounding throughout 1990—in, for instance, Gerald Sirkin's "Multiculturalists Strike Back," Arthur Schlesinger, Jr.'s "When Ethnic Studies Are Un-American," Dorothy Rabinowitz's "Vive the Academic Resistance," and editorials titled "The Ivory Censor" and "Politically Correct."[3]

Academics, however, were already drawn into this debate during the mid-1980s when they began responding to publications of the National Endowment for the Humanities (NEH). Chairman William J. Bennett's "The Shattered Humanities" (1982) and *To Reclaim a Legacy* (1984), on the decline of humanities teaching and research, drew mainly defensive comments printed in the *Chronicle of Higher Education*.[4] But Chairman Lynne V. Cheney's barrage of reports—*The Humanities and the American Promise* (1987), *Humanities in America* (1988), *50 Hours* (1989), *Tyrannical Machines* (1990), and *Telling the Truth* (1992)—on the fallen state of the

---

Reprinted by permission from *Social Text* 36 (Fall 1993):40–80.

humanities, elicited many thoughtful articles and a pamphlet issued by the American Council of Learned Societies.[5]

In 1987, when Cheney's first report was published, mass-market books attacking liberalized higher education began to appear at the impressive rate of two per year: e.g., E. D. Hirsch, Jr.'s *Cultural Literacy* (1987), Allan Bloom's *Closing of the American Mind* (1987), Charles Sykes's *Profscam* (1988) and *The Hollow Men* (1990), Page Smith's *Killing the Spirit* (1990), Roger Kimball's *Tenured Radicals* (1990), and Dinesh D'Souza's *Illiberal Education* (1991).[6] By 1991, the Right had hyped the failings of liberalized higher education in numerous conservative and mainstream periodicals. The *New Republic, Commentary,* and *Academic Questions* had forums on the subject,[7] syndicated columnist George Will fired off columns for the *Washington Post* and *Newsweek,*[8] and D'Souza published in a half-dozen venues, including the *Atlantic Monthly, Forbes,* and the *American Scholar.*[9]

Progressive academics who responded to the attack made the proverbial mistakes of too little and too late. By and large, they replied to the conservative arguments, ignoring the issue of how so many of them had suddenly appeared in print.[10] Limited by their training, they came to the attack through texts and focused on its textual features—the rhetoric, the ideas, the validity of claims[11]—not realizing that once the attack was textualized so widely it was a fait accompli. Moreover, since most of them were not reading right-wing periodicals in the mid-1980s, they did not notice the strategy for the attack percolating there and later spreading to mainstream periodicals. The strategy involved producing criticisms that demonized liberal and left types, an anticommunist technique used by the Old Right in the 1950s, and targeting these criticisms to particular audiences, a direct-mail technique developed by the New Right in the early 1980s.

Chairman Cheney, for instance, tried the strategy out during a talk at a 1988 meeting of the American Council of Learned Societies (ACLS):

> When I become most concerned about the state of the humanities in our colleges and universities is not when I see theories and ideas fiercely competing, but when I see them neatly converging, when I see feminist criticism, Marxism, various forms of poststructuralism, and other approaches all coming to bear on one concept and threatening to displace it. I think specifically of the concept of Western civilization, which has come under pressure on many fronts, political as well as theoretical. Attacked for being elitist, sexist, racist, and Eurocentric, this central and sustaining idea of our educational system and our intellectual heritage is being declared unworthy of study.[12]

Cheney's conceit—that a new academic "gang of four" (feminists, Marxists, multiculturalists, and theorists) was betraying the national cultural heritage—was not just the idiosyncratic rhetoric of an outspoken public official. Rather, it was taken from an already crafted conservative political discourse. As early as 1986, right-wingers had laid out the argument that "tenured radicals" had embarked on a wholesale demolition of the Western cultural tradition and the U.S. universities charged with preserving it. Raising the specter of 1950s communism and 1960s radicalism, such articles as Stephen H. Balch and Herbert London's "The Tenured Left" (1986), Russell Jacoby's "Radicals in Academia" (1987), Chester E. Finn's "The Campus: 'An Island of Repression in a Sea of Freedom'" (1989), and John P. Roche's "Academic Freedom: The New Left Vigilantes" (1989) portrayed the activities of progressive academics as at once McCarthyite and revolutionary.[13]

Conservatives were the most prolific in attacking academic feminism in academic periodicals and feminist positions on such issues as abortion, rape, and sexual harassment in academic and general periodicals. While their discussions of feminism ranged from the serious, though not always accurate (e.g., Virginia R. Hyman's "Conflict and Contradiction: Principles of Feminist Scholarship") to the vitriolic (Carol Iannone's "Literature by Quota"),[14] most differentiated an acceptably moderate equal-rights feminism, which has been embraced by a large part of the public, from lesbian, Marxist, and poststructuralist feminisms, which they linked to academic radicalism.

They were less successful in the battle against academic theory because they had, by and large, to rely upon conservative academics to conduct it. Those who supported traditional kinds of theory were reluctant to condemn the whole enterprise, and those who criticized particular theoretical trends found it harder work (and certainly less fun) to enter these complex discourses than to demonize types. While Peter Shaw's "Declining Discourse" (1988) denounced Marxist criticism without meaningfully engaging it and Joseph Epstein's "Academic Zoo: Theory— in Practice" (1991) read like a *People* magazine account of the names in New Criticism and new theory, most conservative academics grappled awkwardly with deconstruction.[15] Finally, even the *New Criterion*, a conservative art journal edited by Hilton Kramer and managed by Kimball, weighed in on politics, a subject that conservatives believed had no place in such a journal. In the fall of 1991, it devoted several opening commentaries to the politics of the academic left—"The Counter-Revolution Abroad, the Cultural Revolution at Home," "Post-Communist Radicalism and the Cultural Revolution," and "The Academic Left Strikes Back."

The attack on multiculturalism has been the broadest because the opening of the curriculum to previously excluded races and cultures overlaps with other efforts in the academy and society that conservatives oppose: for instance, African-American and gay activism, affirmative action, and hate-speech codes. During the past four years, they have published dozens of articles critical of multiculturalism, Afrocentrism, and alleged reverse racism on campus in *Commentary, National Review, New Republic,* and other periodicals. Most bear provocative titles that ridicule these projects (e.g., Edward Alexander's "Race Fever," Brian Hecht's "Dr. Uncool J: The Sun-Man Cometh to Harvard," and Fred Siegel's "The Cult of Multiculturalism") or that appropriate antiracist rhetoric in order to turn public sentiment against antiracist projects (e.g., Andrew Sullivan's "Racism 101," D'Souza's "New Segregation on Campus," and Thomas Short's "'New Racism' on Campus?"). Honors for the most obfuscating rhetoric go to Nathan Glazer's attack on multiculturalism titled "In Defense of Multiculturalism."[16]

The many publications that could be listed in a comprehensive bibliography on this subject omit two dimensions of the attack: first, thousands of criticisms voiced by conservatives in television and radio interviews, op-ed pieces, letters to the editor, and newsletters; and second, numerous actions taken by citizens and government officials to regulate liberalized higher education. For instance, the former Secretary of Education attempted to regulate accrediting associations and prohibit scholarships for minority students, the former NEA acting chairman rejected grants for artworks with erotic content, the former NEH chairman directed the flow of funding into traditional scholarship and away from the new critical discourses, and the National Association of Scholars (NAS) has been soliciting and referring to legal centers cases of alleged infractions against conservatives on college and university campuses.[17] I emphasize actions in order to point out that most academics have thus far mistakenly assumed that the debate is the attack. The debate, however, is only part of the attack.

The purpose of this chapter is not to survey the debate, even though it has been far more extensive than the American public and academics know.[18] Nor is it to enter into the debate, though its claims are vital as so many academics have pointed out. Rather, the purpose is to show that the Right has manufactured the attack on liberalized higher education by means of a right-wing apparatus dedicated to making radical cultural change. Making radical cultural change is essential to a conservative movement determined to impose its vision of America on all of us.

II. The Conservative Movement and Cultural Production

After the triumph of Roosevelt and the New Deal, conservatives described themselves as "the Remnant"; they were, in the words of one, "obscure, unorganized, inarticulate."[19] The establishment of the *National Review* by William F. Buckley, Jr., in 1955 "laid the foundations for everything that followed."[20] This magazine provided conservatives with "a recognized forum for conservative ideas"[21] and helped them make the transition to an interventionist approach to American politics. Also founded under Buckley's auspices in 1960, the Young Americans for Freedom (YAF) gave young conservatives practical experience in organizing: it held rallies, founded clubs on college campuses, and "'mobilize[d] support among American youth for conservative political candidates and legislation.'"[22] The Goldwater campaign in 1964 produced a new generation of conservative campaign workers as well as the list that served as the basis for Richard Viguerie's subsequent work of direct-mail fundraising.[23] By 1970, the *National Review* had a circulation of 100,000 and YAF had 50,000 members.[24] These mobilizing and direct-mail skills spurred the further development of conservative infrastructure during the 1970s, in particular the proliferation of conservative interest groups, the formation of PACs, and the rise of the Christian Right culminating with the founding of the Moral Majority (1979) by Robert Billings, Jerry Falwell, Ed

McAteer, Howard Phillips, Richard Viguerie, and Paul Weyrich. Less known, however, was another development during this same period: the founding of New Right institutions such as the Heritage Foundation by Edwin Feulner, Jr., Phillip N. Truluck, and Weyrich (1973), the Committee for the Survival of a Free Congress (now the Free Congress Foundation) by Paul Weyrich (1974), the National Journalism Center by M. Stanton Evans (1977), and the Leadership Institute by Morton Blackwell (1979).[25]

Thus, between 1955 and 1980, the Right became a powerful political movement. It had built a coalition of conservative strains (Old Right, neoconservative, New Right, Christian Right, libertarian, free-market and supply-side economics, etc.) and an infrastructure of national organizations, interest groups, churches, and corporate councils. Despite rifts in ideologies and priorities among its various constituencies,[26] the coalition became a political force by organizing cadres of campaign workers, PACs, lobbying groups, and eventually the dominant faction of the Republican Party. Today the conservative movement, the term now preferred by many of its members, is intent on strengthening the coalition by training the "Third Generation" and organizing the grass roots.[27] During these same decades, the Right also enlarged its infrastructure with foundations, think tanks, media, training institutes, and legal centers that began to focus their resources on cultural change.

Conservative Agendas for Education

With the election of President Reagan in 1980, conservatives were finally in a position to use the government to make national cultural change, and they began with education. Their interventions took the form not of critiques, which imply academic analysis, but of agendas, which imply political action. Initially, they produced two agendas for education. The centrist agenda, formulated by neoconservatives, traditional liberals, and policy analysts at the American Enterprise Institute, charged that "federal intervention to promote educational equity was excessive" both in placing equity before excellence and in pursuing it with little regard for the costs involved. The agenda called for a reordering of public-education goals so as first to "*promote economic growth* for the nation," next to "help *preserve a common culture* by teaching students the basic values upon which American capitalism is based," and only then to support educational equity.[28] By contrast, the radical Right agenda, formulated by conservative Christians and policy analysts at the Heritage Foundation, charged that a liberal-humanist monopoly of universities and federal agencies had brought about a decline "of quality teaching and academic standards." Its more drastic aim was to reverse progressive change by defederalizing education (abolishing the Department of Education, eliminating the federal funding of education, and reducing equity regulations and enforcement) but at the same time increasing the regulation of university research sponsored by federal agencies.[29]

The themes of the radical Right agenda were sketched out in *A New Agenda for Education*, a booklet that followed the format of Heritage's other agendas, such as

Mandate for Leadership, by combining analysis and action recommendations to the Reagan administration. In the introduction, Eileen M. Gardiner, an education policy analyst at Heritage, argued that America's traditionally local system of education had given way to a centralized system beset by various ills (increased costs, decreased quality, corruption by special interests) that defederalization would reverse.[30] The five essays on primary-secondary education criticized teacher tenure, teachers' unions, state certification, affirmative action and equal opportunity programs, value-neutral (i.e., secular-humanist) education, denial of federal funding to private and religious schools, and compensatory, handicapped, and bilingual education. The one essay on higher education argued that the mission of universities had been perverted by the postwar growth and liberalization of higher education. Universities, rather than pursuing truth and providing liberal-arts education, now were designed "to remedy social inequalities."[31] The author concluded that "the federal government cannot help universities pursue their educational tasks; democratic government is not, and should not be, an appropriate sponsor for liberal arts training. But while it cannot help, the government can certainly hurt."[32]

The list of recommendations in the last chapter was devised to make government helpful in implementing the radical Right agenda and continues to guide conservatives today as, for instance, they lobby for state school-choice plans and a federal voucher system, litigate reverse-discrimination cases, promote standardized testing, and propose restrictions on teachers' unions and accrediting associations. Though the agenda recommended radical changes in education, it did not tackle the larger matter of cultural production. How, then, did the Right get from a recommendation to defederalize education to a theoretically driven transformation of cultural production?

Cultural Conservatism

In the mid-1980s, a group of conservatives associated with Paul Weyrich, president of the Free Congress Foundation (FCF), undertook a project called "cultural conservatism," which was to be the template for a new American politics. Turning away from the conservative preoccupation with economics, FCF designed cultural conservatism as a response to "activist movements built around values, life-styles, and other non-economic issues." Recognizing these movements as "the vanguards of a profound political change," it predicted that "the politics that carry us into the twenty-first century will be based not on economics, but on culture."[33]

FCF read the issues raised by the vanguard movements as evidence "that America has been suffering from cultural drift ... [a] gradual emptying of a nation's values of their content, not by some violent overturning, but by slow evaporation in which the form is left—in rhetoric and often in manners—but the substance disappears."[34] The symptoms of drift included conspicuous consumption, a "me-first" ethic, demands to eliminate racism and homophobia, scientific proposals to achieve zero-population growth and eliminate male aggression as the source of war, decreased religious and parental influence, deterioration of school education, women's and critical-legal studies, and rock videos. Blamed for it were the 1960s cultural radicals and a newer cast of characters, such as yuppies and welfare recipients, produced by liberal largesse.[35]

Eager to cast off "the negative public image of the 'New Right,'" Weyrich distinguished the strains of postwar conservative orthodoxy (Cold Warriors, fundamentalists, libertarians, free-market economists) from cultural conservativism. Whereas they had defined themselves in terms of what they opposed (they were anticommunist, anti-Hoover, antiregulation), cultural conservatism would define itself in terms of what it stood *for* against the forces of the Left.[36] It would promote, for instance, conservative ideas of environmental stewardship and philanthropy to the poor because it recognized these ideas as part of a longstanding Western tradition.[37] This shift would produce a deeper understanding of conservatism by finding ways to affirm those values it had inherited.[38]

Cultural conservatives, according to Weyrich advisor William S. Lind, "seek to conserve traditional Western culture" because it "is *functionally* true"; that is, "it is necessary if our society is to be successful, in terms of what it provides its citizens."[39] They believe in

> a necessary, unbreakable, and causal relationship between traditional Western, Judeo-Christian values, definitions of right and wrong, ways of thinking and ways of living ... and the secular success of Western societies: their prosperity, their liberties, and the opportunities they offer their citizens to lead fulfilling, rewarding lives. If the former are abandoned, the latter will be lost. The essence of cultural conservatism can be reduced further, to a single phrase: traditional values are functional values. If we want a society where things work—where students learn in schools, where products are competitive, where our homes and our persons are safe from crime, etc.—we must, as a society, follow traditional Western values.[40]

Functionality carries five meanings, according to Michael Schwartz, an FCF vice president. First, what is functionally true for society is not the market but culture. Secondly, if cultural values are functionally true, cultural conservatives do not need to convince people that they are good, but only that empirically they work. Moreover, functional values lead to coalition building because everyone wants a society that works. Functionality also allows the Right to appropriate the ideas of the Left—e.g., the appeal of environmentalism—without rejecting them entirely.[41] Last, functionality means that theory must be put into practice. Or, as Weyrich observes, ideas have consequences *only when* they are connected to action. Asking himself how conservatives can "put feet" on their theory, Lind answers that conservatism has to have a positive vision of the America it wants, an agenda, a grassroots movement, and a leader. Cultural conservatism supplies the vision and the agenda.[42]

Cultural conservatism's agenda is to reform the institutions responsible for transmitting Western culture, those that another group of conservative theorists have called mediating structures: families, schools, churches, neighborhoods, labor unions, professional associations, business, service organizations, and the media. "Stand[ing] between the individual citizen and government," these structures are more effective than government in dealing with social-cultural problems because they are more personal and adaptive to individual needs.[43] In their reform, cultural conservatives believe that government should play an important "role in exemplifying traditional values, preaching them, and, in some cases, enforcing them."[44] Thus the FCF agenda "reflects a certain governmental [as well as citizen] activism," and the challenge is to promote this activism without "generating Federal bureaucracies to 'manage' the resulting programs."[45] Accordingly, FCF policy recommendations would increase the federal regulation of institutions, while reassigning some federal functions to individuals. For instance, FCF recommends that the federal government require public schools to teach the basics, test students and teachers, and impose discipline, while at the same time that it legalize school choice, which would give parents tax vouchers to pay for the education of their children in private, religious, or public schools.

Breaking the Liberal Monopoly of Higher Education

To break what they perceived as the liberal monopoly of higher education, conservatives needed to establish a cultural presence in the conservative policy-oriented think tanks and also a conservative presence in the liberalized academic institutions. T. Kenneth Cribb, president of the Intercollegiate Studies Institute (ISI), which promotes cultural conservatism to students and faculty, put it astutely in a lecture to the Heritage Foundation:

> We must thus provide resources and guidance to an elite which can take up anew the task of enculturation. Through its journals, lectures, seminars, books, and fellowships, this is what ISI has done successfully for thirty-six years. The coming of age of such elites has provided the current leadership of the conservative revival. But we should add a major new component to our strategy: the conservative movement is now mature enough to sustain a counteroffensive on that last Leftist redoubt, the college campus. ... We are now strong enough to establish a contemporary presence for conservatism on campus, and contest the Left on its own turf. We plan to do this by greatly expanding the ISI field effort, its network of campus-based programming.[46]

Conservatives realized that the move would not succeed if they used outsiders to force change upon an academy whose independence from external political interference is traditionally acknowledged (though not always observed in practice) in this country. Rather, the move had to occur both within and against the academy.

The organization initially most successful in moving the attack into the academy is the Madison Center for Educational Affairs (MCEA), formed from a 1990 merger of the Institute for Educational Affairs (IEA) and the Madison Center.[47] It has achieved success largely through its Student Journalism Program, which sponsors the Collegiate Network of seventy conservative student newspapers on sixty-six campuses across the country. "With a combined circulation of more than 600,000," the MCEA writes, "Collegiate Network publications remain the most potent catalyst for debate on college campuses."[48] In this assessment, it is correct. Most of the well-known debates on race, gender, sexuality, and leftism in the academy were catalyzed by these newspapers, as the particularly virulent example of the *Dartmouth Review* attests.[49] Less known, however, is that most of the newspapers have published curriculum surveys, the first appearing in the *Brown Spectator, Harvard Salient, Dartmouth Review,* and *Federalist Paper* (Columbia) in 1988, and have attacked curricular innovations, such as the University of Texas composition course.[50]

Generously supporting the Collegiate Network, MCEA makes direct grants to the newspapers (nearly $200,000 in 1991); provides editorial and technical assistance; maintains a toll-free hotline for advice; publishes *Newslink,* a monthly newsletter; distributes free of charge the publications of CN Friends, a group of more than eighty conservative policy organizations and magazines (including the Heritage Foundation, *National Review,* and *American Spectator*); gives monthly cash awards for student writing; holds regional conferences for newspaper staffs; distributes free of charge the "book of the month" (past books include Sykes's *Hollow Men,* D'Souza's *Illiberal Education,* and Chester L. Finn, Jr.'s *We Must Take Charge*); and makes referrals to the Washington Legal Center and the Center for Individual Rights (on CIR, see below). Through another program, Editorial Internships, it provides summer, semester, and year-long internships for college students at federal offices (NEH, Department of Commerce, Office of the Vice President), conservative organizations (Bradley Foundation, Freedom House), and conservative publications (*New Republic, National Interest, Public Interest, Academic Questions, Policy Review*).[51]

Fueling the attack, MCEA publishes the *Common Sense Guide to American Colleges,* which evaluates the academic and political climate at colleges and universities. Its questionnaires ask administrators, faculty, and students specifically about aggressive affirmative action programs, need-blind admissions and need-based scholarships, abortion counseling, special-interest organizations ("women, Asian, homosexual, etc."), campus controversy about Eurocentrism, opposition to a core curriculum, "courses used for political indoctrination," speech and behavior codes, and "an ideologically diverse mix of speakers."[52] The slant, highlighting issues provocative to conservatives, is more apparent in the faculty and student questionnaires, perhaps because they are mailed to NAS members and conservative student-newspaper staffs.[53]

Finally, MCEA provides grants to scholars working on books—among them, D'Souza for *Illiberal Education* and a new book on "the political, moral, and cultural contributions of Western civilization"; Paul Hollander for a book on "the sources of disillusionment with Communist systems"; and Tamara Jacoby for a book on "American race relations" (see note 7). MCEA's interest in "race relations" informs its Diversity Program, which holds national meetings for minority students, featuring such speakers as Clarence Thomas and Linda Chavez, formerly with the U.S. Commission on Civil Rights, and publishes *Diversity: A Criti-*

cal Journal of Race and Culture, a quarterly magazine written "for people who don't remember the 60s."[54] *Diversity* and the Collegiate Network newspapers reformulate and circulate the vanguard-movement issues that FCF believes conservatives must appropriate.

The roster of MCEA associates suggests how movement reticulation is used to bring cultural conservatism into the academy. The founders, officers, and board members all are affiliated with other right-wing organizations. Long-time IEA president Leslie Lenkowsky is now president of the Hudson Institute (a right-wing think tank) and an NAS member. Madison Center founder William J. Bennett was the NEH chairman, is a fellow at the Hudson Institute and the Heritage Foundation, and recently was appointed the chairman of National Empowerment Television, a Free Congress Foundation project. The Madison Center's first president, John Agresto, and MCEA's first president, Chester Finn, are NAS members and former Bennett associates respectively at the NEH and the Department of Education. With such reticulation across right-wing organizations and the federal government, it is no surprise that then NEH Chairman Cheney wrote a feature article, "Depoliticizing the Academy," for *Newslink* (the Collegiate Network's newsletter), provided summer internships at the NEH, and spoke at MCEA conferences.[55] Board members are similarly affiliated: John Bunzel (Hoover Institution and NAS member), T. Kenneth Cribb (president of ISI), Irving Kristol (NAS member; and see note 3), Harvey Mansfield, Jr. (NAS member and NEH National Council member; see below), and Jeremiah Milbank (JM Foundation). MCEA associates, together with representatives from other right-wing organizations, serve on the advisory boards of Collegiate Network newspapers. The *Dartmouth Review* advisory board—which includes Martin Anderson (Hoover Institution), Patrick Buchanan, William Lind (FCF), William Rusher (*National Review*), R. Emmett Tyrrell (*American Spectator*), and the "Old Right" intellectuals M. E. Bradford, George Gilder, and Russell Kirk—is more illustrious than most, but even the *Fenwick Review* (College of the Holy Cross) advisory board includes Buchanan, Rusher, D'Souza, and Michael Novak (AEI). Those newspapers lacking advisory boards do not lack supporters; the *Wake Forest Critic* gives special thanks to MCEA, Joseph A. Shea, Jr. (Center for Individual Rights; see below), and the Heritage Foundation.

The attack on the academy from without and within is only half of the strategy to break what conservatives believe is a liberal monopoly of higher education. The immediate goal is to transform the higher-education system into a free-market economy by weakening liberal institutions and strengthening conservative ones. These moves are supposed to work together to create a marketplace of competing institutions—public and private, Christian and secular, conservative and liberal. If all institutions are placed in a market economy, their viability can be determined by those who, through their individual choices, can reorient the market. That conservatives have reasonable hopes of creating and reorienting the market is expressed by Michael P. McDonald, president of the Center for Individual

Rights (see below). He is opposed to litigation requiring academic institutions to
be hospitable to a diversity of opinion on their campuses because

> a sounder view would emphasize not the diversity *within* each institution but the di-
> versity *among* them. The goal should be to maximize the range of choices, particularly
> with regard to educational mission. Instead of having courts superintend higher edu-
> cation, we should rely on contractual remedies and informed individual choice to
> safeguard against political zealotry and oppression. A private university with a repu-
> tation for and a record of intolerance will not for long retain good scholars—or moti-
> vated students. Administrators and faculty at the diminishing number of institutions
> that value traditional scholarship should concentrate on building and preserving
> their academic programs, not on opening them up to every passing fad. The simple
> exhortation to "build and preserve" and keep the courts at bay may sound harsh to
> the victims of PC zealotry. But the Supreme Court and Congress have already
> breached the walls of institutional academic freedom in cases involving claims of ra-
> cial discrimination and sexual harassment. By doing so, they have opened a Pandora's
> Box of litigation: any academic who is denied an appointment or a promotion or ten-
> ure—and who happens to be female or a minority—can march into court with a
> prima facie legal case.[56]

The obvious rationale against litigating to achieve a stronger conservative presence on campuses—that it is a double-edge sword—is not the one I want to emphasize. Rather, the implicit rationale informing McDonald's position is that conservatives can use the free-market economic model as a strategy for seizing at least
some means of cultural production and then competing effectively in that market.

How will they do so? On one hand, they will "build and preserve" conservative
institutions, as McDonald suggests, and, on the other hand, they will weaken liberal ones. Already, as education activists, they have won seats on school and university boards, pressured textbook publishers, and formed groups (i.e., Accuracy
in Academe) that monitor education in order to make its content more conservative. As education lobbyists, they promote school-choice legislation in order to
shift the decision-point for funding education from the federal government,
which has refused to support private and religious schools, to parents, who would
be free to do so. Their claim that not only conservatives but also inner-city minorities are dissatisfied with public schools suggests that one result of school-choice
would be to depopulate and thereby defund public schools. While higher-education funding is a more complicated situation, a number of conservative proposals—such as reducing student aid, prohibiting minority scholarships, permitting
competing accrediting associations, and awarding federal funding to conservative
projects—would weaken the liberalizing trends in the academy and redirect resources to conservative institutions. Such projects, I will argue next, are products
of the same right-wing apparatus that produced the PC debate.

III. The Right-Wing Apparatus

Given its agenda for cultural conservatism and its free-market strategy, we should
see conservatism not merely as a reticulated movement, but as a massive appara-

tus consisting of several institutional systems variously articulated to produce cultural change. The systems, which I review next, are think tanks, training programs, foundations, grassroots organizations, and legal centers.

The Think-Tank System

While some conservative think tanks existed before 1975, notably the Hoover Institution (1919), the American Enterprise Institute (1943), and the Heritage Foundation (1973), dozens of national ones were established by the mid-1980s and have been augmented in recent years by some fifty-five state-level think tanks. The state think tanks, regional legal centers, and National Rifle Association belong to the Madison Group, which was launched by the American Legislative Exchange Council (ALEC), an organization of 2,400 conservative state officeholders that "hopes to wrest control of state government from what it sees as Leftist domination."[57] Although state think tanks vary in their projects, they strongly support free-market enterprise and privatization of everything from education to garbage. Modeled on the Heritage Foundation (which holds annual training meetings for state policy activists), the state think tanks aggressively market their policy recommendations and themselves to state governments (for Heritage marketing, see below).[58]

National think tanks were originally conceived as "planning and advisory institutions" on government policy that would influence the "nation's formal political processes"[59] by publishing policy studies, holding seminars for political and business leaders, and banking the resumés of potential conservative appointees to government and judicial positions. The most influential ones during the Reagan and Bush administrations were AEI and Heritage. In 1985, for instance, AEI "had 176 people on staff, ninety adjunct scholars, and a budget of $12.6 million. Thirty-four people from AEI were named to administration posts," and, more important, their ideas were being turned into policy.[60] Heritage had "a staff of 105, a budget of $10.5 million, and thirty-six of its people had been appointed to administration jobs."[61] The traffic also has flowed the other way, with Reagan administration officials becoming think-tank staff and fellows. Among the Distinguished Fellows now at Heritage are Richard V. Allen, former Assistant to the President for National Security Affairs; William J. Bennett, former NEH Chairman and Secretary of Education; and Edwin Meese III, former Attorney General.[62]

Although AEI subsequently was defunded and retrenched because its right-wing backers judged it too centrist,[63] Heritage has continued to expand. In 1991, it had 145 people on staff, 22 fellows and scholars, more than 50 adjunct scholars, and a budget of $19.3 million,[64] which is remarkable for its wide base of support: 50 percent of its income was contributed by 170,000 individual donors solicited through direct mail, 25 percent by foundations, and 13 percent by corporations, with the remaining 12 percent derived from investments and sales. Among the foundations supporting Heritage (as well as other right-wing organizations) are Lynde and Harry Bradley, Adolph Coors, Samuel Roberts Noble, John H. Olin, Reader's Digest, and Sara Scaife.[65]

To produce and distribute its ideas, Heritage draws on the experts listed in *The Annual Guide to Public Policy Experts* and its own nearly 200 publications a year. In 1990, the *Annual Guide* listed "1,500 conservative scholars whose expertise [was] catalogued in 70 subfields," and in 1992 it listed 2,000 scholars whose expertise was catalogued in 77 subfields. Beginning in 1993, the *Annual Guide* will be available on CD-ROM, and all Heritage publications will be available on a subscription computer network.[66] As these numbers suggest, Heritage has been as effective in distributing as in producing its ideas. Edwin J. Feulner, Jr., president of the Heritage Foundation, explains: "We don't just stress credibility. ... We stress an efficient, effective delivery system. Production is one side; marketing is equally important."[67] The delivery system consists of four marketing divisions; Public Relations markets ideas to the media and the public; Government Relations to Congress, the Executive branch, and government agencies; Academic Relations to the university community, Resource Bank institutions (including state think tanks), and the international conservative network; and Corporate Relations to businesses and trades. Division marketing is coordinated at twice-weekly meetings of the senior management, but policy research drives the marketing process.[68]

How the marketing works, according to Blumenthal's research, is that "every congressional staffer is in the Heritage computer. So are about 3,500 journalists, organized by specialty. Every Heritage study goes out with a synopsis to those who might be interested; every study is turned into an op-ed piece, distributed by the Heritage Features Syndicate to newspapers that publish them."[69] The goal is to get the message to the media and the public, who, in turn, get it to policymakers. Feulner's comments are not fanciful capitalist rhetoric. Through the Heritage marketing model, adopted by other organizations, the Right has deployed, in the words of one writer, an "ideas industry"[70] in which a cadre of professional right-wingers use think tanks, interest groups, and media to produce and distribute conservative ideas.

To cite a specific example, in June 1989 Heritage published *A National Health System for America* detailing its Consumer Choice Health Care Plan, a "market-based pricing system" of health insurance. According to the plan, the existing system of government- and employer-provided health insurance would be replaced by tax relief that would encourage individuals to cover routine medical expenses and buy catastrophe insurance. "Under such a system," Heritage claims, "prices would be set through the market choices of those who can afford to buy their own health-care protection. In the present system, prices are set arbitrarily by government and health-care providers, divorced from market initiatives."[71] By the summer of 1992, the Heritage plan "was ranked as one of the three options seriously being considered by Washington policy-makers, and won high praise from *The Economist, New Republic, National Review,* and *Forbes.*"[72]

How was the Heritage plan transformed from a 127-page monograph to a leading option? First, Heritage gave an exclusive to the *Washington Post* and, when the story appeared, was contacted by the media. Then, simultaneously, it made a number of moves to market the plan. Public Relations distributed news releases, the monograph, and the *Washington Post* story to 40 nationally syndicated columnists, 600 opinion-page editors, and 1,100 health-care reporters at every major daily paper in the nation. Government Relations delivered the monograph, the *Washington Post* newsclip, and a cover letter to members of Congress and health-care staffers, and the authors of the monograph held meetings with congressional staffers and HHS officials to explain the plan. As newspaper endorsements appeared, they were sent to Congressional delegations from the appropriate states (e.g., the *Tampa Tribune* endorsement went to the Florida delegation).[73] Similarly, Corporate and Academic Relations distributed materials to their audiences. In addition, Heritage also distributed research papers favorably contrasting its plan to other health-care plans and targeted overviews of the plan to the elderly and low-income minorities. Next, it released a study of the plan's financing, which, according to Lewin/ICF computer projections, would reduce total health-care spending by $11 billion in the first year, and distributed this study to the media and legislators. Presumably, the final phase will be Heritage-organized lobbying for the plan once it is introduced as congressional legislation.[74]

This example not only details the marketing process, but also suggests a shift in focus. Although Heritage, as a staff member pointed out, originally focused on "bombs and bucks" (i.e., foreign and economic policy), it launched several cultural projects in the late 1980s at the behest (and through the funding) of conservative foundations that it should pay attention to the breakdown of families, communities, and values.[75] These projects include the Bradley Scholars, the Conservative Curriculum, the Salvatori Center for Academic Leadership, and the Cultural Policy Studies Program. The purpose of the latter project is "to bring cultural issues into the mainstream of political debate, and to articulate the traditional values that should more fully influence American culture." William J. Bennett, recently named Distinguished Fellow in Cultural Policy Studies, is "examining how federal policies and programs affect American culture, and, in turn, how American culture affects federal policies and programs."[76] The members of its bimonthly Working Group represent other conservative organizations: think tanks (AEI, Hudson Institute, Ethics and Public Policy Center, Center for Educational Policy), media (Media Research Center, WABC Radio, *National Review*), grass roots organizations (Eagle Forum, Citizens Democracy Corps, Traditional Values Coalition [TVC]), and the federal government (staff from the offices of former Vice President Dan Quayle, Senator Jesse Helms, Representative William Dannemeyer, and HHS). The Working Group provided the former vice president with resource materials on Murphy Brown's single motherhood and the Los Angeles riots, helped to raise the congressional debate on speech codes on campus, and, through the TVC, was instrumental in Justice Clarence Thomas's confirmation.[77] The structure and work of the Cultural Policy Studies Program indicate that Heritage has applied its research-and-marketing advocacy model in the cultural arena.

This brief summary shows that cultural conservatives have used think tanks to produce the "expert" knowledge they could not generate from within the academy. They have done so by conflating "expertise" as pertains to knowledge produced by scholarly methods and "expertise" as pertains to the aura of authority surrounding those who produce this knowledge. In this way, the think tanks have constituted an "academicized" aura of authority upon which conservatives have capitalized to advance their political agenda. In actuality, as one writer remarks, most national think tanks grew from "the ideological combat and policy confusion of the past two decades" and "are geared toward political activism and propaganda, rather than toward scholarship,"[78] but they market their ideas through a scholarly apparatus of journals and seminars as if they were the products of scholarship. The result is not merely the misrepresentation of think-tank knowledge as scholarly knowledge but also a deterioration in the value of academic disciplines. Peter Weingart explains that when "scientific" knowledge is produced in these other institutions, science loses "a common frame of value-orientations and beliefs as well as a common basis of interests among scientific and technical experts. Their involvement in politics, which has been interpreted as a 'scientification' of politics, turns out to be the 'politicization' of [academic] science at the same time. The professional status of [academic] science with its sharp delineation from other social institutions, its self-governance with respect to quality standards, criteria of relevance and a code of ethics becomes subject to political conflicts."[79] Although Weingart stresses the changes to academic science (the erosion of its self-governance and in turn its standards), I wish to stress the changes in the economy of knowledge production. When "scientific knowledge," which has been produced by academic institutions, also seems to be produced by think tanks, the likely result is competition among "scientific" knowledges in policy-making and public arenas. Since science is generally regarded as having great authority, the competing "scientific" knowledges are likely to be readily consumed by policymakers and other publics without much critical analysis to differentiate them.

Although think tanks can be used to break the academic monopoly on the production of "expert" knowledge, they do not have the capacity to produce the "experts" themselves. Indeed, when Patrick Buchanan recommended establishing the Heritage Foundation, he argued in a 1972 memo to President Nixon "that the most pressing need" for conservatives "was to create 'a new "cadre" of Republican governmental professionals who can survive this Administration and be prepared to take over future ones.' As Buchanan saw it, one of the main difficulties was 'credentialitis.' "[80] Think tanks do not produce "experts" because they do not control the training and credentialing practices that early in this century moved within the purview of the higher-education system. Consequently, conservatives have appropriated these practices by establishing training institutes.

The Training-Program System

Next, I will discuss two training institutes, the Leadership Institute and the National Journalism Center, that overlap in their ideologies, goals, and programs.

The purpose of the Leadership Institute (LI), founded by Morton Blackwell in 1979, is to increase the number and effectiveness of conservative activists, which it does through nine schools that offer training programs in youth leadership, grass roots organizing, organizational leadership, direct-mail fundraising and mobilizing, preparation for the Foreign Service examination, Capitol Hill staffing, legislative management, broadcast journalism, and student publications.[81] Notice that four schools train conservatives for the movement and five train them for the professions. LI pursues the double strategy of strengthening the conservative movement by putting *professionals* into it and weakening the liberal professions by putting *conservatives* into them. This strategy is reflected in its recruitment of students through conservative organizations and publications[82] and its Job and Talent Bank that places "philosophically sound, technically proficient" conservatives in public-policy positions.[83] Can the strategy succeed? LI offered thirty-three training programs in 1992 and graduated a record 1,002 students in 1991, for a total of 3,950 from 1987 through 1991.[84] Its 1990 estimated income was $1,119,180, and its wide base of support resembles that of the Heritage Foundation: sixty-one percent of its income is from individual donors, twenty-five percent from foundations, seven percent from restricted contributions, and the remaining seven percent from school income and interest.[85]

The purpose of the National Journalism Center (NJC), founded in 1976–77 under the auspices of the Education and Research Institute (ERI), is to "help talented young people break into the media." NJC, which believes that media training should occur "within the framework of traditional educational values,"[86] provides six weeks of training in journalism and "common-sense economics" (students write weekly "spot news" stories, attend Friday seminars, and complete a magazine story), followed by six-week internships at NJC's four dozen outlets. The program is designed to correct what NJC sees as the liberal bias of journalism as it is taught in universities and practiced in the media, and to supply college graduates with the experience they lack when they apply for entry-level journalism jobs. Offering the program four times a year to a total of sixty to eighty students, NJC estimated in 1990 that "500 of our alumni are working in media and media-related posts" at AP, UPI, ABC, CBS, CNN, C-SPAN, Copely News Service, the *Washington Post, Washington Times, Wall Street Journal, Detroit News, Los Angeles Times, San Francisco Chronicle, Seattle Times, Richmond Times-Dispatch, Phoenix Gazette,* a number of magazines, and virtually every conservative periodical.[87]

The Internal Revenue Service has granted these two institutes the tax-exempt status of educational organizations. Section 501(c)(3) of the *Internal Revenue Code* allows exemption to "corporations and any community chest, fund, or foundation, organized and operated exclusively for religious, charitable, scientific, testing for public safety, literary, or educational purposes" and denies exemption to organizations in which "a substantial part of the activities" consists of "carrying on propaganda, or otherwise attempting, to influence legislation" or "participating in, or intervening in, any political campaign on behalf of (or in opposition to) any candidate for public office."[88] An organization not operated exclusively for tax-exempt purposes and engaging in the proscribed activities is termed an "action" organization, whether, for instance, it attempts itself to influence legislation or "urges the public to contact, members of a legislative body for the purpose of proposing, supporting, or opposing legislation," or even "advocates the adoption or rejection of legislation." The term "legislation" includes action by Congress, state legislatures, local councils, and public referendum, initiative, constitutional amendment, or a similar procedure.[89]

While claiming to be nonpartisan in that they support no parties, candidates, or legislation, LI and NJC are not nonpolitical. Their political work is not, insofar as I have observed, to directly influence legislation and elections but rather to influence those who mediate these processes—the media, political organizers and activists, and conservative citizens. For instance, in a direct-mail letter asking for a tax-deductible contribution to LI, Representative Dick Armey plays on conservative fears about the liberal media and professionalizing practices in journalism:

> ... While you read this letter, left-wing journalism professors are preparing their new crop of media radicals. ... College journalism departments in every single state graduate a steady stream of young left-wingers. And send them out to manage the news.
> ... Upon graduation, these young liberals move to professional journalism. That's how they perpetuate the Left's dominance of the media.[90]

By contrast, LI, he writes, "*trains young conservative activists to lead the fight against big media liberal bias on and off campus.*"[91] In other words, LI's function is to produce conservative activists who will influence the media and through them influence political processes. While one might argue that Representative Armey's rhetoric may not reflect LI's practice, my observation of LI's Broadcast Journalism School suggests that it does.

In practice, the Broadcast Journalism School insisted on the liberal bias of mainstream media and the need to counter it. The book, one third of the readings packet, and some of the handouts given to the students asserted only one point of view—that the media have a liberal bias.[92] While the term "bias" appeared in the title of only one of the sessions,[93] the presenters in several sessions promoted this point of view. For instance, in the "Interviewing" session, Tim Goeglein, Press Secretary to Senator Dan Coats, explained that media bias occurs not because liberals get together and decide how to run the country, but rather because the kind of people the media attract—those from broken homes and with social problems—have liberal interests. When a student asked whether conservatives are trying to change media coverage or trying to change the profession, Geoglein replied that if you do the second, the first will follow.[94]

Video newsclips shown at the school were used to reinforce the claim of media bias rather than to critically evaluate it. For instance, Brent Baker, Executive Director of the Media Research Center, showed a newsclip on the Earth Summit in Rio and argued that it represented only one point of view. Most scientists, he asserted without any supporting evidence, do not believe that increased levels of

CO_2 are caused by environmental pollution; rather they believe that increased CO_2 is occurring naturally and that the resulting warmup has some good consequences, such as extending the growing season in Alaska. "Fair and balanced" news coverage, he argued, would report that liberal environmentalists have one opinion concerning the effects of CO_2 and scientists have another. His argument rests on a rhetorical slippage: it implicitly portrays liberal environmentalists as political activists who have opinions and pits them against scientists who have facts. This argument not only is partial in that it fails to present full and fair coverage of the positions and the facts pertinent to them, but also is part of the deprofessionalizing strategy pursued by LI and NJC (see below).

While "fair and balanced coverage" is a phrase I heard frequently at the Broadcast Journalism School, it did not characterize the session on "Office Politics" conducted by Amy Noble, Special Projects Manager at the Federal News Service.[95] Her session consisted almost entirely of a role-playing exercise. Giving the students a script from a McLaughlin show on the *Webster* case, Noble had them play out conservative strategies that local news teams might use in responding to the pro-choice position. The strategies—defending the pro-life position, attacking the pro-choice position, etc.—all asserted the pro-life position. Missing were "fair and balanced coverage" and critical analysis of both positions, so that in actuality the exercise was political, not educational, training.

My observation of the NJC's Friday seminar on "common-sense economics" reporting confirms this institute's similarly conservative political practice. While NJC staff stress that reporting should deliver accurate, balanced, and complete information, the seminar I attended belies this standard. Jeff Tucker, associate editor of the *Free Market* (a newsletter published by the Ludwig Von Mises Institute) and an NJC alumnus, cited poll results (whether actual or fictive, I could not tell) on the "fairness" of wage-and-price decisions: e.g., in response to the question, "Is it fair for vendors to raise flower prices on a holiday?" he reported that sixty percent of Moscovites and eighty percent of New Yorkers said it was unfair. Ridiculing New Yorkers as more socialist than Moscovites, Tucker's explicit point was to equate liberal and socialist economics, and his implicit point was to convey their inferiority to conservative free-market economics. As the FCF has observed elsewhere, "Liberals have been perceived as people concerned primarily with fairness, with seeing that the fruits of prosperity were shared by all segments of society. Conservatives were seen as those concerned mainly with economic freedom and with increasing the common prosperity by spurring economic growth."[96] Thus, in the second part of his talk, Tucker asserted that in a free market the price system "equilibrates" consumer desires with what is being produced. "Fairness," he argued, has to do not with pricing decisions that may prevent some consumers from buying products but rather with the freedom of parties to contract on the market. Rhetorically, his appropriation stripped "fairness" of its liberal moral considerations and made it an operating condition of the conservative free-market system. Substantively, his simplistic account of conservative free-market economics was unaccompanied by critical analysis or alternative economic models, and student questions, rather than challenging the account, only elicited further elaboration of it.[97]

These brief examples suggest that LI and NJC are not primarily educational organizations and should not have tax-exempt status. The *Internal Revenue Code* stipulates that "an organization may be educational even though it advocates a particular position or viewpoint so long as it presents a sufficiently full and fair exposition of the pertinent facts as to permit an individual or the public to form an independent opinion or conclusion. On the other hand, an organization is not educational if its principal function is the mere presentation of unsupported opinion."[98] Armey's opinion on left-wing dominance of the media, Baker's opinion on the effects of CO_2 and the status of liberal environmentalists, Noble's pro-life role-playing exercise, Tucker's "common-sense economics," as well as many other instances that could have been cited—all exemplify the presentation of unsupported opinion and the failure to give full and fair exposition that, according to the *Internal Revenue Code,* disqualify an organization for educational status and tax exemption. LI and NJC are, in actuality, political organizations engaged in political contest. As William Forrest, then an LI vice president put it, "The outcome of political contest over time is determined by the number and effectiveness of the activists on either side. ... To some extent, what we do at this Institute is to try to increase the number and effectiveness of the activists who are conservative." The LI, he added, does what is not done by higher-education institutions; conservatives believe that these institutions serve only certain political views and not others. That's what the fight is about.[99]

LI and NJC are also professionalizing institutions intent on breaking the academic monopoly of professionalization. Paradoxically, they use antiprofessional critique both to attack academic professionalization and to advance their own brand. How do they manage this sleight-of-hand? Speaking at a Friday seminar, Ralph Bennett, senior Washington editor of *Reader's Digest,* warned NJC students not to think of journalism as a profession; there isn't much about journalism, he explained, that you can't learn during two weeks on the job. As an editor, he is less interested in potential employees' training in a journalism school than in their grounding in literature, history, and the Bible. Without such grounding, he opined, journalists are the slaves of whoever gives them information.[100] Chris Warden, an NJC editor, likewise added that journalism is not a profession but a craft. A profession has a body of knowledge unique to its practice, whereas journalism does not. Aspiring journalists "can learn the techniques, skills, tricks of the trade" easily because they are almost formulaic. What they need is general and common-sense knowledge.[101] The general knowledge, it would seem, is conservative, and the common-sense knowledge is the free-market economics explained by Tucker.

By describing journalism as an easily learned craft and thus deprofessionalizing it, LI and NJC delegitimate university training (no need for universities to train students in what are only technical skills) and legitimate their own training (superficial skills can be learned in a few weeks). At the same time that they attack academic professionalization, they use their superficial programs to professionalize cadres of young conservatives by giving them credentials to move into the professions. Moreover, their goal of breaking the liberal monopoly of professions articulates to the larger conservative goal of breaking the liberal monopoly of higher education. Such articulation is enabled not only by rhetoric and practices, but also by the flow of money that supports them.

The Foundation System

In the mid-1980s, conservative foundations put their resources behind the shift to cultural and academic change.[102] This shift can be seen by examining recent funding patterns. One way to look at funding patterns is in terms of a range of grantees and grantors. Here is a grantee sampling for 1989 of some of the organizations mentioned in this chapter.[103]

> *American Spectator:* total $234,000—Bradley, $29,000; Coors, $10,000; Noble, $10,000; Olin, $25,000; Scaife, $115,000; Smith Richardson, $45,000
> *National Review:* total $342,000—Bradley, $200,000; Olin, $42,000; Scaife, $100,000
> *New Criterion:* total $245,000—Newhouse, $20,000; Olin, $100,000; Scaife, $125,000
> Center for Individual Rights (for 1989): total $115,000—JM, $25,000; Smith Richardson, $90,000; (for 1990): total $165,000—Bradley, $25,000; Olin, $50,000; Smith Richardson, $90,000[104]
> Free Congress Foundation: total $710,000—Bradley, $330,000; Coors, $150,000; DeMoss, $90,000; McKenna, $15,000; Noble, $100,000; Olin, $25,000
> Institute for Educational Affairs (before MCEA merger): total $411,902—Achelis, $20,000; Bodman, $30,000; Bradley, $118,000; Coors, $12,000; Kirby, $25,500; Olin, $121,402; Ryder, $15,000; Scaife, $60,000; Warner-Lambert, $10,000
> Madison Center (before MCEA merger): total $555,000—Bradley, $525,000; Olin, $30,000
> Leadership Institute: total $115,000—Bradley, $45,000; Coors, $25,000; Murdock, $45,000
> National Association of Scholars: total $611,200—Coors, $10,000; Olin, $125,000; Smith Richardson, $176,200; Scaife, $300,000
> National Journalism Center: total $110,000—Coors, $25,000; O'Donnell, $25,000; Olin, $25,000; Reader's Digest, $35,000
> National Endowment for the Humanities Jefferson Lecture: total $30,000—Bradley, $15,000; Olin, $15,000

The obvious pattern is that a handful of right-wing foundations—particularly Bradley, Coors, JM, Noble, Olin, Scaife, and Smith Richardson—support those publications and organizations that have been instrumental in the attack on liberalized higher education.

But the grantees are only part of the story. The particular cultural projects funded, Paul Gottfried explains in a book chapter appropriately titled "Funding an Empire," are those that carry out the agenda of foundations controlled by neoconservatives. Originally established by paleoconservative (or anti–New Deal) families, these foundations have been taken over by neoconservative staff who now make decisions to fund those projects that advance cultural conservatism. Gottfried, himself a traditional conservative, writes:

> Without the administrative staffs of Bradley, Olin, Smith Richardson, and Sara Scaife, there would be no operative agenda of "cultural conservatism" being implemented in New York and Washington. While cultural conservatives—i.e., critics of modern society—would undoubtedly still have a forum, there would be no organized activity for positions that foundation heads have decided to call "culturally conservative." ... The shaping of cultural conservatism is now bringing economic benefits to political activists who have discovered a market for "values." For example, the head of the Free Congress Foundation, Paul Weyrich, receives hundreds of thousands of dollars annually from the Bradley, Olin, and Roe foundations. In return, Weyrich goes beyond functioning as a mere congressional lobbyist and serves as a spokesman for an activist political agenda based on "Judeo-Christian values." Breaking with the traditional conservative emphasis on limited government, he calls for governmental programs to promote cultural conservatism across the country.[105]

Gottfried adds, "In their own view, neoconservatives and their allies have seized foundations to influence culture and in turn shape politics. Observing the Left's 'long march through the institutions,' neoconservatives have begun their own march, producing official positions on educational, religious, and aesthetic questions and hiring or coopting advocates to publicize their stands."[106]

Another way to look at funding patterns is in terms of one foundation. Over the years, the Olin Foundation has generously funded conservative academic projects—for instance, conservative institutes (e.g., the Social Philosophy and Policy Center at Bowling Green State University, the Center for the Study of Social and Political Change at Smith College, and the Olin Center for Inquiry into the Theory and Practice of Democracy at the University of Chicago), academic lecture series, and also professorships at various universities for conservative scholars, who in turn train conservative graduate students, some supported by Olin postdocs. In 1989, Olin awarded the following amounts to these few institutions selected from a more comprehensive listing: Boston University, $817,352 (some to Peter L. Berger); George Mason University, $258,102 (some to James C. Miller III and Walter L. Williams); Harvard University, $1,261,745 (some to Harvey C. Mansfield and Samuel P. Huntington); Yale University, $2,118,598 as four three-year grants; University of Chicago, $1,495,934 (some to Allan Bloom); Stanford University, $1,190,533; and University of Rochester, $2,583,000 as a seven-year grant.[107] To cite a longitudinal example, "between 1986 and 1989," Allan Bloom, neoconservative University of Chicago professor and author of *The Closing of the American Mind,* "received from Olin over $3 million in mostly unrestricted gifts."[108] Gottfried makes the well-supported claim that the neoconservative professors associated with these academic projects have trained, or otherwise supported, many of those neoconservatives who now staff the very foundations that support their projects.

Moreover, detailing the "sumptuous lifestyle" enjoyed by recipients of foundation largesse, he points out that "neoconservative academics endowed by the four sisters [Bradley, Olin, Scaife, Smith Richardson] complain of their suffering at the hands of left-wing faculties, but few humanities scholars on the Left dispose of comparable financial resources. There can be no doubt that the widely published socialist scholar Judith Shklar received less financial support in the late eighties than her neoconservative colleagues in the same political science department at Harvard."[109]

A third way to look at funding patterns is in terms of the range of grantors to one grantee. Significant annual donors to the Heritage Foundation are classified in two categories: Associates, who give an annual gift of $10,000 or more, and Founders, who give an annual gift of $100,000 or more. For 1991, its 141 Associates include: corporations (Abbott, Amway, Ashland Oil, Bristol-Myers, Chase Manhattan Bank, Chevron, Dow, DuPont, Exxon, Ford, General Motors, Johnson and Johnson, Lilly, Lockheed, Mobil, Nestle, Pfizer, Philip Morris, Procter & Gamble, Quaker Oats, RJR Nabisco, Searle, Sears Roebuck, Squibb, Winn-Dixie Stores); corporate foundations (Alcoa, Amoco, FMC, GE, Hilton, Merck, Sunmark, UPS); other foundations (Anschutz, Brady, Gerstacker, JM, Kirby, Lauder, Lennon, Martin, McKenna, Pope, Taylor, Van Andel, Walker); and many individuals. For 1991, its twenty-five Founders included the usual right-wing foundations (Bradley, Coors, Noble, Olin, Pew, Reader's Digest, Scaife), as well as individuals and corporations associated with them. Donations from Coors, for instance, came from the Adolph Coors Company, the Adolph Coors Foundation, Mr. Joseph Coors, and Mrs. Holland Coors.[110]

Finally, funding patterns are telling in terms of the academic programs they support, such as two new ones at Heritage. The Bradley Resident Scholars Program, funded by the Bradley Foundation and established in 1987, brings young scholars who are "fully committed to an academic career" to Heritage "for periods of from five to ten months to conduct research, teach seminars, deliver public lectures, and learn firsthand about the policy process." They are usually selected from those working in the social sciences and humanities because the program "has a special interest in research on American political, social, and cultural institutions and the relationship of those institutions to the public policy process."[111] A 1991–92 Bradley Scholar, Laurence Jarvik, launched the conservative campaign to privatize public television not only through Heritage lectures and papers[112] but also through *Comint: Journal of the Committee on Media Integrity,* a quarterly newsletter published by the right-wing Center for the Study of Popular Culture in Los Angeles, which, under the direction of David Horowitz and Peter Collier, also promulgates its ideas through monographs and *Heterodoxy,* the new right-wing scandal-sheet attacking the academy. The Center is supported by the Bradley, JM, Olin, and Scaife foundations, as well as the National Association of Scholars, one of whose most vocal members, Christina Hoff Sommers, serves on the editorial board of *Comint* and contributes to *Heterodoxy.*

The purpose of the Salvatori Center for Academic Leadership, established in 1991 through a five-year $1 million grant from the Henry Salvatori Foundation, is to train conservatives as academic leaders. The Center selects "twenty-five young faculty and doctoral candidates in the social sciences and the humanities" to be Salvatori Fellows for two years. They participate in a summer colloquium and a spring Leadership Conference, which brings together "scholars, administrators, and leaders of organizations working for the renewal of American higher education."[113] Through such training, the leaders are expected to define the issues that, according to conservatives, higher education needs to address.

To define higher-education issues, Heritage employs the inside/outside strategy of raising the debate in academic venues, such as *Academic Questions* (the NAS journal) and its own Leadership Conference, and also through journalists and legislators.[114] Among the issues Heritage is defining are those listed in the Salvatori Center's Statement of Purpose: "the wholesale abandonment of our Western heritage," "the attack on standards today ... from the 'tenured radicals' on the faculty," and "those principles of free enterprise, of civil and religious liberty, and of human excellence that have lifted America to its present eminence." The Leadership Conference held in March 1992 featured, among others, Professors Abraham Miller, Peter Shaw, and Alan Gribben (all NAS members) on a panel titled "PC vs. Academic Freedom: Do Universities Know the Difference?"; and Edwin Meese III, Hadley Arkes (a Heritage Bradley Resident Scholar), and Michael Greve (Executive Director, Center for Individual Rights) on another titled "PC and Civil Liberties: Is Litigation the Answer?"[115] This interest in alleged violations of conservative academics' rights is a topic I shall address after discussing how the attack on liberalized higher education is advanced by grass roots organizing.

The Grass Roots System

Foundation resources may support the nonacademic institutionalization of cultural conservatism, conservative professionalizing practices, and the attack on higher education, but the ideas, practices, and attack also have to be legitimated by academics themselves. The work of legitimation is done by the National Association of Scholars (NAS), which presents itself as a grass roots academic organization. The NAS, which took its current title in 1987, evolved from a predecessor organization called the Coalition for Campus Democracy, which was founded in 1982 under the auspices of the right-wing Committee for the Free World and the IEA, whose associates were neoconservatives Irving Kristol, Midge Decter, Elliott Abrams, and William Simon, current president of the Olin Foundation. The NAS is, as the Coalition was, led by Stephen Balch and Herbert London and funded by right-wing foundations.[116] For FY 1990–91, the NAS received $520,611 from Bradley, Coors, JM, Olin, Scaife, Smith Richardson, Madison Center, and anonymous donors. For FY 1991–92, it estimated revenues of $682,830 from Bradley, Coors, Olin, Scaife, Smith Richardson, Joyce, Madison Center, and anonymous donors.[117]

The complex structure of the NAS—a national organization with some three thousand members, approximately thirty-five state chapters, campus chapters, caucuses within the disciplines, and international affiliates—performs several functions. In its scholarly guise, it holds conferences, publishes a journal, *Academic Questions,* and makes pronouncements about academic culture. Meanwhile, its political activities are wide-reaching. National headquarters mobilizes the membership to lobby government officials and churn out writings on the excesses of "tenured radicals." Its research center assembles the stories of alleged conservative victims of left-academic abuses and also is rumored to compile data on left academics. State chapters establish a conservative presence on campuses and give the appearance of grass roots faculty organizing, although, as is true for the Minnesota Association of Scholars, some were founded by nonacademic political conservatives. Through these activities, the NAS gives legislators and the public the impression that a substantial academic constituency opposes the liberalizing trends in higher education. But more insidious, its scholarly trappings "academicize" the products of the "ideas industry." By trading on the authority of scholarly knowledge, it legitimates cultural conservatism's ideas in the eyes of the public and thereby advances cultural conservatism's agenda.

The Regulatory System

Increasingly using the conservative legal centers that have sprung up across the country, conservatives are turning to the courts to change higher education. For instance, the Center for Individual Rights (CIR) was founded in 1989 by two former staff members of the conservative Washington Legal Foundation: Michael P. McDonald, CIR's president, and Michael S. Greve, its executive director. It differs from the Washington Legal Foundation, the Landmark Foundation, and other conservative legal centers by specializing in academic cases and entering them in the early stages rather than at the appeals level. By the time a case reaches the appeals level, Joseph A. Shea, Jr., a CIR counsel explained, it is "set"; the case has been crafted and the mistakes made. CIR, by contrast, helps to resolve a case before it reaches litigation or to craft it for litigation. To that end, it advises its clients on the rules of "self-defense." The first is to assume that one is battling alone. The second is to respond to all accusations, confront all accusers, get the accusations in writing, and appear on talk shows so the public can see the accused as a person with an opinion. The third rule is to document everything, thereby preparing to go to court even if the case is unlikely to end up there.

CIR focuses on academic cases where university administrators or influential department members are hostile to conservative faculty perspectives or to conservative student organizations, views, and acts. Most of its clients, according to Greve, CIR executive director, are " 'live white males' " targeted by the Left as politically incorrect,[118] and many have been referred by the NAS and MCEA.[119] Perhaps best known are two of the cases the CIR has won: *Levin v. Harleston,* in which Professor Michael Levin, an NAS member who has published "articles suggesting that blacks, on average, are less intelligent than whites," sued City College for creating a "shadow section" to steer students away from his course; and *Wide Awake v. University of Virginia,* which challenged the University of Virginia's refusal to allow student activity fees to fund a religious magazine.[120]

But more important for understanding CIR's activism are cases settled out of court. Among the faculty cases cited by Shea is a professor at the University of Alaska who was criticized as racist for observing in a public speech that she was under equity pressure to graduate unqualified Native American students.[121] The CIR newsletter explains it this way. When "someone, somewhere, filed a Title VI civil rights complaint" against the professor with the Office of Civil Rights (OCR), the CIR argued that the professor's "utterance constituted pure speech that could not possibly give rise to a Title VI violation," but OCR investigated the complaint. "Only after a lot of undignified foot-stomping and the usual threat of a lawsuit on our [CIR's] part, OCR concluded that an 'exchange of views' addressing issues of race or discrimination was not a violation of federal civil rights laws. Due to our vociferous protests, OCR reached this difficult conclusion in a mere twelve weeks."[122] Among the student cases is a conservative student group at Portland State University that refused membership to a lesbian-feminist student, who with her friends attended meetings and, according to Shea, attempted to "overwhelm the membership and change the group."[123] When the group refused membership to the student, she charged it with discrimination and the university, according to CIR, threatened to deregister and defund it. CIR and a "cooperating attorney" took up the case: "For several months, the University refused to budge, and we were looking forward to bring [*sic*] this matter to the attention of a federal court. Regrettably, we never got a chance; after mulling things over, University officials and the State AG [Attorney General] got round heels and keeled over. We take them any way we get them."[124]

Shea was frank about litigation: "Court is not something to be avoided; it may be the forum where truth comes out. Remember that academic 'goons' (repressors on campus) don't respond well to attorneys, who don't take facile answers. Remember, too, that educators and administrators are loathe to get on the stand; when they do, they tend to give convoluted answers rather than factual ones."[125] He returned to this point at a later date: "When you put some of these people on a witness stand and you ask questions for as long as you want to and you can demand truthful answers (or the witness goes to jail for contempt), that is a very enlightening experience for all involved."[126] As his comments and the CIR's newsletter suggest, both litigation and its threat are powerful weapons, though differently so. The threat of litigation is a powerful weapon for a university's out-of-court settlement with a CIR client because universities are reluctant to incur the costs of litigation. But the threat is even greater in the courtroom because there the attorney, not the administrator, knows how to speak the authorized discourse of simple, factual "truth" and thereby is able to strip the university of its authority to explain what are complex academic matters. The de-authorization of the university that would occur in a CIR-type case where a court rules for a plaintiff alleging discrimination would seem to contradict the authorization of the university that has occurred in numerous cases where courts ruled against plaintiffs alleging discrimination against a class (i.e., of women). In the former, a court would find that the university has discriminated against an individual; in the latter, the courts have found that the university, as a decentralized aggregation of departments, by definition could not discriminate against a class. While the two situations appear to be essentially different, what actually happens is similar. In both, the authority of the court, whether denying or affirming the university's position, supersedes the authority of the university and does so by failing to come to grips with the complexity of academic process.

The CIR has an annual income of $450,000, mostly supplied by the Bradley, JM, Olin, Scaife, Smith Richardson, and Wiegand foundations, and a staff of five.[127] However, its reach is more extensive than its budget suggests, because it arranges for attorneys, many from prestigious law firms, to represent its clients on a *pro bono* basis and obtains *amicus curiae* briefs from prominent organizations, such as the American Association of University Professors and the New York Civil Liberties Union. The CIR strategy of establishing judicial precedents for cultural conservatism is likely to be successful in a federal court system now packed with Reagan and Bush appointees.

To cite one more example of the conservative use of regulation to leverage change on liberalized higher education, then Secretary of Education Lamar Alexander, with the help of conservative appointees to his National Advisory Committee on Accreditation (in particular NAS members Christina Hoff Sommers and Martin Trow[128]), attacked the diversity standards of the Middle States Association. Alexander recommended that Middle States be de-authorized, that accrediting agencies be federally regulated, that credentialing be provided by a number of competitive agencies from which institutions may choose, and that institutional eligibility for federal student aid not be contingent upon accreditation. When Middle States agreed under pressure to make diversity standards optional for institutions, some commentators saw this "compromise" as the beginning of a federalization of peer accreditation.[129] In light of cultural conservatism's agenda, these attempts to reconstruct higher education through judicial precedent and government regulation must be seen not as responses to left-wing political correctness but as steps in the implementation of the right-wing agenda.

Some Products of the Ideas Industry

Roger Kimball's *Tenured Radicals* (1990) and Dinesh D'Souza's *Illiberal Education* (1991), to mention two popular attacks on liberalized higher education, should be seen as "ideas industry" products supported by right-wing foundations and "academicized" by the National Association of Scholars.

Soon after coming to this country in 1978, D'Souza attended Dartmouth College. He was a founder and editor of the *Dartmouth Review* (an MCEA Collegiate

Network student newspaper) when it stole and quoted from private correspondence of gay students. Next he was an editor of *Prospect,* a magazine funded by
conservative Princeton alumni, when it attacked women's studies and described,
without permission, the sex life of a female undergraduate student. After writing a
biography of Jerry Falwell, a founder of the Moral Majority, he was a domestic
policy analyst in the Reagan administration and an AEI employee.[130] His work on
Illiberal Education: The Politics of Race and Sex on Campus was supported partly by
a $30,000 grant from Olin, funneled to him in 1988 by the IEA,[131] by $70,000 from
Olin in 1990, and by another $20,000 from Olin, funneled to him by the Madison
Center (recall that the IEA and Madison were merged as MCEA).[132] The IEA, according to one journalist, served for years "as a 'clearing house,' making matches
between those [conservatives] who need money and those [conservative foundations and corporations] who have it."[133]

Much of Kimball's *Tenured Radicals: How Politics Has Corrupted Higher Education* appeared, before being published as a book, in the *New Criterion,* a conservative art journal managed by Kimball and edited by Hilton Kramer. The *New Criterion* is supported by the same foundations that fund right-wing think tanks and
political organizations. The Bradley, Olin, and Scaife foundations together contributed $300,000 to the journal's budget in 1986 and $325,000 each for 1987 and
1988. Notwithstanding conservative complaints about the politicization of scholarship, this art journal regularly promotes the neoconservative political agenda:
for instance, the editor's introductions to the October and November 1991 issues
include attacks on the "American academic-political Left," the American Council
of Learned Societies (ACLS), the Modern Language Association (MLA), and
Teachers for a Democratic Culture (TDC), as well as several individuals by name.
The contradiction of a conservative art journal advancing a political agenda is explained by Harvey Mansfield, a conservative scholar who opposes women's studies and African-American studies because they are "openly and blatantly political." Recently appointed to the NEH council and himself a recipient of Olin
money, Mansfield observes, "It's ironic that conservatives have to use politics to
rid the campus of politics, but we do." He intends to use his position on the NEH
Council to "take a stand against what is happening in the American academy." [134]
Mansfield's instrumentalism is typical. Once they were published, D'Souza's and
Kimball's books were promoted by right-wing organizations and reviewed by
right-wingers, while D'Souza and Kimball themselves went on the conference and
TV circuits. All along, they have been trained and supported by the neoconservative political interests whose views they present in their work, and that work
has been produced and marketed by the "ideas industry."

To reframe the attack on liberalized higher education, I now return to an economic model, this time not the free-market one that guides conservative strategy
but a traditional model of production. Cultural conservatism may be seen as the
template for attack. The articulated systems—think tanks, training institutes,
foundations, grass roots organizations, and legal centers—are the manufacturing

apparatus. The articles, opinion pieces, letters, and news stories, as well as a range of actions, are the individual products. The conservative journals and books, the think-tank seminars, and the grassroots lobbying efforts, together with the mainstream media, are the distribution system. The constitution and uses of this apparatus exemplify vertical articulatory practices. These vertical practices involve constructing institutional nodal points to leverage changes in national and local institutions, which in turn can be used to (re)constitute individuals as subjects and agents of a conservative society.

IV. The Future of Cultural Conservatism

My field research in conservative organizations indicates that the Right will intensify its attack on liberalized higher education in three areas. It will continue to manufacture conservative victim stories, such as those that have already appeared in NAS publications, the Collegiate Network newspapers, *Heterodoxy,* and the columns of conservative journalists. From print, the stories will progress to legal centers and conservative courts, not only constituting a media reality but also changing case law and thereby relocating some of the academy's authority over academic matters in judicial and governmental institutions.

Moreover, the Right will attempt to revert liberalized curricula to conservative ones. Besides the Collegiate Network newspapers' curriculum surveys and the Heritage Foundation's "Conservative Curriculum" program, conservatives have launched several projects, including a curriculum study undertaken, according to President Balch, by the NAS research division; attacks on liberalized curricula published in *Academic Questions* and presented at NAS conferences; a proposal for a traditional liberal-arts curriculum printed in *NAS Update;* and traditional curriculum projects funded by the NEH under Chairman Cheney. According to the National Humanities Alliance, "A major theme of Lynne V. Cheney's chairmanship at NEH has been education reform and central to that focus has [*sic*] been programs (1) to assist humanities teachers to become more knowledgeable about and enmeshed in the study of the subjects they teach, and (2) to help schools and colleges improve content and coherence in humanities curricula."[135] My hunch is that until a liberal successor to Cheney takes office NEH funds will be used to support conservative "curriculum reversion" projects, and, in any event, conservative foundations will certainly support these projects.

Finally, long before the 1992 presidential election, conservatives began to shift their attention away from Washington and to states, cities, towns, and counties, with the aim of organizing the grass roots and making local interventions. We can expect existing right-wing organizations, academic and nonacademic, to multiply their local chapters and increase their memberships. More powerful than these organizations in mobilizing a grassroots movement, however, are three technologies deployed by conservatives: (1) direct mail, which has long been used not merely to raise money but to inform and mobilize recipients about conservative issues; (2)

Town Hall, a national computer subscription network established jointly by the *National Review* and the Heritage Foundation, which links individuals and groups through such features as news bulletins, discussions, and on-line publications; and (3) National Empowerment Television (NET), aired by the Free Congress Foundation to some sixty state affiliates and currently broadcasting four monthly programs—"Family Forum Live" on family-values issues, "Campus Connection" on higher-education issues, "A Second Look Live" on African-American issues, and "Empowerment Outreach" on conservative issues.[136] The local groups and national technologies are the conservative infrastructure for performing those horizontal articulatory practices that early feminists performed in consciousness-raising groups, where, by sharing their experiences and feelings, they bound themselves together in sisterhood. Through horizontal practices, the Right can (re)constitute both traditional conservatives and newly targeted populations as grassroots agents of conservative change, thereby doing two things necessary to sustain the movement. It will be able to diffuse conservative consciousness more widely throughout society, and it will be in a position to make wide-ranging interventions. For instance, it will be able to lobby state legislatures, alumni, and interested local publics on the failings of particular universities and colleges, thereby using these groups to leverage changes on the institutions by withholding funds from them and demanding their further regulation.

The continued success of conservatives in attacking and reforming liberalized higher education depends upon their ability to gain more control over all aspects of the higher-education system—universities and colleges, academic publishing, public and private academic funding sources, state and federal government. The signs that they have gained some control at the national level have been scattered and ominous. The appointment of Carol Iannone, who joined Lynne Cheney, Gertrude Himmelfarb, and other conservatives on the board of the Woodrow Wilson International Center; the firing of NEA chair John Frohnmayer and the appointment of NEA acting chair Anne-Imelda Radice, who rejected projects recommended for funding by peer-panels; the recent appointments of several NAS members to the NEH National Council; the appointment of conservatives to the board of FIPSE; the appointments of Carolynn Reid-Wallace and Christina Hoff Sommers to positions at the Department of Education—all of these show NAS and other conservative leaders gaining more control over the national apparatus that can force radical changes on liberalized higher education. The election of President Clinton may slow but will not stop conservatives because they can still use the growing grassroots movement and their own organizations to make change through legislatures, courts, and local bodies.

Doing so, they use academic rhetoric and professionalizing practices to hide their politics, but their politics, make no mistake about it, consist in courses of practical action to impose a right-wing America—political, economic, and cultural—on all of us. Any effective response from those who are unwilling to live under the right-wing regime will also require practical action: coalition-building across the Left and the moderate center; effective presentation of progressive higher-education values to other communities; electoral politics supporting progressive, liberal, and moderate candidates; restaffing of government agencies; and the acquisition of legislative, lobbying, media, and fundraising skills. In short, to have a hand in determining the future of cultural conservatism, progressive academics must engage less in debate, which we have been trained to believe is decisive in the academic world, and more in activism, which the Right has shown us is decisive in the political and cultural world.

NOTES

I am grateful to James Maertens, Larry T. Shillock, and the editors of *Social Text* for their helpful comments on this chapter.

1. "Taking Offense," *Newsweek*, 24 December 1990, 48–55; "Upside Down in the Groves of Academe" and "Academics in Opposition" (on the National Association of Scholars), *Time*, 1 April 1991, 66–69.

2. Richard Bernstein, "The Rising Hegemony of the Politically Correct," *New York Times*, 28 October 1990, 1, 4; John Searle, "Storm over the University," *New York Review of Books*, 6 December 1990, 34–42; and "Opening Academia Without Closing It Down" (a forum), *New York Times*, 9 December 1990, E5.

3. Gerald Sirkin, "The Multiculturalists Strike Back," *Wall Street Journal*, 18 January 1990, A14; "Campus Culture" (on PC at Vassar and Yale), *Wall Street Journal*, 16 February 1990, A12; Thomas Sowell, "Affirmative Action: From Bad to Worse," *Wall Street Journal*, 6 March 1990, A20; Arthur Schlesinger, Jr., "When Ethnic Studies Are Un-American," *Wall Street Journal*, 23 April 1990, A14; "The Ivory Censor" (an editorial), *Wall Street Journal*, 9 May 1990, A14; John H. Bunzel, "Inequitable Equality on Campus," *Wall Street Journal*, 25 July 1990, A12; L. Gordon Crovitz, "Moral Cowardice at Dartmouth," *Wall Street Journal*, 5 October 1990, A18; Joe Segall, "When Academic Quality Is Beside the Point," *Wall Street Journal*, 29 October 19990, A14; Dorothy Rabinowitz, "Vive the Academic Resistance," *Wall Street Journal*, 13 November 1990, A22; and "Politically Correct," *Wall Street Journal*, 26 November 1990, A10. Sowell and Bunzel are fellows at the right-wing Hoover Institution. Rabinowitz is a long-time member of the New York-based neoconservative group that includes Norman Podhoretz, Midge Decter, and Irving Kristol. Podhoretz is editor of *Commentary* and a director of the Committee for the Free World. Decter, the former editor of *Commentary*, is executive director of the Committee for the Free World and a board member of the Heritage Foundation. Kristol, a former editor of *Commentary*, is a director of the Committee for the Free World and a fellow of the American Enterprise Institute. His son William Kristol was chief of staff for William J. Bennett when he was Secretary of Education and was chief of staff for former Vice President Quayle and is a member of the Heritage Foundation Cultural Policy Studies Working Group (see below). See Christopher Hitchens, "A Modern Medieval Family," *Mother Jones* (July/August 1986), 52–56, 74, 76. For their further connections to conservative organizations and individuals, see Sidney Hook, "Three Intellectual Troubadours," *American Spectator* (January 1985), 18, 20–22; and Paul Gottfried and Thomas Fleming, *The Conservative Movement* (Boston: Twayne, 1988), 59–76. Information on William Kristol from "Black Conservative Expected to Fill Education's No. 2 Post," *Washington Post*, 18 March 1987, A19; and author's interview of John M. Slye, Re-

search Assistant, Cultural Policy Studies Program, Heritage Foundation, Washington, D.C., 11 June 1992.

4. William J. Bennett, "The Shattered Humanities," *Wall Street Journal,* 31 December 1982, 10; and *To Reclaim a Legacy: A Report on the Humanities in Higher Education* (Washington, D.C.: National Endowment for the Humanities, 1984). A Reagan appointee with ties to right-wing organizations, Bennett is currently a Distinguished Fellow at the Heritage Foundation and Chairman of the Board of the Free Congress Foundation's National Empowerment Television. He was a board member of the Institute for Educational Affairs (IEA) and the founder of the Madison Center, two organizations that merged in 1990 to become the Madison Center for Educational Affairs. Information from *The Heritage Foundation 1991 Annual Report* (Washington, D.C.: Heritage, 1992), 25; author's interview of Michael Schwartz, Senior Vice President, Free Congress Foundation, Washington, D.C., 10 June 1992; author's interview of Caroline J. Pyott, Vice President, Madison Center for Educational Affairs, Washington, D.C., 2 April 1992; and Peter H. Stone, "The I.E.A.—Teaching the 'Right' Stuff," *The Nation,* 19 September 1981, 231–35.

5. Lynne V. Cheney, *The Humanities and the American Promise: A Report of the Colloquium on the Humanities and the American People* (Charlottesville, Va.: Colloquium on the Humanities and the American People, 1987); *Humanities in America: A Report to the President, the Congress, and the American People* (Washington, D.C.: National Endowment for the Humanities, 1988); *50 Hours: A Core Curriculum for College Students* (Washington, D.C.: National Endowment for the Humanities, 1989); and *Tyrannical Machines: A Report on Education Practices Gone Wrong and Our Best Hopes for Setting Them Right* (Washington, D.C.: National Endowment for the Humanities, 1990). George Levine, Peter Brooks, Jonathan Culler, Marjorie Garber, E. Ann Kaplan, and Catharine R. Stimpson, *Speaking for the Humanities* (New York: American Council of Learned Societies, 1989). Also a Reagan appointee, Cheney consistently nominated conservatives to the NEH National Council and obtained funding for the annual NEH Jefferson Lecture from right-wing foundations: the Olin Foundation contributed $10,000 and the Bradley Foundation $10,000 for the 1988 Jefferson Lecture, delivered by Robert A. Nisbet (*Foundation Grants Index,* ed. Ruth Kovacs, 19th ed. [New York: Foundation Center, 1990], 526, 764); Olin contributed $12,000 and Bradley $10,000 for the 1987 Jefferson Lecture, delivered by Forrest McDonald (*Foundation Grants Index,* 18th ed., 519, 715); and Olin contributed $15,000 and Bradley $10,000 for the 1986 Jefferson Lecture, delivered by Leszak Kolakowski (*Foundation Grants Index,* 17th ed., 512, 710).

6. E. D. Hirsch, Jr., *Cultural Literacy: What Every American Needs to Know* (Boston: Houghton Mifflin, 1987); Allan Bloom, *The Closing of the American Mind* (New York: Simon & Schuster, 1987); Charles Sykes, *Profscam: Professors and the Demise of Higher Education* (Washington, D.C.: Regnery Gateway, 1988); Sykes, *The Hollow Men: Politics and Corruption in Higher Education* (Washington, D.C.: Regnery Gateway, 1990); Page Smith, *Killing the Spirit: Higher Education in America* (New York: Viking, 1990); Roger Kimball, *Tenured Radicals: How Politics Has Corrupted Our Higher Education* (New York: Harper & Row, 1990); Dinesh D'Souza, *Illiberal Education: The Politics of Race and Sex on Campus* (New York: Free Press, 1991). These authors, with the possible exceptions of Hirsch and Smith, all had financial and institutional connections to the Right—Bloom as the frequent recipient of grants from the Olin Foundation; D'Souza as a recipient of Olin grants and an habitué of AEI, Heritage, MCEA, and Leadership Institute programs; Kimball as managing editor of the *New Criterion,* itself supported by the Olin, Scaife, and Bradley foundations;

and Sykes as an author published by the right-wing Regnery Gateway press. For an account of Smith's quarrels with academe, see his biographical entry in the *1990 Current Yearbook*, ed. Charles Moritz (New York: H. W. Wilson, 1990), 565–70.

7. "The Derisory Tower" (an editorial); Ken Emerson, "Only Correct" (a "campus report" on Wisconsin); Jeff Rosen, "Hate Mail" (on Yale); Jacob Weisberg, "Thin Skins" (on Oberlin); Stephen R. Barnett, "Get Back" (on Berkeley); Jim Sleeper, "In the Mix" (on CCNY); Tamara Jacoby, "Psyched Out: Why Black Students Feel Torn"; Dinesh D'Souza, "Sins of Admission"; Richard Blow, "Mea Culpa"; "Ugh! Oops" (a lexicon of politically correct terms); Fred Siegel, "The Cult of Multiculturalism"; and Irving Howe, "The Value of the Canon"—all in *New Republic*, 18 February 1991, 5–6, 18–47.

8. George Will, "Poisoning Higher Education," *Washington Post*, 21 April 1991, B7; "The Cult of Ethnicity," *Washington Post*, 14 July 1991, C7; "Catechism of Correctness," *Washington Post*, 20 October 1991, C7; "Literary Politics," *Newsweek*, 22 April 1991, 72; and "Curdled Politics on Campus," *Newsweek*, 6 May 1991, 72.

9. Dinesh D'Souza, "Sins of Admission," *New Republic*, 18 February 1991, 30–33; "Illiberal Education," *Atlantic Monthly* (March 1991), 51–58, 62–65, 67, 70–74, 76, 78–79; "The Visigoths in Tweeds," *Forbes*, 1 April 1991, 81–86; "Multiculturalism 101," *Policy Review* 56 (Spring 1991), 22–30; " 'PC' So Far," *Commentary* 92, no. 4 (October 1991), 44–46; and "The New Segregation on Campus," *American Scholar* 60, no. 1 (Winter 1991), 17–30.

10. For an excellent article on this point, see Charles A. Radin, "Conservatives Send Their Agenda to Colleges," *Boston Globe*, 12 November 1990, section 3, 1.

11. The following are extremely thoughtful, if limited, replies. On ideas and the invalidity of claims, see Michael Bérubé, "Public Image Limited: Political Correctness and the Media's Big Lie," *Village Voice*, 18 January 1991, 31–37. On the inaccuracy of charges, see Rosa Ehrenreich, "What Campus Radicals?" *Harper's* (December 1991), 57–59, 61. On the illogic of arguments and invalidity of claims, see Jamin Raskin, "The Fallacies of 'Political Correctness': I," *Z Magazine* (January 1992), 31–37. On rhetoric, inaccuracy of charges, and ideas, see Cathy N. Davidson, " 'PH' Stands for Political Hypocracy," *Academe* (September–October 1991), 8–14.

12. Lynne V. Cheney, "Scholars and Society," a speech to the American Council of Learned Societies, New York, 15 April 1988; printed in the *ACLS Newsletter* 1, no. 3 (Summer 1988), 5–7; quotation, 6.

13. Stephen H. Balch and Herbert London, "The Tenured Left," *Commentary* 82, no. 4 (October 1986), 41–51; Herbert London, "Death of the University," *Futurist* 21, no. 3 (May–June 1987), 17–22; Russell Jacoby, "Radicals in Academia," *The Nation*, 19 September 1987, 263–67; Chester E. Finn, Jr., "The Campus: 'An Island of Repression in a Sea of Freedom,' " *Commentary* 88, no. 3 (September 1989), 17–23; Paul Hollander, "From Iconoclasm to Conventional Wisdom: The Sixties in the Eighties," Stanley Rothman, "Professors in the Ascendant," and Aaron Wildavsky, "The Rise of Radical Egalitarianism and the Fall of Academic Standards," all in *Academic Questions* 2, no. 4 (Fall 1989), 31–38, 45–51, 52–55; and John P. Roche, "Academic Freedom: The New Left Vigilantes," *National Review*, 8 December 1989, 34–35.

14. See, for instance, Carol Iannone, "Feminism and Literature," *New Criterion* 4, no. 3 (November 1985), 83–87; Elizabeth Lilla, "Who's Afraid of Women's Studies," *Commentary* 81, no. 2 (February 1986), 53–57; George Gilder, "Sexual Politics," *Chronicles* (June 1986), 1–15; Carol Iannone, "The Barbarism of Feminist Scholarship," *Intercollegiate Review* 23, no. 1 (Fall 1987), 35–41; James Nuechterlein, "The Feminization of the American Left," *Commen-*

tary 84, no. 5 (November 1987), 43–48; Virginia R. Hyman, "Conflict and Contradiction: Principles of Feminist Scholarship," *Academic Questions* 1, no. 1 (Winter 1987–88), 3–14; Carol Iannone, "Feminist Follies," *Academic Questions* 1, no. 1 (Winter 1987–88), 45–47; Brigitte Berger, "Academic Feminism and the 'Left,'" *Academic Questions* 1, no. 2 (Spring 1988), 6–15; Carol Iannone, "Analyzing a Feminist Whine," *American Spectator* (May 1988), 30–31; Carol Iannone, "Feminism vs. Literature," *Commentary* 86, no. 1 (July 1988), 49–53; Ruth R. Wise, "Living with Women's Lib," *Commentary* 86, no. 2 (August 1988), 40–45; Peter Shaw, "Feminist Literary Criticism: A Report from the Academy," *American Scholar* 57, no. 4 (Autumn 1988), 495–513; Margarita Levin, "Caring New World: Feminism and Science," *American Scholar* 54, no. 1 (Winter 1988), 100–6; Steven Hayward, "Feminism as a Festering Ideology," *New Perspectives* (Winter 1988), 53–54; Jeffrey Hart, "Report from a Phallocrat," *National Review*, 24 February 1989, 45; Nicholas Davidson, "The Myths of Feminism," *National Review*, 19 May 1989, 44–45; Barbara Amiel, "Feminism Hits Middle Age," *National Review*, 24 November 1989, 23–25, 59; Herbert I. London, "Leveraging Feminism at Barnard," *Academic Questions* 3, no. 2 (Spring 1990), 5–6; Nicholas Davidson, "Feminism Deconstructs Itself," *National Review*, 20 August 1990, 42–43; Carol Iannone, "Literature by Quota," *Commentary* 91, no. 3 (March 1991), 50–53; Katherine Kersten, "What Do Women Want? A Conservative Feminist Manifesto," *Policy Review* 56 (Spring 1991), 4–15; letters on the Kersten article in *Policy Review* 57 (Summer 1991), 83–91; Norman Podhoretz, "Rape in Feminist Eyes," *Commentary* 92, no. 4 (October 1991), 29–35; Steven Goldberg, "Feminism against Science," *National Review*, 18 November 1991, 30, 32–33; Kenneth Minogue, "The Goddess That Failed," *National Review*, 18 November 1991, 46–48; and Naomi Munson, "Harassment Blues," *Commentary* 93, no. 2 (February 1992), 49–51. All of these journals are supported by right-wing foundations. For 1989, the "old conservative" *National Review* received $342,000 from Bradley, Olin, and Scaife; and the right-wing Rockford Institute, which publishes *Chronicles*, received $185,000 from Coors, Kirby, and Smith Richardson. For 1989, the right-wing Intercollegiate Studies Institute, which publishes the *Intercollegiate Review*, received $275,000 from Bradley, Coors, Kirby, Shelby Cullom Davis, Olin, Noble, and Scaife; and in 1990, it received $411,200 from Bradley, JM, Olin, and Scaife. In 1990, the neoconservative *New Criterion* received $405,000 from Bradley, Olin, and Scaife; the neoconservative *Commentary* received $50,000 from Bradley and Olin; and the "old conservative" *American Spectator* received $160,000 from Bradley, Olin, and Scaife. Funding of the National Association of Scholars, which publishes *Academic Questions*, and the Heritage Foundation, which publishes *Policy Review*, is discussed in detail below. *American Scholar*, published by Phi Beta Kappa, is edited by the neoconservative Joseph Epstein.

15. Peter Shaw, "Declining Discourse," *Society* 23, no. 3 (March–April 1986), 11–13; Joseph Epstein, "The Academic Zoo: Theory—in Practice," *Hudson Review* 44, no. 1 (Spring 1991), 9–30. Also see Peter Shaw, "The Politics of Deconstruction," *Partisan Review* 53, no. 2 (Spring 1986), 253–62; James W. Tuttleton, "Authority in English Studies," *Academic Questions* 2, no. 4 (Fall 1989), 81–88; Nino Langiulli, "Sifting the Rubble at Yale," *Academic Questions* 3, no. 1 (Winter 1989–90), 77–84. Peter Shaw, "Making Sense of the New Academic Disciplines," Susan Shell, "No Angst and All Play: Today's Cheerful Assault on the Humanities," and Charles L. Griswold, Jr., "Ideology and the Humanities: Questions Whispered to Dissenters"—all appeared in a symposium in *Academic Questions* 3, no. 3 (Summer 1990), 22–39. Books include Peter Washington, *Fraud: Literary Theory and the End of English* (London: Fontana, 1989); John M. Ellis, *Against Deconstruction* (Princeton: Princeton University

Press, 1989); and David Lehman, *Signs of the Times: Deconstruction and the Fall of Paul de Man* (New York: Poseiden, 1991).

16. Thomas Short, "A 'New Racism' on Campus?" *Commentary* 86, no. 2 (August 1988), 46–50; Lawrence Auster, "The Regents' Round Table," *National Review*, 8 December 1989, 18, 20–21; Edward Alexander, "Race Fever," *Commentary* 90, no. 5 (November 1990), 45–48; Andrew Sullivan, "Racism 101," *New Republic*, 26 November 1990, 18, 20–21; "Race on Campus" (a forum), *New Republic*, 15 April 1991, 23–25; D'Souza, "Multiculturalism 101: Great Books of the Non-Western World," *Policy Review* 56 (Spring 1991), 22–30; Midge Decter, "E Pluribus Nihil: Multiculturalism and Black Children," *Commentary* 92, no. 3 (September 1991), 25–29; Nathan Glazer, "In Defense of Multiculturalism," *New Republic*, 2 September 1991, 18–20, 21; D'Souza, "The New Segregation on Campus," *American Scholar* 60, no. 1 (Winter 1991), 17–30; Mary Lefkowitz, "Not Out of Africa: The Origins of Greece and the Illusions of Afrocentrists," *New Republic*, 10 February 1992, 29–36; Fred Siegel, "The Cult of Multiculturalism," *New Republic*, 18 February 1991, 34–36, 39–40; Brian Hecht, "Dr. Uncool J: The Sun-Man Cometh to Harvard," *New Republic*, 2 March 1992, 11–12; and Lawrence Auster, "The Forbidden Topic," *National Review*, 27 April 1992, 42–44. For attacks on affirmative action, see Walter E. Williams, "Race, Scholarship, and Affirmative Action," *National Review*, 5 May 1989, 36–40; Thomas Sowell, "'Affirmative Action': A Worldwide Disaster," *Commentary* 88, no. 6 (December 1989), 21–41; Abigail M. Thernstrom, "On the Scarcity of Black Professors," *Commentary* 90, no. 1 (July 1990), 22–26; Frederick R. Lynch, "Surviving Affirmative Action (More or Less)," *Commentary* 90, no. 2 (August 1990), 44–47; and Chester E. Finn, Jr., "Quotas and the Bush Administration," *Commentary* 92, no. 5 (November 1991), 17–23.

17. On accreditation, see Courtney Leatherman,, "Role of Accrediting Agencies Questioned Following Storm of Criticism and Debate," *Chronicle of Higher Education,* 19 February 1992, A15–16; and the discussion below. On minority scholarships, see Scott Jaschik, "Secretary Seeks Ban on Grants Reserved for Specific Groups," *Chronicle of Higher Education,* 11 December 1991, A1, A26–27. On the NEA, see "NEA Head Vetoes Grants for Sexually Explicit Art," *Minneapolis Star Tribune,* 13 May 1992, 13A; Kim Masters, "Can Arts Chief Take Bold Steps and Tread a Fine Line?" *Minneapolis Star Tribune,* 15 May 1992, 7A, 9A; and "NEA Panel Protests Actions by Chairman," *Minneapolis Star Tribune,* 16 May 1992, 7A, 9A. On soliciting cases of alleged discrimination, see "Research Center: Information Needed," *NAS Update* 2, no. 2 (Fall 1991), 5. On referrals to legal centers, the information comes from author's interview of Joseph A. Shea, Jr. Associate General Counsel, Center for Individual Rights, Washington, D.C., 8 June 1992.

18. Those wishing to sample the debate should see Michael Keefer, "'Political Correctness': An Annotated List of Readings," *ACCUTE Newsletter* (Fall 1991), 1–13; *Debating P.C.: The Controversy over Political Correctness on College Campuses,* ed. Paul Berman (New York: Laurel, 1992); and *Beyond PC: Towards a Politics of Understanding,* ed. Patricia Aufderheide (St. Paul: Graywolf, 1992).

19. Albert Jay Nock, quoted in Sidney Blumenthal, *The Rise of the Counter-Establishment: From Conservative Ideology to Political Power* (New York: Times Books, 1986), 13. For general accounts of the rise of the conservative movement besides Blumenthal, see Jerome L. Himmelstein, *To the Right: The Transformation of American Conservatism* (Berkeley: University of California Press, 1990); Paul Gottfried and Thomas Fleming, *The Conservative Movement* (Boston: Twayne, 1988); and Gillian Peele, *Revival and Reaction: The Right in Contemporary America* (Oxford: Clarendon, 1984). For accounts of conservative leaders,

see *Watch on the Right: Conservative Intellectuals in the Reagan Era,* ed. J. David Hoeveler, Jr. (Madison: University of Wisconsin Press, 1991); and *American Conservative Opinion Leaders,* ed. Mark J. Rozell and James F. Pontuso (Boulder: Westview, 1990).

20. Himmelstein, *To the Right,* 68.

21. Ibid., 65–66.

22. Ibid., 67.

23. Ibid., 65–69.

24. Ibid., 67, 69, 70.

25. Peele, in *Revival and Reaction,* does a good job of differentiating the Old Right, neoconservatives, New Right, Christian (or religious) Right, and other constituencies. By the term neoconservatives, I refer to a loose group of intellectuals—both academic and nonacademic, many centered in New York City, many of them Jewish or Catholic, many self-avowed liberals until disaffected by the left movements of the 1960s and/or Great Society programs of the 1970s—who publish in such journals as *Commentary, Public Interest, New Republic,* and *New Criterion.* By the term New Right, I mean a populist and at the same time professionalizing movement that formed interest groups, founded right-wing institutions, established political and campaign organizations, and employed new technologies, such as direct-mail solicitation. A number of those involved in these activities might also be described as the Religious Right—including fundamentalist and orthodox (e.g., Catholic, Jewish, and Mormon) denominations. The term New Right was often used, from the late 1970s through the mid-1980s, for all conservative constituencies, but seems to be giving way now to the terms "conservatism" and "conservative movement" in the discourse of conservatives themselves.

26. For excellent brief accounts of the differences and commonalities, see Amy Moritz, "Family Feud: Is the Conservative Movement falling Apart?" *Policy Review* 57 (Summer 1991), 50–54; and Jacob Weisberg, "Hunter Gatherers," *New Republic,* 2 September 1991, 15–16.

27. See, for instance, Tim W. Ferguson, "What's Next for the Conservative Movement?" *American Spectator* 20, no. 1 (January 1987), 14–16; Amy Moritz, "It's Time We Led: Conservatism's Parched Grass Roots," *Policy Review* 44 (Spring 1988), 22–25; and "Building the New Establishment: Edwin J. Feulner, Jr. on Heritage and the Conservative Movement," an interview by Adam Meyerson, *Policy Review* 58 (Fall 1991), 10, 12, 15–16.

28. See Fred L. Pincus, "From Equity to Excellence: The Rebirth of Educational Conservatism," *Social Policy* 14, no. 3 (Winter 1984), 51–53.

29. See Fred L. Pincus, "From Equity to Excellence," 50–56; David L. Clark and Mary Anne Amiot, "The Disassembly of the Federal Educational Role," *Education and Urban Society* 15, no. 3 (May 1983), 367–87; Terrel H. Bell, "Education Policy Development in the Reagan Administration," *Phi Delta Kappan* 67, no. 7 (March 1986), 487–93; and *A New Agenda for Education,* ed. Eileen M. Gardiner (Washington, D.C.: Heritage Foundation, 1985), 79–80 and elsewhere.

30. *A New Agenda for Education,* vii; also vii–x.

31. Philip F. Lawler, "Higher Education Today," in *A New Agenda for Education,* 47, 52.

32. Ibid., 58.

33. *Cultural Conservatism: Toward a New National Agenda* (Washington, D.C.: Institute for Cultural Conservatism/Free Congress Research and Education Foundation, 1987), 1.

34. Ibid., 5.

35. For a typical conservative understanding of cultural radicals, see Michael Levin, "The Radical View of the World," in *Cultural Conservatism: Theory and Practice*, ed. William S. Lind and William H. Marshner (Washington, D.C.: Free Congress Foundation, 1991), 45–59.

36. See William S. Lind, "What Is Cultural Conservatism?" *Essays in Our Times* 2, no. 1 (March 1986), 1–2; and Paul M. Weyrich, "Cultural Conservatism and the Conservative Movement," in *Cultural Conservatism: Theory and Practice*, 19.

37. See William S. Lind, "Introduction," *Cultural Conservatism: Theory and Practice*, 2; and Weyrich, "Cultural Conservatism and the Conservative Movement," 19–31.

38. Author's interview of Michael Schwartz, 10 June 1992.

39. Lind, "What Is Cultural Conservatism?" 3.

40. Lind, "Introduction," 1.

41. All information following the quotation is from the author's interview with Michael Schwartz, 10 June 1992.

42. Author's interviews of Michael Schwartz and William S. Lind, 10 June 1992.

43. See *Cultural Conservatism: Toward a New National Agenda*, 24. For the theory of mediating structures, see Peter L. Berger and Richard John Neuhaus, *To Empower the People: The Role of Mediating Structures in Public Policy* (Washington, D.C.: American Enterprise Institute, 1977); and *Democracy and Mediating Structures*, ed. Michael Novak (Washington, D.C.: American Enterprise Institute, 1980).

44. Lind, "What Is Cultural Conservatism?" 7.

45. *Cultural Conservatism: Toward a New National Agenda*, 25, 26.

46. T. Kenneth Cribb, "Conservatism and the American Academy: Prospects for the 1990s," Heritage Lectures Series #226 (Washington, D.C.: Heritage Foundation, 1989), 7.

47. For further information about the IEA, Madison Center, and MCEA, see Peter H. Stone, "The I.E.A.—Teaching the 'Right' Stuff," *The Nation*, 19 September 1981, 231–35; Lawrence J. Delaney, Jr., and Leslie Lenkowsky, "The New Voice on Campus: 'Alternative Student Journalism,'" *Academic Questions* 1, no. 2 (Spring 1988), 32–38.

48. *Madison Center for Educational Affairs 1991 Annual Report* (Washington, D.C.: Madison Center for Educational Affairs, n.d.), 4.

49. The PC issue was first raised by the *Vassar Spectator*, according to Robert L. Lukefahr, Jr. (author's interview of Lukefahr, Senior Program Officer, Madison Center for Educational Affairs, Washington, D.C., 2 April 1992). For typical coverage of PC issues, see the *California Review* (University of California, San Diego) 11, no. 1 (October 1991); *Michigan Review* (University of Michigan), 23 October 1991; and *Amherst Spectator* 7, no. 2 (Winter 1991). For articles on Collegiate Network newspapers, see John Kent Walker, "Ivy League's New Conservative Press," *Boston Globe*, 14 December 1982; Chris Chinlund, "Conservative Papers Relish Stirring Debate," *Boston Globe*, 18 December 1983; David Kupperschmid, "Campus Papers Written by Righters: Conservatives Give a New Edge to College Journalism," *Philadelphia Inquirer*, 1 January 1985, A6; Renee Loth, "The Times, They Are A-Changin'," *Boston Globe*, 19 January 1986, section 3, 14; Sidney Blumenthal, "Conservative Debate Style, Tactics after Dartmouth Incident," *Washington Post*, 5 February 1986, A3; Diane Curtis, "Conservative Group's Hand in Campus Journalism," *San Francisco Chronicle*, 25 April 1989, A1; and Larry Gordon, "Papers Proliferate: The Right Presses Case on Campus," *Los Angeles Times*, 1 May 1989, section 1, 1.

50. Information on surveys from author's interview of Robert L. Lukefahr, Jr., 2 April 1992; and on curricular innovations from author's interview of David S. Bernstein, Pro-

gram Officer, Madison Center for Educational Affairs, Washington, D.C., 2 April 1992. For one example, see the attack on Professor Bruce Nelson's History 33 by the *Dartmouth Review*, 12 June 1991, 10–11.

51. Information from *Madison Center for Educational Affairs 1991 Annual Report*, 6–9, 16–17; *Madison Center for Educational Affairs 1990 Annual Report*, 4–8, 9–10; and author's interviews of Patty (Caroline J.) Pyott and Robert L. Lukefahr, Jr., 2 April 1992.

52. Information from the "Administration Questionnaire," 9 pp.; "Faculty Questionnaire," 7 pp.; and "Student Questionnaire," 7 pp., used for preparation of the second edition of *The Common Sense Guide to American Colleges*, ed. Patty (Caroline J.) Pyott (in preparation), sent to author by Patty (Caroline J.) Pyott, 18 May 1992.

53. On Finn, Lenkowsky, and NAS president Stephen Balch's involvement in the *Guide*, see Carol Innerst, "College Guide to Rate Teaching, Ethics, Value," *Washington Times*, 22 January 1990, A5; and Innerst, "New Guide Rates GU, GWU as Free from 'PC,'" *Washington Times*, 15 July 1991, A3.

54. Information from *Madison Center for Educational Affairs 1991 Annual Report*, 12–13; and author's interview of David S. Bernstein, 2 April 1992.

55. Lynne V. Cheney, "Depoliticizing the Academy," *Newslink* 6, no. 6 (February 1991), 1, 6. Other information on Cheney from *The Madison Center for Educational Affairs 1990 Annual Report* (Washington, D.C.: Madison Center for Educational Affairs, n.d.), 9–10, 15.

56. Michael P. McDonald, "A Lawyer's Brief against Litigating Academic Disputes," *Academic Questions* 5, no. 4 (Fall 1992), 16.

57. See "Burgeoning Conservative Think Tanks," a special issue of *Responsive Philanthropy* (Spring 1991), 20 and elsewhere.

58. See John K. Andrews, Jr., "So You Want to Start a Think Tank: A Battlefield Report from the States," *Policy Review* 49 (Summer 1989), 62–65.

59. James A Smith, *The Idea Brokers: Think Tanks and the Rise of the New Policy Elite* (New York: Free Press, 1991), xiii.

60. Blumenthal, *The Rise of the Counter-Establishment*, 37.

61. Ibid.

62. *The Heritage Foundation 1991 Annual Report*, 34.

63. See Sidney Blumenthal, "Hard Times at the Think Tank for American Enterprise Institute, a Crisis of Money and Conservatism," *Washington Post*, 26 July 1986, D1.

64. Number of staff members (145) from author's interview of Charles L. Heatherly, Vice President for Academic Relations, Heritage Foundation, Washington, D.C., 6 April 1992; however, the annual report lists some 160 staff members. Other information from *The Heritage Foundation 1991 Annual Report* (Washington, D.C.: Heritage Foundation, 1992), 28–29, 34–37.

65. *The Heritage Foundation 1991 Annual Report*, 28–29.

66. For 1990 data, see Smith, *The Idea Brokers*, 200–2. For 1992 data, see *The Annual Guide to Public Policy Experts*, ed. Robert Huberty and Barbara D. Hohbach (Washington, D.C.: Heritage Foundation, 1992). CD-ROM information from author's interview of Charles L. Heatherly, 6 April 1992. Computer network information from author's interview of Jeanne Allen, Director of Town Hall, Heritage Foundation, Washington, D.C., 11 June 1992.

67. Blumenthal, *The Rise of the Counter-Establishment*, 49.

68. Author's interview with Cheryl A. Rubin, Director of Public Relations, Heritage Foundation, Washington, D.C., 11 June 1992; and Cheryl A. Rubin, letter to the author, 2 July 1992.

69. Blumenthal, *The Rise of the Counter-Establishment*, 49.

70. See Smith, *The Idea Brokers*.

71. "Conservatives Unveil Plan for National Health-Care System," Heritage Foundation News Release, 1 June 1989, 4; "New Study Shows Heritage Consumer Choice Health Plan Would Provide Universal Coverage, Control Costs," Heritage Foundation News Release, 3 March 1992, 1. Also see *A National Health System for America*, ed. Stuart M. Butler and Edmund F. Haislmaier (Washington, D.C.: Heritage Foundation, 1989); and Stuart M. Butler, "A Policy Maker's Guide to the Health Care Crisis, Part II: The Heritage Consumer Choice Health Plan," Heritage Talking Points (a policy papers series), 5 March 1992.

72. *The Heritage Foundation 1991 Annual Report*, 4.

73. According to a Heritage Foundation list, twenty newspapers, five syndicated columnists, and four magazines endorsed the plan by name and another sixteen newspapers agreed with it in principle (Cheryl A. Rubin, list sent to author, 2 July 1992).

74. Author's interview of Cheryl A. Rubin, 11 June 1992.

75. Author's interview of John M. Slye, Research Assistant, Cultural Policy Studies Program, Heritage Foundation, Washington, D.C., 11 June 1992. See also "Building the New Establishment" (Feulner interview), 9.

76. *The Heritage Foundation 1991 Annual Report*, 25.

77. Information on the Cultural Policy Studies Working Group, as well as a list of its members, came from the author's interview of John Slye.

78. Smith, *The Idea Brokers*, xv–xvi.

79. Peter Weingart, "The Scientific Power Elite—A Chimera: The De-Institutionalization and Politicization of Science," in *Scientific Establishments and Hierarchies*, ed. Norbert Elias, Herminio Martins, and Richard Whitley (Dordrecht: Reidel, 1982), 73.

80. Smith, *The Idea Brokers*, 197.

81. All information, unless otherwise noted, from author's interview of William Forrest, Vice President for Programs, Leadership Institute, Springfield, Va., 9 June 1992; assorted program announcements from William Forrest; and *The Leadership Institute Prospectus* (Springfield, Va.: Leadership Institute, n.d.).

82. Author's interviews of William Forrest, 9 June 1992; and at the Broadcast Journalism School, Leadership Institute, held at the Free Congress Foundation, Washington, D.C., 13 June 1992.

83. Direct-mail letter, Lisa M. Kruska, Job and Talent Bank Director, Leadership Institute, n.d. (Spring 1992), 2.

84. Representative Dick Armey, direct-mail letter, Leadership Institute, 8 June 1991, 5; and *Building Leadership: The Newsletter of the Leadership Institute* 6, no. 1 (1992), 1, 5.

85. *The Leadership Institute Prospectus*, 22–23.

86. Date of founding and second quotation, author's interview of Chris Warden, Editor, National Journalism Center, Washington, D.C., 3 April 1992; quotation and other information from author's interview of Mal Klein, Associate Editor, National Journalism Center, Washington, D.C., 3 April 1992.

87. *E&RI 1990 Annual Report* (Washington, D.C.: Education and Research Institute, n.d.), 1, 6–9; and a montage of newsclips, National Journalism Center, n.d.

88. *United States Tax Reporter Internal Revenue Code*, vol. 1 (New York: Research Institute of America, 1992), first quotation, 2318; second quotation, 2328.

89. *United States Tax Reporter Internal Revenue Code*, vol. 18 (New York: Research Institute of America, 1992), 35, 117.

90. Armey, direct-mail letter, 8 June 1991, 3 (all quotations).

91. Ibid., 6 (his italics).

92. The book given to students is *And That's the Way It Isn't*, ed. L. Brent Bozell III and Brent H. Baker (Alexandria, Va.: Media Research Center, 1990), 339 pp. The readings are: "America's Biased and Abusive News Media," *New Dimensions* (April 1990), 22–27, 30–34, 37–43; "Koppel and Turner on the Ten Commandments," *New Dimensions* (April 1990), 44–46; Bruce Herschensohn, "The Information Brokers," *New Dimensions* (April 1990), 48–50; David Shaw, "Abortion Bias Seeps into News," *Los Angeles Times,* July 1990, n.p., 8 pp.; David Shaw, "Abortion Foes Stereotyped, Some in the Media Believe," *Los Angeles Times,* 2 July 1990, n.p., 5 pp.; David Shaw, "'Rally for Life' Coverage Evokes Editor's Anger," *Los Angeles Times,* 3 July 1990, n.p., 5 pp.; David Shaw, "Can Women Reporters Write Objectively on Abortion Issue?" *Los Angeles Times* (no other information), 3 pp.; David Shaw, "'Abortion Hype' Pervaded Media after Webster Case," *Los Angeles Times,* 4 July 1990, n.p., 6 pp.

93. "Bias in Broadcast News," seminar conducted by Brent Baker, Executive Director of the Media Research Center, an organization devoted to exposing the liberal bias of the media.

94. Author's observation of the Broadcast Journalism School, Leadership Institute, held at the Free Congress Foundation, Washington, D.C., 13–14 June 1992.

95. Author's observation of the Broadcast Journalism School, 13–14 June 1992.

96. *Cultural Conservatism: Toward a New National Agenda*, 1.

97. All information, unless otherwise noted, is from the author's observation of the seminar on common-sense economics, National Journalism Center, Washington, D.C., 3 April 1991.

98. *United States Tax Reporter Internal Revenue Code,* vol. 18, 35, 119.

99. Author's interview of William Forrest, 13 April 1992.

100. Ralph Bennett, Senior Washington Editor, *Reader's Digest,* from author's observation of the Friday Seminar on Journalism, National Journalism Center, Washington, D.C., 3 April 1992.

101. Author's interview of Chris Warden, 3 April 1992.

102. For information on conservative foundations and what they have funded, see Paul Gottfried, *The Conservative Movement,* rev. ed. (New York: Twayne, 1993), esp. chapter 6, "Funding an Empire"; David Warner, "Scaife: Financier of the Right," *Pittsburgh Post-Gazette,* 20 April 1981, 1, 6–7; "History of Coors: Right Wing on Tap," *National Boycott News* 2, no. 4 (Spring–Summer 1989), 163–65; Russ Bellant and Chip Berlet, "How Coors Family Funding Undermines Democracy," *Guild Notes* 14, no. 5 (November 1990), 1, 6–7; Russ Bellant, *The Coors Connection* (Boston: South End, 1991); "Mixing Beer and Philanthropy to Undermine Progressive Causes," *Responsive Philanthropy* (Spring 1992), 16, 10–12; Jon Weiner, "Dollars for Neocon Scholars," *The Nation,* 1 January 1989, 12–14; Sara Diamond, "Endowing the Right-Wing Academic Agenda," *Covert Action Information Bulletin* 38 (Fall 1991), 46–49; and "Foundations Are Four Times More Liberal Than Conservative: Capital Research Center Reports to the Nation, But Do You Believe It?" *Responsive Philanthropy* (Fall 1991), 1, 12–13.

103. Unless otherwise noted, all funding information is from the *Foundation Grants Index,* ed. Ruth Kovacs, 20th ed. (New York: Foundation Center, 1991). This edition lists grants reported in the tax year 1990 and usually paid in 1989 (though sometimes paid in 1988 or 1990). On cross-checking this listing against selected foundation annual reports, I

concluded that the *Foundation Grants Index* does not always provide complete information.

104. The Center for Individual Rights was founded in 1988 and began operating in 1989. Information on 1989 funding from the *JM Foundation 1989 Annual Report* (New York: JM, n.d.), 23; and *Smith Richardson Foundation Annual Report for 1989* (n.p., n.d.), 4. Information on 1990 funding from the *Report of the Lynde and Harry Bradley Foundation, August 1988–July 1990* (Milwaukee: Bradley, n.d.), 16; *John M. Olin Foundation 1990 Annual Report* (New York: Olin, n.d.), 9; and *Smith Richardson Foundation Annual Report for 1990* (n.p., n.d.), 4.

105. Gottfried, *The Conservative Movement*, 124. For an account of the neoconservative takeover of the foundations, see 128–31; and for an account of the neoconservative takeover, through foundation funding, of think tanks and other organizations, see 131–38.

106. Ibid., 125.

107. *Foundation Grants Index*, ed. Ruth Kovacs, 19th ed. (New York: Foundation Center, 1990), 524–28.

108. Paul Gottfried, "Populism vs. Neoconservatism," *Telos* 90 (Winter 1991–92), 186.

109. Gottfried, *The Conservative Movement*, 140.

110. Lists of Associates and Founders, dated 31 January 1990, given to the author by John M. Slye, 11 June 1992.

111. All quotations from the Bradley Resident Scholars Program application form, 1992–93 academic year. Additional information from *The Heritage Foundation 1991 Annual Report*, 18.

112. See, for instance, Laurence Jarvik, "Making Public Television Public," *Backgrounder* #873, 18 January 1992; "Monopoly, Corruption, and Greed: The Problem of Public Television," Heritage Lectures #379, 25 February 1992; and "After Privatization: Public Television in the Cultural Marketplace," Heritage Lectures #383, 21 May 1992.

113. Quotation and information from *The Heritage Foundation 1991 Annual Report*, 19; and the Salvatori Center for Academic Leadership application brochure, 2–4.

114. Author's interview of Charles L. Heatherly, 6 April 1992.

115. Quotations and information from the Conference Program, Second Annual Leadership Conference for Academic Excellence and Salvatori Awards Dinner, Washington, D.C., 27–28 March 1992, which also contains the Statement of Purpose.

116. See Sara Diamond, "Readin', Writin' and Repressin'," *Z Magazine* (February 1991), 45–49; and Diamond, "Endowing the Right-Wing Academic Agenda," 46–49.

117. From income and expense statements drawn up by the NAS.

118. Denise Magner, "Law Firm Goes to Bat for Campus Conservatives," *Chronicle of Higher Education*, 25 September 1991, A5.

119. Author's interview of Joseph A. Shea, Jr., 8 June 1992; Magner, "Law Firm Goes to Bat," A5; *Docket Report* (First Quarter 1992), 7; and *Wake Forest Critic* (March 1992), 2.

120. Information taken from the CIR's *Docket Report* (First Quarter 1992), 1, 4, 6; Anne Kornhauser, "The Right Versus the Correct," *Legal Times*, 29 April 1991, 15; and Magner, "Law Firm Goes to Bat," A5.

121. Author's interview of Joseph A. Shea, Jr., 8 June 1992. Also see Kornhauser, "The Right Versus the Correct," 1, 14, 15; and Magner, "Law Firm Goes to Bat," A5.

122. "Amendment I v. Title VI in the Matter of Judith Kleinfeld," *Docket Report* (Spring Quarter 1992), 4.

123. Author's interview of Joseph A. Shea, Jr., 8 June 1992.

124. "Conservative Alliance Re-Membered: *Conservative Student Alliance v. Portland State University*," *Docket Report* (Second Quarter 1992), 4.

125. Author's interview of Joseph A. Shea, Jr., 8 June 1992.

126. Author's interview of Joseph A. Shea, Jr., Center for Individual Rights, Washington, D.C., 17 November 1992.

127. Kornhauser, "The Right Versus the Correct," 15; Magner, "Law Firm Goes to Bat," A5.

128. See Scott Jaschik, "Education Secretary Names 5 to Panel on Accreditation," *Chronicle of Higher Education,* 6 November 1991, A31–32.

129. See Scott Jaschik, "Some Accrediting Groups May Be Allowed to Use 'Diversity Standards,'" *Chronicle of Higher Education,* 15 May 1991, A1, A20; Robert H. Atwell, "The Dangers of U.S. Intervention in Accreditation," *Chronicle of Higher Education,* 20 November 1991, A52; Scott Jaschik, "Education Secretary Wants to End the Role of Accrediting in Student-Aid Eligibility," *Chronicle of Higher Education,* 27 November 1991, A1, A2; "Federal Panel Postpones Vote on Recognition of Middle States Group," *Chronicle of Higher Education,* 27 November 1991, A27; Scott Jaschik and Robert R. Schmidt, Jr., "College Accreditors Spur Use of Quotas, Federal Officials Say," *Chronicle of Higher Education,* 4 December 1991, A37, A43; Scott Jaschik, "Middle States Moves to Compromise on Diversity Rules," *Chronicle of Higher Education,* 18 December 1991, A25, A29; "Middle States' Decision on Diversity Standards Seen Enhancing Federal Role in Accreditation," *Chronicle of Higher Education,* 8 January 1992, A24, A36; "U.S. May Toughen Its Rules Governing Accrediting Groups," *Chronicle of Higher Education,* 12 February 1992, A23, A30; and Courtney Leatherman, "Role of Accrediting Agencies Questioned," *Chronicle of Higher Education,* 19 February 1992, A15–16.

130. See Dinesh D'Souza and David Corn's letters to the editor, *The Nation,* 8 July 1991, 38; and Louis Menand, "Illiberalisms," *New Yorker,* 20 May 1991, 101-7.

131. *Foundation Grants Index,* ed. Ruth Kovacs, 19th ed. (New York: Foundation Center, 1990), 526.

132. Fact sheet, Teachers for a Democratic Culture, n.d. (ca. December 1991); information taken from the 1990 annual report of the Olin Foundation.

133. See Stone, "The Ideology Front: The I.E.A.—Teaching the 'Right' Stuff," 231–35; and Lawrence J. Delaney, Jr., and Leslie Lenkowsky, "The New Voice on Campus: 'Alternative Student Journalism,'" 32–38.

134. Karen J. Winkler, "A Conservative Plans to 'Sound the Guns' at NEH," *Chronicle of Higher Education,* 16 October 1991, A5.

135. John Hammer, memorandum to NHA [National Humanities Alliance] Members and Friends, 13 February 1992, 4.

136. Information on Town Hall from the author's interview of Jeanne Allen, 11 June 1992; and "Town Hall Can Benefit You," Heritage Foundation letter, n.d., 2 pp. Information on National Empowerment Television from the author's interviews of Michael Schwartz, Senior Vice President, Coalitions for America Broadcasting Network, Free Congress Foundation, Washington, D.C., 11 June 1992 and 24 November 1992.

4

Blowback: Playing the
Nationalist Card Backfires

GERALD HORNE

THERE IS MUCH hooting and hand-wringing about what in the academy has been called "identity politics." By this some mean the increased focus in the past quarter-century on, for example, Women's Studies, Ethnic Studies, Gay and Lesbian Studies. It is ironic that those who condemn this development do not seem to recognize that events they personally helped to trigger contributed to bringing this very same "identity politics" about. Simply put, the erosion of left influence—especially in class-based organizations such as trade unions—inevitably created fertile ground for various forms of nationalism, as is happening today in Eastern Europe and elsewhere. "Cold War liberals" with their trenchant anticommunism went to extraordinary lengths to root out black leftists; it was a scorched-earth policy that left some progressive organizations destroyed or weakened. I have detailed this unfolding process in *Black and Red: W.E.B. Du Bois and the Afro-American Response to the Cold War, 1944–63*, and *Communist Front? The Civil Rights Congress, 1946–56*.[1] In this vacuum arose various forms of nationalism; in the African American community particularly this process accelerated after 1956, a year that witnessed the launching of the FBI COINTELPRO schemes aimed at black progressives and the Suez War, which increased support among blacks of Nasser's Egypt and Islam itself. It was at this juncture that the Nation of Islam increased its membership.

It was at this juncture as well that the "civil rights movement" began to grow in strength, as U.S. ruling elites could be assured that significant change could be brought to the Deep South especially without the danger of competent black leftists' being able to divert the historical process toward changes in property relations and redistribution of the wealth. The civil rights movement helped to engender a women's movement growing out of the Student Non-Violent Coordinating Committee (SNCC) and a feminist focus that fortunately still persists; this trend was linked to and inspired by similar developments in the Chicano-Mexi-cano movement, particularly after the student massacres in Mexico City in 1968. These movements grew to maturity often without the kind of nurturing they could have and should have received from Paul Robeson, Claudia Jones, and too many others who had been silenced or marginalized. When racist authorities bru-tally assaulted protesting civil rights demonstrators, an explanation that could ex-plain this bestiality in terms of capitalism and imperialism had withered and was being replaced rapidly by a narrative that focused on "white devils." Now, today, those who cheered on the marginalizing of the black Left are lamenting the rise of various forms of nationalism among blacks, be it progressive or xenophobic, and lamenting more the "identity politics" that is often influenced by nationalisms.

If I had been "present at the creation" in the post–World War II era of the Red Scare among blacks, I would have objected; but, alas, I was barely born. I would have objected when Walter White, Roy Wilkins, Eleanor Roosevelt, and the Na-tional Association for the Advancement of Colored People (NAACP) board purged W.E.B. Du Bois from leadership. I would have objected further to the in-fluential articles penned by Arthur Schlesinger Jr., with their absurd claims that the Communist Party was "sinking tentacles" into the NAACP, then as now the preeminent mass organization among African Americans. This culminated in its tumultuous 1950 Boston convention, where stringent anticommunist resolutions were passed, leading to a purge of some of its more militant and progressive mem-bers. This in turn caused a rupture in relations between militants and radicals of various ethnicities. This forced "Balkanization" created favorable conditions for the rise of militant separatist movements pursuing agendas that we are now told threaten the very integrity of the nation.

The Rise and Fall of the Black Left

A more complete outline of the fate of the black Left can be found in the above-noted texts along with my *Black Liberation/Red Scare: Ben Davis and the Commu-nist Party.*[2] For purposes here, it is sufficient to note the following: During the 1941–1945 period the NAACP was a self-avowed anti-imperialist organization. This orientation was reflected in the growth in its ranks. In 1940 the NAACP had approximately 40,000 members; five years later it had over 400,000—a level which it has yet to exceed. Part of this growth was due to the tireless labor of the legend-ary Ella Baker, who galvanized this organization from her position as NAACP leader; she went on to play a founding role in both SNCC and Martin Luther King's Southern Christian Leadership Conference. But part of it was certainly due to the international situation obtaining as well.

The fact that the United States was in an antifascist alliance with Moscow from 1941 to 1945 created favorable conditions for the erosion of the right wing's preem-inent Cold War tool, anticommunism—just as the erosion of the Cold War was a prime factor in the right wing's losing control of the White House in 1992. During

World War II Warner Brothers deemed it fitting to produce and distribute the film *Mission to Moscow,* the now reviled work that hailed Josef Stalin and even went so far as to represent positively his view of the so-called purge trials. Naturally, the filmmakers had a lot of explaining to do once the Red Scare began. But at that moment when Moscow was absorbing the brunt of the Nazi onslaught in Leningrad and Stalingrad, Warners was seen as performing a highly patriotic duty. On the other side of the class and race barricade, a similar influence was felt. It was during those halcyon days that the NAACP invited Du Bois, who had left the organization in a huff ten years earlier in 1934, back to the organization he had helped to found. That he was a self-proclaimed "socialist of the path" was not a major stumbling block at that time.

Du Bois pushed the Truman administration forcefully on the question of decolonization of Africa, the establishment of a state of Israel (a development that Washington was somewhat hesitant about initially), and the predicates of the new Cold War strategy generally. The problem was that Cold War liberals like Eleanor Roosevelt and Arthur Schlesinger Jr. had influence in the highest councils of the NAACP, and they objected to the influence of Du Bois and a coterie of black radicals once the Cold War was launched. They were able to prevail on Walter White and Roy Wilkins, the two top executives of the NAACP, to switch from the alliance with the black Left that had obtained during World War II to a position of anticommunist hostility. Thus, by 1948 Du Bois had been sacked by the NAACP board, in part because of his desire to continue bringing human rights violations committed against African Americans before international bodies such as the United Nations. Malcolm X turned to the UN in 1964 after leaving the Nation of Islam; a few months later he was murdered. Internationalism came with a heavy price, while those who had purged Du Bois and murdered Malcolm continued and continue to live on quite well, thank you.

Du Bois began to have difficulty finding publishers and journals courageous enough to publish his now controversial ideas. Whereas previously he had taught at a number of historically black institutions and lectured at many other universities and colleges, he became less of a presence on college campuses. Though this was a draconian perversion of civil liberties, those Cold War liberals who wielded influence within the American Civil Liberties Union and related groupings—particularly Schlesinger—did not speak up in opposition; in fact, in books such as *The Vital Center,*[3] Schlesinger provided intellectual sustenance for these regressive policies. At the same time, Du Bois's friend Paul Robeson was barred from bringing his "premature multiculturalism"—his magnificent concerts—to halls and campuses across the nation. He was barred from the developing medium of radio though he had been a frequent presence on these airwaves before the onset of the Red Scare and the Cold War.

By 1946–1947, Ben Davis, an African American Communist leader, had been elected and reelected, representing Harlem, to the New York City Council. His predecessor was Adam Clayton Powell, who endorsed him. Davis was born in Atlanta in 1904 to Ben Davis Sr., who was one of the more affluent blacks in the nation, publisher of a newspaper, and a leading Republican Party official. Davis Sr. had close ties to Booker T. Washington and seemed to embody his presumed philosophy of attaining economic success as an antidote for racism. The problem, of course, was that the racist terror—the Ku Klux Klan, the Knights of the White Camelia—that raged across Afro-America in the early twentieth century often targeted *precisely* blacks of means and accomplishment, for it was they who seemed to belie the very notion of white supremacy. So, after Herbert Hoover was elected president in 1928, though Davis had stumped for the ticket as usual, the GOP decided to purge him and other blacks. African American leaders like Davis were seen as an impediment to attracting white voters in the South. So he was ousted politically, harassed economically, and wound up losing much of his fortune during the Depression.

Ben Davis Jr. had attended Amherst and Harvard Law School with Charles Hamilton Houston, the mentor of Thurgood Marshall. It was expected that he would follow his father's path and Houston's path—that is, be progressive and even militant but within the framework of accepting the basic economic premises of U.S. society, presenting no direct challenge to capitalism or imperialism. Davis Jr. demurred. He became a marxist; he joined the Communist Party.

In 1943—yes, during World War II—he was elected to the city council with the support of Lena Horne, Duke Ellington, Langston Hughes, Teddy Wilson (the pianist and so-called marxist Mozart), and thousands of other residents of New York City. He stayed on the council until 1949, when he was ousted unceremoniously, perhaps illegally, as he became one of eleven members of the party leadership convicted, fundamentally, for teaching marxism (though in the popular imagination they were convicted for conspiring to overthrow the government by force and violence). By 1951 he was in federal prison in Terre Haute, Indiana. When he was released in 1956 he was entering a new world that was to be shaped by the Montgomery bus boycott led by Martin Luther King Jr. and the revelations about Stalin presented at the Twentieth Congress of the Soviet Communist Party.

One of Davis's close friends was Claudia Jones. Of Afro-Trinidadian heritage, she too was a Communist leader. By 1948 rumblings had already begun about deporting her. This happened after she had been convicted and jailed in West Virginia for violating the same federal statute that had ensnared Davis. She was deported to the U.K., where she became a leader of the burgeoning black population there, helped to found a newspaper, and influenced a generation of progressives who were to make a major contribution to intellectual and political life in London—but by the 1960s, like Davis and others of that ilk, she was barely known to a new generation of militants.

In 1948 William Patterson decided to take over the leadership of the Civil Rights Congress (CRC). His wife, Louise Patterson, also played a leading role with this left-led grouping, at the time as well known as the NAACP. She, like her husband, was close to Langston Hughes and a number of writers and artists who supported

CRC causes. CRC was not only defending Jones, Davis, Du Bois, and Robeson but taking up the cudgels for countless African Americans, Chicanos, Puerto Ricans, Asian Americans, Indios, et al., facing racist persecution. It defended organized labor at a time when Taft-Hartley and other laws had this important entity under siege. A few years later Patterson had to defend himself against various charges; he did not prevail and wound up in prison. By 1956 CRC had been liquidated in the face of an all-out assault from the Subversive Activities Control Board. Though Patterson was to play a role in the formation of the Black Panther Party, many of the post-1960s militants were hardly aware of his legacy. In part this was because of a Red Scare miasma of distortion of the record of the Left championed by figures such as Schlesinger.

In 1948 the man who was to become Malcolm X was penning a letter to the Nation of Islam (NOI), a small religious sect, requesting membership. By 1956 the towering Harlem figures of Davis, Robeson, Jones, and Du Bois had been persecuted, isolated, marginalized. Associating with them or with their ideas was verboten. What concerned elites was on the surface their reluctance to distance themselves from Moscow and socialism and beneath the surface their ideas about wealth redistribution. The Stalin revelations, coming as they did as the black Left was being pounded, were also a factor. But at the same time that these shocking stories from Moscow about brutalization were hitting the airwaves, another event was to give a boost to various Islamicist sects with regressive ideas about fundamental issues concerning race.

The aggression against Egypt by Israel, the U.K., and France provided an image of a heroic African—and Islamic—nation facing down intervention—or, as the NOI narrative might have it, the righteous Moslems facing down the "white devils." Simultaneously, left forces, including the black Left, were split, with some taking the side of Tel Aviv. This was not the case for the quintet focused on here, but pro-Israel views were disproportionately held by a number of prominent Jewish-American leftists. This contradiction was played on by COINTELPRO as it sought to worsen relations among comrades. This led to charges of black "anti-Semitism" or at least insensitivity and Jewish racism. Out of this confusing matrix emerged a heightened profile for the NOI.

Playing the Nationalist Card

In the 8 February 1993 *Los Angeles Times* Alexander Cockburn writes of how the Israeli leadership promoted the xenophobic nationalism of Hamas as it sought to undermine the secular and leftist Palestine Liberation Organization (PLO).[4] A little-known but profound aspect of the general policy of U.S. elites in particular has been to pursue such initiatives at home and abroad. Part of this process involved discrediting and undermining the black Left; in this Schlesinger played a pivotal role. The other part involved manipulating narrow nationalists against progressive nationalists to the detriment of the latter.

In January 1969 at the University of California at Los Angeles, for example, members of the narrowly nationalist US[5] organization murdered two leftist members of the Black Panther Party, Alprentice "Bunchy" Carter (whose bright daughter Danon was a student of mine just a few years ago) and John Huggins. The issue was control of an Afro-American Studies program. This murder, this bit of intellectual brigandage, stands as a metaphor for what has taken place ideologically over the past forty-five years in this nation: an initial wave of leftists was persecuted with the active participation of Schlesinger and other elites; then a new wave of 1960s radicals was murdered by various combinations of manipulated nationalists and law enforcement personnel. At UCLA and other campuses this set the stage for the rise of various forms of xenophobic nationalism that now Schlesinger tells us must be eliminated (along with progressive varieties as well).

What is being said here is quite simple and descriptively obvious. The fact that one has to restate the thesis for clarity's sake only further underscores the full extent of the brainwashing and ideological massaging that has occupied this nation. Yes, there is a connection between the 1940s purges and the 1960s murders. Yes, these dastardly acts help to explain the strong influence of various forms of xenophobic nationalism among certain sectors in the black community. And, yes, those who engineered the purges and created the conditions that led to the murders now complain with ill grace about the distorted nationalism that has filled an ideological vacuum. To repeat, black leftists like Du Bois, Robeson, Davis, Patterson, and Jones were ousted from influence beginning in the 1940s. In 1966 the lengthened shadow of the Left, the Black Panther Party, was born, with Patterson playing the role of midwife. These organized black left forces were hammered into submission, and it is not the black community alone but the nation itself that pays the price.

Again, elites in the United States and elsewhere have found it easy to choose between various forms of nationalism on the one hand and progressive leftism on the other. Presumably, the former could present a threat to life, whereas the latter—more important—presents a challenge to property relations. Equally important is the fact that even when xenophobic nationalist forces build strength among blacks, the effect at times is to deflect the attention of potentially militant blacks away from the political debate about, for example, spending the public treasury on education and toward the separate debate about dipping into one's own pocket after paying taxes to support an alternative black school system. Right-wing elites in particular appreciate fewer participants' sitting at the table to debate the expenditure of millions.

Naturally, this domestic policy is reflected in the choice of foreign policy options abroad. It is well-known that certain Israeli elites backed the so-called fundamentalist Hamas over the past years as a counterweight to the secular and presumably more threatening PLO. This policy has been underwritten by Washington. In Angola, UNITA postures on a black nationalist platform and, in fact, massacres the melanin-deficient when it seizes territory administered by the

MPLA government in Luanda. This has not prevented melanin-deficient ultrarightists in South Africa from supporting UNITA, nor has this immeasurably eroded UNITA's support in Washington.

It is not just the melanin theorists and the "sun"-people and "ice"-people theorists that Schlesinger is targeting. Though the rise of these forces is intimately bound up with the Schlesinger-boosted project of restricting the black Left, the "anti-multiculturalists" plan to whip up revulsion against distorted reactions to racism by narrow nationalists and then demagogically turn this revulsion against progressives of various stripes. Not surprisingly, U.S. elites abroad have sought to manipulate narrow nationalists against progressive forces, in a manner not unlike what has transpired in Afro-America for the past decades. In Cyprus there has been active and tacit support over the years by U.S. elites of Turkish separatists and xenophobes. In Angola there has been support of the "tribalistic" Jonas Savimbi, who has the gall to pose as "antiwhite" in Luanda in order to gain adherents. Playing the "color card," he charges that his opponents come mostly from the ranks of the "mixed-race." In the former Yugoslavia, U.S. elites over the years backed anticommunist "nationalists" who now have emerged as advocates of the very same policies that now are being denounced as horrific.

In other cases U.S. elite opposition has stressed undermining of the Left in particular nations more than boosting of xenophobes, but the result has been similar. India, whose relations with the United States during the Cold War were always complicated because of its close ties with Moscow, is an example. The state of Kerala has been a showcase for some decades as a Communist-led alliance has ruled and initiated significant reform in such critical areas as literacy, women's rights, land reform, and population policy. Instead of seeking to build on and bolster these admirable efforts, the United States has treated Kerala like Allende's Chile. This attack on the Left, again, has provided favorable conditions for the rise of regressive Hindu fundamentalists who now threaten the existence of the state.

The use of regressive nationalism as a tool against the Left is one of the oldest of elite tactics. Regressive nationalism serves to distance, for example, African Americans from potential allies. As blacks are mostly working-class, this translates into difficulties in building working-class organizations to resist the entreaties of capital. It can also be a barrier on campuses. Likewise, the "white nationalist" and white supremacist ideology given such a boost by George "Willie Horton" Bush and Ronald "Welfare Queen" Reagan has played a similarly disruptive role. This is all an advanced form of the oldest tactic of all, divide and conquer.

One theory used to explain U.S. aggression in Vietnam speaks of the motivation of U.S. rice agribusiness interests in attempting to hamper the growth of a potential rival. Similarly, one explanation for U.S. policy in the Balkans has been that Washington is not upset with a raging conflict on the borders of some of its more vigorous rivals in the global economy, Germany, France, and the European Community. Again, in India one sees a nation that has been able to produce a supercomputer to rival the $25 million Cray (U.S.) model at a fraction of the cost

and software to rival what is being produced here. Other U.S. business interests
are not pleased with past limitations on repatriation of profits from India and
limitations on their entering this vast market. Separatist tendencies, threats from
neighboring Pakistan, and the like, serve as useful chastening and softening-up
for India, in their opinion, just as dividing the antielite front of African Americans, Latinos, Asian Americans, Euro-Americans, Indios, and others is helpful in
repelling progressive change.

This policy of playing on difference while denying this is going on (and, in fact,
proclaiming the exact opposite) is about to have a "blowback" effect. (This is the
term often used to describe, for example, the emergence of CIA disinformation
planted abroad in U.S. media markets or the domestic impact of collaborating
with Nazis abroad.) In the fall of 1992 there was some press coverage of Serb
Americans and Croat Americans clashing in the streets over the conflict raging
thousands of miles away in their homeland (*New York Times*, 18 September 1992).
More recently there has been increasing conflict between Armenian American and
Jewish American organizations because of Armenia's alignment with Iran in its
conflict with Azerbaijan and the latter's alignment with Israel.

The construction of "whiteness" has been one of the key points of stability of
the U.S. empire. This concept has been flexible enough to incorporate the Jewish
community and those of Italian descent, though early theorists of hegemonic ideologies such as Social Darwinism would have objected to this bold maneuver.
Anticommunism was also useful in binding together many Euro-American ethnic
groupings, for example, Albanian Americans, Greek Americans, Hungarian
Americans, and German Americans. Many of these believed that they had a common bond with others with families or compatriots on the other side of the "Iron
Curtain." "Captive Nations" days were a time for many assemblages of commonality. The fact that the U.S. elite was pushing fragmentation in Eastern Europe while
pushing "white solidarity" at home was acceptable as long as Communists were in
power. But now there is the danger of a blowback effect, a spreading of ethnic tension exported from across the Atlantic among "whites" in a manner not seen in
this nation for some time. This is a greater threat to the integrity of this nation
than much of what Schlesinger prates about, and I wish he would speak to these
white folk about it. Combined with the longer-standing nationalisms of minority
communities, however, these tendencies do raise intriguing queries about the future of this nation.

The *California Courier*, the weekly publication of the large Armenian American
population in this state—which has given us William Saroyan and former Black
Panther attorney Charles Garry—has been covering intently the raging conflict in
their homeland. Iran has been helpful in breaking the stranglehold of the Turks
and Azeris in their blockade of this small nation. This is helpful, since Armenia is
now struggling through a major economic crisis of virtually biblical proportions.
However, Israel has been assisting the Azeris, perhaps in partial response to the
Iranian involvement. The *Courier*, as a result, before the November 1992 elections

denounced Representative Stephen Solarz of Brooklyn—a major backer of the Zionist lobby—as the "Congressman from Istanbul." He was defeated.

What does this signify? Can we expect that in the future more international conflicts will have domestic manifestations? Can we expect Armenian and Jewish Californians to squabble in the streets of Los Angeles just as Serbian and Croatian Wisconsinites have rumbled in the streets of Milwaukee? What does this all mean in terms of one of the most pressing race questions of all, the construction of "whiteness" in the United States? If "whites" in the United States begin to engage in difficult arguments inspired by complex international events, what will be the impact on African Americans, Chicano-Latinos, Asian Americans, and Native Americans? Is this truly an example of a blowback effect?

The Sun Rises in the East

There is another example of a possible blowback effect that could have significant impact on people of color. I refer to the rise of the economies in Japan and China and what this signifies in terms of the global correlation of forces. "Greater China," the People's Republic of China combined with the economies of Hong Kong and Taiwan, is predicted to have within years an economy larger than that of the United States. Can we continue to discuss white supremacy in the old way when there has been one of the more significant shifts in the past five hundred years in terms of "non-European" control of capital? Is it fair to say that there are those who would like to see Tokyo or Beijing replace Moscow as the enemy capital of choice? The best-seller penned by scholars affiliated with the Heritage Foundation, *The Coming War with Japan*,[6] outlines what some right-wing elites view as looming just over the horizon—a devastating bloodbath. This is the future that some are preparing for; a question is what the domestic impact of this developing tension will be in a nation such as the United States that lacks widespread class consciousness and barely contains simmering ethnic conflicts? When Japan ousted the British from what is now Malaysia during World War II, unlike London it sought alliance with the indigenous Malay population, theretofore despised. Tokyo made similar overtures to African Americans during the interwar years. Do these historical lessons have any contemporary relevance?

Former U.S. Senator Paul Tsongas during his unsuccessful race for the Democratic nomination for president was fond of posing the rhetorical query, "Who won the Cold War?" "Japan and Germany" won this conflict, he would add, despite the United States's having spent trillions of dollars and borne the main burden of this epochal conflict. Though this Cold War "victory," which has left the nation virtually bankrupt, has not improved the material condition of most of us, there are those who persist in proclaiming otherwise. The defeat of George Bush at the polls was one response to this question. In any case, the fact remains that despite much talk about the "sole remaining superpower," tensions have risen sharply between Washington and erstwhile allies in Berlin, Brussels, and Tokyo.

88

GERALD HORNEGERALD HORNE

Yet, it does appear that tensions with Tokyo have taken on much more of an ethnic flavor, particularly in California. This should not come as a surprise. John Dower in *War Without Mercy*[7] details the racially coded discourse that has characterized U.S.–Japanese relations for much of this century. In his 1991 dissertation "Afro-Americans and Japanese, 1905–45," Reginald Kearny shows that during the first four decades of the twentieth century, Japan was at the heart of African American discourse on race. Du Bois, Marcus Garvey, and Booker T. Washington disagreed about much, but they agreed that Japan's very existence undermined the central tenet of "white supremacy," namely, that only Europeans could construct advanced capitalist societies.

Black nationalism, whose existence in this nation has been facilitated by the crushing of the black Left, historically has maintained more than a passing interest in Japan. Garvey sent funds to Japan after it was hit by a massive earthquake; like most black leaders in New York at that time he was friendly with officials at the Japanese consulate, and officials from Tokyo were often on the dais during his Harlem rallies. Karl Evanzz, in his worthwhile book *The Judas Factor: The Plot to Kill Malcolm X*,[8] suggests that the Black Dragon Society of Japan had a hand in the formation of the Nation of Islam itself in the 1930s. Certainly the NOI's idea of the "black man" as an "Asiatic black man" stems directly from this context of the centrality of Japan among African Americans.

It was the onset of World War II that helped to stem this sentiment, and not necessarily because there was black revulsion over Pearl Harbor. In fact, there was much fear that many blacks would sympathize unduly with Tokyo, and a number of NOI leaders went to jail rather than fight in the war. Just as the fear that racism was a handicap during the Cold War led to civil rights concessions, likewise a factor in the postwar erosion of Jim Crow is this idea that maltreatment of blacks helps to create an enemy within the gates that antagonists like Japan can play on. Racially bigoted statements by certain Japanese elites have harmed Tokyo's image among many African Americans. But, as is reported in the 8–14 July 1992 *City Sun*, the Brooklyn-based black weekly, ultraright radicals from Japan have been making a serious attempt to increase their influence in the black community—and not without success, given the horrific conditions faced in inner cities nationwide.

Conclusion

A concerted attempt has been made by U.S. elites to blunt an effective class-derived discourse in this nation. This has been done legislatively by making it difficult—via the Taft-Hartley Act, the Landrum-Griffin Act, and various state laws—for progressive unions to flourish culturally (e.g., via the Hollywood "blacklist") and economically (e.g., making it difficult for radicals to find work). This has been a largely successful effort. But when blacks, for example, could no longer rely on class-based formations such as CIO unions, this only meant that they had to rely more on their own ranks, which created fertile soil for various forms of nationalism. Arthur Schlesinger didn't like the class approach, and he doesn't like the race approach. He expects African Americans, who come from an entirely different tradition—historically and politically—to be liberals like himself, but this is a difficult project indeed. And it has not happened.

Yes, there has been a splintering of the United States. This is in part because of the neglect of numerous peoples and movements by elite perspectives and in part because of the weakening of class-based organizations that have brought people together across racial, gender, and other boundaries. We have seen how playing on ethnic difference has been part of the tool kit of U.S. elites for some time now and this too has played a role in the rise of nationalism. But U.S. elites will discover in this new world they have helped to create that the tactics they launched in the 1940s, when Schlesinger red-baited the NAACP, will boomerang wildly as we stagger into the twenty-first century.

NOTES

1. Gerald Horne, *Black and Red: W.E.B. Du Bois and the Afro-American Response to the Cold War, 1944–63* (Albany: State University of New York Press, 1986), 58; Gerald Horne, *Communist Front? The Civil Rights Congress, 1946–56* (Rutherford, N.J.: Fairleigh Dickinson University Press, 1988).

2. Gerald Horne, *Black Liberation/Red Scare: Ben Davis and the Communist Party* (Newark: University of Delaware Press, 1994).

3. Arthur J. Schlesinger Jr., *The Vital Center: The Politics of Freedom* (Boston: Houghton Mifflin, 1949).

4. Alexander Cockburn, "Rabin Shows True Colors on Dark Saga," *Los Angeles Times,* 8 February 1993, A2.

5. "US" (as opposed to "them") was led by Maulana Karenga. See Kenneth O'Reilly, *"Racial Matters": The FBI's Secret File on Black America, 1960–1972* (New York: Free Press, 1989), 306–308.

6. George Friedman and Meredith Le Bard, *The Coming War with Japan* (New York: St. Martin's Press, 1991).

7. John Dower, *War Without Mercy* (New York: Pantheon Books, 1986).

8. Karl Evanzz, *The Judas Factor: The Plot to Kill Malcolm X* (New York: Thunder's Mouth Press, 1992).

5

The Entrepreneurship of the New: Corporate Direction and Educational Issues in the 1990s

EVAN WATKINS & LISA SCHUBERT

THE EDUCATIONAL RHETORIC of the eighties seemed full of a vocabulary of "return." Schools were encouraged to "return" to standards of assessment and accountability, to go back to the basics, to rediscover the heritage of Western culture and tradition, and so on. What exactly the country was to return *from* included among other things the "excesses" of political correctness and multiculturalism, as if some invisible pendulum had swung "too far" and was overdue for a compensatory trajectory. Working as we do in a university English department, in the midst of a now immense range of instruments for cultural critique, we found such discourse almost constructed for the purposes of laboratory experiment in critical analysis, made to order for the instruments at hand, with of course the bonus that its very pervasiveness ensured the political relevance of critique. What might have seemed even in the immediate past a relatively local intradepartmental quarrel over hiring decisions or curricular change, say, could now assume the larger dimensions of engagement with already mobilized political forces across any number of sectors in the social field.

We have no intention of denying the political relevance—or the larger implications—of ostensibly local debates in this newly drawn social landscape. But we are convinced that politically useful critique also has to question the notion of a "return" itself rather than focusing exclusively on the frequent distortions of what political correctness and multiculturalism are really all about or decoding the race/gender/class significations masked by "return" appeals. Although it is true enough that "return" rhetoric has simplified and distorted the issues that arose in public debates about political correctness and multiculturalism and unquestionably true that "return" is a coded assault on already politically disenfranchised groups, it seems to us a mistake to assume that "dominant politics" is then unequivocally invested in restoring the power balances that existed somewhere in "the past," before PC and multiculturalism. It's an all too easy assumption to make, since it conforms to the familiar claims of oppositional politics as dedicated to social change—to creating new and alternative possibilities against all the pressures for preserving existing configurations of social relations. As we have suggested, a rhetoric of return appears tailor-made for oppositional political critique playing to oppositional self-perceptions of being in the vanguard of change. To that extent, return rhetoric becomes an agreed-upon designation of ideological positions, however much its values and exact meanings are debated.

Yet it's worth remembering that despite such visible and familiar arguments as William Bennett's in *To Reclaim a Legacy* (1984), public discussion of education initiated within the terms of Reaganite hegemony has by no means always been oriented around a rhetoric of return. The "business community," in publications like the *Wall Street Journal, Fortune, Forbes,* and *Business Week,* has argued long and hard that a public education system in the United States requires a drastic overhaul if it is to teach the *new* worker skills necessary in a rapidly changing and increasingly competitive climate of global business. It is particularly important for those of us who teach in the disciplines of the humanities to attend carefully to these arguments and their agendas. In comparison with Bennett's claims or those advanced by Allan Bloom, Roger Kimball, and others, these business-oriented proposals are much less likely to find expression in some version or other within humanities departments. Not only the self-perceptions of radical political critique but also the internal structure of humanities departments works to emphasize the political weight of return rhetoric, at the cost of minimizing the challenges represented by, among other things, business-community interest in educational reform.

Educational policy in any case is located in the midst of what has been historically the field of greatest tension within Reaganism: on the one hand, economic imperatives that have emphasized corporate "restructuring" and diversification, technological innovation, participation in a global marketplace, and so on, and on the other, so-called social-issues imperatives that have emphasized the importance of the family, the authority of moral guidance and religious belief, and correspondingly the rampant dangers represented by homosexuals, feminists, militant blacks—the familiar gallery of Reaganism's social villains. Educational policy marks a territory where these divergent concerns must meet, if often conflictually, since implementation of both economic and social-issues imperatives requires educating children for a desired *future.* (Thus in a sense, even the most insistent rhetoric of return might be understood more accurately in educational terms as a kind of "back to the future" program.) Insofar as intraacademic debates about multiculturalism and political correctness look first to issues that are explicitly social, political, and cultural, they play in the same field, as it were, as social-issues Reaganism. In contrast, multiculturalism—or "diversity," as it is usually called in discussions of corporate management—appeared first to economic Reaganism as precisely an economic issue. As a result, corporate interests in educational reform enter educational territory, including the debates about multiculturalism and political correctness, from a rather different angle indeed.

Yet educational policy is obviously a matter of social, political, and cultural issues no less than economics. Further, and while the initial excitement over "supply-side" and the like seemed to identify a "pragmatic," profit-oriented side of Reaganism often remote from the fundamentalism of the Moral Majority, there were any number of early indications that the imperatives that would drive corporate change also involved a new priority, if initially couched in negative terms, for explicitly political and cultural concerns. Affirmative action was identified as unwarranted government "political" interference in business practices, for example, while the pressures toward "sensitivity training" and "diversity workshops" were viewed as a time-wasting drag on corporate efficiency.

At the same time, however, globalization meant the necessity of doing business with people from other cultures. The relocation of production plants outside U.S. borders created "problems" of dealing with a "native" workforce. Domestically, the increasing reliance on contracting work outside the corporation and a "leased" workforce within it created similar "problems" with "nonnative" workers in the United States. And the enormous numbers of mergers, acquisitions, and leveraged buyouts posed the difficulty of also merging what often turned out to be surprisingly different "corporate cultures." All of this functioned during the eighties to make *cultural* issues, no less than economic concerns, very high indeed on the agenda of how to prepare "corporate America" for the rapidly approaching twenty-first century. Diversity could not be viewed as just a "problem" imposed by government interference that might be "solved" by cosmetic attention in sensitivity workshops or as part of a regrettably necessary exoskeleton of affirmative-action hiring procedures. Managing diversity profitably would require wholesale changes in the very assumptions that shaped corporate culture.

In the face of these changes in the interest and organization of major corporations, it seems to us no longer very useful to image a simple division between economic and social-issues Reaganism or even to construct elaborate ways of marking out what was a certain ideological congruity. Economic Reaganism has mutated into its own version of *linked* programs for economic and cultural change that are not a matter of "return" in any sense. What these programs involve, and how they legitimate their images of the future, should be a matter of considerable concern in trying to anticipate the directions of educational reform.

In what follows we want to focus on the emergent process of restructuring corporate culture in the terms suggested by human resources analysis and the thematics of "managing diversity" and then, if briefly, connect these directions to what is often referred to as school culture reform, likewise already visible in such things as Bush's America 2000 agenda and Clinton's notion of educational "choices."[1] The premise is a simple one: to whatever extent a public educational system in the United States was both created for and modeled on industrial corporate organization, changes in that organization toward a postindustrial, "service" economy will be a powerful force shaping future changes in education. To see the actual historical development of public education in these terms is not the whole story by any means, and as a result, to project the future of educational institutions by way of looking to corporate reorganization will hardly yield an infallible guide. At best, it will only help identify pressures and potential directions of reform. Thus we don't intend by this emphasis our own form of return to any version of economic determinism, which in any case was always just bad philosophy with little relation to economics. In part, the rationale is simply some sense that when corporate interests pay this much attention to "culture," it's perhaps time for the rest of us to pay some attention to economics. We think that focusing on emergent changes in corporate organization will help to locate issues that should engage educators considerably more than a continual and often virtually hypnotized stare at return rhetoric.

A Culture of Diversity

In 1987–1988 John Fernandez, a former manager with AT&T and later president of Advanced Research Management Consultants, conducted a massive survey of employee attitudes toward "diversity" in the workplace, involving over 30,000 respondents and including often quite lengthy discussions among the some 2,000 employees who had attended Fernandez's workshops in managing diversity. In an article summarizing some of the results, Fernandez and Dubois (1990) report that racism, sexism, and ethnocentrism are still very much in evidence on shop floors and in boardrooms. Consequently, they argue that U.S. companies must make every effort to change their managerial practices to accommodate diversity rather than suppress it or pretend that the "problems" of employing women and people of color have already been resolved. Active accommodation, they claim, will ease conflicts among employees that potentially could hinder productivity and, more important, maximize the productive potential of the cultural resources offered by a diverse workforce. "We must emphasize," they write,

> that companies that are willing to accommodate diversity will reap rewards in traditional dollars-and-cents terms as they listen to their most valuable resource: people. We predict that those corporations that refuse to attend to pressing employee concerns will be split by conflict as they find potential workers more difficult to find and much more apt to work in organizations where they are fully appreciated. (p. 206)

A national study published in 1987 by the Hudson Institute entitled *Workforce 2000* lends demographic support to many of Fernandez and Dubois's suggestions. By the year 2000, the report claims, native white males will account for only 15 percent of the "net new" employees in the United States. Native white women (42 percent), native nonwhite women (13 percent) and men (7 percent), and immigrant men (13 percent) and women (9 percent) are expected to fill the vast majority of the new jobs created. And of existing employee positions, white males will soon account for less than one-third (Hudson Institute 1987, quoted in Morrison 1992, 14). With potential workers coming from so many culturally diverse backgrounds, corporations that refuse to accommodate diversity not only will find it more difficult to reduce the kind of employee conflicts Fernandez found prevalent in his survey but may find it difficult to hire a workforce at all.

Thus companies willing to accommodate diversity will "reap rewards in dollars-and-cents terms," as Fernandez and Dubois contend, because they will save themselves the cost of frequent employee turnovers, reduce the risk of conflicts that deflect attention from the pursuit of corporate objectives, and in general improve employee morale and investment in the company. But this new emphasis on diversity claims to offer more than a sort of "loss prevention" cost-reduction safeguard. A diverse workforce has clear competitive advantages as well, since women and people of color can offer insights and ideas that would not be tapped in the "old boy" network. As any number of recently published books such as Sondra Thiederman's *Profiting in America's Multicultural Marketplace* (1991) testify, a culturally diverse workforce can help secure an increasingly diverse market for corporate products and services. Not only do women know better than men what women "need," for example, but they know best how to play on their insecurities to sell it to them. And with the aggregate spending power of African Americans, Asian Americans, and Hispanics estimated at $424 billion in 1990 and projected to soar to $650 billion by 2000 (Copeland 1988, quoted in Morrison 1992, 16), corporations have every incentive to invest in previously disparaged "efficiency drags" such as diversity training to pursue the potential marketing edge offered by a diverse workforce.

Corporate attention to demographic trends, to the increasingly intense competition for market presence among diverse cultural groups, and to the competition for highly qualified "nontraditional" workers indicates that management has recognized the importance of accommodating diversity. What is not yet clear, however, and currently a subject of debate is the kind of corporate change and retraining this new emphasis necessitates. Since the entrance of women and people of color into the labor force in large numbers creates new and intense pressures, as Fernandez's survey documents, the success of "cultural diversity" in the corporate environment will depend upon "managing" these pressures adequately. Hence John Preston, the CEO of Avon Corporation, adds one caveat to his otherwise upbeat assessment: "More and more, corporations and organizations of all kinds are awakening to the fact that a diverse work force is not a burden but their greatest potential strength—*when managed properly*" (Preston 1991, ix, emphasis added).

By now a vast array of recently published books, including Fernandez's own *Managing a Diverse Work Force: Regaining the Competitive Edge* (1991), have attempted to define what managing diversity entails. Yet there's little if any consensus understanding of the concept within the field. In Ann Morrison's *The New Leaders: Guidelines on Leadership Diversity in America*, for example, what Fernandez calls managing diversity appears rather differently, and for her less patronizingly, as "the multicultural approach." As is typical in situations requiring new definitional constructs, it has often proved easier to identify what managing diversity is *not* than to agree on what it is. A recent course offering for faculty, professional, and classified staff at the University of Washington, "Developing an Organizational Diversity Plan," thus begins by distinguishing "the differences among affirmative action, valuing differences, and managing diversity" (University of Washington 1992, 16) as corporate strategies for integrating women and people of color.

These particular distinctions derive from the work of R. Roosevelt Thomas Jr., the founder of the American Institute for Managing Diversity and the consultant whom James Preston credits with having successfully restructured Avon in the mideighties. In *Beyond Race and Gender* (1991), Thomas argues that affirmative action is implemented primarily for legal and ethical reasons. The assumption is that white males constitute the majority of employees in any given workplace and that "others"—categorized collectively by gender and race—are employed either because the company must conform to government regulations or because management feels a moral obligation to provide "equal opportunity" to women and people of color. For Thomas, affirmative action is, then, a reactive strategy "imported" from outside the corporation to solve internal problems. As such it leads to what he calls an "affirmative action cycle," which is "frustrating and virtually unavoidable. ... [a] cycle of crisis, problem recognition, action, great expectations, disappointment, dormancy, and renewed crisis" (p. 21). A company may "react" to the symptoms of crisis—for example, when morale is low or there has been a high turnover of "minority" employees—by initiating a frantic search for the "right" categorically identified person who can ensure the firm's image as an equitable place to work. But because the "action" has simply assumed the feasibility of assimilating collectively defined "others" into an existing corporate culture, the solution only leads to a renewed "cycle of crisis."

In contrast to affirmative action, a valuing-differences approach responds to the felt needs and values of *individual* employees: "Valuing difference programs are geared to the individual and interpersonal levels. The objective is to enhance interpersonal relationships among individuals and to minimize blatant expressions of racism and sexism" (Thomas 1991, 24–25). According to Thomas, the intent of such an approach is to be the perfect complement to an affirmative action emphasis on collective, group identifications that categorically distinguish women and people of color from white males. Whereas affirmative action imposes legal and ethical obligations from outside to incorporate culturally diverse "groups" into the company, valuing differences attempts to break the "cycle of crisis" with programs that raise awareness of the culturally unique contributions each individual has to offer.

For Thomas, however, valuing differences remains like affirmative action a reactive strategy, simply a complementary way of addressing what is nonetheless perceived as "the problem" of incorporating women and people of color into the company. Whether by legal mandate or ethical obligation, the goals of affirmative action are extrinsic to the corporation, which isn't in the business of writing legal codes or devising ethical systems. And although employees are obviously important to corporate business, their individual qualities as revealed through a program of valuing-differences workshops are not exactly what the company exists for either. With both approaches, severally or in combination, the company merely "reacts" to what is perceived as a human resources "problem" whose correction at best can only set the company back on course.

Through this process of defining affirmative action and valuing differences, Thomas arrives at a kind of double negative, as it were, to identify managing diversity as a positive program. Managing diversity "doesn't seek to give relief to a system's negative consequences by adding supplementary efforts" (1991, 26); rather, it "is a holistic approach to creating a corporate environment that allows all kinds of people to reach their full potential in pursuit of corporate objectives" (p. 167). That is, unlike either affirmative action or valuing differences, managing diversity requires no extrinsic guidelines or imperatives. It is intrinsic to the "natural" operating assumptions of a corporation in the pursuit of profit. Thus in using terms such as "natural creation of a diverse work force" and "natural upward mobility for minorities and women" (p. 28), Thomas doesn't mean that this new picture of the corporation now conforms to some universalized norm of "human nature." He means that hiring and promotion practices appear fully congruent with the "nature" of the corporation, which of course involves making money. "True, all groups will benefit," he argues, "whether they are different in terms of age, lifestyle, gender or race. But their benefit is not the driving motivation. Managing diversity presumes that the driving force is the manager's, and the company's, self-interest" (p. 168).

In order for hiring and promotion practices to appear fully congruent with the nature of the corporation, however, the definition of diversity must expand—"beyond race and gender," as Thomas's title implies—to include difference "with respect to age, functional and educational backgrounds, lifestyle preferences, tenure within the organization, personality traits, and ways of thinking" (p. 170). White men are also constituted as "different" in this new approach and included with everyone else rather than segregated as often happens in diversity workshops. Morrison makes a similar point with respect to what she calls the "multicultural approach":

> In this approach, diversity has a broad meaning that encompasses sex and ethnic groups along with groups based on such attributes as nationality, professional discipline, or cognitive style. In contrast to the assimilation model, this approach assumes that the organization must change and the norms must accommodate a wide range of workers. The explicit goal is to strengthen the organization by leveraging a host of significant differences. (1992, 7)

By revamping the corporate culture to recognize all differences that employees have to offer while selectively valuing only those differences that contribute to corporate success, managing diversity claims to offer the possibility of acquiring and promoting a diverse workforce "naturally," as an intrinsic part of corporate objectives.

Lest Thomas's view be understood as a version of economic determinism pointing invariably to "the last instance" of profit, however, it is important to stress that his understanding of managing diversity is as thoroughly cultural as it is economic. The point for Thomas is that managing diversity *integrates* economic and cultural priorities, recognizes their mutual dependence from within, and thereby maximizes the productive potential of the company. The collectively based categories of affirmative action and the individual attention of valuing differences thus reemerge in the nature of the diverse corporation as an expression of its human resource potential. Indeed, in contrast to what Thomas calls "the old top-down, directive style" of management, in which managers concentrated on performing the "tasks" of the corporation while relegating employee concerns about diversity to human resources departments, this new managerial strategy is based on an "empowerment model." As Thomas explains, "In this model, the duality between 'business issues' and 'people issues' is absent. Instead, the empowerment of employees is linked directly to or integrated with business objectives" (1991, 47). By means of a "radically" altered corporate environment in which employees are "empowered" to pursue corporate ends, managing diversity identifies people rather than raw materials or capital or technologies as a company's most powerful "leveraged" resource.

To "sophisticated" cultural critique a management strategy that claims to privilege human resources may itself seem little more than a disguised return rhetoric doing its usual job of legitimating invidious practices under the banner of "the human." Yet to a certain extent, in ways necessary to understand for the purposes of effective critique, human resources thinking is closer to academic postmodernism than to any lamely residual nod toward "humanistic" discourse. In trying to move beyond the categorical, group-based identifications embodied in affirmative action guidelines and the individualizing programs of valuing differences, this new conception of "human resources" addresses what might usefully be recognized as a kind of collective multiplicity. That is, Thomas's simultaneous critique of affirmative action and valuing differences suggests that the "subject" of human resources analysis is no more a vestige of the metaphysically "human" than the "decentered subject" now so familiar in poststructuralist theorizing. Each person in Thomas's new corporate environment is understood to occupy what such a poststructuralist terminology might identify as "multiple subject positions," involving determinations of race, gender, age, lifestyle, and so on.

The analogy can't be pushed too far, however, since despite the similarities that permit the use of terminology borrowed from our own academic field, these positionalities locate finally a collective *resource* rather than the experientially based, "decentered" multiplicity of poststructuralist theorizing. Thus although not transcendently "human," they are positions that Thomas would image as "beyond race and gender" because immanently corporate; each position in its shifting, contingent, flexible adaptation to continually changing circumstances contributes to the collective goal of "leveraging a host of significant differences," in Morrison's phrase, "that strengthen the organization." That is, differences *as diversity* matter in relation to the maximizing of resources. Not all differences count equally on all occasions. What constitutes "significant differences" involves a politics of selection that is neither some damped-down, "co-opted" version of the postmodern nor a return to "traditional" humanism.

Neither is it merely a deceptive extension of those familiar corporate attempts in the early eighties to circumvent affirmative action guidelines and minimize the importance of diversity workshops. Indeed, the theorizing of diversity expresses the commitments of an emergent corporate culture to include women and people of color as an invaluable resource. Unlike affirmative action or valuing differences, however, managing diversity is not *about* women and people of color. It is about managing. "Managing diversity," Thomas reminds us, "presumes that the driving force is the manager's, and the company's, self-interest" (1991, 168). Thus the practices that regulate the process of inclusion begin not with the question of how to deal with women and people of color but with what Thomas's attention to diversity has already "presumed," a politics of *management* selection that defines company "self-interest" and the resources that might contribute to the realization of that interest. We want to turn, then, from the theorizing of diversity by management consultants such as Thomas and Fernandez to the work of human resources analysis in a "case study" of a corporate merger that describes in some considerable detail how the principles that guide management selection are being altered. As an integral part of a much larger process of change over the last decade, it is the new corporate politics of selection evident in the merger that is likely to influence educational proposals for the future and hence what opportunities actually become available to women and people of color to "participate" in a diverse workforce.

Merging and Selection

One of the more familiar and visible business changes in the eighties was the enormous increase of mergers and acquisitions, nearly doubling by the middle of the decade and involving triple-digit billions of dollars. The financing of these "events" has attracted the most attention, especially as they often depended on leveraged buyouts and the virtually complete transformation of the so-called junk-bond market (with now, as one of the delayed effects, the burgeoning of a whole new sector of financial specialists to engage in "unleveraging" staggering debt burdens and a new legal sector of specialists to rewrite the permissible itineraries of junk-bond movement). Much of the merger/acquisition activity involved unrelated (in terms of product-identification) corporations, reinforcing a perception of an increasingly "decentralized" and global business network, and the unencumbered movement of legal/management/finance specialists across both corporate and national borders.

In a number of cases, however, mergers involved firms offering directly competing products and services, where the financing—while obviously crucial—produced nothing by way of the dramatic action narratives of "corporate raiders" and little of the speculative possibilities of junk-bond float. Financing was largely secondary to the immense and immediate problems of how to reorganize the new corporate structure quickly to maintain market presence. These problems were not financial but "people" problems: Who would do what? Who would stay, and where? Who would go, and under what severance conditions? They were, in sum, problems involving the principles of selection for the collective multiplicity of a new corporate workforce. Cultural diversity in the sense of profoundly different racial, ethnic, gender, and age groups was not an explicit issue in most of these mergers, nor was it in the example we want to focus on, the Baxter Travenol and American Hospital Supply merger in 1985 to form the Baxter Healthcare Corporation. Corporate culture was the central concern but in circumstances that, like the incorporation of diversity, require a revised politics of selection intrinsic to the objectives of the new corporate entity. That is, the Baxter-American merger offers a compact model of change in the politics of selection—a model whose principles are already being extended by human resources analysis to define not only new management objectives but, more important, the larger process of education and training necessary for diversity to be mobilized as a corporate resource.

Anthony Rucci, the senior vice president of human resources for Baxter Healthcare; Frank LaFasto, manager of human resources for Baxter; and David Ulrich, management professor at the University of Michigan, have provided a lengthy summary discussion of the transition process in "Managing Organizational Change: A Merger Case Study" (1990). For our purposes, the most revealing aspect of the merger involved an early key point established by the transition teams with respect to "people selection": the principle of selecting "the best person regardless of company" (1990, 148). Although the idea seems unexceptional, it in fact was not at all common practice in merger reorganization. More typically, the acquiring firm—in this case Baxter—would fit specific individuals into its organization if their expertise seemed valuable or sometimes simply dismiss wholesale much of the acquired firm's personnel. If "practical" enough in circumstances of a generally shrinking market and the correspondingly necessary downsizing of the corporation, in a rapidly growing field of health care supplies such policies made little sense.

How to determine "the best person" in the new circumstances of the merger, however, was by no means clear. Although providing similar products to the health care industry, Baxter and American had operated very differently:

> American Hospital Supply Corporation was characterized by a decentralized operating structure that included multiple operating units with a fully integrated operating philosophy. By contrast, the pre-merger Baxter organization was a much more cen-

tralized and functional operating style with few autonomous operating units and functional responsibilities such as human resources and finance reporting directly to the corporate headquarters. (Rucci, LaFasto, and Ulrich, 1990, 146)

A person skilled in the team organization of one of American's autonomous units might not be skilled at all in guiding a project through the levels of a premerger Baxter hierarchy and might not in any case be willing to work in circumstances that could seem a constraint on decisionmaking authority.

Thus, as important as it was, the principle of "selecting the best person" could not yield an answer to whether decisions should be made on "a strictly individual basis" or on considerations of "group" identifications or values. Nor would an affirmative-action assumption of group identities or a valuing-differences assumption of individual uniqueness supply useful corrective guidelines, because in the circumstances *both* key terms—"individual" and "group"—were the very terms that required definition. Every "individual" interviewee and every "individual" interviewer in the selection process was already and from the beginning also a *Baxter* individual or an *American* individual, who then had to occupy at least the double "subject position" of premerger American or Baxter and postmerger Baxter during the negotiations. Further, the interviewers on the selection teams had no guarantees themselves that they would eventually become part of the new organization. Even "fit" with the postmerger Baxter collective couldn't simply be assumed as a criterion, since postmerger Baxter had yet to be defined and in its details could be defined only through the very process of setting up employee screening processes and interpreting their results. "Selecting the best person" likewise yielded no guidelines for understanding the relation between past performance and projected future performance. What might constitute optimum performance had, precisely, a "functional"—as yet to be determined—and not an "intrinsic" content.

Before "selecting the best person" could be implemented, it was necessary to identify in some detail the corporate "philosophy" of the new Baxter as a "hybrid" organization that involved "decentralizing," on the American model, "those decisions that had a substantive impact on the customer" but for "those areas not seen as critical to customer interface" moving closer to a Baxter-like centralization of authority (Rucci, LaFasto, and Ulrich 1990, 146). It was necessary to determine the composition of screening teams for selection at each level of the new structure— no easy task in itself, since Baxter and American had been often bitter competitors for forty-five years, and part of the corporate lore of each company included many tales of "sinister" behavior on the part of the other. And finally, it was necessary to devise considerably more elaborate "interview" procedures for selection that could generate reasonably accurate predictions of how interviewees would function in the new organization. At the level of concrete detail, in other words, looking at such a process helps explain what exactly is involved in one of Thomas's key principles distinguishing the education for a managing-diversity perspective:

change begins with the very "roots" of corporate culture and always requires a continual and explicitly constructed definition of what it's all for.

How "the best person" was selected in the merger transition is important to understand, because it is a process that has a rather direct equivalent in educational institutions. "Selecting the best person" also expresses a primary educational task of transforming a multiple, diverse student population in the schools into a *workforce* trained and sorted out "appropriately" to the job tasks available. As both feminist and marxist critiques have amply demonstrated, it is a selection process that has operated in all kinds of skewed and discriminatory ways behind the facade of "merit." The Baxter-American merger model, however, profoundly alters the rationale for selection. The politics of selection is no longer based, like merit, in a claim of determining intrinsic qualities of the person. Instead, it becomes a function of the identification of what "significant differences" would best serve the emergent corporate entity. Further, and although the corporate-culture differences addressed by the model are by no means the same as racial-ethnic or gender or sexual-preference or age differences, preserving a rhetoric of selecting the best person nevertheless permits the model to be extended by human resources analysis to *any* form of diversity and difference. Like merit, "the best person" exhaustively codes the available field in the selection process. But in contrast to the rationales for merit decisions, "the best person" is contingently defined for the occasion by the merger process.

For all that it thereby uncouples determinations of "the best person" from familiar, stable ideological codings of merit, a text like "Managing Organizational Change: A Merger Case Study" admittedly lacks the visceral excitement of the postmodern novel for academic literary theorists. And it offers little obvious scope for the political delights of attacking Roger Kimball and the rest with their amplified "return" noises about the imminent collapse of Western civilization. But in many ways it's a lot more important, because it and others like it will have a lot to do with where, under what conditions, and to whom you might in future be teaching postmodern novels and what kinds of jobs, if any, those students who have benefited from your careful instruction will get. As Fernandez and Dubois— if perhaps melodramatically—point out, educational commitments and educational reform must be very high indeed on the agenda of managing diversity:

> if we start investing in education from every source (private donations of various types and funding from all levels of government), we can truly have a literate country and a labor pool of qualified candidates. If we ignore the statistics about workforce composition and education, we will have a severe shortage of qualified workers and a country that continues to have large pockets of extremely disadvantaged people of color. (1990, 208)

Fernandez and Dubois conveniently manage to ignore, however, the way in which this "reformed" vision of larger educational purpose nevertheless continues to embody a politics of selection in terms that by no means guarantee expectations of "advantageous" social change for "large pockets of extremely disadvantaged people of color." Although managing diversity would rewrite the conditions of what constitutes social "advantage" and "disadvantage" through educational training, curricular structure, institutional organization, and selection processes, it nonetheless remains a politics of power, of control over human resources, and to some very great extent of social disenfranchisement, now increasingly finding expression in and through a process of educational reform.

Flexibly Specialized Education

"Flexible specialization" is a complex concept that describes the differences between mass production of standardized goods with predominantly unskilled labor and the manufacture of specialized goods for segmented buying publics employing fewer and very highly skilled workers. This flexibly specialized form of production might be implemented by small businesses or the autonomous operating units of large corporations. In either case, however, it is very much rooted in and dependent on the resources available in a particular region. Thus Michael Piore and Charles Sabel's influential inaugural text *The Second Industrial Divide* (1984) describes in some detail the links between corporations and their regional locations, emphasizing the interconnected ensemble of social relations and institutional resources that identify the specificity of a region. Resources, they argue, typically will involve not only one or more major research universities but the whole complex tributary web of educational suppliers to the university.

For our purposes, the concept of flexible specialization permits a kind of double-exposure image of projected directions of educational reform. On the one hand, it widens the lens significantly beyond the frame of "radical" corporate-culture change that Thomas emphasizes in his managing-diversity programs for re-educating corporate management. Although Thomas understands well enough that implementing a managing-diversity approach takes more time than a day-long diversity seminar, he neglects to consider its dependence on resources beyond the corporation.[2] Even as reorganized in Thomas's terms, a company after all can "naturally" acquire a diverse workforce only if it has well-established connections to educational institutions that "naturally" make such a workforce available. Thus, as Fernandez and Dubois argue, corporations have every incentive "to invest in the communities from which they hope to draw workers" (1990, 238).

On the other hand, however, flexible specialization frames a close-up of how the characteristics of educational institutions may vary from one region to another as the forms of specialized manufacture vary. "Universal" education, general standards of skills and training, institutional uniformity of educational opportunity—such concepts have relatively little long-term use in generating limited pools of highly skilled workers. In order to gain the kind of corporate support for education that consultants like Fernandez recommend, educational institutions themselves, no less than corporations, will have every reason to "flexibly specialize." A corporate politics of selection, that is, becomes in larger terms an educational policy of training different people differently.

In his reconceptualizing of Labor Department classificatory indices of the workforce in *The Work of Nations* (1991), Robert Reich argues that a system developed in the industrial economy of mass production in the thirties which still distinguishes between hand labor and machine operatives is completely inadequate to describe current workforce divisions. The select, highly skilled employees envisioned by the literature of flexible specialization, for example, would be identified by Reich as "symbolic analysts." Rather than being trained to perform specific tasks, symbolic analysts are trained in the conceptual operations of "problem-finding" and "problem-solving." That is, their skills are themselves "flexible," capable of being turned to *whatever* new and continually shifting occasions appear. Reich argues that symbolic analysts are in fact the primary "resource" of "human capital," filling the pages of human resources analysis with hymns to corporate progress.

Even very successful regional sectors, however, will have a population composed not only of such symbolic analysts but also of what Reich calls "routine producers" and "in-person servers," the two other large, general divisions of the workforce in his revised classificatory scheme. Routine producers are engaged in specific and repetitive tasks, whether in the corporate office, the warehouse, or the "home-shop" subcontracting firms that supply much of the labor for specific product runs for large corporations such as Baxter Healthcare. Although, as Reich admits, routine producers continue to decline as a relative percentage of the total workforce, in absolute terms their numbers remain enormous, and to whatever diminished extent their work remains indispensable to corporate productivity. In-person servers, in contrast, are a rapidly growing percentage of the workforce, as necessary as routine producers and no less tied to the regional location. It is of course their "services" that exempt symbolic analysts from much of the tedium of their working lives.

Reich is, then, by no means confident that the high priority of education—as a key to changing corporate culture, as the "tools" available for realizing the potential of human resources, and institutionally as a vital element in the regional web—automatically implies anything like a higher level of education for everybody linked to a highly rewarding and well-paid job.[3] A great many "people skills" may in fact be necessary to an in-person server who rushes McDonald's hamburgers from one office complex to another, and even more such skills if the product is taco sushi instead of hamburgers on the run. It's possible that the server may speak two languages with some remarkable fluency—three including "street" or "'hood." But it's not very likely that that person will be eagerly recruited by the local research university (or local community college, for that matter), the local autonomous operating unit of the now flexibly specialized, downsized, and flattened management hierarchy of recently acquired corporation X, or even the firm supplying a leased workforce to that operating unit.[4] That is not the person who leaps immediately to mind to fill what human resources environmental scans project as a growing number of soon-to-be-empty "skill positions."[5] Such "diversity" is not attractive or indeed even *noticeable* in the landscape of the scan. Skilled though the person may be, s/he has a long way to go in the entrepreneurship of self-marketing.

"Entrepreneurship" is a term made famous during the early years of Reaganism, signifying an emphasis on individual economic initiative, the encouragement of "small business" enterprise, and so on. But like a great many other terms it has itself changed, and it has generated offspring such as the currently fashionable "intrepreneurship," used to designate managerial in-house innovations in employee relations, including treating employees as if they were customers. Marquette Bank, for example, like a number of corporations, has extended a classic bank sales tactic of gifts to attract new customer savings accounts by giving gifts and savings bonuses to employees who generate new ideas that translate into a greater client base. The example is a particularly telling one, for even in its earlier and more directly economic usages "the entrepreneurial spirit" was typically imaged as a matter of recognizing possibilities for new product and service niches in the market. That is, it was already *consumer*-oriented, grounded in a combination of market research analysis and "intuitive flair" for recognizing the occasion. "Successful entrepreneurs," Richard Crawford argues in *In the Era of Human Capital,* "are not risk takers but rather opportunity takers who are constantly looking to shift resources—both human and financial—to areas of higher return" (1991, 128). As a result, Crawford adds, any "good entrepreneurial strategy has to be market based and driven" (p. 129).

Thus, as its meanings have evolved, "entrepreneurship" has more and more come to identify the flip side, as it were, of human resources attention to people resources and selection: What is good human resources management within the corporation translates into entrepreneurial success when directed toward the corporation's clientele, its customers. Correspondingly, what human resources analysis focuses on from a management perspective as a matter of intrepreneurship with respect to managing a workforce might well be understood from a workforce perspective as the skills of entrepreneurial self-marketing in *getting* a good job. You must learn to treat your potential employer as a customer, a consumer of the services you have to offer. It doesn't then take a great leap of logic to see one driving force behind projected directions of educational reform as training in precisely such skills. That training will teach you how to be the kind of employee who will benefit the most and yield the greatest productivity under the new conditions of corporate organization.

All of this has of course a familiar ring to anyone aware of the reciprocal interest in job training between educational institutions and corporations that has existed throughout the history of public education in the United States. As Watkins (1993) has argued, however, to the extent that the reciprocity is familiar it should be a reminder that, as corporations change, what is expected in terms of educational training will change as well. And the changes we have been describing in corporate practices and organization are considerable. In one sense, to be sure, schools have always been expected to provide the "service" of job training and its corresponding cultural conditioning. Thus in marxist critique, for example, an educational system is often understood, crudely, as an "apparatus" for ideological (re)production. These new circumstances, however, permit not only an image of educational reform as training new and different workforce skills but, more important, a redefinition of education itself as a service marketer and distributor, making available a student "service" where and when it is needed for regional consumers.

Recent proposals for educational reform attuned to business interests such as those collected under a school-culture approach are then not open even to the very sophisticated versions of marxist "reproduction" critique in quite the same way. Schools aren't understood as factories processing student "raw material" into the finished product of good, docile workers who know their place. They are entrepreneurial service firms, ever sensitive to indices of marketability that locate new sectors of consumer "needs" and "demands" and dedicated to educating students accordingly. Students, again, are the product-services marketed by the schools. Thus "selecting the best person" in the schools becomes less and less a matter of fine-tuning instruments to detect the precious metal of inherent student potential encased in the slag ore of each individual sample of student work (or, in marxist terms, "reproducing" what is already defined as precious). What is "precious" and "the best" becomes openly and admittedly functional, as in the Baxter-American merger model—defined in and through the interactive and continually changing consumer context of who contracts for the schools' services and managed by the educator as entrepreneurial strategist. As we have argued, educational institutions in these circumstances will have every incentive to "downsize" and "flexibly specialize." (The Edison Project and Channel One are only two of many recent examples.) Their institutional structure and market presence, too, will depend on seizing the occasion of possible new market niches.

This large redefinition of educational organization and function isn't really a return to anything, as familiar as certain aspects of it are. It's a vision of a postindustrial education for a postindustrial economy. It doesn't set out to "return" combatively from multiculturalism or even political correctness or simply to incorporate and isolate their thematics procedurally in order to get on with business. It's part of a vision that offers itself instead as a larger and more comprehensive way of organizing a desirable and "diverse" social world. As Piore and Sabel's work on flexible specialization emphasizes, corporate innovation in this vision is not necessarily at odds with very conservative and even "traditional" social values of a regional center. Nor is it necessarily inconsistent with a region of rapidly changing social values. Thus school-culture reform as it appears in Bush's *America 2000* agenda may appear relatively "conservative," in Clinton's education for choices more "progressive," for neither managing diversity nor school-culture reform can afford to be incompatible with the region's specific and powerful clientele.

But as Watkins (1990) has argued at length, they are altogether incompatible with the hopes and expectations of huge groups of the population—with Reich's routine producers and in-person servers no less than with the populations of "urban ghettos"—who are designated as obsolete, products of a now dysfunctional internal culture, the throwaway waste of change. The proposed educational reforms will after all target these groups not for reform but for disposal and recycling. Waste management is also a service the schools will be expected to supply while at the other end supplying the bright new human-resources capital of the diverse workforce of the future. *That's* the situation that must be changed, not the minds of our collegial William Bennett clones.

Terms such as "multiculturalism" and "political correctness" identify now familiar contested territories but, as we have argued, territories beginning to be occupied by groups with little interest in a "return." It's true enough that the relative freedom of an academic position permits flight to as yet unnamed open spaces at the first signs of an approaching squall line of "co-optation," let alone the massive redefinitional powers of "managing diversity." But not everybody has that luxury; not everybody can afford to see the "co-optation" of terms and territories as a cue to exit stage (farther) left rather than as a necessary struggle just under way. And from the perspective of those who can't afford it, such freedom of academic movement is just another name for that no less familiar educational pattern of the eighties, white flight to the 'burbs.

NOTES

1. "School culture" (or "student culture") is one of a number of terms for an assumption that the assessment of student knowledges and skills affords a direct index of the "learning environment" available in the school. Thus if it could be documented—as both Bennett's (1984) and Cheney's (1988) reports claim to do—that students were deficient in knowledge areas generally recognized as crucial, the primary reason would be found in an inadequate school environment. The answer to those deficiencies would then be a thoroughgoing reform of "school culture" rather than changes in educational funding or in the political and economic conditions of the larger social world that students inhabit. (Bush's recommendation for standardized skill testing in his America 2000 agenda, for example, drew on school-culture reasoning by claiming that such tests simply assemble the necessary data on which to base decisions about educational reform policies.) Like the concept of "corporate culture" in human resources analysis, school culture locates a specific ensemble of interconnected relations between economic and social priorities. (For a further discussion of the term and its implications, see Watkins 1993.)

2. As Schubert (1993) argues, the corporate restructuring of the past twenty years and the new managerial strategies that ensued have necessitated a reeducation process that will teach not only company executives but the general populace a whole new set of priorities and assumptions associated with the new corporate culture. This reeducation process is already visible in popular culture, where white men are increasingly depicted as "cultural managers," employing women and people of color from around the world to achieve "company" objectives.

3. Indeed, in the last section of his book, Reich implores the symbolic analysts, as the top fifth of income earners, to "pay their fair share" for benefiting from the labor and services of routine producers and in-person servers. Since the symbolic analysts have the money, education, and political leverage to understand and influence the public policies that have resulted in the widening divergence in incomes between the top one-fifth and the lower four-fifths—"the growing difference in their working conditions, the regressive shift of the tax burden, the growing difference in the quality of primary and secondary education available to their children, the growing disparity in their access to higher education, [and] the increasing difference in recreational facilities, roads, security, and other local amenities available to them" (1991, 282)—they must vote to increase their own rate of taxation.

Reich's tone in this section, however, is one of desperation verging on futility, as he has just outlined how symbolic analysts spend their weekdays "problem-finding" and "problem-solving" with people all over the world while spending their weekends in suburban enclaves sheltered from the public policies that continue to distance the lower four-fifths from any hope of a financially secure future.

4. "Flattened management hierarchy" identifies both the elimination of a number of "middle management" positions and the streamlined decentralization of decision-making authority. Thus as an index of relative "progressiveness" in Dennis Kravetz's (1988) study, for example, it signals corporate willingness to alter organizational structure in response to changing market conditions. Kravetz claims an impressive statistical correlation between such indices of progressiveness and annualized company profits in a comparative analysis of some 150 firms—most of which were in the *Forbes* 500 list—between 1984 and 1988.

5. "Environmental scan" is a term introduced by human resources analysis to describe a multilayered profile that combines an attention to demographic trends, "lifestyle" changes and accommodations, educational directions and resources, technological innovation, market shifts, and so on, insofar as they might affect the composition, availability, skills, expectations, and commitment of a potential workforce.

WORKS CITED

Bennett, William J. *To Reclaim a Legacy: A Report on the Humanities in Higher Education.* Washington, D.C., 1984.

Cheney, Lynne V. *Humanities in America: A Report to the President, the Congress, and the American People.* Washington, D.C., National Endowment for the Humanities, 1988.

Copeland, Lennie. "Valuing Workplace Diversity: Ten Reasons Employers Recognize the Benefits of a Mixed Work Force." *Personnel Administrator,* November 1988, 38–40.

Crawford, Richard. *In the Era of Human Capital: The Emergence of Talent, Intelligence, and Knowledge as the Worldwide Economic Force and What It Means to Managers and Investors.* New York: HarperCollins, 1991.

Fernandez, John P. *Managing a Diverse Work Force: Regaining the Competitive Edge.* Lexington, Mass.: Lexington Books, 1991.

Fernandez, John P., and Jacqueline A. Dubois. "Managing a Diverse Workforce in the 1990s." In *Human Resource Forecasting and Strategy Development,* ed. Manuel London, Emily Bassman, and John Fernandez, 205–245. New York: Quorum, 1990.

Hudson Institute. *Workforce 2000: Work and Workers for the Twenty-first Century.* Indianapolis: Hudson Institute, 1987.

Kravetz, Dennis J. *The Human Resources Revolution: Implementing Progressive Management Practices for Bottom-Line Success.* San Francisco: Jossey-Bass, 1988.

Morrison, Ann. *The New Leaders: Guidelines on Leadership Diversity in America.* San Francisco: Jossey-Bass, 1992.

Piore, Michael, and Charles Sabel. *The Second Industrial Divide: Possibilities for Prosperity.* New York: Basic Books, 1984.

Preston, James P. "Foreword." In *Beyond Race and Gender,* by R. Roosevelt Thomas Jr., ix–xi. New York: AMACOM, 1991.

Reich, Robert. *The Work of Nations: Preparing Ourselves for 21st-Century Capitalism.* New York: Knopf, 1991.

Rucci, Anthony J., Frank M.J. LaFasto, and David Ulrich. "Managing Organizational Change: A Merger Case Study." In *Human Resource Forecasting and Strategy Development,* ed. Manuel London, Emily Bassman, and John Fernandez, 141–154. New York: Quorum, 1990.

Schubert, Lisa. "Managing a Multicultural Work Force in *Robin Hood: Prince of Thieves.*" *Centennial Review* 37:3 (Fall 1993): 571–592.

Thiederman, Sondra. *Profiting in America's Multicultural Marketplace.* New York: Lexington Books, 1991.

Thomas, R. Roosevelt Jr. *Beyond Race and Gender: Unleashing the Power of Your Total Workforce.* New York: AMACOM, 1991.

University of Washington. "Training and Development: Autumn Catalog, 1992." Seattle, 1992.

Watkins, Evan. *Throwaways.* Stanford: Stanford University Press, 1993.

PART TWO

RESPONDING TO THE ANTI-PC ATTACKS

The Campaign Against Political Correctness: What's Really at Stake

JOAN WALLACH SCOTT

IF THERE WERE any doubt that the production of knowledge is a political enterprise that involves contest among conflicting interests, the raging debates of the past few years should have dispelled them. What counts as knowledge? Who gets to define what counts as knowledge? These are difficult problems, never easy to resolve, but it is the function of universities to grapple with them.

Those who deny the existence of these problems and would suppress discussion of them are not without their politics; they simply promote their orthodoxy in the name of an unquestioned and unquestionable tradition, universality, or history. They attack those who challenge their ideas as dangerous and subversive, antithetical to the academic enterprise. They offer themselves as apostles of timeless truths when in fact they are enemies of change. The cry that politics has recently invaded the university, imported by sixties radicals, is an example of the defense of orthodoxy; it is itself a political attempt to distract attention from the fact that there are serious issues at stake and more than one valid side to the story in the current debates about knowledge.

What we are witnessing these days is not simply a set of internal debates about what universities should teach and what students should learn. Journalists and politicians have joined the fray and added a new dimension to it. There is much more at stake in their campaign against "political correctness" than a concern with excessive moralism, affirmative action, and freedom of speech in the academy. Rather, the entire enterprise of the university has come under attack, and with it that aspect that intellectuals most value and that the humanities most typically represent: a critical, skeptical approach to all that a society takes most for granted.

The far-ranging scrutiny of university practices—curricular change, admissions standards, fellowship awards, disciplinary codes, hiring and tenure procedures, teaching loads, "useless" time spent on research, accreditation standards—attempts to delegitimate the philosophical and institutional bases from which social and cultural criticism have come. We are experiencing another phase of the ongoing Reagan-Bush revolution that, having packed the courts and privatized the economy, now seeks to neutralize the space of ideological and cultural nonconformity by discrediting it.

Academics ought to be alarmed at the onslaught, for the conservative agenda would deny us our most valuable—and pleasurable—activity: thinking hard about everything, from obscure texts to our present condition, and teaching others how to think that way. The current situation requires this kind of critical thinking. It calls for an attempt to understand what is going on, to enter the fray, not necessarily by choosing sides exactly as they have been defined by others but by analyzing the entire situation and looking for new ways to address questions about the production and transmission of knowledge in increasingly diverse and, for that reason, necessarily conflicted academic communities. This chapter aims less at taking sides—though you will have gathered already that I am not neutral—than at provoking thoughts about what is needed to guarantee the future of universities as centers of inquiry and critical reflection.

Since provocation can take many forms, there are five parts to this chapter, each a preliminary mapping of a complex and contradictory field.

Paranoids, Fetishists, and Imposters

I was tempted, in a fit of rhetorical excess, to follow the sensationalist lead of Camille Paglia and call this entire chapter "Paranoids, Fetishists, and Imposters." What better way to characterize the small band of publicists who have taken it upon themselves to banish "political correctness" from the academy and with it affirmative action, multiculturalism, curricular innovation, and all serious attention to those *institutional* structures of inequality that produce racism, sexism, and other forms of discrimination? I would have used the terms *paranoids, fetishists,* and *imposters* not as epithets but as diagnoses, because they seem to me to capture something of the doubleness at play in the publicists' game. Such an analysis would have gone something like this:

Paranoids project their own fears outward. The sense of one's own weakness and instability becomes the perception of an external danger; instead of acknowledging the limits, even the fictional qualities of their power, paranoids attribute these to a threat from outside.

The result is an extreme polarization. On the one side there is a flawless, innocent victim, on the other an aggressive, destructive force. Much of the critique of multiculturalism and "political correctness" is structured exactly in these terms. The danger is depicted as coming from outsiders, often minorities ("minority" in the publicists' usage alludes to those who have lost in democratic elections and so are justifiably outside; in that way the issue is shifted from race and discrimination to individuals and democracy), people who are somehow sore losers and seek revenge by attacking the university, Western civilization, democracy, its representatives and its values.

Rarely is the historical inhospitability of universities to various minorities mentioned. To read Dinesh D'Souza one would never know that Jews were deliberately excluded from university faculties until after World War II, that women were until recently systematically denied appointment at most research universities because of their sex, and that blacks were not admitted as students or hired as faculty at many public and private universities until the 1960s. Nor would they know of the campaigns he participated in during the past decade to make blacks, women, and homosexuals unwelcome at Dartmouth and Princeton.[1] One would think only that universities were completely accessible communities for those excellent individuals who deserved to be in them until the radicals arrived.

Rarely, too, are the difficulties of minorities acknowledged to have been produced by the democratic institutions that are being ardently defended. Reading the *New Republic*'s 18 February 1991 special issue on campus racism one forgets that racism is a problem internal (but not unique) to democracy and Western civilization; instead, those proposing reform are depicted as outsiders whose agenda will only subvert an essentially good system. The danger to society or at least to the university, one concludes from reading that issue, is not its own racism but an alien multiculturalism that is being imposed "from outside."

Fetishists worship an object that both avows and obscures the real stimulus to their desire. The displacement of erotic attention from, say, the female genitals to the foot covers their shame about their initial desire but allows them to pursue it by substituting a part for the whole.

In the current controversies, the publicists have substituted "tradition" (the embodiment of taste, culture, and cumulative wisdom) for the white male privilege they so deeply desire and want to protect. To read their accounts of "tradition," one would not know that it is largely invented and always contested and that what has counted as tradition has changed from generation to generation. Canons are, after all, heuristic devices for exemplifying the literary or the philosophical or the artistic, not—as the publicists would have it—timeless and unique repositories of human truth.

The fetishizing of "tradition" allows the publicists to present a particular version of culture—one that gives priority to the writing and viewpoints of European white men—as if it were the only true version without, however, acknowledging its particularity and exclusiveness. This kind of practice, which discounts and silences the voices and experiences of others, is profoundly undemocratic. In the

guise of protecting an objectively established "tradition," the publicists can disavow any association with undemocratic practices while still engaging in them.

Imposters are those who pretend to be what they're not. Those they imitate are
the objects both of their deep desire and their jealous resentment. Their imitative
behavior conveys both admiration and hatred.

In the current situation, those leading the campaign against the university and
making judgments about its theoretical debates are posing as knowledgeable
scholars and hoping to be mistaken for them. Serious intellectuals have only to
read the self-assured, hopelessly ill-informed, and simply wrong descriptions of
deconstruction, psychoanalysis, feminism, or any other serious theory by the likes
of D'Souza, Richard Bernstein, David Lehman, Roger Kimball, Hilton Kramer,
George Will—and even Camille Paglia—to understand the scam. They will recognize people for whom teaching has no real value, for whom literature is a pawn in
a political argument but not a passionate commitment to the play of language and
the pleasure of reading.

It is in their ambivalent stance of attraction and resentment that one can detect
the imposters. The superficiality of their accounts, their large generalizations
based on a few scattered (but repeatedly cited) examples, and their obvious ignorance of the topics they write about suggest that their project is motivated not by
serious intellectual concern but by another kind of personal and political agenda.

For those who have some familiarity with the operation of universities and with
the intellectual matters under discussion, the imposters' writings are an embarrassment, lacking as they do any serious historical and philosophical foundations
and all grasp, therefore, of the issues. But their anger at the very scholars they long
to emulate, as well as their superficial comprehension of what is often difficult,
specialized, and abstruse writing, seems to have worked in some quarters. That is
partly because the publicists have assumed another persona besides that of the intellectual: they pretend to represent the common man—whom, as elitists, they
also loathe. They claim to speak for a democratic public that knows truth when it
sees it, that is suspicious of elitism and shrewd in its ability to detect falsehood.

That marginal intellectuals, conservative journalists, and disaffected scholars
are taken to represent this public is hardly credible from one perspective; from another—that of history—it becomes understandable. The fraud works because it
taps into a deep tendency in American culture, that of suspicion of and hostility
toward intellectuals, a tendency of long standing that is ever available for political
battles. An examination of that tendency provides perspective on the appeal that
the paranoids, fetishists, and imposters seem to be having these days. And it shows
why thinking about the small band of publicists only in clinical terms, focusing on
them as the key to the current "crisis," is not enough.

Anti-Intellectualism in American Life

In 1962, as McCarthyism waned, the economy expanded, and hopes ran high for
social justice, Richard Hofstadter published a book that attempted to explain in

broad, historical terms "the political and intellectual conditions of the 1950's" (Hofstadter 1962, 3). Hofstadter argued that the anti-intellectualism of that time, expressed in contempt for "eggheads" and carried out by malicious inquisitions into the activities of university professors, was not new but a recurring feature of American life. "Our anti-intellectualism," he wrote, "is older than our national identity, and has a long historical background" (p. 6).

Hofstadter defined anti-intellectualism as "a resentment and suspicion of the life of the mind and of those who are considered to represent it; and a disposition constantly to minimize the value of that life" (p. 7). What was most feared about intellectuals was their critical relationship to society, their insistence on independence, and their freedom from practical restrictions. "The intellect is always on the move against something: some oppression, fraud, illusion, dogma, or interest is constantly falling under the scrutiny of the intellectual class and becoming the object of exposure, indignation, or ridicule" (p. 45). This has led intellectuals to support movements for social justice, to embrace avant-garde artistic experimentation, to question government policy, and to challenge assumptions about what counts as nature, science, morals, and politics.

Suspicion of intellectual work and its critical impulses has come from many quarters: from evangelical religious leaders who stressed the power of spirit over reason, heart over mind; from those cultural leaders who saw American uniqueness in its closeness to nature and the land; from businessmen who extolled masculine practicality, efficiency, and a cult of action; from politicians who insisted that education serve the needs of democracy by providing a common denominator of "useful knowledge" for all citizens; and (most interesting from our perspective) from educational reformers whose egalitarianism associated intellectual work with elitism and whose sense of democracy focused on developing the inner resources and personality of the child.

According to Hofstadter there has been a paradoxical relationship between democracy and anti-intellectualism that has led to the consistent undervaluation of teaching as a profession and of critical intelligence as a national resource. The result is a chronically impoverished educational system that prefers rote learning to the cultivation of critical thinking and that—as is now about to be the case—would rather spend money on national testing than on substantive programs or teachers' salaries. Periodic cries of alarm about the lack of preparation of students—the inability of the United States to compete with Germany in the heyday of its industrial development, with the Soviet Union at the time of Sputnik, or now with Japan in these days of economic competition—lead again and again to proposals for reform; but even in these periods the proponents of Hofstadter's vision of education as the cultivation of intellect have a hard time making themselves heard.

One of the fascinating aspects of Hofstadter's analysis is the point that anti-intellectualism is often expressed by those in some way responsible for education. It is sometimes incorporated by intellectuals themselves into anxiety about the social utility (the relevance) of their intellectual work. It is often, too, expressed in proposals for undergraduate reform: the perpetuation of an ossified classical curriculum in liberal arts colleges in the early nineteenth century in the name of "tradition" is one example Hofstadter offers. In those times, for patrician or "mugwump culture," reform meant resistance to change, the inculcation of "correct taste" and "sound morals"—"and taste and morals were carefully defined in such a way as to establish disapproval of any rebelliousness, political or esthetic, against the existing order. Literature was to be a firm custodian of 'morality'; and what was meant by morality was always conventional social morality" (p. 402). The point was to curb any independent creative critical spirit, to prevent that unlimited, sometimes necessarily excessive, experimentation with new forms and ideas that Hofstadter sees as the hallmark of intellectualism.

Today's "mugwumps" are not defending a declining patrician class but pushing an orthodoxy that is fundamentally anti-intellectual in the name, of course, of educational improvement. William Bennett's report on humanities education in America, called *To Reclaim a Legacy* (1984), laid the foundations of an argument that has been taken up by conservatives within and outside the academic establishment. In it he bemoaned the fact that the classic texts of Western civilization were being criticized and sometimes replaced by texts of lesser quality and dubious importance. A legacy was being lost, he warned, one that consisted of timeless truths and values that must be transmitted intact from generation to generation.

Lynne Cheney's reports since she took over as chairman of the National Endowment for the Humanities (NEH) have elaborated these themes. In 1988 she attacked the "politicizing" of the humanities by groups asking that their experience be included in representations of history and literature. Their demands, she wrote, ignored the timeless truths, "transcending accidents of class, race and gender, [that] speak to us all." In 1990, Cheney wrote *Tyrannical Machines: A Report on Educational Practices Gone Wrong and Our Best Hopes for Setting Them Right.* In it she continued to stress timeless truths, defining the primary role of education as the transmission of them. Although the report pinpoints a number of genuine problems in schools and universities, its solutions rest on a vision of education that illustrates many of Hofstadter's points.

For example, although research is acknowledged to be an important function of universities, it is also blamed for diverting professors' attention from teaching. In itself this is not inaccurate; many universities reward only publication as professional achievement. But it is the definition of teaching that reveals the report's anti-intellectual agenda. Teaching involves the diffusion and transmission of knowledge, Cheney maintains, not its production (1990, 27, 37). What counts for her as knowledge is uncontested; it is information purveyed through "comprehensive treatment of important subjects," "rigorous and coherent curricula," and a core curriculum. The fact that standards of importance and comprehensiveness are variable and have always been contested is not mentioned. (I don't think, for example, that we would all agree on what a "coherent" curriculum would look like.) Rather, Cheney tells us, the test of a university's commitment to teaching is the existence of requirements for broad-based courses that will introduce students to "the great deeds and ideas that have shaped the world" (p. 41). (Are "great" deeds self-evidently so?) There is no value placed on the interpretation of texts, the exploration of new ideas, or the opening of the mind to new ways of thinking. Rather, teaching means the induction of the student into a set of received values and ideas. The word "critical," in Hofstadter's notion of the dissenting, nonconformist spirit, is translated by Cheney into a question of taste, an ability to appreciate (she quotes William James here) the "excellent and the durable," to "admire the really admirable" and to scorn "what is cheap and trashy and impermanent." These attitudes, she says, must be shared by citizens of a democracy; they provide the wisdom needed to make sound political and personal judgments and to secure the future.

The tone of Cheney's report is judicious and calm. It bears little resemblance to the hysterical pronouncements of members of the National Association of Scholars, who, using the language of the followers of Senator Joseph McCarthy, talk about fending off the "barbarians" who are storming the gates of academe and who would deprive us of our individual freedom. Yet, if Hofstadter is right, and I think he is, Cheney and the NAS and the highly visible band of journalists and publicists who are promoting the conservative agenda have in common the intention to control thought, to prescribe its contents and boundaries, to police its operations, and above all to rein in the critical spirit that must be unfettered in a truly free society. That this is all done in the name of democracy is, according to Hofstadter, a characteristic of anti-intellectualism.

All of this ought to give us pause, for there can be no democracy worthy of the name that does not entertain criticism, that suppresses disagreement, that refuses to acknowledge difference as inevitably disruptive of consensus, and that vilifies the search for new knowledge (about, say, the place of minority history in "general" history courses).

In typical paranoid fashion, the leaders of the campaign against change in the universities have labeled all critics and advocates of change "thought police." And while it is surely true that there are within universities—on the left and the right—people who would impose their ways of thinking on everyone else, they do not represent the majority, and they have never gained control. One of the tricks of the publicists has been to conflate serious criticism and intolerant dogmatism under the label of "political correctness" and thereby discredit *all* critical efforts. The worse aspect of this conflation is that it misrepresents intellectual life and intrudes upon it by, for example, mobilizing extensive support in the form of alumni gifts (such as George Bass's to Yale) to support courses whose content will uphold "the values of Western civilization" as defined by conservative scholars.

What is being so misrepresented in all of this is the way universities actually operate. They are, of course, political institutions in which individuals and groups compete for predominance and resources. But they are also unusually open spaces in which criticism and self-criticism can flourish. The more open the space, the better the process works; the more constricted the space (as it becomes when anti-intellectualism is ascendant), the less well the self-correcting mechanisms operate. These mechanisms involve a set of procedures and standards for argumentation and research that require a certain familiarity and expertise. Those who lack this familiarity and expertise (whether they work inside or outside the university) cannot claim to understand or speak for academic life; indeed, when they do speak about it they misrepresent and distort it.

At the heart of intellectual activity there is a commitment to pursuing truth, however provisional it is understood to be. Indeed, truth can be defined as an ever-receding horizon—not a fixed quality that can ever be finally known—that is approached through a communal enterprise of hard work, conflict, and argument. This communal enterprise, which at its best does not rest on or expect consensus, takes place in classrooms, seminars, lectures, faculty meetings, and conferences that are scenes of exploration and disagreement—places where critical ideas are tried out, often in extreme, dogmatic, and outrageous form, and where, ideally, despite enormous differences, opinions are exchanged and ideas expressed. The appearance at the meetings of the American Historical Association or the Modern Language Association of critical papers with sexually explicit titles and provocative interpretations, however many of them there are, doesn't mean that a new orthodoxy is being enforced; rather, it means that ideas are being tested and the horizons of knowledge expanded. The preoccupation of some humanists with poststructuralist theory is similar. Their sometimes highly abstract articles, full of technical language, don't signal the end of the possibility of simple communication among scholars; rather, they are an attempt—hotly contested—to bring new kinds of philosophical ideas to older enterprises.

It was in the university, after all, that "political correctness"—as a behavior, as a critique of doctrinaire leftist attitudes, and as a subject of scholarly analysis—was produced. Left there, it would have been dealt with as another form of academic dispute. In the hands first of the *New York Times* reporter Richard Bernstein and then of other journalists, joined by conservative scholars, businessmen, and politicians, it has become a political "crisis" of "major proportions." This kind of pressure on universities, mobilizing as it does deep-seated anti-intellectual sentiment, is far more dangerous to the academic enterprise than debates about the limits of free speech, the rights of minorities, and the politics of knowledge.

Diversity

Universities have changed dramatically since the 1960s, and much of the present controversy has roots in those changes. In 1960, 94 percent of college students were white; the figure was 96 percent for private universities. Of the remaining 6 percent, one-third attended predominantly black institutions. A number of public and private universities did not admit blacks at all, and some of the most highly regarded centers of learning did not admit women. Colleges tended to be white male enclaves for students and faculty: 63 percent of college students were men, 90 percent of Ph.D.'s were men, and 80 percent of university faculties were men. (When I was a graduate student in this period, the Woodrow Wilson Foundation stated explicitly that no more than one-fourth of its graduate fellowships would be awarded to women.) In 1991, 20 percent of college students were nonwhite or Hispanic and 55 percent were women (Menand 1991). Women made up over one-third of all graduate students and were even more highly represented as Ph.D. candidates in the humanities; they represented about 27–28 percent of university faculties.

The change in university populations follows in part from a general increase in college attendance during the past several decades, and this has been accompanied by changes in recruitment policies. The expansion of the university has not so much altered admission policies as added more considerations to them and made them more visible. Admission, even to the most prestigious schools, was never based on merit alone, although that is the myth being advanced now in the antiuniversity campaign; rather, merit was one among many factors that included athletic skill, wealth, geographic location, and family connections to alumni, the famous, and the powerful. The special treatment that came with high social status never seems to have been seen as a compromise of university standards. (One has to wonder why it was that, for example, the test scores of blacks were stolen from the admissions office at Georgetown Law School and published by disgruntled conservatives while those of alumni children or influential politicians were not. One can only conclude that the call for a return to a meritocracy that never was is a thinly veiled manifestation of racism.)

The new populations in the universities bring with them histories of their own that have not been part of the traditional curriculum; their presence challenges many of the prevailing assumptions about what counts as knowledge and how it is produced. This is so first because of the sheer numbers, as well as the new kinds, of students and faculty on campuses. Is critical thinking possible when masses of students are attending college instead of only the children of elites? Is critical thinking advisable for the masses of students, or should they (as the reports of Bennett and Cheney suggest) be given a prescribed education that they will passively receive? Can critical thinking take place in communities that are no longer elite and homogeneous?

There have also been, in recent decades, major political and philosophical developments that have changed the way we think about relationships of difference in the world. These include decolonization of the Third World and the emergence of national identities that positively value histories and cultural practices once obscured or demeaned by colonizers who equated European standards with civilization; philosophical critiques of universalism and foundationalism and of the idea of community as a consensual, homogeneous institution; and analyses of power and difference that call attention to how "we" construct ourselves in relation to "others" (West 1987). If, in earlier generations, minorities adjusted to college life by assimilating to prevailing standards and accepting as universal norms that had not previously been their own, now they have the means to question the very notion of universality and insist that their experience be taken into account.

But how is this to be done? Perhaps it is better to ask the question more historically: How has it been attempted? How have universities attempted to accommodate their different and "diverse" populations? How have demands for new approaches to knowledge been received? In some ways, the overall process today is not very different from previous contests about knowledge: there has been pressure for change and powerful resistance to it as well as accommodation. But there are also differences. Contests about knowledge are now understood to be political not only because they are contests but because they are explicitly about the interests of groups (rather than the opinions of individuals) in the substance and form of what counts as knowledge. It is the question of group interest and power that has been introduced into the knowledge debates and so "politicized" them in new ways. Although it sometimes takes extreme and tendentious forms, the explicit discussion of interest is, I think, inevitable, and it is not only minority voices that are responsible for this politicization.

A crucial point, one regularly overlooked in hysterical pronouncements about the takeover of the curriculum, is that power is unequally distributed—those demanding change must contend with disciplinary and pedagogic practices that are institutionalized, command resources, and claim to have truth, rigor, and objectivity on their side. The emergence of separate courses and programs of women's studies, African American studies, Chicano studies, and the like, testify to this situation: they were created in the face of the refusal of departments to include material on these groups in existing courses and in an effort to demonstrate that they were subjects worth studying. The programs and courses, in turn, taught and attended largely by members of the groups being studied, underscored the differences in perspectives and interests that existed across the curriculum.

They also gave rise to a series of observations, highly contested but quite serious in their philosophical as well as practical implications, about the relationships between knowledge and group identity. Does one have to be of the group to care about its history? To teach its literature? Are intellectual perspectives expressions of particular social standpoints? Does understanding require firsthand experience? What are legitimate grounds for objecting to the exclusion of whole realms of experience from so-called mainstream courses in the humanities or social sciences? What gives authority to claims for inclusion? Is it possible to teach mainstream courses from a perspective different from the one traditionally taken?

There are many answers being offered to these questions, even if the sensationalist press only reports the insistence by some blacks or women that they are uniquely qualified to teach black history or women's literature. And since they are not easy questions, the discussions are necessarily full of conflict. What is least reported these days is the fact that the disciplines, too, have exclusionary notions about who is capable of teaching what. History departments regularly refuse to consider for positions in general American history, for example, scholars who write on women or African Americans (or homosexuals or other particular groups), arguing that they are not generalists, unlike those who are no less specialists but have written about national elections or politicians' lives—subjects that are taken to stand for what the whole discipline is about. Recently a literature department at a major university proposed to hire in a generalist slot a scholar some of whose work was in feminist theory. The department's argument that feminist theory was central to its mission was rejected as implausible by the administrative oversight committee, which turned down the recommendation.

These kinds of decisions distinguish between general and particularized knowledge according to gendered, racial, and ethnic criteria, but they refuse to acknowledge that these are the terms of definition. In so doing, they perpetuate the balkanization of knowledge, creating the conditions that necessitate separatist claims on the part of excluded groups and fuel their frustration and anger. My point is not to justify separatism or to endorse standpoint epistemologies. Rather I want to suggest here that separatism is a simultaneous rejection and imitation of the powerful and must be understood in the context of the university's accommodation to diversity.

The nature of the university's accommodation to diversity can be seen in the words used to describe campuses and curricula: "diversity," "multiculturalism," "pluralism." All take into account the existence of different populations with different needs and interests, but none of them registers the fact that difference is not simply a state of separate being but a hierarchically constructed relationship. Being black or female or gay isn't inhabiting or acknowledging membership in a preexisting sociological category; rather, it is being constituted in a particular subject position, and this constitution (or interpellation) is always in process.

An example of the relational nature of difference comes from a comment made by a white middle-class student who lived in a predominantly Latino dormitory at Stanford:

> "Sometimes I'd get confused," she said, because she never knew when a simple comment she made would offend someone else. She finally appreciated the difference between herself and the Hispanic students when one of them asked her what it felt like to be an Anglo. "I'd never heard anyone use the word Anglo for me before. ... Where I came from no one was Anglo; everyone was just Irish Catholic. But after being [here] awhile I realized that an Anglo can be an Anglo only if there's someone who's not. (de Palma 1991, 7)

A pluralism or multiculturalism that fails to recognize that difference is a relationship of power achieved through a process of signification encourages separatism. Indeed, it provides the conceptual basis for an essentialism that denies the historicity of processes of differentiation. Each group claims a fixed, transcendent identity and argues for its unique ability to present and interpret itself. It then establishes its own canon, its own history, thereby denying the relational nature of difference and the interconnectedness—however asymmetrical and oppressive—of different groups.

S. P. Mohanty, taking up an argument made by Cornel West against a notion of separate canons, of new canons entirely replacing old, puts it this way:

> How do we negotiate between my history and yours? How would it be possible for us to recover our commonality, not the ambiguous imperial-humanist myth of our shared human attributes, which are supposed to distinguish us from animals, but, more significantly, the imbrication of our various pasts and presents, the ineluctable relationships of shared and contested meanings, values and material resources? It is necessary to assert our dense particularities, our lived and imagined differences; but could we afford to leave untheorized the question of how our differences are intertwined and, indeed, hierarchically organized? Could we, in other words, afford to have *entirely* different histories, to see ourselves as living—and having lived—in entirely heterogeneous and discrete spaces? (1989, 13)

His answer is obviously no. Instead he calls for an alternative to pluralism that would make difference and conflict the center of a history "we" all share, "a history whose very terms and definitions are now being openly contested and formulated" (p. 25).

Individualism

University populations began to change in the 1960s and 1970s, a period in which concerns for social justice were widespread and plans were implemented to increase the possibilities for equality. Affirmative action was based on the notion that certain classes of individuals had historically been treated differently from others not on the basis of merit or ability but because they were perceived to be members of groups with undesirable traits and characteristics. Affirmative action took into account these historic prejudices and attempted to reverse some of their most pernicious effects not by reversing discrimination but by extending to blacks and women access that had historically been reserved for whites or men *as groups.*

The conceptualization of the problem in terms of groups was difficult in a society with deep individualistic strains, but, partly because there are also deep egalitarian impulses that could be appealed to, it was not impossible. In the 1980s and 1990s the ideological pendulum has swung back to individualism. The courts are reversing affirmative-action decisions, a president has vetoed civil rights legislation, and the history of discrimination as evident in statistics or group experience is being denied. All this is being done in the name of justice for individuals, who are conceived to be entirely equal units living in a cultural and historical vacuum.

The logic of individualism has structured the approach to multiculturalism within the university on many sides of the question. The call for tolerance of difference is framed in terms of respect for individual characteristics and attitudes; group differences are conceived categorically and not relationally, as distinct entities rather than interconnected structures or systems. Administrators have hired psychological consulting firms to hold diversity workshops that present conflict resolution as negotiation between dissatisfied individuals. Disciplinary codes that punish hate speech justify prohibitions in terms of the protection of individuals from abuse by other individuals, not in terms of the protection of members of historically mistreated groups from discrimination. The language of protection, moreover, is conceptualized in terms of victimization; the way to make a claim or to justify one's protest against perceived mistreatment is to take on the mantle of the victim. And everyone, whether an insulted minority or the perpetrator of the insult who feels he is being unjustly accused, becomes an equal victim before the law. Here we have not only an extreme form of individualizing but a conception of individuals without agency.

There is nothing wrong, on the face of it, with teaching individuals about how to behave decently in relation to others and about how to empathize with each other's pain. The problem is that difficult analyses of how history and social standing, privilege and subordination are involved in personal behavior entirely drop out. Chandra Mohanty puts it this way:

> There has been an erosion of the politics of collectivity through the reformulation of race and difference in individualistic terms. The 1960's and 70's slogan "the personal is political," has been recrafted in the 1980's as "the political is personal." In other words, all politics is collapsed into the personal and questions of individual behaviors, attitudes and life styles stand in for political analysis of the social. Individual political struggles are seen as the only relevant and legitimate form of political struggle. (1989–1990, 204)

Paradoxically, individuals then generalize their perceptions and claim to speak for a whole group. This individualizing, personalizing conception has also been behind some of the identity politics of minorities; indeed, it gave rise to the intolerant and moralizing dogmatism that was dubbed, initially by its internal critics, "political correctness."

It is particularly in the notion of "experience" that one sees this operating. In much current usage of "experience," references to structure and history are implied but not made explicit; instead, personal testimony of oppression replaces analysis and explanation, and it comes to stand for the experience of the group. The fact of belonging to an identity group is taken as authority enough for one's speech; the direct experience of a group or culture—that is, membership in it— becomes the only test of true knowledge. The exclusionary implications of this are twofold: all those not of the group are denied even intellectual access to it, and those within the group whose experiences or interpretations do not conform to the established terms of identity must either suppress their views or drop out. An appeal to "experience" of this kind forecloses discussion and criticism and turns politics into a policing operation: the borders of identity are patrolled for signs of disapproval or disagreement, and the test of hostility or support for a group becomes less one's political actions and relationships of power than one's words.

I do not want to suggest that language has no bearing on relationships of power; far from it. Instead I want to warn against the reduction of language to words, the reduction of "experience" to an idea of unmediated, direct access to truth, and the reduction of politics to individual interactions. Furthermore, I do think that different groups have different experiences and that they offer new perspectives on knowledge that have been neglected and must be included. It is true that whiteness and femaleness set conditions of possibility and an interpretive frame for my life that they don't for a black woman or any man. But if, as S. P. Mohanty (1989) has suggested, our histories are entwined in one another, then no group is without connection or relation to any other, even if these are hierarchical, conflicted, and contradictory relationships. Groups are not isolated, separate entities, nor are individuals. I don't believe that my subjectivity sets complete limits on my ability to think about things and people other than myself, in part because who and what I am has something to do with how I am differentiated from them.

That kind of thinking about others is hard; I sometimes must be pressured to do it, and the terms of encounter with others who challenge the way I am used to thinking are not always pleasant and calm. Civility and politeness probably cannot be expected to characterize these exchanges. But the encounters are at least possible when the issues are framed as issues of cognition and not of personality, when analysis and interpretation are the medium of exchange, when ideas are what is traded (however heightened the rhetorical expressions of them), and, above all, when the encounters are understood to be taking place not between discrete individuals or atomized groups but between people who share a history, however contradictory it is.

Is it possible for universities to be centers of intellectual conflict when there are differences that cannot be resolved? I think so, but only if diversity is not conceived in individualistic terms and if "community" is redefined.

Community

If universities are to adapt to the new conditions of diversity, the notion of community according to which they operate must change. Some of the extraordinary tensions evident on campuses these days stem from attempts to impose universalist ideas of community that presume homogeneity and that stress consensus and shared values on a situation in which differences seem fundamental and irreducible. The consensual idea assumes that some commonality of interest allows "us" to articulate our common concerns and regulate our disagreements; those who do not accept the consensus are necessarily outside the community. This is the idea that, in the name of a common culture, is invoked by those who defend the superiority of Shakespeare to, say, Toni Morrison (as if anyone were insisting that contemporary literature entirely replace "the classics"); it is the idea that underlies some disciplinary codes as well as some of the most extreme demands for "political correctness." This vision of consensus ultimately requires, indeed imposes, homogeneity—not of persons but of point of view. It rests on a set of exclusions of "others."

Something else is needed in these days of diversity and difference, and not only for the university. But the university is the best place from which to search for a different understanding of what a community might be. First of all, universities can be seen already to exemplify an alternative. They are, after all, places where separate and contingent, contradictory and heterogeneous spheres of thought have long coexisted; the grounds for that coexistence are acceptance of difference and an aversion to orthodoxy. This doesn't mean that there aren't continuing battles for resources, influence, and predominance; indeed, these kinds of politics are the way differences are negotiated. It does mean that there is ultimately no resolution, no final triumph for any particular brand of thought or knowledge.

Second, within the universities, the humanities in particular offer the possibility of thinking about difference and community in new ways. There is one approach within the humanities, to be sure, that would reify a particular canon as the defining mark of our common humanity. But there is another, more complicated approach, equally available in the very fact that humanities is "humanity in the plural." Jonathan Culler puts it this way: "A particular virtue of literature, of history, of anthropology is instruction in otherness: vivid, compelling evidence of differences in cultures, mores, assumptions, values. At their best, these subjects make otherness palpable and make it comprehensible without reducing it to an inferior version of the same, as a universalizing humanism threatens to do" (1987, 187). Add to this the fact that interpretation is the name of the game in the humanities, that meanings are always contested, reworked, revoked, and redefined, and there is at least a basis for thinking about communities in which consensus cannot prevail. Thought in these terms, the humanities become a starting point for discussion of the reconceptualization of community in the age of diversity.

I do not have a blueprint for that idea of community, but I think that there are points it must address. Here is a partial list:

1. "Community is not a referential sign; but an appeal to a collective praxis" (Van Den Abbeele 1991, xiii). Community is not an essence, but a strategically organized set of relationships.
2. Differences are often irreducible and must be accepted as such. The introduction to a new book on community puts it this way: "What we have in common is the commonality of our difference" (Van Den Abbeele 1991, xxv).
3. Differences are relational and involve hierarchy and differentials of power that will be constantly contested.
4. Conflict and contest are therefore inherent in communities of difference. The play of difference is unavoidable and is not a game; it is both the basis for and the necessarily destabilizing aspect of community.

Christopher Fynsk, following Jean-Luc Nancy, suggests that the French word *partage* inform our notion of community (1991). *Partage* means both to divide and to share; this double and contradictory meaning insists on what Fynsk calls "openings to the other" as a condition of existence. In contrast, conformity that rules out the other, substituting one set of beliefs for another, brings us the regime of yellow ribbons and American flags as the test of patriotism. It leads students to condemn dissent, as one student recently did at Princeton, as treasonous and un-American.

Partage is a more difficult concept than consensus, but a better one, I submit. It accepts difference as a condition of our lives and suggests ways we might well live with it. It lets us accommodate one another as we strive on a large scale for what is already possible in the classroom, at least in classrooms such as the one described by Elsa Barkley Brown. For her, teaching African American women's history is not

> merely an intellectual process. It is not merely a question of whether or not we have learned to analyze in particular kinds of ways, or whether people are able to intellectualize about a variety of experiences. It is also about coming to believe in the possibility of a variety of experiences, a variety of ways of understanding the world, a variety of frameworks of operation, without imposing consciously or unconsciously a notion of the norm. (1989, 921)

Can we achieve this kind of opening to difference in our teaching? Can universities become the place where communities of difference—irreducible and irreconcilable difference—are conceptualized and exemplified? This is the challenge we all face in the next years. It is a challenge that must be taken up even in the face of outrageous, threatening, and punitive attacks. It is a challenge that requires the kind of critical intellectual work universities are supposed to encourage. Such critical work, is after all, the university's *raison d'être* and its highest form of achievement.

NOTES

This chapter was originally the keynote address at the Mellon Fellows' Conference on Scholarship and Society, Bryn Mawr College, 15 June 1991. It was published in *Change* in a slightly different version in November/December 1991. I am thankful to the many students there who demonstrated their commitment to critical inquiry by asking hard questions and refusing to let me off any number of philosophical and political hooks. Their comments make this revision a far better version than the original talk. I am also grateful for their suggestions to Alison Bernstein, Sylvia Schafer, and Catharine Stimpson. My biggest debt is to Tony Scott for the many long discussions we had as I prepared this chapter. When I got stuck he was always willing to help; his insights have immeasurably enriched my own.

1. Editors' note: For a revealing account of the race-baiting and gay-baiting practices of the *Dartmouth Review* when D'Souza was editor, see David Corn, "Beltway Bandits," *The Nation*, 13 May 1991, 620, and "Corn Replies: I Was Too Gracious," *The Nation*, 8 July 1991,

38. On D'Souza's similar activities at Princeton, see Louis Menand, "Books: Illiberalisms," *The New Yorker*, 20 May 1991, 101–107.

WORKS CITED

Bennett, William J. *To Reclaim a Legacy: A Report on the Humanities in Higher Education.* Washington, D.C.: National Endowment for the Humanities, 1984.
Brown, Elsa Barkley. "African-American Women's Quilting: A Framework for Conceptualizing and Teaching African-American Women's History." *Signs* 15 (Summer 1989), 921–929.
Cheney, Lynne V. *Humanities in America: A Report to the President, the Congress, and the American People.* Washington, D.C.: National Endowment for the Humanities, 1988.
———. *Tyrannical Machines: A Report on Educational Practices Gone Wrong and Our Best Hopes for Setting Them Right.* Washington, D.C.: National Endowment for the Humanities, 1990.
Culler, Jonathan. "Excerpts from the Symposium on 'The Humanities and the Public Interest,' Whitney Humanities Center, April 5, 1986." *Yale Journal of Criticism*, no. 1 (Fall 1987), 186–191.
de Palma, Anthony. "Campus Ethnic Diversity Brings Separate Worlds." *New York Times*, 18 May 1991, 7.
Fynsk, Christopher. "Community and the Limits of Theory." In *Community at Loose Ends*, by the Miami Theory Collective. Minneapolis: University of Minnesota Press, 1991.
Hofstadter, Richard. *Anti-Intellectualism in American Life.* New York: Knopf, 1962.
Menand, Louis. "Books: Illiberalisms." *The New Yorker*, 20 May 1991, 101–107.
Mohanty, Chandra Talpade. "On Race and Voice: Challenges for Liberal Education in the 1990's." *Cultural Critique* 14 (Winter 1989–1990):179–208.
Mohanty, S. P. "Us and Them: On the Philosophical Bases of Political Criticism." *Yale Journal of Criticism*, no. 2 (Spring 1989), 1–31.
Van Den Abbeele, George. "Introduction." In *Community at Loose Ends*, by the Miami Theory Collective. Minneapolis: University of Minnesota Press, 1991.
West, Cornel. "Minority Discourse and the Pitfalls of Canon Formation." *Yale Journal of Criticism*, no. 1 (Fall 1987):193–202.

7

Illiberal Reporting

ALICE JARDINE

I found, during my recent campus travels, that I can still pass for a student.

—Dinesh D'Souza, *Illiberal Education*

I DIDN'T HESITATE for a moment when the smiling, conservatively suited young Indian man asked me if he could sit in on my feminist theory class at Harvard one fall 1989 afternoon. Mine is, or has been, an open classroom, which in practice means that as long as the students duly enrolled do not suffer, anyone who wants to visit on occasion may do so. Little did I know that two years later I would be named by that selfsame "student," Dinesh D'Souza, one of the Neo-Con Stars of 1991, in his best-selling book *Illiberal Education: The Politics of Race and Sex on Campus.* Little did I know that two years later I would begin my classes by asking representatives from the American Enterprise Institute or the National Association of Scholars or other nonstudents to please identify themselves; would begin my courses by cautioning students that in these times it was wise to establish the identity of whoever questioned them about the what and why of their lives and choices at Harvard, because they might be taped and/or quoted without their knowledge or consent, as some students claimed after the publication of D'Souza's book.

Of course, I also could not have foreseen how a thin media narrative about something called "political correctness" could so rapidly and expeditiously become the connective subtext for a series of terrifying televisual specta-tales (the Gulf War, the Hill/Thomas hearings, the William Kennedy Smith trial) about the dangers menacing, both externally and internally, our suddenly quite fiftyish American Way of Life. As in the fifties, the Big Threat is located Over There—then in Korea, now in Iraq—and then brought Back Home. As in the fifties, Back Home is the terrain of intellectuals and artists and of their institutional affilia-

128

tions—the universities (always among the first on the hit list of reactionary movements), the National Endowment for the Arts, public media, sundry governmental bodies—where "rampant conspiracies" of power-hungry liberals, women's groups, civil rights groups, and homosexuals are allegedly utilizing the two big categories of race and sex to destroy the very fabric of Western civilization.

For the Right, the links between the "external" and "internal" threats remain clear. As D'Souza puts it, "One reason for this increasing radicalism [back home] is that, with the collapse of Marxism and socialism around the world, activist energies previously channelled into the championship of the proletariat are now 'coming home,' so to speak, and investing in the domestic liberation agenda" (D'Souza 1991, 214).

Much could obviously be said about the larger right-wing agenda and strategy in which Dinesh D'Souza apparently hopes to become more than a bit player. In particular, the timing of these media attacks on "cultural issues" such as multiculturalism and political correctness must be seen in the context of the continuing (economic) war of the Right against all those who are raising questions about, for example, the military budget in the post–Warsaw Pact/Comintern era; about deregulation in the light of the savings and loan and banking crisis; about fossil-energy policies in the age of environmental devastation; about the appropriate funding focus and approval process of medical research (especially with regard to the AIDS epidemic); about health insurance; about housing policy; etc., etc. In particular, I think it is worth noting the ways in which the neoconservative D'Souza and his right-wing fellow-travelers are projecting onto the Left the mirror image of their own "political correctness" agenda: homophobia, racism, sexism, and of course, ever finessed, classism/elitism. My interest here, however, is more local: to trace the connections between Dinesh D'Souza's political orientation and his rhetorical approach, between how he appears and what he intends, and between what he says and what he means, especially as these relate to an area of my intimate concern and knowledge, namely his description and analysis, in *Illiberal Education,* of that selfsame class of mine he attended in the fall of 1989. The issue of what is concealed and what is overt, of the relationship between what is said and what goes unsaid in D'Souza's general campaign-to-discredit—of what is being manipulated and hidden under the apparently "open," "commonsense," "balanced," "forthright" speech and presentation of a Dinesh D'Souza—raises questions and images of the covert agent, of the intellectual spy, of infiltration, of a certain provocateurship, of flying false colors, and of adopting a rhetorical style to match.

Illiberal Education purports to be a critique of the "rhetorical excesses and coercive tactics of the Politically Correct" and of multicultural activists who have "split the university on moral grounds," producing balkanized tribal enclaves "without a shared commitment to the goals of liberal learning." Again, "It is in liberal education, properly devised and understood, that minorities and indeed all students will find the means for their true and permanent emancipation" (D'Souza 1991, 23). As the title itself indicates, the book positions itself as a defense of liberal edu-

cational values against illiberal influences and of a "higher obligation to truth unfettered by ideological predisposition" (p. 204). The casual reader might therefore
be easily misled into presuming that D'Souza is in reality himself a liberal, openly
committed to the classic liberal values of unconstrained dialogue and open process. And therein begins our tale.

As Deep Throat said of the Watergate quest to establish agency: "Follow the
money"—and D'Souza's patrons establish his actual political affiliations pretty
straightforwardly. While accusing everyone in sight of having an ideological
agenda, he himself works for two quite unusual "public" organizations: the National Endowment for Democracy and the American Enterprise Institute. Both
were set up by Reagan; both are funded by Congress; both have a history of conservative bias. Although taxpayers provide their funding, these organizations do
not report to anyone. D'Souza is also heavily involved with the National Association of Scholars, whose board of advisers includes Jeane Kirkpatrick, Irving
Kristol, and John Silber. His other credentials include student editorship of the
far-right *Dartmouth Review*, an admiring biography of Jerry Falwell, the conservative televangelical minister, and stints as a domestic policy analyst in the Reagan
White House and as a solicitor of the Catholic vote for the Bush/Quayle campaign.

Of course, these personal economic and political signifiers do not necessarily
tell us what D'Souza really believes, but they do point to a large discrepancy between D'Souza's rhetorical self-presentation (defender of liberal educational
values) and his actual history (conservative political activist and employee). More
important, perhaps, they point to a pattern of intellectual feint that is repeated in
Illiberal Education itself. I think it important to understand this pattern, for
D'Souza and his associates are currently polishing their "reasonable," "apolitical,"
"middle-ground" image in order to escalate their appeal to a fundamental anti-
intellectualism in the name of something they call "merit." In this way they hope
to discredit the younger generation currently moving up the academic and artistic
ladders, a generation working with an altogether differently difficult conceptual
and pragmatic "New World Order" from the one D'Souza and his employers want
to design. (I can't help but wonder what would have happened to me if I hadn't
had tenure and had been "named" in a best-selling neoconservative book.) I think
it important to understand the intellectual sleights of hand that have allowed the
neoconservative forces to build up a McCarthyite wave of fear upon which they
hope to ride their candidates and agendas into office—a fear primarily targeted at
a traditionalist, white, especially male population that within a brief quarter of a
century will itself be a minority in this country.

What I want to look at more closely is what has made D'Souza not just a well-
coached and well-rewarded spokesperson but a best-selling storyteller in the era
of Reagan-Bush and beyond it—and that turns on his enactment of certain
tried-and-true rhetorical strategies. Some are obvious: exaggeration, binary
framing, and a naive, indeed simpleminded, model of representation. The con-

servative political agendas being pushed by D'Souza (e.g., the dismantling of affirmative action) cannot be directly addressed, so they are first carefully hidden behind "commonsense" expositions of what are described as other people's political "problems."

Illiberal Education is neatly compartmentalized in this regard. Each chapter of the book is devoted to one major "episode" or "problem" represented by one major (widely perceived as elitist) university: "Admissions Policy" at Berkeley, "Multiculturalism" at Stanford, "The Search for Black Pharaohs" at Howard, "The New Censorship" at Michigan, "Subverting Academic Standards" at Duke, and—in climax—"The Teaching of Race and Gender" at Harvard. The "problems" at these universities then become, through a series of not only inflated but downright inaccurate narratives, exemplary of "problems" said to be sweeping the rest of the country—a wildly exaggerated statement, and one patently ridiculous to anyone actually involved with trying to put race and gender on the intellectual map at all. Remarkable for its omission in D'Souza's "problem" taxonomy is class, which occasionally rears its ugly head in futile and unfair affirmative action programs but does not apparently merit its own analysis the way race, sex, and censorship do. Just as obvious is D'Souza's thick-headed tendency toward polar and reductive rhetorical framing: for example, there's something called Western civilization—which, of course, all au courant multiculturalist people are against—and then there are all those other unnamed cultures and societies that didn't abolish slavery and don't understand freedom and democracy.

All of this pointed framing, combined with the high level of factual inaccuracy in D'Souza's writing, lead to the difficult question of how to respond, if not in an equivalent sound-bite style, at least in a style that will not bore the reader to death with repetitive "not true, not accurate, not fair, not. ..." Like Kate Stimpson, when I read D'Souza's version of current, intensely complex, intellectual, pedagogical, and political issues, I am often torn "between laughter, because it is so foolish; anger, because it is so false; and frustration, because it is so hard to answer" (Stimpson 1991, 382).

But the real perniciousness of D'Souza's rhetoric seems to me to be grounded in his appropriation of the rhetoric of fifties McCarthyism under the McCarthyite guise of defending liberal, democratic Western values. I do not mean this in some metaphorical or abstract sense; I precisely mean that D'Souza recapitulates many of the specific rhetorical devices that Joe McCarthy used so tellingly to discredit and intimidate those artistic and intellectual communities that were resisting the political consolidation of what Dwight Eisenhower later called "the military-industrial complex."

Having just spent several months intensively researching the McCarthy hearings for a book I am writing on the 1950s, I can attest to the fact that—contrary to the current omnipresence of the "McCarthyism of the Left" sound bite—it is the similarities between D'Souza's methodology and that of the McCarthyites that are truly astounding. Especially notable is the self-positioning as defender of the

American way and the repetitive calls for "reasonable people" and the "middle ground" to prevail. (Surely D'Souza must have studied the same videotapes of McCarthy that I have!) What D'Souza does, as did McCarthy before him, is draw together a hodge-podge of items that are verifiable on the level of detail, decontextualize them, and then reassert them within a new code system of his own right-wing making. As did McCarthy, he proceeds by insinuation, a kind of accusation by coding. One becomes "guilty by suspicion" and convicted by association. He especially prides himself on his access to informer gossip—his book abounds with expressions like "for those who visit the American classroom today" (instead of "for those who question students after class under false pretenses") that are right out of the McCarthy transcripts. There is a kind of "hysteria of description" contained within a "paranoia of naming." When one looks closely at his prose and asks, What are his assumptions here? What is it that is bad or dangerous in his mind? one finds little but an elaborately coded network of commonplaces, a connotative code system whose interpretive community would seem to be based in some notion of a normal, down-home, bullshit-detecting, commonsense individualism that refuses to be caught up in all these hyper-intellectual but parochial approaches to scholarship and policy.

So, in the passage on pp. 208–210 where my class is named as typifying the "distinctive perspective" of Women's Studies, itself "typical" of a "balkanization" of intellectual work, D'Souza develops his critique not by direct commentary or analysis but by a detailed description of the "color" and "atmosphere" of the class. Within his rhetorical strategy, this stylized description is in itself presumed to be evidence and conviction for anyone able to read the codes. For example, just so that no one will miss the point, D'Souza starts his description of my class with "political rally" in the first sentence:

> The atmosphere in Jardine's course resembled a political rally. The seminar group was almost entirely female: twenty-five women versus [sic] three men. Headbands and turquoise jewelry, loose long shirts, and pins advertising various causes filled the room. There were no blacks in the class; a couple of the women were Asian. The mood in Jardine's class, while not exactly festive, was bustling, energetic. A student went to the board and put up a poster of a "Fifty Foot Woman"; everybody smiled at this emblem of female power. (D'Souza 1991, 208)

He proceeds like this for a couple of pages, with plenty of direct quotes (a tape recorder?) and a selective wealth of descriptive detail. Space limitation unfortunately prevents me from providing the full text of these rhetorical flourishes, analyzing their often multiple codes, or addressing in like detail his use of this approach in other sections of his book.

For each set of D'Souza code words, there is what is insinuated to be the case—and it's bad:

- class "almost entirely female" = "lesbian" and/or "not objective," biased;
- "headbands"/"turquoise jewelry"/"loose long shirts"/"pins" = uh oh, the 1960s/1990s, with hippie multiculturalism rearing its standards-debasing

head (the long shirts probably also carry a light semantic valence of "lesbian");
- "no blacks" = racist despite the progressive rhetoric, an example of feminist
hypocrisy, feminists unable to speak to/for minorities;
- mood of class is "bustling, energetic" = "feminine," not serious, like a
kitchen not a classroom;
- poster of a "Fifty Foot Woman" = antimale, film, popular culture, not serious;
- "emblem of female power" = antimale, more lesbianism/goddesses.

This kind of thing carries on throughout the book and contributes to its weari-
some, repetitive quality. Again and again D'Souza sets up detailed anecdotes
whose force depends almost entirely on accepting his insinuating code structure;
reject the code and the argument falls apart. And there is such a limited number of
codes. I'm not quite sure what to attribute all this to, but I do know that there is
something about this rhetorical strategy, something about the combination of
D'Souza's glibness, carelessness, ignorance, and arrogance parading as humility—
while he attempts to trash some of the best and most painfully wrought insights
and advances of the postwar period—that I find truly offensive.

What is crucial here is that the book is finally saved for the "average reader" because D'Souza uses these repetitive code systems to tell a story—one that works at
all only because of his heavy reliance on what Roland Barthes once called "the reality effect." The realist writer hopes that by providing "the details" (name, date,
place, title, brand, quoted dialogue, etc.) he or she becomes authorized to generalize, even universalize, about—lots of things, but especially about "the human condition." D'Souza tries to do the same thing. His overinsistence on empirical description, facile anecdotes ("I was there," like the Berlin Wall souvenir T-shirts two
years later), the complete lack of careful thought about or analysis of the data he
collects, turn his "truth-full" nonfiction book into a piece of failed realism, a
potboiled roman à thèse.

D'Souza has an embarrassingly naive vision of how the language and logics of
representation work—his favorite terms are "resembles," "is representative of,"
"typical of," "typifies," etc.—and whereas this is consistent with his "common-
sense" rhetorical stance it dramatically damages his ability to address persuasively
the complex issues that are his chosen foil.

In fact, given that his chosen mode of writing depends for verisimilitude on the
accuracy of reported details, it is remarkable that anyone believes anything in this
book at all. At least in the section where I am described in such a paradigmatically
McCarthyite manner, he simply gets most of his "factual details" wrong, leaving
me to wonder about other "episodes" to which I do not have such unequivocal access. (Basically, he can't decide whether he's a journalist or an analyst but tends toward the former as he gets swept away in a millennial style of breathless revelations.) The way in which he omits significant details altogether makes me wonder
if he ever stops to think about what he has just said as he rushes ahead with his

"self-evident descriptions." His smug self-satisfaction with what he has "learned" by attending the class but missing the course makes him a slightly ridiculous— and thoroughly unreliable—narrator:

1. I am not, as he calls me, "a professor of Women's Studies."
2. The seminar he describes is not a Women's Studies course but rather an advanced seminar in the Department of Romance Languages and Literatures.
3. The title of the course is not "French Literary Criticism" but, rather, "Feminist Literary Criticisms"—a very different matter.
4. He states that my class was "fairly representative of numerous Women's Studies classes [he] attended, at Harvard and elsewhere." This is just silly, but a good example of his tendency to project a monolithic orthodoxy onto the fields he dislikes. My seminar was no more representative of Women's Studies (or, for that matter, literary criticism) courses at Harvard (or anywhere else) than any course, anywhere, can be said to be "representative" of an entire field, especially one so new, rapidly evolving, and highly contested.
5. D'Souza was for some reason irked when a student "put up a poster of a 'Fifty Foot Woman'" on the board, and "everybody smiled at this emblem of female power." But this was not just any old poster of "a" fifty-foot woman. This is what happens when you attend the class but miss the course. The student had brought to class the famous movie advertisement for the 1958 American film *The Attack of the Fifty-Foot Woman* as a footnote to the discussion of "high and low culture" we had begun the week before. This follow-up discussion was with reference to Andreas Huyssen's important and widely read article "Mass Culture as Woman" (1986).
6. One of D'Souza's longest paragraphs in his trashing of my class describes a quite brilliant presentation by a graduate student of Bessie Head's novel *Maru*. But contrary to his account, the "female student"—he seemed to want to name so many unsuspecting students in his book, one wonders why D'Souza didn't name her too—didn't just "imply," she actually said that *Maru* is also about lesbianism in many important ways.
7. A strange paragraph about missing penises has a hysterical edge to it: "Throughout these descriptions one female student offered ribald one-liners about a man who lost his penis, penises that were cut off, accidents in which every part of the victim was recovered—except the penis. These brought loud and unembarrassed laughter from the professor and other students." What I believe he is referring to here is the ten-minute discussion the class devoted each week to a review of some of the major Greek and other Mediterranean myths in preparation for a close reading of the French novelist Hélène Cixous. This was a separate discussion, not one continuing "throughout these descriptions." Here I can only postulate that D'Souza is playing a game with either himself or his readers—one knows

not which. The myth under discussion was that of Osiris, the most popular of all Egyptian deities, whose body was rent into fourteen pieces by Typhon and scattered throughout Egypt. His wife Isis buried each piece as she found it, and thus Osiris came to be worshipped in many cities. However the phallus was never found, so Isis made an image of it, an image that the Egyptians use at their festivals and tourists scurry to buy at souvenir shops.

Is it possible that D'Souza, loud defender of the canon, has not read, at the very least, Frazer's *The Golden Bough?* This failure to recognize or contextualize the Osiris myth is all the more surprising given his devout Catholicism (we musn't forget that he was, after all, director of the Catholic vote for the Bush campaign). Osiris—hardly the "victim" D'Souza remembers—is widely considered to be the mythical model for Jesus Christ. This "great civilizer," this "king," was persecuted, "crucified," and resurrected and henceforth "presided as judge at the trial of the souls of the departed, who received the reward of virtue in a life eternal or the appropriate punishment of their sins" (Frazer 1922, 426). The fascinating connections between the births, lives, and deaths of Osiris and Christ have even been discussed on television by Joseph Campbell. But enough. Here, as elsewhere in his book, the issue is whether D'Souza's accusatory innuendos are grounded in his ideology or his ignorance. And I trust that the ways in which this mythical narrative of missing body parts could lead a class of young people to giggles are obvious.

8. In his mocking of my reading of Marguerite Duras's novel *Le Ravissement de Lol V. Stein,* D'Souza gets the title of the novel wrong by repeating an error made by its English translator, an error whose significance was the very topic I discussed during the class in question. This could perhaps be dismissed as a trivial detail, except that what he does is leave out of the title the famous "V"—Lol Stein's middle initial. I must admit I am amused by this unselfconscious omission, given D'Souza's longish deadpan ridiculing of my discussion with the students of the major importance of this letter to the overall logic of Duras's text. "One student asked if Duras intended any of this; it seemed so remote from the language of the novel. 'I've met Duras,' Jardine said. 'I think all of this was massively unconscious. Massively.'" Well, I've met Mr. D'Souza, too, and I am quite sure that his surprising omission was also massively unconscious. Massively.

9. In D'Souza's list of the poststructuralist authorities to whom I referred during class, only the woman needed to be marked by a sign of sexual difference: "Foucault, Derrida, Julia Kristeva, Lacan." Is this singling out based on merit? On a fondness for Julias?

10. Finally, the last paragraph of D'Souza's pastiche of my class speaks volumes about his attitude toward young people of a persuasion and circumstance different from his own:

> Talking with students after class, I found that they took all of this with ex-
> treme seriousness; there was not a hint of irony in anything they said.
> Comfortable, well-fed, and obviously intelligent, their conspicuous em-
> bitterment with and alienation from American society were hard to com-
> prehend. Besides, whatever the malady, it was hard to imagine it being
> remedied by this sort of intellectual fare, so esoteric and yet so vulgar, so
> free-wheeling and yet so dogmatic, so full of political energy and yet ulti-
> mately so futile. (1991, 210)

The students in that class were not all "comfortable" and "well-fed"—although
they were, I grant, "obviously intelligent." A number of those students were incest
survivors; several were anorexics; the majority were on scholarship, many from
working-class backgrounds; all of them were more than competent to decide for
themselves which intellectual frameworks helped them best to understand their
various forms of "embitterment with and alienation from" the culture in which
they were living. Although they may not have experienced the vaunted hardships
of D'Souza's native Bombay (indeed, it is not clear to what degree D'Souza himself
experienced them), his presumption to generalize about those young people, to
speak in their name, to mock the reality of their cultural embitterment turns his
own intellectual bullying against him: it is his own posture that is "vulgar," "free-
wheeling," "dogmatic," and, finally, thank goodness, "futile"—for the best students will always recognize empty polemicism when they encounter it.

As has often been noted, when small minds encounter large ideas, violence is
often the result, violence to the other—other facts, other representations, other
ideas—all of which become alien, foreign, threatening, subversive, in this case,
"un-American." Early on in the book D'Souza notes that unfortunate acts of bigotry and extremism have been performed on both sides of the political divide he
addresses. But this moment of real balance is almost immediately undermined as
he proceeds to an extremely illiberal and unbalanced discussion of the issues, all
the while masquerading as a liberal, commonsense skeptic visiting the revolutionary centers of American academe. In the final analysis, D'Souza's ingenuous and
precocious schoolboy style, his "Look, the emperor has no clothes" straining for
his employer's approval, is a style well suited to entertaining the Washington Press
Clubs in which he currently appears to spend so much of his time. It is an altogether less useful style with which to try and engage the complexities of social and
psychic life.

D'Souza has so thoroughly obfuscated his conservative agendas behind a rhetorical stance purportedly defending the values of liberal education that it is hard
to know where he really stands. But hey, I for one have long since abandoned the
notion of a "higher obligation to truth unfettered by ideological predisposition."
And I'm afraid that in large part this abandonment is due to the painful lessons
learned through the saturation of our modern and postmodern history with the
illiberal politicking and rhetorical imposturing of people—most of them men—
like Dinesh D'Souza.

WORKS CITED

D'Souza, Dinesh. *Illiberal Education: The Politics of Race and Sex on Campus.* New York: Free Press, 1991.

Frazer, James. *The Golden Bough.* New York: Macmillan, 1922.

Huyssen, Andreas. "Mass Culture as Woman." In *After the Great Divide: Modernism, Mass Culture, Postmodernism.* Bloomington: Indiana University Press, 1986.

Stimpson, Kate. "Big Man on Campus." *The Nation* (30 September 1991), 382.

8

Political Correctness, Principled Contextualism, Pedagogical Conscience

EVAN CARTON

I cannot get a hold on what is meant by a direct pragmatic political usefulness which might be unrelated to the classroom.

—Gayatri Chakravorty Spivak, *The Post-Colonial Critic*

THE REFRAIN of the recent conservative assault on developments in literary and cultural study in the years since women, minorities, Vietnam protesters, uncloseted gays and lesbians, feminism, marxism, and poststructuralism achieved footholds in the American academy is by now thoroughly familiar. As Lynne V. Cheney, chair of the National Endowment for the Humanities, sounded it in 1988: "the key questions [in the professional lives of contemporary literary critics] are thought to be about gender, race, and class, and truth, beauty, and excellence are regarded as irrelevant" (Cheney 1988, 21). In short, the assailants claim, proper disciplinary objects, inquiries, and standards have been taken hostage by left-wing politics.

One strategic (and, I think, to some degree substantive) mistake that many progressive literary intellectuals have made in defending ourselves against this charge is our indiscriminate wielding of poststructuralism's bluntest axiom: the interestedness of all discourse and knowledge. In this defense, or countercharge, the aesthetic—and, likewise, the cognitive, the pedagogical, the disciplinary—*is* the political. Those who wish to keep "literary" values from "politicization" are, thus, either undeconstructed formalists who are too dense or lazy to have thought through New Critical orthodoxies or out-and-out reactionaries who are too disingenuous or self-deceiving to acknowledge their own ideological interests.

What such charges and countercharges tend to share is the myth of a disciplinary Fall from formalist innocence (or ignorance) to poststructuralist guilt (or self-knowledge), one that is willful and unfortunate for its assailants, necessary and fortunate for its defenders. In light of the power of this narrative, which I believe to be an inadequate and a damaging one in both its inflections, it may be useful to begin by considering the *political* metaphor by which the principal architect of the formal academic discipline of literary study and its formal aesthetic object made his case for *literary* value. In his 1941 book *The New Criticism,* John Crowe Ransom characterized the poem as a "democratic state"—a state in that it was a constituted structure that functioned as a whole in accordance with certain governing principles and practical limitations but democratic in that it was "weakly regulatory," restrained itself from "a really imperious degree of organization," and encouraged its constituent members (words, images) to "retain their personalities," to "display energy in unpredictable ways," and even to "[disrespect] whatever kind of logical content" its own overall structure sought to enforce (Ransom 1941, 43, 224, 270). Half a century later, we may see a number of ironies in Ransom's representation of New Criticism's verbal icon not only as a political space but as a space, however contained, of resistance. Yet, to the extent that we take our engaged critical theories and practices to have subverted the formerly imperial poetic object and self-mystifying disciplinary state of Ransom and his contemporaries, we misrepresent both his practice and ours and, as I will argue, *depoliticize* the pedagogical space they share.

Ransom clearly understands the poem's "local texture" and the reader's "poetic experience" to be modes of resistance (Ransom 1941, 224, 280). If what they resist is not totalitarianism per se (although the use of the figure of the "democratic state" in 1941 implies as much), then it is at least the totalizing and objectivizing power of instrumental scientific discourse or of what Allen Tate, whom Ransom quotes, calls "the positivistic attitude that has captured the modern world" (p. 201). Ironically, by virtue of its objectification of the literary work and its postulation and policing of a scientific literary criticism, Ransom's antipositivistic project became our representative of positivist hegemony. Ironic, too, is his use of the worldly image of the democratic state to characterize an object and an activity in which he arguably sought an escape from the political world. But Ransom's image remains instructive, in part because it names the form of domination to which its subversive energies succumb—the self-protective structure that must contain its own constitutive "poetic" or "democratic" elements lest it "fail ingloriously in the business of a state" (p. 43)—and in part because it speaks to tensions in the state of our progressive critical practice that we have rarely named ourselves. Our antiaesthetic, democratic textualism also harbors the empiricist demand that language be indexed to the reality of natural (read: political) phenomena, and our system of critical notation is, in a sense, designed—like that of the logical positivists—to reduce the distortion between linguistic description and the objective (read: social, or historical) world.

The state of contemporary literary study is neither one of intellectual sin, as Cheney would have it, nor one of political grace. Ransom's figure of the democratic state is an apter representation because it defines a structural tension that, differently contextualized, informs academic criticism and pedagogy both in his historical moment and in ours. Although we may no longer see the poem as the necessary site of Ransom's dialectic of antinomian freedom and marshaled power, I suspect that his poetic ideal, as quoted above, accords fairly closely with a pedagogic one—a vision of the space and dynamic of the classroom—that many of us do hold. Moreover, the image of different constituents occupying the same structured space aptly conveys our multiply (and inconsistently) constituted disciplinary identity and the multiply articulated space of our work as scholars, teachers, administrators, and authorized institutional representatives. Finally, I find Ransom's figure of the democratic state to be significant for its suggestion that the mediation between imperious organization and unpredictable particularism, between "logical content" and "local texture," between hierarchy and heterogeneity is not only an inescapable but a valuable task and for its implication—to which I will return—that resistance is a process, not a product.

In 1991, debating Dinesh D'Souza on the issues of multiculturalism and affirmative action, I traced the connections between the media assault on academic multiculturalism and "political correctness" and the deep pockets and larger ideological agendas of some of the most reactionary organizations, institutions, and politicians in America. I claimed, with historian Maurice Isserman, that "the 'Political Correctness' Scare of the early 1990s was less a reflection of the political slant on American campuses than it was of the triumph of the Right virtually everywhere else in American society" (Isserman 1991, 82), and argued, adapting an observation by literary critic Cathy Davidson, that *Illiberal Education*'s underlying refrain was simply "Willie Horton's gonna get your alma mater" (Davidson 1991, 12). In the same year I wrote for the journal *Tikkun* an essay originally entitled "Counterterrorism at Home and Abroad: The Multicultural Abyss and the Gulf," in which I explored the fears, motives, and rhetoric commonly exhibited in Operation Desert Storm and in the coincident mobilization against the academic Left, which I called "Operation Campus Storm." I believed then, and believe now, that it is legitimate to place the battle over academic politics in these national and global contexts. But an almost unavoidable consequence of this globalizing move is a kind of sublimation of our professional activity, a disengagement from the specific sites and local textures that any adequate account of the politics of our practice must engage. In this essay, therefore, I propose to remain closer to home—for me, the English department of the University of Texas. My effort will be to take up, and take seriously, the institutional and pedagogical sites and investments of my professional identity and to examine the ways in which these sites and investments at once constitute and complicate the space of my politics.

In my department, those of us whose critical and pedagogical practice is informed by progressive political commitment have good reason to know that the rumors that we have captured the academy—let alone America's cultural agenda—have been greatly exaggerated. These rumors have been cynically and

systematically exaggerated here to legitimate (or, more often, to disguise) a conservative backlash that in recent years has taken such forms as the following: the
presidentially imposed disqualification of assistant and associate professors from
serving on, or participating in the election of, the departmental executive committee; the dean's rejection of a job candidate (who had emerged from a rigorous
and democratic recruitment process as the consensus choice of a generally traditional group of male Americanists and who would have become the only woman
in the department with a primary interest in the American literary canon) on the
sole grounds that her appointment would exacerbate the department's putative
loss of "ideological balance"; and the university administration's repeated interference with or dictation of curricular changes in the rhetoric and composition
program, in violation of established principles of academic freedom, faculty governance, and due process.

Under such conditions of external assault, self-examination is difficult and may
provide little usable ammunition. Still, in the most notorious battle that my department fought in the late 1980s and early 1990s, our proposed implementation
of a revised freshman composition course (English 306) in which students would
have learned principles of critical thinking and writing by analyzing legal cases
and debates that revolved around issues of race, gender, and other forms of social
"difference," the foreclosure of the planners' process of self-examination by ideological attacks from the outside contributed to the plan's and the department's defeat.

Even before the syllabus for the course, "Writing About Difference," had been
completely drafted, opponents had taken to the newspapers and airwaves and begun letter-writing campaigns to alumni to condemn "Marxism 306" and its abandonment of punctuation in favor of polemic. These were false characterizations of
the course, which sought to offer students substantive occasions for writing, to
provide practical models of argumentation, and to prompt participatory critical
discussion of tangible social and legal questions in American public life. With respect to the politics of American public life, English 306 was never intended to enforce a single position and would not have imposed an authoritative ideological
content. Yet, in conceiving the course with reference to the politics of American
public life and in having from the start to defend it in that large rhetorical arena,
the planners allowed the terms and configurations of that politics to eclipse or replace those (different ones) of the classroom. Constructing the syllabus around
case law, especially federal and state Supreme Court decisions, the course committee hoped to avert the charge of left-wing coercion that they feared the inclusion of significant amounts of social criticism would elicit. Ironically, however,
this means of avoiding the appearance of authoritative ideological content produced a syllabus that, in this pedagogical situation, would have been coercive and
authoritarian in form. That is, the imposing scholarly and disciplinary trappings
of the case law, as experienced by uninitiated readers, would have discouraged the
dialogic engagement that the planners sought. More probably, students would

have been rendered passive by the technical apparatus, unfamiliar data, and specialized language of the readings, which, within the politics of the classroom, would have enhanced the teacher's structural dominance, however scrupulously he or she might have sought to resist assuming ideological authority.

Our "writing about difference" in literary and social texts is more advanced, I believe, than our thinking about difference in our own professional context. My account of the planning of English 306 was meant to illustrate a powerful temptation of engaged disciplinary practice: the conflation of overlapping but different (and differently) political sites and subject positions that we simultaneously occupy. The temptation is especially strong for some of our most ambitious graduate students, whose worst intellectual moments, it seems to me, proceed not from polemical self-righteousness about what a colleague of mine likes to call "the facts on the ground" but from confusion by the many different facts and kinds of facts that currently compete on and for the disciplinary ground and from frustration by the complexities, limitations, and mediations of their own engagement (as readers of texts in classrooms, intellectuals, and preprofessionals who also occupy various ethnicities, genders, class and regional positions, and sexual orientations) with those facts.

Anyone who teaches in a graduate English program, I suspect, will have observed this impulse to escape the multiple and problematic situatedness of cultural and political meaning and of its academic interpretation. I offer two examples from my own graduate classes. Rosellen Brown's novel *Civil Wars* (1984) traces the shifting grounds of political commitment in the lives of two veterans of the civil rights movement. Passionate, full-time activists when they married in 1964, Teddy and Jessie Carll find their political lives diminished and their marriage disintegrating in the new South of 1979. Teddy, once a courageous, nearly martyred white movement leader and intimate of Carmichael and King, is driven by a mixture of unrelinquished idealism, insatiable guilt for his racist heritage, and a lust for personal heroics to manipulate and then neglect his family in a quixotic attempt to revive the movement in its early dramatic phase and reclaim a sense of his own historical significance. Jessie, attempting a feminist redefinition of "the political" that might validate a social practice within more local and even familial contexts, discovers a sexual chauvinism and a self-absorption in her husband that his disappointments have intensified—qualities that, in retrospect, she sees more clearly in other male movement leaders. The novel subtly and sympathetically (in my view) explores the multiple and sometimes incompatible bases of personal identity: racial, regional, sexual, economic, psychological, genealogical, ideological. Most of the students, however, were scandalized by Teddy, whose inability to separate his political principles from his personal needs and desires they found "despicable," and some, taking the critique of Teddy's sexism by his unwaveringly committed, egalitarian, and integrationist wife to be tantamount to authorial repudiation of the civil rights movement and of political activism in general, found the whole novel "offensive."

In my current course, "Americans Abroad/Aliens at Home," in which we are juxtaposing modern American international and intercultural narratives with contemporary cultural criticism and postcolonial theory, Henry James's *The American Scene* (1968), a very different text, elicited the same judgment for much the same reasons. Neither Ross Posnock's recent demonstration that James unsettled his genteel contemporaries by complicating, satirizing, and at moments directly resisting—even as he self-consciously confessed his susceptibility to—the nativism and nostalgia with which they greeted "the alien" nor my own efforts to remove some of the semantic obstructions to a serious engagement with James's cultural critique (including the not entirely facetious suggestion that we read the text's every "vulgar" as "hegemonic") shook many students' conviction that James was an unmitigated racist and classist. Curiously, though, what seemed to intensify the general hostility was James's very mitigations of his own judgments—his meticulous specifications of the difficulties, ambivalences, and limits of his own positionality as participant-observer in the scene, as alien native and as "restless analyst."

In an essay that we read later in the semester, "Can the Subaltern Speak?," Gayatri Chakravorty Spivak argues that "the task of the first-world subject of knowledge ... is to resist and critique 'recognition' of the Third World through 'assimilation'" and charges such an analyst with the responsibility to maintain "a vigilance precisely against too great a claim for transparency" (1988, 292–293). Postcolonial critics, Spivak suggests, must accept that "to confront them [the "heterogeneous Others," or James's "aliens"] is not to represent [speak for] them but to learn to represent [image] ourselves" (p. 289) and must understand the site of theory to be one of an "inaccessible blankness circumscribed by an interpretable text" if they are to resist the tendency of "the complicity of the investigating subject (male or female professional) to disguise itself in transparency" (p. 294).

Spivak's injunctions, and even her key figures of transparency and textually circumscribed blankness, may be seen to inform James's practice in *The American Scene.* I do not mean, of course, to equate Spivak's and James's personae or their politics, but in their vigilance with regard to "the complicity of the investigating subject" and their resistance to what Spivak terms "ferocious standardizing benevolence" (p. 294) and James calls "our pale poetic" (1968, 198) or "the wholesale varnish of consecration, that might have been applied, out of a bottomless receptacle, by a huge white-washing brush" (p. 127), they perhaps have more in common than either would care to admit. James's confrontation with the Other involves incessant identification of himself as a professional intellectual, a spectator, a member of an elite class, a white male—positions that he occupies not in the complacent knowledge or hope that they preclude or exempt him from engaging with others but in the recognition that they problematize any such engagement. This recognition, a number of passages from *The American Scene* suggest, entails the acceptance of limits on what James can know, the acknowledgment of an "inaccessible blankness" at the center of his lavishly interpretive text. And it entails

self-limitations on what he can speak—as when he implies that certain critiques
of urbanization and waste that may be available to Indians, or of the history and
culture of the American South that may be available to blacks, are not properly ar-
ticulable by him.

My students' hostility toward Brown, James, and the two works discussed above
bespoke their discomfort with the problematics (upon which these works insisted) of their own subject positions and institutional positions as engaged intellectuals. More generally, I believe, such discomfort is the product of a profound
tension in the predominant model of disciplinarity and professional identity in
current literary study. This tension may be dramatized by citing and complicating
a passage in Stanley Fish's *Doing What Comes Naturally* (1989). Amidst 570-odd
pages of dualism-busting, Fish offers a rare disciplinary distinction between legal
and literary interpretation. The discipline of law, Fish writes, demands "that
judges give remedies and avoid crises," while in literary studies "exactly the reverse" obtains. There, "the rule is that a critic must learn to read in a way that
multiplies crises, and must never give a remedy in the sense of a single and unequivocal answer to the question, 'what does this poem or novel or play mean?' "
This rule, he goes on, is "inherent in the discipline's deepest beliefs about the objects of its attention, in its deepest understanding of what literary works are for—
for contemplation, for the reflective exploration of complexity, for the entertainment of many perspectives, for the *suspension of judgment*" (p. 137).

In fact, our current critical theories and practices are invested both in protecting Fish's distinction and in exploding it. Walt Whitman wrote that the poet
"judges not as a judge judges but as the sun [does]," but what contemporary literary intellectuals want (arguably, Whitman wanted the same) is to judge both as a
judge and as the sun. In Fish's terms, our reigning ethos is at once an ethos of generative crisis (of complexity, multiperspectivalism, free play) and an ethos of remedy (of political consequence and moral judgment). Edward Said articulates this
tension in essays with suggestive titles such as "Traveller or Potentate?" and attempts to stake out a mediatory or integrative position in "Secular Criticism,"
cautioning on one page that "criticism modified in advance by labels like 'Marxism' or 'liberalism' is, in my view, an oxymoron" and allowing on the next that
"were I to use one word consistently along with *criticism* (not as a modification
but as an emphatic) it would be *oppositional*" (1983, 28, 29).

I take Said's distinction between "modification" and "emphatic" to introduce a
difference between what I would call *oppositional product*, which I associate with
the business of the state (or counterstate) and the provision of remedy, and *oppositional process*, the sustenance of local democratic energies and of interpretive crisis. To acknowledge a difference, even an opposition, between oppositional process and product, moreover, is to recognize that the "oppositional" is not a
freestanding substantive but a matter of position, relation. And in no site of the
discipline of literary study is the teacher-critic's positionality and the relation be-

tween oppositional product and oppositional process more problematic than in the classroom. My paradigmatic figure for this problem, which is sure to have confronted anyone who embraces the principles of contemporary pedagogy and criticism on the left, is that of the eager disciple who looks up from his notebook and asks me, "How do you spell 'hegemony'?"

In the spring of 1992, as a means of formally and collectively exploring the kinds of issues I have raised here, I organized a graduate-faculty colloquium in my department under the rubric "Pedagogy and Values." Fourteen graduate students, all assistants or instructors in freshman- and sophomore-level classes, and ten faculty members presented papers in a series of six sessions with titles such as "Pedagogical Styles, Discourses, and Principles," "Political Crises in Class," and "The Engaged Instructor: Conscience or Coercion?" Our department's recent history had demanded that those who studied and taught in it confront in the most immediate ways difficult questions about the relations between theory and practice, politics and pedagogy, and the colloquium illustrated that such confrontations had borne intellectual, curricular, and ethical fruit. Several speakers, for instance, outlined appealing models of self-reflexive and counterhierarchical pedagogical practice that made use of the theoretical resources of critical postmodernism and, often, of the technological resources of the department's two computer-mediated classrooms. One colleague found that the use of the Interchange Network democratized the classroom and empowered students, allowing for what he called "heterogeneity without hierarchy." Another, drawing on the theories of classical rhetoricians and neopragmatists, sought to articulate principles for an engaged instruction that promoted "morality without dogmatism." But it quickly became apparent, as the uneasy relationship between these two phrases may suggest, that all of our responses to the questions around which the colloquium was structured tended to reproduce rather than resolve the disciplinary tension that I have described as a simultaneous ethos of crisis and ethos of remedy.

Hierarchy, however nondogmatically advanced, is intrinsic to morality in the simple sense that morality is the elevation of some attitudes, positions, or behaviors above others. Moreover, the heterogeneity invited by democratic principles and democratizing technologies in the classroom does not necessarily counter—in fact, may enhance—dogmatism and intolerance. Nowhere were these complications better exposed than in several powerful papers, presented by lesbian graduate instructors, on the panel entitled "Sexual Orientation(s) in the Classroom." One of these papers, which analyzed transcripts of computer-mediated student exchanges on texts that represented gays and lesbians or involved questions of sexual orientation, argued that the radically egalitarian—and interpersonally depressurized—computer classroom did facilitate open, inclusive, diverse, and humane discussion. But subsequent speakers strikingly testified to the ways in which classes that are less hierarchically organized, whether as a consequence of professorial ideology or instructional technology, can facilitate and even encourage heterosexism and homophobia and can be complicit in the denial of an expressible gay subject position.

In particular, one presenter recounted a painful occasion on which she chose to tolerate intense and increasingly demagogic, if widely participatory, homophobia in a computer-mediated discussion, thus silencing herself and perhaps contributing to the silencing of some gay students, rather than risk alienating her class early in the semester. The decision to cede the elevated and authoritative teacher's voice did not, in this instance, promote heterogeneity. Nor did it undo hierarchy so much as it allowed one traditionally hierarchical structure, the hierarchy of socially approved and disapproved sexualities, to replace or occupy another, that of the teacher-centered classroom. Professorial dogmatism was resisted but, arguably, at the cost rather than in the service of morality. As another panelist put it, professorial fidelity to a counterhierarchical classroom may unreasonably place on the most embattled students the burden of doing some of the most difficult pedagogical and political work, the identification of heterocentrism and heterosexism in class discussion. Moreover, it may deprive students of their traditional—and legitimate—investment (economic, intellectual, and emotional) in the idea of the teacher as a source of authority. This point suggestively echoed a question to the theorists of democratic pedagogy that had been posed at a previous session of the colloquium and received as a conservative caveat. The question was "How do you deal with the issue of mastery, of what the instructor has to impart?" In light of the subsequent session on "Sexual Orientation(s) in the Classroom" this question took on new dimensions: What if one of the things the instructor has mastered more successfully than most of her students is her susceptibility to irrational prejudice? What if one of the things the instructor has to impart is a commitment to heterogeneity or a sense of justice?

A week or so before our departmental colloquium began, a controversy erupted in the university's College of Liberal Arts that dramatized as powerfully as any incident I have encountered the tension between what I have called the overlapping but different (and differently) political sites and subject positions that socially engaged academics occupy. I will close by describing that controversy, recounting my initial response to it during the colloquium, and attempting, with the help of some challenges that were raised by others, both to situate and to critique that response. In performing this final representation and self-representation, I wish not to hierarchize the institutional, pedagogical, and broadly social sites and investments of our professional identity but to argue for their continuing mediation, as the title of this essay seeks to multiply and mediate the injunctions—political correctness, principled contextualism, pedagogical conscience—of PC.

Over his desk in his teaching office, a Latino graduate instructor in another department of the College of Liberal Arts displayed what he described as an erotic AIDS awareness poster (Fig. 8.1). The poster presents a grainy black-and-white image of two naked young men of color in a passionate embrace. One man stands,

FIGURE 8.1

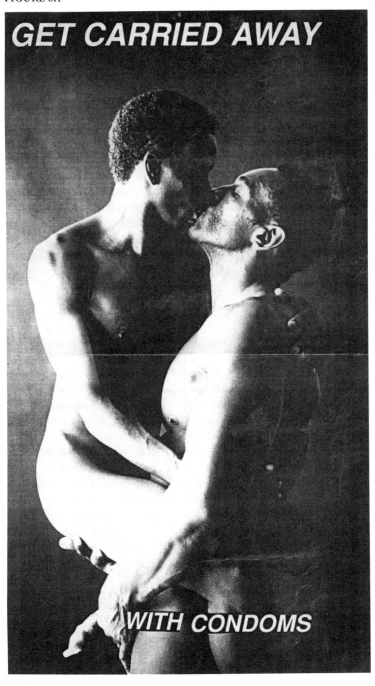

supporting the other—who is off the ground, legs locked around the waist of the standing lover whom he kisses—with his right arm and hand beneath the other's thigh. The left hand of the standing figure holds his own erect, condom-sheathed penis. At the top of the photograph, a block-letter caption reads GET CARRIED AWAY. At the bottom are the words WITH CONDOMS. Following a complaint about the poster, the dean of the college ordered the graduate instructor to remove it.

The public debate that followed tended to pit the discourse of individual expressive freedom against what the dean called "the case for limited censorship" grounded in a discourse of community standards and legitimate restrictions on the individual. As the debate intensified, charges of institutional heterosexism were countered by suggestions that the poster's display may have violated the university's policy against sexual harassment. What these positions on either side shared, it seemed to me, was the contextualization of the incident within one or another broad social struggle (freedom of speech, gay rights, freedom from sexual harassment) and a privileging of the space of that struggle over a space that undoubtedly is informed by all of these contests and others but that is not synonymous with them. That space—the most literally relevant and conceptually problematic space here, I suggested—was a pedagogical one. On the basis of my understanding of the claim and the dynamics of the pedagogical space, I argued that an instructor ought not to display this poster in his teaching office. (As I pointed out at the colloquium, this position is not identical, and does not entail agreement, with the university's demand that the poster be removed.)

Colleagues who supported or defended the poster's display made a number of indisputable points: the poster did convey an urgent AIDS awareness message; the society accords little public space for affirmative images—of which the poster counts as one—of same-sex love; the pervasive discomfort of gays in a heterocentrist and heterosexist society far outweighs the occasional discomfort of straights. But such points, in my view, again worked to elide a distinction between the space of our pedagogy and the space of our larger political relations and social commitments, a distinction that must constantly be interrogated, I held, but must not be effaced. My argument was that, in the faculty office, the relations of power that govern the pedagogical situation hold sway over other, doubtless quite different, relations of power in the general society and culture. In combination with the inherent inequality of the student-teacher relationship and with the circuit of desire that necessarily informs it (the desire to win admiration, to win approval, to provide what is needed, to give what is wanted, to move, to please, to bond), the display of the poster, however unintentionally, manipulated and threatened to disable the pedagogical enterprise in ways that I felt a commitment to principled contextualism and pedagogical conscience disallowed.

In taking this position, I noted its dependence on the fact that the pedagogical space at issue in this instance was the office and not the classroom. Drawing on an explanation by one of the speakers on "Sexual Orientation(s) in the Classroom" of her policy of balancing productive discomfort with student safety in her teaching (safety, she said, is students' knowing they can speak; discomfort is their not having to like what they hear), I suggested that the classroom offered a space in which students and instructor might engage the poster, the issues it raised, and their responses to it with the balance of safety and discomfort in force, whereas the office did not. In the office, the invitation to student speech and the conditions of safe speech are diminished. The poster hanging on the wall there is not the same "text" that it would be in the classroom or, indeed, in any more public space. In the context of the faculty office, I contended, other and even perhaps more obviously available meanings of the poster—its AIDS prevention message, its affirmation of gay sexuality—are likely to be eclipsed by its unjustified exacerbation of the unequal power relations between teacher and student. The context of the office even tends, ironically, to cancel otherwise crucial differences between the poster at issue and one (which most of the supporters of this poster's display would have assailed) that depicted white, opposite-sex lovers in the same pose and under the same caption: the verbal and visual imperative of either one ("get carried away"), I argued, is certain to constitute, for many students, an intimidating and unproductively discomforting desublimation of the politics of desire that inform the teacher-student relationship.

When I first drafted this response for the colloquium on "Pedagogy and Values," I marked my ambivalence about it, and my anxiety about articulating it, by writing, in midargument, "I find myself posing objections to almost everything I say here but that seems a better reason to go on than to stop or than never to have started." I still (ambivalently) would argue this position, but I have come to recognize that my representation of the issues raised by the poster's display was produced with, and to some degree depended upon, minimal self-representation—minimal analysis and articulation, that is, of the position *from* which (rather than that *of* which) I spoke. My argument had contested what Spivak would call the assumption of "transparency" by the pedagogical subject—the lack of an account, on the part of those who defended the display of the poster, of the specific institutional relations of power that inform an instructor's communication with students, govern the semiotics of faculty office space, and in this instance situationally shaped the poster's meaning. But, in making it, I had been transparent to myself in my failure to observe the ways in which my constructions of "an instructor's communications with students," of "faculty office space," and of the pedagogical "politics of desire" were not normative representations of institutional relations of power within the academy but products of the even more specific and differentiated positions within those institutional relations that I personally occupied.

In a general way, of course, I was aware that my interpretive foregrounding of the potential abuse of power in the poster's display was connected to my privileged status—as white male heterosexual tenured professor—in every dimension of my social and institutional identity. That status allows (requires) me to experience my position in relation to my students as one of undivided empowerment such as the position of a gay, female, nonwhite, or even untenured instructor might not be. Mine is also a subject position that, whatever my political principles or affiliations, abstracts me from the most immediate kinds of investment in gay and AIDS activism. Although I sensed that my own situation inclined me to the reading of the event that I produced, however, I needed others to begin to show me how some of the very terms of my reading depended on that particular professorial situation rather than on other actual and possible ones.

For instance, one graduate student pointed out, my implicit model of the faculty office was that of the private space assigned to tenure-track and tenured professors at my institution, not that of the space shared by three or four graduate instructors (the kind of office in which the poster was displayed), one that generally accommodates a number of bodies and conversations at once and is always subject to public intrusion. My imaginative privatization of the space of the poster's display in turn enhanced my conviction that the sexual dynamics of the teacher-student relationship would be likely to inform its reception. Moreover, as several women colleagues argued, the sexual dynamics that concerned me most typically described the relation or potential relation between a male figure of authority and a younger female. Were these dynamics relevant to the effect of this poster within a pedagogical space or to a situation in which the instructor himself was a graduate student, not much older than those in his class? Would I have the same objection to the poster's display over the desk of a female instructor? And, finally, might not any individual instructor, irrespective of gender or sexual orientation, establish a relationship of sufficient openness and trust with students as to enable them to encounter the poster on the instructor's office wall freely and safely?

In an interview published under the title "Criticism, Feminism, and the Institution," Gayatri Spivak argues for the need of politically engaged teachers and critics to "become vigilant about our own practice," to "situate it at the moment" (1990, 11). "One thing that comes out" of the effort to situate critical and pedagogical practice, not only within the frame of one grand narrative or another but at the moment of its institutional and interpersonal production, Spivak continues, "is that you jettison your own purity as a theorist" (p. 12). Both my critique of the display of the AIDS awareness poster and the questionings and qualifications of that critique presented above have sought to exemplify the process of jettisoning theoretical and ideological purity that it seems to me the most responsible and fully engaged criticism and pedagogy must sustain. This process entails the vigilant articulation of the resistances, as well as the opportunities for integration, brought about by our simultaneous occupation of pedagogical and political spaces, institutional and larger sociocultural positions, differently constructed, empowered, and constrained identities. To acknowledge and address these resistances is to take seriously both our pedagogy and our politics and, however frustrating "at the moment," perhaps ultimately to enhance both.

WORKS CITED

Brown, Rosellen. *Civil Wars.* New York: Knopf, 1984.

Carton, Evan. "The Self Besieged: American Identity on Campus and in the Gulf." *Tikkun* 6 (July/August 1991):40–47.

Cheney, Lynne V. *Humanities in America: A Report to the President, the Congress, and the American People.* Washington, D.C.: National Endowment for the Humanities, 1988.

Davidson, Cathy N. "'PH' Stands for Political Hypocrisy." *Academe* 77 (September/October 1991):8–14.

Fish, Stanley. *Doing What Comes Naturally: Change, Rhetoric, and the Practice of Theory in Literary and Legal Studies.* Durham: Duke University Press, 1989.

Isserman, Maurice. "Travels with Dinesh." *Tikkun* 6 (September/October 1991):81–84.

James, Henry. *The American Scene.* Bloomington: Indiana University Press, 1968.

Posnock, Ross. *The Trial of Curiosity: Henry James, William James, and the Challenge of Modernity.* New York: Oxford University Press, 1991.

Ransom, John Crowe. *The New Criticism.* Norfolk: New Directions, 1941.

Said, Edward W. *The World, the Text, and the Critic.* Cambridge: Harvard University Press, 1983.

Spivak, Gayatri Chakravorty. "Can the Subaltern Speak?" In *Marxism and the Interpretation of Culture,* ed. Lawrence Grossberg and Cary Nelson. Urbana: University of Illinois Press, 1988.

———. "Criticism, Feminism, and the Institution." In *The Post-Colonial Critic,* ed. Sarah Harasym. New York: Routledge, 1990.

9

Not Born on the Fourth of July: Cultural Differences and American Literary Studies

GREGORY S. JAY

THE SCENARIO has become familiar. After a long history of apparent uniformity and consensus, a nation suddenly collapses. Political institutions and ideological arguments that had once been its supposed foundation are blown down like a house of cards. Beneath the appearance of a monolithic history and singular future there abruptly bursts forth the reality of irreconcilable differences. Citizens increasingly see themselves primarily as members of particular regional, ethnic, religious, economic, or sexual groups rather than as individuals with a common society, culture, or system of beliefs. A shrinking economic pie and a ferocious struggle for limited resources polarizes citizens into competing interest groups. Political correctness (PC) and identity politics become pervasive practices and accusations. Where once the identification of the individual person with the universal national spirit was seen as an equalizing force that promised the eventual participation of all in directing the country's fate, now this universalism is roundly condemned as an ideological ruse that obscures the subordination of disempowered groups exploited by a hegemonic elite. The political culture descends into exchanges of condemnation, recrimination, and even gunfire; the fracturing of any sense of commonality leads to an appalling cynicism and lack of compassion. Argument centers on proving who has been the most victimized and who the most reprehensible. The classic question of politics—"What is the common good?"—is replaced by the question "What's in it for me and my friends?"

Citizens of the United States may take this scenario as describing such former nation-states as the Soviet Union or Yugoslavia or as pertinent to current tensions in Britain or Germany. Yet it also, with many qualifications, mirrors the social and political dissensus characteristic of the United States as the twentieth century gives way to a postcolonial, postmodern, multicultural future. Since global patterns link the cultural crises in the disparate parts of the world, the forces driving cultural change in the United States ought to some degree to be interpreted from such an international perspective. For example, we see around the world different nations struggling to find a way to balance the claims of individuality, ethnic or racial solidarity, democracy, economic development, and nationalism. The principles of self-determination and freedom abstractly embodied in theories of democracy clash with the desires of cultural, ethnic, or religious groups to create social systems predicated on their own traditional beliefs. Perhaps most significant, the globalization of the labor force and the mobility of international commodity capitalism create economic competition that often exploits the resources of patriotic nationalism and of racial, ethnic, and gender bigotry.

Postcolonialism often leaves former dependent states in splintered ruins, while the former imperial powers themselves suffer internal breakdowns that partly stem from an influx of postcolonial refugees. At the level of political ideology, any recourse to the rhetoric or policy of universalism, humanism, and common culture seems bankrupt from the start, victim of its own record of hypocrisy and bad faith. Yet the economic interdependency of the globe's regions continues to increase, defying the tide of tribalism as multinational corporations continue to transgress political borders. Likewise the technology of communication, from personal computers and fax machines to the prospective fiber-optic "information highway," does not respect the lines drawn by factions on a map as the exchange of images and consumer goods bridges peoples to create commonalities in the practices of their everyday lives. My computer can connect me to the world, though of course my ownership of one says something particular about my privileged place in the universe.

Across the globe, one question repeats itself: Is the elemental unit or agent of political theory and culture to be the individual or the social group? A series of corollary questions follows: How do we respond to the fact that the creation of any national identity always involves the exclusion of certain citizens, whether through the subtle omission of their beliefs from the culture's dominant institutions or through the violence of outright genocide? Is democratic freedom possible for the individual if the social or political culture treats the individual according to how that culture values the group to which it assigns that individual? Can a person resist such oppression individually, or only through changing the way the group is represented? Switching from questions of theory to conditions of history, can the nation-state be a viable political or cultural entity now that the technology of industrial production, transportation, and communication makes global mobility so pervasive? Are such categories as race or ethnicity any longer viable as fundamental components of cultural identity? Or have our crises precisely been the product of wrongly thinking we could transcend such categories in appeals to universal principles (whether those of marxism or Western humanism)?

In trying to frame the current cultural discord in the United States today, then, I submit that the situation here is not unique, though it does have a very specific and unusual history. The history of our discords must be remembered if we are not to treat the present crisis as a kind of biblical Fall from a previous Eden of communal harmony. I believe the divisions in American culture today can only be understood historically, and understood first of all as a symptom of the nation's recurrent historical amnesia. As a nation we do not like to remember the past. Freedom from the past, after all, has been our national myth, and that innocence has often been a key to our achievements. We tell ourselves that we received our unique identity in a moment of revolutionary forgetting, when we declared ourselves independent of the old world. We think a new world can be made because we have shed the old world and renamed ourselves. At some time or another, every American has been Jay Gatsby. Unfortunately, we have gone on fabricating stories about ourselves through repeated acts of amnesia, forgetting our own divisive history in the process of creating our common future. How else could a nation of immigrants wake up one morning to a debate over the meaning of multiculturalism?

What so many insurgent groups in the United States today have in common—from African and Native Americans to women, the working-class, recent Asian immigrants, and gays and lesbians—is their insistence that we have an ethical and political responsibility to remember our history differently. That is why the debates over school and university curricula are so important and so symptomatic, since they reflect the argument that the history of oppression in America has been a function of the oppressive character of the way history has been represented and taught, in mass media and popular culture as well as in the schools. Revisionists go beyond debating ideas to focus attention on the material institutions that produce cultural identities, and so the agitation of political activists has surprisingly joined forces with the skepticism of poststructuralist academics anxious to deconstruct the ideologies of Representational Man.

If politics is in some degree essentially about the distribution of power, and if knowledge about the powerless tends to be biased or simply left out, then redressing the imbalance will be seen by some as a "political" rather than an "academic" matter. But teachers cannot help the fact that they inherit schools, textbooks, and ideas that reflect the biases of the past. Surely it is the responsibility of teachers to correct those biases as best they can. These educational biases are in part caused by the way that political power has been distributed in the United States, so as to largely exclude people whose perceived identity (seen in terms of race, ethnicity, class, sexual orientation, or gender) does not conform to the politically correct line. This political motive behind traditional educational biases means that those who seek to tell the story differently will inevitably be accused of "politicizing" the curriculum when in fact they are simply trying to point out the effect that politics has already had on what we study and what we value.

We should not have been surprised, then, when the exaggerated story of political correctness gained such rapid and powerful ascendancy in the public sphere. The same structural and ideological biases that dominated higher education also shaped the personnel and policies of the major broadcasters, magazines, think tanks, and government officials. Even "marxists" and other "left" intellectuals joined the ranks criticizing feminists, multiculturalists, and literary theorists, for these academic movements challenged the cultural politics of the Old Left as well. Thus from all sides we heard about how a conspiracy of tenured radicals, leftover 1960s activists, feminists, and minority scholars has succeeded in taking over U.S. colleges and universities, imposing upon them a uniform ideological program of neomarxist totalitarianism that rejects Western civilization in favor of Afro-centrism, deconstructive nihilism, Hollywood films, Harlequin romances, and MTV. We are routinely told that the agents of political correctness have brought politics into the ivory tower, indoctrinating their students and tolerating no opinions that do not match their own. This ludicrous exaggeration of the power of groups that are still very much on the margins reflects the degree of fear on the part of the establishment that these groups and their concerns may actually now be winning some influence.

Such attempts to blame progressive intellectuals for imposing a standard of political correctness on our campuses perversely misrepresent the truth of history, which is that educational institutions have always been partly in the service of dominant social and political institutions. After all, most colleges are owned and run by churches, corporate boards, and governmental bodies. Where were today's born-again champions of democracy, freedom of thought, and evaluation by merit during all the years that women were denied admission to many of the nation's top colleges and universities? Where were they during all the years that Jews, blacks, and others were similarly discriminated against? Why were the *Atlantic, Time, Newsweek,* the *New York Times,* and the rest of the media relatively silent during the decades when curriculum and teaching practices amounted to a "thought police" on behalf of white Anglo-Saxon males? Who cried out *then* about "political correctness" on campus? In contrast, how many conservative students or professors have been denounced by multiculturalists at Senate hearings or executed, like the Rosenbergs, for treason? The only new McCarthyism in town, sad to say, is still the old one, though now it is busy discovering feminists, black studies scholars, and poststructuralists under every bed.

Although literary study should not become a branch of political science, we should not complacently imagine that culture and politics have no ties that bind. Contrary to some accusations, it was not the irrelevance of work done by activist academics and critical theorists that precipitated the crisis at the universities. Rather, it was the increasingly irrelevant character of higher education that prompted the move toward multiculturalism. The virulent campaign of the anti-PC crowd testifies to exactly how relevant the reforms are, how precisely they have hit the target, and how far the powers-that-be will go in protecting their privileges. Just take a look at the success with which the Reagan and Bush administrations reversed the gains made by women and minorities since the 1960s and you can imagine what conservatives have in mind for education. Defunding and "privatization" have already gone far in destroying the autonomy of schools. Perhaps the Clinton administration will stall or reverse these policies, though its opponents have a powerful ideological and financial machine already attacking such a prospect. As for free speech, it was the justices of the Supreme Court of the United States who ruled that doctors at clinics receiving federal funds may not even mention abortion to their patients. *They* are the real thought police, and they remind us of the court that decided, in the Dred Scott case, that blacks had no rights that a white man need respect. Fortunately the Supreme Court does not yet have jurisdiction over our course syllabi; if they do extend their political control from the womb to the classroom, there are apparently many opinions we will be forbidden to express.

The politics of PC in American culture, then, unfolds as part of a contradictory global transformation that has local effects. Whereas the internal history of American higher education explains some of the present controversy, that history in turn belongs to a larger history that shapes it and that today overdetermines the campus as a site of racial, economic, political, and social unrest. I want to review that larger history in an effort to better situate present debates over the politics of cultural identity.

Born on the Fourth of July?

In a previous essay on the need for a multicultural practice in the teaching of the literature of the United States, I questioned the existence of "American" literature, pointing out that most efforts by critics to invent it had relied upon nationalistic agendas that were ultimately political rather than aesthetic or cultural.[1] At the level of critical theory, one can deconstruct the various interpretive paradigms that were used in the past to fabricate the illusion of a singular "American" literature. At the historical level, one can easily show that the diversity of written texts produced in the colonies and the United States always amounted to a multicultural dialogue rather than a single voice of the national spirit. In the words of the *Heath Anthology of American Literature,* "From its start, the New World community was multiracial and multicultural. ... The New World, comprised of defined spheres of influence over territories claimed and counterclaimed by European sovereign powers, early offered signs of the necessary mingling of red, white, and black that remain its earliest, best promise."[2] The United States became a postcolonial nation on that famous Fourth of July and went on to become a rarity—a former colony that would itself become an imperial, colonial power. Throughout its history, however, this lack of a homogeneous or pure racial, ethnic, or cultural origin meant that the United States would have to struggle to produce a common national culture, even if this meant violently repressing the differences within its borders.

Since the Revolution of 1776, literary journalists, critics, and artists have repeatedly called for a uniquely "American" literature. All about them, however, that uniqueness was already taking the form of a polyvocal, even multilingual, writing that would continually resist formulation into a homogeneous canon. But, as Paul Lauter has concisely demonstrated, literary critics at the colleges and universities largely succeeded during the period from 1920 to 1970 in drastically narrowing the canon of authors and works and in creating textbooks, curricula, departments, professional organizations, and interpretive studies based on that canon.[3] Throughout this era, from the early essays of Van Wyck Brooks through the decisive works of Vernon Louis Parrington, F. O. Matthiessen, Richard Chase, and Lionel Trilling (who, like Nathaniel Hawthorne, really was born on the Fourth of July), definitions of the American literary canon hinged on the critic's search for a usable past and were motivated by the desire to construct a set of authorizing cultural documents to give foundation to specific notions of a democratic culture.

In retrospect we can see how limited those notions were, especially as they tended to depend on an ideology of American individualism that emptied the human being of his or her material, historical features—such as race, class, gender, and sexuality. The tendency to focus on common human traits and conditions is of course understandable when one considers the historic diversity of wave after wave of immigrants who, to this day, continue to alter the physical and cultural face of the United States (as today postcolonial immigration also brings a crisis of cultural identity and social power to such traditionally homogeneous nation-states as England, France, and Germany).[4] Born during the height of the European Enlightenment, the United States was founded on philosophical doctrines that emphasized the universal rather than the particular. This philosophy produced a legal system of justice predicated on the ethos of an abstract human subjectivity equally shared by all rational creatures. The ringing phrases of Thomas Jefferson's language in the Declaration of Independence forever linked the establishment of the nation to that humanistic idealism.

"We hold these truths to be self-evident, that all men are created equal, that they are endowed by their Creator with certain unalienable Rights, that among these are Life, Liberty, and the pursuit of Happiness."[5] The *subject* of the Declaration of Independence—grammatically and politically—is the rhetorical "we," produced in discourse and on paper before it appears in reality. This "we" creates the theatrical illusion of a preexistent, univocal subject who originates and speaks the revolutionary utterance. But this utterance is what rhetoricians call a "performative" speech-act: it performs an action as well as declaring a set of facts. The "we" of the American people is born during this performance. We become our own subjects, subject no longer to King George but to the higher "Laws of Nature and of Nature's God." As Jay Fliegelman points out, the Declaration represents the Revolution as both an unavoidable necessity *and* a free act of will, exhibiting an uneasy dialectic between mechanical determinism and individual agency characteristic of the period.[6] The Declaration speaks predominantly in the passive voice of what is "necessary for one people" to do after such "patient sufferance" of the willful actions against them of the king. By making their invention of their own rebellious subjectivity sound like a necessity imposed upon them, the colonists mitigate their guilt and obscure the artificial character of the union they declare.

In this "unanimous declaration" we hear of "one people," of "the Right of the People" and "their duty" to—among other things—commit treason. Although the agency of the human action narrated by the Declaration anthropomorphizes the body politic, imagining it as a collective of different persons, this subject nonetheless speaks with one voice, as if it were a particular individual with rights and duties. Was this presumption ethical, especially considering how many particular people had no voice in this utterance? "Jefferson's statement of equality" in the sense of being equally made by God with moral faculties, explains Fliegelman, "was far from a racial call for social equality."[7] The Declaration postulated an abstractly equal and universal human subjectivity despite the historical exclusion from it of Indians, slaves, women, and those men who did not own property. The words of the Declaration continue to haunt the moral and political life of America, and subsequent generations have both embraced and repudiated them.[8] At the origin of the United States, then, we find an ethically troubling contradiction between enabling fictions of universalism and stubborn realities of particularity and exclusion. What the next centuries bring is not simply a history of hypocrisy, however, but a series of appropriating subversions as those who were left out of the original declaration use its own utopian terms both to challenge and to expand the practices of American democracy.

The original draft of Jefferson's Declaration contained a long, hypocritical, and self-serving condemnation of the king's encouragement of the international slave trade and of the crown's policy of offering manumission to slaves who rebelled against their rebellious masters. But even Jefferson and his colleagues quickly recognized the folly of citing the king's offer of freedom for slaves as an example of the tyranny they opposed; the passage was dropped, though a veiled reference to the crown's instigation of "domestic insurrections" was inserted.[9] When the Constitution of the United States was eventually negotiated, it counted enslaved Africans as two-thirds of a person for the purpose of determining the representation of districts and states in Congress. These slaves, of course, had no vote themselves; nor did women and most unpropertied men, for that matter. The Declaration and the Constitution presented Americanness as a revolutionary identity or ethos for all, but the reality and power of citizenship were in practice restricted.

Even before 1776, protesting slaves in Massachusetts were using the language of the Enlightenment, claiming that "we have in common with all other men a naturel [sic] right to our freedoms." In a subsequent petition of January 1777, slaves in Massachusetts were already appropriating the Declaration of Independence and Jefferson's phrases as they made two claims that would characterize abolitionist (and later women's rights) literature: (1) that African Americans were entitled to equal status as human beings and (2) that the oppression of African Americans vividly resembled the oppression suffered by the colonies at the hands of King George. These petitioners claimed to "have in common with all other men a Natural and Unaliable Right to that freedom which the Grat parent of the Unavers hath Bestowed equalley on all menkind and which they have Never forfeited by any Compact or agreement whatever"; they further expressed "their Astonishment that It have Never Bin Consirderd that Every Principle from which America has Acted in the Cours of their unhappy Difficultes with Great Briton Pleads Stronger than A thousand arguments in favours of your petitioners" seeking freedom from slavery.[10]

Black and white abolitionists throughout the early 1800s continued to throw the slave owner Jefferson's words back in the face of the political establishment and to make that one sentence ("We hold these truths to be self-evident, that all men are created equal") the most often and ironically quoted text in abolitionist literature. David Walker's 1829 *Appeal to the Coloured Citizens of the World,* perhaps the most fiery antislavery pamphlet before the speeches of Frederick Douglass, pointedly singled out Jefferson for analytic ridicule. Walker responded at length to Jefferson's assertion of the racial inferiority of blacks in his *Notes on the State of Virginia.* He also quoted the first two paragraphs of the Declaration verbatim and asked, "Compare your own language ... with your cruelties and murders inflicted by your cruel and unmerciful fathers and yourselves on our fathers and on us. ... I ask you candidly, was your sufferings under Great Britain, one hundredth part as cruel and tyrannical as you have rendered ours under you?"[11] When in 1853 William Wells Brown wrote the first novel by an African American, he called it *Clotel, or The President's Daughter.* Brown based his novel on the rumors that Jefferson had fathered two mulatto slave daughters who were subsequently sold south. The epigraph on Brown's title page was Jefferson's by then notorious sentence about equality from the Declaration of Independence.[12]

The summation of this tradition of antislavery responses to the Declaration was the escaped slave and abolitionist leader Frederick Douglass's spectacular oration "What to the Slave is the Fourth of July?," pointedly delivered on 5 July 1852:

> What to the American slave is your Fourth of July? I answer, a day that reveals to him more than all other days of the year, the gross injustice and cruelty to which he is the constant victim. To him your celebration is a sham; your boasted liberty an unholy license; your national greatness, swelling vanity; your sounds of rejoicing are empty and heartless; your denunciation of tyrants, brass-fronted impudence; your shouts of liberty and equality, hollow mockery; your prayers and hymns, your sermons and thanksgivings, with all your religious parade and solemnity, are to him mere bombast, fraud, deception, impiety, and hypocrisy—a thin veil to cover up crimes which would disgrace a nation of savages. There is not a nation of the earth guilty of practices more shocking and bloody than are the people of these United States.[13]

Sadly, some in the United States today would probably dismiss Douglass's speech as merely the hot air of political correctness, for they are dedicated to that very historical amnesia and hypocrisy that Douglass condemns. The apostles proclaiming the univocal, superior virtues of "Western civilization" seem to forget the role of slavery and the voices of people like Douglass in the history of that civilization. That forgetting is unethical and lies close to the heart of the immorality running through the traditional curriculum.

In analyzing racism in the United States, we ought to remember its economic motive, for this determines its role in building the civilization. Like most discourses of bigotry, this one results in profits for one group at the expense of another. More specifically, the rhetoric of Negro inferiority helped justify a system that kept wages for labor at an artificially low—even nonexistent—level. Slavery presents the extreme example of bigotry, for here the subject is not simply represented as a deficient or perverse individual: this subject is not a subject but *property*. As the Boston Tea Party suggests, the Declaration of Independence declared the independence of (some) men to own property and the dependence of their rights as citizens on that freedom to acquire, sell, and possess property. Insurrectional classes (slaves, women, immigrants, etc.) will be subjected to discrimination to the degree that it profitably regulates their relation to (or as) property. For such classes, declaring independence of the Master means taking back their own bodies as property and claiming the political power that comes with the freedom to control property. The original language behind the Declaration, after all, had listed "life, liberty, and property" as the citizen's trinity. The cultural and political history of the United States was and continues to be conditioned by this codependency of freedom and property, with the attendant complicating relation of freedom to wage labor.

Critical economists have argued with some persuasiveness that the enormous and rapid growth of wealth in the U.S. economy resulted mainly from the successive exploitation of low-wage labor performed by indentured servants, slaves, women, and a wave of different immigrant populations. At the close of the twentieth century, multinational corporations now find this labor abroad, often for pennies a day. Workers in the United States find themselves competing with the populations the West once colonized; domestically, cultural separatism increases as discrimination works to bar certain groups from gaining access to the increasingly small pool of higher-paid labor. Although the American ethos states that prosperity for all is available through hard work, work is not available for all Americans. To the degree that the structural necessity for an underclass in capitalism comes to overlap with groupings by cultural identity, economic strife may take the symbolic form of ideological warfare, from debates over Negro and female inferiority to the more recent uproar about multiculturalism and feminism.

It was no accident that Frederick Douglass gave his speech in response to an invitation from the Rochester Ladies' Anti-Slavery Society. For decades the causes of women's rights and antislavery had been closely linked, as women played a key role in advancing the work of abolitionism in the North. Indeed, the association of the condition of women with that of the slaves goes back at least to 1776. In a famous exchange of letters during the months prior to the signing of the Declaration, Abigail and John Adams gave rare witness in writing to a debate that doubtless raged in many households. "I long to hear that you have declared an independency," wrote Abigail, "—and by the way in the new Code of Laws which I suppose it will be necessary for you to make I desire that you would Remember the Ladies." Observing to her husband that "your sex are Naturally Tyrannical," she asked for specific laws to protect women from the "cruelty and indignity" suffered under the "unlimited power" of husbands: "If particular care and attention is not paid to the Laidies we are determined to foment a Rebelion, and will not hold ourselves bound by any Laws in which we have no voice, or Representation." John Adams responded, "As to your extraordinary Code of Laws, I cannot but laugh." Exploiting the witty tone of Abigail's letter to his own end, he noted that the revolutionaries had been accused of fomenting a general anarchy and a disruption of traditional social hierarchies: the Tories claimed that children, apprentices, students, Indians, and Negroes all grew "insolent to their Masters." "But your letter," he continued, "was the first Intimation that another Tribe more numerous and powerful than all the rest were grown discontented." He went on to say, "We know better than to repeal our masculine systems," and he repeated the myth that men were the victims of what he called the "Despotism of the Peticoat." He jokingly (perhaps) accused King George's government of instigating rebellion among the women as it did among "Tories, Landjobbers, Trimmers, Bigots, Canadians, Indians, Negros, Hanoverians, Hessians, Russians, Irish Roman Catholicks, Scotch Renegadoes."[14] By this argument, the same made by Jefferson in the Declaration's struck passage on slavery, the Founding Fathers meant to declare their independence from women as well as from King George. Their construction of the American political ethos carefully separated a masculine claim to inalienable (property) rights from claims made by the groups whose clamoring for representation they thought ought to be squelched. John Adams's sarcastic linking of women's claims to those of Negroes, Indians, and other oppressed groups would, of course, return as a serious political argument in the hands of feminists and abolitionists in the nineteenth century and remains a logical connection for many cultural analysts to this day.

By the late 1820s, women were increasingly apt to compare their situation to that of the slaves, all the more so when women's attempts to speak in public and exercise political power were met with contempt, ridicule, and violence. One of the first of these women, Angelina Grimké, herself the daughter of a slave owner, wrote Catharine Beecher in 1837 that "the investigation of the rights of the slave has led me to a better understanding of my own." Using the ideological rhetoric of sentiment, domesticity, and Christianity, Grimké established equality on the basis of morality: "Human beings have *rights,* because they are *moral* beings: the rights of *all* men grow out of their moral nature; and as all men have the same moral nature, they have essentially the same rights. … My doctrine, then, is that whatever it is morally right for man to do, it is morally right for woman to do."[15] This radical feminist assertion of the ethos of a common moral nature intends to override the particular discrimination against the character of women and blacks used to define their subordinate social and political place. In 1845 Margaret Fuller underscored how American's declaration of "national independence be blurred by the servility of individuals," and she too drew the by-then standard analogy between women and slaves: "As the friend of the negro assumes that one man cannot by right hold another in bondage, so should the friend of Woman assume that Man cannot by right lay even well-meant restrictions on Woman."[16]

As Barbara Bardes and Suzanne Gossett point out in *Declarations of Independence: Women and Political Power in Nineteenth-Century American Fiction*, women's rights activists and women novelists in the nineteenth century often took up Jefferson's rhetoric for their own subversive purposes.[17] The participants in the historic 1848 Women's Rights Convention in Seneca Falls (which Frederick Douglass attended) left this account of preparing their manifesto, which they would call the Declaration of Sentiments:

> And the humiliating fact may as well now be recorded that before taking the initiative step, those ladies resigned themselves to a faithful perusal of various masculine productions. The reports of Peace, Temperance, and Anti-Slavery conventions were examined, but all alike seemed too tame and pacific for the inauguration of a rebellion such as the world had never before seen. ... After much delay, one of the circle [Elizabeth Cady Stanton] took up the Declaration of 1776, and read it aloud with much spirit and emphasis, and it was at once decided to adopt the historic document, with some slight changes such as substituting "all men" for "King George."[18]

In substituting "all men" for "King George," the women turned the strategy of universalization to their own ends, the same strategy that had left them out of the original Declaration when the men's reference to "men" obscured their exclusion of women. To these rebellious ladies, all men were King George. The women's strategy recast the figure of the oppressor, from the particular tyrant King George to the universal tyranny of men over women. And in *their* Declaration, the women boldly rewrote Jefferson's most famous line: "We hold these truths to be self-evident: that all men and women are created equal." By rewriting, with a significant difference, the words of the founding document of the nation's cultural identity, the women of Seneca Falls gave voice to something repressed at the nation's origin, even something whose repression was constitutive of that origin. Their Declaration became an uncanny return of the repressed, producing a mocking echo within the univocal expression of American truth, replacing his-tory with her-story. The women's version stated: "The history of mankind is a history of repeated injuries and usurpations on the part of man toward woman, having in direct object the establishment of an absolute tyranny over her."[19] The women of Seneca Falls exposed the masculine ethos of the Founding Fathers even as they invoked the values of liberty (not least of all in the liberties they took with Jefferson's text).

By the 1850s, an ironic reference to the Declaration of Independence was standard to the rhetoric of the women's rights movement. Sara Parton, who under the pen name of Fanny Fern became perhaps the most famous woman journalist of her day, delighted in satirizing the injustices of patriarchal tyranny from the bedroom and parlor to the houses of prostitution and publishing. In a column of 30 July 1859 for the *New York Ledger,* Parton wrote as if in conscious imitation of Douglass as she took up the theme of women's relation to the promises of the Founding Fathers:

> "FOURTH OF JULY." Well—I don't feel patriotic. Perhaps I might if they would stop their deafening racket. Washington was very well, if he *couldn't* spell, and I'm glad we are all free; but as a woman—I shouldn't know it, didn't some orator tell me. Can I go out of an evening without a hat at my side? Can I go out with one on my head without danger of a station-house? Can I clap my hands at some public speaker when I am nearly bursting with delight? Can I signify the contrary when my hair stands on end with vexation? Can I stand up in the cars "like a gentleman" without being immediately invited "to sit down"? … Can I go to see anything *pleasant,* like an execution or a dissection? … Can I be a Senator, that I may hurry up that millennial International Copyright Law? Can I *even* be President? Bah—you know I can't. *"Free!"* Humph![20]

Fanny Fern didn't feel patriotic because, in many detailed ways, she did not live in the land of the free. The nation that existed because of the Declaration treated her like a criminal and a child, denying her the most mundane as well as sublime rights. In her commentary on this column, Lauren Berlant argues that "to Fern, citizenship is not an abstract condition or privilege: it is a relay to protection and legitimation under the law and in the public sphere, which includes the world of the arts and the more banal experience of the body in the marketplace," including "the absurdity of the degree to which society regulates juridically what women wear and what they say."[21] In contrast to the Enlightenment notion of a universal political citizen with equal rights, Fern portrays the specific ways that society and the law address women and their bodies, disciplining their freedom with an oppressive protective custody. Implicitly, as some feminist legal scholars argue today, women's freedom cannot result from the simple application to them of a doctrine of rights developed on the model of a masculine citizen but must be crafted to address the specifics of women's particular condition in a patriarchal society. Whereas "freedom" remains a universal abstract token of women's desire, the realization of freedom (or of its absence) takes place only in particulars—in the wearing or not wearing of a hat, in the public display of emotion, in standing on an omnibus, in watching an execution or dissection, in getting paid for one's work, in being president. In a democracy, part of our ethical responsibility (by which I mean our responsibility to others) involves asking what freedom will look like for particular citizens, not simply for the citizen in the abstract.

For women in antebellum America, it was property rights, not the vote, that dominated the agenda as women considered the particulars of their lack of freedom.[22] Under the legal doctrine of coverture women lost their property rights under marriage, even their rights to their children. Upper- and middle-class women found this an increasingly inconvenient and shameful state of affairs, as did lower-class women who began to receive wages for labor (such as shoebindery and needlework) that had once been remunerated through barter. The late 1840s saw the first legislative acts guaranteeing property rights for married women. At the same time, women in the manufacturing industries continued to complain about the artificially low wages paid them under the ethos of domestic ideology that defined them first as wives and mothers and paid them wages calculated to compensate the family for time taken from domestic chores. Men were paid under the "head of household" rubric, and so domestic ideology blocked any notion of equal pay for equal work. Women could not be independent of the patriarchal home without a wage, but if they left the home for outside work they found themselves paid as if they were wives or mothers or daughters. True citizenship for women would mean the right to hold property and the achievement of a just wage. Any "political" rights granted in the absence of these reforms was of little worth and deceptive, for it would throw a cloak of respectable universal citizenship over the particular reality of women's inequality in a patriarchal society. The claim of women to the universal principles of freedom and equality, however, provided a rhetorical and utopian lever by which to move men off the pedestal of privilege they had erected for themselves.

What the antislavery and women's rights literature demonstrates is that every attempt to rectify a past injustice involves some appeal to universality and that these claims usually produce more rather than less social and cultural discord along with any actual progress they achieve in the treatment of individuals. When women and African Americans appropriate Jefferson's voice, they decenter the national rhetoric by having it spoken through an unauthorized body. This (un)ethical appropriation of language and ideas seems to express the extension of universality to the formerly excluded subject, but the ironic embodiment this entails seems to underscore the limits of pluralism. Women and African Americans cannot lay claim to equal rights in the abstract without eventually upsetting the practical distribution of social power and cultural authority. Equal rights cannot be painlessly achieved by rhetorical or legislative fiat; some persons have had their bodies, wealth, and rights taken from them, and undoing this injustice means depriving a once-dominant group of the privileges and resources it has taken for granted as its own rights. This redistribution of wealth and power must also be formulated in moral terms, as a general ethos of justice to which we submit regardless of our own particular self-interest.

Can Cultural Identity Be Ethical?

The Enlightenment rhetoric of universality portrays a relatively harmonious society, but that peace obscures the interdependence of rights and powers. The resistance of men and slave owners to the women's rights and abolitionist reformers, like the resistance in the United States today to affirmative action, Indian treaty rights, or gays in the military, stems from a real understanding that the application of universal principles results in particular change. Since the original postulation of a universal subject had actually been predicated on an unequal distribution of social power among particular cultural groups (by race, class, gender, etc.), the response of those oppressed will necessarily be double-edged: on the one hand, they will claim membership in the very universal category of humanity from which they have been excluded and entitlement to the rights that go with it; on the other hand, they will insist on affirming the value of the particular social group to which they feel tied and whose fate has largely determined their destiny as individuals. Somewhat paradoxically, we understand universal rights by recognizing the historical, concrete, and contingent lives led by individuals in real social classes. In theoretical circles today, this is known as the debate between the advocates of "identity politics" and their opponents (whether liberal humanists upholding Enlightenment individualism or poststructuralists opposed to essentialism).[23]

In the heat of these disputes it is vital to remember that no group can be formed without postulating some quality, experience, or factor *universal* to members of the group; likewise any universality that does not have a basis in, and a respect for, the particular qualities and experiences of human lives as actually lived will be worthless and probably an unintended ally when dominant groups force their will on a society. Ultimately cultural identity is not something inherent to an individual but a meaning that persons give themselves or others as a result of social determinations and subjective choices. Cultural identity is an ethos. It follows that social change requires altering the systematic, material, and impersonal forces that condition the lives of individuals *and,* at the same time, respecting the freedom of individuals to determine the character of their being as subjects.[24]

The rigidity of the sides in the dispute over identity politics might be eased by concentrating more on its material basis, on how cultural assimilation and the "melting pot" lose their ideological credibility when times are tough. During the past thirty years the United States has experienced a steady decline in the number of entry-level manufacturing jobs that require few skills and offer good wages and a chance for some upward mobility. To this diminution of the manufacturing base one should add the cutbacks in government jobs programs begun under Ronald Reagan and continued by Bush and the Democratic Congress. These kinds of jobs were a vital channel for the assimilation of every immigrant group before today, including the large numbers of African Americans who moved north into industrialized cities after the 1890s. The growing underclass has become more difficult to assimilate into the economy, whatever the social or ethnic group of the individual. As a result, racism, anti-Semitism, and overt acts of bigotry are on the rise nationwide. Symptomatic are Bush's Willie Horton ad, the terrorism of antichoice activists against women's rights, and the appalling spectacle of Nazi candidate David Duke's winning the majority of the white vote in Louisiana's governor's race largely on the basis of an appeal to poor and middle-income whites who were told that they could blame economic hard times on Jews, blacks, and women. The immorality of our politics feeds at the trough of material despair. The economic crisis has precipitated a cultural crisis of scapegoating, separatism, selfishness, cynicism, and rank exploitation of anxieties and fears. Social and immigrant groups that cannot look forward to assimilation turn more readily to insisting on the preservation of what cultural identity they do have, since no route toward a common identity or common culture appears open. In an era of scarcity, competition for jobs, houses, college admissions, and other necessities takes the shape of group conflicts as individuals band together to strengthen their hand in the struggle for a piece of the shrinking pie. Scarcity also makes it vastly more difficult to redistribute wealth in order to right past injustices such as the denial of equal opportunity to women and minorities.

Individuals belonging to social groups that have been the regular victims of bigotry and discrimination fight even harder to get some small increase for themselves and step up the ferocity of their denunciation of the group that has benefited from their exploitation or oppression. Whites, particularly men, often respond to this challenge to their dominance in the same way as they respond to the general decline of economic opportunities: they look for a scapegoat and portray themselves as the true victims, fortifying the walls of prejudice and selfishness rather than building bridges of common cause and compassion. On the one hand, women and minorities see the discrimination against them as groups more clearly than ever and so tend to respond as alienated communities of interest that have no common bonds. On the other hand, middle- and lower-income whites, especially men, react to the reduction of their own economic opportunities by irrationally blaming feminism and affirmative action programs as if these were responsible for the disappearance of entry-level manufacturing jobs, government employment, and retail expansion. Thus one should greet the current tendency to portray white men as the unfairly victimized targets of left-wing hate groups by pointing out its faulty moral logic and the continuing position of predominance most white men have in U.S. society. If reforms in society and education and government result in targeting the privileges white men have had for so long, it is not out of a personal hatred of them for their gender or their race but out of a political analysis of the unjust distribution of social power and knowledge.

At the colleges and universities, a similar story unfolds. The momentum of the civil rights and women's movements of the 1960s created a variety of institutions and ideas, mostly on the periphery of the academic center, to remedy past intellectual injustices through collective action. Autonomous though usually precarious and underfunded programs in Women's Studies, Black or African American Studies, and similar innovations brought identity politics into campus administration and curriculum. Throughout the Reagan and Bush years, however, the moneys and political support for these programs dried up, along with financial aid for the poor and victims of discrimination. Twenty-five years after the Civil Rights Bill, black enrollment in higher education actually began to decline despite affirmative action programs. The fall into poverty of northern black industrial communities that lost their share of the wealth produced by urban manufacture (now exported to the Third World) had a devastating impact on the ability of blacks to attend college. By 1990, after a decade of expanding requirements, tuition raises, and cuts in financial aid, white students too began to feel the economic pinch, and massive numbers of white college students began taking part-time jobs to pay their way through school. Again, many whites irrationally blamed affirmative action programs for the decline in college opportunities and course offerings rather than pointing the finger at the government officials who stole from the poor and middle-class and gave to the rich under Reagan's regime. Young Americans of college age now stare hungrily at each other, seeing not friends or compatriots in a common culture but competitors in a grim struggle for money and power.

In debates on multiculturalism and the diversity of educational offerings, one sometimes encounters objections to the constant reiteration of "race, class, and gender" as seemingly the only categories requiring revised representation. Why, critics ask, should we restrict ourselves to this holy trinity? What about all the other, theoretically infinite, kinds of differences that separate people, such as region and religion? Why not affirmative action to ensure representation of evangelical Christians or Irish Americans or short people (the "vertically challenged," as some wags put it)? The answer lies, I think, in the connection between our knowledge about social groups and the relative power that social groups have in a given culture. Within the context of the United States, a strong argument has been made that acts of bigotry and discrimination against people on the basis of their race, class, and gender (including sexual orientation) are the most prevalent in our history and society. These groups—persons of color, women, the poor, gays and lesbians—are on the whole less socially powerful and more easily targeted than other groups. Although abstract ideas about justice and equality might suggest the arbitrariness of privileging race, class, and gender, a *historical* understanding of the particular history of the United States shows the dominant role these categories have played. The fact that everyone can claim to be a victim of some prejudice does not mean that all have been *equally harmed* or that *degrees of oppression* are insignificant.

The lack of power of specific social groups has been reflected in the way they have been represented in educational materials and institutions (if at all), and this misrepresentation (or lack of representation) in turn reproduces their social disempowerment. So the reiteration of "race, class, and gender" does not follow from some wrongheaded assertion that only these groups have suffered or that only these groups have cultural riches that require study and appreciation. Rather, the argument is that the traditions of other groups during America's history have relatively more access to representation and so do not require so much energy to gain a place in the fabric of some larger culture or political entity. In this way, we can understand why questions of educational purpose and scholarship cannot be easily disentangled from political questions, especially when an education often provides the most ready access to better-paid jobs and social power.

We should also remember that cultural and economic assimilation in the United States has historically been relatively easy for those of European descent, more difficult for those of Hispanic descent, and virtually impossible for those of African descent. Native Americans, of course, were placed beyond the pale and subjected to genocide. Assimilation of Asian Americans remains problematic even as they form powerful economic groupings in California and Hawaii. Racial prejudice, then, the ancient human habit of making one's own personal identity dependent on the illusion of feeling superior to someone else, continues to be decisive in American life. Today there is a demographic swing toward growth in those very sectors of the population that have been traditionally the most difficult to assimilate. This has contributed to the ever-stronger tendency to see the nation as a conglomerate of distinct social and cultural groups rather than as a social contract among highly individual and independent persons.

Indeed, many now question whether assimilation should be a goal at all, since it usually means the assimilation of less-empowered groups to the cultural values and institutionalized powers of dominant groups. The cities of Los Angeles, New York, and Chicago are increasingly made up of racially and ethnically distinct neighborhoods, composing together a kind of multicultural metropolis. A recent article on demographics in California was titled "Los Angeles: Capital of the Third World." As the cultural critic Todd Gitlin observed at a recent conference at the University of Michigan, there has been an almost complete reversal of the political landscape as concerns the old debate between universalism and particularism.[25] Whereas in the eighteenth century liberal progressives of the Enlightenment swore allegiance to a common humanity transcending material particulars, today leftist reformers insist that political change must start with, and always respect, the unbridgeable differences between heterogeneous peoples. At this rate, we will soon have difficulty finding anyone who was born on the fourth of July, who thinks of him- or herself as "simply an American."

Obviously academic scholars can only indirectly affect the fundamental economic factors that are accelerating the breakdown in cultural consensus in the United States. As educators we can work vigorously to change the policies and material practices of our own institutions, seeking to make them more democratic, more respectful of cultural diversity, and more in the service of the broadest possible spectrum of American society. We should not protest injustice in faraway places and ignore its persistence in our own backyards. As intellectuals or cultural historians, we can object to the language of novelty commonly used about the "disuniting of America."[26] We can point out that the consensus was never very comprehensive in the first place and that acceptance of it was often not a matter of choice. We can also celebrate the multicultural demographics of the American population as something to be proud of and something requiring a new vision of the nation's history and purpose. Reversions to nationalistic patriotism, whether in the political sphere or in formulas for cultural history, should be strenuously resisted. Intellectuals have a responsibility to remind the public at large of how such patriotism has historically been used as a weapon of violence against many of our own citizens and as an excuse for telling lies about our past.

At the same time we ought to be critical of any undialectical endorsement of identity politics or cultural separatism, since these repeat at the local level many of the same blindnesses that nationalism perpetuates at the state level. Rather than taking sides in disputes between fixed positions, we should be encouraging encounters that focus on how the ways we represent our differences affect the way we value each other and the access each of us has to social and economic opportunities. We may want to challenge the centrality of "identity" itself in arguments about culture, for example, by considering the difference between "having" an identity and living by an ethos. At the colleges and universities, cultural difference must be a central focus of the agenda, though it should not become the pretense for naive pluralism or uncritical celebrations of ethnic traditions. Here the poststructuralist critique of identity proves politically useful; the uncritical assertion of the value of one's personal or cultural identity is not ultimately a sufficient response to those who have, on the basis of their own identity politics, repressed and denied one's identity. When we talk about rescuing those "differences within" that systems of totalizing identity whitewash away, that goes for the differences within the self as well as within the community or state.

Although a first step may be to recognize and respect someone else's difference from me, that realization still tends to leave me in the privileged position: I have the luxury to decide to be tolerant or understanding, the power to be condescending. The structure of superiority is left intact. More crucial, the sense of my own settled and unquestioned identity is also left intact and all the "otherness" seen as belonging to someone else. The next step, and it is an ethical as well as a political one, is to see my own subjectivity *from the other's point of view* and to open up a dialogue with the differences within. The exploration of otherness and cultural identity should have as its goal an achieved sense of *my own* strangeness, my own otherness, and of how my assumed mode of being emerged historically; I could have been someone other than I think I am, and maybe I am.

An experience of the relativity of cultural values can lead to an ethical moment of self-criticism. I call this moment ethical in part because in it we submit ourselves to the judgment of a principle larger than our own self-interest. We hold our cultural identity and its practices to the standard of justice, and we ask how our mode of being affects the lives of others. Slavery and patriarchy were, after all, popular because they served the self-interest of a ruling class. What justifies struggles against that ruling class? Merely the desire of other classes too for power? Power to do what? For whom? To what end? These are questions, again, of "the good," and they cannot be reduced solely to questions of power. In a pure clash of forces for power, there is no reason to prefer either side. Rather, a real political philosophy requires that we be able to argue that one arrangement of power is unjust, immoral, unethical, and therefore even those who benefit from it ought to be persuaded or constrained to give it up.

Thus I believe that ethical imperatives inform political change, since concepts of justice and of rights depend on a moral grounding. Self-interest and the acquisition of (or resistance to) power cannot found a community or a political philosophy; the former cannot do justice to social relationships involving conflicting self-interests, and power without a concept of the good is only instrumental and thus nihilistic. Social inequalities will not be alleviated without structural changes in the government and the economy, to be sure, but these cannot be motivated or justified except through what are ultimately moral arguments about the evils of unbridled self-interest and the irresponsibility of the will to power. Demonstrating these points will involve careful historical argument about the particulars of a social legacy as well as scrupulous theoretical debate about what constitutes the good universally and in a given instance. A discourse on ethics remains vital to the ongoing process of creating mechanisms that do justice to the competing claims of different cultural groups and of individuals who in their everyday lives often differ with themselves. The importance of this ethical moment needs to be reasserted and restored in the current climate, where "the political" (often vaguely if at all theorized) reigns. In the agency and decisions of the ethical subject the competing demands of the universal and the particular seek their only practical justice. In the ethical the subject's responsibility toward the social meets the subject's responsibility toward the individual. In ethics decisive acts of judgment become synonymous with the realization of human character and social existence. To get beyond the accusations and scapegoating and name-calling, unless we acknowledge our ethical political responsibility to each other we can expect an endless history of self-righteous violence.

Cultural criticism, to be worth the effort, must have an affirmative dimension, though this may take complex, even ironic, forms, as my discussion of the subversive affirmations of the Declaration of Independence has demonstrated. Ralph Ellison continues this tradition in the "Epilogue" to *Invisible Man,* where his narrator gives this final gloss to his grandfather's deathbed injunction to "overcome 'em [whites] with yeses, undermine 'em with grins, agree 'em to death and destruction":

> Could he have meant—hell, he *must* have meant the principle, that we were to affirm the principle on which the country was built and not the men, or at least not the men who did the violence. ... Did he mean to affirm the principle, which they themselves had dreamed into being out of the chaos and darkness of the feudal past, and which they had violated and compromised to the point of absurdity even in their own corrupt minds? Or did he mean that we had to take the responsibility for all of it, for the men as well as the principle ... ? Was it that we of all, we, most of all, had to affirm the principle, the plan in whose name we had been brutalized and sacrificed ... ?[27]

Meditating in *Shadow and Act* on the black writer's contradictory relation to the American dream and its fictional tradition, Ellison observes that "though as passionate believers in democracy Negroes identify themselves with the broader American ideals, their sense of reality springs, in part, from an American experience which most white men not only have not had, but one with which they are reluctant to identify themselves even when presented in forms of the imagination."[28] As I see it, the tradition of radical reform in American literary and cultural studies says yes to democracy in just the double-edged way Ellison describes. This affirmation obligates us to engage in complex and difficult acts of identification and imagination. On occasion we must affirm that which we have not experienced or, in politics, say yes even when the Supreme Court, from Dred Scott to yesterday, says no. We need an ethos that is accountable to history's horrors, that dreams of a community of stories, that is merciless in exposing the practices of injustice, that emphasizes the responsibility of individuals to each other, and that acknowledges that power without a vision of the good is a hollow goal.

NOTES

1. Gregory S. Jay, "The End of 'American' Literature: Toward a Multicultural Practice," *College English* 53:3 (March 1991):264–281. See also the five readers' comments and my response in the February 1992 issue of *College English;* I have adapted some of the material from that response for this essay.

2. Paul Lauter, ed., *Heath Anthology of American Literature,* vol. 1 (Lexington, Mass.: D. C. Heath, 1990), 19.

3. Paul Lauter, *Canons and Contexts* (New York: Oxford University Press, 1991), esp. 22–97.

4. By this remark I do not mean to minimize the cultural diversity that always characterized these geographical regions to some extent; one need only consider the history of the Jewish people in Europe for a lesson in the long-standing relationship of racism to the construction of nation-states.

5. The faculties of rationality and the moral sense were often used to construct this subjectivity (and to define those groups outside its borders). The essential study here is certainly Garry Wills's *Inventing America: Jefferson's Declaration of Independence* (New York: Random House, 1978). But Wills, in my judgment, often goes a bit far in exonerating Jefferson for his prejudices and racism (see chap. 15, for example, where Jefferson's often prurient remarks on the inferiority of Negroes are implausibly balanced by his sentimental respect for the moral sense of slaves). As I shall show, Wills exaggerates the "obscurity" into which the Declaration fell and underestimates the degree of influence its ideas immediately had among disenfranchised portions of the new American population.

6. See Jay Fliegelman, *Declaring Independence: Jefferson, Natural Language, and the Culture of Performance* (Stanford: Stanford University Press, 1993). Fliegelman's brilliant book reached me some two years and three drafts into this essay. I was glad to find, at least in my own view, considerable agreement in our readings.

7. Fliegelman, *Declaring Independence,* 197.

8. A strong case can be made that the political theory of the Declaration of Independence represented a minority opinion and an aberration in the mainstream of American thought and that by the first decades of the nineteenth century a new, conservative consensus had taken hold that repudiated the assumptions of Jefferson's language. See, for example, Larry E. Tise, *Proslavery: A History of the Defense of Slavery in America, 1701–1840* (Athens: University of Georgia Press, 1987).

9. See Wills, *Inventing America,* chap. 5, and Fliegelman, *Declaring Independence,* 189–200.

10. Herbert Aptheker, ed., *A Documentary History of the Negro People in the United States,* vol. 1, *From the Colonial Times Through the Civil War* (New York: Citadel Press, 1951), 8, 10.

11. David Walker, *David Walker's Appeal, in Four Articles, Together with a Preamble, to the Coloured Citizens of the World, But in Particular, and Very Expressly, to Those of the United States of America* (1829), ed. Charles M. Wiltse (New York: Hill and Wang, 1965), 75.

12. William Wells Brown, *Clotel, or The President's Daughter* (1853), ed. William Edward Farrison (New York: Carol Publishing Group, 1989); reprinted in William L. Andrews, ed., *Three Classic African-American Novels* (New York: Mentor, 1990).

13. Aptheker, *Documentary History,* 334. For an account of the speech's context, see William S. McFeely, *Frederick Douglass* (New York: Norton, 1991), 172–173. The complete text of the address may be found in John W. Blassingame, ed., *The Frederick Douglass Papers,* series 1, *Speeches, Debates, and Interviews* (New Haven: Yale University Press, 1982), vol. 2, 359–388.

14. Letters of John and Abigail Adams, 31 March and 14 April 1776, in Lauter, *Heath Anthology of American Literature,* 930.

15. Angelina Grimké, "Human Rights Not Founded on Sex," in Lauter, *Heath Anthology of American Literature,* 1835–1836.

16. Margaret Fuller, "Women in the Nineteenth Century," in Bell Gale Chevigny, *The Woman and the Myth: Margaret Fuller's Life and Writings* (New York: Feminist Press, 1976), 243, 248.

17. Barbara Bardes and Suzanne Gossett, *Declarations of Independence: Women and Political Power in Nineteenth-Century American Fiction* (New Brunswick: Rutgers University Press, 1990).

18. Mari Jo Buhle and Paul Buhle, eds., *The Concise History of Woman Suffrage: Selections from the Classic Work of Stanton, Anthony, Gage, and Harper* (Urbana: University of Illinois Press, 1978), 92.

19. Buhle and Buhle, *Concise History,* 94.

20. Fanny Fern (Sara Payson Willis Parton), *Ruth Hall and Other Writings* (New Brunswick: Rutgers University Press, 1986), 314–315. See also her earlier piece on "A Little Bunker Hill": "I hope no female sister will be such a novice as to suppose it refers to any but *masculine* rights" (p. 243).

21. Lauren Berlant, "The Female Woman: Fanny Fern and the Form of Sentiment," *American Literary History* 3:3 (1991):442.

22. See Bardes and Gossett, *Declarations of Independence,* chap. 3, "Women and Property Rights." They conclude by observing that the passage of married women's property laws focused mainly on land, at midcentury benefited primarily wealthier women and did little to mitigate the economic exploitation of wage-laboring women.

23. For a fine commentary on these issues see Diana Fuss, *Essentially Speaking* (New York: Routledge, 1989).

24. See Jeffrey Escoffier, "The Limits of Multiculturalism," *Socialist Review* 91:3–4 (1991):61–73.

25. For a related discussion, see Todd Gitlin, "On the Virtues of a Loose Canon," in Patricia Aufderheide, ed., *Beyond PC: Towards a Politics of Understanding* (St. Paul: Graywolf Press, 1992), 185–190.

26. See, for an example of how not to understand America today, Arthur Schlesinger Jr.'s *The Disuniting of America: Reflections on a Multicultural Society* (New York: W. W. Norton, 1992).

27. Ralph Ellison, *Invisible Man* (New York: Vintage, 1952), 16, 574. Ellison's references to the ideals of the Founding Fathers show how the African American tradition of ironically citing July Fourth and the Declaration continued into the twentieth century, where it also shows up in texts such as Audre Lorde's *Zami* and Alice Walker's *The Color Purple.*

28. Ralph Ellison, *Shadow and Act* (New York: Random House, 1964), 25. For more on the role of ethics in debates over the politics of culture and the canon, see my "Taking Multiculturalism Personally: Ethnos and Ethos in the Classroom," in Jane Gallop, ed., *Pedagogy: The Question of Impersonation* (London: Routledge, in press).

10

Take Back the Mike: Producing a Language for Date Rape

GRANT FARRED

In "Whose Story Is It Anyway?" Kimberlé Crenshaw, in remarkably simple terms, accounts for Anita Hill's "inability" to convince the United States Senate of the validity of her experience. As a black woman, Anita Hill was beyond the pale of the two dominant narratives, race and gender, invoked at the Clarence Thomas confirmation hearings: "Underlying the legal parameters of racial discrimination are numerous narratives reflecting discrimination as it is experienced by black men, while the underlying imagery of gender discrimination incorporates the experience of white women."[1] Excluded from the category of "racial discrimination" because she is a woman and denied access to "experience" of "gender discrimination" on the basis of her race, Professor Hill was rendered without a narrative, vocabulary, set of tropes, or easily identifiable metaphors.[2] In the unfolding of the Hill-Thomas media spectacle, the black woman's story had no public currency, and she could not, in several important ways, be "heard" by an American populace glued to its TV screens, much less have her "evidence" understood, because this captive audience had never encountered a narrative produced out of so unusual a conjuncture of race and gender.

To mainstream America, Anita Hill told an unfamiliar tale the nuances and subtleties of which had been effectively censored from the range of public discourse. Judge Thomas, on the other hand, traded—all too cynically—in and on the familiar. Ironically deployed though it was, as several commentators have noted, "high-tech lynching" was sound-bite perfect for mass consumption; Thomas strategically recalled the memory of white racism, thereby racializing the hearings and evacuating the Senate of the moral authority to question him, the latest victim in a long history of white aggression against black men.[3] For Anita Hill, however, explicit re-creations of sexual harassment of a black female lawyer by a black male judge did not play at all well with any constituency—black, white, male, or female—because her experience could not be accommodated "within the dominant images of sexual victimization."[4] Since she was neither a white woman nor a black man, Hill could not be listened to, let alone comprehended or supported, in this Senate-cum-paralegal forum.[5]

Thomas's successful bid for confirmation as Supreme Court justice demonstrates the urgency of developing a discourse that can represent the experiences and locations of specific unarticulated communities in the American public's political and cultural imaginary. As an instance of narrative production, Anita Hill's testimony registers the inadequacy of the existing race/gender paradigm and implicitly calls for a discursive structure that takes account of black women's experiences. One of the legacies of Anita Hill's struggle is that she displayed for the American public the formal and informal means by which the dominant race and gender narratives restrict ideological and political refashioning; by challenging Thomas in an arena that was hostile to her testimony and incapable of comprehending the violent nature of sexual harassment, Hill encountered the boundaries of her fledgling narrative. However, by engaging the confirmation process as political institution, she alerted her audience to a sense of the possibilities available to those challenging these structures.[6] "Race" and "gender," she demonstrated, cannot be invoked as unproblematic cultural markers that are in and of themselves politically or strategically sufficient. Her ability to speak her traumas in the full glare of the national and international media—to stage her experience of sexual harassment as public spectacle—facilitated the drawing together of several different but equally important stories: black women's struggles, feminism, and victimization by sexual harassment.

For members of these three constituencies, Hill's testimony represents an enabling political intervention in this moment of backlash against women. As Susan Faludi explains, women in general and feminism in particular have been forced to adopt a conciliatory, even defensive, posture in the face of a sociopolitical hostility that is currently widespread: "Instead of assailing injustice, many women have learned to adjust to it."[7] "Adjusting" to the "injustice" of Clarence Thomas's sexual harassment, however, was only a partial experience for Anita Hill. The prospect of a Supreme Court Justice Thomas represented for Hill a "*threshold* of irreversibility,"[8] to use Etienne Balibar's phrase, a point at which she could no longer operate in a mode of "adjustment"; instead, she adopted the strategy of exposing her former employer, which enabled her to "assail" him implicitly in what turned out to be the most telegenic of forums. It is in that moment of radical transition, from accommodating her experience within a patriarchal structure to articulating it in another, that Anita Hill's testimony furnished us with a new, though still formative, language that inserts the black woman's experience where the dominant narratives historically displaced her and enables us to critique more incisively the "injustices" she suffered. Hill's intervention, furthermore, established sexual harassment as a recognizable category of social violence, a development that unleashed sociopolitical (and economic) forces far beyond the constituencies of women, feminists, or even victims of sexual harassment. Within weeks, if not days, Fortune 500 companies set up sensitivity training centers, news programs starting doing sexual harassment polls, reported cases of harassment skyrocketed, and law firms hired more sexual defense counselors. Whereas Anita Hill struggled to give victims of sexual violence an identifiable public narrative, her testimony inadvertently created an industry that centered on sexual harassment. Deliberately misheard by the Senate, the ideological import of her testimony reverberated all too clearly and loudly in social forums beyond Capitol Hill.

The professor's articulations map an intricately deployed politics of offense. In extrapolating from Crenshaw's reading of Hill, then, the task is not so much to "assail" the black patriarchy or white feminists (though these remain important tasks) as it is to attend to the "insufficiencies" and exclusionary nature of the dominant narratives; in doing so, we must investigate the processes by which these narratives have been able to naturalize silences around groups such as women, rape victims, minorities, and the gay and lesbian communities. As a black woman structurally disenfranchised by the narratives she was trying to operate within, Hill was left with little choice but to embark upon the process of constructing a new, potentially oppositional discourse. A black, middle-class, female Reagan appointee, Hill was problematically implicated in the very structures that disempowered her. Therefore, considering how conversant she was with the legal apparatus, her failed intervention into the Thomas nomination process emphasizes the urgency with which counterhegemonic communities must construct, popularize, and deploy their own narratives in the broader public domain.

It is particularly necessary for feminists, in the wake of "1991, a year defined by date-rape trials, harassment hearings, abortion battles, and gender wars,"[9] to find ways that secure greater currency for the vocabularies that women are developing to describe themselves, their experiences, and their locations in the sociopolitical landscape. (In producing such a discourse, feminists are, for example, challenging designations such as "welfare mothers" and "battered wives," terms introduced by social scientists and repressive state agencies that implicitly refuse to acknowledge, name, and criminalize patriarchal violence. Instead of talking about "battered wives," the state should be acting against "battering husbands," thereby creating a new, identifiable category of male violence.) If Hill's intervention into the confirmation hearings represented a "defining moment in the backlash debate,"[10] then feminists must take advantage of the media attention to represent themselves publicly and define their experiences.[11] Although it is undoubtedly important for feminists to pull off a narratological coup to prevent the prospect of their being Anita-Hilled by those who tell the most widely understood and frequently recounted stories, it is equally important to investigate how the "backlash" ideology is invested in certain tales and to analyze the means by which those tales get told.

From the Courtroom to the Campus

The need for feminists to define women's experiences and to produce a narrative out of their encounters is nowhere more urgent than in the discourse surrounding date rape on American college campuses. It is in large measure because these young women have no publicly recognizable vocabulary for talking about date rape that a recent sociological study of a Southern campus found that the "majority of females who report unwanted sexual experiences do not define these experiences as rape."[12] Although "date rape" is a feminist term that has only in the past decade inched its way, encountering much resistance, into the popular consciousness, it is nonetheless profoundly disturbing to learn that the majority of college women who are victims of male aggression and violence do not name those experiences "rape." Yet, it is precisely the phenomenon of what we might term "familiarity," or acquaintance of varying intimacy with the assailant, that accounts for women's reluctance to describe their "unwanted sexual experiences" as acts of violation. The "rape" of women has traditionally been understood as perpetrated by the unknown assailant, not by teachers, clergymen, "friends, family members, or fellow students."[13] Acknowledging that men with whom one is familiar are equally capable of such violence "domesticates" rape. Most important, such a rethinking means that the experience of having been raped by an acquaintance constitutes a very specific form of violation that can only be thought of and understood by making an epistemological break: expanding and reconfiguring the category of "rapist" so that it can now potentially include intimates such as friends, neighbors, and lovers. For the woman who has been date-raped, the naming of the act as "rape" can also possibly lead to the recognition that the very social contract of gender is founded on violence—that in fact all social relations contain the potential for violence.[14]

In producing a reconfiguration of rape it is also necessary to politicize the sites in which such acts of violence occur. The domestic space, which in patriarchal terms resonates with metaphors of intimacy, sanctity, and security for women, is now radically transformed into a location that is always already threatening and unsafe for women. Therefore, the central quality of "in-timacy," which is supposed to mark the domestic "inside" off from the public "outside" (the normative space in which women are violated), is emptied of its patriarchal guarantees; the domestic is thereby transformed into a site of potential violence against women. The architectural division of inside and outside into "safe" and "unsafe" collapses in the face of such a spatial politicization of date rape. Rather than acting as inverse mirror reflections of each other, the inside and the outside produce a continuum of potential threat and aggression. The college campus, a self-contained, autonomous universe, with its large numbers of young people under intense pressure to conform to a special variety of "intimacy," pretends to a particular brand of domesticity that renders the distinction between the inside and the outside, the intimate and the public, unclear. However, if the entire university consti-

tutes a private space vis-à-vis the adjoining community, then it could also be argued that the university simultaneously defines itself—the campus, libraries, the
dorms, the labs, and so on—as an idiosyncratic public sphere within its realm of
privacy.

By situating itself so problematically between the public and the private discourses—now locating itself in the public by speaking to concerns beyond the
campus, now invoking a notion of its peculiar privacy by eschewing certain public
controversies, and often straddling the two modes—the university has ensured
that date rapes that occur on college campuses have become the focus of intense
scrutiny in both spheres. The Take Back the Night marches make this point admirably. In these marches college students take the issue of sexual harassment back
and forth between the campus and the adjoining community, seeking to address
victims of harassment in both communities, demonstrating how permeable the
town/gown boundary is. Furthermore, the university's desire to occupy multiple
locations has problematized the notion of which authority, the state's or the university's, obtains in instances of violence against women. It is difficult to account
for the university's ability to arrogate to itself the power to perform authoritatively
in such cases except in terms of its acting *in loco parentis,* itself an infantilizing
gesture that attempts to contain the violence by domesticating it. The strategy of
containment serves the purpose of "damage control," enabling the college to protect its reputation but certainly constituting a dubious practice that effectively
denies rape victims access to the legal channels available to the public of which
they are incontrovertibly members. By blurring the lines between the university's
and the state's power with regard to violence against women, the university insin-
uates itself into a position of authority that can criminalize or decriminalize rape.
By preventing the state's authority from following its course, the university
thereby appropriates to itself the power to redefine "rape" on campuses and to locate that definition outside the criminal mainstream.

As a phenomenon of violence, therefore, campus rapes are diminished as
crimes against women; ultimately we might ask how date rape is to be distinguished from other campus misdemeanors such as plagiarism or alcohol abuse.
At the point where the two forms of authority should be converging and reinforcing each other so that a student found guilty of rape can be both convicted and ex-
pelled, state and campus are separated so that one form of authority is excluded
and the other ameliorates the violent practice itself. By distinguishing the university's authority from the state's, I do not mean to suggest that it is only the university's obfuscatory tactics that are preventing the state's legal apparatus from dealing effectively with the problem of date rape. Victims of date rape have as much
difficulty in obtaining legal recourse in a courtroom as they do within the offices
of the campus authorities; it is as difficult to get a conviction of a rapist as it is to
get university administrators to acknowledge date rape as a political problem and
to legislate countermeasures. However, in tracing how the two forms of power operate, how they overlap and confuse each other's boundaries, we are left with the

recognition that both institutions are steeped in the patriarchal tradition; there-fore, they seem to complement each other's capabilities to the point that they rein-force each other in militating against the women who are the victims of this vio-lent practice. Although it is not possible here to elaborate on the purely legal rami-fications of this debate, we can engage the issue of how violence against women on college campuses has been recast in a specifically cultural form that makes possi-ble a different articulation of these concerns: date rape as the gender wing of the political correctness campaign in the American university.[15]

If the dominant understanding of rape has been "forced intercourse against a person's will and without her, or his, consent," then the notion of "date rape" has done much to expand and complicate our definition. In this regard, a social en-gagement such as a date—which carries its own domestic resonances—becomes politicized so that a man inviting, or agreeing to, participation in this long-stand-ing custom is required to acknowledge the woman's sexual and political enfran-chisement: she, as much as her male companion, has the right to set the limits for the physical intimacy that may or may not follow. Recognizing a woman as agent in the context of such a social interaction requires a rethinking of the concept of the date: a woman's participation in the social ritual does not necessarily consti-tute a tacit agreement to sex afterward. Any intimacy, and the degree thereof, that follows has to be negotiated by the two parties, whatever the nature of the "ex-changes" that characterize the date. If the man chooses to pay, he marks his ideol-ogy as patriarchal, but that in no way confers upon him the right to extract a "re-payment" from his date in the form of sex if she does not consent. The anti–date rape movement represents an attempt to nuance the issue of consent so that a woman is empowered to intervene at any point in the engagement: intimate ex-changes between two parties do not inexorably have to culminate in the sexual act.

A woman can participate in physical intimacy without fulfilling the consum-mation narrative. Anti–date rape activists emphasize the potential for a woman to intervene where the patriarchal discourse of consummation insists on the inevita-bility of the fully scripted sexual encounter. In challenging the narrative of inexo-rability the anti–date rape community is responding, in part, to earlier defenses of "implied" though never articulated consent invoked by rapists, who claim that the smallest sign of acquiescence or lack of resistance, a kiss, an embrace, a "tease," or "provocative" attire, constitutes "consent." The consummation narrative effec-tively disenfranchises women by suggesting that they are incapable of represent-ing their desires; it thereby empowers men because it allows them to project their sexual desires onto women's bodies, ideologically legitimating the fulfillment of a patriarchally scripted narrative by whatever means necessary. "Consent" as a de-fense has nowhere more been opportunistically invoked than in a recent case in Austin, Texas, in which the victim asked her assailant to wear a condom for fear of contracting AIDS. The twenty-seven-year-old accused, Joel Rene Valdez, told the *Austin American-Statesman* (and, presumably, the grand jury), "'If she didn't want to, why would she give me the condoms?'"[16] Valdez's defense and the fact that the first Austin grand jury did not indict him demonstrate how the patriarchally inclined legal system is prepared to read "consent" even in an instance in which the victim, despite being threatened by a knife-wielding assailant, was sufficiently resilient and politically skilled to convince the rapist that a condom would, at one level, "protect" both of them against AIDS, sexually transmitted diseases, and her against an unwanted pregnancy. What is remarkable about the woman's behavior is that she was able to act effectively while under extreme psychic and physical duress. Her "insisting" on the right to protect her body (in the medium and long term) even as she was completely vulnerable was a distinct form of political agency. The public, the media, and, most important, the legal system should have, as Cassandra Thomas, director of the Houston Rape Crisis Center and president of the National Coalition Against Sexual Assault, pointed out, "applaud[ed] the victim for her fast thinking."[17] Instead, women's groups had to protest the grand jury's decision and pressure the state prosecutors to present the case to a new jury. Ironically, it was the woman's restricted agency, her "request" that the assailant wear a condom, that provided the jury with the grounds to pronounce "consent." Therefore, as agents women make themselves more, not less, vulnerable to the dictates of the law, which reads complicity into their attempts to protect their bodies. At both ends of the socio-legal spectrum, therefore, as a "provocatively dressed tease" or a partial agent, women are easily construed to be "consenting." As Lynn Thompson Haas, director of the Austin Rape Crisis Center, put it: "We still have a long way to go destroying the myths that women are asking to be raped or deserve to be attacked."[18] Women's very agency thus disempowers them in the face of the law even as they resist patriarchal violence.

It is in response to such ideological, psychic, and sociopolitical pressures that the women's movements on American campuses are addressing Sharon Marcus's rhetorical question, "Whose 'no' means 'no'?"[19] by enfranchising women so that their "no" means exactly that. Women are sexual agents in touch with their bodies and fully capable of articulating their sexual desires: a woman's uncoerced no is thereby afforded the same discursive status as her uncoerced yes. A woman who is ambiguous as to whether she wants to have sex is also, in this way, afforded a certain agency in that she is unsure, not implicitly acquiescent. She can be persuaded to become a sexual partner, but she can also refuse. Jon Carroll, writing on the Valdez case, said it most incisively: "Aren't people allowed to experience ambivalence, even to change their minds?"[20]

My argument, then, is that insistence on the rhetorical and agential equivalences between a woman's consent and her dissent represents an important tactic within the anti–date rape strategy. A woman can voice her intentions, and when her articulations are willfully disregarded this constitutes a violation of her subjectivity, sexual and otherwise. By deliberately misrepresenting a woman's words, such as reading a maybe as a yes or a no as a maybe, men revert to a patriarchal and colonialist mode of violence which reserves to itself the right to impose and script meaning. In claiming the power to define, men enact gender "inequalities anew" and show that a "rapist's ability to accost a woman verbally, to demand her attention, and even to attack her physically depends more on how he positions himself relative to her socially than it does on his allegedly superior physical strength."[21] Implicit in Marcus's argument is a critique of the violent "physical," but, more important, she attacks the ideological and linguistic means by which the patriarchy has appropriated power to itself, causing a rape or, for that matter, any other form of sexual harassment to play out a script of gendered inequities. The anti–date rape movement has read this power imbalance back into heterosexual relations, revealing how it attempts to rob women's speech of authority and limit their room for maneuver in a context such as a date so that they can be "accosted" or compelled to give their "attention" involuntarily and exposing how such a social script tacitly encodes the capacity for violence against women. Rape, therefore, is not an aberration but the forced culmination of that social document.

The struggle around the practice of date rape on campus has focused primarily on the definition of "rape" and the agendas of the anti–date rape feminist movements and of cultural conservatives who regard these movements as simply a ruse to impose politically correct (read radical/leftist/feminist/gay/lesbian-inspired) speech and behavior codes on campuses throughout the country. In attacking the anti–date rape activists, the cultural Right has been unable to focus on the issue of defining "rape" and instead insists on revealing the "hidden" feminist agendas of its antagonists.[22] Neil Gilbert, a New Right professor of social welfare at the University of California at Berkeley, contends that "researchers are inflating rape statistics to gain attention and money for rape-prevention and counselling centers."[23] Notwithstanding the fact that date rape studies have only within the past few years achieved any public visibility and that researchers without the means to conduct more complete studies tend to produce conservative estimates that in themselves undermine claims upon university administrations, it is extraordinarily cynical—though not lacking in political expediency—for a "social welfare" scholar to make such tautological links between statistical data and the need for resources for the victims of sexual abuse.

Because the very term "date rape" is a recent, though now a disproportionately embattled, addition to the feminist vocabulary and sexual harassment codes are newcomers to university policy, "rape-prevention and counselling centers" have only recently begun to appear on some college campuses. Gilbert implicitly attempts to deny the seriousness of date rape on campuses by depicting the researchers who attest to its prevalence as irresponsible sensationalists merely out to grab a disproportionate share of the university's resources. The very politics of date rape is therefore rendered worthy of nothing but public suspicion and, if possible, interrogation. What Gilbert's critique engenders, furthermore, is a shift in focus from date rape as a problem of violence against women to date rape as a social construction, specifically via "inflated statistics" and wasted university resources. In this regard, of course, Gilbert is an ideologue who practices cultural politics by renovated conservative means. Rather than invoke "traditional values" as George Bush did, Gilbert works in the cultural mode popularized by Jesse Helms, the senator from North Carolina, whose economistic logic requires us to think about the "proper" way to spend taxpayers' dollars. The struggle against the radicals, the liberals, and their campus insurgents can, in Helms's and Gilbert's terms, be conducted by a very simple strategy: if you take away their funding, they will be organizationally paralyzed—to wit, the campaigns against abortion and "pornographic art." By centering statistics in the discussion of this social phenomenon, Gilbert seeks to shape the ideological contours of the date rape debate. Because "statistics" as a form of political analysis enjoys wider currency than an investigation of the discourses that underwrite date rape, we run the risk of talking about violence against women in terms of the statistical frequency of the problem rather than how patriarchal discourse, endemically violent, (c)overtly sanctions it.

Gilbert's recourse to number-crunching as a counterexplanation and his commitment to statistics represent an effort by the cultural conservatives to delimit the possible questions and types of inquiries of this debate. When Gilbert casts aspersions upon the agenda of the anti–date rape activists, he is deploying yet another tactic in a series of strategic attacks on the feminist movement as it constitutes itself on university campuses: defining the debate by focusing on those terms that resonate most familiarly with the general public (to invoke the North Carolina senator again, no public dollars for projects that do not coincide with "our"— that all-inclusive New Right pronoun—definition of the mainstream).[24] By making this move, it is possible to talk about a "new" issue in "old" ways, eliminating the element of unfamiliarity and with it the opportunity to frame a different set of questions in a distinct vocabulary. This is not to say that statistics should not constitute an integral part of the anti–date rape movement's linguistic repertoire, but it can be used only if its history is engaged and the practice itself is relocated within the feminist discourse.

It is because the conservatives recognize the diversionary importance of statistics in their strategy against the campus feminists that the New Right has emphasized it so repeatedly. By focusing on statistics, the New Right can quite comfortably drop its customary ruse, the mantra of "keep politics out of the classrooms" in whatever guise—gender, race, class, sexual orientation—and conduct politics in the ideological dress of those they regard as the new insurgents. The Berkeley scholar and his conservative colleagues have, in the terms outlined above, waged a (successful) campaign against the credibility of the anti–date rape movement by simply talking about the validity of the date rape statistics. A recent study demonstrates the way in which the New Right has been able to reformulate the terms of the date rape debate; the sociologists involved report a progression "from the discovery of a new social problem in 1987 to a debate over the actual existence of a problem in 1991."[25] It is exactly because the cultural conservatives have been able to undermine the "actual existence" of date rape as a "problem in 1991" that they may now be sufficiently empowered on some campuses to divert funds away from the rape prevention and counseling centers that the survivors so desperately need.

The New Right, recognizing that this cultural struggle is being waged on several fronts and in many discrete forms simultaneously, has conducted its campaign by recruiting allies who most closely resemble their opponents. However, as Susan Faludi points out, the cultural conservatives have simply flipped through their old strategy files: in "time-honored fashion, anti-feminist male leaders enlisted women to handle the heavy lifting in the campaign against their own rights."[26] Camille Paglia, one of the prominent newly created antifeminist feminists, has been all too ready to engage this project, pronouncing without a trace of irony that "the important issue of sexual harassment, one of the solid innovations of contemporary feminism," has been "used and abused for political purposes." (It therefore follows that, for Paglia, "Anita Hill is no feminist heroine.")[27]

However disparaging Paglia and her conservative colleagues have been about the "important issue of sexual harassment," their engagement with the practice and their antagonistic dialogue with campus feminists speaks of its significance as a question within the political correctness debate. Therefore, when the Paglias and the Kimballs speak to this issue, they provide the anti–date rape movement with an opportunity to intervene in the process of narrative production. Utilizing the ideological space created by the opponent to give voice to one's own position is a crucial strategy for groups that lack the material resources to struggle on an equal basis. It is in this vein that Andrew Ross, understanding that radical communities have long been embattled on university campuses, urges that these groups seize the political possibilities created by the political correctness debate: "As a result of the PC debates, the actually existing left, especially within the universities, has at last gained recognition, but at the cost of becoming a visible, and potentially vulnerable, target. We may not welcome the conditions of our newfound visibility, but we ought to be prepared, in time-honored fashion, to make some history under conditions not of our own choosing."[28] Those communities who constitute the "Left" will have to learn quickly, in Ross's marxian terms, to operate in "conditions ... not of [their] own choosing"; just because feminists or gays or the anti–date rape contingent do not own the playing field does not mean that they should not be(come) active participants or that they cannot tamper with the rules. At the very least, leftists must contest the markings of the terrain.

Both Ross and the feminist theorist and historian Joan Scott "want to make history," and Scott also identifies "visibility" as important in conducting an unequal struggle. The resistance movement must have a public face so that it constitutes a presence, a forceful image that is indistinguishable from its linguistic articulations. "Making the movement visible," Scott writes, "breaks the silence around it, challenges prevailing notions, opens new possibilities for everyone."[29] Ross and Scott are both attentive, in their different ways, to the possibility of threat or backlash against leftist movements that engage in the spaces of the dominant culture. Ross's language anticipates a certain hostility, asserting as he does that this "newfound visibility" will render radical groups a "potentially vulnerable target." Through his articulation Ross gives us a sense of the direct confrontation of unequal forces, since the oppositional communities lack the resources and the experience (and maybe even the strategies, initially) to conduct this struggle. Scott focuses the contestation by reminding us that the increased visibility "opens possibilities" not just for the Left but for everyone. Visibility constitutes a tactic for producing a certain kind of public image within a larger struggle; although it is important that radical campus groups have made themselves more "visible," the Left can hold onto this advantage only as long as it makes the "new possibilities" work strategically for it against conservative forces that are determinedly contesting the same political space. By qualifying their articulations of "visibility" so assiduously, both Ross and Scott emphasize the responsibilities incumbent upon resistant communities to use effectively the spaces that have been achieved.

The anti–date rape campus movement, however, has shown a particular ability to perform several of the functions contained within the outlines of this visibility paradigm. While Ross's readings have been useful, it seems to me that Scott's terms are more ideologically congruent with the activists' problematic. In the essay on which I have been drawing, Scott interrogates that often invoked but seldom critiqued phenomenon of lived human reality in such a way that her work becomes invaluable for engaging the very vocabulary within which the anti–date rape movement has to conduct its struggle. As a historian, she is particularly attentive to the need to focus attention upon a problem around which there has long been silence. At the most basic level, the anti–date rape movement has had to identify both the existence of such a silence and the effects that silence has had on women and would continue to have if the practice were not opposed. For Scott, the interventions of the campus activists perform a necessary historical function because they "document the existence of those institutions in all their variety and multiplicity, to write about and thus render historical what has hitherto been hidden from history."[30] The campus activists therefore not only interrogate the silence(s) that have remained outside of the dominant narrative and locate them within the historical but produce for feminism a particular kind of discursive visibility by rendering their movement historical. The anti–date rape activists are writing their experiences into the annals of campus history, observed by their peers, their professors, and the university authorities. Those who struggle to combat date rape are producing a script that includes a reading of patriarchy, resistance, and, most important, presence where there had only been hegemonically authored historical absence. In refusing to remain hidden from history any longer, therefore, the anti–date rape movement has been able to emerge from the patriarchal shadows into history with a recording of its own narrative.

Take Back the Night Marches: Spectacular Resistance

In constructing a discourse that seeks to resist violence against women, the challenge for the anti–date rape activists is to make clearly visible to their fellow students that the sites of violence on the campus are frighteningly familiar: the walkways of the campus, dorms, library stacks, lecture theaters, and so on. These "old" spaces therefore have to be defamiliarized and recast in a form that renders them visible as sites of violence against women. Scott's understanding of how knowledge is constructed through visibility is particularly incisive: "Knowledge is gained through vision; vision is a direct, unmediated apprehension of a world of transparent objects. In the conceptualisation of it, the visible is privileged ... seeing is the origin of knowing."[31] Recognizing that visible is privileged, the anti–date rape movement has sought to produce visibility as a political spectacle: the Take Back the Night marches enunciate the ubiquity of violence against women on campuses and thus perform an ideological task that approximates Anita Hill's intervention into the confirmation hearings, an enabling moment for feminists in all contexts. Hill made sexual harassment a visible category of social violence by constructing herself as a "face" who had experienced it. By making her charges Hill immediately drew attention to herself, as (black) woman, lawyer, and victim of sexual violence with a traumatic tale to recount in public. In the Take Back the Night marches "survivors" (for the greater part women) gather in their numbers on university campuses in candlelight vigils to remember their experiences of violation.[32] By staging their marches in the dark of the early spring nights, these women increase their visibility by the spectacle that they create. Their candles offer little in the way of real light but serve as dramaturgical props, drawing attention to the cause of those holding them. The darkness, lighted by meager flames, and the indistinct marchers themselves contribute to a heightened sense of the drama of the event.

The march as spectacle confounds our notion of the visible because it is staged in a context, the night, where it is barely visible, hard to recognize distinctly, available to the viewer only in outline and silhouette. It is thus spectacle as anti-aesthetic, staging concealment rather than revelation. In several ways the march, as self-reflexive nonspectacle spectacle, serves as an appropriate metaphor for the anti–date rape struggle itself. Despite its existence as a widespread campus problem, date rape is concealed, if possible, by the university authorities. If that is not possible, then the university administration attempts to play down its prevalence. Underestimating the significance of the problem is an effective way of formally recognizing it without allocating to it any of the resources required. It is a means of dealing with the problem by gesture almost utterly devoid of substance. Although the march takes place at night, its temporality does not locate it outside the formal aegis of the administration. Rather, the march is fixed within the formal orbit of campus life because it deliberately brings into focus, in terms of both visual and oral narrative, issues of university administration—the adequacy of security personnel, campus lighting, the availability of emergency telephones—that are not as crucial to preventing sexual violence during the day, the more easily identifiable temporality of the administration. By drawing attention to security during a Take Back the Night march, the anti–date rape activists are attempting to ensure greater vigilance on the part of the university authorities that will, in turn, translate into increased safety for heterosexual women, gay men, lesbians, and other minority communities. In a somewhat ironic fashion, the marches are simply reminding the administration of its responsibility toward certain constituencies within the university community; it is implicitly being held accountable for the violence that it is either refusing to address or addressing inadequately.

By forming a community and claiming the night as a safe space for themselves, the women are rejecting temporal restrictions on their mobility. The anti–date rape movement, having inverted and complicated the inside/outside dichotomy that used to serve as the dominant architectural metaphor for the campus, employs marches to politicize temporality in much the same way. The night, a period which is supposed to represent extreme female vulnerability and therefore presumed to be beyond occupancy (certainly mass occupancy), is taken back by women so that their agency, time of expression, social investigation, and political practice are unrestricted by the clock. The hour or minute or second that separates the day from the night, a period of (relative) safety from potential violence, is erased by the marches, which bring into focus and interrogate the conditions of a historical logic that has produced these arbitrary divisions. Take Back the Night marches seek to account for the patriarchy's ability to naturalize the night as a nonfemale sphere by designating it unsafe for women (or safe only for women outside of patriarchal protection, such as prostitutes). As the anti–date rape movement has "familiarized" rape and rendered the spatial inside/outside opposition problematic, the marches constitute the temporal arm of that struggle.

The marches, however, serve another crucial political purpose in that they produce women's resistance on campus as a spectacle: hundreds of (mostly female) marchers with candles gathering to protest violence against women. Through the Take Back the Night marches, campus feminists, along with gay men (another constituency rendered particularly vulnerable by the night), attempt to make themselves visible in those moments when they are, in terms of the dominant script, supposed to be absent, out of view, or out of harm's way. Because it has been so successful in focusing women's political energies and drawing attention to the cause of sexually abused women, the march has recently been adopted as a strategy by gay and lesbian activists. As a community, gay men particularly are exposed to a form of homophobic violence that is even more censored from the public imaginary than violence against women, and they are finding marches an effective way to combat gay bashing and to establish themselves as a distinct community. After an attack on three gay men by marines in a Capitol Hill bar in 1990, the National Gay and Lesbian Task Force planned a march for 6 July to protest it. The march was used by the task force to publicize the attack as gay bashing, since the police had refused to record the assault as such (despite evidence from witnesses that affirmed its homophobic basis); it was also designed to give gays and lesbians increased visibility and, finally, to historicize the antagonistic relationship of marines and gay men in the Capitol. By spectacularizing their historical vulnerability ("The reason people are so riled up about this is because it's been going on for 20 years," according to Sue Hyde of the task force),[33] gays and lesbians were attempting to secure their right to occupy a public space such as a bar without fear of harassment or violence and, also, to have the legal state apparatus categorize gay bashing as an identifiable form of political violence. Through the Take Back the Night marches, therefore, the women's movement has enfranchised other groups who are victims of harassment and violence by providing strategies for countering those practices.

Furthermore, the marches are especially significant in that the women establish themselves in both "communities"—those who make up the town and those who don the gowns—by walking from the campus into the town and back. By adopting this strategy, they link their movement to the two sites where they are socially active and refuse to respect the arbitrary spatial and ideological boundaries that separate one from the other. The campus marchers thus have the potential to forge a relationship between themselves and women in the town community, since they are in all likelihood giving voice and physical expression to conditions that also affect the women in town. The Take Back the Night marches thus constitute an instance of community building as women invalidate spatial, temporal, and ideological borders. By transgressing the town/gown split, the march impacts the sociopolitical imaginary, leaving the town with a set of queries and uncertainties about the spectacle itself.

During the march the women move between asserting their physical presence and displaying their vulnerability in the face of the elements, symbolized by the flickering candles. How do we account for the political incongruency in this literal/metaphorical split? Why are these women utilizing a symbol[34] that evokes a patriarchal understanding of female vulnerability at night, a notion totally contrary to their radical agenda? For the marchers the candle is not so much contradiction as strategic deployment. The visual impact of the candle's scant light serves as a reminder of how youthful, lacking in resources, and embattled their movement is. In this way, the candle constitutes a form of passive resistance, a strategy that relies on producing itself as spectacle in full view of its antagonists. The candle-bearing aspect of the march emblematizes women's pacifist resilience, eliciting attention without the threat of aggression. Therefore, the incongruence between the symbolic vulnerability of the candle and the assertiveness of the marchers, rather than indicating an ideological tension, metaphorizes the march as an act of resistance that is complicated, rather than split, along pacifist/activist lines. Read inversely, the meager light emitted by the candles is vastly disproportionate to the women's real and symbolic determination to (quite literally) take back the night one flame at a time. The march, therefore, with its determination to cross and recross spatial, ideological, and temporal boundaries, to "take" the campus's walks and the town's streets, implicitly to form a coalition of town and gown women, to claim the night by making it resemble the day, represents the activist and tacitly confrontational characteristics of the protest. If the dominant culture insists on naming the day a "safe" period for women, then the women will transport light, understood to confer safety, into the night so that they can claim those moments too for the activities they practice by day; if the night can be artificially lighted, then it can also be made to accommodate women's bodies safely, and this tension only serves to increase the arbitrariness of the divisions. By staging their resistance in a temporal locale that normally excludes them, women stake a dramatic claim to their right to extend other social functions into that locale without fear of violence.

The Take Back the Night marches thus constitute, for the campus date rape "survivors" and their supporters, an ideologically complex practice that enacts women's resistance. The symbolism of the march, however, is heavily overlain with a narrative structure of personal testimony. At various points during the event, as Ruth Shalit reports, the marchers will stop and give the "survivors" an opportunity to deliver their personal testimonies: "One by one, they ... grab the microphone, clear their throats, and begin: 'My name is ———, and I'm here to take back the night.'" In several instances, the trajectory of Take Back the Night has developed from the purely personal recounting of the violence to a participation in the larger discourse of the political correctness debate: the survivors "linger in the spotlight, interspersing their narratives with ... denunciations of the university administration, of male cultural hegemony, of Western society in general. The more ardently political the testimony, the more affirming the response tends to be."[35]

The marchers make these denunciations of the various authorites—university administration, male cultural hegemony, and Western society in general—because they recognize that their struggle directly or indirectly engages these political realities in the forms of male-dominated university administrations, fraternities, and patriarchal dorm socialization. Because the university administration has a patriarchal history that it is only starting to reflect upon, issues such as women's safety have not been attended to, thus implicating the institution in the patterns of violence against women. The march enables women publicly to forge links between their long experience of such violence and the university authorities' responsibility for dealing with the problem. As an articulation of male cultural hegemony, the university is predicated upon an exclusion of others (women, minorities, and gays and lesbians) that has to be engaged by developing practices that engender female resistance. By locating themselves within the more general campus political debate in new and compelling ways, the marchers have been able to draw on and situate themselves within the narratives and histories of other groups in the PC movement, thereby diversifying both their resources and the range of the questions and ideologies of radical groups on campuses.

By aligning themselves with the radical elements of the cultural debate, the Take Back the Night marchers are attempting to secure the march as a space for progressive feminists. More and more, however, radical feminists find themselves defending the march against the incursions of right-wing forces who want to reconceptualize the politics of the event in their own terms. According to a conservative rape victim, the Take Back the Night march "is being turned into a vehicle for something that has nothing to do with rape or sexual harassment. … 'The whole point of the march is to give women a space, and that can't happen if you set a political agenda.'"[36] The insistence on "depoliticizing" the march represents the conservative ideological campaign to contain the narrative of rape. The only articulation of rape as an act of political violence that this victim will allow is the anecdotal, the trauma of personal recollection, that marks the outer limits of her political expression. For such conservative critics, to forge extraanecdotal connections is to politicize the march because it locates the experience of rape within the network of patriarchal power relations that has a history of systematic violence against women. The current attractiveness of the anecdote for conservatives, of course, can be partly explained in terms of its practice by those in the New Right vanguard, such as D'Souza, Paglia, and Kimball, who have refined this form of political storytelling into a self-sufficient political narrative that is beyond critique or interrogation. In a context such as the march, the valorization of the anecdote is a particularly effective ploy, as it all too expediently implies that to critique the testimony is insensitive and an attempt to "invalidate" the experience of the victim when the actual task of analysis is to forge broader ideological connections with the effects of patriarchal structures. This resistance to politicizing the march speaks to the extent to which campus feminists have to contest every space from which to articulate their position, even, ironically enough, those that they were instrumental in institutionalizing. Contrary to claims that the march is "being turned into a vehicle that has nothing to do with rape or sexual harassment," the anti–date rape activists demonstrate that "rape" and "sexual harassment" have never constituted acts of violation in and of themselves but are expressions of the gendered nature of violence that originates from a web of patriarchal power relations.

It is because they make feminist issues unmistakably visible that the marchers provide a substantive intervention into campus politics; women's experiences and struggles are thus rendered "real"—all too "real," for some of the survivors—and an all too widespread part of college life. By appropriating the term "survivor," associated most closely with those who "survived" the Holocaust, campus feminists achieve access to an especially evocative articulation of both a history of violence suffered and the resilience of those who reproduced themselves as political subjects. In naming themselves "survivors" the Take Back the Night marchers are locating their movement within an ideological trajectory with powerful linguistic resonances. They are ensuring that gender will be engaged as a campus political issue by symbolically and articulately reenacting the experience of sexual violence. The march produces the gender struggle as political metatheater by simultaneously invoking and producing for consumption the images of violence that have led to this performance of painful public recollection. By recording their testimonies, the survivors register the urgency of their political agenda. Through their individual and collective stories they display to their audiences the importance of instituting counseling programs, making funds available for the establishment of rape-prevention centers, and publicizing the marches themselves. The march emphasizes the importance of dealing with gender as both a discrete category of political analysis and experience and one that is intimately connected with others. Although the march unremittingly invokes the "reality" of the experiential, it also fixes gender as discursively inseparable from the PC debate as a whole. By introducing, defining, and deploying such a highly charged term as Take Back the Night within the PC debate, the anti–date rape movement is working to produce a vocabulary that speaks of women's experience and to them in a particular way.

These women, and campus feminists in general, thus have linguistic means for talking to each other and to others; their vocabulary, furthermore, has resonances in several public spheres, and therefore they have a set of terms available for describing the political task of the anti–date rape movement. In addition to crafting new ones, however, the movement has redefined the terms "survivor" and "personal testimony" and located them within the orbit of feminism, particularly campus feminism. The terms, however have been claimed in such a way as to inflect them with a political agenda unimaginable to its other users. The activists have enriched the date rape vocabulary by redefining the political utility of these central two terms within the narrative. The Take Back the Night campaigners have thus created a lexicon for feminist resistance by taking and remaking words, fashioning out of them a specifically feminist discourse. Most important, however, those who have endeavored to take back the night via spectacle have also grabbed the mike and given us the words to speak so that the visual and the oral conjoin to produce mutually reinforcing narratives.

NOTES

1. Kimberlé Crenshaw, "Whose Story Is It Anyway? Feminist and Antiracist Appropriations of Anita Hill," in *Race-ing Justice, En-gendering Power: Essays on Anita Hill, Clarence Thomas, and the Construction of Social Reality*, ed. Toni Morrison (New York: Pantheon Books, 1992), 404.

2. Wahneema Lubiano's essay "Black Ladies, Welfare Queens, and State Minstrels: Ideological War by Narrative Means" (in Morrison, *Race-ing Justice*) is, like Crenshaw, especially useful for naming the narrative possibilities available to black women and critiquing the limitations of these ideological apparatuses. "It is difficult to conceive of a 'normal,' an unproblematic, space," Lubiano writes, "in our historical moment for black women outside of the demonic-narrative economy of the welfare queen or the betrayal-narrative economy of the black-lady overachiever—both figures about which Moynihan [in the Moynihan Report] warns" (p. 333).

3. In executing this rhetorical maneuver, Thomas was able to play what Andrew Ross calls the "Black Panther card." In asserting, "I will not recognize the 'white justice' of this court," Thomas achieved a "mock self-representation as victim" ("The Private Parts of Justice," in Morrison, *Race-ing Justice*, 48, 54). See also Kendall Thomas's "Strange Fruit" (in Morrison, *Race-ing Justice*, 364–389).

4. Crenshaw, "Whose Story Is It Anyway?," 407.

5. However, if Anita Hill could not be "heard" or was deliberately "misheard" by several of the distinguished gentlemen, her intervention in the confirmation process returned in a form that these public servants recognized all too well—electoral politics. Hill's testimony resonated across the spectrum of American political life in a way that Crenshaw's critique, written before the 1992 elections, could not fully anticipate. Although these subsequent historical developments compel us to amend Crenshaw's readings, we are also in a position to reflect upon the possibilities Hill opened up. It is in large measure because of Hill's dramatic TV appearances that the 1992 elections were subtitled "The Year of the Woman." Her testimony created a heightened sense of political awareness around the question of women's position in American life, and that gave rise to a renewed interest in the role of "mainstream feminism" in this society. Crenshaw's critique of the exclusionary means by which the dominant narratives operated is valid as a reading of the hearings, but the campaigns of Carol Moseley Braun, the black senator for Illinois, and Lynn Yeakel, a white woman who ran unsuccessfully against incumbent Pennsylvania Senator Arlen Specter, suggest that Hill's stance has initiated a process that is redefining the dominant narratives of "race" and "gender." Both women relied extensively on the public memory of Hill's courageous testimony and her "feminist" tendencies in their campaign strategies. Moseley Braun's election in particular represented a rare historical moment, made possible by Hill, in which a black woman could foreground or at least not be overly handicapped by both her gender and her race. Moseley Braun represents the exceptional narratological confluence of these predominantly discrete categories, inherited from Hill but denied to the law professor during the hearings.

6. Kimberlé Crenshaw, Wahneema Lubiano, and Christine Stansell ("White Feminists and Black Realities: The Politics of Authenticity," also in Morrison, *Race*-ing *Justice*) offer important readings of the potentialities and restrictions of the dominant narratives within which Hill is working.

7. Suan Faludi, *Backlash: The Undeclared War Against American Women* (New York: Doubleday, 1992), 57.

8. Etienne Balibar, "The Nation Form: History and Ideology," in *Race, Nation, Class: Ambiguous Identities*, trans. Chris Turner (New York: Verso, 1991), 88.

9. Nancy Gibbs, "The War Against Feminism," *Time*, 9 March 1992, 52.

10. Gibbs, "War Against Feminism," 54.

11. In stressing the importance of large-scale feminist involvement in such a project as providing a language for talking about the Thomas-Hill hearings and giving it ideological shape, Lawrence Grossberg points to "the increasing presence (even as popular figures) of new conservative intellectuals, and the threatening implications of the power of a popular new conservatism" (*We Gotta Get out of This Place: Popular Conservatism and Postmodern Culture* [New York: Routledge, 1992], 3).

12. G. David Johnson, Gloria J. Palileo, and Norma B. Gray, "'Date Rape' on a Southern Campus: Reports from 1991," *Sociology and Social Research*, 76:2 (January 1992):37.

13. This phrase is borrowed from a letter written to a Princeton University newspaper. *The Nassau Weekly* (5 December 1991), by David Ellison, Eva-Lynn Jagoe, Isabel Karpin, Gitanjali Maharaj, David Thomson, and myself in response to an article on date rape by a fellow Princeton graduate student that appeared in the *New York Times* (20 November 1991). I would like to thank my fellow signatories as well as Wahneema Lubiano and Raphael Allen for their support in developing this essay, which in some measure grew out of that intervention into campus politics.

14. See Teresa de Lauretis's "The Violence of Rhetoric: Considerations on Representation and Gender," in *Technologies of Gender: Essays on Theory, Film, and Fiction* (Bloomington: Indiana University Press, 1987).

15. "Date rape" of course constitutes only one gender issue within the PC debate, even though I implicitly include under this rubric "sexual harassment." Other aspects of the gender struggle include the commitment to redress the male/female imbalance on college campuses, ensuring that feminist issues gain proportionate panel representation at conferences, and so on.

16. "Condom-Rape Case Brings an Outcry," *USA Today*, 15 October 1992.

17. "Beyond the Risk of Rape," *Washington Post*, 16 October 1992.

18. "Condom-Rape Case."

19. Sharon Marcus, "Fighting Bodies, Fighting Words: A Theory and Politics of Rape Prevention," in *Feminists Theorize the Political*, ed. Judith Butler and Joan W. Scott (New York: Routledge, 1992), 387.

20. "The Subtle Message of the Big Knife," *San Francisco Chronicle*, 29 October 1992.

21. Marcus, "Fighting Bodies," 390, 391.

22. At Stanford University, the local chapter of the conservative National Association of Scholars (NAS) "adopted a resolution calling for the withdrawal of Stanford's policy on sexual assault," which states that "sex by force or coercion through the use of drugs or alcohol is absolutely unacceptable" at the university ("Critics: Withdraw Sexual Assault Policy," *Stanford Observer*, March-April 1992). Steeped in New Right rhetoric, the Stanford NAS's chairman insists that the new sexual harassment policy is "making people nervous because they feel there's an agenda behind this" (*Stanford Observer*, March-April 1992).

23. "A Berkeley Scholar Clashes with Feminists over Validity of Their Research on Date Rape," *Chronicle of Higher Education*, 26 February 1992, A35.

24. Gilbert's disregard for the problem of date rape on U.S. campuses can be gleaned from the title of his essay in the Spring 1991 issue of *The Public Interest*, "The Phantom Epidemic of Sexual Assault."

25. Johnson, Palileo, and Gray, " 'Date Rape' on a Southern Campus," 38.

26. Faludi, *Backlash*, 239.

27. Camille Paglia, *Sex, Art, and American Culture* (New York: Vintage Books, 1992), 46.

28. Andrew Ross, "PC is Here to Stay," *Progressive Review* 10:2 (November 1991):11.

29. Joan Scott, "Experience," in Butler and Scott, *Feminists Theorize the Political*, 23.

30. Ibid.

31. Ibid., 24.

32. "Vigil" is only one way to describe the marches, which differ from campus to campus, being dynamic, even celebratory, in some places and decidedly somber in others.

33. "Fighting on Hill Involving Gay Men, Local Marines Heightens Tensions," *Washington Post*, 21 June 1990.

34. The flickering candle is also, interestingly enough, the insignia for Amnesty International.

35. Ruth Shalit, "Radical Exhibitionists: When Rape Victims Become Actors in Campus Political Theater, Someone Inevitably Gets Hurt," *Reason*, July 1992, 37.

36. Ibid., 41.

11

The Institutional Response to Difference

JEAN E. HOWARD

WHEN SPEAKING OF political intervention in the academy, we need to recognize how diverse are the institutions and places of work included under that rubric. Initiating political action within different branches of that academy requires a hardheaded calculation of what most *needs* to be done and what *can* be done at various sites: the community college, the private liberal arts campus, the urban city-run university, the Ivy League, the Big Ten. For the moment I work at an Ivy, and it is a very specific kind of workplace. For example, an urban-based, elite school like Columbia can provide an excellent base from which to speak as a "public intellectual." TV stations and journals of opinion abound in the city, and a Columbia affiliation often grants access to these resources to respond to a Roger Kimball, an Allan Bloom, or a Camille Paglia and to forward an alternative cultural agenda. But as a total educational apparatus Columbia is probably one of the more politically conservative institutions in this country, judged by such simple but important criteria as the number of women and minorities on the faculty or the number of courses in which feminist, queer, or African American modes of making knowledge are foregrounded. At the undergraduate level commitment to a "core" siphons off a huge amount of institutional teaching resources, and alumni nostalgia for that core—at an institution dependent on an annual fund and hefty gifts to endowment—helps to hold in place a curriculum whose adequacy for the social and intellectual realities of the 1990s is never rigorously interrogated. At the graduate level, overspecialization, fear of intellectual vulgarity, and an ideology of professionalism work more strongly than at many other academic sites to keep the knowledge-making enterprise safely within bounds: up-to-date but not radical and not activist in the sense of linking academic work to social and institutional change. Yet Ivies educate people who will wield disproportionate amounts of power in the culture at large. They produce not just a corporate elite but an academic elite in the specific sense of Ph.D.'s hired at other prestigious schools. In such a context, left faculty have to ask hard questions about priorities for political work. At an Ivy it is undoubtedly easier to be "radical" in print or on the airwaves or at a conference in Paris than to effect progressive change within the structures of the institution where one works. Yet having one's radical politics "elsewhere" allows the institution to get credit for tolerating, even for promoting, diversity and dissent on its faculty while keeping radical scrutiny away from the fundamental structures of the institution itself. In such a context—and I suspect in many others—there needs to be vigorous debate on the left about what is the most pressing political work for particular faculty to undertake.

Consequently, while I am committed to Gerald Graff's basic premise that the public and well-financed assault on "political correctness" in the academy needs to be answered strenuously and in an organized fashion by left intellectuals, that imperative does not lessen the need for continued work on transformation *of the academy itself.* Bruce Robbins is right that left intellectuals must accept that collectively we have had an impact on changing the educational apparatus and that our real successes have, in fact, fueled the political correctness attacks.[1] Nonetheless, these achievements are not spread evenly across the educational spectrum, and they are fragile. If the truth is told, most of us, perhaps especially those who work at elite schools, are employed at institutions that have been radicalized far too *little.* It is imperative to continue that process of radicalization even while learning to speak more directly to the "public" under the umbrella of organizations such as Teachers for a Democratic Culture.

In the struggle to make the academy more democratic, the question of how to acknowledge and incorporate "difference" has become a major point of contest, one being taken up now in part under the rubric of multiculturalism. Simply put, proponents of multiculturalism want education to acknowledge the plurality of traditions making up American culture and the existence of a world beyond the borders of Europe and America. Although some schools have tried to make multiculturalism a curricular reality, at most campuses multiculturalism is at present more discussion topic than fact. Consequently, at this inaugural moment it is worth thinking critically about just what one wants to achieve by promoting multiculturalism and how, more generally, the institutional response to "difference" might go beyond the liberal agenda of giving voice to the silenced and embrace a more radical agenda of promoting a restructuring of social relations and a redistribution of cultural and economic resources.

A good place to start is with the vision of the university of the future articulated by Stanley Aronowitz and Henry Giroux in *Postmodern Education.* They praise educational initiatives that attack what they see as the central modernist notion of a legitimate "center" to the project of knowing, a vantage point from which to establish control and to determine hierarchies. For them, the increasing number of programs and courses in gender studies, minority or ethnic cultures, and popular culture signals the welcome end of the dominance of Eurocentric, white, masculine, heterosexual knowledge. In a university with no dominant canon or paradigm for knowing, students from many different class and ethnic backgrounds could, for example, lay claim to their "own" knowledge and not have to transform themselves imaginatively into versions of white middle-class students, and white middle-class students would, by exposure to courses requiring attention to difference, have the assumed primacy or centrality of their culture destabilized and relativized.[2]

These are important goals, and most schools are very far from promoting the empowerment of the marginalized so passionately advocated in Aronowitz and Giroux's work. Yet there are also pitfalls to any straightforwardly pluralist appropriation of their vision. The chief dangers, it seems to me, lie in (1) a balkanization of the academy such that interconnections between different spheres of knowledge and power can never be forged in order to effect more than local change and (2) an embrace and celebration of difference that effaces the constructed and politically interested nature of most, if not all, culturally significant categories of alterity. Perhaps most ironic is the possibility that promoting awareness of cultural difference *can* be used to quite unmistakably regressive ends in a late-capitalist global economy. I think of a wonderfully crass example from the *New York Times*. In an article entitled "For Coke, World Is Its Oyster," a reporter interviewed the president of Coca-Cola about the problem of finding new markets for his product. The answer, he said, lay in going global. "When I think of Indonesia—a country on the equator with 180 million people, a median age of 18, and a Moslem ban on alcohol—I feel I know what heaven looks like."[3] This man is aware of difference, all right; specifically, he is aware that in Islamic culture the use of alcohol is prohibited by religious law. But he uses this knowledge as the basis for a marketing strategy that will transform these Indonesians into American-style consumers of Coca-Cola. One of the dangers of a globally inflected multiculturalism is that it can very easily serve the ends of multinational capitalism. To know the other is to be able the better to enmesh him or her in the tentacles of globally organized production and consumption. Emphasis on the difference of the "non-West" can thus be necessary preparation for colonial encounters in an age when force by itself no longer can do the work of imperialism.

Equally dangerous, I think, is the possibility that the creation of space for the study of differences (ethnic difference, sexual difference, religious difference) will blunt internal dissent by giving various identity-defined groups a share in a pluralist academy. Those familiar with histories of women's studies and African American programs know the effort it takes to keep such programs from becoming places where the radicalized and alienated talk to one another while the rest of the campus goes on its usual way. Aronowitz and Giroux imagine a postmodern academy in which all sense of a "center" of legitimate knowledge has been replaced by the democratic eruption of many knowledges speaking to the plural realities of a plural culture. From my vantage point I see a core of centered knowledge very much in place and around that center various marginal spaces where other knowledges are produced and often contained.

I think this may potentially be less the case at some community colleges and some urban public institutions than at schools higher up in the prestige network.[4] There are obvious reasons for this hope. Community colleges and city universities "skill" the working classes, immigrants, border people. The stakes in this process are enormous. Through the university these social groups can be readied for the employment that will keep them off the welfare rolls and make them into responsible citizens who will take up economically productive, if not very exalted, places in the social hierarchy. But—and here is the point to be pressed—concentrations of immigrants, border people, working-class students whose material histories have cut them off from access to many kinds of cultural and economic resources are a radical resource if, in the university of the future, they learn to assess how their "differences" are produced and used in a social system that is not equally open to all and that they might challenge. A critical concept of difference is not one that simply accepts and celebrates difference but one that examines its *production*, its *political uses*, and, in an oppositional sense, *its potential role in positive cultural transformation*.

In *How Capitalism Underdeveloped Black America,* Manning Marable undertakes such an analysis. He argues that from the beginning of the slave trade to the present moment white America's successes have rested on the subordination and exploitation of African Americans.[5] In light of this analysis, crucial differences between blacks and whites such as differences in income level, in places of residence, or in access to resources such as health care are seen to be produced by man-made material practices, not just by prejudice, and by a social system premised on economic and social inequality. Similarly, cultural phenomena—religion, cuisine, speech, music—appear not as exotic signs of innate otherness but as aspects of resistance and survival in conditions of oppression. Moreover, in Marable's analysis, black and white cultures cannot be studied in isolation, the point being that they are interdetermined, though unequally so, in that the development of one is premised on the underdevelopment of the other. For Marable such an analysis ends with a redefinition of what equality and democracy should mean in the sites where we live:

> [By] equality I do not mean "equal opportunity" as defined by the Urban League and the Federal bureaucracy, as a means toward integrating minorities and women into the hierarchies of the state and civil society. Equality implies a theory of justice which assumes that all parties within the state should have free access to the state apparatus, can reform existing economic and social institutions, and can enact laws that promote a more humane society.[6]

I am using Marable here as a synecdoche for what I call a critical concept of difference that would underwrite a left, rather than a liberal pluralist, concept of multiculturalism, whether posed in global or in domestic terms. Schematically, such a critical conception of difference rests on the following assumptions: that differences are for the most part produced, rather than innate, if only in the sense that cultures choose to *mark* or *notice* at certain times some differences from all the thousands of possible variables; that concepts of difference usually serve interested ends; that they are linked to material practices such that a simple linguistic erasure or destabilization of the terms of difference is not sufficient to erase their real effects in history; that devalued terms of difference can be seized as points of resistance; that the goal of studying difference is not a celebration of human diversity but the creation of the material conditions for a more just world in which difference is severed from practices that enforce inequality and exploitation.

In sum, what is necessary is not the simple acknowledgment of difference within a curriculum and an educational apparatus that has excluded such an acknowledgment, important though that may be to relativizing what Aronowitz and Giroux posit as dominant thought, the thought of the center. Also necessary is a way of teaching difference that aims for the transformation of society and resists the appropriation of the study of difference to the ends of the global marketplace.

A final question not to be dodged is who is to teach this knowledge. Are black scholars to teach about African American difference, gay scholars about marginalized sexualities, and so on? Social identity guarantees nothing, I would argue, about a person's ability to promote a critical knowledge of the production of difference in contemporary society. It is a truism that all women aren't feminists, nor are all practicing homosexuals gay activists or all members of the working class socialists. The workings of ideology and the relative advantages of certain members of any marginalized group are partial explanations of this fact. But it is also true that the social labels *woman, queer, black* have been used as categories upon which exclusions have been based—exclusions from, among other things, higher education and higher-education faculties. These labels have been part of systems of oppression with real material consequences that can be transformed in part only by changing the sex, race, and sexuality ratios in places of privilege such as the one that employs me. We must eschew several forms of naïveté: the assumption that social identity guarantees a politics or a particular critical perspective and the assumption that social identity is irrelevant to making political choices. "Enlightened" members of privileged groups must not think we have done anything like enough if we teach a critical theory of difference and have no tenured colleagues who are black, gay, female, etc. And, I want to suggest, we must, at the particular sites where we work, be continually assessing what is the most urgent political work to do and not confuse the difficult with the unimportant or what is individually satisfying or comfortable with what is collectively necessary.

NOTES

1. Bruce Robbins, "Introduction: The Grounding of Intellectuals," in *Intellectuals: Aesthetics, Politics, Academics*, ed. Bruce Robbins (Minneapolis: University of Minnesota Press, 1990), ix–xxvii.

2. Stanley Aronowitz and Henry Giroux, eds., *Postmodern Education: Politics, Culture, and Social Criticism* (Minneapolis: University of Minnesota Press, 1991), esp. chap. 2, "Postmodernism and the Discourse of Educational Criticism," and chap. 5, "Border Pedagogy in the Age of Postmodernism."

3. Roger Cohen, "For Coke, World Is Its Oyster," *New York Times,* 21 November 1991, D1 and D5.

4. At the Modern Language Association meeting at which I presented an early draft of this chapter, I was asked if I was not romanticizing the community college or the urban public university. Obviously this was not my intention. In many ways such schools are the most dedicated to integrating students into the existing social order. I simply meant to indicate that the composition of the student body invites, under certain conditions, politicization as well as "normalization."

5. Manning Marable, *How Capitalism Underdeveloped Black America* (Boston: South End Press, 1983), esp. 1–19.

6. Marable, *How Capitalism Underdeveloped Black America,* 17.

12

Culture Wars and
the Profession of Literature

VINCENT P. PECORA

IT IS PERHAPS more than obvious that relations today between aesthetics, politics, and the profession of literature are afflicted by a deep sense of insecurity, one that reflects real practical change in all three areas. Some would say that this insecurity is a happy development, one that, once everyone becomes conscious of it, will allow for a more genuinely pluralistic and decentered cultural life. Since no grand cultural narrative is possible any longer, no one voice can command the field. Others would lament the same state of insecurity as typical of traditional intellectuals and would claim that, if true, it represents nothing more than a return to the decidedly repressive and apolitical pragmatism of much professional life after the House Un-American Activities Committee in the 1950s. And a third group—one whose voice has been on the rise for some time and to which I want to turn my attention for a moment—has discovered both the apparent hegemony of European-influenced theoretical discourse on one hand and the apparently radical climate of academic politics on the other, has concluded either that one entails the other (as do Roger Kimball and Dinesh D'Souza) or that one ironically precludes the other (as does Camille Paglia), and has proclaimed the need to rediscover an authentically American sensibility wherein all the women are strong, all the men are good-looking, and all the children are above average.

Now, Garrison Keillor, for all his escapist nostalgia, plays with his audience's conventional fantasies of the genuine and the normal in America—hence the gender-reversed modifiers of his slogan. Keillor, that is, knows that what he sells is a myth, a fantasy that never really existed even for those who believed it or believe it still. A thinker like Camille Paglia, unfortunately, seems to be hardly so well informed. Her paranoid vision is an intellectual mélange celebrating Ayn Rand–like American will to power, "infantile in its beaming, bouncing egotism"—a phrase that suggests not so much the parodic gestures of Jerry Lewis, who is one of

Paglia's examples, as the more sinister infantilism of the fundamentalist Jerry Falwells and Jim Bakkers with their Cheshire Cat grins. Worse, Paglia promotes an eerie nationalism filled with *ressentiment:* "American G.I.'s (including my uncles)," she cries, "got shot up rescuing France when she was lying flat on her face under the Nazi boot. Hence it is revolting to see pampered American academics down on their knees kissing French egos."[1] As if this were not enough, her discourse is also dressed up in a patronizing rhetoric of solidarity with those truly American symbols of pop-cultural vitalism—rhythm-and-blues singers, preferably black ones—who embody a positive and enduring libidinal energy otherwise squandered by the counterculture of the 1960s.

It is not only Norman O. Brown's kitsch philosophy of psychic liberation—*Life Against Death, Love's Body*—that Paglia champions against the "spinsterish" ideas of the French but Elvis Presley and, skipping no beats, Aretha Franklin, Levi Stubbs, James Brown, Gladys Knight. "Black artists," she croons, "are the American paradigm of vivid, vibrant personality, dramatic self-assertion, and spiritual magnitude of the individual voice."[2] On the one hand, Paglia might be said to suffer from nothing more serious than a terminal case of Big Chill syndrome. From this perspective, she emerges as a flower child in a time warp, one who read Marcuse (though he is cited nowhere in her magnum opus) and held onto the worst parts of *Eros and Civilization.* Pitting the trickster Prometheus who serves the reality principle against the feminine Pandora or the feminized Orpheus, who serves the pleasure principle, and quoting Brown for support, Marcuse declares: "The beauty of the woman, and the happiness she promises are fatal in the workworld of civilization."[3] It is *Sexual Personae* in a nutshell, but it also neatly summarizes why so much of Marcuse rings hollow in a world where many women would prefer to be something other than the object that promises men happiness when the working day is done—though Paglia has surely found an audience for her message.

On the other hand, however, hers is the disease that Frantz Fanon—another French-speaking spinster, perhaps?—discovered in the white American sensibility forty years ago. Quoting Senghor, Fanon ironically recalls the double bind created by his discovery of negritude as a strategy of resistance.

> I made myself the poet of the world. The white man had found a poetry in which there was nothing poetic. The soul of the white man was corrupted, and, as I was told by a friend who was a teacher in the United States, "The presence of the Negroes beside the whites is in a way an insurance policy on humanness. When the whites feel that they have become too mechanized, they turn to the men of color and ask them for a little human sustenance." At last I had been recognized, I was no longer a zero.
> I had soon to change my tune.[4]

In her confused reading of contemporary American intellectual life, Paglia issues nothing less than a call to return to those halcyon days of 1952, when women again began to promise happiness to American men, as long as it was outside the workplace, and when a young Fanon struggled to figure out why the vocal vibrancy of negritude should place him in such a compromised position in spite of its obvious force. "There is a quest for the Negro," he writes further on, "the Negro is in demand, one cannot get along without him, he is needed, but only if he is made palatable in a certain way."[5] The personal and political impasses that Fanon confronts in addressing the questions of colonialism, racism, and psychic identity are *real* (not merely theoretical) impasses, in the face of which Paglia herself indeed remains childlike and innocent.

Many would say that attacking Paglia is an effort wasted on an inconsequential ranter. Like other denouncers of theory and/or politics in the humanities, from Sykes to Bloom to D'Souza, Paglia is, for some, popular but transient. Like her academy-bashing comrades, the claim goes, she will only be granted more credibility than she merits if she is awarded a serious and direct response. Other academics, even bona fide former counterculturalists like Todd Gitlin, have felt compelled to admit that there may be some truth to the claims made by Kimball, Bloom, et al., and that a complacent university system ought to acknowledge its errors and clean up its act.

I would claim, on the contrary, that the right-wing attack on the humanities in the American academy is quite threatening to intellectual independence, that this attack is alive and well in spite of a recent electoral defeat at the national level, and that it needs to be taken very seriously indeed. It does not take a dissertation's worth of research to discover what is at the heart of this attack, but neither are the underlying motives perfectly transparent. The university in America—and the life-world and social status associated with a professional career within it—have been changing for some time now, and there are more than a few professors and wanna-bes unhappy with these developments. There is, in short, a tremendous amount of bitterness and resentment now aimed at the humanistic disciplines in the university and at those who serve as scapegoats for the unhappy. (Like the Jew who is still held to be the cause of economic catastrophe in Poland today, where for all intents and purposes Jews no longer exist, "deconstruction" or "French theory" or "marxism" is most theatrically indicted precisely in those institutions where it no longer exists or has never appeared at all.) Whence this bitterness and resentment? What is its etiology?

Aesthetic Education and Its Vicissitudes

It is a common error, I think, to treat these effects as nothing more than the incidental complements of right-wing groups that have finally felt authorized by the successes of the Reagan-Bush era to retake the bastions of learning. Undoubtedly, something like this revenge of the Republican Guard is involved, but not always. Camille Paglia is a perfect counterexample: the angry ex-hippie denied a prestige position who winds up teaching some undifferentiated subject called "humanities" even though she is convinced that she is the only member of her generation whose intellect survived the sex, drugs, and rock 'n' roll of the 1960s. But it is the rage of this group that is in fact out of all proportion to the task of saving our culture that they have assigned themselves. (Many universities contain literature departments that hardly need to be "retaken" by the Right in any case, since it was in actuality the American public that swerved left and then right again while the departments have remained blissfully constant.) More often, it is in fact a particular university only belatedly coming to grips with deeply entrenched and outmoded traditions that suddenly seems to be in need of being saved from a left wing with quite limited power. Stanford, dominated by the tower of its Hoover Institution and protected by the pastoral atmosphere of its plantation, was a semifeudal anomaly ripe for conflict during Reagan's tenure. In the end, what should really surprise us about such curricular dissent is that it took so long to occur in such places. (Brown University, one will remember, went through major academic reform in the 1969–1970 academic year.)

But even the peculiar vicissitudes of often haphazard and nonsynchronous curricular reform are insufficient to explain the anger of the conservative unhappy consciousness. The etiology of the bitterness must finally be traced both to sociological and to structural transformations within humanistic disciplines in the American university. By sociological transformations I mean changes in the racial and ethnic makeup of the student bodies of most of our universities and (much slower) changes in the gender, racial, and ethnic makeup of their faculties. D'Souza's profound ignorance of the history of his own subject matter, Louis Menand has written, "makes it impossible for him to evaluate what he has observed":

> In 1960, a year well within the memories of most senior professors and university administrators, ninety-four per cent of college students were white. (At private institutions, the figure was a little over ninety-six per cent.) Of the students making up the remaining six per cent, a third attended all-black or predominantly black institutions. Sixty-three per cent of college students were men; almost nine of every ten Ph.D.s awarded were awarded to men; and nearly eighty per cent of university faculty were men. Some of the most prestigious private colleges in the country did not admit women, and there were several public universities (not to mention private ones such as Duke) that did not admit black students.[6]

Menand's larger point seems to me irrefutable—that what is taught and how it is taught will rarely reflect, in spite of all goodwill, "the interests and perspectives of the people who were not there." At the root of the conservative unhappy consciousness is in many ways a broad demographic transformation of the university, one that brings with it portents of intellectual and curricular change far more threatening than those carried by returning GI's onto campuses in the 1950s. Figures like D'Souza attack threatening ideas—whether political or "theoretical"—even when these ideas have a marginal presence, because to attack a threatening shift in the gender and racial constitution of the university would be too egregious (and, in D'Souza's case, ironic) a sign of the intolerance that fuels their resentment.

If such sociological changes should in one way be obvious (though they are often not) and imply obvious consequences, in another way they are fraught with discrepancies and surprises. The percentage of black male undergraduates in our universities relative to the black male population has actually declined over the past two decades. Henry Louis Gates Jr. has enjoyed great academic success, but there may be fewer black men in the auditorium to hear his words than one might expect. Worse, it is still clear that equal education does not automatically breed racial or gender equality in the workplace. Nevertheless, I think one can assume that demographic transformations, in spite of periodic reversals, will continue to occur and will exert an even greater pressure on the curriculum than heretofore. There are, for example, more African Americans, Asian Americans, Mexican Americans, and Native Americans pursuing advanced degrees in the humanities than ever before, and this is having an important effect on the kinds of things that are studied.

The structural transformations within the humanities take place on two levels, and I wish to describe them, at least initially, as inherently neither good nor bad but rooted in a most basic way in the social infrastructure of American life—that is, in the administered capitalist economy that sustains American society as well as in the social and cultural conflict that reproduces itself in the university, sometimes in highly veiled or symbolic form. On one level, a subtle yet fundamental change has occurred in the way humanistic studies are actually organized. The last quarter-century has seen an increase of agreed-upon modes of specialization; the fragmentation of fields, accompanied in many cases, ironically, by a greater uniformity of training methods and formal standards; the expansion of permitted kinds of "knowledge" along with an increased and leveling access to such knowledges; new relations to public (that is, "popular") discourses, such that academic scholarship has paradoxically become more focused on popular media as objects of study even as it has drifted farther away from a popular audience; new constitutions of research paradigms; the blurring of disciplinary boundaries; and important shifts in the organic relations between disciplines. The right wing's often repeated worry, for example, that the denunciation of Eurocentrism is in reality a rejection of essential "human" values as well as of an entire system for producing knowledge must be situated, if its hysterical nature is to be properly understood, in a context that includes not only the shifting racial and ethnic balance in American society and the altered significance of American power in "post"-colonial geopolitics but also the increasingly rationalized production of knowledge in institutions of higher learning—which has been going on for quite some time. This context must be understood to have a somewhat arbitrary internal articulation: the new demographics and geopolitics are not in themselves responsible for new modes of organization in the humanities, which follow relatively autonomous paths of growth and decay. Nevertheless, all these changes belong to the same historical moment in American education and need to be treated accordingly.

On the second level, there is an equally profound though far less noticeable alteration in the way cultural capital—"distinction," as Pierre Bourdieu might say—is accumulated through humanistic study, an alteration that is the result of the ever increasing importance of technological knowledge in the world marketplace on one hand and the shifting position of art and of the modes of legitimation of aesthetic "taste" on the other. Beyond the geopolitical consequences, the Gulf War also confirmed for the American people—that is, if any still needed to be convinced—that those who can design, use, and televise weapons (putatively) smart enough to destroy incoming missiles at the speed of sound are in possession of an almost sacred knowledge, one rivaled only by the wisdom possessed by research scientists searching for a cancer cure. What is at issue here, then, is not simply a purely technical "division of labor" within the humanities, one that merely repeats and extends already accomplished divisions between the sciences and the humanities and within the latter, such as those that occurred amid much debate in the mid-nineteenth century. Rather, as Louis Althusser insisted, there is no purely technical division of labor within a capitalist economy, even a highly rationalized one. Each division, each new field of knowledge, takes its place in a hierarchy of knowledges through a process often filled with struggle and contention. With each new and more powerful home computer that appears on the market, the forms of cultural capital of the computer user are slightly altered.

At the same time—and this brings me to the issue of the aesthetic per se, and thus to one of the supposed cruxes of this essay—an important shift may be occurring in where and how cultural capital is produced, certified, conferred, exchanged, and reconfigured. For Bourdieu the educational institutions, and especially the university, have been *the* primary sites for the production and reproduction of cultural capital in the modern era. That is, Bourdieu drew his conclusions from a model (one perhaps more persistent in France, especially the France of the 1960s, when much of his research was done, than elsewhere) in which the university retained primary responsibility for the maintenance and transmission of cultural capital through its humanistic disciplines, especially those organized around art, literature, and music. Although there is ample room for other forms of transmission in Bourdieu's analysis—hereditary or familial circuits being the most obvious and most effective after the demise of royal courts—the school is an indispensable broker in the market of cultural capital and *the* broker for the bourgeoisie created by a capitalist economy.

Now, I would claim that the conservative cultural critics—from E. D. Hirsch with his now comic reification of the cultural goods to Paglia with her nonsensical glorification of nineteenth-century belles-lettres (has she really read Pater carefully, one wonders?)—in fact wish to defend their inherited vision of university education as *the* mode of production of cultural capital. On one hand, there is the threat of what might be called simple revisionism. This is the arena in which all the debates about the canon get played out. At stake is what objects, books, performances—one might also say *whose* objects, books, performances—really get to count as cultural capital. If Alice Walker is "authorized" by university training often enough and long enough, then both knowledge and "appreciation" of her work will begin, however slowly, to represent cultural capital and will begin to circulate in all the social venues where cultural capital is itself useful instead of, or at least on a par with, a knowledge and appreciation of Walter Scott or Walter Pater. Though this is a significant change, one that I would call both positive and necessary, I hope that I will not be misunderstood if I insist that by itself it is after all neither the most fundamental threat to the aesthetic order dear to the conservative cultural critics nor one that the university will find impossible to accommodate.

New specialties will be added to the curriculum, a certain amount of retraining will occur, and—perhaps most of all—new faculty will be hired. And, as I noted above, the ongoing rationalization of the discipline will continue. It may well be that within a decade or two a doctorate in "English Literature" will no longer possess any agreed-upon meaning. I do not claim that this will occur without struggle and debate or that there will not be political victories and defeats along the way. Nor would I claim that there is any way to measure the desirability of such an outcome. Rather, the point is that this sort of change still takes place within the already accepted processes of disciplinary rationalization and division of labor that are fundamental to capitalist development and to its ideological institutions. The primary conflict here will be the status—again, no technical division without hierarchy—of the new disciplines or specializations. But, at least in these debates, the university will remain the locus of the production of cultural capital.

What I want to suggest on the other hand is something more far-reaching and hence more threatening to the conservative cultural critic's view of the university, something that is also rooted in infrastructural transformations but that has at least the potential to open up new areas of social-symbolic contestation. That is, it may be that we are also witnessing in disciplinary changes within art, literature, and music—all traditional carriers of cultural capital—the slow decline in the power of the university to create, legitimate, and preserve cultural capital in aesthetic forms and to convey it to its students in exchange for the price of admission. The academic cultivation of aesthetic response, especially when it occurs as if untouched by social interests, has often been made to serve politically conservative ends. Simply acquiring the "good taste" that comes with aesthetic training can help to create allegiance to class formations that take it upon themselves to preserve not only the cultural heritage but the social status quo itself from attack and transformation.

This is not to say that all representations or celebrations of the aesthetic are inherently antiprogressive in character, as a long tradition of criticism from Georg Lukács and Theodor Adorno to Virginia Woolf and Toni Morrison surely implies.

But one must at the same time admit that any program of aesthetic education that ignores the relations between aesthetic form, ideological substance, and the social basis of their significance may be doomed (or designed) to put aesthetic response to politically conservative ends. What is slowly evaporating, for a number of reasons, is the ability of the university to maintain its innocence, to serve any longer as the locus of production of pure aesthetic value and aesthetic experience. This fall from grace threatens both the prestige of the scholar and the humanistic rationale behind the academic study of works of art, things even left-leaning intellectuals are loath to give up. At stake is the power of a university education to bestow through humanistic training the marks of a certain elite class distinction—that is, good taste—and hence implicit moral and political authority.

Of course, the university will still function as a site of the production and exchange of cultural capital in other forms. "Knowledge," after all, no matter how related to immediate, instrumental application, will continue to represent a form of cultural capital, and the university will continue to have a fundamental role in the production of scientific and technical knowledges of all types. But like the putatively apolitical appreciation of aesthetic form, knowledge in the hard sciences has, with certain definable exceptions, managed to steer blissfully clear of the problem of social value that, for many, is the raison d'être of humanistic study. Thus, the "social sciences," especially those, like sociology, in which a certain strain of scholars has rooted the production of human values in historically determined social life, are routinely attacked from the right. It is no accident that it is precisely such sociological disciplines that are understood by the conservative cultural critic to have made damaging inroads on the belletristic study of literature. It is also no accident, then, that these extraliterary disciplines have come to be understood by many "theoretically" informed critics—who eschew belletrism's transcendence of the social—as essential to a less mystified reading practice.

Nor, finally, is it an accident that the political debates over the function of the humanities within the university have invaryingly focused on those disciplines, such as literature, or those cross-curricular inventions, such as Western Civilization or Humanities, in which what is often at stake, whatever the "moral" veneer applied, is the supposedly intrinsic "quality" of the text. In the Western Civilization curriculum, for example, this sense that a text is inherently significant and of essential value, no matter what the specific field of knowledge by which it is classified and through which it acquires its specific force as "knowledge," can only be an aesthetic judgment, precisely because the very purpose of the Western Civilization course is to detach individual works from a disciplinary (or instrumental) climate of evaluation and to resituate them in an apotheosized tradition—"sweetness and light," as Matthew Arnold aptly named it—that has value *in and of itself.* No student reads Machiavelli's *The Prince* in a Western Civilization course because it is necessary to specialized work later on in the field of political science. One reads *The Prince,* often as a freshman, in such a course even if (perhaps because) there is a real probability that one will *never* pursue additional study in political science. One reads it because, in the minds of many, no matter how good one is at designing smart bombs or clever computers, one will not be considered truly "educated"—which does not at all mean "informed," or "smart," or possessing a specific kind of "knowledge" but rather signifies primarily that one has accumulated a certain supply of cultural capital. One may never refer to, or even remember, *The Prince* after that Western Civilization course—indeed, one may never have to acknowledge how subversive of reified Western "values" the texts in such a course might actually be—but one will have been "educated." And it is precisely the power of the university to produce cultural capital in this purely "aesthetic" sense—like the disinterested Kantian appeal of the beautiful "for its own sake"—that is in question, along with the moral and political distinction this capital represents.

The Future of an Institution

Finally, beyond revisionism and the broader decline of aesthetic education, both of which only partially modify the university's traditional mission to produce cultural capital in its humanities programs, there are even larger transformations looming on the horizon for departments of language and literature. These transformations are almost completely dependent on economic changes in the university, in government funding, and in an increasingly debt-ridden American society. Within the next ten years, it is possible that two big alterations will occur in the study of literature. First, universities will find it difficult to maintain administratively distinct departments of language and literature, each with its own national and linguistic reason for being. (This has indeed already occurred on some campuses.) "Literature" may become a single department containing a grand hodgepodge of disparate pursuits, capped by a wide array of graduate degrees individually marked to reflect myriad subdisciplines. Even the category "literature" may be subordinated to something broader called "cultural studies."

Second, the present system of scholarly interchange and evaluation in literature departments—dependent, essentially, upon the book-length monograph—may disappear. What evolved in the middle of the twentieth century, especially in America, was a very cozy network of exchanges that took place between university departments filled with scholars, the university presses, and the university libraries. Scholars wrote books, the presses published them, the libraries bought them, and the university in turn used the book as evidence in evaluating the scholar. For several decades, this system has been almost self-sustaining; that is, university presses could be assured that library sales alone would allow them to break even on a publication, which in turn allowed the university to use such publications as the criteria for promotion and tenure and further assured the scholar a permanent home for his or her scholarship. As most editors will point out today, this neat system is crumbling. Although university libraries may have bought between eight hundred and a thousand copies of a new monograph twenty years ago, they often purchase only two hundred to four hundred copies today. Presses have met the challenge by simply publishing more books in smaller numbers, but this is a superficial remedy at best.

If, because of both internal and external forces, the cultural distinction of humanistic study is withering, and if, primarily because of wholesale economic shifts, the system of departmental autonomy and scholarly exchange that supported the humanities as a kind of specialized expertise is slowly collapsing, it seems apparent that humanistic education will be asked to function ever more obviously as a service adjunct to the hard sciences and technology. Research and scholarly discussion—essential to the "life of the mind" in universities—will be curtailed; ever more reified modes of "truth" will be promulgated by professors supposedly dedicated to teaching. Ironically, it is precisely this trajectory that the conservative attack on higher education (including Paglia's), putatively intended to save the humanities from themselves, has supported. The more that humanistic scholarship is held up for ridicule as a "scam," the easier it will be to relegate the education that grows from it to the ashcan of history. No one can predict with certainty the actual result of battles that lie ahead. The important point to recognize is that only by confronting such developments with candor, only by acknowledging that the internal structure and practice of humanistic disciplines cannot be held aloof from the broader social forces at work at this time, can an adequate defense of humanistic inquiry be mounted. Trying to return to an anachronistic model of academic life is worse than absurd—it's suicidal.

What, finally, does all of this mean today for the profession of literature? It reveals that the heated argument over things like tradition and the canon of great works, the entire debate over literary quality and universality, may represent more than just another of the revisions of taste that occur periodically within the discipline. What critics like Hirsch and Bloom and Kimball make clear is the underlying worry that the professoriat as they knew it is slowly losing its grip on the control of culture in America and that only a repressive return to an earlier era will save it. Indeed, some professors of literature have for much of this century dealt with their already anachronistic position as cultural authorities by emphasizing a technical knowledge of the arts rather than openly celebrating the privileged access to taste and culture they supposedly embody.

Paglia is a good example of the regressive desire to recover traditional forms of cultural distinction in the halls of the academy. For all her supposedly visceral embrace of American popular culture and "its sacred poetry of the body," she inevitably reveals her disdain for the average American mind and her nostalgia for the strong, cultured *Doktorvater,* managing to confuse deconstruction with a hatred of high culture in the process.[7] (One wonders if she has ever read J. Hillis Miller on his love of canonical masterpieces.) "In the United States, deconstruction is absurd, since we have never had a high culture of any kind. Far from being overliterate, we are still preliterate."[8] Even as she praises an untutored American art of the streets, she condemns "ignorant professors, who have substituted 'expertise' for breadth and depth of learning in the world history of art and thought."[9] The point, I would claim, is surely not that breadth and depth of learning are of no use to the scholar but that the nature, purposes, and cultural status of such "learning" are themselves on trial as humanistic disciplines develop in the last decades of this century. Given that Paglia safely dismisses today's academic politics as "secondhand" and irrelevant, one might want to ask what "breadth and depth of learning" actually represent for her—other than a manifestation of cultural capital in its purest, most repressive sense. And no patronizing praise of African American popular music should be allowed to shield her from such a question.

More important, the question of the relation between aesthetics and politics will only become more pressing and more fraught with contradiction in the years ahead. Simply acknowledging that in the future the university may have less of a monopoly on the process by which cultural practices are legitimated or suppressed—on the maintenance of cultural capital—will hardly make the role of culture in contemporary American social and political conflict less important or more transparent. And here—despite Henry Louis Gates Jr.'s recent warnings about rampant academic Fanonism and despite the glaring problems with gender and sexuality in *Black Skin, White Masks*—I would like to return to Fanon, who, in his confrontation with the unresolved tensions in Sartre's understanding of negritude, touches on something crucial in the role of culture in contemporary American society, something that Bourdieu seems not to understand very well at all.

In the middle of *Black Skin, White Masks,* Fanon squares off against his mentor Jean-Paul Sartre and confronts a crucial knot in the relations between the professional intellectual, the aesthetic, and the pressing political questions of his time. It is a confrontation that encapsulates not the very broad and often quite abstract issues that I have been raising in this essay but something far more particularized, personal, probably irresolvable, and perhaps all the more deeply political in the balance than anything I have said so far. And it suggests, for me, where the important struggles will continue to occur within the academy in the immediate future.

You will no doubt recall the scene. Fanon, personally caught between racial polarities, between national identifications, between languages, and between what we might still today call world views, discovers that at the precise moment in which he feels that he has finally recovered some stability in his self-understanding, his great white intellectual father has already taken it away from him. "I wanted to be typically Negro—it was no longer possible. I wanted to be white—that was a joke. And, when I tried, on the level of ideas and intellectual activity, to reclaim my negritude, it was snatched away from me. Proof was presented that my effort was only a term in the dialectic."[10] What follows in the text is a long quotation from Sartre's *Orphée Noir*, which ends as follows:

> The position of negritude as an antithetical value is the moment of negativity. But this moment is insufficient by itself, and the Negroes who employ it know this very well; they know that it is intended to prepare the synthesis or realization of the human in a

society without races. Thus negritude is the root of its own destruction, it is a transition and not a conclusion, a means and not an ultimate end.

Fanon responds: "When I read that page, I felt that I had been robbed of my last chance. ... Help had been sought from a friend of the colored peoples, and that friend had found no better response than to point out the relativity of what they were doing."[11] What Fanon discovers is that Sartre, "that born Hegelian," has suddenly forgotten that the negativity of that negative moment must be absolute, that there can be no easy "intellectualization of the *experience* of being black," no already achieved theoretical sublation of the moment of consciousness and identity that Fanon recognized in the literature of Césaire and Senghor.

Fanon is caught between forms of resistance to hegemony offered by an aesthetic practice (such as negritude) that offers intellectual identity to those previously denied it and the lure of a totalizing theory (such as Sartre's), developed by the dominant intellectual class, that makes "romantic," personal, and idiomatic relations to the aesthetic appear suspect. But the position in which Fanon finds himself here remains a crucial site of contestation in the profession of literature today. In the critical writings of Barbara Christian, bell hooks, or Henry Gates Jr. himself, one will find Fanon's dilemma reproduced and worked through. True, Bourdieu's questions about class formation in the academy will likely remain as intractable as ever. The only way to imagine a world in which a university education, with or without aesthetic training, would not serve class interests is to imagine a world in which the university's resources were available to all on an equal basis, and it is clear what that would require. But changes in racial, ethnic, and gender demographics, combined with a host of structural transformations in and outside the academy, do offer real and new possibilities, even within the institutionally sanctioned purposes of the profession. And it is precisely these opportunities that must be safeguarded against the ravages—indeed, the institutional death wish—of a fairly well orchestrated right-wing assault.

The trick, ironically, may be to avoid allowing the tangible and particular choices that need to be made, from hiring and admission to curricula, to be too quickly subsumed by the grander political visions of the Sartrean—or, in today's world, "theoretical"—variety. In spite of all the long-range changes in literary study that I thought I could point to earlier, the fundamental questions to be asked about the relation of aesthetics, politics, and professional life in the coming decade will be as specific, as direct, as concrete, and often as personal as those raised by Fanon. It will not, I think, simply be a matter of waiting and watching or of producing more theoretically sophisticated readings of presumably important texts, whether already acknowledged as such or soon to be. There is no magical correspondence, for example, between the intellectual and political hygiene achieved by generating one Althusserian or Derridean interpretation after another and the diverse, complicated, and contradictory efforts that will be required to maintain the practical viability and moral responsibility of humanistic inquiry. To sustain itself, what progressive change demands most of all, even in the rarefied halls of a university, is imagination and practical understanding, not theoretical formulas or political shibboleths.

A worldly and informed intellectual is still the best defense against the scare tactics and witch hunts of the Right. But the attributes of such an intellectual cannot be fixed outside of history any more than culture itself can. "I do not come with timeless truths," wrote Fanon, even as he resisted the this-too-will-pass-away attitude of Sartre. It is no longer sufficient—if it ever was—to maintain one's expertise in a literary field or one's familiarity with the great books. Nor is it possible to hold up the reified image of the traditional scholar imbued with what Paglia calls "breadth and depth of learning," as if there were one such model for this learning, as Paglia implies, waiting to be emulated in nineteenth-century Germany. More than ever, intellectuals committed to progressive change in the humanities will have to cross frontiers. They will have to be willing to acknowledge interests and perspectives and ways of knowing that may not be "their own" with the faith that the good and the true are not so brittle as to be unable to withstand radical inquiry. What the literary academy faces is a time in which the study of literature itself will be forced to justify its aims, its methods, and its priorities in response to questions that have not been asked with such force since its formal inception in the middle of the nineteenth century. Only those fixated in a sort of pre-Oedipal relationship to the profession will insist that the questions not be asked or despair that they cannot be answered.

NOTES

1. Camille Paglia, "Ninnies, Pedants, Tyrants, and Other Academics," *New York Times Book Review*, 5 May 1991, 29.

2. Ibid., 29.

3. Herbert Marcuse, *Eros and Civilization* (Boston: Beacon Press, 1974; first published 1955), 161.

4. Frantz Fanon, *Black Skin, White Masks*, trans. Charles Lam Markmann (New York: Grove, 1967), 129.

5. Ibid., 176.

6. Louis Menand, "Illiberalisms," *The New Yorker*, 20 May 1991, 104.

7. Paglia, "Ninnies, Pedants," 33.

8. Ibid.

9. Paglia, "Ninnies, Pedants," 1.

10. Fanon, *Black Skin, White Masks*, 132.

11. Ibid., 133.

13

Political Correctness and the Attack on American Colleges

PAUL LAUTER

THE MAIN NEWS Americans were taught about colleges during the last few Bush years was that they had been infected with a galloping moral disease, "political correctness." Talking with academics across the country and visiting over twenty campuses, I came to think that the charges of PC were fundamentally a smokescreen designed to discredit higher education. Behind that screen, conservatives have implemented a well-orchestrated and well-financed campaign to cut budgets, downsize universities, and thus sharply restrict access to higher education. This process has particularly hurt the "new" student populations that began to arrive on campus late in the 1960s. More broadly, higher education in the United States is undergoing a revolution in structure and function as profound as that which, earlier in this century, converted it from the province primarily of a tiny group of white gentlemen into a broad-based institution of social inclusion.

The construction of the monster PC depends upon highly partisan interpretations of a series of campus events.[1] The extraordinary cutbacks in higher education can, however, be documented in painful detail. The State University of New York suffered $60 million in cuts in 1991–1992; 1,150 faculty and staff jobs were lost, and over thirty academic programs were closed. Meanwhile, tuition for New York State residents soared from $1,350 in 1990–1991 to $2,650 in 1991–1992, still a bargain compared with tuition at the state's private institutions but a major strain on the budgets even of middle-class families.[2] The City University of New York,

Reprinted by permission from *Radical Teacher* 44 (Winter 1993):34–40.

where enrollments have grown by about 5 percent since 1970–1971, suffered a cut of some $350 million, or 33.5 percent, in state and city funding during this period—that is to say, the costs of CUNY have been privatized.[3] The University of Connecticut absorbed cuts of $47.5 million in four years with the consequent loss of about 600 jobs—and, of course, few pay raises for employees. Tuition, which in 1988–1989 was $2,293, went up by 42 percent to $3,902 in 1991–1992; in fact, with additional fees, higher room and board, and other expenses, the rise in costs to students was about double. With the imposition of a new state income tax, such increases priced the university out of the range of many theoretically "middle-class" students.[4]

Nowhere, perhaps, were the cuts more dramatic than in California. In 1992–1993, the University of California system lost $224 million, or 10.6 percent of its total state appropriation, leading in May 1993 to an across-the-board pay *cut* of 5 percent. Meanwhile, the California State University system, largest in the nation, lost $125 million, or 7.6 percent of its 1991–1992 budget—totals more damaging to the four-year colleges than to the UC system because they are far more dependent on state funds. (Institutions like Berkeley and UCLA receive under 20 percent of their funding from the California budget.) According to an April 1993 draft report for the California Assembly Committee on Higher Education: "In only the past two years, the state has withdrawn more than $550 million from its $6.5 billion in annual support for higher education. The workforce of the two public universities has shrunk by 6,800 faculty and staff (or 7.2 percent of the total)—the only sector of state government employment to have declined—in the last ten years." Similarly, the California Community College budget faced a 29 percent cut in 1992, which was offset by raising fees per credit hour from $6 to $10 (a further increase to $30 was proposed) and by a set of budgetary devices—such as charging $15 per term for parking.[5] For those who already held a degree but wished to return to community college for retraining, the cost climbed to about $50 a unit.

The impact of these cuts was most striking at institutions like San Diego State and San Jose State. At San Diego, where state funding was down 16.2 percent in two years, enrollments were cut by 17 percent. Whole departments, such as sociology, were threatened with elimination, and only a strenuous organizing campaign prevented professors with up to twenty years of seniority from being laid off. Still, some six hundred jobs were lost, most part-time and many untenured faculty were dropped, and students often found it impossible to enroll even in courses required for graduation—such as basic English—or for their majors.[6] San Jose, which eliminated virtually all part-timers and even teaching by early-retirees, reduced its student ceiling by 15 percent; still, even classes at 7:30 A.M. were overenrolled. Statewide, Cal State officials projected the elimination of some 10,000 students from the university rolls. Meanwhile, in the community college system, "over 100,000 potential students, most seeking job retraining, were unable to obtain courses" they needed in fall 1991 because classes were filled or eliminated, and at least an equal number were, in 1992, unable to pursue their courses of study at their local colleges.[7] California community colleges were for the first time actually turning students away from their doors.[8]

Viewed nationally, the picture is equally grim. In 1990, state funding showed "the lowest two-year growth since the figures were first collected in 1958."[9] In seventeen states, including Florida, Illinois, and Ohio, apart from New York and California, appropriations were actually lower than two years before. Overall 1990 totals, including states that were then increasing funding, were about 1 percent less than in 1988.[10] After 1990, things got worse: funds for higher education were "cut in 30 states, affecting two-thirds of all public colleges and universities."[11] These cuts and the consequent sharp raises in state college tuitions affected students in most economic groups: in forty states, public-institution tuitions rose at a faster rate than personal income.[12] Many showed two straight years of double-digit increases in tuition, a rate three times that of inflation.[13] According to *Business Week,* private college tuitions were rising faster than medical costs, with public colleges not far behind; in fact, "college costs as a share of median family income jumped from 26.6% to 39.9% for a student at a private school and from 12.1% to 15.9% at a public one."[14]

What is particularly striking about these figures is perhaps less the size of the cuts, the rapid rise of public tuitions and fees, or even the laying off of faculty and staff than the *disproportion* of the cutbacks. In Ohio, for example, the 1992–1993 budget called for a cut of $170 million in the overall $1.8 billion university budget—a harsh measure, to say the best of it. What catches my attention, however, is the fact that 54 percent of Republican Governor George Voinovich's budget cuts came from higher education, although higher education accounted for only 12 percent of the overall state budget.[15] Ohio's governor was by no means distinctive in using higher education as the fall-guy for state budget cuts. C. Peter Magrath, president of the National Association of State Universities and Land-Grant Colleges, asserts that "state support for higher education is deteriorating. ... In a lot of states, where 10 years ago 18 percent of the state budget was going to higher education, now it's down to 14 percent."[16] In California, education funding in 1992 was down from 15.5 percent of the state budget in 1985 to 12.4 percent. In Illinois, colleges received 23.5 percent of state funds in 1968, 18.3 percent in 1990.[17]

The federal government has also disinvested in higher education. During the 1980s, funding for student aid programs rose to some extent, although the basic Pell grants have never been funded at their authorized levels. Indeed, in the last Bush year, drawdowns on Pell grants put the fund $1.4 billion in arrears; part of the dispute over President Clinton's stimulus package concerned the appropriation of funds for this program. More and more students have turned to such grants as states have ended long-established programs such as New York's Regents' Scholarships, which helped generations of students through both public and private institutions. And, as the federal government has sought funds for other programs, it has depleted moneys available for programs like work-study, on which many middle-income students depend.[18] Similarly, for better or for worse, federal support for university research programs has eroded. Although it is no doubt true that a few research universities ripped off taxpayers through excessive indirect-cost procedures, the effect of recent changes has been to cut budgets even further, especially at less prestigious (and less wealthy) institutions.

Many faculty members have gone without raises and thus fallen farther and farther behind economically and significant numbers especially of part-time employees (and thus usually of women) have lost their jobs, but the greatest impact of these sharp cuts has been upon students. Virtually every story in the popular press or in higher-education trade journals tells some variation of a now-familiar tale: monster sections such as an eleven-hundred-student introduction to political science at the University of Illinois; students sitting on the steps of packed auditoriums; library hours cut back and acquisitions curtailed; students unable to get into English 101 after five terms of trying (in 1991, in fact, twelve hundred San Diego State students failed to get into *any* of the classes for which they had registered)[19]; major requirements taught only every second or even third year; planned elimination of programs such as aerospace engineering at San Diego and threatened deep cutbacks of traditional departments such as sociology even at Yale. The Minnesota system closed a campus; the University of Massachusetts (where state funds were cut 30 percent in three years) shut the accessible downtown Boston campus; the City University of New York's chancellor proposed "consolidating" certain departments so that not every campus would offer all traditional subjects, such as philosophy; the State University of New York at Old Westbury tried to retrench one of the nation's few African American music programs—at a college that is half minority. The pattern is clear enough, but one statistic is even more striking: in 1976 it took students an average of 4.6 years to graduate with a bachelor's degree; in 1992 it took an average of 5.5 years.

What has been less evident is the process one might describe, in a term borrowed from industrial union contracts, as "bumping." As private institutions have become increasingly expensive, upper-middle-class students not eligible for aid have turned in large numbers to the flagship institutions of state systems, which remain significantly cheaper than privates. "Since there are only a limited number of slots at the flagships," Arthur M. Hauptman points out, "the wealthier kids from suburban schools with better grades and better test scores squeeze out poorer kids, who then go to a state college or a community college or the regional, private liberal arts college that will offer them $5,000 in aid. Or they don't go to college at all." That, Hauptman claims, "undermines the mission of public schools: to broaden access to higher education by subsidizing colleges with taxpayers' money."[20] Such a "bumping" process not only limits the life chances of many middle- and working-class students but undermines opportunities for poor and particularly minority students even to attend college. *Business Week* concludes that "middle- and working-class students are being squeezed out of the nation's best, most expensive schools to compete for slots at public colleges—where prices are also rising year after year."[21]

Furthermore, as costs have risen and aid packages have increasingly been limited, students who do stick it out emerge from college with enormous debts. It is not unusual for a student to complete a B.A. with a debt of $20,000 or more; in fact, median debt more than doubled between 1977 and 1992, from about $2,000 to $4,800.[22] What has been occurring here is not only the undermining of the mission of public institutions but the privatization of the costs of attending college.[23] For an increasing number of students, moreover, the combination of increased costs, the difficulty of getting courses they need, and the problem of finding a job that will enable them to attend college even part-time leads to a decision to drop out—indebted, discouraged, and bitter.

The American education system has always, in part, been a means for stratifying society. Schools used to sort students—primarily on the basis of class characteristics—into variously named tracks (college-bound, general, or commercial) or into "ability" groups. Now, colleges are being made to play an increasing role in such class stratification.[24] Between the 1970s and 1992 the proportion of students from high-income families who attend four-year colleges rose from 54 to 60 percent; among lower-income families the proportion remained at 27 percent.[25] Among households in the upper half of income, 26 percent of students took a four-year college degree in 1979, and that figure was up to 31 percent in 1992; among students from the lower income half, the proportion had fallen from 14 percent to 13 percent.[26] In other words, the gap between upper-income and lower-income educational levels is steadily, if slowly, increasing.

Even these discouraging figures do not tell the full story, however. The University of Arizona has been less affected by cuts than some; its budget was up about 1 percent in 1991. Yet it has canceled remedial math and language classes for the 40 percent of incoming students who need them. Many of these are Latino first-generation-to-college students. They may still take such courses off campus, but their costs will not be covered by financial aid packages. Such measures—and Arizona is by no means alone in implementing them[27]—are often presented as desirable efforts to raise academic "standards," but so long as schools, shattered communities and families, and a drifting economy fail to prepare many students to do academic work, these measures will in fact sharply restrict access to higher education, especially for poor and minority students. Indeed, the chancellor of the California State University has expressed concern that the impact of current policies, particularly as they are applied to public four-year colleges, will be to "shut the door just as people of color are reaching to open it."[28]

One might argue, of course, that the plight of higher education is indeed sad but that, after all, things are tough all over, from Sears to Boeing. But, as I have pointed out, public institutions of higher education have taken a disproportionate hit. Furthermore, it is simply not the case that public funds are *not* available for some projects, even for some connected with colleges and universities. The state of New York managed to build a new stadium at the University in Buffalo for the World University games. Other institutions making cuts in programs have installed Astroturf on their football fields or draperies in the homes of their presidents. At a Colorado campus, the salary of the football coach is reported to be some $360,000 a year, far more than the president's. UCLA bought memberships in a fancy club for some of its elite staff. Moreover, of all college costs, those for administration have increased by far the most rapidly.[29] The Department of Education reports that between 1975 and 1985 nonteaching professional staff expanded by 61 percent, whereas the faculty grew by only 6 percent.[30] And all of this says nothing about the federal funds that continue to be poured into the savings and loan and other banking scandals, not to speak of outer space, Star Wars, and the supercollider and the cabinet jaunts that marked the last days of the Bush administration. It is *not* simply the invisible hand of the market that has decreed such outrageous cuts in higher education. On the contrary, spending choices have been made by people carrying out definable projects: the cuts in higher education that I have chronicled reflect *political* decisions.

To argue in this direction is, of course, to raise a question: What political goals can possibly be pursued by cutting higher education? We may begin answering this question by examining a postelection op-ed article from the *New York Times* by Charles Murray, a fellow at the right-wing American Enterprise Institute. In the article, Murray offered advice on educational policy to the new president and his secretary of education, Richard W. Riley:

> *Giving qualified students a chance at college is something we already do well.* More than three-quarters of the nation's top students already go to four-year colleges. The number of top students who don't go to college because of lack of money is minuscule. It is fine to make it possible for every qualified student to go to college, but there is not much room for improvement. If Mr. Clinton's loan plan succeeds in significantly expanding enrollment, it may well damage university education: campuses will be flooded with still more students who are not ready for college-level material. That this view is elitist does not make it wrong.[31]

I need to set some facts against Murray's use of slippery, subjective terms like "qualified" and "top." About 80 percent of American young people now graduate from high school. "Fewer than 30 percent receive bachelor's degrees and/or continue on to graduate school."[32] Thirty percent fewer kids in the economically poorest quartile graduate from high school than in the richest quartile. The gap in the college participation rate is 32 percent; the same gap obtains in the rates of graduation from college, and this final set of figures has not changed over the past twenty years.[33] Such numbers cast Murray's assertions in a different light: the issue is not that they are elitist but that they are profoundly simpleminded as well as dangerously undemocratic. The assumption underlying Murray's argument is that standards of qualification for college work are known, agreed-upon, and universally objective—a notion undermined by the rather differing weights given to a variety of factors by college admissions officers.[34] Moreover, such "qualification" is by no means a constant, essential quality of some young people; the ability to succeed in college changes in individuals over time, in relation to particular institutional environments, and in significant measure in relation to external factors such as the availability of funding. Hidden under Murray's bland assertions is a Thatcherite vision of an American education system designed more systematically than ever to channel young people into levels of the workforce for which they are "appropriately" prepared. Indeed, what the figures I have cited strongly suggest is that colleges and universities have replaced secondary schools as primary mechanisms for sorting people on the basis, mainly, of their class origins.

The Thatcherite vision has, unfortunately, been bought into by many even well-meaning higher-education administrators as well. Chancellor Sheila Kaplan of the University of Wisconsin's Parkside campus writes in a model of administrativese as follows: "In the face of limited resources, we must consider the possibility of reducing enrollments and thus preserving the quality of our enterprises by bringing the number of students served into closer congruence with our available resources." Kaplan goes on to quote the Wisconsin system president, Kenneth A. Shaw:

> The University of Wisconsin System is committed to providing quality in teaching, in research, and in public service. The University of Wisconsin System is also committed to providing access to its quality programs and resources. ... However, when faced with a choice between maintaining educational quality and decreasing access to its programs and resources, the University of Wisconsin System must choose to maintain quality. For if academic programs, research, and public service are not first rate, access to the institutions will be of little value.

"Enrollment management," Kaplan continues, "requires that choices be made and that students with the best chance of success be admitted to the university."[35] In short, Kaplan and Shaw counterpose "access" to "quality" in an artificial opposition in which "access" is bound to be the loser.[36]

What these arguments come down to politically is this: access to colleges and universities was opened to an unprecedented degree in the 1960s. Politically, it is impossible to return to a policy of much more limited access, just as it would be to abrogate other universal "entitlements" put in place during those bad old days. Access can *only* be restricted if one can successfully argue that restriction is a function of economic forces beyond our control and if one can somehow make colleges politically suspect.

Such arguments play nicely into the overall conservative agenda, which emphasizes privatization (of costs as well as services), downsizing of government (in education as in other areas), and letting the "market" operate rather than using government to level the playing field. Moreover, for those committed to the future outlined in the North American Free Trade Agreement, "excessive" access to higher education is an impediment. After all, NAFTA envisages a decline in living standards for many—if not most—American workers, which is surely the only way Americans will be able to stanch the outflow of jobs to lower-paying and lower-cost Mexican plants.[37] The problem with education, especially college and university education and most particularly "liberal arts" education, from this perspective is that it raises expectations far too high. It encourages workers to aspire beyond what the shrinking job market can offer, to think and imagine beyond what labor discipline must impose. An "overeducated" workforce is, to this kind of thinking, as "destabilizing" to the United States as it once was to the state of Kerala in India.

The problem for conservatives then becomes, as Max Sawicky has put it, "not how to devise a better way to deliver services, but how to overcome the political obstacles to cutting public spending."[38] The idea is not to devise means for offering more and better educational services. Rather, as Sawicky quotes the right-wing maven Stuart Butler, "There is one missing ingredient in the campaign for a smaller and more efficient government sector—a political strategy that works."[39]

Enter "political correctness."

The construction of the PC monster was one of the major preoccupations of cultural conservatives, especially during the last days of George II. I use the term "construction" with care, for it rather resembles the way in which the Piltdown Man was produced. One particularly notorious but exemplary instance is provided by the so-called Thernstrom case at Harvard. It is cited as a prime instance of PC not only in the right-wing bible of academic condemnation, Dinesh D'Souza's *Illiberal Education*, but in Lynne Cheney's valedictory pamphlet, given the Pickwickian title of *Telling the Truth*.[40] Cheney's account nicely illustrates the self-referential process by which tales of political correctness were inflated like Macy's parade balloons. To support her account of the heinous attacks on poor Thernstrom's academic freedom, she cites D'Souza, a strikingly primitive article in *New York Magazine*,[41] that offered no independent evidence of anything, and Thernstrom himself in that journal of scholarly objectivity, *Academic Questions*.[42] But she does not cite an article by Jon Wiener,[43] which effectively dismantles D'Souza's initial account by reporting on Wiener's own interviews with the undergraduates supposedly guilty of harassing Thernstrom, with Thernstrom and other Harvard faculty members, and with the Harvard administrators who, according to Thernstrom, did not support him. Wiener's conclusion, to which there has been no substantive response from the Right, is that "almost every element of the story D'Souza tells is erroneous" (p. 384) and that therefore the accounts spread by right-wing mockingbirds like Cheney are equally fallacious—that, indeed, there was no "Thernstrom case."

But of course, it was not only right-wing flacks like D'Souza and Cheney, marginal at best to the academy, who spread such poison through the body politic. Indeed, I suspect that the most damage was done by liberals within academe such as C. Vann Woodward. In an essentially laudatory review of D'Souza's book in the *New York Review of Books*, Woodward offered an uncritical summary of D'Souza's account of how poor Thernstrom was "silenced" and "forced" to stop teaching the class in question. His recanting of what he wrote about Thernstrom appeared only in the collection edited by Pat Aufderheide called *Beyond PC* and published by Graywolf Press in St. Paul, where he admits that he "and others were misled by

D'Souza's account."[44] He does not say how many people may have read him in the widely circulated *New York Review of Books* and how many may have come upon his retraction in the Graywolf Press volume.

My point is not, of course, that political correctness, self-righteousness, and poor scholarship do not exist. Of course they do, as Lynne Cheney's pamphlet nicely illustrates and as any of us who have struggled with the more vapid forms of identity politics can testify. The academy has always had its share of charlatans and lowlifes; they have produced an Aryanized version of the classics, the fake twin-studies that have so corrupted the understanding of intelligence, American literary history without black writers, and my favorite bit of academic nonsense, the "end of ideology"—not to speak of NCAA Division One athletics. But they are no more—well, maybe a little more—representative of the American academy as a whole than, say, Leonard Jeffries's ideas about "ice people" and "sun people." For every abuse of affirmative action—and there have been some, to be sure—I could tell a story of academic favoritism, incompetence, and silliness—indeed, I don't have to, for they're set out in hilarious detail in a book of a quarter-century ago called *The Academic Marketplace*—long before affirmative action or anything like it had been thought up as an effort to right the previous obliquity of segregated schooling. For every instance of preferential admission by gender or race I could cite the multiplying thousands of instances in which preferences like those for alumni children became de facto tools for sustaining segregation and privilege. For every instance in which students of color have chosen to gather among themselves I could cite hundreds of instances in which they have been segregated by regulations, threats, and the legacy of racism with which we all live.

I can excuse D'Souza his ignorance; he, after all, wasn't around when Karl Shapiro wrote of the University of Virginia in those good old 1940s days: "To hurt the Negro and avoid the Jew/Is the curriculum."[45] I can excuse D'Souza, but not people like the former dean of Yale College, who proclaimed that the climate in his and other universities was worse than it had been in those good old days of black exclusion, Jewish quotas, and McCarthyite firings of big, bad Commies—those good old 1950s when the barber at Indiana University's Union claimed he "just didn't know how to cut a Nigra's hair" and the subtitle of the Western Civilization course I once taught—and loved—was the distinctly unideological "The Origins of Christian Civilization." Those were good days, all right, when Yale's eighteenth-century English literature program produced recruits for the CIA—including its director of counterintelligence—not to speak of the methodological base for the CIA's gathering and deployment of information and the intellectual grounding of its Cold War ideology.[46] I can regard these people who have gone around talking about "tenured radicals," the left-wing takeover of the university, and the rest of the PC line as little other than a fifth column, for the practical effect of these attacks on the university, particularly by those within it, has been to threaten our colleagues' jobs, our students' access to education, and the usefulness of learning to the nation's future and to support the worst know-nothings hanging on in statehouses across the country.

But all of this has come to seem to me ancient history—BC, so to speak. It is *boring*, like most right-wing scholarship, and without its promotion from the White House, the PC monster seems to be deflating like the Snoopy balloon the day after Thanksgiving. It may still be useful to understand how political correctness has been deployed, to use Stuart Butler's language, as the "missing ingredient in the campaign for a smaller ... government sector—a political strategy that works." It may be useful to show how precisely those individuals—like William Simon—and organizations—like the Olin, Scaife, and Coors Foundations—that have promoted the conservative agenda have also been the major financial sources for those talking up the PC threat. It may also be useful to point to other factors that have helped produce the constriction of college budgets: to cite just three, an aging population that no longer wishes to pay for other people's education, the narrowing of states' discretionary choices about where to spend money produced by Reagan-Bush mandates to carry on programs shifted to localities from the federal budget, and the push for international "competitiveness"—shared by Reaganites and Clintonites alike—that has led to efforts to decrease domestic consumption and thus wages and public spending.[47] No doubt it would also be useful to think about ways in which university education can be made more cost-effective. But I want to suggest that our primary problem is at least as much to organize as to analyze.

Those of us who are committed to broadening educational access and who believe in the value of multiculturalism and sex and gender equity need, I believe, to persuade Americans, as we have not successfully done, of the value of what we and our students do in colleges and universities. Many people have become skeptical of that enterprise—indeed, in traditional American fashion, of intellectual work generally. In fact, one might argue that the real crisis of higher education has to do with the sharp decline of its authority, most particularly its cultural authority. To an increasing number of Americans, including our students, universities mean little more than a stamp on one's life passport—important but not all that serious. For them, the flickering screen, the boom box, the Boss and the Dead—not to mention the Pistols, the Michaels, Madonna, Chuck-D, Ice T, the Nike ads, and (God save the mark) Roseanne—define the shape of culture. And the color of money. This is not altogether bad, given the imperial versions of culture that until recently predominated in colleges and universities. Yet we need to stop to consider what it might mean for youthful values to be increasingly established by the media, by a network of print, video, and advertising organized primarily around considerations of profit.

Some of the findings in Alexander Astin's recent book *What Matters in College?* are strikingly relevant here. Astin reports that "student acceptance of the idea that the chief benefit of a college education is to increase one's earning power is positively affected by ... living at home, majoring in engineering, and a peer environment characterized by a Lack of Student Community." Such student attitudes are further associated with the number of hours spent watching television, "a particularly interesting effect," Astin comments, "given the great emphasis on acquisitiveness and materialism that one finds in most commercial television programming."[48] By contrast, an institution's "Humanities Orientation" negatively affects such attitudes; also negatively associated with this set of beliefs are the number of hours spent talking with faculty outside of class, the number of courses a student takes that emphasize writing, and similar factors. Astin's statistics illuminate a common wisdom about collegiate experience: that definable factors can influence students' political, social, and cultural outlooks. We might, then, argue that current fiscal policies in higher education are, especially in public education, decisively eroding precisely those features of academic life that foster humane values alternative to those of "acquisitiveness" and "materialism"; that the erosion of contemporary academic cultural authority is no accidental by-product of financial cutbacks and culture wars but one of their objectives; and, further, that such a shift is a mark not of rational economic progress but of social ill-health.

It is because I have a certain faith in the value of intellectual work and in the academy that I've helped begin an organization called—perversely it seems to some—the Union of Democratic Intellectuals. It would be hard to cram more conflicted words into a title, but the main reason for the name UDI isn't linguistic perversity, however appealing that has often seemed to be to academics. The reason is located precisely in the union of intellectual work with a democratic polity. Our responsibility—especially when we are well-situated in universities—is to sustain, to nourish, to develop that union. The responsibility of intellectuals, after all, does not cease with the final footnote; it takes us into communities, into politics, into organizing.

The "crisis" of the university we face may in fact prove an opportunity. It can be an opportunity not only to help renew the struggle for broadened access but to debate the question of access to what. It should be an opportunity not only to reassert the value of diversity in curriculum, students, and staff but to discuss how we can press for concrete measures to ensure that real diversity, at every level, begins to be realized as it never has been. Certainly it is an opportunity to extricate ourselves from the defensive postures into which many twisted this last twisted decade and to take up the tasks of shaping the debate rather than being defined by other people's sound-bites. Above all, it must become an opportunity to identify alternative directions for college education; precisely because we can no longer assume that jobs or departments or even institutions will continue, intellectuals must rethink the work we do in universities and colleges and the work such institutions do in the rapidly underdeveloping economy of the United States. Will universities be ever more elaborate mechanisms for sorting and dividing Americans—and foreign elites as well—or can they become instruments for democratizing society and culture? The answers are not foreclosed but depend upon our imagination, energy, and willingness to organize.

NOTES

1. See below on the Thernstrom "case" at Harvard for an illustrative example.

2. Andrew L. Yarrow, "At UConn Costs Squeeze Its Students," *New York Times*, 16 August 1992, 42.

3. Jeannie Cross, "Higher Education Under Attack," *Empire State Reports* 18 (August 1992):31.

4. Yarrow, "At UConn, Costs Squeeze Its Students," *New York Times*, 16 August 1992, 37, 42. Yarrow's subhead conveys the essence of his story: "Many in Middle Class Face Crisis over Fees."

5. Kit Lively, "California Colleges Worry About How to Live with Deep State Cuts," *Chronicle of Higher Education*, 9 September 1992, A25.

6. Sonia L. Nazario, "Funding Cuts Take a Toll at University," *Wall Street Journal*, 5 October 1992, B1, B11.

7. "Important Trends for California Community Colleges, 1992," Report prepared for the Board of Governors' Retreat, 23–25 April 1992. See also Lively, "California Colleges," A25.

8. Anthony de Palma, "Community Colleges Forced to Restrict Access, and Goals," *New York Times*, 11 November 1992, 1.

9. Edward Hines, *State Tax Funds for Operating Expenses of Higher Education* (Washington, D.C.: National Association of State Universities and Land-Grant Colleges, 1990), as cited by Arthur M. Hauptman, "Meeting the Challenge: Doing More with Le$$ in the 1990s," *Educational Record* 72 (Spring 1991):8.

10. Mary H. Cooper, "Paying for College," *CQ Researcher* 2 (20 November 1992):1003; Robert M. Sweeney, "Report of the States: 1992 Annual Budget and Fiscal Survey of the AASCU Council of State Representatives," American Association of State Colleges and Universities, 1992.

11. Nazario, "Funding Cuts," B1.

12. Gordon Van de Water, "Public Tuition and State Expenditures for Higher Education, 1984–1988," NCSL (October 1991).

13. Cooper, "Paying for College," 1003.

14. *Business Week*, 24 May 1993, 112.

15. Joye Mercer, "Drop in State Support Leaves Ohio Colleges Wondering How Much Farther They Can Fall," *Chronicle of Higher Education*, 9 September 1992, A23.

16. Quoted in Cooper, "Paying for College," 1013.

17. Nazario, "Funding Cuts," B1.

18. Thomas J. DeLoughry, "Recession Takes Toll on U.S. Student Aid," *Chronicle of Higher Education*, 10 June 1992, A1, A20–21.

19. Nazario, "Funding Cuts," B11.

20. Quoted in Cooper, "Paying for College," 1004.

21. *Business Week*, 24 May 1993, 154.

22. Cooper, "Paying for College," 1007.

23. As Rita Rodin, a spokesperson for CUNY, pointed out, the City University, long free, began to charge tuition in 1976 and raised its tuition by a total of $53 million for 1992. "The upshot is that 'a greater portion of the burden [of financing CUNY] is falling on students. …'" Cross, "Higher Education Under Attack," 34–35.

24. This is not a new development but the extension of a role colleges have increasingly played since a significant proportion of American youth began attending after World War I and especially since very large numbers of Americans began attending after World War II. For useful earlier analyses of the sorting functions of higher education, see Ivar E. Berg, *Education and Jobs: The Great Training Robbery* (New York: Praeger, 1970); Samuel Bowles and Herbert Gintis, *Schooling in Capitalist America: Educational Reform and the Contradictions of Economic Life* (New York: Basic Books, 1976); Christopher Jencks and David Riesman, *The Academic Revolution* (Garden City: Doubleday, 1968); and Paul Taubman and Terence Wales, *Higher Education and Earnings: College as an Investment and a Screening Device* (New York: McGraw-Hill, 1974).

25. Charles F. Manski, *Parental Income and College Opportunity,* Democratic Study Center, 26 August 1992, quoted in Cooper, "Paying for College," 1004–1005.

26. U.S. Census Bureau figures cited by Nazario, "Funding Cuts," B1.

27. See, for example, "The Battle for City University," *Lingua Franca* 3 (January-February 1993):1, 24–31. 62.

28. Nazario, "Funding Cuts," B1.

29. "College Education: Paying More and Getting Less," Staff report to the Select Committee on Children, Youth, and Families, presented at hearings on 14 September 1992, 3. To be sure, many of these administrative expenses, such as for security and utilities, are quite legitimate. It would be hard, in my judgment, to maintain, however, that huge presidential salaries and burgeoning administrative staffs are uniformly necessary. At the same time that the president of San Diego State initially announced layoffs for hundreds of faculty, he gave himself a five-figure raise—just a small instance of how the greedy culture of the 1980s has infected educational institutions.

30. *Business Week,* 24 May 1993, 113.

31. Charles Murray, "Bad Lessons," *New York Times,* 8 January 1992, p. A25.

32. Peter Smith, "Beyond Budgets: Changing for the Better," *Educational Record* 72 (Spring 1991):27.

33. Ibid.

34. Amy Lang has informed me about a decision at the Massachusetts Institute of Technology to increase the weight given to verbal scores on the Scholastic Aptitude Test. That adjustment alone moved the proportion of women in the entering class upward by about 20 percent. It was, I should note, motivated less by the Institute's desire to diversify its student population than by the fact that computer science had been overwhelmed by student enrollments; women, however, seldom went into computer science, and so an increase in the female population served to relieve enrollment pressures without "lowering standards."

35. "Maintaining Quality in the 1990s: How Will We Pay?" *Educational Record* 72 (Spring 1991):17.

36. Both Kaplan and Arthur M. Hauptman, "Meeting the Challenge," note the danger to minority enrollments of the cuts they cite, but neither presents any concrete plan or, indeed, more than a vague hope that such cuts will not roll back previous gains (such as they have been).

37. As a leaflet issued by the Jobs With Justice Fair Trade Committee of Boston puts it, "Economists at Skidmore College and the University of Massachusetts have estimated that by the year 2000 investment in Mexico would reach over $50 billion costing the US more than 450,000 jobs and a 2.3% decline in wages."

38. Max Sawicky, "What's NEWP? A Guiding Theory of the New Right," *Social Policy* 22 (Winter 1992):9.

39. Ibid.

40. Dinesh D'Souza, *Illiberal Education* (New York: Free Press, 1991); Lynne V. Cheney, *Telling the Truth: A Report on the State of the Humanities in Higher Education* (Washington, D.C.: National Endowment for the Humanities, 1992).

41. John Taylor, "Are You Politically Correct?" *New York Magazine*, 21 January 1991, 32–40.

42. Stephan Thernstrom, "McCarthyism Then and Now," *Academic Questions*, Winter 1990–1991, 14–16.

43. "What Happened at Harvard," *The Nation* 253 (30 September 1991):384–388; reprinted in Patricia Aufderheide, ed., *Beyond PC: Toward a Politics of Understanding* (St. Paul: Graywolf Press, 1992), 97–106.

44. C. Vann Woodward, "Freedom and the Universities," in Aufderheide, *Beyond PC*, 43. To his credit, Woodward acknowledged and accepted some of the criticisms directed at him in *NYRB*'s letters column. But the Thernstrom case remains a source of conflict. I might add that I find it hard to understand why a teacher would not use student inquiries—or even complaints—about the content of his course as a basis for discussing and clarifying his objectives.

45. Karl Shapiro, "University," in *Collected Poems 1940–78* (New York: Random House, 1940), 10.

46. See a wonderful essay by William H. Epstein, "Counter-Intelligence: Cold-War Criticism and Eighteenth-Century Studies," *English Literary History* 57 (1990):63–99.

47. The most useful analysis of the economic relationships between national economic policies and the fiscal crisis of higher education is Ernst Benjamin, "Higher Education and the Fiscal Crisis: From Defense to Offense," *Footnotes* (AAUP) 13 (Fall 1992):4–5.

48. Alexander W. Astin, *What Matters in College?* (San Francisco: Jossey-Bass, 1992), 153–154.

14

English After the USSR

RICHARD OHMANN

As I HAVE WATCHED the geographical, economic, and ideological map of the world changing almost beyond recognition in recent years I have felt very much a spectator, yet of a drama that would surely involve me and you as at least bit players, one that would change the terms of our lives in general and our professional lives in particular. How? I had only the vaguest ideas. I needed to think about it, read, talk with others. An invitation to speak to Chicago-area English instructors and another to write for this volume gave me the chance I wanted. I gave my Chicago host a title that would make me face my confusion at its deepest level, "English After the USSR," and allowed myself a few weekends to consider the strange-sounding conjuncture. Here are the speculations that ensued, as amended by welcome advice from friends and editors.

To start with, what are some of the issues close to where we work—close to those committee meetings, stacks of papers, and other urgencies of life in English these days—that one might wish to grasp in relation to a large movement of history? I think of the questions and conflicts that surround our teaching of writing, from those about the nature and politics of literacy itself, including something called "cultural literacy," to the ever-increasing demand for vocationally useful writing, professional writing, business writing, technical writing, and so on. I think of the infusion of new technologies *into* writing, bringing as always utopian hopes and monstrous fears. At the border between our two professional territories, the guerrilla war between privileged literature and underprivileged composition simmers on, even while writing instruction makes stronger claims to professional standing. Meanwhile, the professional standing of both groups is under assault as budget cuts make the hiring of temporary and part-time workers seem imperative to administrations, creating a two-class divide between tenure-track

Reprinted by permission from *Radical Teacher* 44 (Winter 1993):41–46.

faculty and others, closely connected to the divide between comp and lit instructors, and as those budget cuts drive the workloads of many regular faculty members up to a level that calls into question the premise of a dual commitment to teaching and research and the more basic ideal of every profession: that it control the conditions of its own work. Finally, I'd name as another set of issues very much on our agenda in the field of English, partly because they are on some rather more influential agendas, those having to do with canons, with cultural authority, with the multiplicity of cultures and identities and entitlements in this society: in short, the debates that have burst into the public arena under the headings of multiculturalism and political correctness. These are questions that clamor for attention on the job and are thematized at conferences and in volumes like this one.

I seek paths of connectedness between them and the world-historical events toward which my title gestures, more than the disbanding of the Soviet Union, of course: the abandonment almost everywhere of the project that called itself socialism or communism; the tectonic-plate shifts in relations among capitalist societies; the proliferation of new nation-states even as many commentators are ready to declare the nation-state itself a vestigial remnant; and the emergence not of a new world order, I think, but of the conviction that some such order is slouching toward Bethlehem to be born.

I am looking, then, for ties between global dislocations and our local concerns in English. It may help to begin, however, by positioning our work in an intermediate sphere, that of *this* nation-state's recent history, making clear as I do so my commitment to the idea of hegemony as an instrument for thinking about domination and resistance. Though the concept of hegemony was developed within marxist thought, I think it has use for anyone who believes that some groups have relatively entrenched power and privilege in each society while others pursue their life chances in ways that challenge that power. A signal advantage of the idea is its use in understanding societies like ours in which inequality is not *primarily* maintained by naked force but rests on a measure of consent, with force in the background.

In a working hegemony, power filters through innumerable laws, institutions, daily practices, attitudes, and needs, so that except to those directly under the heel of the policeman it feels less like rule than like what Gramsci called common sense. It saturates experience, consciousness, and customary relations with other people to the extent that inequality and domination seem normal or invisible. In this process, education helps reproduce the inequities of the social order but does so in ways widely accepted as fair and natural. The ideology of equal opportunity and merit rewarded has been quite serviceable toward that end, through large parts of our history, obscuring the decisive advantages of family position and wealth, the differential access of young people to cultural capital and networks of privilege, the politics of tracking, and the operation of the hidden curriculum to discourage and derogate those not adapted by birth and rearing to the culture of school. When the system is working smoothly, not just its main beneficiaries but also its victims understand their life chances and trajectories as resulting from differences in individual ability, effort, choice, and luck.

No hegemony stays automatically in place or unproblematically retains its appearance as common sense. As Raymond Williams put it, "a lived hegemony ... has continually to be renewed, recreated, defended, and modified. It is also continually resisted, limited, altered, challenged by pressures not at all its own. ... At any time, forms of alternative or directly oppositional politics and culture exist as significant elements in the society."[1] Surely we are living in a time of strenuous effort to renew, re-create, defend, and modify the hegemony of dominant groups in the United States.

The reconstructive effort, including the PC campaign, seems to me to be overdetermined in obvious and less obvious ways. There is the long decline of American capitalism since the postwar boom began to taper off at the end of the 1960s while European and East Asian economies rapidly expanded (about which more later). Also, just when the economic system was reaching the limit of its ability to improve material life for each successive generation, 1960s political movements came along to demand more equal shares in the distribution of goods and in political power. Whatever the willingness of those in charge to respond to such demands, economic stagnation made it impossible to accommodate these new claimants, even to the extent that the white, male industrial workforce had been grudgingly accommodated during the 1940s and 1950s. But the new movements did establish the state as a place to contend over entitlements and fix the social categories—African Americans, women, Latinos, and so on—by whose fortunes the legitimacy of the social order would in part be measured; hence, for instance, the widespread perception of the Rodney King affair and the Los Angeles riots not as isolated outrages but as symptoms of profound social failure.

Sixties movements had also enabled that kind of perception through later decades by insisting that the Vietnam War, white supremacy, male domination, environmental damage, and so on, were expressions of systemic malaise rather than separate problems to be solved by liberal management. Comprehensive analyses—marxist, feminist, ecological—gained currency and remained available as challenges to mainstream common sense even through the right-wing resurgence of the 1980s. Needless to say, these strains of critical thought took root especially in universities. Among their targets were the educational system itself and the official knowledges it produced and purveyed. Taken together, challenges to the authority of high culture, to bourgeois political economy, to the exclusions and blind spots of traditional history, to Eurocentrism, to male and heterosexist assumptions in many disciplines, and to the power relations embedded in the educational institution and its pedagogies amounted to a running contest over cultural capital. Far from hegemonic even in universities (only about 5 percent of faculty members and 2 percent of students place themselves on the "far left"), these projects have at best constituted a weak counterhegemony.

One more point: as the contemporary university system took shape in the post-war period it became a much more critical site of social reproduction than before and a central locus too for the vastly expanded professional-managerial class whose activities mediate and shore up the system in innumerable ways. The 1960s showed that the loyalty of this class, especially of its youth, is far from secure, so the questions of who might function as organic intellectuals of the professional-managerial class and what forms its cultural capital might assume have taken on a good deal of political importance—the more so in a time when the place one may hope to attain in the social hierarchy depends more and more on access to education.

If you accept this highly abbreviated and mainly political history you will be no more surprised than I that those seeking to defend and re-create the domestic hegemony of our system and its elites have chosen to engage in battle over the content and practices of education, higher education in particular. Why that battle has taken such specific forms as the assault on "political correctness" and multiculturalism is not so obvious. In exploring this question, I want to begin stalking, from a distance, my announced prey, that which is named vaguely enough by the prepositional phrase "After the USSR" in my title. The devious pursuit will take me first, with dizzying simplification, back over the same twenty-five years of our history, this time tracing a path more economic than political.

It has been clear for quite a while that long before the Soviet empire began to quake its productive system had weakened and ossified and that American capitalism too had run into a difficult patch. The trouble began to show—it had of course been brewing for longer—about 1970. This was a time marked in memory for many of us as the year the academic job market collapsed. Less parochial changes were also under way. National unemployment has never again dropped to anywhere near the level of 1969 (below 4 percent) and has stayed instead within a couple of points of a rate about twice that. Real wages, which had risen steadily since 1940, stalled for a few years after 1970 and then declined about 10 percent—a dull number but one realized in the lives of millions in terms of second jobs, more spouses entering the job market, kids working more after school, families struggling to stay even, young people facing expectations lower than those of their parents. You or I could cite many other indices of the decline—they're in the news and on the lips of pundits and politicians. The balance of trade went negative in 1975 and has gotten much worse. The dollar faded against stronger currencies from the early 1970s on. The federal debt began its notorious rise in the late 1970s; so did personal debt, with corporate debt following a few years later. Profits as a portion of national income sagged after 1968. And so on. I hope it is clear from these dates that the trouble is not an artifact of the Reagan-Bush regime and that I am not here to celebrate the advent of the Clinton administration, which will have little impact on these epochal shifts (though I hope it will smooth out some of the harshness and injustice that became all-but-explicit policy over the previous twelve years).

Meanwhile, the nature of capitalism changed, and not just in the United States. This is a subtler transformation, not so easily captured in a few statistics, yet again everyone who reads at all about such matters knows it's happening. A variety of labels have gained currency to describe parts of it—globalization, finance capital, deindustrialization, the knowledge society, etc. One more that attempts to capture the change at a quite general level is richly analyzed in David Harvey's *The Condition of Postmodernity.* Harvey describes a "sea-change in cultural as well as in political-economic practices since around 1972," a change from what he calls "Fordism" (which I don't think I need describe) to a regime of "flexible accumulation":

> It rests on flexibility with respect to labor processes, labor markets, products, and patterns of consumption. It is characterized by the emergence of entirely new sectors of production, new ways of providing financial services, new markets, and, above all, greatly intensified rates of commercial, technological, and organizational innovation. It has entrained rapid shifts in the patterning of uneven development, both between sectors and between geographical regions, giving rise, for example, to a vast surge in so-called "service sector" employment as well as to entirely new industrial ensembles in hitherto underdeveloped regions (such as the "Third Italy," Flanders, the various silicon valleys and glens, to say nothing of the vast profusion of activities in newly industrializing countries).[2]

We have all experienced the instability and excesses of this casino capitalism—the painful dislocation of the old industrial base, especially in the Northeast and Midwest; the torrent of financial and industrial bankruptcies; the merger frenzy of the 1980s; the 1987 crash and subsequent boom; the internationalization of production, so that even when one wants to "buy American" it's hard to know how; the evolution of a world financial system so intricate that almost nobody can understand it. Again, although we associate many of these upheavals with the Reagan-Bush years, they began well before then and extend far beyond the borders of the United States: one could plausibly see deregulation, for instance, as a *response* to them rather than as their cause.

Furthermore, at least from some stratospheric height where human lives look small, these shifts might even be a *successful* adjustment of the system, a tremendous reinvigoration of capitalism's old project of accumulation. They have certainly thrown the old, popular, labor-based opposition a curve ball in the First World. And I would even suggest that flexible accumulation, as much as Cold War fatigue and political tyranny, helped scuttle the Soviet Union and most of the other "actually existing socialisms," stuck as they were in a stale, rigidly enforced Fordism and unable to compete in a new game whose rules were drawn up elsewhere.

Be that as it may, it is not possible to think clearly about any part of our working lives without seeing them in the context of historical shifts in the world's productive system. And although from here on my ruminations will finally draw closer to their quarry, I want to insist that the demise of the Second World affects our professional lives not as an independent line of causation but as an *additional* force, closely related to changes in world capitalism.

The first of six conjectures I will now venture about English after the USSR is that the events of the last few years in Central and Eastern Europe, Asia, and some other parts of the world that were within the Soviet sphere will feed into, and further, changes already under way in the national and international division of labor. Employers of all sorts have long been responding to increasingly worldwide competition, the weakening of unions, and the dispersed pools of cheap and surplus labor by moving production to wherever capital has the greatest advantage over labor and by breaking up the rigidity of Fordist work regimes. Flex-time, part-time, and temporary labor, subcontracting and outsourcing, job sharing, homework, and piecework, workfare and prison labor and other practices have eroded the old core labor market of full-time, long-term employees and surrounded it with a huge global penumbra of marginal, now-and-then labor. Part of this is no news to those of us teaching English in the United States. More than people in other academic fields, we know firsthand the use of flexible labor—adjuncts, part-timers, moonlighters, and an army of graduate students paid at a national average of around $1,700 per course, usually with no benefits. To look at this from another angle, in the mid-1960s over 90 percent of new humanities Ph.D.s had full-time tenure-track appointments; in recent years the figure has hovered around 40 percent. English has served, it would almost seem, as a small laboratory for innovative uses of flexible labor. Within universities, we stand as a microcosm of the shrinking labor market core and the expanding periphery.

But this is not the full extent of the change. Education is itself, more and more, an internationally circulating commodity. As Nancy Folbre points out, when Texas Instruments hires fifty programmers in Bangalore or Saztec International (a Kansas data-processing company) has most of its work done in the Philippines, they are taking advantage not just of low-wage technical workers abroad but of cheaper *teachers* and cheaper *education* there.[3] (Also, the dual labor market in this country has always been divided in part racially; now the global division of labor reproduces the color line and, of course, the feminization of cheap, peripheral, flexible labor.)

I suggest that the absorption of the USSR, Central and Eastern Europe, more gradually China, and smaller pockets of so-called socialism (is Cuba next?) into world capitalism will greatly enlarge the labor periphery, opening up the possibility of new *maquiladora* schemes almost everywhere and making it less and less urgent from the corporate point of view to improve American education unless political pressure weighs in heavily on the other side.

Two last implications of this conjecture: Obviously, these developments put professions under stress. It's not just a matter of a two-class system, though one can see that widening fault even in strong professions such as law (paralegals, legal secretaries) and medicine (proliferation of low-paid workers around doctors). In English, core professionals themselves find their work more and more driven by imperatives of higher productivity. In every department I've visited recently the full-time people, the *tenured* people, are working harder and having more trouble setting their own professional standards than a decade ago. And finally: in the regime of flexible accumulation knowledge is perhaps the most valuable commodity of all, and its rapid development and circulation are crucial. Universities are increasingly drawn into this regime in ways that reduce their autonomy. They become in effect subcontractors. (The University of California at Berkeley now receives only 15 percent of its funding from the state.)[4] We might wonder how this will affect English, which from the corporate outside looks more and more like an adjunct to the circulation of knowledge, and one among others that may well be cheaper, in the United States and abroad.

To reiterate: across a range of interlinked changes such as these, in the international division of labor, the disappearance of the USSR and other communist regimes is not a fresh cause but may have an accelerator effect on processes already under way. I've spent a long time working toward this first conjecture about English and world events because I felt it necessary to chart the fall of actually existing socialism in tandem with a movement of global and American capitalism. I can be briefer about the other five points. The next one is the most evident. It's that the end of the Cold War itself changes everything in this country. Most of the talk about this has been happy talk—the liberation of peoples, the release from fear of nuclear war, the peace dividend—and I do not want to spoil anyone's day by cynically refusing the grounds for hope. But I do want to flag some questions about the peace dividend and its potential for diverting money to education, thus improving our circumstances in English. I wonder. For decades the peacetime military, the Cold War military, has not just been a *drain* on the economy: it has been a site of knowledge production, an alternative educational system, and a place where very many young people have jobs who otherwise might join the reserve army of the unemployed. The expanding proportion of young people in universities and the lengthening of their stay have served the same purpose and helped adjust the labor market to the boom-and-bust cycle. Were the army and other forces to spill a million or so people back into the private economy, along with those laid off from military production, would the colleges be able to absorb the surplus? And, since the enlargement of the college population, along with the deskilling and exportation of work, has already made for a lot of overtraining and overcredentialing, I wonder how the awkward fit between college education and the job market might be worsened by an additional flow of young people into our institutions. Will we become, even more than now, a machine for sorting out those who will ride the high wave of flexcap into glitzy careers from those relegated to dead-end, insecure jobs in its trough?

Whatever the answers to these questions—and clearly they depend not just on grim economic law but on the politics and movements that will take shape in the near future—one thing is clear: the taxpayer revolts that dotted our landscape in the 1980s and gathered into a national strategy of the Republican Party have set in place a massive reluctance to pay for education and widened the "savage inequalities" of Jonathan Kozol's recent book.[5] Now, the old Sputnik rationale for strengthening American education is gone with the Cold War. Gone, too, is the Cold War rationale for deficit spending, as we heard quite explicitly in the 1992 political campaign. A Ross Perot commercial said, "The enemy is not the red flag of communism but the red ink of the national debt," and the other candidates gave at least lip service to that principle. If anything like the sacrifice that Perot and many businessmen call for in the interest of debt reduction should come about, it's hard to see how funding for the work we do can remain at even its present level.

Yet at the same time, a different rationale for policy comes forward with the fall of the Soviet Union, filling up space occupied by the old one but doing so with needs and ideas that will not play out in the same way at all. Our competition now is not the Soviet behemoth but resurgent Europe, invincible Japan, the Asian gang of four, soon China; and the competition is not military but quintessentially economic. The very national interest has been purified, distilled to its innocent 1920s form: the business of America is business. And that's the premise of my third conjecture about English after the USSR. To be sure, perils to the national interest remain here and there around the globe, and we can expect clean little wars now and then to fight tyranny, restore democracy, *and* defend oil or the like. But mainly the national interest will be spelled out in terms of productivity, competitiveness, efficiency, technological development, and so on.

Where will English be borne by such imperatives? I can hardly guess; I'd be grateful for a conference on the question, where I could hear smart people work through its labyrinthine paths. But for starters I will throw out a fact and a couple of leads. The fact: in the legislative and political arenas, the economic rationale for education reigns almost without challenge. Already in 1989, the education president stated just four goals for his education bill: sustained economic growth, enhanced competitive position in world markets, increased productivity, and higher incomes for everyone. That's it. I don't think that the Democrats' understanding of education's task is much different; nor in fact is that of Albert Shanker. We are talking here not about citizenship in a democracy or about timeless values (though a Lynne Cheney may do so in other venues but about economic measures of success. How does English contribute?

One lead begins with an observation of Evan Watkins in his book on English departments, *Work Time.*[6] He suggests that the abstract form of labor in our field, for students and instructors, is this: "A accomplishes a task of speaking or writing; B evaluates the performance of that task; and C reports the evaluation to A and/or C." He has in mind work in literature, but the formula generalizes pretty well to cover work in composition. "A" may be living or dead, a student or a major author; "B" may be a student or an instructor; "C" may be an instructor or the readership of a journal. The point of looking at our labor in this abstract form is to see how much of what we all perform is a traffic in evaluations. Why? What use is that? I'll compress Watkins's subtle argument almost to the vanishing point by saying that the traffic in evaluations has much to do with the sorting out of young people into various career paths, with the attribution of merit, with a democracy's need to locate and justify social authority anew in each generation, or, if you like, with making inequality seem fair.

That need will persist and intensify, I believe, but what's interesting is that it can be met by widely shifting practices of *concrete* labor, including shifts back and forth between the uneasy cohabiters of English, comp and lit. From the perspective of abstract labor and its uses to the economic system, it doesn't matter whether we spend most of our collective time commenting on themes or writing articles on Kate Chopin; whether our students write seminar papers on Milton or computer-scored tests on usage. This means that the flow of concrete labor is free to respond to whatever specific needs and pressures are out there, insofar as English meets specific needs at all. And of course some of it does. Businesses and bureaucracies want some employees with writing skills. The post–Cold War identification of national interest with business interest should give more force to that need. I imagine that composition will continue to grow in relation to literature as a portion of our work, a process aided by its moderately successful professionalization during the past two decades. But not just composition in a general way: I would expect our concrete labor to slide toward recognizably practical, vocational kinds of writing instruction, as it has been doing: witness the sharp increase of courses and programs in technical, business, and professional writing that I mentioned in my initial list of things to be explained. Some of the work we do is already, in effect, subcontracting for business, and it is altogether compatible with our work in class reproduction.

But that is not enough. We don't do enough for accumulation—for profits—that business is willing to consign to us, or to education in general, the task of matching knowledge and skills up to the job system, and this is the second of my two leads. Business is giving less to public education. It is doing more education internally ($50 million a year at Ford, $30 million at GM, and so on and on). Why not? If the only interest is competition in the new regime of flexcap, why not educate just the workers you need in just the ways you need? Why pay for literature and philosophy? If South Carolina can attract a new BMW plant partly by offering to supply the company with pretrained workers, isn't such an expenditure of state funds more obviously beneficial than increasing support for the state university system?

Privatization moves on quickly in another way, too. We have all been hearing about Whittle Communications and its Channel 1—required viewing, commercials and all, for about 8 million students. Now comes Whittle's Edison Project, backed mainly by Time Warner and a British media firm and headed by former Yale president Benno Schmidt, planning as many as a thousand for-profit schools within a decade.[7] Should the voucher system become a reality, of course, it would open wide the education market to private investment and flexible accumulation. I'm not sure what the place of English might be in this new environment.

My final conjectures have more to do with ideology than with hard economics; I can be both vague and brisk. The fourth conjecture is that with the fall of the Soviet Union the framework of old global politics collapses, and the durable structure of domestic ideology too. Of what use now in galvanizing political emotion is the anticommunism that was the air we breathed for forty years and more? With domestic dissidence pried loose from any illusion of links to the evil empire as it has long been detached in fact, the task of maintaining hegemony in the United States must find a new basis, a new organizing principle. This is a murky and fluid time on the ideological front, but it seems that a broad strategy is gathering force. With internal challenges to domination and privilege no longer graspable as tentacles of communist subversion, the Right and many others turn to an assault on social movements that have in fact grown more and more separate since 1970, when *the* movement began to lose what coherence it had and many of its constituent groups veered toward identity politics and even a politics of lifestyle. The Right has picked up on that change in the forms of dissidence and has mounted one assault after another on entitlements won in the 1960s and 1970s: on affirmative action, women's rights, gay rights, children's rights, workers' rights. On the ideological front this strategy materialized just after world socialism began to crumble in a coordinated attack on multiculturalism and political correctness, specifically targeting colleges and universities and with the crosshairs right on English. I need hardly tell you what bearing this strategy has on issues in our field—on two decades of rethinking canons and cultural authority, on the retrieval of lost texts and forgotten experiences, on the slow and painful effort to dismantle the white, male, heterosexual, upper-middle-class "we" that once put itself forward as universal. "Universities have become saturated with politics," says Benno Schmidt. Lynne Cheney picks up the assertion on the first page of her newest National Endowment for the Humanities report, *Telling the Truth,*[8] and makes it her theme. She attempts to put politics to bed, not counterpose a politics of democratic capitalism to a communist challenge. The Soviet Union merits just one mention in her booklet, as an example of the impoverished life that results from "suppressing thought." Meanwhile, the fundamentalist Right subsumes an older, class-based politics in the crusade for "family values," attacking much the same groups as Cheney but from another flank.

My fifth conjecture is that in spite of the forces arrayed against identity politics, issues of racial and ethnic and sexual identity will continue to sit high on our agenda in English and that the fall of the Soviet Union will make them more heated and volatile. We see in the Balkans, in Central Europe, and in the republics of the former USSR an eruption of ethnic hostilities and national claims unmatched since at least the midnineteenth century; they find parallels in similar divisions from India to South Africa, from Spain to Britain to Canada. Nationalism seems now *the* privileged mode of resistance to domination, even as established nation-states lose their autonomy. The great movements of people across national boundaries, following the imperatives of the flexible labor market, are augmented by movements of refugees. The United States is more a nation of immigrants now than at any time since the immigration law of 1924 shut down earlier migrations. New ethnicities gather; some old ones regroup as their homeland counterparts struggle for nationhood (Ukrainian, Croat, Serb, Lithuanian). Black Americans and other groups seen as *racially* different continue to face repression, discrimination, and the hard choice whether to resist in separatist or in integrationist terms. Gay and lesbian people are finding more of a voice and forming more of a movement: queer politics, Queer Nation, and queer studies gain strength. Asian American Studies appear alongside African American Studies, Chicano Studies, Women's Studies. All these movements overlap with and infiltrate English. Multiculturalism will be with us for some time, its forms changed in ways I can't predict by ethnic wars in the old so-called socialist sphere.

My sixth and last point hardly deserves to be called a conjecture. It's more a series of questions arising from the stunning collapse of the socialist project. To speak a little more personally than I've done so far, people like me in the socialist feminist Left, formed politically in sixties and seventies movements, never had much use for the dreary regimes that ruled the earth from East Berlin to Vladivostok. For us, whatever historical allowances we made, these were deformed alternatives, betrayals or failures of an idea, false utopias. Many of us were saying, from 1989 to 1991, "Good riddance, and hooray for the peoples of that huge region: now maybe we can start afresh to imagine a democratic successor to undemocratic world capitalism, freed up at last from stifling ideas like the dictatorship of the proletariat and the vanguard party." But what will the world be like without any living alternative to capitalism? What can serve as a focus of hope in Latin America if Cuba goes the way of Nicaragua? What can the idea of socialism amount to if nobody is trying to enact it? How can our students imagine any historical narrative that could take us out of the present world crisis if they, like President Bush (in one of the 1992 campaign's debates), encode the events of the past few years as the triumph of freedom and democracy? Now that freedom and democracy have won, why is there all that killing and oppression and greed in the newly free regions? Why are hundreds of millions dying of disease and starvation in the free world? What does this victory mean in our own troubled country? Are we to live happily ever after in consumer heaven, no longer bothered with the nuisance of politics and citizenship? What about the half of our people not invited to the victory bash? What ways do our students have to think their own future, apart from the giddy logic of flexible accumulation, which nobody can understand? If our society and our world need some new social form, how can we imagine it in the cold light of a victory that has left us with no visible other to ourselves?

People my age have taught for forty years within the ideological envelope of the Cold War, for reasons that are, for English, surprisingly specific.[9] I believe the Cold War has confined our thinking and that of our students, our sense of the culture we wish to pass on and criticize, our pedagogies and our hopes for our students, our sense of the possibilities of English, within limits so natural, so tacit, so invisible that it will take us years to figure out what they were and to get new bearings. It's a worthwhile task. The world will be very different when our students are middle-aged, but the course of its change will not follow the master narrative of old marxism *or* the Cold War narrative of democracy victorious in an epic battle against communism. If we and our students are to be agents rather than dupes in the process, we'll need to invent a new narrative. English, where we at least talk about empowerment and imagination, would seem a natural place for the utopian impulse to range; but if the conjectures explored in this essay turn out to be even partly right there will also be much to check the utopian spirit.

NOTES

1. Raymond Williams, *Marxism and Literature* (Oxford: Oxford University Press, 1977), 112–113.

2. David Harvey, *The Conditions of Postmodernity: An Enquiry into the Origins of Cultural Change* (Cambridge: Basil Blackwell, 1989), 147.

3. Nancy Folbre, "The Bottom Line: Business to the Rescue?" *The Nation* (September 1992), 281–282.

4. Kit Lively, "California Colleges Worry About How to Live with Deep State Cuts," *Chronicle of Higher Education*, 9 September 1992, A25.

5. Jonathan Kozol, *Savage Inequalities: Children in America's Schools* (New York: Crown, 1991).

6. Evan Watkins, *Work Time: English Departments and the Circulation of Cultural Value* (Stanford: Stanford University Press, 1989), 83.

7. Jonathan Kozol, "Whittle and the Privateers: Corporate Raid on Education," *The Nation* (21 September 1992), 274.

8. Lynne V. Cheney, *Telling the Truth: A Report on the State of the Humanities in Higher Education* (Washington, D.C.: National Endowment for the Humanities, 1992).

9. William H. Epstein, "Counter-Intelligence: Cold-War Criticism and Eighteenth-Century Studies," *English Literary History* 57 (1990):63–99.

15

The Politics of Political Correctness

NINETIES POLITICS began with the PC wars. The claim may seem surprising. After all, despite some heavy bystander involvement as the result of an insistent media hype and some really cynical political manipulation, at bottom the battles over "political correctness" hardly extended beyond some low-circulation opinion rags, some middle-brow talk shows, and some melodramatic skirmishes within the academy. Nonetheless, I want to suggest how this controversy has been important and speculate about what can be detected in it concerning the state of our political culture.

First, an overarching point: At this time in our history, the values in controversy in the argument over PC can be understood as a diminutive model, a somewhat risible microcosm, of much more consequential conflicts unresolved in our society. What is important about all of these battles is their intractability. They cannot be reconciled or harmonized. There's *no* right position—not only about political correctness but about any number of more consequential or infrastructural disputes—waiting to be discovered over the horizon of some cultural, political, or social epiphany. On the contrary, the conflicts behind the arguments that stress our polity are real. This reality of unresolved—perhaps unresolvable—conflict, in turn, has important implications for any progressive or liberationist politics in the contemporary period.

Liberal ideology often suggests that disagreement reflects misunderstanding. It supposes that political problems can be settled with better information, improved logic, or greater goodwill. In the case of real social conflict I think that's largely wrong. In such situations, what can progressive intellectuals do? Constantly, we emphasize the vitality of difference. But this ratification of diversity has important implications for our politics. We ought never to underestimate the *difference* that difference makes in determining the forms and contents of political life. An entire apparatus inherited from the tradition of an older politics—the *party*, the *analysis*, the *struggle*, most of all the *victory* ultimately to be won—mystifies our contemporary situation by the persistence of the singularities it projects. Such singularities transgress the fundamental condition of politics today. Contemporary politics is constituted in the realization that there is not just "one" of *anything* in the social world today.

What, then, can we do? To begin with, one important job would be to help to generate an analytical structure that moves us past the angry multivalence of contemporary conflict, past the frozen iteration of dispute. We need to progress toward places where some elements of discourse common to the diverse sides of any argument enable us to clarify its sources, the theories sustaining each position, and the resistances on each side to credit or even hear the others' claims to begin with. Today whole classes of conflict concerning fundamental political choices or social values are largely sterile. If we're going to have conflict, we need at least to seek to make it intellectually and politically productive. But beyond such a deck-clearing operation, how can we conceive politics today?

I want to identify three principles that bear upon an analysis of political and cultural conflict in contemporary society. These might help to frame the issues in the PC wars, which were larger than the parochial issues that framed explicit debate. The first principle I want to offer toward a rethinking of this situation relates to the impulse within living systems to value homeostasis and stability. Stability, homeostasis, constancy of the environment put less wear and tear on organisms than change does. It takes a lot of psychological and physiological work to deal with newness. It takes a lot of time and effort to adapt to change. There are powerful implications in this principle for any political process. Of course, this doesn't mean that we should simply submit to homeostasis and save ourselves the trouble of change. Psychological and physiological costs are worth paying as we seek to make the world a more libertarian and egalitarian place. But it will never do to think that such changes have no cost. Change stresses us. New ideas don't just comfortably slip into people's heads in the place of old ones. If we push for change, we can expect that conflict and resistance will result.

Culture is itself a reflection of this fact. Overall we could think of cultures as fundamentally conservative *memory systems*.[1] Cultures are designed to keep things in place. They train bodies how to act in the kinds of situations societies put people in. They discipline thought and language—indeed, they give people language to begin with without their having the slightest say in the matter. By their nature the memory systems that we call "culture" are normed by constancy. They suppose stability, and they exist to reproduce it.

The PC wars—particularly their avatar as media blitz—happened because when some people (however cynically) claimed that the world was turning upside down, many others heard them against the background of their own uneasy experience of change, displacement, and instability. Some people's worlds really did seem to them to be turning upside down. Who was having these perceptions? What determines the degree to which an individual or group feels the pressure of change? Probably the principal factor is the subject's position of domination or subjection within the social formation.

Dominant groups have the privilege of "managing" the way change affects them more comfortably than subordinated groups can. Usually change is something dominant groups themselves decree in response to their own perceived self-interest. And even when this is not so, dominant groups have generally had resources to blunt the effects of change, reserves (whether of economic or of symbolic capital) by which the pressures of the new could be moderated. So, despite the acceleration of change and of stress since the twin revolutions of the nineteenth century, for dominant groups culture has often provided the comfort of familiarity, manageability, and affirmation. I want to call this image *culture as comfort*. I argued that culture carries a homeostatic default assumption. In turn, the notion of culture as comfort internalizes such projections of stability as a *right*. The notion of right makes clear the political resonances in this situation. My first principle thus combines the predilection of culture for homeostasis with the political judgment that, because of their culture-determining power, dominant groups like the American Right since the early 1970s have considerably less tolerance for disruptive change, with interruption of the comfort of homeostasis, than do other social strata.

My second framing assumption is that since the nineteenth century, in contrast to the homeostatic image of culture as comfort, culture has rather been what elsewhere I have called a *field of struggle*.[2] Once the feudal empires of Europe broke up in the progressive capitalization and democratization of life, then "the war of everyone against everyone"[3] became the image of social existence itself. The principle of homeostasis, of culture as comfort, projects the experience of security. But the principle of culture as a struggle in which my interests and my person are at risk projects a diametrically contradictory image. The important point here is that both of these images are true. Their conflict is the inevitable consequence of the conditions of modern life as they have played themselves out in our attempt to achieve the democratizing ideals of the late eighteenth century, most recently as we have tried to assimilate such society-altering practices as multiculturalism, gender neutrality, and authentic egalitarianism. The fight over PC is more serious than many of us have been willing to recognize because it plays out deep impulses and dynamics in our existence.

The two principles that I have referred to collide head-on. Culture as homeostasis and culture as struggle define a powerful contradiction. How can both be right? The answer is at the heart of my analysis here. In the contemporary world, social reality is complex in ways that may be unprecedented. I don't just mean that our world is complicated in the manner, say, of a computer program, however long and intricate it may be. A software program may take years to write and days or weeks to learn to use, but ultimately its reality is that (as we say) it "computes": it functions, it makes sense. The aspect of our social reality that I want to point to here is different. That reality often *doesn't* compute. The different parts of the social order don't seem to order themselves coherently any longer. They rather work at cross-purposes, against each other. To put this in an older philosophical language, the antagonisms in modern society, the desires, interests, and needs of different individuals and groups, seemingly cannot be totalized. We talk of society as a "whole," but in this sense it hardly seems like one. So we live in an experience of contradiction and conflict that is not just apparent but as real as things ever become in social and political existence.

The intensity of this situation has become essential to our society's self-conception in a way that may be new. What accounts for it? There seem to be two principal determinants: (1) the insistence upon recognition and liberation on the part of social groups not only previously subordinated but formerly powerless to alter that state of subordination: real difference is active within contemporary politics in ways that seem systematically unprecedented; and (2) a global and national situation that has eroded our belief that the United States will always have enough savvy and enough resources to solve any problem it sets itself.

The political implications of what I'm terming the complexity of contemporary reality are considerable. The situation means that people of goodwill cannot just assume that if they sit down and reason together, they'll come up with a fix for whatever has brought them into discord. That Enlightenment ideal no longer seems to capture the intractability of contemporary problems. If we take the egalitarian, democratic impulses that have underlain our culture seriously—or even if we just take the demography seriously—it seems there can be no single overall "truth" for our society, for the whole of American culture. And if there's no one right answer, the question of how our society can organize its affairs, distribute its resources, and resolve its conflicts become acute.[4]

If we really are different from one another, if there is no one truth that can hold for all the diverse segments of our society, if our culture really is a site of struggle because no hegemonic view of what ought to be believed or done in social or political situations is shared by the quasi-totality of citizens, then any singular, official, establishment, or obligatory view of things becomes suspect. It can only have been imposed by authority. And that will be true both of the use of official authority (whether of the state or the university) to impose an orthodoxy upon a diverse population and of unofficial efforts to declare a singular view of language or social reality alone acceptable.

We have to distinguish between two issues that were foregrounded in the PC wars and circulated rather thoughtlessly through them: the self-censorship that can occur through a lack of courage to confront divergent opinion and the external censorship imposed by constituted power. These two varieties of inhibition of speech are distinctly different. Is "social pressure" coercive? Obviously: it unquestionably changes behavior, as everything from daily experience to the notorious Milgram experiments demonstrates.[5] Indeed, that is how culture itself works: by socializing those subjected to it to constituted forms of thought and behavior. All groups evolve norms about behavior, language, and ideology. We *always* feel a

RICHARD TERDIMAN

pressure to refrain from expressing ourselves because of opposition or divergence. To think otherwise is a particularly blithe form of Idealism—the notion that ideas (because they are impalpable) have no material force. But they do have force, and inevitably they are exposed to the material force of other ideas. The notion that we have a right to be protected from them—which really means protected from our existence as political beings—is a particularly pure and opaque form of Rousseauist fantasy.

The pressure of other people's ideas and interests is what politics is about. So we could hardly think that such pressure is actionable in itself or automatically requires redress. If we celebrate difference we need to integrate what it means for the conduct of social life. In particular, the presence of pressure or coercion cannot trigger legal protection or ethical protest by itself—or else we would arrest elementary school teachers who make their pupils learn the multiplication tables.[6] Power, as Michel Foucault constantly reminded us, is everywhere, and power is not simply malign. It is integral to society. We have to test its exercise against another standard. The fact that power was deployed, even that anxiety was experienced, is not sufficient to draw any conclusions whatever about the agent of the coercion or the remedy that ought to be offered to its victim. Indeed, what this argument most essentially asserts is that the category of "victim" is fundamentally diverse and can't be assessed on purely subjective grounds. The question then becomes *What sorts of victimization deserve redress?*

This question leads to my third framing principle, by now a familiar one in social analysis: that the deployment of power always occurs within a frame of hierarchy, of greater and lesser domination of the social space and the interactions that occur within it. The principle of hierarchy is crucial for understanding the struggles that stress contemporary society—particularly because the fragmentation of our social environment makes the privileging of any specific set of values problematic in principle.[7] What we can do is assess to what degree the deployment of power in a given situation threatens to *suppress* social or cultural values simply as an effect of power itself. There seems little doubt that progressives of whatever diverse individual persuasion ought still to unite in resisting that sort of subjugation.

In our society dissident voices from diverse loci have been making themselves heard—the more effectively because of the degree to which, after years of intolerance and discrimination, a long series of struggles has begun to legitimize the idea that people ought to be treated equally and respectfully. To be sure, whole segments of the American Right have never really embraced egalitarianism, and they are not comfortable with it now. Fold in the explosive issue of sexuality as recent progressive struggles have done, and all sorts of primitive resistances are stirred in the dominant culture. Then there's the factor of what Daphne Patai has termed "surplus visibility." When groups who have been silenced begin to speak, to make demands, the contrast makes their voices appear too loud to those in dominance and comfortable with homeostasis.[8] Finally, as progressives must acknowledge with whatever chagrin or distress, in the late eighties and early nineties the dissident voices being heard have been expressing themselves against a background of as great a silence on the left as we have seen since the paralysis of the 1950s.

Yet beneath such inertia on the left, American society has been changing in profound ways. If my analysis of the fundamental complexity of American life has any truth to it, then the sorts of arguments the Right has made against PC—tending to close down the possibilities of multiple discourses within the society and substitute forms of traditionally authoritative speech and conduct—were *singularly* inappropriate to the new situation we find ourselves in. The one thing you *wouldn't* expect to do in the multicultural, multiracial, plurigendered society that is building itself before our eyes is to impose *any* one way of doing, or thinking, or understanding anything.

Let me turn now to the Left. I've implied that the PC wars—however mock-epic they seem today—might best be seen not as a pitched battle or a war in place between a static Right and Left but rather as a symptom of the turmoil accompanying the migration of a whole society from one self-conception to another. There was as much confusion as settled ideological conflict determining the arguments and the tactics that characterized this bizarre fracas. One thing that has been particularly strange is how much of the conflict about PC has played out in the realm of language. Usually real social conflict has been a struggle over more infrastructural issues and interests. How can we understand a battle like the PC wars that turned in large part around what you ought to call people?

The PC wars have been fought in the realm of symbols because our cultural discourses and practices aren't yet at the point of foregrounding the substance behind much of this conflict. We're only beginning to register the demographic, economic, legal, and cultural changes that form the background to what we're trying to make sense of today. Consequently we fight about symbols. The reason we have expended such energy in terminological skirmishes is that we haven't yet brought the underlying reality of our conflict into focus. Our society is trying to learn how to deal differently with *difference,* but that effort isn't just about symbols or terminology or language. It's about reframing an entire structure of values and their interaction, a whole way of defining ourselves and our conception of our reality as a society. When that all becomes clearer with the passage of time and the clarification of the real struggle, then much of the terminological fracas that so amused the public will take on its proper proportions as an early sign of an epochal articulation in social change.

With regard to the Left, we need to be frank in our self-assessment. Nothing at this time of transition and confusion is clearer than that analysis of our own place, our own role, and our own relation to the social forces and dynamics that make up the politics in our country must be hardheadedly objective. The old politics doesn't seem self-evident any more. Where is the new politics to come from?

I think that for quite objective reasons we don't and we can't yet have a positive answer to that question. We ought not to conjure one up before the conditions of its emergence and the infrastructure to support it really exist. What we probably need to do is rather to pursue an activity that is one of the most powerful dynamics we have inherited from a long progressive tradition and one whose pertinence I believe can still—can in these unsettled times especially—be counted upon: *critique*. Our politics today can't yet project the positive shape of a new society, the modalities of transformed social relations. We need rather to ground our practice of politics now in our capacity and our activity as critics.

Consequently I want to criticize the Left—from a position of sympathy and participation but also from one of a new skepticism or uncertainty. This attitude arises in the very impropriety of the designation I've been using to this point— "the Left"—to characterize a diverse and dispersed cluster of movements now hardly less variegated or internally conflicted than contemporary politics overall.

I want, then, to argue that (to the extent that you can talk about sides at all) the sides in the PC wars were characterized by an uncanny and unrecognized mirroring. Earlier I suggested that dominant social groups have tended to conceive "culture" in terms of their own experience of domination: as a reassuring structure within which they expected to continue to enjoy the same comfort that their hegemony has traditionally procured for them. We know the historical costs of such a projection. The image of the individual defined by the "Western tradition" to which the Right appealed in the PC wars was stabilized over a long conflictual history of class and gender oppression in the United States, and it has solidified during the past two decades of conservative domination. It is an image of *privilege*. What is the character of the privilege it embodies? Principally, I think, it is the privilege of all dominant ideology, the capacity for automatic and unreflective legitimation, for being unaware of the contingency of your claims.

But in the contemporary world, and in the wake of the PC wars, what's striking in such a projection of dominant ideology is how fragile it seems behind its bravado. It appears that as soon as you call it into question, it panics and bursts into a flurry of defensive fire. That rigidity hardly seems to translate confidence that in a political or social struggle such an ideology can self-assuredly sustain its claims. In its fundamental practice, dominant ideology fears politics—fears the conflict of ideas and interests that make politics to begin with. Such a vision of politics as conflict is all the more pertinent to our sense of society today because our growing multiplicity and heterogeneity have made it difficult to credit the claim of any group to have the right to dominate the social whole.

What made people laugh about PC, the strain of conduct on the left that the Right found it so easy to satirize, can be interpreted as a peculiar and inadvertent mirror image of the narrow rigidity of dominant ideology itself. In making fun of PC, the ruling class was stigmatizing a version of its own self-conception and its own rhetoric. Progressives dreamed of being comfortable too. But in framing its own politics, the Left made a fundamental mistake. It rightly sought to integrate into the structures of the society it projected the extraordinary and heady diversity we're discovering in ourselves as a multicultural nation. But paradoxically the Left put such a perception into practice in the form of its own bristling dogmatism and rigidity—precisely the characteristics of the static, self-satisfied traditional view of U.S. society that they were so rightly contesting on another level. Let me test this paradoxical perception in the following way.

If we project the image of the individual, of the self, that we might derive from the social groups that were satirized by the Right for their enforcement of political correctness, what do we come up with? In the face of the structure of intolerance that the Left has correctly perceived and has been seeking to make our entire society confront, the tactical fragment that became the protagonists of political correctness as it was defined by the Right theorized *not* a politics that opened up a broad social debate about difference but a program to purify rhetoric and language. This rhetoric and the behaviors that were prescribed along with them *presumed* the realization of an egalitarian society before the social toleration of diversity had even been broadly argued about to begin with. In politics, timing is everything. Bad timing, bad tactics. Many would argue that on this score alone, the campaign for PC did harm to its own cause.

It's been widely observed that the PC "language police" never had much support among thoughtful progressives. But despite the manipulated character of the charge by the Right, anyone who's been in the academy in the recent past knows that a rigidifying orthodoxy—of opinion, of language, even in some places of diet and personal hygiene—has taken form and continues to exercise influence.[9] What's wrong with that? The claim I want to make is that—to the extent such an orthodoxy really is acted upon by us in the academy and is not simply a red herring thrown at us by the Right—such a stance is both tactically and strategically a serious mistake. It projects not a vigorous openness to the intellectual and ideological struggle by which social change can occur but rather a stop-in-your-tracks foreclosure of conflict that assumes precisely what has still painfully to be realized by long political work. Hence it forestalls the realization by arresting the very process of contestation and discussion by which such realization could occur.

Of course, progressives were correct in identifying the egalitarian and liberationist objectives to be achieved. The social background of this effort is clear and incontestable. Everywhere, in the form of prejudice and bias, narrow-mindedness, and discrimination, they rightly saw a society in which a dense texture of social abasement was being lived out by minority people and people whose culture diverged from dominant norms. Such people regularly confronted threats to their self-esteem and their dignity. *This* is real. The Left has correctly perceived how far our society still has to go to achieve tolerance of difference.

Conversely, dominant groups have internalized an image of their place and privilege that induces them to ward off any questioning of their claims. Such ideological confrontation would immediately explode the assumptions that are the condition of possibility of domination to begin with. But marginalized groups cannot assume such a privilege, however tempting it might be to imagine that they could suddenly arrogate to themselves the structure of automatic validation and transparent self-evidence that dominant groups have only been able to achieve after centuries of often brutal struggle and repression of their opponents. Women, gays, blacks, and other groups are demanding for their own lives and experiences the degree of validation, of "comfort," that dominant groups have had. That desire is laudable and comprehensible. But it misses a crucial point. The self-assurance of domination was *always* fraudulent. It was always bought at the price of mystifying the reality of disadvantage that sustained it. How could progressives want to achieve that sort of legitimation, or mistake it for authentic dignity?

What's been wrong on the Right has been the inability to countenance any contestation of their hegemony. Look at the depictions of catastrophe and victimization that the reactionaries served up in the PC wars when conservative faculty at Duke, Harvard, Berkeley, or other universities found themselves challenged for what some of their students experienced as racism or sexism.[10] How delicate, how fragile these professors seemed in the face of opposition! Their discomfort was palpable. But discomfort is not an issue of academic freedom—it is the price we pay for living in a complex and internally conflicted society and, particularly, for engaging in vigorous intellectual debate within the university. The Right would like self-protectively to mystify that. It wants its comfort back. But why should the Left imitate such blindness?

Rigidification and dogmatism are habits of thought and practice that work in the interests of dominant power. In imitating that mind-set, it is as if progressives had learned the wrong lesson from the Right and its domination. The last thing progressives should have taken over from their opponents was the traditional upper-class ideal that culture should be comfortable and reassuring for those living within it—particularly at a time when culture is anything but. For progressives such a projection is a conduct of what Nietzsche called *ressentiment*—of reactive frustration and resentment of their more powerful opponents, coupled (in what is only an apparent paradox) with an involuntary adoption of their fundamental view of social privilege. Such a notion misreads the political situation badly. Today the reality of our culture is conflictual. Any representation of it that tends to veil the objective conflict or shut down our perception of it leads us astray.

Much of the Left's rhetoric in the PC wars has thus revolved around a campaign to insist upon equality and justice on terminological levels and thereby to protect people from discomfort—as if we could suddenly slip into privilege and never have to deal with the distressing aspects of our reality. Ideally, of course, that would be wonderful. But such a politics inevitably smacks precisely of Idealism— a promotion of verbal and symbolic behaviors far beyond what the material infrastructure or other levels of social practice could authentically sustain or justify. Can anyone really imagine that if I as a Jew never hear anyone use a derogatory term about Jews, I've somehow been exempted from anti-Semitism or that it has disappeared from social life?

Fundamentally conservative and reactionary positions within American politics still dominate today. Despite the recent election, they still enjoy the privilege of ignoring self-consciousness; they still don't seem particularly destabilized or embattled. Under such circumstances, a progressive politics needs now to remobilize precisely the *critical* capacity that has been central to intellectuals' functioning since the nineteenth century. The last thing we need now is to agitate for shutting down debate, for under such conditions the fundamental and undisturbed hegemony of the American Right can only be reinforced. Rather than proscribing the signifiers of prejudice, which can only increase polarization or drive intolerance out of our hearing, let's get people talking about what they feel about each other; let's bring to bear the possibilities of an authentic confrontation of values and interests. Among many Americans the opening of such a debate—particularly within the university, with its traditions of managing conflict in relatively nonviolent ways—might mobilize a deep sense of ethics about how people ought to be treated. It could inhibit prejudice not by coercion but by a slowly growing understanding that in our diverse society we have to respect difference and learn not automatically to hierarchize it.

So I'd argue that in contradistinction to the terminological purism of certain recent political practices, the Left should shun dogmatic, apodictic styles of framing social rhetoric and norming behavior—not simply out of some nostalgic adherence to liberal, Enlightenment tradition but because a progressive political trajectory must suppose and instantiate such a politics of *de*-normalization. If you want to challenge dominant power, it simply can't be right to shut yourself off from challenge in return. And it is this fantastical projection of a world that has *already* internalized the utopia to which multicultural politics is urging us on that makes the satire of PC so available to its antagonists and so effective as a tactic. Everybody knows that today such a projection is completely off the mark. It makes the Left seem beside the point at the very moment when its fundamental analysis responds to urgent needs in our culture.

Many progressives have understood this instinctively. The great tradition of social protest in this country has always been based upon a principled recognition of the authentic force of the opposition at the very moment it was being confronted. At the same time, a strategy of purifying language as a way of conjuring away the inequities in our society looks more like magical thinking than like real politics. It fails to confront the infrastructural realities that the linguistic ones surely reinforce but can hardly be thought responsible for creating. Hence there's an undeniable and undesirable idealism in any form of PC language policing if it substitutes attention to signifiers, however pervasive or supportive of structures of oppression, for attention to the signifieds and the real material determinants of such oppression itself.

Moreover, by reifying language a certain strain of the Left has gotten itself caught in an extraordinary humorlessness about the contemporary world. By practicing a politics that effectively equates language to reality, some progressives have deprived themselves of the resources of reconceiving reality through the process of language itself. From antiquity to the contemporary period, techniques have operated in comedy, parody, satire, and lampoon as effective mechanisms for putting salutary pressure upon social reality. Certain PC dogmatists would exclude the burlesque—as if our contemporary world were not itself transparently crazy and worthy of representation as such. We'd be silly to think that satire lacked seriousness or that minds can't sometimes best be changed through humor.

The PC wars have brought us many "-isms" to shun, but the one some have called "laughism" is worth looking at in this regard. At the University of Connecticut, the term "laughism" was coined to stigmatize inappropriate responses to ethnic jokes and other un-PC sniggering.[11] But what about the kind of comedy that for my generation Lenny Bruce discovered it was possible to marshal in the service of liberation? Bruce's satire of the prejudices held by dominant society about blacks or Jews or gays was authentically unsettling to those who held such views. And his comedy has surely been one of the preconditions for our perception today of the intolerable stupidity of such intolerance. How did Bruce do it? He transformed perception by reenacting the idiocy of the bigots, by holding it up in such pure and quintessential form that no one could miss it. Bruce's parody mimed prejudice so clearly and devastatingly that some who heard him could never again utter the signifiers of intolerance without feeling shamed. We need to rediscover the resources of such satirical strategies. "Laughism" makes them unavailable to us and to our efforts at social change.[12]

So I'd have more faith in what Thomas Grey termed "life's ordinary rough and tumble" as the right setting and the right mechanism to confront prejudice and foster the legitimation of diversity.[13] When from within our current deeply conflictual reality we project an ideal world in which people are protected from all exercise of power, even from the pedagogical violence that obliges them to memorize their multiplication tables, what happens? What happens when we attempt phantasmically to institute miniversions of such a world within a larger society still rotten with prejudice? Such an expedient provides not solutions but mystifications. And meanwhile the real determinants of discrimination and inequality are not touched at all.

There's another reason, moreover, that I think that progressives within the university ought to resist the impulse to dogmatism, to what Justice Brennan termed the "pall of orthodoxy,"[14] no matter how powerful the provocations emanating from the reactionaries on the other side. Like progressives in general, I think that the university has a *critical* role to play that we ought never to lose sight of. As Michel de Certeau put it, our role is to "reflect on the power [we] lack."[15] Think of us as the *other* side of affirmative culture, the contrary to the self-celebratory chorus that cheers on our society, right or wrong—or fails to think about it at all. Conservatives can play that role on their own. Our job as intellectuals is to say the contradiction, to bring the tools of critique to bear in a wider culture that in the United States particularly has had very little tolerance for contestation. However, as soon as we start articulating a discourse of positivity and of "truth"—particularly at a moment in our history when the theoretical possibilities of such a discourse are profoundly suspect to begin with—we abandon the resource of a stance of criticism without necessarily gaining anything but an ignominious marginalization or co-optation by dominant power.

In saying this I'm not suggesting that we reify a tradition of the "alienated" intellectual. Confrontation and alienation seem to me quite different stances. The former is resolutely activist, and that's what I'm urging here. I'm suggesting that the most significant aspect of our social role in the academy is to subject dominant power and contemporary reality to the techniques of analysis and critique that the university has been honing since the advent of civil society two centuries ago. There's a strong tradition among intellectuals of sustaining such a role as opposition to—even as inimical to—dominant power.[16]

This is the more true given that any projection by the Left of a stance of power that might objectively counter the hegemony of American conservatism at this point in history would seem fatally self-deceptive. Most commentators on the PC wars have agreed that the relative impotence of the Left has been one of the most important preconditions for the rigidification of the ideological battle that we have witnessed. Barbara Epstein's assessment seems to me sane and accurate: "Perhaps today's political correctness bears some relation to the peculiar situation in which progressives find ourselves in the eighties and nineties: we have considerable cultural influence, at least in some areas (notably the university and intellectual circles), but virtually no political clout."[17] This situation poses an important problem of timing. Affirmative, apodictic assertions about the conduct of politics can have widely different strategic value at different stages in a political process. But surely they make the most sense when an authentic shift of dominant power can at least plausibly be imagined. That's not now. At present the context in which the Left sorts out its politics must be reckoned as a time in which progressives have never been farther from such domination. Bill Clinton's election hasn't changed this situation by itself. We still need the Left.

In the PC wars the reactionaries tried to cast progressives in the university as dominant and as radicals. The university *radical?* Let's not be ridiculous. The university is the most successfully conservative and traditional secular establishment in human history. After the Catholic church, no social institution in the world is older than the academy. We didn't become so venerable by chance: the university's function is based upon organizing and propagating a powerful dynamic of homeostasis and of reproduction of the same. As I have suggested, that's not the only dynamic active in academe. But despite the doomsday hand-wringing of the Right, the power of such homeostasis in higher education remains profound. That's why if the society is to continue at all, it needs us. Of course that also means that the university's fascination with itself, with its functioning and its role, cannot simply be interpreted as narcissism. We are central to the operation of our culture; what happens within the university *is* consequential. That's yet another reason why despite their surface silliness the PC wars are worth concerted cultural and social reflection.

If progressives ought to cast their politics in terms of an opening, an invitation to the "rough and tumble" of the conflicts that stress contemporary American society, then what has come to be called "identity politics" has got to be subjected to just as serious questioning as the rightist protestations of intolerable injury to consecrated values that we have been hearing. I understand by identity politics a view that construes the culture of a group (whether based upon race, region, religion, gender, or any other marker) as absolute, as incomprehensible from outside itself, and that views its claims as automatically self-validating. That sort of essentialism immediately closes down the diversity of our modern world of complexity. It projects disconnected and mutually uncomprehending monads. But the fact that the competing claims of distinct groups cannot be harmonized in some transcendent synthesis does not mean that communication cannot flow or knowledge and understanding occur at all.

Back to the rough-and-tumble, then, of our real diversity. It gets acrimonious. Whether we fear that or not, we can't really avoid it. In a world of diversity, we can't prevent the conflicts that come from authentic disagreement, nor should the university seek to forestall the discomfort of authentic difference. It would be like demanding that the real world leave us alone. On the contrary, we need to go out and understand that world, we need to change it. So to move on to where we must go, we have to open the academy and our whole society to the confrontation with what we truly already are. To my mind, such a progressive initiative makes more sense than the flattening of meanings and the freezing of behaviors that has sometimes been the by-product of political correctness. We're moving toward a future that would resolve the inequities and the irrationalities that as intellectuals and as citizens we have been training for two hundred years to stigmatize and to overcome. The best thing about political correctness is that it has put politics back on our agenda. It's time for an authentic debate of ideas and values, time to begin to confront the real conflicts that are the essence of our present.

NOTES

1. For Yuri M. Lotman and B. A. Uspensky, culture *is* precisely such a memory: "We understand culture as the *nonhereditary memory of the community.* ..." ("On the Semiotic Mechanism of Culture," *New Literary History* 9:2 [1978]:213). See my *Present Past: Modernity and the Memory Crisis* (Ithaca: Cornell University Press, 1993), 3.

2. See my *Discourse/Counter-Discourse: The Theory and Practice of Symbolic Resistance in Nineteenth-Century France* (Ithaca: Cornell University Press, 1985), 25.

3. Thomas Hobbes, *Leviathan* (Paris, 1651), pt. 1, chap. 4.

4. This image of politics in the contemporary world owes a lot to the paradigms of certain recent theorists. In particular, I'd mention the work of Ernesto Laclau and Chantal Mouffe, particularly their book *Hegemony and Socialist Strategy* (London: Verso, 1985).

5. See Stanley Milgram, *Obedience to Authority* (New York: Harper and Row, 1974). For a discussion, see Frederic Schick, *Having Reasons: An Essay on Rationality and Sociality* (Princeton: Princeton University Press, 1984), 97–100, 110–114.

6. Pierre Bourdieu and Jean-Claude Passeron have gone so far as to term the exercise of even this sort of pedagogical authority "symbolic violence." See their *Reproduction in Education, Society, and Culture*, trans. Richard Nice (London: Sage, 1977), xi and passim; and Terdiman, *Discourse/Counter-Discourse*, 64. But we can agree that such a term, however evocative, is inevitably metaphorical. What it registers is the omnipresence of *power* in society.

7. In an authentically clarifying essay intended to sort out the competing civil rights and civil liberties claims often muddled in the controversies about regulation of campus speech and conduct, Thomas C. Grey makes a telling point. He observes that though legislation prohibiting discriminatory speech must necessarily be content-neutral on its face, in fact such structural neutrality is rarely mirrored on the level of content *because of the existence of hierarchies of the sort I'm referring to here.* Specifically, codes of campus conduct typically contain language prohibiting the use of epithets "commonly understood to convey direct and visceral hatred or contempt for human beings on the basis of their sex, race, color, handicap, religion, sexual orientation, or national and ethnic origin" (the quotation is from Stanford University's "Discriminatory Harassment Provision," which Grey drafted). However, Grey notes a crucial point: "As best I can see, there are *no* epithets in this society at this time that are 'commonly understood' to convey hatred and contempt for whites *as such*. … The denigrating epithets covered by the Stanford provision are able to inflict the serious and distinctive injuries characteristic of legally prohibited invidious discrimination because they strike at groups subjected to longstanding and deep-rooted prejudices widely held and disseminated throughout our culture" ("Civil Rights vs. Civil Liberties: The Case of Discriminatory Verbal Harassment," *Social Philosophy and Policy* 8:2 [Spring 1991]:81–107 at 95–96). Such a situation *practically* delineates precisely the sort of asymmetry I am referring to here.

8. See "Surplus Visibility," in *Beyond PC: Toward a Politics of Understanding*, ed. Patricia Aufderheide (St. Paul: Graywolf Press, 1992), 123.

9. For evidence of such a perception among those sympathetic to the progressive goals of multiculturalism and gender equality, see several of the essays in Aufderheide, *Beyond PC*; Miles Harvey, "Politically Correct Is Politically Suspect," 144; Barbara Epstein, "Political Correctness and Identity Politics," 148; Todd Gitlin, "On the Virtues of a Loose Canon," 187.

10. See, for example, C. Vann Woodward, "Freedom and the Universities," in Aufderheide, *Beyond PC*, 43.

11. See Harvey, "Politically Correct Is Politically Suspect," 146.

12. I examined some older strains of such socially reformist deployment of humor in "Counter-Humorists: Strategies of Resistance in Marx and Flaubert," *Discourse/Counter-Discourse*, chap. 4.

13. "The decisive question is not whether the harassment constitutes speech or action, but whether it is widespread and serious enough to go beyond what the courts judge must be tolerated as part of life's ordinary rough and tumble" (Grey, "Civil Rights vs. Civil Liberties," 85).

14. Quoted by Nat Hentoff, "'Speech Codes' and Free Speech," in Aufderheide, *Beyond PC*, 51.

15. *The Writing of History,* trans. Tom Conley (New York: Columbia University Press, 1988), 8.

16. Though written from a political point of view very different from mine here, Edward Shils's reflections on this point are interesting and confirm the existence of such a tradition. See "Intellectuals and Responsibility," in *The Political Responsibility of Intellectuals,* ed. Ian Maclean, Alan Montefiore, and Peter Winch (Cambridge: Cambridge University Press, 1990), 257–306 at 264–265; see also 276–277.

17. "Political Correctness and Identity Politics," in Aufderheide, *Beyond PC,* 153.

PART THREE

AFTER PC: REDESIGNING DISCIPLINES & INSTITUTIONS

16

Neither Impugning nor Disavowing Whiteness Does a Viable Politics Make: The Limits of Identity Politics

GEORGE YÚDICE

WHEN YOU PURCHASE your ticket to the 1993 Whitney Biennial Exhibition, you are given a button on which is printed one or several of the words in the statement: "I CAN'T IMAGINE EVER WANTING TO BE WHITE." I had no idea that I had been given the button that reads "WHITE" as I automatically attached it to my shirt pocket, assuming that it bore the museum logo. Engrossed in the show, I did not notice what was on the buttons that the other patrons wore until I spotted an acquaintance wearing the button with the word "IMAGINE." I immediately thought of John Lennon and wondered about the connection between 1960s and 1970s counterculture and the identity-politics feel of the exhibition. Was it, I imagined, a way of suggesting that the source of the counterculture, as Michele Wallace has argued, was in the challenges to the mainstream culture by "others," especially people of color?[1] It was only when I added my button to the others in the box at the exit that I grasped the statement in its entirety and realized that it was part of the show. This canny installation, *Museum Tags: Second Movement (Overture) or Overture con Claque—Overture with Hired Audience Members*, by Daniel J. Martinez, forced me to reflect on the statement and everything I had just seen.

What a strange sensation it was to think about walking through an exhibition of work that challenged the "authority" of whiteness while wearing a label that dredged up an archaic ambivalence about my ethnoracial identity! As a child of Salvadoran immigrants, growing up in El Barrio and in East New York, Brooklyn, in the 1950s, I had to navigate a sea of uncertainties around ethnoracial identity. At that time the U.S. ethnoracial order was characterized by a white-black distinction, with people of differing degrees of "whiteness" or "nonblackness" (as cultural constructs, of course, rather than "real" colors) such as Jews, Sicilians, and quite often "Hispanics" of different nationalities variously absorbed into the

255

white classification. The double anxiety of immigrant status and "lesser" or dubious whiteness among these competing ethnicities frequently erupted into violence. A gang of Italian American toughs known as the New Lots Boys would mer-
cilessly beat the blacks who risked coming to the elevated train stop on my block,
which was a kind of ethnic crossroads. The New Lots Boys policed this crossroads
and marched under the El with signs that read "S.P.O.N.G.E." ("Society for the
Prevention of Niggers Getting Everything"). By the time (summer of 1965) the
number of blacks in the area approached that of Italian Americans, there was a
riot and several people were killed. Mayor John Lindsay called on the leadership of
the different parties, including the Gallo brothers as the most significant arbiter,
to negotiate a truce, and the violence was ended.

It was tough living on that crossroads, and I myself painfully experienced prejudice aimed not only at "spics" but also at "guineas" and "kikes." *Plus ça change:*
Violence is still the order of the day, despite all the multicultural rhetoric and the
gradual formation of three or four panethnicities that will perhaps provide some
kind of system of checks and balances. As Richard Alba and others have argued,
these panethnicities have emerged in the wake of the civil rights struggle with the
consolidation of diverse peoples of European and African background as European Americans (whites) and African Americans (blacks), respectively, on the one
hand, and the sundry national groups that constitute Latinos, Asian Americans,
and Native Americans, on the other.[2] This emerging ethnoracial order does not
and cannot, of course, uncontradictorily accommodate the full spectrum of
groups that make up the United States. Where do Arabs, Turks, Brazilians, and
others fit in? Will they, like square pegs, be jammed into the rounded classifications of white, black, Asian, or Latino? Furthermore, the difficulty of accommodation is also evident in the reluctance to be considered part of a U.S.-constructed
panethnicity on the part of many immigrants from Latin America and Asia.[3]
Ethnoracial relations vary according to region, and intra-panethnic strife is evident in clashes between Puerto Ricans and Dominicans in Quisqueya Heights,
New York City, or Central Americans in South Central Los Angeles and Chicanos
in East Los Angeles. Such struggles also characterize the interaction between new
immigrants from Europe (particularly those from the fragmented former Soviet
bloc, who are here to make a living and feel no responsibility whatsoever for the
current state of racial affairs in the United States) and historical "racial minorities," as is evident in the strife between Hasidim and Puerto Ricans in Williamsburg, Brooklyn, or between African Americans and recent Albanian immigrants
in the South Bronx. Nevertheless, I accept in a general way the argument that the
tendency is toward the construction of Euro-American, African American, Asian
American, and Latino panethnicities.

I can't say that all this went through my mind right there in the museum as I reflected on the statement, but it was there bubbling in the background. My insights
into whiteness are derived from my own experience of the shifts in the ethnoracial
order since I was a child. Certainly the ambivalences that I felt as a boy have di-

minished after over a decade and a half of participation in the Central American solidarity movement and in the discursive construction of Latinoness, a conflictive one, in fact, that has in turn generated ambivalences of its own that are difficult to resolve. Racial or ethnic belonging for "Latinos" (and many whom I have interviewed confirm this) is quite variegated: "we" are of all races and national backgrounds, yet "we" are lumped together in the categories "Hispanic" and "Latino," which also enable a degree of leverage in the U.S. ethnoracial political and social systems. The experience of whiteness for someone like myself includes negotiating the conflicting signals sent by the state, the market, and sundry social institutions as Hispanics have gone from no particular classification in the data-gathering devices of these instances to a situation in which several classifications were tested (Spanish-surnamed, Spanish-speaking, Spanish American heritage or nationality of origin, Hispanic, etc.), settling for the time being on Hispanic versus non-Hispanic white, non-Hispanic black, and non-Hispanic Asian. Anyone who has had to live through this muddle cannot but be highly aware of the constructed character of ethnoracial identities. And it is, in part, by taking advantage of this awareness, by examining the overdetermined character of identity, that its pitfalls (primarily the subordination of differences of class, gender, race, sexual orientation, linguistic formation, and national provenance) can be more easily discerned and, ideally, avoided. Although I certainly subscribe to *Latin* culture (for better or worse, I *am* a Latin from Manhattan), Latinoness does not have the hold for me that, say, blackness or Jewishness does for many African Americans and Jews. I was not born a Latino (there was no such category in 1947), and my relative acceptance of the term is more a result of political agency, which in turn is nourished by cultural practices and interpretive processes. I agree with Howard Winant's argument that, despite the arbitrariness of factors that work to create one category rather than another, ethnoracial categorization will remain strong in the United States,[4] precisely because it is probably the major way (along with affiliations based on gender and sexual orientation) in which political but also social and cultural gains are made in a society in which rights are increasingly theorized and negotiated in relation to group ethos despite the fact that the legal system has its historical foundation in the rights of the individual.[5] The current order of things, however, is racked by many problems, not the least of which is the "problem of whiteness."

So let's get back to the statement "I can't imagine ever wanting to be white." I mused on my way out of the museum that not everyone would accept it. David Duke would certainly contest it. And how are we to understand Michael Jackson's gradual whitening, not only in terms of skin color but also nose shape and hair texture? Is he a wanna-be the way, say, Mose Allison or Marky Mark seem wanna-be blacks? How do we approach these questions in an era of nonessentialist identities? And given the new ethnoracial order of things, how do I relate to my own ethnoracial identity? I can remember that, in contrast to what it must have been like for someone who was sure of having the social passport of whiteness, as a boy in the 1950s I felt subject to attacks on my worth as a person whenever I was called a spic. Some people, evidently concerned about my feelings and thus not wanting to stigmatize me with an "inferior" identity measured in units of melanin, negotiated the "problem" for me by construing me as "Spanish," "doing me the favor" of raising me a few notches above the bottom of the racial ladder presumably occupied by blacks. I eventually rebelled against the disavowal of this "difference" that I shared with other people like myself and felt pleasure in rubbing my indigenous forebears in the faces of those who would whitewash me and in foiling the strategies of those who wanted to "pass." Over the years, then, my evolving racial consciousness led me away from someone who *could* imagine wanting to be white through someone who did not *want* to, to someone, now, who has become more interested in exploring and exploding what it means to be white or black or otherwise in this country.

"White," like "Latino," is evidently a construction whose overdetermination is not seriously explored, one most often impugned by critics as usurping the ground of normalcy, centrality, dominance. It should go without saying that many individuals do not assume the white supremacy of this stereotype. The point of this essay is that it is in the interest not only of whites but perhaps even more of those who are constructed (and construct themselves) as other than white to transform the ethnoracial order in which they collude in reproducing the centrality of whiteness. That entails not only placing other cultural formations center stage, so to speak, but also teasing apart the link between whiteness and unmarkedness that confers both privilege (within the status quo) and liability (among emergent ideologies of "difference"). The privilege comes from occupying the "naturalized" position in a social system in which whiteness, like right-handedness, is taken to be the standard. The liability ensues from the lack of an increasingly valued (some might say commodified) "difference" or "markedness," which many whites are lamenting more and more (examples abound, but the case of white supremacist youths' longing to have their own ethnic identity should serve as a caution to those who would mark whiteness as just another ethnic category). The current contradictions and attempts to reconfigure race in the United States have to do not only with justice and the demands of subordinated groups but also with the pressures of globalizing economic, political, and social forces. As Stuart Hall has argued, U.S. capital, "in order to maintain its global position, ... has had to negotiate and by negotiate I mean it had to incorporate and partly reflect the differences it was trying to overcome."[6] He then goes on to privilege marginality as the position from which these groups "reclaim some form of representation for themselves," thus forcing their partial incorporation. But marginality, as I have argued elsewhere, is itself a problematic platform for social change, often compelling many nonmarginals to disavow privilege with the contradictory result that the privileged (e.g., Deleuze and Guattari, but especially their numerous academic epigones) become advocates of a radical "becoming minor."

Exploring and exploding whiteness means, for me, imagining nonracist and nonnormativist ways of being white, although the very idea may produce the fear in some that once the centrality of whiteness against which they partially construct their own identity politics is, if not eradicated, then at least mitigated, the rug of their political effectiveness and cultural legitimacy (viz., marginality and related notions) will have been pulled out from under them. New patterns of immigration, for example, are producing situations in which the racial common sense of white = privilege and black/people of color = subordination is being traversed by claims that challenge not the privilege of whiteness but the way of construing the subordination of a generalized "people of color." In Dade County, Florida, for example, "many American-born blacks ... seem perplexed ... by th[e] tendency of black Cubans, Dominicans, Panamanians, and Puerto Ricans to define themselves not by the color of their skin, but by their language and culture."[7] The organizer of an African American boycott of tourism in Dade County aimed at Miami's Cuban-dominated government, which had snubbed Nelson Mandela, complained: "You can't just tell if you look at somebody. I can be walking down a street and I say, 'Hey, brother,' and they speak back to me in Spanish." The fact is that Hispanics in Miami have become the dominant group, causing discontent among both blacks and whites. This situation calls for new responses and accommodations that, if they are to get at some important root causes, have to be examined not only nationally but also in the context of globalization.

The diversification of the ethnoracial order of the past decade and the changes in immigration, economics, and demographics that made this possible have not led to change in the understanding of white and black in the United States. Discussion of whiteness is almost always evaded by turning to its "other," blackness. The two are imbricated in each other's representations, but the emphasis is on the "other," and this not only on the part of white critics but even more so on the part of those "others" who understandably want to move their own heritage center stage. Consequently, whiteness remains elusive—even more elusive than blackness, whose invisibility in today's media and commodity public spheres seems to be an exaggeration. My reading of the 1980s and 1990s—of the conspicuous racialization of political elections; of Howard Beach, Bensonhurst, Rodney King and the Los Angeles riots; of the media salience of black sports figures like Magic Johnson and Michael Jordan; of the spate of "black" TV sitcoms like *The Cosby Show, Fresh Prince of Bel Air,* and *In Living Color;* of the not improbable displacement of rock by rap as the national music (according to *Billboard,* three of the top twenty pop albums are rap albums);[8] of the rappification of MTV (and not only on MTV/Yo Raps), the emergence of Black Entertainment Television (BET), and the mainstreaming of rap in one commercial after another on TV—runs counter to the denial that a significant transformation of the media has taken place.[9] It is, after all, very big business. But, according to bell hooks, for example, "Since most white people do not have to 'see' black people (constantly appearing on billboards, television, movies, in magazines, etc.) and they do not need to be ever on guard, observing black people, to be 'safe,' they can live as though black people are invisible and can imagine that they are also invisible to blacks."[10]

The days of this invisibility are over, which is not to say that the situation of working-class and unemployed blacks and other minorities has gotten any better because of greater representation. There is no necessary connection between a politics of recognition of difference and a politics of equitable distribution of wealth and services. As Peggy Phelan points out, it is a rather mystified perspective that expects increased visibility to equal increased power.[11] Furthermore, as Isaac Julien has argued,[12] countering stereotypes by projecting "positive images" does not address the kind of ambivalence that I have tried to capture in the account of my reaction to Martinez's installation on whiteness at the Whitney.

I would like to suggest, also, that the generation of positive images facilitates *strategies of disavowal* among whites of the inequities of a racially divided world, acknowledgment of which is "burdensome because it implicates white people as the undeserving beneficiaries of structural social inequalities. It forces people to confront the need for social change. White people cannot, in the face of such inequality, afford to rest on their laurels without a certain sense of guilt. *The Cosby Show* in this sense is extremely seductive."[13] "Enlightened racism," according to Jhally and Lewis, is a strategy of disavowal that works by acknowledging the problem and at the same time considering it eliminated: "Racism, in other words, is seen by white Cosby watchers as a disease that has been essentially cured; the society requires no further medicine."[14]

My purpose in this essay is *not* to argue that we continue to live in a white supremacist society—that has been and continues to be argued quite cogently by numerous, even mainstream critics. I prefer to approach the problem from the other end: what are the strategies of disavowal, and how can we construct a nonracist, nonnormativist imaginary that whites, blacks, Latinos, and others would want to embrace? I would like to participate in this discussion with a critique of multiculturalism and identity politics, for they have, in my opinion, contributed to strategies of disavowal. Except for the "far Right," which would rather fight on behalf of whiteness than resort to disavowals, it seems to me that many whites nowadays—at least those who have nothing to lose by opting out of whiteness—can imagine not ever wanting to be white with the relative ease that Martinez's installation at the Whitney points up. Some may actually seek to gain, as in (my reading of) Michael Lerner's "Jews Are Not White." Basically, he argues that Jews' roots in difference and oppression disqualify them from any imputation of "privilege": "It is impossible to imagine that any other people that had one out of every three of its members murdered in the past 50 years would be seen as 'privileged'—except by those who in some way covertly sympathized with the murderers."[15] Lerner evidently needs to be reminded that privilege is not wholly voluntaristic but is accorded to you: if you are perceived as white, then you get all the privileges of membership. Privilege is also relative; it operates in relational systems whose positions shift across time and space, and in the United States of the 1970s, 1980s, and 1990s Jews are privileged by comparison with Latinos and African Americans. But, of course, what Lerner seeks is an equal footing with so-called people of color in the new, multicultural mode of production of value. That is, he *wants in* and needs to legitimate himself as different (a Jew, not a white) before those who are brokering the emerging system, whose password is "difference":

> To reject the fantasized concept of "whiteness" and instead recognize the complex stories of each cultural tradition, not privileging one group over another [here it's not whiteness but difference that carries value], but insisting on hearing and reclaiming everyone's stories. But this is not how it functions today. Today it is merely the tool of elite minority intellectuals seeking to establish themselves inside the intellectual world that has too long excluded them. And in that context, Jews must respond with an equally determined insistence that we are not white, and that those who claim we are and exclude our history and literature from the newly emerging multicultural canon are our oppressors.

I do agree with Lerner that multiculturalism is frequently brokered by "minority" intellectuals who too easily construct their arguments vis-à-vis whiteness. The solution, however, should not be to declare oneself "not white" and thus gain entry to the emerging system of value. It smacks of hypocrisy, opportunism, and racism. Isn't it a kind of racist passing in reverse?

Just as there has been an explosion of claims to marginality, Lerner's argument for declaring nonwhiteness can be taken up by others. If all white people declared themselves nonwhite and, on the basis of their "cultural difference," however they might construe it (one gay man that I interviewed declared himself nonwhite on the basis of his queerness), sought entry into the value system of multiculturalism, would that solve the problems of unemployment, lack of health care, unequal quality of education, etc.? Rather than declaring nonwhiteness, which is not really an option for many whites in precarious positions (e.g., the unemployed working-class), there needs to be a rearticulation of whiteness. As white supremacy comes under attack, the white working class is left with nothing but its own resources in a time of diminishing expectations. And *difference* is not an asset that they can easily claim. They feel that blacks and "others" have difference and culture and they don't. And without such a cultural means to self-valuation it is unlikely that they will abandon practices of "otherization." But identity politics as it is currently construed does not permit them a "difference" on the basis of which, especially if they are male and straight, to opt out (the "easy solution"). More significant, it does not permit the construction of a new antiracist and nonnormativist social imaginary that doesn't call for whites to change "on behalf of" others or to "wanna-be."

Perhaps the most eloquent testimony to this dilemma is Diana Jeater's attempt, in the British context, to come to grips with her own "crisis in white self-esteem": "there is a significant body of young, or youngish, white people in Britain's urban centres who don't feel they have an 'ethnicity,' or if they do, that it's not one they feel good about. I want further to suggest that this feeling bad is not a very useful response to the issue of contemporary racism, or indeed to anything else, and that there must be more to being 'white' than this."[16] Multiculturalism and identity politics have not constructed an imaginary for whites who want to participate in the extension of citizenship to all (Lerner's position only corroborates the bias that whites need not apply, except, perhaps, as cheerleaders or simulators of marginality). As Jeater complains, whites are seen as wanna-bes or as guilt-ridden liberals who want to do good to counteract their relative privilege, often seeking the acceptance or admiration of blacks and other oppressed peoples. In Jeater's case, it must be acknowledged that she is not seeking the admiration of blacks or any kind of reward for "political correctness." She clearly recognizes that there *are* whites who "wanna-be" black—because it means living more "relevantly" or intensely or with "soul" rather than the blankness of white that Richard Dyer refers to in connection with *Jezebel*[17]—but what she seeks is an opening in identity politics that will allow her to be "white" *and* oppositional: "The 1980s saw the institutionalization of 'identity politics' in the thinking of the Left. Everyone had to have an identity to anchor their politics. And the problem with being white was that it did not seem to bestow an identity which could be linked to any kind of oppositional politics."[18]

This lack of a vision for whites qua whites has its complement in blacks' suspicion that whites become antiracist because they somehow fundamentally wanna-be. This is the gist of Stuart Hall's "welcome to the club" of postmodern marginalization, a kind of generalized synecdoche of black: "envy is a very funny thing for the British to feel at this moment in time—to want to be black! Yet I feel some of you surreptitiously moving towards that marginal identity. I welcome you to that, too."[19] Jeater does not fall for the backhanded welcome. She clearly aims to be progressive and antiracist without being construed as wanting to be an "honorary black":

> It's nice to be welcomed, of course, but I think it's important to understand who is being welcomed to what. If our sense of ourselves as "white" has become problematic, because the cohesion of our polity has broken down, "whiteness" has become synonymous with the state's preferred modes of citizenship, and many of our political and cultural references have come from groups defined by their exclusion from that polity and by extension from "whiteness," does this mean that we are, or want to be, "honorary blacks"? Or does it mean that there is something wrong with the way we think about "whiteness"?[20]

Yes, of course, there *is* something seriously wrong about the ways in which whiteness has been normalized, but there is also something wrong with the "easy" ways of opting out of the positions of privilege that many whites differentially "enjoy." The label "wanna-be" implies that such a strategy of disavowal is looked upon with suspicion. In the United States, except for the Right and neonazis, most whites *appear* to feel that there is no God-given or good reason for being white.

That makes whiteness all the easier to disavow, as was demonstrated in a course on race relations in the military that was the focus of a *Frontline* documentary.[21] I have interviewed dozens of white youths and people in their thirties and forties on this issue. Invariably when I ask them about *their* whiteness and how they negotiate it in "our" progressive context (multiculturalism, identity politics) where it isn't advantageous to occupy the "norm," they tell me how difficult it is for their acquaintances or their students or their parents to overcome racism. Or they tell me a story about how some kind of metonymic logic of displacement—their having grown up among blacks or having had a black lover or knowing rap backward and forward—although not of course being a stand-in for black experience has made it possible for them to feel "comfortable" or "normal" about black culture. Black is not, of course, their only point of reference; sometimes it's Chicano or queer. It is as if hanging out with blacks or Chicanos or queers got one off the hook of one's relative privilege as a white. White, in fact, has become a convenient carpet under which to shove the problem of privilege and disavowal. And even Asians and, increasingly, Latinos (despite their relatively low income) are being seen by blacks as permitted a relative privilege not accorded to them. This is evident, again, in the Los Angeles riots or in the black-Latino struggle in Dade County, where the same lawyer who started the tourism boycott mentioned above argues that many Hispanics are just white people who happen to speak Spanish.[22]

The compulsion to disavow is inevitable as whites seek to avoid being on the wrong side of the *us and them* divide that identity politics continues to enforce, as in Ruby Rich's differentiation between enthusiasts of deconstructive postmodernism (*them*—are we to imagine that they are all white and heterosexual? what do you do, then, with Gayatri Spivak or Craig Owens?) and those who are "finally attaining positions of authorship" (*us*, that is, "women, queers, the *other* races").[23] It is hardly surprising, then, that whites look for ways to get on *our* side, as some "white ethnics" (Jews, Italian Americans) have tried to do by appealing to a history of discrimination that might establish a bridge to the "other." But this is a bridge that tends to be constructed on the "backs" of the "others" (to use Gloria Anzaldúa's phrase), mistaking the experiences of these "others" for one's own—a maneuver that does not go uncriticized:

> Most of the white Jewishwomen in the class did not want to identify as white (I'm not referring to the Jewish women-of-color). Some declared that they felt they "belonged" more to the women-of-color group than they did to the white group. Because they felt isolated and excluded, they felt that their oppressions were the same or similar to those of women-of-color. Some *mujeres-de-color* questioned the concept of "same" oppressions and claimed that all oppressions were being collapsed into one. The problem was that white women and white Jewishwomen, while seeming to listen, were not really "hearing" women-of-color and could not get it into their heads that this was a space and a class on and about women-of-color.[24]

The new ethnoracial order has thus construed all Euro-Americans as central and dominant in much the same ways in which "WASPs" once were by "ethnics," and they are subject to the same critiques. And their opting out of whiteness is no more convincing than if non-Jewish Germans had told Jews that they too felt like Jews. Nor is this option available to all. The "easy solution," then, implies a strategy of "becoming minor" or "marginal," a superficial maneuver that suggests that nothing is at stake in one's identity if one can easily disavow it. Declaring oneself marginal without experiencing the hardships is, like ubiquity, a feature of privilege. Nor is the "difficult solution" (i.e., engaging one's white identity as a function of the "dominant culture," which can result in hostility or guilt) much better, for it leaves no project, no positive imaginary for the self. As Jeater argues, it is necessary to *reinvent* whiteness as the "possibility of a radical white identity that isn't guilty, doesn't eat roast beef, and isn't trying to be black." That entails, she adds, rethinking the metaphors by which we now understand identity, particularly *center* and *margin*.[25] The danger is, of course, that once we are all supposedly reconfigured as neither "central" nor "marginal," there will no longer be a moral basis on which to demand that "others" be listened to.

How are we to go about this arduous endeavor? Jeater recommends adopting Homi Bhabha's notion of a "Third Space" of *hybridity* to characterize non-essentialist *and* nonintegrationist identities. Bhabha elaborates on this idea in his catalog essay for the 1993 Whitney Biennial, positing postmodern interstitiality, the "expanded and ex-centric site of experience and empowerment," particularly that of "women, the colonized, minority groups," as subversive of the epistemological foundations of any centrality or supremacy: "The wider significance of the postmodern condition lies in the awareness that the epistemological 'limits' of those ethnocentric ideas are also the enunciative boundaries of a range of other dissonant, even dissident histories and voices—women, the colonized, minority groups—the bearers of policed sexualities."[26] For reasons that will become more evident, I find Bhabha's endorsement of hybridity seductive but ultimately ineffective. Suffice it to point out that by remaining within the realm of the aesthetic-as-such—which I understand him to define as the space where the "'foreignness' of cultural translation" is foregrounded[27]—he severely limits the practicability of hybridity in strategies for infrastructural change. It seems to me that Bhabha expects the "displaced" or "foreign"—the unhomely, as he calls it in another essay—to be redeemed by an aesthetic practice that requires what Peter Bürger has called the "autonomy of the institution of art"[28] rather than a practice that forces this institution into encounters and conflicts with other institutions:

> In order to appear as material or empirical reality, the historical or social process must pass through an "aesthetic" alienation, or "privatization" of its public visibility. The discourse of "the social" then finds its means of representation in a kind of *unconsciousness* that obscures the immediacy of meaning, darkens the public event with an "unhomely" glow. There is, I want to hazard, an incommunicability that shapes the public moment; a psychic obscurity that is formative for public memory.[29]

To argue that classic aesthetic distancing (whose counterparts are the Russian Formalist *Ostranienie* and the Freudian *Verfremdungseffekt*) is the means by which colonized or subaltern "otherness" makes itself present—Bhabha writes "begins its presencing," an allusion to Heidegger's notion of "unveiling"—is to misunderstand how two orders of sociality—aesthetics and politics—interact. Literary theory is rife with these assimilations of social problems to philosophical and aesthetic categories: Heidegger's homelessness versus homeless people, Kristeva's abjects versus social "deviants," Freud's uncanny versus the parent-to-child power differential, French feminists' play of the signifier versus women's sexuality, and so on. It is only by sleight-of-hand, I would argue, that the aesthetic can be made to redeem the "disadvantaged" side of this dubious equation. What Bhabha understands as aesthetic alienation is among the phenomena that keep "otherness" separate from the outsiders and oppressed of everyday experience. A more effective understanding of the imbrication of aesthetics and social action, what I have elsewhere called "practical aesthetics,"[30] would move the discussion in to the examination of how institutions function in relation to public spheres, precisely the spaces in which citizenship, in all its cultural dimensions, is struggled over. Such a practice would permit not the extension of marginality to all that provokes Hall's ironic "welcome to the club" but rather an understanding of how cultural practice can work to change institutional relations.

But let's return, again, to the question of whiteness. I would like to explore how "liberals" and the "far Right" differentially deal with the problem of race. It is evident that for some—the conservative wing of the Republican Party, the religious Right, and sundry neonazi groups—the defense of whiteness is a crucial political issue. These groups wage a synecdochal politics against affirmative action that supposedly benefits all those who deviate in one way or another from a phantasmal norm: the black "underclass," lesbians and gays, non-English-speakers, and so on. For the Right the defense against "degeneracy" is based on moral outrage. But white liberals and many white leftist/progressives (God knows how to characterize what was once the "Left") have also expressed dissatisfaction with affirmative action because it diminishes the chances of maintaining their status in lean times. Their defense is phrased in terms of "quality," the argument that blacks and other so-called minorities are undeservedly getting jobs and promotions on the basis of their race, ethnicity, or gender. (As one critic argues, however, affirmative action may actually function as a palliative that employers can use to let down unsuccessful white applicants "gently"; they can simply say that they are forced to hire minorities.)[31] Although whites might argue that they get short shrift on account of their color, none of them have made a case for the importance of whiteness to their identity. None have expressed anxiety that whiteness will lead to exclusion, humiliation, or disrespect. If the Right seeks to enforce white heterosexual supremacy, liberals rely on it to maintain their status.

But I am not, for the moment, interested in pursuing this line of argument, which has been amply rehearsed not only in the writings of multiculturalists and others involved in identity politics but even in the most mainstream of media, such as Hollywood movies, network TV, the *New York Times, Time,* and *News-*

week. For example, a recent issue of the latter carries as its lead article an essay entitled "White Male Paranoia? Are They the Newest Victims—or Just Bad Sports?" that trivializes what has been a crucial movement to expand citizenship to people of color and other subordinated groups. The author, David Gates, implies that politics is but a simple game of role playing, of playing the victim, a sport whose stakes are of no more consequence than childish sore-losing. The cover features the ragged face of Michael Douglas, who, in *Falling Down,* portrays the unemployed, middle-aged white male D-Fens whose sanity gives way because the world he once knew has all but come apart. His reaction is to take revenge on Chicanos, Koreans, blacks, panhandlers, and other disadvantaged groups. The mainstream liberal press, of course, has been nothing but critical of the film. John Rosenthal, on National Public Radio, had no trouble seeing through the thinly veiled attack by still dominant white males on subordinated groups. *Newsweek* exposes the myth of white male oppression by citing a string of statistics meant to demonstrate that, complain as they might, white men still hold most of the power:

> White males make up just 39.2 percent of the population, yet they account for 82.5 percent of the Forbes 400 (folks worth at least $265 million), 77 percent of Congress, 92 percent of state governors, 70 percent of tenured college faculty, almost 90 percent of daily newspaper editors, 77 percent of TV news directors. They dominate just about everything but NOW and the NAACP; even in the NBA, most of the head coaches and general managers are white guys.[32]

Still and all, no argument is made on behalf of the cultural importance of whiteness beyond seeing it, as do many critics (James Baldwin, Frantz Fanon, Joel Kovel, Richard Dyer, bell hooks, Thelma Golden), as a transparent backdrop whose power resides in the assumption of that transparency—whiteness—as the "natural" way of being, a measure against which blacks and whites' "others" do not match up.[33]

I would like to argue that, despite the public onslaught of the Right and the closeted anxiety of some liberals, the challenge to whiteness leaves most so-called whites largely unfazed. This is even the case in a noted progressive such as Barbara Ehrenreich, who, although fully aware of diverse groups' struggles to gain space in the United States, rather easily opts out of whiteness for a "race of 'none'" embodied in a family tradition of progressive values:

> The more tradition-minded, the newly enthusiastic celebrants of Purim and Kwanzaa and Solstice, may see little point to survival if survivors carry no cultural freight—religion, for example, or ethnic tradition. To which I would say that skepticism, curiosity and wide-eyed ecumenical tolerance are also worthy elements of the human tradition and are at least as old as such notions as "Serbian" or "Croatian," "Scottish" or "Jewish." I make no claims for my personal line of progenitors except that they remained loyal to the values ... of our ancestors.[34]

Ehrenreich, of course, does not *have* to seek value on the basis of ethnicity since, as an unmarked white, she has the privilege—denied to others—of opting out.

This is a significant departure from the racial climate in which Baldwin wrote *The Fire Next Time*, when "challenging the white world's assumptions, was putting [the challenger] in the path of destruction."[35] Now, at the Whitney, we can all wear that challenge on our shirt pockets or lapels with relative impunity. This is not, of course, to say that some white critics do not get hysterical. In his review of the Whitney Biennial, for example, Michael Kimmelman shrieks, in the staid *New York Times*, of all places, "I hate the show." His arguments are predictable, most of them having been leveled at iconoclastic art throughout history: the artists demonstrate no talent or skill; the works are driven by content, particularly political sloganeering, rather than form; openly moralistic, they lack wit and provide no pleasure; and so on.[36] Evidently, Kimmelman and I saw two very different shows. Wit and pleasure: how else can one describe Mark Rappaport's *Rock Hudson's Home Movies* (1992), which takes sequences from Hudson's films and splices them in such ways that they can be read, with the help of the first-person voice-over, as expressions of the actor's gayness, or Pepón Osorio's installation *The Scene of the Crime (Whose Crime?)*, which uproariously confounds notions of taste, as Coco Fusco observes in her catalog essay.[37] Rather than Kimmelman's diatribe against the "sound, fury, and little else" of such work, we might apply Cuban critic Gerardo Mosquera's description of Flavio Garciandía's kitsch-art, "Bad Taste in Good Form," which enables discernment of an ethos and an aesthetic will to which the backlashing, normativist critic is deaf, blind, and dumb:

> The painter ... is working in a new style based on images drawn from the festive and ornamental kitsch of cities. He doesn't criticize kitsch but rather "recuperates"—not entirely without humor—some stereotyped signs (e.g., the "tropicalizing" representation of coconut trees). He reworks the abstract ornamentations used in everyday decoration by the nonprofessional (in homes, murals, feasts, etc.) and decorations in "bad taste" designed by the professional (stands, carnival floats, textiles, etc.). Composed of a scandalous hodgepodge of forms that can be considered neither geometrical nor informal, these designs may be the result of a "savage" assimilation of "civilized" forms, the natural and original product—i.e., the imaginary—of "mass culture" or even a naive degeneration of "primitivization" of elements drawn from "mass culture." We're dealing here with an astonishing morphology which surrounds us everywhere without causing the slightest surprise and which has stimulated this artist to produce painted collages, installations, and books.[38]

The "we" of Mosquera's commentary escapes the critic whose limited range of experience keeps him from appreciating and understanding the workings of a taste that straddles different institutional settings and public spheres, not to speak of national contexts. Kimmelman's observation that the Biennial has fostered a "negative critical consensus" makes me wonder whether the lessons of multiculturalism and identity politics are likely to fall on fallow ground. Despite all its claims to the contrary, identity politics perpetuates the *us and them* distinction (with good reason, since whites should not pretend that they suffer the same oppression) that makes liberals like Kimmelman "feel battered by condescension."

Multiculturalists and advocates of identity politics, such as bell hooks, argue that "there must exist a paradigm, a practical model for social change that includes an understanding of ways to transform consciousness that are linked to efforts to transform structures."[39] Hooks also argues that blacks and other people of color should not be expected to do the "work of challenging and changing their consciousness." I agree with the general tenor of the complaint that subordinated peoples have to do not only the manual labor but even the work of reproducing sociality. This is an argument that has also been applied to the work done by women to keep conversations going, as many feminist sociolinguists have explained. But if black and white, center and margin are inextricably imbricated, the way out of the bind of normativism is not to refuse to collaborate. The very difficulty of imagining a new social order that speaks convincingly to over 70 percent of the population requires critics to go beyond pointing out the injustices and abuses and move on to an agenda that will be more effective in transforming structures. What good is it to fight against white supremacy unless whites themselves join the struggle? The potential cultural rearticulation that multiculturalism and identity politics point to will be realized only if the "norm" is set aside in the process.

The Limits of Identity Politics and the Call to Rearticulate Whiteness

Let me attempt to characterize the current status of multiculturalism and identity politics. It seems to me that the lines of struggle around the politics of identity embodied in multiculturalism have been drawn quite clearly and that "progressivism" in the United States is now defined in relation to those who believe that true democracy means the recognition not only of the rights of all citizens, especially of so-called minorities and identity groups hitherto relatively disenfranchised in social and political matters, but, just as important, their history and their culture. Indeed, the shift to a politics of identity since the civil rights era has been accompanied by the increasing importance of defining needs and rights on the basis of the cultural ethos of given groups.[40] It is on this basis, furthermore, that subordinated groups have been able to challenge even the agendas of progressive political associations composed largely of whites, such as feminist and environmental organizations.

Conversely, the different varieties of identity politics—based on differences of race, gender, sexual orientation, and so on—generally thought of as progressive or leftist have also come under criticism, if not outright attack, by many left intellectuals and activists. It goes without saying that the recognition of cultural diversity they proclaim would be attacked by the various groups on the right, but fear of diversity is not the basis on which they are held to be suspicious by the Left. Enough has been written on the topic in the past two or three years to make the criteria for suspicion familiar: identity groups seem to be relatively easily co-optable by the media and institutional structures of power; they can "degenerate" into culturalist agendas relatively deprived of a politics that translates into effective redistribution of resources; they often ignore class, economic, and other infrastructural issues; they are fragmented with respect to each other and thus do not offer a principle of solidarity on the basis of which a new social vision can be projected across the entire spectrum of society; they are often constituted on the basis of a lack of sensitivity to fundamental identity factors of other groups, for example, the presumption that Latino or African American identity, especially in its nationalist projection, is masculine and heterosexual.

Although I fully subscribe to these critiques, I also have the general impression that many of them have been or are in the process of being taken to heart by progressives. White feminists have had to rethink their agendas on the basis of what lesbians and women of color have argued about the politics of sexuality, the family, the workplace, and so on. Likewise, AIDS activism has been questioned as a gay-defined problem, and it too has brought about a recognition of homophobia within communities of color, including the black church. I could go on, but I think that identity politics has gone at least one step beyond where it was when the aforementioned criticisms were made. This is not to say that racism, sexism, and homophobia among "progressives" have disappeared. But there are other, quite resistant impasses to worry about, such as confronting class issues, environmental problems, immigration, the military, and foreign relations, although many intellectuals and activists have begun to deal with these as well. In what follows, I would like to venture some thoughts on what might transform identity politics into a more viable politics. But first a bit of contextualization.

Many adherents and progressive critics of identity politics have acknowledged that a rightist coalition has over the past two decades wrested hegemony from liberals who during the civil rights era worked with more radical social sectors, negotiating concessions as they were deemed necessary. These concessions were, of course, internationally conditioned, for, as Manning Marable and others have argued, the specter of communism, together with its clearly antiracist platform as embodied in anticolonial movements, would have entailed a much more violent struggle than that which saw the end of de jure segregation.[41] Liberalism tolerated the identity politics that emerged with civil rights, extending from the black movement to feminists, Chicanos, Nuyoricans, Native Americans, Asian Americans, and gays and lesbians. But the counterattack has succeeded in good measure in rearticulating the terms of identity politics, presenting them as "choice," "reverse discrimination," and "quotas" and, most important, appropriating the idea that rights—affirmative action, abortion, school prayer, official language—are open to redefinition and rearticulation. Even "political correctness," which was a left way of ironizing its seriousness and self-righteousness, has been wrested away. In other words, sundry groups on the right—which Howard Winant (1990) has grouped into *neoconservatives* (intellectuals seeking to intervene in policy debates, especially to turn around the ideas of "group rights" and "equality of result"), the *new Right* (grass-roots movements often linked to religious fundamentalism, for example, the "Moral Majority" of the 1980s) and the *far Right* (a motley mix of bigots and racists with a modernized wing led by the likes of David Duke)— found that they too could engage in identity politics, affirming such values as a Eurocentric common culture, whiteness, English, the integrity of the family (which was more symbolic than actual, stressing compulsory heterosexuality), the work ethic, U.S. global hegemony, and so on. As the working classes of the United States found themselves in economic straits and as U.S. interventions abroad were portrayed as patriotic duty by the media under the domination of the state, the Right's populist agenda became palatable to the white working and middle classes. Ultimately, even the small but increasingly influential conservative sector of African Americans and Latinos—for example, Thomas Sowell, Clarence Thomas, Richard Rodriguez, and Linda Chavez—have bought into the Right's project without even having to abandon their blackness or Hispanicity.

At this very moment of economic crisis and job flight to the so-called Third World under free-market policies, there seem to be serious weaknesses in the Right's hold over the white middle and working classes. Clinton's victory over Bush corroborates this weakness, although his foot-dragging and backtracking on his promises of reform, not to speak of his embrace of conservatives like David Gergen, also confirm the precariousness of progressivism. Current progressive or leftist racial identity politics are not coherent enough, in my opinion, to win over the majority of "middle-of-the-road" citizens that may be necessary for radical infrastructural changes. And a coalition of feminists, African Americans, Latinos, Asian Americans, and gays and lesbians is neither easy to establish nor sufficient on its own. Furthermore, these groups are not monolithic entities, and the Right is certainly capable of winning over a substantial percentage of them, as is evident in recent mayoral elections. In Los Angeles, for example, Richard Riordan won at least 50 percent of the Latino vote in his successful bid for mayor in 1994, and in New York Herman Badillo's decision to run for comptroller on Republican Rudolph Giuliani's ticket in the mayoralty race was meant to reduce Dinkins's portion of the Latino vote.

Many have called for a new common sense as an alternative to that dissemi-nated by the Right, but no broad social vision has emerged that has the power of the civil rights movement of the 1960s. At best, I can only think of multicultural-ism as the basis for a new common sense, a new progressive populism. But multi-culturalism has all the drawbacks that I have mentioned with respect to identity politics and even more.

In the first place, multiculturalism is firmly rooted only in the schools and uni-versities, with some significant spillover into the media and the art world and some influence in the business world. And it is precisely in these spheres that lib-eralism continues to condition the articulation of multicultural agendas. But that is precisely its greatest weakness. Liberal multiculturalism is potentially little more than a symbolic mechanism of homeostasis for the powers that be; it could become a U.S. version of Brazilian "racial democracy," that is, visibility and equality in matters of symbolic representation and continued unjust distribution of resources.[42] It places emphasis on what I have elsewhere called an "I'm okay, you're okay" embrace of difference but withdraws in horror when—as in Afrocentric definitions of blackness and the Latino project to disseminate the Spanish language throughout the public spheres of schools, advertising, and the airwaves of the electronic media—those differences are proclaimed with an underlying assumption that white people have no legitimate grounds on which to assume an analogous identity based on subalternity. The so-called new ethnicity that emerged in the 1970s as a reaction to the identity politics of people of color—whereby Irish, Polish, German, etc., Americans nevertheless sought to construct community on the model of such racial minorities—did not survive the 1980s. If anything, whiteness as a broad category has emerged as the basis for one brand of reactionary cultural politics of the late 1980s and 1990s, especially among youth. Like the new "men's movement" led by Robert Bly, "white activism" has spawned groups of varying ideological stripes on many college campuses. Activism on the basis of white identity, of course, is what fuels the far Right, embodied in the populist movement of David Duke.

The premier issue of the journal *Race Traitor* promises much—"to win over the majority of so-called whites to anti-racism": "ABOLISH THE WHITE RACE—BY ANY MEANS NECESSARY ... THE KEY TO SOLVING THE SOCIAL PROBLEMS OF OUR AGE IS TO ABOLISH THE WHITE RACE."[43] Its program, however, seems more wishful thinking than carefully thought-out strategy. The editors do make one point that I find suggestive: "The existence of the white race depends on the willingness of those assigned to it to place their racial interests above class, gender or any other interests they hold. The defection of enough of its members to make it unreliable as a determinant of behavior will set off tremors that will lead to its collapse."[44] By this they do not, of course, mean that they are conspiring to exterminate millions of people. Rather, they appeal to the notion of abolition as it was used in the antislavery movements of the nineteenth century. The analogy is as follows: just as some Northerners and Southerners abjured slavery, leading to its collapse by defecting from the status quo, so also will the defections from whiteness by some late-twentieth-century whites lead to the collapse of white supremacy. "It is our faith—and with those who do not share it we shall not argue—that the majority of so-called whites in this country are neither deeply nor consciously committed to white supremacy; like most human beings in most times and places, they would do the right thing if it were convenient."[45]

This is where *Race Traitor*'s political savvy breaks down. Their project lacks a notion of articulation; simply having faith that whites of goodwill under convenient circumstances will defect from their racial formation is to ignore that (1) we are living in a time of diminishing expectations and (2) what binds together a social order is an overdetermined configuration or constellation of ideologemes: democracy, individuality, free enterprise, work ethic, upward mobility, and national security are articulated in complex ways that do not simply split apart when any one of them is challenged. Social formations tend to undergo processes of rearticulation, according to Ernesto Laclau,[46] rather than the kind of upheaval that *Race Traitor* seeks.

I have already suggested that cultural-political common sense is moving from a discourse based on individual rights to one based on group rights. Another ideologeme that is undergoing change is the notion of national security, which in the wake of the demise of the Soviet Union is increasingly being reoriented toward economic and immigration issues. The North American Free Trade Agreement features prominently in this transformation, for it is imagined as having an impact on the right to a job in the United States. *Race Traitor* is evidently forgetting that the increasing percentage of Latin Americans in the United States is leading to situations, as in Los Angeles and Miami, in which African Americans tend to be further removed from job opportunities, even if those are menial. This drives a wedge right through such traditional tenets of political common sense as the unity of the Right, on the one hand, and the solidarity of people of color in the struggle for empowerment on the other. The "new" and "far" Rights can be expected to seek greater policing of U.S. borders while free-market conservatives advocate open borders in keeping with the compromises arrived at with the Mexican government—which, by the way, is increasingly taking an interest in Chicano politics and, through its consulates in major metropolitan centers, playing an active role in the evolution of Latino identity politics. On the African American front, the request to Senator Orrin Hatch by the Black Leadership Forum in July 1992 not to repeal the sanctions against the hiring of undocumented workers is symptomatic of the state of racial affairs among blacks and Latinos.[47] A recent *New York Times*/CBS News poll found that "black Americans were nine percentage points more likely than whites to see immigrants taking jobs away,"[48] a suspicion that is even leading some blacks to question whether Latinos should qualify for protection as a nonwhite disadvantaged group. It is only by taking into consideration all of these factors and the ideologemes that they generate that one can get a reliable idea of how the racial formation is operating in any given period.

In this context, one can look at multiculturalism as an emerging common sense that has the capacity to reconfigure the ensemble of ideologemes that gives the United States its self-understanding. This common sense is, of course, contested terrain. Elsewhere I have criticized multiculturalism for its global pretensions, which are not necessarily at odds with the U.S. government's involvements abroad, particularly in Third World countries. For the United States to retool as a global nation, white supremacy will have to be transformed, if not abolished, although not, perhaps, in the ways desired by *Race Traitor*.

The foregoing observations lead me to suggest reconsidering the place of whiteness within multiculturalism. Such a move is difficult, to say the least, especially since the constitution of the identities of people of color is based partly on the rejection of white privilege. The sleight-of-hand by which whites—of every national and class descent—are thought to share a common European-derived hegemonic culture has made it impossible, as Jeater argues, to construct a contestatory white identity on a par with that of African Americans, Native Americans, and Latinos. Those tendencies of multiculturalism that are willing to take class into consideration do, of course, open up such a possibility, but there is no viable articulation of identity on the basis of even a white working-class cultural ethos. With the folkloric exception of the rural working class, with their country music, whiteness cannot be said to have a viable basis for constituting identity. And country music has recently undergone a transformation that has displaced it as an exclusively working-class cultural phenomenon. In any case, whites have not been devalued and excluded from the distribution of services and material and symbolic goods on the basis of their whiteness; only rightist hype makes that claim along the lines of a rhetoric of "quotas" and "reverse discrimination." At the moment there are no grounds for a white identity within a radical multiculturalism.

It is incumbent upon multiculturalists, then, to project a new democratic vision that makes sense to the white middle and working classes. But identity politics have been at their weakest, in my opinion, in articulating such a vision. Each identity group has articulated its own agenda, with nods to the agendas of other groups also perceived to have been oppressed on the basis of their racial, ethnic, and sexual identity. Multiculturalism is at its strongest in disseminating the representations of these identities and on this basis legitimating needs claims and their satisfaction. After all, it is people of color, women, gays and lesbians, and other subordinated groups who are on the front lines of the downward slide of life chances. But this should not be seen as a point of contention around which groups divide, claiming greater victimization and thus construing themselves as more deserving of compensation than this or that other subordinated group. It is an opportunity, rather, for subordinated groups to occupy positions of leadership in multiracial and multigroup coalitions struggling to increase and democratize the distribution of resources. This may sound a bit Pollyannaish, especially in light of the painful racial and sexual conflicts throughout the United States epitomized in New York by Puerto Ricans pitted against Hasidim in Williamsburg, blacks against Koreans in Flatbush, and other examples cited above. But these conflicts, it seems to me, point not to a weakness in the struggle over resource distribution that I advocate but rather to the limitations of an identity politics that does not look at the larger picture: the relationship between identity groups and institutions, the relationship among institutions (e.g., the academy and business), the relationship between these institutions, the state (the military and the welfare bureaucracy), and the economy, and the articulation of all of these relationships in a global context. I am only trying to make the obvious point that identity politics and its academic ideology multiculturalism must go beyond a politics of representations, understood as the critique of omitted and distorted representations, to a critique and an intervention in the institutional supports of these representations and their immersion in state and economic rationalities.

The problem is that multiculturalism has no place in it to legitimate the claims of over 70 percent of the population—the white working and middle classes—who also have to face the shrinkage of educational, employment, and other social and economic resources. As Manning Marable argues, "We need to keep in mind constantly that 60 percent of all welfare recipients are white; that 62 percent of all people on food stamps are white; that more than two-thirds of Americans without medical insurance are white."[49] Whiteness, then, is not only a matter of social and cultural privilege; we all know that it is also an economic advantage, that constructions of race correlate with and reproduce class positions. But it is more than this; it is also about the very mechanisms—instruments such as census questionnaires, polls, etc.—on which institutions, be they educational, legal, civic, or even recreational, rely in order to achieve self-understanding. Whiteness is even an issue in foreign affairs, underlying decisions that favor economic aid, say, for Eastern European countries over aid for Latin American, African, or Asian countries. It is an important factor in immigration policy, the negotiation of free-trade agreements with Mexico and other Latin American countries and the relation of these agreements to the shrinking U.S. labor market, and so on.

I don't want to suggest that multiculturalists have completely disregarded these issues; it does seem to me, however, that they have gotten short shrift in the much more vociferous call for "whites" to recognize the history and demands of people of color, a call in which whiteness is taken for granted. After arguing that we must all understand each other, one writer, for example, asserts:

> Those from the dominant culture and class [meaning middle-class whites] must cease naming our [meaning people of color's] experience for us, outside of our participation. Instead, if they sincerely wish to express solidarity for the self-determination of people of color, they must work to use their influence to support in concrete ways our struggles for a place to work, speak, and affirm our existence.
>
> There must be an active commitment by those from the dominant culture to work in their own communities to challenge the forms of injustice which result from racism, classism, sexism, homophobia and other forms of institutional oppression.
>
> There must exist a clear understanding by all that the struggle of people of color is not one that is limited to the domain of the intellectual, the academic or the realm of ideology, but rather that it is a struggle that is ultimately linked to the material, to the heart, and to the spirit.[50]

These are desiderata that I share. But for radical multiculturalists to share them is not the problem. The problem is, rather, how to get liberals and the so-called dominant class and culture, especially white youth, to share them as well. I am afraid that accepting the hegemonic white construct is not the best means. This is a dilemma that Kathy Dobie explores in an essay on disaffected white youth who opt to embrace white supremacism:

> If ethnic identity and ethnic suffering are valued now, what's a mongrel white kid to do? (Most of the skin[head]s are some hodgepodge of Western European ancestry that ceased to mean anything a long time ago.) "What about *our* history?" they yell.

They don't seem to see themselves as part of the big white backdrop that people of color have charged against for ages, making a mark here and there. They're just blanks. Because of their white skin, they've escaped hyphenation. They're just American kids, not African-American or Asian-American or Mexican-American. Yet it makes them feel rootless, all alone, without a flag to defend. They want an ethnic community, too—but what is it? What can it be for a white American kid?[51]

One thing it cannot be is an ethnic identity analogous to that of people of color and other subordinated groups who have had to bear the brunt of diminishing expectations. The conditions for mobilizing white youth to fight for a progressive culture cannot be provided convincingly by continually telling them that they must forget their own interests on behalf of those of others. On the contrary, rather than forget their whiteness in order to focus on the plight of others, they must rearticulate it; the basis for their relative privilege must be uncovered and replaced with an understanding of how life chances have diminished under free-market policies not only for people of color but for themselves too. It must be demonstrated that their opportunities to get ahead in the world are diminished not because of affirmative action but rather because of the abandonment of the social contract under the Reagan and Bush administrations and, more generally, under the logic of late capitalism, which now brings us the North American Free Trade Agreement.

Such a rearticulation also means that whites must be called upon to take notice of how their whiteness functions in the world. Most multicultural appeals to whites are like Antonia Darder's demand that the dominant class not "name our experience for us, outside of our participation"; no call is made for the interpellated white "you" to participate in rearticulating the whiteness of the dominant class. One interesting strategy in this regard has been addressed by Frank Kirkland, who argues that white youth should not be held responsible for what previous generations have done; they should take responsibility now in the present for the cultural capital they assume with their identity.[52] There is more to assuming an identity than simply "taking up" or "wearing"; assuming also has the sense of "taking" and "usurping." When these are combined with still another sense, "taking for granted," assuming an identity comes to mean "usurping something by taking on an identity and taking it for granted."

Not taking one's identity for granted is also an important feature of an interesting new group within multiculturalism and identity politics, Italian Americans for a Multicultural United States (IAMUS). Formed initially to counter the Columbus quincentenary celebrations, IAMUS aims to recuperate some of the progressive traditions of Italian and Italian American history (Giuseppe Garibaldi, Carlo Tresca, Anna LoTresca, Vito Marcantonio) and to construct new ones, such as political and cultural alliances with people of color and progressives. Although not oriented as expertly in iconoclastic public-sphere actions as ACT UP, IAMUS similarly transgresses the boundaries that separate institutions. Its activities include educators, high school and college students, artists, writers, and journalists who contribute to the multicultural debates in a panoply of venues and intervene as community organizers, human service professionals, social workers, and labor activists in political debates on health care and labor.[53]

Kirkland's and IAMUS's arguments take us a bit farther than the garden variety of multiculturalism, but they may still not be convincing enough for so-called whites to perceive their relative white-skin privilege and begin to rearticulate it. For that I think they must feel that something is at stake for them. This is where identity politics segues into other issues, such as tax deficits, budget cuts, lack of educational opportunities, lack of jobs, immigration policies, international trade agreements, environmental blight, lack of health care insurance, and so on. These are areas in which middle- and working-class whites historically have had an advantage over people of color. However, today that advantage has eroded in certain respects. Although there is certainly a lot of truth to the claim that environmental blight is very often environmental racism (environmental crimes such as the dumping of toxic waste being more prevalent in communities consisting predominantly of people of color), many forms of environmental blight affect everyone. The quality of the water or the air in many U.S. cities can be uniformly bad, and white women who work at McDonald's or Burger King lack health insurance just as do people of color who work in the service industry or are unemployed. Similar problems can be raised with respect to the military. Although abolishing discrimination on the basis of any identity feature is an important step forward and the march on Washington in support of lifting the ban on lesbians and gays in the military was admirable, a progressive politics requires attending also to the function of the institution (e.g., policing the world on behalf of capital) in which one seeks equal status. Again, recent debates about affirmative action on behalf of women and "minorities" in the FBI have included nothing whatsoever about how that agency often represses the civil rights of citizens, including members of the racial minorities that are increasingly being hired.

If multiculturalism is to be a more effective intellectual movement, that is, if it is to help in making identity politics more viable and consequently keep the academy open for people of all walks, then it is crucial that it connect with the issues I have mentioned. This is the most convincing way for those who up to now have simply assumed whiteness to feel solidarity with those who have suffered deprivation as members of subordinated groups. Without these links it seems to me that multiculturalism runs the risk of becoming simply a symbolic articulation of diversity. This is a serious danger, in my opinion, for if the cultural politics that underpins multiculturalism remains at the level of representations, then claims can always be made—as in Brazil—that everyone is recognized. What good would it do to study the culture of blacks, Puerto Ricans, Native Americans, etc., if they were channeled into community colleges and at best four-year colleges under siege or into the new programs that business is devising with government to train minorities for service-sector jobs.[54] Indeed, there are now business school programs in the "management of cultural diversity,"[55] not to put so-called minorities

on a par with whites but rather to make them functional within the service economy in the new global order.

Cultural Politics and the Academy

I would like to conclude with a brief reference to cultural studies in Latin America,
for despite its drawbacks this movement can in some ways serve as an example for
our own practice. I should say, parenthetically, that the lack of interest in cultural
studies traditions other than those of Britain and the United States (with a nod to
Australia and to India's Subaltern Studies group) only reproduces the assumption
of an analogous "taking for granted" that I spoke of before in relation to whiteness, as if cultural studies only existed in the Anglo-American world.

The main difference between cultural studies in the United States and in Latin
America is that here they are being consolidated around a politics-of-representa-
tion paradigm wherein injustice based on race, class, and gender discrimination is
thought to be reparable at the discursive level and there they are more involved in
problems of resource distribution and engaging communities' relation to the
state, to national and transnational capital, to environmental issues, and so on.
Basically, citizenship—cultural as well as social and political—is construed in relation to access to resources, without slighting the role of the cultural but rather
shifting it from its traditional aesthetic enclave and understanding it as a way of
legitimating claims to resources. The difference between these two traditions is
due to several factors. First, the emerging cultural studies movement in Latin
America is led by social scientists who have questioned their role as adjuncts of
the state, that is, as legitimaters of the paradigms of knowledge production and
problem solution that have foundered in the wake of what in Latin America is
called the "lost decade" of the 1980s: dictatorships, (re)democratization, external
debt and restructuring in line with neoliberal economic policies dictated by the
United States (some of which are the very same problems we are experiencing
here as well). Secondly, the crisis in the social sciences is due not only to the
poststructuralist, postmodernist, deconstructive turn that has been so influential
in Latin America as in the United States but also to the incapacity of the state and
the economy to meet the demands for more egalitarian distribution of resources.
These are demands that cannot be mollified by a politics of representation unsupported by the legitimating semiotic spillover from an expanding consumer economy. In other words, a politics of representation is viable only where there is a
generalized consumer economy that can create the impression that citizenship is a
function of buying power. Since there are no viable consumer economies in Latin
America, consumption has become the occasion for political struggles, including
identity politics, as in the cases of indigenous peoples, shantytown dwellers,
working-class women, participants in the informal economy, and so on.

The economic and political upheavals of the 1970s and 1980s have brought
about a paradigm crisis in the social sciences that has caused anthropologists and

sociologists to rethink their roles vis-à-vis the state and the citizenry. The Mexican anthropologist Guillermo Bonfil refers to this paradigm crisis in assessing the viability of anthropology in the current context.[56] He argues that anthropology in Mexico emerged in the 1930s as an adjunct of the Cardenista state's project of national integration. What, then, is the space for anthropology now that the state is brokering Mexico's integration into a transnational arrangement, most immediately the North American Free Trade Agreement, which is just the first stage in the United States's Enterprise for the Americas Initiative, energetically pursued by many Latin American governments? So long as anthropologists were an integral part of the state's national project, they were able to have some leverage in policy decisions. Now, Bonfil suggests, anthropologists ought to "ally themselves with society," that is, alter their relation to their informants and involve themselves in projects that serve communities and social movements.

Such a "reconversion" of the anthropologist's practice has important repercussions on cultural studies. Bonfil's suggestion is already being carried out, in fact, by other intellectuals who conceive of cultural studies not only as the study of culture but as *intervention in and collaboration with* social movements. Here the interrelations between politics, cultural politics, identity formation, institution building, and the reconversion of citizenship come together. For example, Elizabeth Jelin (1991) and other members of the Centro de Estudios de Estado y Sociedad have been working with victims of human rights violations in a project to open up the Argentine legal process to conceptions of law that take into account cultural and identity factors. Jelin's premise is that the concept of citizenship in a democratic society must take into consideration symbolic aspects such as collective identity and not just a rationalized rights discourse. In this regard, she comes quite close to Nancy Fraser's concept of the correlation between identity and the struggle over needs interpretations. According to Fraser, the conflicts among rival needs claims in contemporary society reveal that we inhabit a "new social space" unlike the ideal public sphere in which the better argument prevails. The struggles over needs interpretations involve the viability of experts who oversee state bureaucracies and other institutions that administer services, the legitimacy of claims made by groups on the basis of a cultural ethos, and the " 'reprivatization' discourses of constituencies seeking to repatriate newly problematized needs to their former domestic or official economic enclaves."[57] To Frazer's spheres we would have to add the traditional aesthetic enclaves that would relegate individual's practices, on the basis of taste, to elite or popular forms regulatable by state apparatuses. In this way, the difficulties of Bhabha's aestheticist approach to redressing injustices referred to above can be obviated.

Jelin posits three domains in which citizenship is produced: (1) the intrapsychic, which is the basis for intersubjective relations, (2) public spheres, and (3) state relations with society, from authoritarian to participatory, taking into consideration as well forms of clientelism, demagogy, and corruption. The main question is how to foment a democratic ethos. Jelin's answer is by expanding public spheres, that is, those spaces not controlled by the state in which practices conducive or oppositional to democratic behavior are constrained or promoted. The proliferation of public spheres will ensure that not just one conception of citizenship (e.g., rights and responsibilities) prevails. The task of the researcher, then, is to work in collaboration with groups to create spaces in which the identity and cultural ethos of those groups can take shape. Such a cultural studies project becomes part of the struggle to democratize society just as the state is brokering free-market policies such as the privatization of public and cultural space.

The Latin American example may be useful for U.S. cultural politics, for it is in the creation of such public spheres that identity politics and struggles over resources can work in tandem. This is the greatest challenge to multiculturalism. Not only must teachers and professors learn about the heterogeneous histories and cultures of their students; they must also link these representations of group history and identity to the current struggles over resources. Only thus will there be change in the historically hegemonic function of the university as a "factory for producing rationalizations of elite behavior while curtailing investigations of why society works as it does."[58]

An example in the United States of such a linkage is the Southwest Organizing Project (SWOP), a multiracial, multiissue community organization whose purpose is to "empower the disenfranchised in the Southwest to realize social, racial, and economic justice."[59] This organization has taken on the mainstream environmental advocacy groups and gotten them to understand that environmentalism is of concern not only to whites but to people of color, who are most often on the front lines with regard to pollution, toxic waste, and so on. What makes SWOP so important is that its leaders are largely Latinos and other people of color, including Native Americans, whose land claims "have often been overlooked by Chicano activists pressing the land claims of their own people." Its work demonstrates that the very same identity groups involved in the politics of representation support viable political struggles over resources. It is incumbent upon multiculturalists in the academy to make such efforts known when addressing the history and culture of so-called minorities.

Another example is provided by the Ganados del Valle cooperative, also in New Mexico, which has taken on the Nature Conservancy's project to create wildlife preserves that not only fail to recognize Chicano land claims but also disregard the "cultural traditions embedded within the family and friendship networks of the community" that form part of their agropastoral practices.[60] Ganados del Valle was able to demonstrate that the kind of conservationism promoted by mainstream environmentalists had racist and elitist aspects that ultimately run counter to the interests of the entire citizenry:

> The implications for the future of the environmental movement in the U.S. are clear: either conserve culture and nature together and establish a long-term blueprint for cultural and ecological survival, or enjoy the temporary delusion of a victory for the preservation of a (non-existent) pristine nature, and ignore the broader threat of

(and unresolved struggle against) an ever expanding, urban industrial capitalist system. The mainstream environmentalist position must be characterized as the "gardens in the midst of blight" model of environmental politics—a model that insults the land ethics and naturalist sensibilities of the Chicanos of Tierra Amarilla.[61]

It is arguments such as those of SWOP and Ganados del Valle, not simply the claim that all we need to fight is white, Eurocentric cultural imperialism, that have the power to incorporate the white middle and working classes into struggles led by coalitions that include people of color and that benefit the citizenry rather than capitalist corporations. Whites must feel that they have a stake in the politics of multiculturalism and not simply see themselves as a backdrop against which subordinated groups take on their identity. The question may be raised whether the rearticulation of whiteness and the incorporation of whites into struggles over resource distribution do not lead to the deconstruction of other racial and identity groupings and thus weaken the basis on which people of color in the United States have waged their politics. Rearticulating whiteness does not necessarily lead to a weakening of the identity of people of color and other oppressed groups, but it does create the possibility that many more issues will be perceived no longer as exclusively "white" concerns but also as matters of importance to ethnoracially and sexually minoritized groups and vice versa. Shifting the focus of struggle from identity to resource distribution will also make it possible to engage such seemingly nonracial issues as the environment, the military, the military-industrial complex, foreign aid, and free-trade agreements as matters impacting local identities and thus requiring a global politics that works outside of the national frame.[62] Of course, such a politics is meaningless unless it can be articulated among diverse constituencies and to the location of power and capital in the state. In *City of Quartz*, Mike Davis has mapped the ways in which urban ethnoracial politics and a myriad of global forces brokered by the U.S. state are imbricated:

> The privatization of the architectural public realm, moreover, is shadowed by parallel restructurings of electronic space, as heavily policed, pay-access "information orders," elite data-bases and subscription cable services appropriate part of the invisible agora. Both processes, of course, mirror the deregulation of the economy and the recession of non-market entitlement.[63]

The erosion of public space, the bunkerization of the wealthy, the segregation of ethnoracial groups, the political economy of drugs, the expendability of youth, the absolute permeation of everyday life by consumerism from the richest to the poorest, even a religious schism between right-to-lifers (Archbishop Mohanty) and Christian liberationists (Father Olivares)—all of these phenomena are shaped by global forces that greatly *exceed* although they certainly do not exclude the question of whiteness. It is incumbent upon multiculturalists and identity-politics activists, if we are going to make a difference, to take our politics beyond, without placing all the blame on or fostering disavowal of, the white (straw)man at which we have aimed so many of our efforts. I CAN'T IMAGINE EVER WANTING TO

BE WHITE. This statement makes me *think*, but it does not encourage me to imagine; in fact, it admits to a failure of the imagination. But why not imagine the circumstances under which one might *want* to be white—or black, or brown, or queer, or none of the above?

NOTES

1. Michele Wallace, "Reading 1968 and the Great American Whitewash," in *Remaking History*, ed. Barbara Kruger and Phil Mariani (Seattle: Bay Press, 1989), 97–109.

2. See Richard D. Alba, *Ethnic Identity: The Transformation of White America* (New Haven: Yale University Press, 1990); Yen Le Espiritu, *Asian American Panethnicity: Bridging Institutions and Identities* (Philadelphia: Temple University Press, 1992); Juan Flores and George Yúdice, "Living Borders/Buscando America: Languages of Latino Self-Formation," *Social Text* 24 (1990):57–84.

3. See Suzanne Oboler, "The Politics of Labeling: Latino/a Cultural Identities of Self and Others," *Latin American Perspectives* 75:4 (Fall 1992):18–36.

4. Howard Winant, "Amazing Race: Recent Writing on Racial Politics and Theory," *Socialist Review* 23:2 (1993):161–183.

5. On the opposition of group and individual rights and possible solutions to this seeming aporia, see Kristie McClure, "On the Subject of Rights: Pluralism, Plurality, and Political Identity," in *Dimensions of Radical Democracy: Pluralism, Citizenship, Community*, ed. Chantal Mouffe (London: Verso, 1992), 108–127, and Martha Minow, *Making All the Difference: Inclusion, Exclusion, and American Law* (Ithaca: Cornell University Press, 1990). McClure identifies three generations of pluralist debate in the United States (turn of the century to World War I, 1950s and 1960s, 1980s and 1990s), each of which was "articulated in opposition to unitary, monolithic or totalizing conceptions of the political domain, particularly in so far as these presume some singularly sovereign or unique agency overseeing or determining political processes and/or social relations" (p. 115). Such pluralist debates actually run counter to the myth of the melting pot, for they view the "'subject of rights' as a site of multiple and intersecting group memberships or identities within that social plurality, only one, and by no means necessarily the most significant, of which is that of formal citizenship in the state."

Minow offers a kind of sublation of individual rights and group identity (for which she uses the term "relational strategies"): "It is only contradictory to defend both rights and relational strategies in a conceptual framework that poses either/or solutions and reads any focus on human interconnection as a retreat from liberalism to feudalism. We are more inventive than that. It is a mistake to infer that relational strategies are inconsistent with rights. An emphasis on connections between people, as well as between theory and practice, can synthesize what is important in rights and what rights miss. Especially when located as a historical response to patterns of assigned status, rights present an important critical tool to challenge persistent relationships of unequal power. The shortfalls in traditional rights analysis, for those who question assignments of difference and legacies of stigma, are its insistence on proof of similarity with a given 'norm' and its defense of the private power of people entrusted with the care of others. Here, relational strategies can help. Rights can be reconceived as a language for describing and remaking patterns of relationships. Rights can be understood as communally recognized rituals for securing attention in a continuing struggle over boundaries between people. ... Infused with attention to relations between theory and context, parts and wholes, selves and others, and observer and observed, the language of rights can enable rich contests over whose version of reality should prevail, for now" (pp. 382–383).

6. Stuart Hall, "The Local and the Global: Globalization and Ethnicity," in *Culture, Globalization, and the World-System: Contemporary Conditions for the Representation of Identity,* ed. Anthony D. King (London: Macmillan Education, 1991), 32.

7. Larry Rohter, "As Hispanic Presence Grows, So Does Black Anger," *New York Times,* 20 June 1993, 1, 11.

8. Cited in Alison K. McLaurin, "Listening Closely to Rap Music's Message," *The News and Observer,* 22 April 1993, 5B. Readers should recall Paul Gilroy's observation that there is such a boom in hip-hop product that he "can't keep up with [it] anymore. I don't know if anyone can. There is simply too much of it to be assimilated, and the kinds of judgments we make have to take that volume into account. It's a flood. ..." (Paul Gilroy, "It's a Family Affair," in *Black Popular Culture: A Project by Michele Wallace,* ed. Gina Dent (Seattle: Bay Press, 1992), 309.

9. If we want to discuss invisibility, representation of Latinos is almost nonexistent in the mainstream media, and what there is, is most often caricaturesque. Despite the populational parity of blacks and Latinos, the United States is still imagined in its public spheres as a society that defines itself in black and white, so much so that discussions of the Los Angeles riots, even to this day, tend to overlook the black-Chicano and Chicano–Central American tensions that flared in the months before and after them. *La Prensa San Diego* (15 May 1992) ran an editorial pointing out that although Central Americans played a major role and "a substantial number of Hispanics [were] killed, shot and/or injured, every major television station was riveted to the concept that the unfolding events could only be understood if viewed in the context of the Black and White experiences." Jack Miles, in whose essay "Blacks vs. Browns: The Struggle for the Bottom Rung" (*Atlantic Monthly,* October 1992) this editorial is cited, qualifies *La Prensa*'s self-serving register by noting that "the editorial ended by declaring 'the established Mexican American communities' to be 'the bridge between Black, White, Asian and Latinos'" (p. 51).

But my argument is *not* about competing misrepresentations or victimization; in fact, it implies the opposite: the need to construct affirmative imaginaries that do not derive their main legitimacy from countering victimization, a process that renders identity beholden to it.

10. bell hooks, "Representing Whiteness in the Black Imagination," in *Cultural Studies,* ed. Lawrence Grossberg, Cary Nelson, and Paula Treichler (New York: Routledge, 1992), 340.

11. Peggy Phelan, *Unmarked: The Politics of Performance* (London and New York: Routledge, 1993), 7.

12. "The project of producing positive images is an impossible one. Though it may have the best intentions of redressing imbalances in the field of representation, it is bound to fail as it will never be able to address questions of ambivalence and transgression" (Isaac Julien, "Black Is, Black Ain't: Notes on De-Essentializing Black Identities," in Dent, *Black Popular Culture,* 261.

13. Sut Jhally and Justin Lewis, *Enlightened Racism: The Cosby Show, Audiences, and the Myth of the American Dream* (Boulder: Westview Press, 1992), 87.

14. Ibid., 90.

15. Michael Lerner, "Jews Are Not White," *Village Voice,* 18 May 1993, 34.

16. Diana Jeater, "Roast Beef and Reggae Music: The Passing of Whiteness," *New Formations* 18 (Winter 1992):107.

17. Dyer explains that after Julie, the protagonist of *Jezebel*, learns the behavior befitting a proper (and therefore presumably white) lady, it is her black maid Zette who must express her feelings and desires: "She no longer expresses feeling—she 'lives' through Zette. Zette has to express excited anticipation, not in speech, but in physical action. ..." The upshot is that "it is black people who bodily express her desire" (Richard Dyer, "White," *Screen* 29:4 [Autumn 1988]:58).

18. Ibid., 114.

19. Stuart Hall, "Minimal Selves," in *The Real Me: Postmodernism and the Question of Identity* (International Communication Association *Documents*, no. 6 [1987]), 44–46, quoted in Jeater, "Roast Beef and Reggae Music," 115.

20. Jeater, "Roast Beef and Reggae Music," 115.

21. "For 16 weeks, a group of blacks, Hispanics, and whites takes an intensive U.S. military race-relations course." (National Public Television, 15 June 1993).

22. Rohter, "Hispanic Presence," 11.

23. B. Ruby Rich, "The Authenticating Goldfish: Re-Viewing Film and Video in the Nineties," in *1993 Biennial Exhibition* (New York: Whitney Museum of American Art/Abrams, 1993), 94.

24. Gloria Anzaldúa, "*Haciendo caras, una entrada:* An Introduction," in *Making Face, Making Soul—Haciendo Caras: Creative and Critical Perspectives by Women of Color,* ed. Gloria Anzaldúa (San Francisco: Aunt Lute Foundation Books, 1990), xx.

25. Jeater, "Roast Beef and Reggae Music," 121, 122.

26. Homi Bhabha, "Beyond the Pale: Art in the Age of Multicultural Translation," in *1993 Biennial Exhibition* (New York: Whitney Museum of American Art/Abrams, 1993), 66.

27. Ibid., 69.

28. Peter Bürger, *Theory of the Avant-Garde,* trans. Michael Shaw, foreword Jochen Schulte-Sasse (Minneapolis: University of Minnesota Press, 1984).

29. Homi Bhabha, "The World and the Home," *Social Text* 31/32 (1992):141–154.

30. George Yúdice, "For a Practical Aesthetics," *Social Text* 25/26 (1980):129–145.

31. David Gates, "White Male Paranoia?" *Newsweek,* 29 March 1993, 49.

32. Ibid.

33. James Baldwin, *The Fire Next Time* (New York: Dial, 1963); Frantz Fanon, *Black Skin, White Masks* (New York: Grove, 1967); Joel Kovel, *White Racism: A Psychohistory* (New York: Pantheon, 1970); Dyer, "White"; bell hooks, "Overcoming White Supremacy," *Z,* January 1987, 24–27 and "Representing Whiteness in the Black Imagination," in *Cultural Studies,* ed. Lawrence Grossberg, Cary Nelson, and Paula Treichler (New York: Routledge, 1992), 338–346; Thelma Golden, "What's White ... ?" in *1993 Biennial Exhibition* (New York: Whitney Museum of American Art/Abrams, 1993).

34. Barbara Ehrenreich, "Cultural Baggage," *New York Times Magazine,* 5 April 1993, 16.

35. Baldwin, *The Fire Next Time,* 41.

36. Michael Kimmelman, "At the Whitney, Sound, Fury, and Not Much Else," *New York Times,* 25 April 1993, H1, H37.

37. Coco Fusco, "Passionate Irreverence: The Cultural Politics of Identity," in *1993 Biennial Exhibition* (New York: Whitney Museum of American Art/Abrams, 1993), 83.

38. Gerardo Mosquera, "Bad Taste in Good Form," trans. [George] Y[údice] Espínola, *Social Text* 15 (1986).

39. hooks, "Overcoming White Supremacy," 27.

40. In addition to McClure, "On the Subject of Rights," and Minow, *Making All the Difference*, see Flores and Yúdice, "Living Borders/Buscando America," and Yúdice, "For a Practical Aesthetics," which make this argument, drawing in part on Howard Winant's claim that the "new" social movements emerged from the aftermath of civil rights and on Nancy Fraser's analysis of the turn from the politics of rights to that of "needs interpretations." See Howard Winant, "Postmodern Racial Politics: Difference and Inequality," *Socialist Review* 20:1 (January–March 1990):121–147 and Michael Omi and Howard Winant, *Racial Formation in the United States: From the 1960s to the 1980s* (New York: Routledge and Kegan Paul, 1986); Nancy Fraser, "Women, Welfare, and the Politics of Need Interpretation" and "Struggle over Needs: Outline of a Socialist-Feminist Critical Theory of Late Capitalist Political Culture," in *Unruly Practices: Power, Discourse, and Gender in Contemporary Social Theory* (Minneapolis: University of Minnesota Press, 1989):144–160, 161–187, and "Rethinking the Public Sphere," *Social Text* 25/26 (1990):56–80.

41. Manning Marable, "Multicultural Democracy: Toward a New Strategy for Progressive Activism," *Z*, November 1991, 89.

42. Without reducing race criteria to those of class, it should be pointed out that the notion of "racial democracy" emerged in the first three decades of the twentieth century as Brazil underwent the transition from a largely plantation society to an industrialized one in the southern states. In order for Brazil's project of modernization to succeed, intellectuals and state technocrats considered it necessary to integrate, at least at the level of representation, blacks and mixed-race groups. It was immigrants of European descent, however, capable of assimilating into the middle class and even the elite sectors, who took the lion's share of resources in accordance with white-skin privilege. This difference between integration-via-representation and assimilation-into-the-common-wealth accounts for the fact that African-based cultural forms such as samba—through which Brazilianness came to be defined from this period on—could be popular while the vast majority of blacks and browns continued (and continue) to live in dire poverty. The contradictory functions of Brazilian samba (space for Afro-Brazilian cultural practices and yet hegemonic interpellation of the nation through it) should sound a cautionary note regarding the currency of U.S. rap. Greg Tate, in the preview issue of *Vibe*, touted as the "new mainstream" in Michel Marriott's "Hip-Hop's Hostile Takeover: Rap Joins the Mainstream" (*New York Times*, 22 September 1992, B12), does more than sound a cautionary note; he considers hip-hop the "invitation to party for the right to demagoguery" in a society that, like hip-hop itself, has lost whatever potential it had for a vision and an agenda: "I have yet to hear a rapper say that commodity-fetishism is the true God of this nation" (*Vibe*, September 1992, 15).

43. Editorial, *Race Traitor*, 1 (Winter 1993):1.

44. Ibid., 2.

45. Ibid., 3–4.

46. See Ernesto Laclau, "Towards a Theory of Populism," in *Politics and Ideology in Marxist Theory* (London: Verso, 1979), 143–198.

47. Miles, "Blacks vs. Browns," 58.

48. Seth Mydans, "A New Tide of Immigration Brings Hostility to the Surface, Poll Finds," *New York Times*, 27 June 1993, 1, 16.

49. Manning Marable, "Multicultural Democracy: The Emerging Majority for Justice and Peace," in *The Crisis of Color and Democracy: Essays on Race, Class, and Power* (Monroe, Me.: Common Courage Press, 1992), 251.

50. Antonia Darder, "Building Alliances with People of Color," *School Voices* (March 1992):9.

51. Kathy Dobie, "Long Day's Journey into White: Skingirls and White Power, a Guided Tour of the Aryan Nation," *Village Voice*, 28 April 1992, 29.

52. Frank Kirkland, workshop on "Rethinking Politics, Power, and Organizing," City University of New York Black Student Alliance Conference on Race in the Postmodern Era, 4 April 1992.

53. See George De Stefano, "We Don't Need a Macho Hero," *New York Newsday*, 9 October 1992, 56, 58. IAMUS can be contacted c/o PACE, 79 Leonard St., New York, NY 10013; (212) 274-1324.

54. *Time*'s recent prognosis for higher education sees the demise of many small liberal-arts schools and the increase of new schools geared to business interests, especially "two-year community colleges emphasizing service-oriented courses" (13 April 1992, 54).

55. See the advertisement in *Hispanic Business* (November 1991) for Columbia Business School's Executive Program on "Managing Cultural Diversity": "A 5-day executive program on managing cultural diversity in the workforce—the most critical issue corporate America will face in the next decade" (p. 76). The curriculum of such programs includes such books as Christopher A. Bartlett et al., *Managing the Global Firm* (New York: Routledge, 1990), John P. Fernandez, *Managing a Diverse Workforce: Regaining the Competitive Edge* (Lexington, Mass.: Lexington Books, 1991), Philip R. Harris and Robert T. Moran, *Managing Cultural Differences* (Houston: Gulf, 1987), David Jamieson and Julie O'Mara, *Managing Workforce 2000: Gaining the Diversity Advantage* (San Francisco: Jossey-Bass, 1991), Albert Koopman, *Transcultural Management: How to Unlock Global Resources* (Cambridge: Basil Blackwell, 1991), George F. Simons et al., *Transcultural Leadership: Empowering the Diverse Workforce* (Houston: Gulf, 1993). Some of these are reviewed in L. A. Kauffman, "The Diversity Game: Corporate America Toys with Identity Politics," *Village Voice*, 31 August 1993, and Scott L. Malcomson, "We Are the Worldview: A Brief Guide to Right-Wing Multiculturalism," *Village Voice Literary Supplement*, September 7, 1993, 21.

56. Guillermo Bonfil Batalla, "Desafíos a la antropología en la sociedad contemporánea," *Iztapalapa*, 11:24 (1991):9–26.

57. Fraser, "Women, Welfare, and the Politics of Need Interpretation," 157.

58. Editorial, *Z*, May 1991, 3.

59. See Elizabeth Martinez, "When People of Color Are an Endangered Species," *Z*, April 1991, 63.

60. See Devon Peña, "The 'Brown' and the 'Green': Chicanos and Environmental Politics in the Upper Rio Grande," *Capitalism, Nature, Socialism* 3:1 (March 1992):93.

61. Ibid., 101.

62. I address some of these problems in "We Are *NOT* the World," *Social Text* 31/32 (1992), 202–217.

63. Mike Davis, *City of Quartz: Excavating the Future in Los Angeles* (London: Verso, 1990), 226.

17

The Campus Culture and the Politics of Change and Accountability: An Interview with Thomas P. Wallace

RONALD STRICKLAND

Editors' note: Thomas P. Wallace is president of Illinois State University. He has been a sharp critic of the growing tendency among state legislatures to underfund public institutions of higher learning, and he has proposed innovative steps to preserve access for lower- and middle-income students. More recently, Wallace has criticized the academy's inherent resistance to change and to the current demands for "accountability."

RONALD STRICKLAND: Your critique of conventional funding practices for state universities and your critique of faculty resistance to most forms of accountability address a general crisis in public higher education. What, in your view, are the most urgent problems facing the universities?

THOMAS WALLACE: The academy has not learned from its own history! The evidence of economic and social change in America during the past forty years mandates modification of the academic culture and embracing new accountabilities. These changes range from an examination of who should pay what portion of the cost of a public university education to the role that the faculty should play in the application of academic expertise to promote the economy, to solve social problems, and to develop, in general, broad opportunities that will benefit society.

For example, let us examine the issues of public higher-education finance. There has been enormous growth in American higher education during the past forty years, with greatly expanded institutional missions, academic programs, and student support services as well as the inherent higher costs. The basic financial strategies of the past no longer work for public higher education, as state legislatures cannot or will not provide the necessary resources to support a mature national public higher-education system. The result has been that student access to all educational options has suffered and will continue to decline unless there is an overhaul of fiscal policies and practices. Students have been increasingly segmented according to family income into two-year and four-year commuter colleges and residential universities, resulting in some public university student bodies' now having higher average family incomes than those of some private colleges. In reality, some public higher-education options are too expensive for many families, while higher-income families who could afford to pay a higher percentage of their education costs enjoy significant state subsidies as a result of tax revenues received by public institutions. This situation is not equitable, nor does it result in the appropriate funding base for the institutions.

I have argued that much higher tuition must be charged in order to collect a greater percentage of the full education cost from students who can afford to pay it. With this approach a significant portion of the added tuition revenues would be used for grants to low-income and lower-middle-income families to help them pay the higher cost of attendance. Public institutions would have a higher "sticker price," and the "real cost" would vary more dramatically within an institution's student body on the basis of the student's ability to pay.

This high-tuition/high-financial-aid strategy can provide additional operating dollars for the public institution, shield lower- and middle-income families from tuition increases, and limit the need for additional state tax support, which is and will continue to be in short supply.

R.S.: Many faculty members would, I think, welcome the sort of innovative funding strategy you've proposed as a way to preserve the integrity (in both senses of that word) of the university in the face of what is sometimes seen as a concerted effort by conservative state and federal legislators to roll back the gains in access and educational quality made by public universities since World War II. Yet, for many of these same faculty members, your call for the academy to accept a higher degree of social accountability would raise fears of even greater intrusions into the academy by state and federal government. How would you respond to this concern?

T.W.: I would approach these issues as a natural evolution of American social and economic change—a systemic adaptation—during an era of great expansion in public higher education. Such societal change should have moved more rapidly, having a more noticeable and constructive impact on or drawing a response from the academic culture, and should inherently have been expected to produce new external expectations and accountabilities for the academy. Of course, resistance to attempts to change the historic academic culture is not surprising, since what is seen as evolution and orderly constructive change by one person appears to be revolution and chaos to another.

The higher-education literature describes the historic academic culture, involving the philosophical views and prerogatives of faculty toward campus governance, accountability, and institutional change. Whereas some of these basic conditions of the academic culture are formal in nature, others exist as elements of an underground code of conduct. Peter Seldin defines the academic culture as "the unspoken language that tells administrators, faculty, staff and students what is important, what is unimportant, and how they are expected to do things. In a sense, it is the ropes to know and the ropes to skip" (1988, 75).

Although such views address the realistic and important politics that affect institutional change, the force of new external pressures and expectations on higher education today has subjected the traditional campus culture to heightened stresses and conflicts between administration and faculty as well as between higher education and its external publics. The increased cost of higher education (related to cost-plus pricing or budget incrementalism), the growth in scope and size of administration, consensus internal management, and the scope and magnitude of faculty noninstructional activities have created financial and public relations problems. The expectations of legislators, governors, system governing boards, and state coordinating boards of higher education regarding accountability for such activities as economic development, applied research, industrial training, adult education, and more cost-effective delivery of instruction via technology are not receiving adequate responses from higher education. The institutional change inherent to this new agenda is difficult to implement because of the traditional academic or campus culture that is solidly ingrained in the higher-education enterprise.

R.S.: I'd like to pursue your critique of the "traditional campus culture" as a force that inhibits the academy's ability to respond to recent global economic, technological, and social transitions. What, specifically, is wrong with the "traditional campus culture"?

T.W.: First, it must be established that a university, particularly a public university, has some responsibility to society and even perhaps to the taxpayers for becoming engaged in the problems and the opportunities of the day. This does not mean the periodic educational fads or fashions but significant social, cultural, and economic issues. If this is a reasonable assumption for the role of the academy, then one could view evolution as conforming necessarily to changing conditions that theoretically can be positive for society while not prostituting the academy. The resistance of the academy to change is not, per se, an undesirable condition but indeed one of its strengths. But this assumes that resistance reflects thoughtful and full consideration and not simply a situation in which people take more delight in debating issues than in seeing positive benefits of change.

There are major issues before American society that need the attention of our universities. For example, in order to survive in national and international competition, American business has embraced innovation and entrepreneurship to produce higher-quality products at reduced unit cost. The current trend toward reduced personnel costs accompanied by higher levels of productivity found in technology-oriented businesses is in direct contrast to the outdated smokestack-industry philosophy found in the academy, where more people and higher expenditures are required for increases in the quality and quantity of a product or service. Peter Drucker has offered the following view of the new technology: "Management is the new technology that is making the American economy into an entrepreneurial economy. It is also about to make America into an entrepreneurial society. Indeed, there may be greater scope in the United States—and in the developed societies generally—for social innovation in education, health care, government and politics than there is in business and the economy" (1985, 171). The traditional campus culture, however, resists this sort of innovation. As Henry Levine has argued, "universities are not technologically progressive because there are few incentives to be so at the level of those who make instructional decisions. That is, it is simply not in their interest" (1989, 3). The view is also true for many staff members whose responsibilities are administrative and this view is not restricted to "instructional decisions." In the academy, attempts to invest in technological advancement can very easily be thwarted by the politics of the campus culture.

R.S.: As you know, many academics see business-derived concepts like "entrepreneurship" as inappropriate to the mission of the academy. Some observers, including several of the contributors to this volume (see the essays by Richard Ohmann, Paul Lauter, Richard Terdiman, Jean Howard, and Evan Watkins and Lisa Schubert), acknowledge the primacy or importance of the vocational mission of the academy while attempting to resist various unwanted effects and conditions of that mission, such as the tendency for the university to work principally in the interests of the business sector and to hold in place existing and inequitable social hierarchies of race, gender, and class. At the same time, some of the most prominent conservative critics of the academy (such as William Bennett, Allan Bloom, Dinesh D'Souza, and Lynne Cheney) have all but ignored the vocational mission of the university. The widely publicized conservative attack on "political correctness" and multiculturalism in the university projects a vision of the university as primarily a site for the transmission of a cultural heritage rather than a site for career preparation. Your own characterization of the problems facing the university seems to cut across the lines of these politically charged positions. Do you see elements of resistance to necessary change—reactionary elements of the "traditional campus culture"—in the attitudes of progressives who are wary of increased corporate control of the university in the new postindustrial order or in the attitudes of conservatives who decry the decline of tradition in an increasingly multicultural society? How would you respond to the progressive faculty member who resists Drucker's call for academic entrepreneurialism as an impediment to democratic and egalitarian progress or to the conservative faculty member who resists entrepreneurialism as a threat to traditional values?

T.W.: The fear that technological progress equates to vocationalism in its usually negative context is unfounded in the type of change that I envision. First, it should be pointed out that universities have always had the mission of preparing students for careers. In American colonial times, the colleges stated their missions as preparing clergy, politicians, and gentlemen. C. P. Snow took great delight in reminding his colleagues at Oxford of the university's emphasis on career preparation. However, let us examine the new elements of today's job market beyond simply a new or modified knowledge base. The role of general education is even more important today than ever before as the new and evolving career opportunities place greater reliance on higher-order thought skills involving analysis, problem solving, critical thinking, and other elements that are or should be the foundation of general education. For the average faculty member, designing and teaching general education courses is far from the top of the list of most favored activities! Greater emphasis is required and must be placed on graduating thinking students or, as one writer suggested with the title of a book, *Thinking for a Living*. Smarter people devise smarter economic products; uneducated people can't build them or manage them satisfactorily! Products of our economy are increasingly composed of a higher knowledge content produced by thinking people and are composed less of a natural-resources content produced by uneducated people.

R.S.: What, in your view, are the strengths and weaknesses of the available models for addressing the academy's resistance to accountability?

T.W.: Successful organizational changes in institutional culture involve attitudes, behavior, and leadership as well as incentives and rewards for those who are engaged in the enterprise. There are examples within and outside education of successful alteration of the campus or organizational climate, culture, and accountabilities. The steel, agriculture, and automotive industries have altered the business climate and the methodologies of the American workplace. However, the new attitudes and behavior learned by business in the past few decades from the changing global economy have had little if any impact on the academic culture or on the management and financial principles and strategies that drive American universities. Regardless of the type of enterprise, these elements of good management and change fundamentally apply.

American higher education today is affected by national and regional economic conditions, an aging and largely unmarketable senior faculty, changing national and state political oversight roles for education, and declining national values particularly related to tax support for education and other human services and changing student demographics. These and other factors should have a greater effect on the culture of higher education and should long ago have altered traditional views, practices, and outcomes of the university enterprise. Leadership is a central necessary ingredient for guiding change and establishing new accountability in an evolving culture or organization.

Successful leadership at various levels can take many forms, from a quiet behind-the-scenes style to the one-person show. However, successful leadership, regardless of form, is ultimately related to a futuristic vision or plan, broad campus ownership of the vision, and a financial strategy that usually involves enhanced resources and institutional reallocation focused on a limited high-priority agenda.

During the past few decades a few institutions, notably Stanford University and Carnegie-Mellon University, have successfully completed developmental phases that significantly changed them and achieved the status and funding of nationally recognized first-tier universities. The principles that appear to have driven the administrative and faculty leaders during this period of significant change were not consistent with the historic academic culture. These universities identified their academic areas of expertise and potential strength and over the years "stuck to their knitting." They achieved greatness by matching their strengths and institutional aspirations to external opportunities, needs, and potential funding.

Stanford's development from 1955 through 1975 is an example of what can be achieved by visionary leaders who overcome barriers to institutional change by clever campus politics and competent work. Stanford identified the comparative and competitive advantages that would ensure a world-class academic program, hired the best faculty, and marketed its vision of the future to those outside the university who had the resources to finance the new Stanford. This successful evolution of an individual campus culture to embrace strategic thinking has spread to other high-quality but mostly major research universities. Unfortunately, these fundamental principles of selected academic themes or priorities and broad campus responsibility for financial accountability and resource acquisition have been mostly applied to the research function and not to the other two basic academic functions of instruction and university outreach.

Many of the elements of the historic academic culture that are under siege or being evolutionized are those discussed in the strategic planning literature as the concepts and practices of a new type of leadership and long-range planning. In 1983 George Keller published the highly acclaimed volume entitled *Academic Strategy: The Management Revolution in American Higher Education.* Keller's treatise entered the market at a time when a new strategic thinking was just beginning to be discussed nationally as a potentially important new planning concept. The popularity of this work was also due to the author's ability to capture the frustrations, experiences, and thoughts of many administrators who were trying to guide their institutions through different and difficult times. Higher education was entering an era in which the campus environment, both internally and externally, did not seem conducive to the academic culture or the attitudes and planning models of the past. Interestingly, Keller's work was not a detailed methodology for conducting an institutional strategic planning process but a philosophical and outcomes-oriented volume directed toward the reality, politics, and potential of American higher education in a new era. As such, it provided much-needed therapy for many practicing administrators who identified with Keller's description of evolving external demands on higher education and his analysis of internal problems associated with the elements of the historic campus culture in America.

R.S.: How does faculty participation in shared governance relate to the conflict between the traditional campus culture and the new entrepreneurial academy that you've described?

T.W.: Campus governance has evolved toward a more collegial process; thus, campus politics as well as formal decisionmaking has increasingly reflected more of a shared-governance philosophy. Numerous institutional committees today have broader representation and functions, often extending beyond the faculty, students, and administration. The traditional model of strong, top-down administrative planning is disappearing from the higher-education culture. This increased degree of collegiality is reflected in a text by R. G. Cope appropriately entitled *High Involvement Strategic Planning: When People and Their Ideas Matter*. Cope acknowledges that "there are many individuals who are content with the norms, goals, and structures to which they have become accustomed. They don't want anything changed. Their security rests with the present. They resist change." Still, Cope argues that greater shared governance can have beneficial effects: "A central tenet is this: successful organizational strategies do not result from plans, management systems or formulas narrowly conceived. On the contrary, successful strategies evolve from leaders—who may or may not be supervisors—who think about the enterprise as a whole and act in ways that meet stakeholder needs and build on strengths" (1989, 3).

Cope's thesis is attractive and reflects the idealistic view that those who care greatly about the future of the university will develop a vision for the future that will serve the institution well. The challenge to the institutional leadership is to ensure that a majority of such talented people are appointed or elected to the university's task forces dealing with institutional change. Also, although this political approach may ensure a consensus agenda, decision, or plan, the nature of the process does little to inspire ownership among those who will have the responsibility for implementing it. This point is of even greater significance if those who are to implement the plan are responsible for acquiring new resources or reallocating existing resources, which, of course, is becoming more and more prevalent in higher education.

Another analysis—that of R. H. Waterman—suggests that in today's environment ad hoc committees are best suited to problem solving: "The real action in organizations occurs outside 'the proper channels.' ... Simply put, ad hoc organizational forms are the most powerful tools we have for effecting change. A manager who can launch a task force, keep it on track, and get results without uprooting sound bureaucratic infrastructure ... that is the manager with a bright future" (1990, 4–5). This concept of adhocracy is based on the theory that organizations need "adaptive, problem-solving temporary systems of diverse specialists linked together." The success of ad hoc structures in higher education is predicated on the belief that faculty, students, and staff acting together can forge worthwhile ideas into desirable programs and activities without being influenced by the usual politics that slow progress within the "bureaucratic infrastructure." However, this approach replaces one type of politics, that of the official administrative infra-structure, with another, that of the campus underground. The ad hoc group's re-sponsibility for outcomes, implementation, and sources of funding is minimal; it can create without concern for responsibility or retribution. Unfortunately, both Cope and Waterman tend to assume that formulation of the appropriate plan or the decision is the end result, and they avoid the implementation problems and the mass avoidance of responsibility by academic administrators that are created by their methodologies.

As administrators have increasingly embraced the politics of safe involvement, the equilibrium for institutional decisionmaking has shifted more toward faculty responsibility. Also, opportunities for department chairs and deans to be entre-preneurial and for institutional committees and faculty governance systems to make important but difficult decisions have increased as institutional decision-making and control have shifted away from central administration. However, the shift toward high faculty involvement and authority has not been matched by an equal shift toward increased accountability, responsibility for implementation, or support of difficult decisions and their impact on the institution. Academics have done a terrible job of professional self-regulation compared with the professions of law and medicine, for example. And it is questionable whether increased in-volvement in institutional management has resulted in improved decisionmak-ing, increased institutional productivity, or quicker responses to institutional op-portunities. The campus politics involved in making recommendations and *in the planning for change* is a separate issue from *the implementation of change*.

The absence of incentives and rewards at all levels of the university for making difficult decisions related to improving cost-efficiency and effectiveness and to generating additional revenues is a central political problem associated with the traditional campus culture and the resistance to institutional change. The envi-ronment of public higher education does not include the fear of bankruptcy or the motivation of financial rewards found in business. As a result, individual self-mo-tivation that goes beyond meeting the minimum instructional expectation and that accepts responsibility for enhancing university revenues or improving in-structional cost-efficiencies is not a common element of campus culture among most faculty and administrators. Academic responsibility usually ends at the stage of planning for the consumption of resources in the name of quality, which most frequently necessitates hiring more people and/or a reduction of an individual's formal instructional or administrative responsibilities.

The leadership role of the campus CEO has changed significantly in the past few decades. Today the CEO must influence with persuasion rather than domina-tion or rigid control. Modern high-involvement politics must balance the leader-ship implementation responsibilities of the CEO with the independent faculty prerogatives. Such an equilibrium necessitates delicate political and substantive discourse between the two parties. In practice, the CEO's role has increasingly be-come more circumspect as the probability of presidential survival in office has been generally recognized to increase as the CEO becomes less involved and less responsible (i.e., as CEOs also practice the politics of safe involvement). As one writer describes the CEO's dilemma, "The chances of being held responsible for a negative outcome are greater than the chances of being rewarded for a success" (Hannaway 1989, 56).

R.S.: Given these formidable obstacles to change, what is your view of the prospects for improving accountability in the academy, and what needs to be done?

T.W.: Let us approach the question by discussing the necessity for dealing with the politics of implementing change and how change can productively be used to guide constructive, organized evolution toward accomplishing a shared institutional vision. First, charting a course of change and productivity can enable an institution to achieve its future vision of success defined in terms of mission, strengths, academic niches, goals, and opportunities. As I've argued, within universities, discussion of change, increasing productivity, and cultivating and seizing new external opportunities can be and often are thwarted by the politics of the campus culture. Cohen and March (1974) described the university climate as a "prototypical organized anarchy." Birnbaum expands on this theme:

> The concept of the organized anarchy suggests that colleges and universities often make choices through a process of "garbage-can decision making." Problems, solutions, and participants form steady streams that flow through the organization as if they were poured into a large can. When one tries to make a decision, other people or issues in the can may become attached to it because they are contemporaneous, even though they may not appear to be logically connected. (1989, 31)

The model of such an "organized anarchy" involved in "garbage-can decision making" is hardly an environment from which to expect large-scale institutional change, increased productivity, and enthusiasm for addressing an important national agenda for higher education.

The internal difficulties in dealing with institutional change are significant and time-consuming and require a great deal of personal and institutional compromise. The inertia of the system itself is often the primary source of the problem. In such an environment, many participants oppose changes because the status quo is comfortable. In addition, many participants who embrace the concept that change is necessary and healthy for the institution decline or limit participation as a result of the realities of the campus climate with regard to change.

However, even when solutions and approaches to higher education's problems are identified and gain internal support, the external political system increasingly prevents experimentation and implementation of identified futuristic directions and programs. This is particularly true of public universities, which have increasingly become overmonitored, overcontrolled, and bureaucratized by external bodies at great expense in dollars and in lost opportunities. These external bodies, having a life of their own, construct their own views on the nature, format, and outcomes for institutional success and related financial management. The national trend of rapid growth and increased involvement of state multicampus governing boards and their related staffs has superimposed a significant and growing external political system on the historic campus political culture that has ramifications for institutional change and productivity. The influence of state executive and legislative branches of government has grown to include most elements of university operations.

The loss of campus control of decisionmaking to external bodies has diluted the authority and responsibility of the administration and the faculty. This diffusion of internal and external authority and leadership responsibility justifies Birnbaum's application of the label "organized anarchy." Kerr and Gade described accurately the variety of current problems: "fewer decisions can be made because of more veto power; ... those decisions that can be made are made more slowly due to extensive consultation and confrontation; ... there is less of a central vision for the institution and more of a congeries of competing visions; ... nobody is in charge" (1986, 143). Business leaders, alumni, legislators, and other groups are increasingly critical of higher education's perceived unwillingness to change and to embrace accountability. One could safely forecast that the priority for higher education will continue to slip in the minds of those external to the academy, particularly if universities continue to weaken themselves and lose credibility. Other public agenda items such as roads and bridges, health care, the elderly, K–12 public education, and prisons are higher priorities for state and federal funding. The reluctance of universities to embrace change parallels the reluctance to respond to external calls for institutions to be accountable and to increase productivity. As Henry Levine suggests, some of the most stubborn obstacles to increased productivity are rooted in the academy's structural resistance to accountability:

> The glacier-like movement toward raising productivity among colleges and universities is attributable to the large scope of control over resources and activities (de facto property rights) held by academic departments at decentralized levels of the organization and to the lack of incentives. Colleges and universities have not generally harnessed the self-interest of faculty and other academic decision makers by creating meaningful incentives to raise productivity. (1989, 9)

Universities must recognize and incorporate measures of departmental, student, and institutional productivity as well as address incentives for productivity for individual faculty members and departments. Institutional success will depend on the degree that the campus culture embraces a driving lust for excellence and a higher expectation of innovation and accountability.

The campus culture must evolve to accept a greater broad-based campus responsibility for success of the enterprise to balance the historic shared-governance role that provides the faculty with almost complete formal and informal decisionmaking authority. Modern external pressures for change and accountability in higher education are extreme and unrelenting and will prevail to some degree. The major unanswered question is the nature of the accommodation that higher education is willing and able to make to protect a positive and prosperous future position in American society.

WORKS CITED

Birnbaum, R. "Responsibility Without Authority: The Impossible Job of the College President." *Higher Education Handbook of Theory and Research* 5 (1989):31–56.

Cohen, M. D., and J. G. March. *Leadership and Ambiguity: The American College President.* Boston: Harvard Business School Press, 1974.

Cope, R. G. *High Involvement Strategic Planning: When People and Their Ideas Matter.* Cambridge: Basil Blackwell, 1989.

———. *Strategic Planning, Management, and Decision Making.* Washington, D.C.: American Association for Higher Education, 1981.

Drucker, P. F. *Innovation and Entrepreneurship: Practices and Principles.* New York: Harper and Row, 1985.

Hannaway, J. *Managers Managing: The Workings of an Administrative System.* New York: Oxford University Press, 1989.

Keller, G. *Academic Strategy: The Management Revolution in American Higher Education.* Baltimore: Johns Hopkins University Press, 1983.

Kerr, C., and M. Gade. *The Many Lives of the Academic President.* Washington, D.C.: Association of Governing Boards of Colleges and Universities, 1986.

Levine, H. M. *Raising Productivity in Higher Education.* Philadelphia: Higher Education Research Program of the University of Pennsylvania, 1989.

Seldin, P. "Academic Culture." In *Year Book of American Colleges and Universities 1986–87,* ed. Thomas Kurian. New York: Garland Press, 1988.

Waterman, R. H. *Adhocracy: The Power to Change.* Knoxville: Whittle Communications, 1990.

18

Public Policy and Multiculturalism in America: Educational Rhetoric and Urban Realities

A. R. LATEGOLA

My professor tells me that I am an unrepentant materialist. Thus (so as not to disappoint her), I would like to begin this piece with a little geopolitical orientation. The urban neighborhood in which I am currently living and doing my Ph.D. fieldwork is the Paradise/Mayfair neighborhood, located in Northeast D.C. Most D.C. residents see the city as bifurcated into two seemingly neat semiotic halves: West/East, White/Black, Splendid Imperial Rome/Decaying Urban War Zone, etc. Anything east of the Anacostia River seems as foreign to whites living in Northwest or the suburbs of Virginia as the planet Mars. I have found that even people who have lived in the District all of their lives, when I asked them for a ride home after a night out, could not find their way into the Paradise/Mayfair neighborhood without a Department of Defense–length logistical briefing (although, strangely enough, getting out never seemed to be a problem).

This is, needless to say, an ideal position from which to observe all of the various cultural paradoxes and contradictions that interlace the edifices of the "capital city." Washington, of course, very much exemplifies the "world city" in its "core" Northwest sector. It is the hub of international political and economic activity of every sort imaginable. When I attended the Inaugural Parade, there were people in the crowd from a dazzling array of ethnic backgrounds that would make any Benetton advertiser drool. Here we have the "corporate" vision of multiculturalism—a free-floating plurality of tastes, cultures, and styles that all can adopt or

This work was made possible by a Graduate Fellowship from the National Science Foundation. The views portrayed here are those of the author and in no way represent the views of the National Science Foundation.

purchase depending on their desire at the moment; a tourist's-eye view of aesthetic global "difference," and all combined with the happy, fuzzy feeling that we are all really the same deep down inside (we all love a parade, right?).

This idyllic vision of postmodern globalism, however, jars with the realities of life east of the Anacostia River. Indeed, many of the arenas in which the term "multiculturalism" has been deployed seem to have had virtually no impact on life in the Paradise/Mayfair neighborhood. The furor over "debating political correctness" and the supposedly corroding effects of the discourse of equality and rights have not altered the fact that every single resident of Paradise Manor has an income below the median income of Washington, D.C., and that nearly one-third live at or below the poverty level. The "canon wars" have not altered the fact that there is virtually no significant commercial development in this area other than liquor stores and supermarkets. These conditions have been more or less constant, regardless of what has happened at the levels of educational and political discourse.

I would like to examine one of the most prominent policy arenas in which I have seen the concept of multiculturalism deployed: the debate over "political correctness" within the American public school system. Robert Reich states that "Americans love to get worked up over American education. Everyone has views on education because it is one of the few fields in which everyone can claim to have had some direct experience"; he adds, however, that "those with the strongest views tend to be those on whom the experience has had the least lasting effect" (1991, 226). I would like to look at the main lines of reasoning around which these curriculum debates have centered and consider why it is that they have yet to get at the main social dynamics that might make multiculturalism meaningful for school-aged youths—something other than yet another empty political euphemism in a seemingly intractable debate.

Why Do We "Educate"?

To begin with, it may be instructive to take a look at exactly what role education has played within the modern state (particularly in the United States) and how this role has set the stage for the conflict surrounding multiculturalism in education.

Public education has been the centerpiece of American and European democracies since their ideological inception in the Enlightenment Age. According to philosophers such as Locke and Rousseau, in order for a liberal democracy to work the body of the governed (and the governing) had to be composed of educated citizens who were loyal to the nation. In order for there to be an ample supply of educated citizens, a system of state-sponsored public education needed to be installed so that all citizens would have equal access to the knowledge thought necessary to make them effective participants in their government. According to Robert Reich, this knowledge had a specific character: "By the last decades of the nineteenth century, in Europe and America, children were expected to attend free public schools, where they studied their nation's history and heroes, learned to write and speak the national language correctly, and pledged their allegiance to the nation's flag" (1991, 18). Michel Foucault also traces the development of mass-based modern public education to the needs of the modernist, industrial, state-based economy. Since the new industrial mode of production demanded the precisely coordinated, streamlined use of masses of able-bodied laborers, the new mode of education had to provide the training that these future citizens and foot soldiers of the capitalist state would need in order to be "productive"—it was to be the education of what Foucault calls the "disciplinary society" (or what Weber before him called the "Iron Cage Society"): "Generally speaking, it might be said that the [pedagogical] disciplines are techniques for assuring the ordering of human multiplicities ... in short to increase the docility and utility of all [human] elements within the system" (1979, 218). The precision-based industrial economy and the military state that protected it and provided civil order had to be based in an education that atomized children in a streamlined process that has characterized American pedagogy up until the present: "American schools mirrored the national economy, with a standard assembly-line curriculum divided neatly into subjects, taught in predictable units of time, arranged sequentially by grade, and controlled by standardized tests intended to weed out defective units and return them for reworking" (Reich 1991, 226). Thus, the public schools filled their charges with the knowledge necessary to be good citizens, appreciative of their country's history and culture, and trained them to respond to the demands of the captains of industry who would lead their nation to prosperity.

So why is this mode of education currently coming apart at the seams? Educational conservatives such as Allan Bloom (1987), Roger Kimball (1990) and Arthur Schlesinger Jr. (1992) pin the blame on the "ethnic upsurge" and the ascent of the "cult of the individual" in the 1960s and 1970s. According to these scholars, during the wars over equal representation in the curriculum the basic principles of logic and scientific objectivity central to classical education were completely lost. However, according to Molefi Kete Asante, one of the best-known proponents of multicultural curricula in the public schools, "educational experience should reflect the diverse cultural heritage of our system of knowledge. ... Such is not the case and cannot be the case until teachers know more about the African-American, native American, Latino, and Asian experience" (1992, 305).

From here, the debate over multiculturalism in the public schools seems to center not so much around multi- versus monocultural curricula as around notions of cultural pluralism versus cultural particularism. Diane Ravitch, Asante's leading nemesis in the public school debate, seems to have no problem with multiculturalism per se: "Today, pluralistic multiculturalism must contend with a new, particularistic multiculturalism. The pluralists seek a richer common culture; the particularists insist that no common culture is possible or desirable" (1992, 276). Thus, the debate at the public school level is not so much whether or not to teach multiculturalism as how to package it. Under pluralistic multiculturalism, the American nation-state would still be the main framework within which students learned history, grammar, math, etc.; however, that frame would be modified by adding elements of African American history, Native American culture, etc. Asante's multiculturalism is not content with adding minorities and mixing. Instead, the Afrocentric curriculum that he proposes would place African culture, history, and technological achievements at the center of the curriculum in predominantly African American school districts (several school districts across the country, including Atlanta, Detroit, and Washington, D.C., are currently developing Afrocentric curricula [Ravitch 1992, 279]).

In her critique of the canon debate, Katha Pollitt points to the faulty assumption (shared by all partisans) that there is a magical one-to-one correspondence between reading-list ideologies and child behavior patterns: "Read the conservatives' list and produce a nation of sexists and racists—or a nation of philosopher kings. Read the liberals' list and produce a nation of spineless relativists—or a nation of open-minded world citizens. Read the radicals' list, and produce a nation of psychobabblers and ancestor-worshippers—or a nation of stalwart proud-to-be-me pluralists" (1992, 210). From Pollitt's argument it would appear that a concern for ideology is still very much alive and well on all sides of the canon debate. What has been lost is an idea of where concrete school conditions and pedagogical practices fit into all this furor.

Ravitch seems to glimpse that there is a common set of underlying material conditions surrounding the PC debate in the public schools: "They [students in Black and Latino districts] would fare better in school if they had well-educated and well-paid teachers, small classes, good materials, encouragement at home and school, summer academic programs, protection from the drugs and crime that ravage their neighborhoods, and higher expectations of satisfying careers beyond the school" (1992, 289). However, this insight gets lost amid ungrounded (bordering on paranoid) speculation that "particularism" will result in "arousing distorted race pride in children of all races, increasing racial antagonism and producing fresh recruits for white and black racist groups" (p. 290).

Even supposedly progressive theorists such as Asante seem to fall all too readily into this trap. As Patty Lather (1991, 16) states, a "liberating" curriculum can all too easily become oppressive and one-dimensional when served as pedagogical medicine to be memorized within a mass-based, assembly-line school environment: "tied to their version of truth and interpreting [student] resistance as 'false consciousness,' too often such pedagogies fail to probe the degree to which 'empowerment' becomes something done 'by' liberated pedagogues 'to' or 'for' the as-yet-unliberated, the 'other,' the object upon which is directed the 'emancipatory' actions." In the end, what the discourse of the canon wars has ignored is that there has always been much more that affected students' ability to become "good, productive citizens" (whatever these may be) other than the literary diet prescribed during the course of their education. As we shall see, students' chances after high school are determined more by where they are educated and what pedagogies are used in that process than on what particular books they are forced to read and regurgitate.

Education Within the Global Economy: The Death of the State School and Pedagogical Triage

If we are educating our children to ensure that they will be productive, working members of society, the past decade has demonstrated that even this correlation is misleading. Within the context of an increasingly decentered world economy, being a faithful and diligent worker does not necessarily mean being "productive" in relation to other workers around the world. According to Robert Reich, there will be three main job categories in the globalized economy of the future: symbolic-analytic services, in-person services, and routine production services (1991, 174). The characteristics of these categories may be summed up as follows:

Symbolic-Analytic	*In-Person*	*Routine Production*
Varied	Repetitive	Repetitive
High autonomy	High supervision	High supervision
Globally marketed	Locally marketed	Globally marketed
Nonhierarchical	Hierarchical	Hierarchical
Teamwork	Management	Management
Manipulation of symbols/language, problem solving	In-person services	Manipulation of raw materials/assembled goods
Critical thinking, creativity, initiative	Loyalty, punctuality, pleasant demeanor	Loyalty, punctuality, predictability

Unlike the days of the New Deal, when a "good, honest [white] man" could work "his" way up from the bottom of the industrial hierarchy into a well-paid, skilled, unionized job (with his faithful wife keeping house in the background), the low-end jobs of the New World Order are dead ends. As the workforce has become increasingly automatized and deskilled, the middle rungs of the occupational ladder have been removed, leaving symbolic analysts (mostly white males) at the top and in-person servers (mostly women—all racial backgrounds) and routine production servers (mostly women of color) at the bottom of the global hierarchy (Reich 1991, 175–179).

As the job categories of the future have become cemented into these stratified slots, so has the type of education given to the children who are expected to fill their ranks. Since, according to Reich, the main character traits of in-person servers and routine production servers are punctuality and docility, "a standard American education, based on the traditional premises of American education," discipline, coordination, and maximum efficiency, "will suffice" (1991, 175). For these children, knowledge will consist of a list of "facts" (whether mono- or multicultural) that they are expected to memorize by rote and regurgitate upon command. Here, the partisans of the canon debate have tended to rail about what set of "facts" will be fed to children in the public school system and missed the most important lesson of the "information highway" age: that the memorization of static "facts" is an obsolete practice. Information and technology are being transferred and communicated at such a fast pace that, once one set of historical or scientific "facts" is memorized, it is likely to become obsolete in the face of new data, studies, or debates within its field. Thus, since the pedagogy of the "standard American education" is largely obsolete, the only thing that it will be good for is to keep children somewhat busy and off the streets for about thirty hours a week. It will be preparing them for jobs that require punctuality, docility, and endless repetition but have little or no chance of upward mobility or reward for individual initiative.

The education of the future symbolic analyst, however, is a very different thing:

> On the advanced tracks of the nation's best primary and secondary schools ... the curriculum is fluid and interactive. Instead of emphasizing the transmission of information, the focus is on judgement and interpretation. The student is taught to get behind the data—to ask why certain facts have been selected, why they are assumed to be important, how they were deduced, and how they might be contradicted. ... The symbolic-analytic mind is trained to be skeptical, curious, and creative. (1991, 230)

If the writings of emancipatory-education theorists are correct (Giroux 1981, Freire 1985, Shrewsbury 1987, Culley and Portuges 1985), this is ideally the sort of education that every child should have—one that treats the student as an active, inquisitive investigator within the learning process rather than the object of a one-dimensional curriculum served up as "medicine." However, this sort of education also requires an enormous amount of energy and resources on the part of the budding symbolic analyst's parents and teachers: "Their parents are interested and involved in their education. Their teachers and professors are attentive to their academic needs. They have access to state-of-the-art science laboratories, interactive computers and video systems in the classrooms, language laboratories, and high-tech school libraries. Their classes are relatively small; their peers are intellectually stimulating" (Reich 1991, 227). Needless to say, an education like this is a "positional good" (Hirsch 1976)—a good or service whose availability depends on one's social status and income. Rather than having access to "more" or "better" facts per se, these students have access to the tools, technology, and training that will allow them to access, evaluate, and manipulate a wide range of "facts" in order to engage in problem solving, planning, and other creative enterprises.

Symbolic analyst parents worry ceaselessly about their children's education, because if the children aren't secured places among the elite ranks of student symbolic analysts they will have to go to the public schools and feed from the common educational trough, which will not (so the parents think) give them the skills or attention they need to compete for entrance into the more elite four-year colleges of the country. Even though a 1989 study in Fairfax County, Virginia, cited in the *Washington Post* indicated that there was no difference in test scores between English-proficient students who attended schools with high immigrant populations and those who attended more homogeneous schools, middle-class parents in the area have still been extremely edgy about the demographic shift. One local woman commented, "I feel I pay a lot of [tax] money, and I want my child to have as much attention as she needs. I don't want to come off as a bigot either. I guess it's good old maternal instinct" (Brown 1992, A10).

When symbolic analyst parents are faced with increasing diversity in the classroom, their reaction (as it was in the pre–civil rights past) has been flight. A recent article in the *Washington Post* detailed the worries of parents in the suburbs of Arlington and Alexandria, Virginia, cities that have seen a 25 percent and a 50 percent increase since 1982 in the number of students in area schools who speak English as a second language (Brown 1992, A10). Apparently flight from the public schools is now a result not only of perceived racial difference but of class difference and ethnic difference as well. According to Harold Hodgkinson, director of the Center for Demographic Policy, "This is really not a white phenomenon. It's a middle-class phenomenon, and middle-class parents don't want anything bad to happen to their kids' education. ... Whites have fled inner cities since the '60's and '70's. Now black parents are following that. In Prince George's [County], you get black parents who are concerned about kids in class who don't speak English" (Brown 1992, A10). Robert Reich has also made this argument; however, he is careful to note that "in America, economically motivated segregation often results in de facto racial segregation" (1991, 276).

In reaction to successful desegregation efforts in the more grossly inequitable state school systems (particularly in California and Texas), irate property owners (predominantly white) pushed through legislation that made up the "tax revolt" of the late 1970s (exemplified by California's Proposition 13). However, it has recently become apparent that the massive property tax rollbacks of the 1970s are threatening to gut the state school system as a whole. In response, middle-class property owners have come up with a new secession strategy: "You equalize, we privatize" (Folbre 1992, 282). The privatization of middle-class education has become an increasingly broad trend, as symbolic analyst parents have abandoned the increasingly poor and trouble-ridden public schools in their districts rather than investing their time and energy to work out collective solutions to improve them.

The newest wrinkle in this trend has been the "voucher" movement, which gained much of its momentum under the Bush administration's America 2000 education plan (Kozol 1992, 274). Instead of expanding government spending on public schools that would serve a large cross section of children, the government would give out vouchers for children to attend the private schools of their parents' choice. According to Jonathan Kozol, even liberal commentators bought into this logic by espousing "market choice and competition in the public schools while reassuring us that we can ward off any threat of private-school vouchers" (1992, 277). John Chubb, a vocal proponent of the voucher system, has elaborated on its logic, baldly demonstrating his contempt for the concept of public, democratic education:

> Excellence in public schools, says Chubb, is undermined because so "many students come from families that put little or no emphasis on education." The virtue of the voucher-funded schools that he proposes ... is that, like private schools today, they would be attractive to the kinds of kids whose parents are "informed," "supportive," and "encourage education." Children of the other kind of parents—"parents who may cause problems"—are, he says, "the ones most likely to drop out." (Kozol 1992, 277)

As Kozol comments, "Strip away the fancy language here and we are looking at a social Darwinist scenario, a triage operation that will filter off the fortunate and leave the rest in schools where the children of 'better' parents do not need to see them" (p. 277).

In addition to the imminent possibility that outright privatized segregation will obliterate the public school system is the other danger that the students of schools bankrolled by corporate sponsors will become the captive audiences for intensive marketing campaigns for their products, whether or not they are healthy for the children at whom they are aimed. Chris Whittle, founder and chair of Whittle Communications, is one such corporate education sponsor. He plans to open two hundred for-profit schools by 1996, but his sponsorship comes with an explicit commercial price tag. According to Kozol, "Whittle's commercials for Snickers, Burger King, and other products on Channel One, shown in 10,000 schools, are required viewing for almost 8 million students daily—more than a third of all teenagers in the nation's schools" (1992, 274). Thus, in the schools of the New World Order (or Brave New World, as the case may be), students are taught not only how to be good, docile workers but how to be good, docile consumers. In this context, the debate over a Eurocentric reading list versus a multicultural one may be the least of our worries.

In addition to evaluation of current pedagogical techniques, an understanding of the current public educational system requires a long, hard look at the political and economic struggles that go into shaping the locality (geopolitical) in which the educational process takes place. Public schools do not appear out of nowhere. They are created and maintained within a very specific local economy, which is in turn affected by larger global economic trends. The political economy in which these educational arenas are structured and maintained, in turn, has a profound effect on how they will "perform" (or *what* they will "perform") in the process of creating "good citizens." As we shall see, the whole notion of the "place" where citizens are created and grow up is rapidly changing, and with it the idea of what a "citizen" is to begin with.

The Politics of Place:
Where the "Savage Inequalities" Start Out

As Diane Ravitch briefly observed in her discourse, the quality of children's life chances depends not only on what is put into their heads during the maturation process but also on the kinds of material and institutional resources that are available to them and their families. These life chances and resources are profoundly affected, in turn, by the political economy that structures the job opportunities and public services available in any given locale. Thus, any attempt to revitalize public education must be linked with a comprehensive agenda for urban revitalization and economic empowerment for the parents of public school children.

In *Urban Fortunes: The Political Economy of Place* (1987), John Logan and Harvey Molotch examine the dynamics of this political economy over time and in considerable detail. What their work reveals is that, in spite of the allegedly successful hijacking of the American agenda by the "politically correct" Left, the fundamental processes that cement material inequality into urban life have not changed very much over time, except to accelerate the economic and racial stratification that has always existed there. As Adolph Reed Jr. and Julian Bond note, "mainstream" distaste for multiethnic schools and communities long preceded the "excesses" of any alleged "cult of ethnicity" that emerged after the civil rights period. Pointing in particular to Edsall and Edsall's (1992) *Chain Reaction*, they write:

> For them, the phenomenon of post-war suburbanization had nothing to do with pre-existing racial polarization, and thus the attitude of white suburbanites now is a reaction to what they see as the excesses of the inner city. But the desire to flee from impoverished inner-city populations (and from blacks in general) that the Edsalls describe long preceded post-war suburbanization and was, in fact, one of the forces that drove it. (Reed and Bond 1991, 735)

This fact is amply demonstrated by consulting the original text of the underwriting manual that the Federal Housing Administration circulated to banks in 1938, when banks were looking for potential sites in which to build the New Deal, federally subsidized suburbs of America:

> Areas surrounding a location are [to be] investigated to determine whether incompatible racial and social groups are present, for the purpose of making a prediction regarding the probability of the location being invaded by such groups. If a neighborhood is to retain stability, it is necessary that properties shall continue to be occupied by the same social and racial classes. A change in social or racial occupancy generally contributes to instability and a decline in values. (Judd 1991, 740)

This provision, even though eventually overturned in court, effectively shut non-whites out of the emerging suburbs, since no federal policy was ever developed taking an explicit stand against urban segregation. Thus, as Dennis Judd observes, "Between 1946 and 1959, less than 2 percent of all the housing financed with the assistance of federal mortgage insurance was made available to blacks" (1991, 740).

During the period in which the educational purists allege that the American agenda fell prey to the cultic clamoring of racial and ethnic minorities, comparatively little progress was made for these groups in terms of the political economy that governed their chances of finding adequate housing, employment, or community resources. In fact, in spite of the War on Poverty and the urban agenda of the Johnson administration, conditions for inner-city residents rapidly deteriorated. The urban renewal programs of the early 1960s (referred to by Malcolm X as "Negro removal") were a catastrophe for the urban poor:

> Although improving the housing of the poor was ostensibly the program's key goal, less than 20 percent of all urban renewal land went for housing; over 80 percent went for developing commercial, industrial and public infrastructures. ... In reality, urban renewal destroyed more housing (especially poor people's housing) than it created. As Friedland (1982, 85) calculated, "90 percent of the low income housing destroyed by urban renewal was never replaced." (Logan and Molotch 1987, 168–169)

Likewise, the block grants, revenue-sharing programs, and urban development action grants of the 1970s always seemed to wind up subsidizing upscale private commercial development that did little or nothing to improve the lives of the poor at whom it was targeted: "Only 15 percent of UDAG [Urban Development Action Grants] money was spent under the classification 'neighborhood facilities,' and even this was accomplished only after officials began to place projects like shopping malls in the 'neighborhood' rather than the 'commercial' category" (Logan and Molotch 1987, 170–171).

In the meantime, as low-income inner-city housing was being razed to make way for shining new retail "cores" in downtown areas, suburbanization—a process that was explicitly racially and economically stratified from the very beginning (see Judd 1991)—was continuing apace. The segregation of the suburbs, according to Logan and Molotch (1987), has not been much affected by the post–civil-rights-era reforms either. Although race-based real estate covenants had been ruled unconstitutional, all that was necessary to preserve the lily-white enclaves created by white flight from the city was zoning that might exclude several kinds of development (for instance, low-income housing, rental housing, unrestricted utility access, etc.) while encouraging other kinds of development more geared toward the affluent (large-lot zoning for houses, open space preserves, etc.) (Logan and Molotch 1987, 191). One result of exclusive zoning (in addition to other more subtle forms of economic racism) has been the formation of suburbs that are if anything, more segregated throughout the 1980s: "86 percent of whites live in suburbs with a black population of less than one percent" (p. 194).

In terms of its ramifications for public education, this increasing stratification has led to a situation in which affluent residents increasingly secede into their own urban enclaves, taking their tax resources with them and leaving the urban poor to fend for themselves within an economy of massive federal and state spending cuts (instituted during the Reagan-Bush years) on the educational and welfare programs that they need the most. Logan and Molotch observe of the economic disparities between affluent and poor suburbs that

> working-class residential towns raise more [tax] revenues and spend more money than other communities. They impose higher tax rates and receive more outside financial help. Poor suburbs must pay for higher levels of social welfare services, such as special education programs, income supplements, public hospitals, and housing. They spend two to four times as much as other communities on these functions. (1987, 192)

Thus, suburbanization has effectively created and reinforced a regressive tax structure wherein the inner-city and suburban poor are increasingly bled of the educational and welfare resources that they need the most (which must come from the increasingly miserly state and national purses).

When partisans of the canon debates spend countless hours and pages railing over the ideological content of what children are taught at school, they miss the fact that the most important thing that influences children's life chances is what greets them when they get out of school. Parents who face chronic under- or unemployment, poverty, lack of affordable housing, and limited community resources will justifiably be too exhausted by the end of the day to lavish the same amount of time and resources on their children that symbolic analysts are able to spend. Children also learn from an impoverished urban environment that what they learn in school is irrelevant to an urban existence devoid of entrepreneurial or creative opportunities. When these conditions are combined with a thriving domestic drug and gun trade, the results are lethal for the children of the urban poor. In 1992, 160 teenagers and young adults were killed in the District of Columbia as a result of gun violence (Wilgoren 1993). According to a recent *New York Times Magazine* article, small-caliber semiautomatic handguns have recently made up 30 percent of the guns traced by the Federal Bureau of Alcohol, Tobacco, and Firearms to various crimes across the country: "The cheap pocket guns are found in the hands of small-time drug dealers ... and, increasingly, students in inner-city high schools who believe they have a need for self-defense" (Anderson 1993, 22). Needless to say, it is impossible for children to concentrate on schoolwork and achievement motivation in an urban socioeconomic environment that is discouraging and frightening at best and lethal at worst.

Conclusion: What Is to Be Done?

The advent of the Clinton administration has brought with it a host of promises regarding the overhaul of public education. But which direction is most important to take? What would the elements of a successful education reform be? How would this reform tie in with an urban revitalization agenda? And how would the concept of multiculturalism play into this scenario if it were to be deployed effectively?

To begin with, the debate on public education has to address the question of how it will be financed, because the source of the money will have (as demonstrated above) an enormous impact on what children are "fed" (both informationally and nutritionally) during the course of their school day. In order to stem the rampant resegregation of the school system through privatization, federal spending on education will have to be vastly increased. Part of the problem with public education in the United States is that, since it has always been predominantly paid for through local property taxes, it has always been directly affected by larger trends in urban segregation. According to Margaret Spillane and Bruce Shapiro, "Among the top nineteen industrial nations, the United States ranks seventeenth in spending for public education, and dead last in compensation of teachers. The United States is also the only major industrial nation to promote a radically inequitable school-financing system based on local property taxes" (1992, 281).

One encouraging development in establishing equitable public education has been the Clinton administration's Goals 2000 initiative, which would abandon the voucher strategy and increase federal funding for public schools while leaving an ample amount of ideological elbowroom for local districts to decide how they wish to implement the educational goals outlined in the initiative. However, the program has already come under fire as inadequate even for the beginnings of a reform effort. Stephen O'Connor, a public school teacher who has worked in New York City, Houston, and San Francisco, has commented that "expecting national standards to improve the quality of American schools is like expecting a lame dog to jump merely because you hold a hoop in front of it. After all, it's not as if schools don't already have standards of their own, or know how far short of them they fall" (O'Connor 1993, 704). According to O'Connor, even though Clinton's plan includes $393 million to develop new education strategies and enhance parental involvement, "The $7.5 billion New York City school budget, for example, could absorb [this] amount with hardly a ripple."

One thing that the Clinton plan does recognize, however, is the need for an empowered and mobilized local public to keep the schools responsive to the needs of the children in their particular area. Where most federal school reform proposals have fallen short, however, is in realizing that in order to have an empowered local public it is necessary to have a community of adults whose developmental and institutional needs are met. New modes of low-income development need to be promoted in local communities that empower local residents to own their own businesses and housing (whether individually or collectively) rather than having large-scale outside developers suck all of the dollars right out of these communities in return for a smattering of low-end, service-sector jobs. There also needs to be vastly increased legislative and federal activism in terms of providing gun-control laws with teeth and increasing funding for health-care and community services that can stem the blood-flow from impoverished urban communities. Only when there is an activated, empowered, and healthy local citizenry will there be a local government willing to give them their equitable share of tax-based re-sources—better schools and well-paid teachers being chief among them.

The real challenge, then, is radically reformulating ideas about local commer-cial and residential development in these areas and explicitly tying them in with education programs so that children who live in urban neighborhoods under siege will have an outlet for their talents and creativity before and after they grad-uate and an environment in which they can concentrate on learning instead of on doing daily battle just to survive. In addition, the parents of children who are still in school need a fully developed employment and community service pool in their community that is both fiscally and environmentally sustainable.

Far from being utopian, this kind of rethinking of local development has been one of the top items on the national agenda in recent years and has resulted in a number of innovative projects to rehabilitate impoverished inner-city neighbor-hoods in a way that is empowering to local residents. One recent example from the Clinton administration is the Youth-Build initiative, which would train high-school-aged children in construction skills and give them jobs renovating public housing in their neighborhoods. Under Jack Kemp's leadership at HUD there has also been a significant movement toward cooperative ownership of several apart-ment complexes around the country. In the case of Paradise Manor (mentioned above) the cooperative conversion effort has already served as the springboard for the formation of a number of neighborhood organizations and services, including a community-based construction company (Paradise Builders, Inc.), a support group for young men focusing on conflict resolution and leadership skills (Posi-tive Image), and a high school students' organization that provides college en-trance skills and training, as well as full scholarships to the institution of their choice once they graduate (Young People on the Rise). All except the last of these programs have been initiated and overseen by residents themselves in a housing complex where every household is below the D.C. median income level and 38 percent (as of June 1992) earn $10,000 or less per year.

A cautionary note should be sounded, however, about the plethora of develop-ment initiatives that have recently sprung up under the banner of "public-private partnerships" to increase local tax bases, claiming to have "revitalization" in mind. For many of these efforts, economic "renewal" ends up meaning the mas-sive subsidizing of private developers and corporations with public money. Typi-cally, any kind of benefit to lower-income residents such as long-term employ-ment or neighborhood "empowerment" comes as an afterthought if at all. Los Angeles's Rebuild L.A. Committee, for example, has so far aimed only at "attract-ing jobs" from large-scale for-profit corporations—a tactic that has tended simply to reinforce the conditions of poverty and environmental degradation that fueled the Los Angeles rebellion to begin with (and the Watts rebellion before it): "since all the major industrial companies that left Los Angeles in the past fifteen years—G.M., Ford, Firestone, Goodyear, American Can, Bethlehem Steel, etc.—did so in search of lower wages and corporate consolidation, what can [Peter] Ueberroth

[Chairman of Rebuild L.A.] offer to lure them back except low wages, tax concessions and waivers of environmental regulation, all of which have existed de facto in South L.A. for some time?" (Mann 1993, 409). The lesson of Los Angeles is that conducting more mass-development "business-as-usual" is both insufficient and counterproductive to the long-term goals of creating job security and political empowerment for the urban poor with regard to the quality of life in their neighborhoods. An urban revitalization agenda that will truly bring life into the public schools will have to be one in which development initiatives are conceived and deployed from the grassroots up, putting indigenous ownership of businesses and property squarely at the center of discussion.

In addition to rethinking the built environment that surrounds public schools, the whole approach to public school pedagogy needs to be completely reassessed. As stated above, the ideology behind public education in America has always viewed the student as a patient who needs to be "fed" the proper medicinal knowledge in order to become a good citizen. The recent conflict over multiculturalism has mainly raged over what kinds of knowledge will be fed to children and what kinds of people will be feeding it to them. However, as Pollitt notes, "while we have been arguing so fiercely about which books make the best medicine, the patient has been slipping deeper and deeper into a coma" (1992, 206).

As Robert Reich has pointed out, the main problem with American public schools is not so much that they have gotten worse over time as that "they simply have not changed for the better" within the context of a rapidly evolving global economy (1991, 226). In order to be prepared to function within this economy, the memorization of "facts" will be of secondary importance, because children "will live their adult lives in a world in which most facts learned years before (even including some historical ones) will have changed or have been reinterpreted. In any event, whatever data they need will be available to them at the touch of a key" (p. 229). Thus, in order to function in the information age it is more important that children learn how to access information and how to critique the logic behind it. This is the sort of education that the children of upper-middle-class symbolic analysts receive; however, these fortunate children make up no more than 15 to 20 percent of American children (p. 227). The logic behind increasing the amount of federal funding for equitable public education would be to make the education of a budding symbolic analyst available to children of all backgrounds. Under a stratified voucher system of education, the children of symbolic analyst parents (who are likely to be concentrated in one or two exclusive enclaves in the city) would receive the best interactive and creative education that money can buy; the children of poorer parents would most likely be subject to memorization by rote and Burger King commercials in the classroom. In one Colorado school that has recently accepted the support of McDonald's, the corporation has had the following effect on the curriculum: "At Fairview High School ... pupils study McDonald's inventory, payroll and ordering procedures in math; McDonald's menu plans in home economics; and the company's marketing practice in business class" (Rodd 1992, 276). Thus, corporate-sponsored education would prime less fortunate students to fill the ranks of the unskilled service lumpenproletariat. The argument has often been made, however, that "someone has to do society's dirty work" (in other words, not everyone can grow up to be a symbolic analyst). When we look at the basic skills that make up the repertoire of symbolic analytic work, though, we find a set of skills that could ideally be used by virtually anyone in any context—both on the job and within the community. Skills such as teamwork, problem solving, communication skills, and systems analysis are not only quite relevant to life in the inner city but desperately needed. The challenge, then, lies in revising antiquated, top-down corporate models of development and deploying new models that maximize participation and input at *all* levels, whether developing new businesses, new housing, or new schools. This model would not only expand entrepreneurship opportunities but also enable those with symbolic-analytic skills to tackle personal dilemmas better. After all, a democracy can't be harmed by greater education and empowerment for *all* its citizens, can it? Isn't it better to shift billions of tax dollars to universally advanced public education and grassroots development initiatives than to continue to waste the same amounts warehousing the poor in prisons, dilapidated housing, and crumbling schools? The state of the city and the schools housed within it is dire. Solutions are possible only when we dare to be visionary.

WORKS CITED

Anderson, David C. "Street Guns: A Consumer Guide." *New York Times Magazine,* 14 February 1993, 20–23.
Asante, Molefi Kete. "Multiculturalism: An Exchange." In *Debating P.C.: The Controversy over Political Correctness on College Campuses,* ed. Paul Berman. New York: Laurel, 1992, 299–314.
Bloom, Allan. *The Closing of the American Mind.* New York: Simon and Schuster, 1987.
Brown, DeNeen. "Classroom Diversity Raising Concerns: Language Barriers Worry Parents." *Washington Post,* 23 November 1992, A1, A10.
Culley, Margo, and Catherine Portuges. *Gendered Subjects: The Dynamics of Feminist Teaching.* Boston: Routledge and Kegan Paul, 1985.
Edsall, Thomas Byrne, and Mary D. Edsall. *Chain Reaction: The Impact of Race, Rights, and Taxes on American Politics.* New York: W. W. Norton, 1992.
Folbre, Nancy. "The Bottom Line: Business to the Rescue?" *The Nation,* 21 September 1992, 281–282.
Foucault, Michel. *Discipline and Punish.* New York: Vintage Books, 1979.
Freire, Paulo. *The Politics of Education: Culture, Power, and Liberation.* South Hadley, Mass.: Bergin and Garvey, 1985.
Friedland, Roger. *Power and Crisis in the City: Corporations, Unions, and Urban Policy.* London: Macmillan, 1982.
Giroux, Henry. *Ideology, Culture, and the Process of Schooling.* Philadelphia: Temple University Press, 1981.
Hirsch, Fred. *Social Limits to Growth.* Cambridge: Harvard University Press, 1976.

312 A. R. LATEGOLA

Judd, Dennis. "Segregation Forever?" *The Nation,* 9 December 1991, 740–744.
Kimball, Roger. *Tenured Radicals: How Politics Has Corrupted Our Higher Education.* New York: Harper and Row, 1990.
Kozol, Jonathan. "Corporate Raid on Education: Whittle and the Privateers." *The Nation,* 21 September 1992, 272–277.
Lather, Patti. *Getting Smart: Feminist Research and Pedagogy With/in the Postmodern.* London: Routledge, 1991.
Logan, John, and Harvey Molotch. *Urban Fortunes: The Political Economy of Place.* Berkeley: University of California Press, 1987.
Mann, Eric. "Los Angeles—A Year After (I): The Poverty of Corporatism." *The Nation,* 29 March 1993, 406–411.
Meier, Deborah. "Get the Story Straight: Myths, Lies, and Public Schools." *The Nation,* 21 September 1992, 271.
O'Connor, Stephen. "Death in the Everyday Schoolroom." *The Nation,* 24 May 1993, 685, 702–704.
Pollitt, Katha. "Why Do We Read?" In *Debating PC: The Controversy over Political Correctness on College Campuses,* ed. Paul Berman. New York: Laurel, 1992, 201–214.
Ravitch, Diane. "Multiculturalism: E Pluribus Plures." In *Debating PC: The Controversy over Political Correctness on College Campuses,* ed. Paul Berman. New York: Laurel, 1992, 271–298.
Reed, Adolph Jr., and Julian Bond. "Equality: Why We Can't Wait." *The Nation,* 9 December 1991, 733–737.
Reich, Robert. *The Work of Nations.* New York: Vintage Books, 1991.
Rodd, Ira Emory. "McLunchrooms!" *The Nation,* 21 September 1992, 276.
Schlesinger, Arthur Jr. *The Disuniting of America: Reflections on a Multicultural Society.* New York: W. W. Norton, 1992.
Shrewsbury, Carolyn. "What Is Feminist Pedagogy?" *Women's Studies Quarterly* 15:3 and 4 (1987):6–14.
Spillane, Margaret, and Bruce Shapiro. "Bush's New American Schools: A Small Circle of Friends." *The Nation,* 21 September 1992, 278–281.
Wilgoren, Debbi. "D.C.'s Young Testify to 'Making It the Right Way.'" *Washington Post,* 1 January 1993, B3.

19

'68, or Something

LAUREN BERLANT

To describe this feeling as "nostalgia" is about as adequate as to characterize the body's hunger, before dinner, as a "nostalgia for food."

—Fredric Jameson, *Postmodernism*

"Something Must Be Returned to Us ..."

In 1992 a few women colleagues and I separated from a progressive faculty group we had been in for a number of years in order to write a memo to the group. Our fantasy had been that this committee, the Committee on Critical Practice (at the University of Chicago), might become our home away from home, departmentally and disciplinarily speaking. Our memo expressed frustration that the group had not seen fit to engage seriously the different meanings of progressiveness that operate in the different domains in which we practice as intellectuals, political agents, teachers, and ordinary actors in the world. The committee had been founded on the wish such an analogy expresses: that to be politically on the left would mean that disciplinarily, pedagogically, and institutionally radical aspirations would drive us as well. (I refuse to put radical, progressive, and left in quotes: I think you know what I mean by that refusal.) What bonded the women who wrote together was that the latter two categories—teaching and professional/institutional relations of power, knowledge, and expertise—were underwhelming concerns of our colleagues, for the most part. We began our memo: "For us the main disappointment of CCP has come in its failure to inhabit a space of concrete utopian imagining."[1]

I loved every minute of writing this memo; it was so (*collectively*) *personal*. It was truly joint *authorship*. It was a moment when *feminism* seemed entirely integrated as a political concern with other aspirations for social change (even) less fully supported, at the moment, by movement politics. We knew that some colleagues would find our insistence on institutional practices hopelessly naive: I remember imagining hearing their eyeballs creak as they rolled in sarcastic fatigue while reading. Two weeks after we circulated the document, during which time none of us heard anything by way of response from our colleagues, two close friends from the committee called me to say, "This was the worst memo we have ever read. You are so '68. We have gone through all this already, and watched its failures once, and we're not going through it again." One of them threatened to resign. I believe there was also a chastising sentence about taking "the moral high ground." Another friend reported to me, "You're being characterized all over as '68, a real flower child."

What does it mean to be accused of being '68 in the 1990s? What nuclear button does the word "utopian" push? Why does an insistence on the politics of professionalism elicit such rage and contempt? How is it that a narrative of failure has come to frame that "revolution" with a black edge, an edge that has become a bar to reimagining a radical relation of politics and professional life? What, if anything, does this anxiety have to do with the increasing authority of feminism and with the additional pressures queer politics and multiculturalism have put on the value of knowledge production and intellectual identity? This essay is written on behalf of refusing to learn the lessons of history, of refusing to relinquish utopian practice, of refusing the inevitability of a movement from "tragedy" to "farce" that has stained much analysis of social movements generated post-'68[2]—indeed, to place '68 in a scene of collaborations and aspirations for thinking, describing, and theorizing social change in a present tense whose alterity to what we can now imagine for pragmatic, "possible," or "useful" politics I mean heartily to embrace and promote.

Two kinds of worries frame this effort to think from "'68." One is concerned with the current pressures on intellectuals and identity politicians to adopt a "professional" voice of expertise in some putative "public sphere." I am worrying that the drive to make legitimate a progressive politics in America will force the Left into accepting the rationalizing lingua franca of professionalism over the urges and improvisations of political creativity. I would take such an event to be, among other things, a victory of the New Right's own successful pressure to so overdefine the identity subcultures that threaten the historically dominant classes of the United States that identification as professional or "public" intellectuals would seem, the way nationality has seemed, to liberate one from being fixed negatively in an identity.[3] I am worried that as the popular media attend more closely to the products of academic life, we will become more "careful" to adopt and even to desire the pose of the ethically communicative replicant, the cyborg functionary—not the one Joanna Cassidy plays in Blade Runner, all exotic, powerful, and sensually available in her see-through raincoat, crashing through windows while fleeing some wooden man with a gun, but the bureaucratically and affectively good daughter, played by Sean Young, who lives her exploitation by technologies of memory, capital, and heterosexuality without being destroyed by their contradictions—which are many.

I digress. This is an essay about the political risks of becoming minor—or "'68"—by embracing utopian logics and tonal disruptions of theoretical, descriptive, and analytic norms in and outside of the academy. The stakes are double: one, to confront not only the problems of description, practice, and political imagination we have come to represent as "the new cultural politics of difference";[4] two, to confront, in the mode of a powerful ambivalence, the centrality of waste, failure, loss, pain, and chagrin to the project of inciting transformation itself—not only "what does it mean" to fail but how political breakdown works as something other than a blot, a botched job, a basis for the paternalistic virtue dominant cultures often claim when dissident movements fail.[5] The risk of taking on a politics of hegemony without dominance is a big one, for it seeks to transform the scene of power's intelligibility, not just by changing the kinds of persons who manage it.[6] A "minor" politics would therefore make both "leadership" and "participation" in subaltern and public spheres difficult, the writer/teacher/activist no longer owning a translatable ground of authority to support her claim to "representational" status. It thus risks the loss of whatever cultural capital a decorous intellectual, writer, or speaker might gain, speaking for "diversity" or "difference" from within the legitimating forms of a dominant culture. It tactically confuses the terms in which a minor, sub-, or microculture would achieve self-identity or solidarity in the face of pressures to observe the decorums of engagement with powerful antagonistic public spheres.[7] It risks making an audience apathetic at moments when we want to solicit identifications, alliances, and transformational acts and imagination. It risks boring people. I want to argue, nonetheless, for occupying history on the ground of discourses of possibility and contestatory experimentation, seen here as modes of *practical* politics.

How do we retain a sense of historical significance for thinking the possibilities of any important broad-scale change, especially when the global political context is one of defensiveness, atomization, violent cultural and economic domination, and retreat? And how do we secure the importance of transformation, radical openness, departures from the past for our languages and practices of politics in a time when revolutionary projects are so widely and effectively dismissed? You might see my citation of '68 as the opposite of a departure from older models of change. But this was not an intertext I sought. It is as though I had woken into a dream to find myself being dressed (in an intertextile), or dressed down, in public. Hence this is not an essay *about* "'68." I take the ill-fitting mantle of '68 to stand here for something like the risk of political embarrassment, of embracing undercooked transitional thought about the possibilities and politics of futurity itself. More on that presently.

This essay has another and immediate enunciative context too, from within American academic feminism, which is one place where I live. By "academic" I mean not "irrelevant," as in the "merely academic," but rather one site for a set of practices that traverse a variety of institutional, professional, pedagogical, analytic, and activist contexts. My opening anecdote might suggest that it is women,

women writing together, feminists, who remain at home in the contradictions of professional and political identity. I don't mean to say this specific thing, although anecdote is argument and feminism still does vitalize a powerful and "radical" relationality between political and conceptual movement.[8] But it was in a rush of exasperation after five years of silent and explicit struggle that we withdrew from speech and took up writing. We had felt not at home in traditional disciplines, so we sought alternative political and intellectual spaces in the university; when this act failed, we sought another, developing a Gender Studies program; we acted within a highly conventional understanding of universities as extended families, of departments as ideal "homes," and mistook the memo as a genre of political inter-vention, like an eighteenth-century broadside. Just as our colleagues' repudiation of radical professional activity was tainted with the fear of the farce of a second failed revolution, so too our need to remake the university as *heimlich* must also be captioned "Something is wrong with this picture."

Indeed, as academic feminism continues its institutionalization and its genera-tions of experts become available in the public sphere within which feminism is unevenly an important and a banalizing irritant, we find ourselves further caught in the contradictions of critical liberal consciousness. On the one hand, feminists are still made violently minor in both institutional and everyday-life contexts as less rigorous, more sentimental, more "tribal," more merely subcultural and subnational, more merely lesbian, sexually pathological, or just *sexual,* stuck structurally in an essentializing or navel-contemplating narcissism ("women's studies," "gender studies"). On the other hand, because even the most common-sensed of critics occupies spaces of metadiscourse and other pedagogical privilege (teaching/criticism are privileged tautological activities that breed their own au-thority, after all), questions of *academic* feminism's horizons of possibility—out-side of constructing *identifications*[9]—remain for the most part tacit or underdescribed in academic criticism. American academic feminism also oper-ates out of fear, I believe, of repeating the definitional exclusions, violences, and imaginative lapses of feminism since '68, of repeating American/white feminism's overoptimistic parochialism.[10]

It is because of these fears—of holding unjust authority, of having none but the authority of experience or theoretical self-indulgence, of failing to specify "wom-an"—that feminist cultural studies during the seventies and eighties transformed the horizon of reference that defined the object of feminist work, moving from at-tention to the generic individual woman to a commitment to redescribe gender within geopolitically diverse conditions of women's experience, exploitation, ex-pertise, and exorbitance and to develop points of comparison along the axes of sexuality/nationality/class/race that provide a kind of sloppy intelligibility to the female-gendered bodies that cross them. This involves cultivating importantly nonoptimistic relations to global capitalist forms, to national identities, to liberal promises for universal suffrage. I refer here to important, well-known work by bell hooks, Chandra Mohanty, Biddy Martin, and Gayatri C. Spivak, among others.[11]

This kind of committed work does not simply transform "woman" into a point of comparison between incommensurate and contradictory global systems of gendered signification. By foregrounding the problem of the example in the construction of critical and pedagogical authority, they also avoid the simplifying incitement to "represent" woman as a point of comparison for a variety of hyphenated othernesses that can be strung together. In this multiply situated academic/activist feminist analytic, the consideration of criticism's imperializing force enters explicitly into thinking and teaching about what it means even to construct a comparative notation of women's and of feminism's "minority." These are the sound reasons for the feminist hesitation to theorize, speculate, enter the aggressivity of revolutionary thought: these have to do with the real difficulties of negotiating the pragmatic pressures to counter general misogyny and patriarchalism with specific local countertherapies, discourses, policies, and politics of resistance. The project of specifying the technologies of misogyny must take place in locales; eyes must be kept as well on the incredibly powerful transnational, national, local, private, quotidian sexualizations of power against women that might make a global or multiply allied feminist public-sphere politics not only possible but vital and effectual. But since the scale and terms of specificity such a double vision demands will inevitably involve struggles to redefine the terms and frames of knowledge, expertise, and praxis that frame questions and sites of engagement, this project must be committed to producing risky theories/fantasies: American academic feminism is becoming increasingly loath to do so in the face of the demand to maintain a putative relation to an underspecified (and not nearly Queer enough) "realness."[12]

As this inclination to be situated within particularized "publics" has led to a more affirmative feminist situatedness in varieties of popular activism, pressure to adopt a "professional" relation to pseudotransparent norms of publicity itself must be checked. This involves different issues from the ones outlined in the progressive public-sphere intellectual nexus I describe above. If in that mode the desire to actively engage in intellectual self-translation and public-sphere interaction threatens to reintroduce unproblematized, conventionally framed performances of expertise, in the case of American feminism and public spheres the risk comes from a different will to transparency. Important developments in feminist legal and psychoanalytic theory have joined old habits of women's studies to reinvigorate the aim to produce, as feminists, "safe spaces" in the classroom, departments, journals, and the world. Catharine MacKinnon and other legal scholars, for example, link feminist critical pedagogy to a demand to redefine harmful language and injurious speech to include the "ordinary" pain of being gendered itself; feminist pedagogy theorists frequently see their classes as ideal disorder-free zones.[13] I am worried—to continue my list of worries—that feminists will increasingly identify their ambition to make the world safe for women with an expanding fear of unsettling knowledges, under the guise of an important concern not to create and generate even more pain for women. But embracing "ordinary language" and "safe

knowledge" as things good in themselves will distract us from engaging the impossible, ambitious, and always failing activity that Marx describes enigmatically
as "the poetry of the future."[14]

At the conjuncture of these two pressures to simplify the representation and
imagination of what social change might be and feel like, I seek to affirm the importance of imagining a Left/feminism that refuses to lose its impulse toward a
revolutionary utopian *historicity.* To begin to imagine what scene of politics this
kind of critical commitment to failing/utopia would entail, I would like to tell
some stories about encounters with some sublime violences of contemporary social life, encounters whose sublimity creates, simultaneously, scenes of terrible
failure and courageous impulses of revolutionary futurity. Poaching from many
texts—from Toni Morrison's *Song of Solomon,* Michelle Cliff's *No Telephone to
Heaven,* Carolyn Kay Steedman's *Landscape for a Good Woman,* Gilles Deleuze and
Felix Guattari's "What Is a Minor Literature?"—I will speak about being minor;
about producing and representing local, national, and transnational particularity;
about radically redressing bodies, affect, and authority; about writing criticism;
about reinventing the forms of history in the intimate sensations of childhood,
envy, exile, and political trauma.[15] A little too much like a diorama at a world's
fair, I will read these questions of criticism and identity from locations in 1963,
1979, 1989, and 1993. And above all, I will argue the necessity for preserving,
against all shame, a vitalizing and animating commentary on and relation to the
question of revolution itself, a question about utopia that keeps pushing its way
through a field of failed aspirations, like a student at the back of the room who
gets suddenly, violently, tired of being invisible. ...

Food for Thought

First, a little reading about "what goes down in history." Deleuze and Guattari's
commentary on relations of domination and cultural production in "What Is a
Minor Literature?" represents the political situation of culturally minor or "marginal" peoples but not in the analytic languages of identity politics or political
economy. Rather, it asks how the interiority, the sensations, the erotics, the sensual locations of political marginality might provide an unpredicted energy for
reconfiguring power, identity, and collective knowledge. In this they are aligned
with the project of revitalizing the traditional, premarxian mode of radical social
analysis that Carolyn Steedman advocates in *Landscape for a Good Woman:* "Its
notable feature ... was that its rhetoric allowed the tracing of misery, evil, and un-
fairness to a *political* source, that is, to the manipulation by others of rights, privileges, and money, rather than attributing such perception to a shared consciousness of exploitation. It was a coherent device both for understanding the ordering
of the world in a particular way, and for achieving that understanding without direct *experience* of exploitation."[16] Steedman argues that a radicalized vision of society has long provided a way of explaining not only the structural conditions for

class consciousness but also the "states of unfulfilled desire" and envy that accompany the rageful estrangement from cultural value by which the experience of dominated populations is defined.[17]

"What Is a Minor Literature?" answers its own titular question in three ways. First, a minor literature is a corpus that registers a minority culture's linguistic displacement from a majority culture's authority over the "real." Linguistic distance might involve the invention of vernaculars or of palpable silences or a hypersensuality of the body or language—perhaps graffiti would be an apt example of this quality of the minor. Second, a minor literature registers and performs a collapse of historical or diachronic narrative time into a lyric disruptive present tense, one in which minor individuals experience their activity exemplified in the sheer presentness of their dislocation from traditional referentiality. Think about, for example, the way lost histories, amnesia, and archival violence are central to stories of minor cultures. Third, a minor literature produces a new understanding of authorship and of the relation of the primary to the secondary text. In this context, where everything is political, transcendent originality is inconceivable, because the grounds of power that make transcendence even an imaginary possibility for a ruling class do not exist for a minor culture. Therefore minor authors experience their authorship in the state of dissolved boundaries between themselves and the publics from within which they speak; thus their texts may be understood to be collaborative, ongoing sites of cultural production. Additionally, criticism from a minor culture is a performance of collaborative authorship, for the commentary the minor critic produces is central to the terms with which a people comes to experience itself as itself and as historic, in history.

But minor peoples also experience the banality of power from within the majority lifeworld and feel that "a whole other story," their story, "is vibrating within" the "cramped space" of cultural domination. Minor citizens live within the paper, synthetic, metalanguages of national, racial, class, and gender hegemony—the language of law, of medicine, of nation, of fundamentalisms, and of commodity culture, say—and they also get the crumbs of their legitimation there. Thus although they are displaced persons, in exile from collective narrative control over the language that renders their own story, and although they may be caught in the impossibility of even imagining an "indigenous" language and political community (except in the vernacular sense: *indigenous,* born in a country; *vernaculus,* native, from *verna,* a home-born slave), minor authors have—they are burdened on their very bodies with—historical consciousness that becomes the material whose force can most powerfully split the screen memory of pseudoconsensual national "cultures" into fragments of revelatory data and revolutionary knowledge.

Hence the difference between major and minor cultures is lived, from within the minoritized group, as simultaneously a real relation of domination and a vastly movable barely "cultural" boundary. These two articulations of minor culture explain the ambivalence it generates from the majoritarian perspective: although the fact of marginal culture itself seems tautologically to confirm the stability of social hierarchy, minor culture also figures as a kind of irreducible waste, a set of jumbled signs and practices with respect to which a dominating power can never fully establish itself as the referent or the cultural dominant. We have all seen how dominated exotic microcultures have produced what appears to be confectionery on which major cultures have sought to suck, as though the meat and potatoes of power left them starved for something else, something other: more.[18]

This is what I love about the story Deleuze and Guattari tell about revolution. We can see it developed in two examples. I have suggested that Deleuze and Guattari see the minor culture's political displacement as a disruption on the body. This is evident especially in a competitive relation of speaking to eating. "Rich or poor," they write, "each language always implies a deterritorialization of the mouth, the tongue, and the teeth. The mouth, tongue and teeth find their primitive territoriality in food. ... To speak, and above all to write, is to fast" (p. 62). In other words, the exile of the minor culture from legitimation finds its property either in the body or in the language that takes up the space a homeland otherwise might. (We will return to the marking of eating, writing, and revolutionizing anon.)

Second, "What Is a Minor Literature?" shows how minority reveals itself in distinct linguistic modalities. "*Language stops being representative in order to now move toward its extremities or its limits*" (p. 65). In the vast sorrow of forced expatriation, and with great perverse pleasure, the minor act of reterritorialization, of claiming imaginary property, may be flashingly, movingly experienced in language. In one version of this vehicular, referential, or mythic language, the privileged lushness your minoritized body cannot claim emerges in a sensuality toward the body and of the language itself, becomes an intensive blur that crosses barriers in lush allegory; in the other modality, you write the sparest, non-metaphorical *writing* possible, seeking "to bring language slowly and progressively to the desert. To use syntax in order to cry, to give syntax to the cry" (p. 67). (In the relation between rich and empty calories, the category "food" becomes entirely theoretical, unassimilable: is it possible for a surviving culture to live on what it produces textually amidst the dominant cultural voracity that appropriates the meat, leaves the carcass, seeks the sweets? Of course, this translation of dominated populations into a thing called "minor culture" and the assimilation of relations of dominance to a leitmotif of food exchange is merely "heuristic."

Each of these "minor" possibilities clearly exists within multiple frames of power and can be used to unsettle dominating, jingoistic, or technocratic jargons. But more than that, Deleuze and Guattari argue that "there is nothing that is major or revolutionary except the minor," because only the wish for a postauthoritarian culture can secure the yet unlived grounds of unconstrained social life toward which minor cultures restlessly drive. The paradox of the major/minor can be located in the importance Deleuze and Guattari place on the need to imagine an exoteric freedom, without the old legitimations that made the nation and its identities intelligible. Remaining foreign to a hegemonic imaginary—with its dream of a linguistic ethno-utopia, the privilege of uncontested generalizing and control over reference—requires remaining outside of the dream of enforcing a new master tongue for eating or writing, or singing.[19] The politics of minor culture must occupy and transform the resolutely sensual, must generate passages composed in the registers of excess, the spare and the lush.

Thus minor literatures are literally unsettled, they represent unsettlement, and their expression creates an unsettling wedge: it is this crossing over, suspended in flight between splendor and a hyperrealist refusal of allegory's excesses, that ensures their both productive and deadening failures and embarrassments. This is where Steedman's analysis of fantasies that children and infantilized national classes use to explain their relations to, expectations of, and desires for self-extension in the world comes in. How do minor cultures speak? Steedman argues that fairy tales are the intense explanatory devices children use to register their emplacement, powerlessness, and transformative fantasy; powerful aspirations to commodity ownership are what she designates as the working class's scene of fantasy, a scene of punctures and sutures manufactured to bind them to an otherwise remote but Oz-like *patria*.

The fantastic techniques of displacement Steedman describes, which register the distances between ordinariness and the forms of pleasure and safety that adult, national, and capitalist cultures promise, transform how she might read the politics of minor "language": no longer a mere marker of class and national origin, it here emerges as an archive of gestures that participate in, produce, and explain the ordinary violent taxonomies of social life including but not limited to an engagement with the scene of national culture. Steedman shows how children and the infantilized classes spoken to as children by state authorities and represented by the culture industries of nostalgic national bourgeoisies become the essentialized signs of English innocence and depth, simplicity and real knowledge that adults feel that they must lose a vital, contemporary relation to in order to be "major," national citizens. And in compensation the national culture projects its own anxieties about uniqueness and community into dramas of its own "people's" Otherness; thus, the "national culture industries" of England endow the infantilized classes with the bare-minimum facticity of a "national character" that always threatens to be lost.[20] And perhaps this is the function of minorities in the production of "national nostalgia" (for, say, rural authenticity, the purity of suffering in a working or underclass, or women's "hidden" injuries): that a minor culture's suffering persists allows ineffectual preemptive collective mourning for a whole nation's massive and ordinary systemic failures.

1963: A Holocaust of Little Girls

"Today there is a story which should have caused the sun to eclipse the earth—something … something in the heavens should have objected."[21] What is this story? "Four little colored girls had been blown out of a church."[22] "September 16,

1963. ... In thick dark letters, stark: SUNDAY SCHOOL BOMBED—next line, smaller print: FOUR CHILDREN DEAD. ... 'Addie Mae Collins, 14; Denise McNair, 11; Carole Robertson, 14; Cynthia Wesley, 14.'"[23] Is *that* the story? "Every night now Guitar was seeing little scraps of Sunday dresses—white and purple, powder blue, pink and white, lace and voile, velvet and silk, cotton and satin, eyelet and grosgrain. ... The bits of Sunday dresses that he saw did not fly; they hung in the air quietly, like the whole notes in the last measure of an Easter hymn."[24] This, a personal vision of tattered fabric; next, what fractured icons newspaper readers might have seen: "A stained-glass window. Fragments of images dangle from its leaden boundaries. The face of Jesus is ruined. Dark space where the bomb has torn if off. His hands and crook intact. The legend of the window—willing workers—half there, half absent."[25] And, in another less visual but no less formulaic medium, Martin Luther King preaches, witnessing:

> These children—unoffending; innocent and beautiful—were the victims of one of the most vicious, heinous crimes ever perpetrated against humanity. Yet they died nobly. They are the martyred heroines of a holy crusade for freedom and human dignity. So they have something to say to us in their death. They have something to say to every minister of the gospel who has remained silent behind the safe security of stained-glass windows. They have something to say to every politician who has fed his constituents the stale bread of hatred and the spoiled meat of racism. They have something to say to a federal government that has compromised with the undemocratic practices of southern dixiecrats and the blatant hypocrisy of right-wing northern Republicans. They have something to say to every Negro who passively accepts the evil system of segregation ... to each of us, black and white alike, that we must substitute courage for caution. ... Their death says to us that we must work passionately and unrelentingly to make the American dream a reality.[26]

Perhaps I am not telling this story successfully or rendering fully what the pictures of death "say": but who has? How to narrate? As King says, the story of the little girls says so much "something" that no commentary can fully gloss the heat of the meanings its violence generates. It is this fact about the sublimity of power's effects—that commentary will inevitably "fail" comprehension—that provides the historical, theoretical, and political urgency to generate some cunning radical creativity.

On 16 September 1963, four African American girls, named above, wearing white dresses and white shoes, were talking in the girls' room of the 16th Street Baptist Church in Birmingham, Alabama. There to help lead a service, they were killed by a bomb protesting the organized civil rights resistance to white racism in Birmingham/Alabama/U.S.A. In 1977, Toni Morrison organized the political and narrative climax of *Song of Solomon* around this event; a decade later, in 1987, Michelle Cliff marked a moment in the political education of her character Clare Savage by registering Savage's response to this event. "Something in the heavens should have objected," she thinks—"something," King says, that should have been heard by every American. "Something" here stands for the irreducible violent sublimity of American racism in 1963, 1977, 1987, and beyond: something, a word that holds the place for a demand to produce something like a language—entire novels, songs, lyrics, histories, letters, criticism—that in this instance might attest to the random encounter of systemic racial violence with individuals who happen to be somewhere, at some time, doing, then suddenly not doing, some "thing." Always crucially after the fact, these texts take the "fact" back, so to create a decolonized history of the "something" that *didn't* happen[27]—the "thing" to be specified, endlessly, just beyond what seems possible, the task of a dissident history.

Yet in the "national memory" 1963's most famous racial event, 1963's memorable political moment, is not the holocaust of little girls, this minor flurry of death. It is that singular, now iconic contraction Americans call "the" March on Washington, which took place 28 August 1963. Taylor Branch argues that in 1963 "the" March fused with "the" massacre of little girls to take on "mythic proportions."[28] The mythic proportions of (im)personal violence and mass testimonial resistance in these texts recommemorate the revolutionary racial counterpolitics of citizenship in 1963: that's one part of the story. Another is, of course, the obliteration of the story of the little girls in the blaze of monumentality that marks the "national memory" of the March and of Martin Luther King's speech at the March: Americans call this speech "I Have a Dream."[29] The "Dream" too has been sanctified by violent death. King, only figuratively a prophet, could not have commented there on the future violence to the little girls whose eulogy he would later say. But his speech at the March predicts that among the outcomes of the successful nonviolence and "creative suffering" (p. 219) the civil rights movement practiced had to be the future ordinary happiness of "little black boys and black girls," here functioning literally and as figures for all "God's children" in America (pp. 219–220). "As long as our children are stripped of their selfhood and robbed of their dignity," the United States is no "sweet land of liberty," but the worst thing, a cold desert, providing no consoling warmth of the tropic, just a once-meaningful national allegory.

Thus when King tropes on "My country, 'tis of thee" in "I Have a Dream" he insists he sings it "with new meaning" (p. 219). The new meaning he gives it, on behalf of the child-citizens whose futures depend on the realization of an actually existing racial and economic democracy in the United States, insists on making the spirit of the old wish the song expresses the letter of the law the nation must now adopt and enforce. It is constituted by a forced reduction of allegory into the *real* political time of national culture where the law meets everyday experience. His tactic here is to make literal and practical the utopian foundations of the nation. Let freedom *actually* ring, this minute, in the time it takes for the voices of the marchers to ring through the air(waves). First usurp the temporality of national language; then, decolonize national space; alongside, speak and write.

A few months later, King's commentary on the little girls focuses not on the need to seize the law right now but on the political necessity to misread and to reallegorize death and suffering. But not in a simple way: on behalf of creating at least a prosthetic future, where a real scene of justice might take the place held, here, by the word "something." He speaks of the deaths as a speech-act made collectively by the girls: they have something to say to "us," the survivors. What would it take to "make the American dream a reality"? It would take understanding that "something" must be done, that passive resistance and passive acceptance are entire universes of "passivity" apart. However, the children's deaths do not, in King's rendition, produce one redemptive national allegory. Each subject position—the minister, the African American, the parents of the children, members of the congregation, liberal and racist politicians—has to find and to hear its own allegorical supplement, its own specific gloss on the something that remains unsaid in the eulogy, undone in the nation. Saying, hearing, doing, writing: these relations of practice entirely break down the dichotomy between rhetoric and activism that so hampers a simply mass-mediated political imaginary. It is the purpose of the eulogy to force its stipulated audiences into *creating* the critical allegories that will translate the little girls in a way that unsettles the certainties of privilege, identity, language, and world that complacent (or ambitious) citizens possess. King makes the demand to define "something" a matter of the pedagogy of conscience, a gesture of political translation that radically reconfigures relations among persons, populations, and the laws that govern her/him/them.

For Morrison and Cliff too, allegory is the ground of departure but absolutely not the utopian or the inevitable means for producing a national memory of a nation that does not yet exist: yet as King suggests, it produces a confrontation in the present tense with the violence and waste of national life so that the present tense might not merely be a ground for the end of history/utopia. Allegory is the scene of excess in which we live the failure of official/dominant archives, policies, and argots to grant the diverse conditions in which bodily practices, transcultural encounters, national histories have met, meet, might meet again in the future: it is, indeed, an inheritance promising totality that needs to be split, to be simultaneously embraced and overcome. Therefore its spaces of anomaly open up the possibility for experiencing *change*. The kind of change I imagine these texts generating here signals not an invention of an authentic language of identity in a post-ideological world but rather a commitment to the ongoing fight to *redistort* a whole range of nationally and globally organized scenes of power, in part as a gesture toward not passively dying from fury at the not-random-enough violence of the world that terrorizes, that marks you personally and collectively, as a member of a designated "population." As Spivak says, "we learn the inscription of identity letter by letter."[30] These novels tell different histories of the letter's violences/opportunities: the redescriptive and redemptive activity of fiction/politics no longer appears dismissable, or assimilable, as "mere" rhetoric.[31] Morrison stays within the modernist project, occupying the plural allegories of minority history; Cliff tries to write beyond the nation, beyond the desert, beyond what history can bear to imagine.

Song of Solomon takes on the task of minor literatures and their historic registers of collective rhetorical struggle in ways Deleuze and Guattari might have predicted: cast against the proprieties of the bourgeois table, it is a book full of stark,
fierce, theory-driven politics and, also, a book tumbling over with sweet, milky,
fruity reimaginations of the world, as though the garden in the biblical Song of
Solomon had reemerged as the collective archive of African American cultural
politics in the 1960s. A new historicity is generated in the novel's recoding of the
relation between political and genealogical definitions of African American culture, for the book cuts across a politics of radical violence and the promise of taste
sensations passed down to the present tense through, among other things, character names: Sugarman, Sugargirl, Sweet. My concern here is to trace the techniques
of historical narration in each of these allegorical modes, modes of politics and of
promise, and to see what Morrison makes of the violences, failures, and yet successful transformations wrought in the horizon of identity that Milkman and
Guitar's uneasy and dangerous collaboration begets.

In *Song of Solomon,* Morrison's allegorically named Guitar Banes belongs to a
revolutionary group called Seven Days. The mission of Seven Days is to enact a
black politics of *lex talionis* (eye for eye, life for life) against the racist rage for
death that marks ordinary life in the United States. In apposition to the logic of
Guitar's/Seven Days' radical collective countermemory and counterpraxis, the
novel chronicles the bourgeois historical aspirations of Milkman Dead, the hero
whose attempt to commandeer his own life story organizes the novel. In the
course of the narrative, Milkman pursues a practical and symbolic regrounding in
African American citizenship and culture by making a journey through the family
genealogy "back," as it were, since he has never been there or imagined himself as
having come from there, to the "South."[32] *Song of Solomon* thus reads the state of
race in America through a dialect(ic) that traverses Milkman's collective/personal
identity politics and the revolutionary biblical logic of revenge encoded in Guitar's allegorical group name (Seven Days, in which the Earth was created; seven
members, each of whom is responsible for countering the violence that happens
on "his" day, either in a simple inversion of the logic of creation or else, as I would
argue, signifying a mode of *creation* countering the hierarchies of a racist culture
that does not count black deaths as attenuations of the nation).

We can see in the passage above that Guitar experiences the holocaust of the little girls as a rending of the fabric of black life in general. He sees ghosts of fabric,
not the specifically dead bodies. The tactility and the specificity of the fabric that
haunts him at night evokes the rose petals that fall on the sidewalk in the novel's
opening scene, where a hieroglyph of spectacular death—the death of modernism, of Icarus/Daedalus, figured in the flying suicide of a black man, Mr. Robert
Smith—contracts into itself the birth of Milkman (induced by the trauma of the
suicide, as seen by his mother) and the coming of Pilate, his aunt. Pilate's magical
being—with no belly button, she has only a fictive relation to the bodies and

blood of other humans—produces the song she sings, "Sugarman don't fly away," that links the politically motivated death of the insurance man, the privileged birth of the Milkman, the nationalist politics of Seven Days' men, and the lost sweet violent history of black America. Rose petals, fabric swatches, allegorical song, magical women, all survivors of (patriarchal, national) violence: Guitar elsewhere argues that the death of a black American is not solitary but condenses the death of seven generations, and therefore the narrative he helps produce chronicles multiple holocausts. It is Guitar's purpose to remake into practical/ utopian politics the frozen image, this rigor mortis: fragments of fabric hang in the air "like the whole notes in the last measure of an Easter hymn."

The redemption of the Easter image of the martyred girls in *Song of Solomon* depends, somehow, on Guitar's decision to avenge the little girls by killing Milkman, for Milkman has taken another route, through capitalism, property, and inherited stolen wealth, to imagining his "people's" survival in the United States (though he would never think history politically, and thus his "people" is in some distant elastic relation to the humiliated citizenry Guitar kills for). Milkman unravels the allegory of not the whole notes of the Easter hymn but the nonsense of a folk song that tells the story of his and his "people's" life. It is a song of diaspora, departure, not "home." Its chorus is

> *O Solomon don't leave me here*
> *Cotton Balls to choke me*
> *O Solomon don't leave me here*
> *Buckra's arms to yoke me*
>
> *Solomon done fly, Solomon done gone*
> *Solomon cut across the sky, Solomon gone home.*[33]

In different versions of this song, Solomon is also pronounced Sugarman, Shalimar, *Shalleemone*. Like a student agitated at the sudden disclosure of new knowledges that will happily, painfully unsettle the way he handles the world, Milkman is unbelievably stimulated by the project of decoding and inhabiting this allegory, which he gradually discovers to be about *him*, his *patria*, the history of his *body*, and about the possibility that families don't hyperstabilize identity (as his property-obsessed father had wished were true) but precisely shift the terms of identity around constantly, forcing the name and the knowledge it organizes always to migrate and to become unfamiliar, in the present tenses of history, generation after generation.

In contrast, Guitar is neither textualist, philologist, nor anthropologist; he cares nothing about the history of internal migration, translation, and colonization that becomes the "other" African American history that circulates through the "minor" spaces of the novel. To him, "that's what all human relationships boiled down to: Would you save my life? or would you take it? ... Would you save my life or would you take it? Guitar was exceptional. To both questions he could answer yes" (p. 331). It is important to see how fully the brutal political explicitness of this

question "wins" the novel's narrative from the one it early obsesses on, the inces-
tuous necrophilic identifications of Milkman, his mother Ruth, and her father
that threatened to take the Dead family out of history in the way I, and its name,
have just described. The novel ends not remembering crises of identity and propriety in the bourgeois black family but repeating Guitar's question. Yet this time,
Milkman is the exceptional one, and the undead one, having taken Guitar's lesson:
"'You want my life? … You need it? Here.' Without wiping away the tears, taking a
deep breath, or even bending his knees—he leaped. As fleet and bright as a lodestar he wheeled toward Guitar and it did not matter which one of them would give
up his ghost in the killing arms of his brother. For now he knew what Shalimar
knew: If you surrendered to the air, you could *ride* it" (p. 337). There is a lot left
unsaid here about the politics of *these* freedom riders and of the need Morrison
signals, in and beyond 1963, for African Americans to have a knowing and
undefensive relation to the multiple histories that might still generate startling
changes: a "lodestar" guides those who know how to surrender to its light, the poetry of the future. Morrison leaves *Song of Solomon* refusing to censure the two independently failed encounters with the impossible losses of history. The space
shuttle between the not-opposite but apposite African American historicities in
the novel therefore reoccupies 1963 not in the way of postmodern flatness or modernist psychology but through an accumulation of anomalous languages. It provides a source of generative agency that allows the novel to unsettle its own tacit
present tenses. It suggests a prolegomenon to all future African American politics,
based no longer on the rough hierarchies wrought by the paternalistic censorship
and criticism Guitar and Milkman's father use to order the world but on the suspension of these modes of discipline to reconceive what might be brought into the
kinds of explanation and praxis that are deployed as *politics* itself, despite the
threat of its apparent nonutility. Who is to say, in advance, what tactics will work
to create a wedge that opens up the seemingly certain violences of hegemony production in social life in a way beyond accommodation? I take the rupture of the
novel's own habits of causality, in this Angel of History–like moment of closure, to
be a performative critical pedagogy on the subject of failure/utopia: framed by unresolvable questions, sweet gifts of life, petty and devastating sacrifices, and also a
brutally fixed gaze on the geopolitics and the tattered fabric that amount to the
personal effects of racism and capitalism in the United States.

   To the strains of the *Song of Solomon,* we heed the making narrative of lessons
unlearned in at least two present tenses—1963 and 1977—that have not yet confronted the different ways "something" sensual and political about the actual
American world pulses almost supernaturally to be known; and it is fitting that
the other chronicle of the little girls we have found, in Cliff's *No Telephone to
Heaven,* opens with a pedagogic performance, during a high school current-
events class in New York City. There we find Clare Savage reading aloud from the
newspaper. She sits in front of her class and like a conscientious student waits for
"something" to happen after she and her peers learn of the bloodbath, but no:

"There was no rush of air in the room. No explosion."³⁴ "Something" important about knowledge, history, and revolution is revealed privately to Clare, though: that no allegory of a world in which natural justice naturally avenges catastrophe will do to explain *this* world of nations; that learning of the thing itself does not beget justice either—what a student must do is to produce acts of willful reading, restless acts of glossing, framing, slanting, and making ever more explicit questions about what counts as evidence, explanation, action, and transformation. These epistemologies of violence become foundational for the revolutionary praxis that Clare develops, to which we shall return. She dissolves the knowledge/practice hierarchy in order to usurp the privilege of forcing *something* through into consciousness and corporeality, once something else—in the heavens and the nation—refuses to happen. As we shall see, this "something" is not the unvarnished truth of the unmediated "Real" but rather something else, riskily underdefined. The word that stands in for the pressure on "something" here is "need."

> The next day, June 17, 1963, Clare sees the picture "she needed to see." A girl in a coffin, open. Girl, coffin, platform, all draped in a fine white cotton, like a delicate mosquito netting protecting her from the tiny marauders of a tropical night. A curtain to protect onlookers from the damage. The veiled girl identified in the caption as "one of the victims of Sunday's bombing." ... She cut the picture from the paper and put it in a celluloid pocket in her wallet—to glance at even when they buried the President. (p. 102)

This passage executes a brutally ironic action of veiling and revelation. In contrast to Branch's history, which links the holocaust of little girls to the March on Washington, Cliff links it to the most analogous "national" scene of death in 1963, John F. Kennedy's assassination, which carries with it its own always intensifying visual fascination and memorial power. Clare chooses to affiliate with the "other" atrocious scene of violence fully authorized by a specular economy, and this one too allots to the picture of the unidentified dead black female child the entry into public—or white, national—consciousness of her precise value, here the value of the always already wounded and mourned-for infantilized, eroticized black body. On the one hand, the nameless little girl reminds one of a patrician "lady" visiting the tropics, virtue and body protected from mosquitoes and other locals by a white veil; on the other hand, surely she too is a mosquito just barely irritating the subcutaneous layers of consciousness that give whiteness its precarious hold on prerogative. The picture, thus framed, serves Clare's "need." But for what?

When Clare's father, Boy Savage, catches her looking at the picture of the veiled dead girl instead of at "American history in the making" at Kennedy's death, he takes the picture from her and destroys it, telling her "not to judge this country" (p. 102). Boy knows immediately that the aversion of Clare's gaze constitutes a full-bodied political choice, one that includes the deauthorization of the official United States as the index of her barely developed utopian political imaginary. Thus his admonition is belated: Clare has already memorized the picture, and indeed she has already begun constructing an archive of radical practices that include breaking the idol of utopian nationality for a much more destabilized, transitional vision of what politics must do.

For Boy Savage's generation of immigrants to the United States, the lure of capital makes countermemory or even resentment at racism and labor exploitation taboo, and many of the island immigrants we see make do as they climb the ladder of success from crushingly menial to slightly less menial labor in a precarious economy without safety nets that pits the fortunes of one minority culture against the imputed failures of others. For Clare's mother, Kitty, however, taboo topoi generate new allegory that Clare inherits. Kitty Savage takes on the main burden for originating the minor language of a yet unnamed and unfounded "mother country" whose ethnogenealogy in the novel is complex and whose allegories inhabit many registers. The daughter learns from the mother about what it means to repudiate conventionally indexed aspirations to the "good life," instead risking unsafety and death to regenerate collective life and history in the unclear way of revolutionary instinct we have been pursuing here under the sign of a politics of "something."[35]

Kitty's story, briefly, is that she comes with Boy and Clare to the United States in 1960 to find a "better life" and steps into a cadence of racist violence in which survival entails a two-step of silent absence and vocal passing. Kitty cannot racially pass, though Boy can and does. She cannot and won't, eventually erupting in the semiotic excesses we have come to see as insurgent signs of rupture and creativity in the domains of minor cultures. First, under the pressure of staying true to her natal body and consciousness, Kitty makes long trips through New York to find "the shops from *home*" that make the food she must eat to live (p. 64):

> Kitty mastered the route by subway and returned with mangoes, yams, cho-cho, saltfish, plantains, callaloo, goat-meat, and Jamaican curry to rub it with. She came home with these things laden in her arms, as if to say, Family, this is for you. In these shops she broke her silence, here she felt most the loss of home, of voice, even as she brushed the loose dirt off the yam-skin. ... Resisting a desire to rub the sharp stickiness into her nostrils and around her mouth. (p. 65)

The second way Kitty breaks her silence for survival and entailment's sake moves, as we might have predicted, from the sensuality of *food* and other haunting postcolonial dreams she has to surreptitious rageful *writing*. Kitty works in a dry cleaner's and places in each package of cleaning a little letter to the customer that contains some "philosophy of laundry" (p. 73). At the bottom of each communiqué Kitty writes the signature of the fictive author, a Jane Darwell–like "Mrs. White," whose linkage of love and the sanitary aims to render every laundry-linked housewife a domestic goddess. Kitty feels strongly Mrs. White's iconicity as "such an American image" (p. 73), representing an American ideology of sacred, protected, clean, white domesticity. One day, following a fierce impulse, Kitty "drew a balloon from the upturned mouth of the benign lady and printed within: EVER TRY CLEANSING YOUR MIND OF HATRED? THINK OF IT" (p. 78). Kitty becomes obsessed by writing and dispensing these chilling scripts:

WE CAN CLEAN YOUR CLOTHES BUT NOT YOUR HEART.
AMERICA IS CRUEL. CONSIDER KINDNESS FOR A CHANGE.
WHITE PEOPLE CAN BE BLACK-HEARTED.
THE LIFE YOU LIVE WILL BE VISITED ON YOUR CHILDREN.
MARCUS GARVEY WAS RIGHT. (p. 81)

The final straw: "It was time to end her nonsense once and for all. Once and for all. She took a stack of letterheads and colored in the pink face of Mrs. White. She drew a balloon next to each dark face. HELLO. MRS. WHITE IS DEAD. MY NAME IS MRS. BLACK. I KILLED HER" (p. 83). Sending "her furious Aunt Jemima into the world" has unexpected consequences: the two African American women who work with Kitty are fired for doing what Kitty did, for the boss's hatred of "that kind" and his exoticization of a woman from the islands makes him simply incapable of hearing, speaking to, and specifying actual human beings different from himself. This event, signifying Kitty's failure to educate even one person about racism, causes her to abandon Boy, Clare, and America and return to Jamaica, where she dies—but not before sending Clare the important communication that resonates with all about the burden of little girls that has come before: "I am glad you are studying. ... I hope you make *something* of yourself, and *someday* help your people" (p. 103, emphasis added).

Something to someday: Clare finds the material for her second-generation engagement with national/tribal peoples in a variety of places, all riddled with the specific historical hybridities that mark the postimperial West. One locus of ancestry is found in the official national allegories that have marked the sentimental negativity of imperial politics: in particular, the novel links its impulse toward utopian praxis to the notion England so fully promoted of itself as "mother country" (pp. 109–111). Cliff/Clare rewrites this in the language of embittering oedipalization, showing how still, long after the high imperial moment has passed, Jamaica and other postimperial sites must nonetheless continue to play the game of domination/castration beneath the caretaking skirt of the motherland (scenes of castration and sodomy are central to the novel's exhaustion of patriarchal national politics as a source of emancipatory federation). The first act of the novel is the castration, rape, and pillaging of an old colonial family: the last event is the guerrilla-led disruption of a U.S.-financed film about the Maroon insurrection of 1738 in a blazing counterholocaust directed this time not against the state but against the publicity apparatus that ensures the repetition of violence and counterviolence as national effigies of Jamaica, allied with the paternalistic forms of economic, touristic, and military "help" the poor islands like Jamaica receive as the price of entering the world system at all. "JAMAICA, A WORLD OF CULTURE WITHOUT BOUNDARIES," read the ads that call tourists to the island (p. 6). The boundaries that don't exist, even in the era of decolonization, are sexual, familial, economic, archival: the ideology of the mother country is the ruse used to veil and distract from the scenes of (non)penetration through which colonial domination was managed in Jamaica and elsewhere.

Renouncing dominant corporeal schemas is impossible, as Fanon so dramatically says, without a total making raw of the body:[36] this book shows that even intuitive revolutionary insurgence must visibly scorch the skin, the land, and the archive through word-deeds and body-deeds. Clearly, fetishizing newspaper
pictures of death as Clare does might lead to more amnesiac distortion: the holocaust as done deal, pictures memorializing the completeness of the event, its think-
ability. But Clare sees the picture of the dead veiled little girl as posing Guitar/
Milkman's futile question "Would you save my life or would you take it?" and experiences rage, revolutionary rage, that the question is always posed after the fact
of someone *else's* death.

   Clare Savage's life over the long term links living out 1963 with occupying the
death-filled spaces of New York, London, and Vietnam and, finally, with taking
over the homeland, Kingston, Jamaica, emptied and wasted by colonial powers,
and with redistributing violence into the scene of the world that has banalized,
made forgettable, those events (and there are so many) that ought to have produced *something*—a historic change, somewhere registered as an epistemological,
corporeal, and political sublime. She becomes thus committed to usurping the
privileged deployment of death from imperial and postimperial world powers:
first, she leaves the United States for London to study the classics and to fall in love
with a Vietnam veteran (their love and their dissolution both terribly haunted by
Western history's ghosts). The philosophy of assimilation Clare's father professes
in the United States then becomes the practice of guerrilla camouflage in Jamaica,
where classic, imperial, and mass cultural renditions of colonial death encounter
other revolutionary species and genealogies of the undead, zombies, spirits,
shades, traces that mark the land waiting to work and be worked on behalf of reclaiming Jamaica.[37]

   There is thus a long contextualizing history to tell of *No Telephone to Heaven*—
elsewhere—about the way it closes off nothing but the already exhausted futures
we call "the present tense" that the novel traces from a transnational late 1950s
through the globalized late 1980s in Jamaica, as refracted in the code of imperial
racist culture England and the United States enact as matters of domestic and foreign policy. These relations between the conventional registers of history (Vietnam, civil rights, the failed socialism of Michael Manley, and the failed Maroon
Rebellion against empire in late eighteenth-century Jamaica) and the personal genealogies of characters leaving home as fast as they can are generated by the scene
of revolutionary allegory marked by the wasted bodies of the four Birmingham
girls. As Clare joins the revolutionary guerrilla group that drives the truck labeled
No Telephone to Heaven, she evokes the almost meaningless picture of the girl and
turns her need and her mourning into action: "I know only that the loss, the forgetting ... of resistance ... of tenderness ... is a terrible thing. Look, I want to restore something to these children. ... And of course you are right: what good is
imagination ... whatever the imagery available to it ... to a dying child?" (p. 196).
Yet the "nation" that will be transformed by the textuality of the child-dedicated

counterviolence is not only the geopolitical discursive idea of a "nation" but also the United States, Great Britain, and Europe as the modernist master-referents for political futurity.

In *No Telephone to Heaven* as in *Song of Solomon,* the truth of pan-African history—that not slavery but a profound dialectic between diasporic loss and memorial accumulation constitutes the ongoing Middle Passage from which is generated African American identity[38]—counters powerfully the identity logics of America and the other nations whose imperial histories shift around the same constellation in that "heaven" of empire where so many things do and "something" so often does not happen, where atrocity is processed by the ex post facto *unidentification* or stripping away of the name of the victim, who is reduced to and remembered as a representative identity, a shadow behind a veil. In these texts America is just one more nation whose global activities and internal violences try and fail to organize what characters and "we" can imagine about how agency and futurity can be articulated under the pressures of a pulsating present. This present is of course founded on anachronism, through an archive that ranges from the classics of Western form that Clare studies in London to a period piece about the Maroon Rebellion to *Gone with the Wind* as a *documentary* about race, gender, rank, and fantasy in the United States (its obscene epigraph, "As God is my witness, I'll never go hungry again," might tacitly represent here the documentary truth about the melodrama of beset whiteness that marks U.S. nationality, and there is a story to be told that links it ironically with the refusal to die the death by starvation of political *irrelevance* that minor cultures so often endure; finally, *Gone with the Wind's* intense focus on making the land and language *work* for survival after this one moment of political annihilation predicts the tactical centrality of the "ruinate" Cliff focuses on, the growth of lush barbaric forest over the decorous groves that have come to civilize Jamaica for colonizers and tourists—so "ruined" is the island by the revolutionaries that the novel opens acknowledging its glossary, forcing foreign readers to enter the text/island from the back, as it were). Yet for all of its multinational and syncretic intertextuality, the end of *No Telephone* evokes "The Waste Land" and *Ulysses,* modernist transnational novel and epic. Ending with Shanti (peace, in another language) and Yes (a vernacular performance, yet emptied of political reference), these texts imagine the separation of aesthetics from national history's jagged edges yet affirm the intelligibility of whatever surviving culture remains; Cliff's ending too performs an affirmative ripping apart of time from Jamaica *but in order to occupy the space* that is not yet or ever a ground of "culture." A good-enough mother country in *No Telephone to Heaven* is not a place to return to but an aspiration unimaginable, readable only, and barely that, in the shards of empire and the scraps of failed resistances, revolutions, the lush/spare broken spaces of death that condense/displace the history of all the worlds in which tourism has circulated the pleasures of power, including the world of mass culture, here all summarily vanquished by a constellation of unreadable, broken ex-allegories. Clare's revisionary maternalist drive to debanalize the wounded-icon/dead-child in the newspaper by producing lush ongoing revolutionary/utopian tactics remains, thus, nothing more nor less than a promise: "Captive people have a need for song" (p. 87).

> *O je t'adore, O je t'adore, O je t'adore*
> *Poor-me-one, poor-me-one, poor-me-one*
> *Tres-tonos-son, tres-tonos-son, tres-tonos-son*
> *Kitty-woo, kitty-woo, kitty-woo. …*
>
> *She remembered language.*
> *Then it was gone.*
>
> *cutacoo, cutacoo, cutacoo*
> *coo, cu, cu, coo. …*
>
> *Day broke. (p. 208)*

In the end, Cliff refuses to be caught in the both/and discursive logic of minor cultures. Trying to imagine a language that undoes itself, turning its own words into barely referential phonemes, she takes on the risk of failed communication and failed allegory, breaks the "day" after a revolutionary act with an aubade. But this morning/mourning song performs a violent refusal to write further, a refusal to risk affirming that the island is actually living when we can see how it has been reduced to a confection cultivated and consumed by touristic and imperial drives toward yet more extravagant scenes of pleasure.

Such a suspension of the will to knowledge that accompanies the accommodations made between imperial and colonized cultures (this is where, perhaps, the disjunction between the African American and the Caribbean cases is most visible: the possibility of boundary, the sense of *place* usurped) is graphed onto the body of Harry/Harriet, Clare's gay cross-dressing friend. Harry/Harriet is the postcolonial pedagogue who takes over the maternal muse function in the education of Clare into revolutionary personhood—s/he tells Clare to read C.L.R. James, for example, and to return home to join the struggle against postimperial touristic evacuation of Jamaica. More important, it is s/he, refusing the allegory of gender on her/his body, who leads Clare to the praxis that dedramatizes the minor pleasures Jamaica offers. It is not only that they deconstruct tourist mentalities left and right, though the novel takes much time for pleasure in that. It is that Harry/Harriet's autobiography provides the terms that undo or counter the evacuation of identity we have witnessed in the processing of minoritized persons into semiotic substances for use by dominant cultures—an activity we witnessed, for example, in the newspaper's erasure of names from the little girls of Birmingham whose deaths initiated this process of political upheaval.

Harry/Harriet tells Clare of his rape by a white British officer. He glosses the text of his rape thus:

"Darling, I know it is hard to listen to all this; it is hard to tell. I have been tempted in my life to think *symbol*—that what he did to me is but a symbol for what they did to all of us, always bearing in mind that some of us, many of us, also do it to each other. But that's not right. I only suffered what my mother suffered—no more, no less. Not symbol, not allegory, not something in a story or a dialogue by Plato. No, man, I am merely a person who felt the overgrown cock of a big whiteman pierce the asshole of a lickle Black bwai—there it is. That is all there is to it." (pp. 129–130)

Harry/Harriet bears the burden of registering the transformation of geopolitics in *No Telephone to Heaven* and, as David Roman has argued, thus places an asterisk on the text's apparent ambition, to destroy the instrumental availability of minority bodies for majority pleasures.[39] Her/his point in this passage, though, is to refuse her/his symbolization in the fields of empire, and in two ways. One is in the mode of brutal self-description, a refusal of the consolations of rhetoric; the other is in the profoundly antiformalist regime of bodily practices s/he takes on. First, a cross-dresser who refuses to bury the "cross" in a smooth field of representation (her/his introduction in the novel: "Harry/Harriet puts on a bikini—bra stretched across his hairy, delicately mounded chest, panties cradling his cock and balls— and starts to dance to 'Hey Jude'" [p. 21]), s/he finally adopts "Harriet" and kills Harry, putting off the actual operation until the "revolution" ("But, you know, darling, castration ain't de main t'ing ... not a-tall, a-tall" [p. 168]).[40]

Coupling the diachronic interactivity of Clare and the dead mothers who inspire her to do *something* for other little girls, her "people," and the synchronic antisymbolic praxis of Harry/Harriet, who lives the sexual revolution of the sixties at every moment of her/his circulation in the metropole of Kingston, Cliff swells the stream of the many political anachronisms, uneven developments, and simply vulgar interventions that will undermine the course, the canon, the curriculum, and the customs of history: she comes to echo the anachronistic historiography of the book's epigraph, from Derk Wolcott's "Laventille": "We left / somewhere a life we never found, / customs and gods that are not born again." The year 1963 stands, therefore, as the intertextual catalyst that changes the terms of global/national/local necessity. By speaking slowly, deliberately, deferring "communication" and "persuasion," by defacing the visual regime that brings "life" to Jamaica by including it in the world system of exotic violence and friendly capital, by countering regimes of death with more death, and finally, by refusing the consolations of allegory, *No Telephone to Heaven* attempts and fails to represent the "something" that didn't happen by executing a fantasy of postimperial world cultural system failure, after which "something" else can be felt if not figured but only after the "break"— of the day, of history, and of the novel.

Coda: The Kiss and the Hit

I knew a child once, who was less than three. Her parents were anthropologists. They showed me how their daughter forced them to bless each bite of food she took: she would pick it up, and make them kiss it, and then she would eat it and the kiss they put on it. I was skeptical, thinking that it must have been an invented tradition, something the family formulated as a "product" of the child's so that they could continue to give birth to the child by being symbolically eaten by her (the kiss being the vehicle for the incorporation of the family into the child, a kind of everyday-life DNA) and so that they could tell the child later this story about how much she loved and trusted and found magical her family. The child, in any case, did delight in her ritual and in the happiness it produced for her interlocutors: when for the first time I was chosen to kiss a cookie, I remember, I felt, well, chosen.

Why do I tell you this now, after these magical narratives of failed and partial histories? Partly to open a space of memory for what this essay has not had the capacity to imagine: some remaining horizons of critical historicity whose force in disrupting notions of practical/utopian politics, of failure/success, was a crucial though understated context for this paper.

One of these is the scene of pedagogy, troped in the young girl's coming to see that a first act of magical thinking (around food, as around political trauma) might become a scene of repetition, solicitation, domination, testing, leading to a public-sphere-making reimagination of the world: will you come through for me, kiss my cookie? A sequel to this essay will engage some problems of feminist pedagogy around the question of how identification and identity frame the scene of power and its politics, especially in graduate education that takes place between feminist/women (sometimes Queer, or lesbian) teachers and their feminist/female (sometimes Queer, or lesbian) students.[41] Just as the fantasy of almost contractual equality glosses the scene of magical eating, so too feminists have long hoped that collaborative work with and among students would break down degrading hierarchy, would make the scene of transmission of knowledge more of a kiss than, say, the hit on the back of the neck children of my mother's generation received if they did not eat their (goddamn) dinners.

But it has become clear to me, and to my students (alas), that more must be said about the relation between the "kiss" and the "hit" in the transmission of feminist knowledges and support intergenerationally and about why the humanities fight structurally against "collaboration" in their resolute embrace of authorship as a site of origin for critical texts—an embrace that sets the scene of professional value and expertise in fundamental and fundamentally constraining ways.

Second, the question of utopia/failure, played out in countless scenes (sometimes simultaneous) of gratitude and betrayal between teachers and students in feminist academic communities, emerges in another venue as well: this has to do with the banalization of "politics" into an intellectual/activist split that has made the white Left seem, well, mainly aspiring to generate individual star expert talking heads, compared with the rapid expansion of Queer and multiculturally identified bodies into publics of their own, publics that have become important grounds for emergent cultures of radical expertise that have not given up their sixties-like rages, affects, polemics, nonsense: witness the variety of "experts" (wearing their various styles, skins, and fabrics) brought into the public eye around Bill Clinton's meeting with the "Gay and Lesbian Community" before the Gay and Lesbian March on Washington in April 1993. I have tried to show how "'68" denotes, in the United States, an event whose history is still unfolding, still cluttering the way with little piles of waste and inspiration; its banalized legacy, in the postpolitical rages of professionalism and in the feminist, progressive, and right-wing contest to administer political correctness, must be understood as well as a desire to frame the moment of '68 as no longer historical, as *finished*, and therefore failed.[42] PC, a slur, must be understood as a mode of etiquette: to which I say, in a way I hope dimensionalized by all that has passed between us in this investigation of the sublime productivities of political failure, "something" unspeakable.

NOTES

Like this essay, these notes reveal writing as a collaborative space, of passions and citations. Thus every note that follows begins with a tacit "I take inspiration/language from ..." The project derived from four conversations: with Nick Dirks and Sherry Ortner, on the legacies of '68; with Robyn Weigman, on women's studies and the nostalgic discourse of "home"; with Chris Newfield, on the prospects for intellectuals in the wake of public sphere contention over political correctness in the United States; and with Geoff Eley, on the theory and geopolitics of utopia/failure. I have been also lucky to have ongoing discussions with Arjun Appadurai, Hortense Spillers, Michael Warner, and the Gender Studies Divas of note 3.

1. I thank my great colleagues Leora Auslander, Norma Field, Elizabeth Helsinger, and Martha Ward for permission to quote our work and to remember how patiently and stubbornly we must defer any prognoses of failure, celebrations of success.

2. I adapt this observation from the more general critique of modern national historiographies in Nicholas B. Dirks, "History as a Sign of the Modern," *Public Culture* 2:2 (Spring 1990):25–32.

3. For more serendipitously aligned thought on the subject of identity politics and the New Right, see Kobena Mercer, "1968," in *Cultural Studies*, ed. Lawrence Grossberg, Cary Nelson, and Paula Treichler (New York: Routledge, 1992), 424–449. See also Biddy Martin and Chandra Talpede Mohanty, "Feminist Politics: What's Home Got to Do with It?" in *Feminist Studies/Critical Studies*, ed. Teresa de Lauretis (Bloomington: Indiana University Press, 1986), 191–212.

4. Cornel West, "The New Cultural Politics of Difference," in *Out There: Marginalization and Contemporary Cultures*, ed. Russell Ferguson, Martha Gever, Trinh T. Minh-ha, and Cornel West (Cambridge: MIT Press, 1990), 19–36.

5. See Gayatri Chakravorty Spivak, "Subaltern Studies: Deconstructing Historiography," in *In Other Worlds* (New York: Methuen, 1987), 197–221.

6. Ranajit Guha's exploration of the contradictions of liberal/postcolonial logics of authority describes the ways that, at least in India, state and other forms of social power establish themselves by asserting modes of domination as forms of hegemony, with all the taci

implications of "consent" that the condition of being hegemonic requires, at least in the important realms of self-representation. By inverting the terms I mean to emphasize the contrast between this aim to hold power through the veil of some historically grounded simulacrum of consent and the aim Deleuze and Guattari imagine, which is to imagine cultural and political legitimacy without the ambition to reproduce a total world of nation-state sublimity (Gilles Deleuze and Felix Guattari, "What Is a Minor Literature?" in Ferguson et al., *Out There*, 59–69). See Ranajit Guha, "Dominance Without Hegemony and Its Historiography," in *Selected Subaltern Studies*, ed. Ranajit Guha and Gayatri Chakravorty Spivak (New York: Oxford University Press, 1988), 210–309.

7. These kinds of questions about the problems of translation that arise in the movements of expertise and self-representation between sub- and dominant cultures are almost entirely elided in the best work available now on identity politics and the public sphere. See Nancy Fraser, "Rethinking the Public Sphere: A Contribution to the Critique of Actually Existing Democracy," and Michael Warner, "The Mass Public and the Mass Subject," in *Habermas and the Public Sphere*, ed. Craig Calhoun (Cambridge: MIT Press, 1992), 109–142, 377–401. In contrast, see *How Do I Look? Queer Film and Video* (Seattle: Bag Press, 1991), esp. Cindy Patton and Kobena Mercer, and Chicago Cultural Studies Group, "Critical Multiculturalism," *Critical Inquiry* 18 (Spring 1992):530–555.

8. I take this phrase from R. Radhakrishnan, "Nationalism, Gender, and the Narrative of Identity," in *Nationalisms and Sexualities*, ed. Andrew Parker, Mary Russo, Doris Sommer, and Patricia Yeager (New York: Routledge, 1992), 81.

9. See Chandra Talpade Mohanty, "Cartographies of Struggle," in *Third World Women and the Politics of Feminism*, ed. Chandra Talpade Mohanty, Ann Russo, and Lourdes Torres (Bloomington: Indiana University Press, 1991); Lata Mani, "Multinational Feminisms," *Feminist Review* 35 (Summer 1990):24–41; Lauren Berlant and Elizabeth Freeman, "Queer Nationality," *boundary* 2 19 (Spring 1992):148–180; and Lauren Berlant, "The Female Complaint," *Social Text* 19/20 (Fall 1988):237–259, on the subject of feminism's politics of identification.

10. See, for example, the good analyses of feminism's history of exclusionary violences and contradictions in Alice Echols, *Daring to Be Bad: Radical Feminism in America, 1967–1975* (Minneapolis: University of Minnesota Press, 1989); bell hooks, *Feminist Theory: From Margin to Center* (Boston: South End Press, 1984) and *Talking Back: Thinking Feminist Thinking Black* (Boston: South End Press, 1989); Hortense Spillers, "Interstices: A Small Drama of Words," in *Pleasure and Danger: Exploring Female Sexuality*, ed. Carole S. Vance (Boston: Routledge, 1984), 73–100.

11. This list of already-cited names stands in for a larger cluster of materialist feminist work in the humanities and social sciences that takes the stressful relation between representation and empiricism to be central to a complex analysis of the ways gender, race, and other essentialisms dominate the scene of identity under capitalist and other state systems.

12. See the use of "realness" in the 1992 film *Paris Is Burning*. "realness" is the quality of character the fabulous, creative, and transgressive identity performance contemporary queer subculture supports. I take the risky dialectic of identity logics that queer politics has produced between "gay and lesbian" norms of practical reference and metropolitan or public-sphere-based subcultural identification to be a foundational model for radical politics in and outside of the academy.

13. See, for example, the way the tension plays out in Margo Culley and Catherine Portuges, eds., *Gendered Subjects* (Boston: Routledge and Kegan Paul, 1985); Donald Mor-

ton and Mas'ud Zavarzadeh, *Theory/Pedagogy/Politics: Texts for Change* (Urbana: University of Illinois Press, 1991); *Notes from the Beehive,* special issue on Feminism and the Institution, Differences (Fall 1990); Joan E. Hartman and Ellen Messer-Davidow, *(En)Gendering Knowledge: Feminists in Academe* (Knoxville: University of Tennessee Press, 1991); Patti Lather, *Getting Smart: Feminist Research and Pedagogy With/in the Postmodern* (New York: Routledge, 1991). For a summary of the feminist harmful-speech/harmful-knowledge argument, see Nadine Strossen, "Legal Scholars Who Would Limit Free Speech," *Chronicle of Higher Education,* 7 July 1993, B1–B2.

14. Karl Marx, *The Eighteenth Brumaire of Louis Bonaparte* (New York: International Publishers, 1963), 18. For a suggestive meditation on Marx's enigma, see Terry Eagleton, "Nationalism: Irony and Commitment," in *Nationalism, Colonialism, and Literature: Terry Eagleton, Fredric Jameson, Edward W. Said,* introduction by Seamus Deane (Minneapolis: University of Minnesota Press, 1990), 27 et passim.

15. Michelle Cliff, *No Telephone to Heaven* (New York: Vintage, 1989); Deleuze and Guattari, "What Is a Minor Literature?"; Toni Morrison, *Song of Solomon* (New York: Knopf, 1977); Carolyn Kay Steedman, *Landscape for a Good Woman: A Story of Two Lives* (New Brunswick: Rutgers University Press, 1987).

16. Steedman, *Landscape for a Good Woman,* 119.

17. Ibid., 123.

18. Ibid., 62–64.

19. An important gloss on the text of minor language and fields of domination can be found in Mary Louise Pratt, "Linguistic Utopias," in *The Linguistics of Writing,* ed. Nigel Fabb, Derek Attridge, Alan Durant, and Colin McCabe (Manchester: Manchester University Press, 1987), 48–66.

20. For a history and critical engagement with the mass cultural construction and the annulment of "working-class culture," see Geoff Eley on *Distant Voices/Still Lives:* "The Family Is a Dangerous Place: Memory, Gender, and the Image of the Working Class," in *Revisioning History: Film and the Construction of the Past,* ed. Robert Rosenstone (Princeton: Princeton University Press), forthcoming.

21. Cliff, *No Telephone to Heaven,* 100.

22. Morrison, *Song of Solomon,* 174.

23. Cliff, *No Telephone to Heaven,* 100–101.

24. Morrison, *Song of Solomon,* 173.

25. Cliff, *No Telephone to Heaven,* 100.

26. Martin Luther King, "Eulogy for the Martyred Children (1963)," in *A Testament of Hope: The Essential Writings and Speeches of Martin Luther King, Jr.,* (San Francisco: HarperSanFrancisco, 1986), 221.

27. See Dirks, "History as a Sign of the Modern," 30.

28. Taylor Branch, *Parting the Waters: America in the King Years, 1954–1963* (New York: Simon and Schuster, 1988), 892.

29. Martin Luther King, "I Have a Dream (1963)," in *A Testament of Hope,* 217–220.

30. Gayatri Chakravorty Spivak, "Acting Bits/Identity Talk" *Critical Inquiry* 18 (Summer 1992):790.

31. I take the deployment of allegory in these novels as scenes, in the Freudian sense, of departure/disavowal/misrecognition of and identification with inherited models of privacy, locality, political facticity, and maps of world history. In this sense they occupy and I think quite surmount the breach/bridge of allegorical national politics currently debated

by Aijaz Ahmad, *In Theory* (New York: Verso, 1992), and Fredric Jameson, *The Geopolitical Aesthetic* (Indianapolis: Indiana University Press, 1992).

32. On the ideology and imaginary of the African American south-north migration in Morrison's work, see Susan Willis, *Specifying: Black Women Writing the American Experience* (Madison: University of Wisconsin Press, 1987).

33. Morrison, *Song of Solomon*, 303.

34. Cliff, *No Telephone to Heaven*, 101.

35. Here Cliff demonstrates what Ahmad insists on, that the easy substitution of "nationality" and "collective life" is pernicious and must analytically and politically be resisted. *In Theory*, 106–110.

36. Frantz Fanon, "The Fact of Blackness," in *Black Skin, White Masks*, trans. Charles Lam Markham (London: Pluto Press, 1986), 109–140.

37. This is where we can link up this discussion of allegory, nationality, anomaly, contradiction, death, and the uncanny generative possibilities of *something* with Slavoj Zizek's discussion of intimacy, trauma, and the symbolic orders of democracy in "You Only Die Twice," in *The Sublime Object of Ideology* (New York: Verso, 1989), 131–150. Milkman Dead/Guitar Banes and Clare Savage reimagine themselves, in their allegorical texts, as manifestations of the "sublime body between two deaths" and stage their risky failed overcoming as crucial to keeping revolutionary, life-giving activity alive, though "dead."

38. The Middle Passage that slaves endured to reach the United States figures prominently in contemporary African American writing, to unsettle the narrative origin story about how African American identity derives from slavery, a story told often to wipe out the prehistory of black modernity. Books like Morrison's *Beloved* (New York: Knopf, 1987) and (clearly) Charles Johnson's *The Middle Passage* (New York: Atheneum, 1990) and criticism like Hortense Spillers's "Mama's Baby, Papa's Maybe: An American Grammar Book" (*Diacritics* 17:2 [Summer 1987]:67–80) feature this ultra-geopolitical transition to signal the important impossibility of reclamation, rescue, recuperation to any national narrative. But the Middle Passage's importance to diasporic thinking is, in a sense, as powerfully attested to in the casual aura of its use in *No Telephone to Heaven*. Speaking of Kitty and Boy as they drive through the treacherous South to the only slightly less treacherous North: "They were shipmates, as surely as the slaves who crossed the Middle Passage together. ... This was a huge, a difficult country and each was outside of it" (p. 60).

39. David Roman, "Tropical Fruit: Latino Gay Males in Three Resistance Novels of the Americas," delivered at the American Studies Association, 6 November 1992.

40. Harry/Harriet, modern queer, is the most modern instance of a genealogy of feminized subjects whose bodies bear the visible burden of pornographic sensationalism apparently necessary to produce the universal, disembodied promises of Enlightenment-style nationalities. For a summary of this process, see Lauren Berlant, *The Anatomy of National Fantasy* (Chicago: University of Chicago Press, 1990), 19–56, 135–150.

41. The sequel will be written with Elizabeth Freeman. I have happily or sheepishly inserted the parenthetical sexual categories at her request/demand.

42. I use this managerial language deliberately, to emphasize the bureaucratic impulse behind the taxonomizing chaos generated by identity politics and its ugly imaginary friend, political correctness. I learned this from Christopher Newfield, "What Was Political Correctness? Race, the Right, and Managerial Democracy in the Humanities," *Critical Inquiry* 19 (Winter 1993):308–336.

20

Cultural Studies: Countering a Depoliticized Culture

DONALD LAZERE

I WANT TO RESPOND here to allegations that academic leftists have unjustifiably politicized literary and other humanistic education and, more particularly, that they have used cultural studies as a pretext for propagating marxist or other left ideology. Attacks against leftist political correctness are suspect when they come from right-wing forces like the National Association of Scholars, who would, one gathers, simply prefer to see propagated a version of PC acceptable to their Reaganite corporate sponsors, such as the Olin and Scaife Foundations.[1] Nevertheless, I think these criticisms have some substance to them that needs to be confronted in an honest way, and I also disagree with some of the dominant trends in left cultural studies, so I will try here to stake out a position critical of both the Right and the Left. First I will survey the forces for conservatism in American politics and mass culture since World War II that have justified leftist cultural opposition; then I will show how the same conservative forces have dominated American education, including literature and composition studies, and have justified leftist intervention in those disciplines. I will go on to survey my disagreements with current left theory and concepts of cultural studies and to describe a course I teach that embodies the principles developed to that point. Finally, I will address some of the ethical and practical problems in implementing left-oriented cultural studies.

Many academic sources in the marxist tradition, broadly speaking, have contributed to the focus on the intersections between politics and culture that have recently coalesced into cultural studies—Frankfurt School critical theory, women's and ethnic studies, the Birmingham Center for Contemporary Cultural Studies, and poststructuralist and postmodernist theory, among others.[2] At this writing, the most recent turn that cultural studies has taken is toward incorporation into teaching and academic writing of the notion of the public intellectual and the responsibility of women and men of letters to act as political/cultural critics (of their society in general as well as of educational and other cultural institutions) through journalistic or creative writing, public speaking, and activism. The tradition of the left public intellectual in the United States runs from the nineteenth-century transcendentalists, realists and naturalists, muckrakers and socialists through the literary Left and New York intellectual circles of the early-to-midtwentieth century to the New Left and academic radicalism in the sixties. In the Modern Language Association the Radical Caucus, which emerged out of the anti–Vietnam War movement in 1968, is closer to this tradition than is the Marxist Literary Group, more Eurocentric and theoretical—although the two have converged in recent years (partly out of the imperative to make common cause against the assault by conservatives against the academic Left), as is evidenced by the mix of contributors from both groups in this book. The approach to cultural studies that I will advance here is most akin to the American public-intellectual tradition, though it derives more directly from the immediate conditions of American society and education and specifically from my own long experience of teaching undergraduates in a conservative, middle-class, vocationally oriented university.

I think it fair to say that the revived study of cultural politics in this country since the sixties occurred more or less inevitably as a filling of the vast vacuum left by the unprecedented depoliticizing of American culture and scholarship after World War II; it might be said to amount not to politicization but to de-depoliticization. As for the "leftist bias" in cultural studies, I contend that this bias can be defended on the grounds that the academic critical study of culture is one of the few remaining areas of American society that is, or has the potential to be, a counterforce to societywide domination by conservative corporate, political, and military influences. (Conservatives ridicule sixties radicals for turning to academia as the only avenue hospitable to them anymore; the implication is that conservatives will only be content when *no* forums remain open to the radical Left.) I further contend that the conservative order in America is bolstered by the atomization of public discourse and mass consciousness, which inhibits effective oppositional organization. Thus cultural studies have a mandate to be the "adversary culture" neoconservatives abhor—to combat this atomization with a comprehensive, coherent vision.

In this respect, those of us committed to the political Left and cultural studies ought not to accept the label, tendentiously pinned on us by conservatives (abetted by the excesses of poststructuralist pluralism), as the adversaries of the Arnoldian holistic, disinterested vision of the humanities but should lay claim to being its legitimate successors. I do not think it is doublethink to regard left commitment as compatible with disinterested scholarship, because in this sense being on the left does not mean pushing a doctrinaire political line but rather maintaining a critical viewpoint outside the ideological mainstream and striving for an integrative epistemology in opposition to the atomizing and interest-controlled dominant culture. My position here is a reaffirmation of the tradition of marxist humanism, a variety of leftism that is, I believe, more faithful to the essential Marx—the contemporary of Arnold and other nineteenth-century philosophers of an organic world view—than the structuralist and poststructuralist marxism that has attempted to discredit humanism and organicism on the left. I also submit that the depredations of the Reagan-Bush era have given new currency to basic marxist economics and its relevance for cultural studies, as opposed to the phenomenological and linguistic emphasis dominating recent marxist theory.

In this post–Cold War, postmodern age, one is subject to ridicule, even in many sectors of the Left, for insisting on any remnant of value not only in marxist economics but even in democratic socialism. (It might be argued that the apparent "triumph of free enterprise" has, at least in the West, been due not so much to its ideological or even practical superiority as to the power of international capital to overwhelm or buy off all opposition—but that is not centrally at issue here.) What aspects of the socialist idea remain valid, especially for cultural studies, in contemporary America?

To begin with, most American public discourse is confined to a narrow spectrum whose leftward limit is the Democratic Party version of governance by relatively liberal corporate and military executives, lawyers, and lobbyists now incarnated in the Clinton Administration—albeit with a multicultural spin. Compare America with European democracies that have large socialist or labor parties and presses and in which sharply progressive taxes, socialized medicine, free education in the best secondary, undergraduate, and graduate schools, government family subsidies for home purchases, child rearing, and day care, five-week vacations for all workers, and in some cases a reduced work week—measures still too "radical" to be seriously considered here under Clinton—have long been taken for granted and are not likely to be rolled back much even after socialists lose control of the government as they recently did in France. After François Mitterrand's election in 1981, one-third of the members of the French National Assembly were teachers, who also exert far more power in the Socialist Party than American educational associations do in the Democratic Party. The issue here is not the efficacy of European socialist parties and policies, whose record is mixed at best (though arguably no worse than that of conservative counterparts like Reagan and Bush here or Thatcher and Major in England) but conservatives' ludicrous exaggeration of the power and extremism of both teachers and "the Left" in the United States.

Conservatives' claims of leftist bias in American politics, education, and media are typically engineered through blurring the distinction between Democratic liberal capitalism and socialism, as well as through a trick of selective vision wherein every instance of bias on the Left is cited but none on the Right so that no sense of relative proportion is established. Even if conservatives were correct in every instance they cite of liberal biases, pointing to any number of random instances of liberalism in American politics, education, or media does not necessarily lead to the conclusion that any of these fields, or American society on the whole, is dominated by leftist ideology—especially socialist ideology. Conservatives blithely ignore the multiple ways leftist ideas get neutralized in virtually every area of American public discourse. My anthology *American Media and Mass Culture: Left Perspectives* (1987) was in effect a six-hundred-page catalogue of these ways; here I will only review quickly a few key points from my introductory passages there, then explore their implications for cultural studies.

The conservative critique overlooks all the massive forces that bias our socialization in favor of Americanism, free-enterprise boosterism, organized religion, and the norms of upper- and middle-class white patriarchy. Those forces include the billions of dollars spent every year by corporations and corporate-wealthy individuals on political lobbying and campaign contributions, legal representation, public relations and advertising, news and entertainment media controlled directly or indirectly by ownership and sponsorship, contributions leading to trusteeships in universities and other cultural institutions, subsidized university faculties, research institutes, and academic fronts like the Heritage Foundation, the American Enterprise Institute, the National Association of Scholars, and the Madison Center for Educational Affairs (which funds a network of conservative college student organizations and publications).

In addition to these means of direct social control, and more pertinent to cultural studies, is the conservative influence of what Richard Ohmann once termed "the politics of inadvertence." The American status quo is perpetuated not only through deliberate social control but through the more or less inadvertent effects of the fragmentation of knowledge and communication, the absence of any presentation of political events or opinions within a common understanding of ideologies, and the distractions of entertainment and sports, consumerism, and sheer busyness. For example, the sum total in recent years of liberally oriented American films, television newscasts and dramas, and print media dealing explicitly with political issues is offset by the fact that such expressions still form a minute percentage of the total media output; the dominant climate of apolitical distraction and promotion of commodity consumption dissipates *any* political message, whether of the Left or the Right. As is the case with many social policies, this politically amorphous atmosphere may not be calculatedly engineered by corporate or political powers, yet its conservative results coincide comfortably with their hegemonial interests, so that taking steps to change it is not likely to be high on their agenda.

I've come increasingly to think that the most important but least discussed way in which the American status quo is perpetuated is through habit, routine, and busyness. In the classic opening sequence of Charlie Chaplin's *Modern Times,* the little fellow is working on an assembly line, turning bolts with a monkey wrench in each hand at a frantic pace. His foreman starts haranguing him to speed up even more, and Charlie stops in exasperation to protest; but as soon as he stops, the assembly line moves ahead, the foreman orders him to catch up, and he has to leap ahead on the line and redouble his pace just to get back to his original position. Here is the emblem for the daily lives of virtually all of us except those wealthy enough to hire others to do their busy work for them—which may be the strongest of all the forms of power that wealth can buy.

According to an extraordinary cover story in *Time* (Gibbs 1989), "In 1967 testimony before a Senate subcommittee indicated that by 1985 people could be working just 22 hours a week or 27 weeks a year or could retire at 38. That would leave only the great challenge of finding a way to enjoy all that leisure" (p. 59). After the economic reversals of the past two decades, however, "the amount of leisure time enjoyed by the average American has shrunk 37% since 1973. Over the same period, the average workweek, including commuting, has jumped from under 41 hours to nearly 47 hours. In some professions, predictably law, finance, and medicine, the demands often stretch to 80-plus hours a week" (p. 58). Typical of the mass media in failing to place concrete events in an ideological context, *Time* simply treats these economic developments as if they were acts of God, without analyzing what political policies may have produced them or who benefits from them, for example, the downscaling of wages by American corporations and the growing gap between the rich and the rest of us accelerated by Reaganite economic policies. (See Schor's *The Overworked American* [1993] for a more politically focused analysis.)

Concerning the conservative effects of busyness, no one in our time has improved on Thoreau's attack on the rise of nineteenth-century industrial capitalism in "Life Without Principle": "I think that there is nothing, not even crime, more opposed to poetry, to philosophy, ay, to life itself, than this incessant business" (Thoreau 1950, 712). The rush to get through the day's business keeps people too busy to have the energy to think about changing the system that is keeping them so busy; they are apt to shut out leftist alternatives because they create cognitive overload and a threat to the comforts of routine.

We are all kept on the treadmill by the need to get ahead or, like Charlie, just to keep from falling behind. Students must scramble desperately to get the grade and then the degree, in order to get the job and then the promotion. The work world is much the same whether one goes into business or the professions, the private or the public sector. Whether you are going for CEO, managing editor, or higher political office, for chief surgeon or a law partnership, for tenure or a department chair, you face the same pressures to conform to the will of those above you on the ladder. Few of the debates I have heard about liberal versus conservative forces in American society talk adequately about the subservience of workers, and of students as workers-to-be, to those with the ultimate conservative prerogative—the power to hire and fire.

One of the persistent appeals of socialist theory—and one that deserves to be receiving renewed public attention in light of the present economic regression reported by *Time*—is the possibilities it presents of guaranteeing employment and minimum income, reducing required work time, and ultimately ending the long-established bonds between work and basic subsistence and the corollary power of employer over worker. Yet any possibility of these ideals' even being considered is currently shut out in the United States, precisely because most people are kept too busy working under the present system to give serious thought to an alternative system.

The distractions of busyness are compounded by the confusing absence of a consistent ideology in either the Republican or the Democratic Party and of any agreed-on definition of the basic points differentiating the "liberalism" and "conservatism" within which American public discourse is parochially bound. (In recent presidential elections, candidates have avoided even the limited consistency of identifying their positions with *these* terms.) Among the points ignored by the conservative critique of media and education is that, however liberal or even radical the message of a particular media production, publication, or teacher, its point will be lost if audience members and students lack the understanding of differing political ideologies that will allow them to interpret it within some coherent universe of discourse. (I have illustrated what I mean here about establishing a universe of political discourse in "Teaching the Political Conflicts: A Rhetorical Schema" [1992].)

A good case can be made that the very lack of clearly defined political controversy in the United States is a preferable alternative to countries that suffer from constant, often violent political conflict. We are at the other extreme, though, where any distinguishable ideology is excluded from public discourse because of the attempt by both political parties to appeal to *everyone* rather than to a specific constituency and because of the nonideological, "neutral" stance of American mass media and education. Daniel Bell's proclaimed "end of ideology" in the fifties has degenerated into nationwide ignorance of ideologies. Politicians, the media, and educators alike stampede toward the fanatic middle of the road, where "moderate" is a euphemism for bland evasion of controversy and where "balance" consists of a mishmash of liberal and conservative messages on diverse issues, with no clear-cut exposition of underlying philosophical differences. The result is that those in power easily maintain control in default of any articulated or organized opposition.

The most wide-reaching nationwide outlet for a consistent ideology is Christian broadcasting and publishing, which is a powerful voice for right-wing politics as much as for religion. Otherwise, there is no mass-circulated, nationally accessible equivalent in television, radio, or print of a *Commentary, National Review, In These Times, The Nation,* or Pacifica Radio that might frame current events within a cogent political perspective. (For only one point of contrast, France has two leftist national daily papers: the Communist *L'Humanité* and the *Libération,* which has gone from being the underground paper of the uprising of 1968 to being available today on newsstands nearly everywhere.) The most feasible democratic alternative in the United States to the present media monopolies, a system of broadcast and print communications providing a forum for a full range of ideological positions, is effectively precluded by lack of capital or political support for

346   DONALD LAZERE

a true public broadcasting system. As the purge a few years ago of editors sympathetic to left authors at Pantheon Books confirmed, we have a vicious circle
wherein lack of a profitable or politically sizable constituency for left media precludes their funding—and the lack of left media precludes the growth of that constituency.

Suppose, if only hypothetically, that democratic socialism (not its totalitarian
perversions in communist countries) did in fact present some preferable alternatives to capitalism in America. In the present ideological climate, the vast majority
of the public would never even have access to knowledge of those alternatives.
People suffering from immediate, intense oppression—the situation of the proletariat in Marx's scenario for socialist revolution—need little abstract information
or theoretical sophistication to be persuaded that change is in their interest. In
present-day America, however, the grosser forms of injustice have been greatly reduced, and the majority of the population has been socialized into a mood of at
least passive assent; even as they have lost ground economically over the past two
decades and become increasingly disgruntled, most people have little understanding of the dynamics of the global and domestic forces squeezing them. And they
are all the more unaware of the exploitation of Third World labor and resources
on which the West's relative affluence depends. The information and explanations
necessary for analysis simply aren't widely accessible. Having lived most of my life
in various middle-American communities, I can testify that the Chamber of
Commerce view of reality, in which what's good for business is good for America
and the world, is the only one most people in such communities are ever exposed
to from cradle to grave.

So the status quo of capitalism and nationalism is immediate and familiar,
while socialist (or any other) alternatives are hypothetical, distant, and alien. Socialism entails a completely different system of thought that takes more time to
explain than is available in any area of American public discourse except for advanced scholarship and some intellectual journalism. (A major anomaly of cultural politics in contemporary America is that access to socialist thought has
largely become restricted to intellectuals, especially academic ones, whose own
class position in most cases is ultimately inimical to socialism.) By contrast, the
ideology of capitalism and nationalism is propagated less through theoretical discourse than through constant, saturating repetition of its everyday manifestations. Expositions of socialist ideology would have to counteract the 350,000 propaganda messages for capitalism that American children are exposed to by the age
of eighteen in the form of that many TV commercials, in addition to the immea-
surable daily dosage of socialization in consumerism, the nationalist rituals of
"The Star-Spangled Banner" and the pledge of Allegiance, the influence of organized religion, etc., etc.

Sociolinguists such as Basil Bernstein, Pierre Bourdieu, Claus Mueller, and
Richard Ohmann have developed the hypothesis that the restricted cognitive and
linguistic codes that Bernstein identifies with working-class socialization, and that

have become the dominant mode of modern political and media discourse, make it virtually impossible for the population in general even to conceptualize, have the language to articulate, or concentrate long enough to understand any theoretical alternative such as socialism.[3] A good deal of recent empirical research along these lines strongly confirms Herbert Marcuse's theory of "the closing of the universe of discourse" in *One-Dimensional Man* (1964)—a theory and a book that are certainly due for a revaluation today in face of the reemerging gap in American power and class relations and the declining credibility of opposing pluralistic models of American society like those of both liberal social science (and its neoconservative refinements) and poststructuralism—more about which later.

To the extent that all the above and other forces bolstering capitalism in America involve issues of cognition, conceptualization, and language, they become legitimate and necessary subjects of study in English and other fields of the humanities that are currently merging into cultural studies. I believe that the primary importance of maintaining or reviving a socialist presence today may lie in socialism as an alternative cognitive system rather than as an economic one; thus, socialism might conceivably be discredited as a practical economic model yet retain its value as a critical perspective outside the mainstream of American ideology. Maintaining this presence may be all the more vital in the wake of the recent worldwide "triumph of free enterprise"; this ostensible victory has compounded the complacency of capitalist ideology and rendered it even more impregnable to cognitive alternatives.

Let me give a concrete example of what I mean about socialism as an alternate cognitive system. During the Gulf War, not one of the major national news media, including those that conservatives claim are most leftist, raised the issue of the conflicts of interest resulting from ownership of media corporations by military contractors—most notably ownership of NBC by General Electric, which makes components for the Patriot missile—and ownership of substantial stock in General Electric by the government of Kuwait. The only report I saw of these facts, or consideration of the biases they might produce in NBC's reportage on the war, appeared in *EXTRA!*, the magazine of the radical-left Fairness and Accuracy in Reporting. More broadly, it is quite natural that corporately owned and corporately sponsored media, conservative or liberal, are generally reluctant to air questioning of the role of their parent corporations in the military-industrial-government complex or the international flow of capital and arms—to say nothing of the special interests of these corporations in a myriad of other domestic and foreign issues on which the media they own routinely report. Who could object, simply on the grounds of a free market of ideas, to the premise that capitalist ownership of virtually all our major sources of public information might not be in the best interests of a free society and that a broader range of expression would result from the creation of some mass media with a socialist viewpoint (i.e., to the left of PBS) or at least from making available some prime air time and print space to that viewpoint?

348

Politically Sanitized Education

In a multitude of ways, American education both reflects and reproduces the foregoing conservative traits of American culture. Everyone knows—though few of
the hand-wringing reports on the sad state of liberal education in America acknowledge it—that the real purpose of high school and college education is to
prepare the majority of students to get jobs in business and the professions, so
that in most schools other than the elite prep schools and liberal arts colleges general education and critical thinking are considered boring nuisances. (That the
primary site of the PC controversy has been elite universities indicates that this is a
struggle for ideological domination within the liberally educated upper classes
rather than within the vocationally educated masses.) The majority of university
faculties outside the humanities and perhaps the social sciences, as well as most
administrators and trustees, are more or less overtly in the service of big business,
the political establishment, or the military both in preprofessional training of students and in research or consulting activities. Left teachers constantly fight a losing battle against students' knowledge that they are eventually going to have to tai-
lor their political attitudes to the conservative views of businesses, professions, or
government agencies in order to get and keep a job. No amount of leftist faculty
bias is apt to make a dent in a curriculum geared to uncritical vocationalism, any
more than the reputed leftists in media are apt to make a dent in a system geared
toward distraction and commodity consumption.

Our schools also reflect and reproduce the politics of inadvertent conservatism.
At every level of education we find the same deemphasis of politics and absence of
systematic exposure to a full spectrum of ideologies. I can think of no more telling
symbol of American priorities than the apparently nationwide convention that
high school social science classes are taught as an incidental activity of varsity
sports coaches. The exposition of clear-cut ideological viewpoints gets further
blurred by the convention that teachers and textbooks are expected to be blandly
neutral. (As I remember my days at Roosevelt High in Des Moines, though, the
coaches who taught social science weren't at all inhibited from voicing their right-
wing biases; around 1950 one terrorized us with grim assurances that we would be
in a nuclear war with Russia within five years.)

Comprehensive political understanding is still further impeded by a depart-
mentalized curriculum of unrelated courses each jammed into a few hours a week
for one semester or quarter and each in turn broken up into discontinuous units
corresponding to television's blips of information. Students and teachers alike are
caught on Chaplin's assembly line, too hurried and overworked ever to gain a view
of issues that goes beyond today's exam or exercise. Conservative critics of education claim that the schools and colleges are threatened by teachers pushing left
ideology, but many of those teachers are primarily attempting to combat the absence of *any* coherent exposition of ideas in the curriculum. Moreover, as Paulo
Freire and his American followers like Ira Shor, Richard Ohmann, and others associated with the journal *Radical Teacher* have been arguing persuasively, even the

teaching of left views is likely to be canceled out if the social relations of the class-room itself—with the teacher in an authoritarian role and students set against each other—reproduce the alienation and hierarchies of power within the larger society.[4]

How do university English teaching and scholarship fit into this depoliticized, decentered social and educational context? Beginning with the level of conventional undergraduate instruction, both literature and writing courses are typically structured in the standard discontinuous units of study, using textbook anthologies that reproduce fragmented, serial consciousness—in a random sequence of authors and themes with little ideological cohesion. Most literature courses are organized as chronological surveys of periods and movements, as groupings of readings by genre, or as applications of diverse critical approaches. The explicit or tacit political viewpoint of readings usually receives little glossing in editors' notes; few literature or composition anthologies and handbooks include as part of the apparatus an overview of how authors differ in their political viewpoints. The emphasis prior to the twentieth century on rhetoric and oratory as the center of both literary and writing instruction provided a viable means of incorporating the analysis of political argumentation, but rhetoric has been exiled to academically marginal departments of speech.

In undergraduate literary survey courses, the strong tendency of literary anthology editors has been, at least until the last few decades, to steer clear of political writings. In American surveys, Jack London is typically represented by "The Law of Life" or "To Build a Fire"—rarely by any of his socialist works. Charlotte Perkins Gilman has likewise been represented by "The Yellow Wallpaper" rather than by *Herland* or her socialist works; "The Yellow Wallpaper" is also typical of the preference of anthology editors for stories dealing with mental illness and suicide as reflections of purely personal, psychological conflicts divorced from any political context. The political writings of canonical writers like Thoreau, Mark Twain, and Howells have likewise been played down. (A description in a cable TV guide of *The Mysterious Stranger*, Twain's savage existentialist fable attacking, among other political targets, bigotry and religious hypocrisy in justification of imperialism and war, written out of Twain's anger over the Spanish-American War: "In a film adaptation of Mark Twain's delightful fantasy, a printer's naive apprentice from Missouri daydreams himself into a medieval European castle and meets a magical youth called 44, who displays fascinating powers.") Only little by little over the past two decades have anthologies—preeminently the Heath anthology of American literature edited by Paul Lauter (1990)—introduced more political writings as accommodations to sixties protest movements and canon revision.

To be sure, good politics does not necessarily produce good literature, but that does not justify the extent to which American literary education has excluded politics since World War II. Many English majors, grad students, and professors deliberately or unconsciously turn toward literature precisely as a refuge from politics, and they often join forces with the conservatives in resenting attempts to politicize literary studies. Undergraduates taking lit courses as electives commonly bring to them the attitude of the tired worker who just wants to watch TV for escape; they may never have heard of the New Criticism, but they are amazingly adept New Critics in their aestheticist antipathy to any literature with a political message. The art-for-art's sake aesthetic dominating postwar American literature and literary studies—in combination with the societywide avoidance of politics—has been a crippling force in relation to any literature that does deal with politics. When I teach novels like Rebecca Harding Davis's *Life in the Iron Mills*, Upton Sinclair's *The Jungle*, Simone de Beauvoir's *The Mandarins*, Isabel Allende's *The House of the Spirits*, or even George Orwell's *1984*, I have found it necessary to preface them with lengthy handouts glossing the basic political terminology and historical background these books presuppose in readers. Even so, the completely predictable response of most students is to respond only to the personal conflicts while skipping over or blanking out the political content.

The individualist aesthetic that has dominated postwar American literature and literary criticism has demonstrably impoverished us in relation to literary activity in the rest of the world. The hegemony of New Critical aesthetics (and, more recently, poststructuralist epistemological skepticism) has obscured the simple truth that much important literature has always been engendered by the obligations writers feel to bear witness to, celebrate, or protest the political events of their time. These aesthetics have likewise muted concern about the exclusion of creative writers and literary intellectuals from American political life and, conversely, their indifference to it as a literary subject. Can the most conservative critics deny the sterility of recent white male American literature in comparison with the literary vitality that has been engendered by the struggles of minorities and women in America or by those of politically committed writers in other countries like Vaclav Havel, Milan Kundera, Chinua Achebe, Naguib Mahfouz, Doris Lessing, Nadine Gordimer, Mario Vargas Llosa, Isabel Allende, Gabriel García Márquez, Carlos Fuentes, Octavio Paz, Ariel Dorfman, and Salman Rushdie? (Typically, Phillip Roth's recent attempt to deal fictionally with the Israeli-Palestinian conflict in *Operation Shylock* founders on the narcissism that has constricted his own scope and that of his generation of American writers for the past four decades.)

Poststructuralist Theory: Depoliticizing Politics

On the level of advanced scholarship and criticism, the whole history of literary theory (as well as composition theory) since World War II can be read as an exorcism of the earlier influence of marxism, with one theoretical school after another gaining popularity precisely because each has afforded yet another avenue for evading radical politics. Even movements such as existentialism, structuralism, and poststructuralism that have a strong political dimension in Europe typically lose that dimension in their American adaptations. (I have discussed this topic at some length in my works on the literary reception of Albert Camus in the United States [1973, 1981], particularly in the way the radical political dimension of Camus's writing was either downplayed during the late forties and fifties in favor of his "existential" concerns—likewise with Sartre and Beauvoir—or twisted into an endorsement of American interests in the Cold War.[5])

Bizarrely enough, at the present moment, as cultural studies and other revivals of political approaches gain a foothold in English studies, one can observe the inevitable process at work as even *politics* gets depoliticized. In composition theory, for example, National Council of Teachers of English and Conference on College Composition and Communication conventions and publications are now filled with papers appropriating trendy keywords from Freire and Foucault ("The Politics of ———," "Resistance and Empowerment in ———" whose content is little more than a rehash of conventional approaches to writing instruction.

In literary scholarship, politics typically gets depoliticized in the very process of "theorizing" it. Literary scholars have been so browbeaten by nearly three decades of arcane poststructuralist metacriticism that they seem ashamed to be caught talking about the obvious cultural implications of issues like the work week, tax policy, electoral and international politics, environmentalism, basic literacy, or the effects of mass media unless they can find a way to inflate such topics into jargon-filled theoretical ruminations. As a teacher of three or four sections of undergraduate comp and lit courses per quarter in a non-elite state college (with no teaching assistants), I never could understand why I should need a whole apparatus of Saussurean linguistics, Lacanian psychoanalysis, and phenomenological philosophy to help students deconstruct Proposition 13, political speeches, or the kind of blatant manifestations of sexism, racism, and colonialism to whose criticism deconstruction has been most concretely applied. In spite of repeated efforts, I never could slog through sacred texts like Derrida's *Of Grammatology* (1976) (or even Gayatri Spivak's eighty-page preface thereto), though I always suspended judgment awaiting the collapse of multinational corporate capitalism under the relentless onslaught of deconstruction on the phenomenological front.

My truancy toward reading theory has finally been rewarded, as the past few years have seen a refreshing trend away from poststructuralist theorizing and toward concrete issues in cultural studies, reviving more traditional marxist historical and socioeconomic analysis (a trend I hope I helped promote in *American Media and Mass Culture: Left Perspectives*). Caught up in this tide, heavies like Derrida and Spivak are now writing, admirably, about apartheid and colonialism and claiming that deconstruction from the beginning was not really ahistorical or apolitical but a mode of reading historical or political "texts" and of radical political practice. Even now, however, many American scholars remain in the thrall of the latter-day courtly muses of Europe; they seem to feel that their studies in the most familiar aspects of American culture have to be filtered through the jargon of, and allusions to, the continental pantheon. I constantly encounter grad stu-

352   DONALD LAZERE

dents and young faculty who are steeped in Derrida, Lacan, and Barthes but
haven't read Norman O. Brown, who know Baudrillard but not Daniel J. Boorstin,
semiology but not general semantics. Their laborious analyses of "subject
positionality" are often no more profound than the formulation of Mark Twain's
black boyhood friend: "'You tell me whar a man gits his corn pone, en I'll tell you
what his 'pinions is'" (1967, 188).

The present stage of poststructuralist cultural studies theory seems to boil
down to something like the following: The tradition of Enlightenment rational-
ism and humanism, including marxist versions thereof, has either been wholly
complicit in capitalist and phallogocentric modes of political-cultural domination or else, in spite of its oppositional intentions, resulted in futile efforts to hu-
manize an irremediably inhumane power structure. Thus rational, humanist
thought, language, and culture are themselves the enemy, and they must be
undermined through "valorizing" different cognitive modes, such as those of
women, the working class, gays, and nonwhite and non-Western cultures. A variant on this position is that the key problem may be not rational humanism itself
but only the political-cultural-linguistic hegemony of capitalism and white patriarchy, which should be resisted through multicultural pluralism—heteroglossia
in literature, composition, and media studies as well as in the larger culture—that
can drown out the dominant, monologic voice. Both variants have contributed to
the study of "transgressive" and "counterhegemonial" cultural practices, modes
of popular resistance to or appropriation of commercial culture—hence the proliferation of celebratory studies on Madonna, punk style, rap, Harlequin romances, *Star Trek,* drag queens, etc.

Although I do not want to categorically deny the validity of these ideas or the
specific studies they have produced, I find the more extreme versions of them
flawed on several counts. First, the antirationalist line is glib at best, pernicious at
worst. It is apparently not as evident at the heights of graduate faculties at Duke or
Yale as it is at Cal Poly, but the majority of American students suffer not from an
excess of logocentrism and humanistic culture but from a deficiency in the elements of them that are necessary for self-defense against manipulation by political, economic, and cultural elites. I have taken to giving vocabulary and factual
quizzes in my junior-level class in American literature from 1865 to 1918 since I
discovered that few students could define words in the readings such as *plutocracy,*
demagogue, the spoils system, populism, progressive, and *socialism* or identify any
president during that period or date the Russian Revolution and World War I
within twenty years. It is dreamily romantic to expect that the masses of young
Americans today are eager or able to set their indigenous language and culture in
opposition to the dominant language and culture when they have so little knowledge of the latter to begin with (see my "Back to Basics: A Force for Oppression or
Liberation?" [1992]). One of the unheralded virtues of E. D. Hirsch Jr.'s *Cultural
Literacy* (1987) is his advocacy of the vocabulary of basic political concepts and
ideologies as part of his agenda of what every American needs to know to survive.

Do any of the critics who bash Hirsch, most of them leftists, believe that all students, regardless of class, ethnicity, or gender, ought *not* to be familiarized with these concepts? Jürgen Habermas, maintaining the Frankfurt School tradition, seems to be among the few left theorists today defending a position compatible with Hirsch's.

Second, despite the value of many particular studies of counterhegemonial cultural practices, a danger in their pursuit is the temptation, given the infinite number of such potential topics, simply to make an academic specialty like any other out of doing this kind of study, in the same way that many marxists have become marxologists. Going that route can provide the double gratification of gaining professional advancement for studying whatever pop cult or sexual kink you happen to enjoy while telling yourself that you (or those conducting the counter hegemonial practices) are subverting the political power structure by doing so; however, the proliferation of such studies detached from a unified political perspective quickly becomes yet another way of depoliticizing politics. Likewise for pseudopolitical rationalizations of sexual transgressions, such as Michel Foucault's inflating sadomasochistic orgies in San Francisco gay bars, from which he apparently contracted AIDS, into "'anarchy within the body, where its hierarchies, its localizations and designations, its organicity, if you will, is in the process of disintegrating'" (Wolin 1993, 260).

Finally, even the invigorating recent attention to the politics of gender and racial issues has been moving toward depoliticization in its extreme tendencies toward individualism and pluralism. I have been struck by the fact that my students, who are mostly middle-class whites and not feminists, tend to respond more positively to literature about the personal tribulations of women and minorities than to those that deal with broader political themes (and, as noted above, they invariably focus on the personal rather than the political dimensions of works that contain both). I suspect that this response goes beyond purely aesthetic judgments and reflects the traits of American individualistic socialization, restricting consciousness to personal experience and psychology to the exclusion of the political context in which the personal is formed. These student responses are pertinent to current debates among cultural leftists over whether issues of race, gender, or class should take precedence or, more broadly, whether questions of race and gender can or should be addressed independently of (or in opposition to) a marxist or other master discourse placing race and gender issues in a larger socioeconomic context. (Arguments about whether patriarchy and racism have preceded or superseded capitalism or socialism historically are important, to be sure, but they sometimes obscure the essential relationship of racial or gender issues to political economy.) These debates are further related to those over single-issue political constituencies or identity politics that have fragmented the American Left.

Elizabeth Fox-Genovese has most astutely addressed these problems in relation to American studies:

Since Marxist thought had, until very recently, paid little attention to race, gender, and ethnicity *per se,* scholars who are primarily concerned with African-American, women's, and ethnic culture have some grounds for believing that Marxism does not directly or adequately address the issues that most interest them. But the real problem seems to lie with the general view of Marxism as at least as authoritarian and mechanical as the earlier elitist consensus. For, in general, the new literary studies in race and gender have focused on recovering personal experience rather than a systematic view of the central dynamics of American society and culture. The haste to dismiss Marxism thus merges with a general disinclination to engage general theories of social and cultural relations and leaves many of the new studies hostage to the models that they are attacking.

Rather than engaging the battle for American culture as a whole, many of the new studies have, if anything, enthusiastically embraced fragmentation, variously described as diversity or pluralism. They, accordingly, risk settling for a one-sided reading. At issue is not the importance of recuperating previously excluded voices, and assuredly not the importance of demonstrating the integrity of African-American writer or women's cultures. ... But these discrete cultures developed within a larger society and polity with which, in some measure, they identified. To sacrifice that context is to abandon the attempt to understand the ways in which African-Americans, women, and others related to each other and, especially, to those who wielded cultural as well as social and political power. It is, in effect, to lose the national dimension of the American in American Studies. (1990, 22–23)

Elsewhere warning about possible excesses of multiculturalism and canon revision, Fox-Genovese observes:

At some point the attack on the received canon shifted ground. Increasingly, the attack has been waged in the name of the individual's right to education as a personal history, a parochial culture, and a private epistemology. The worst of it is that the "radical" critics of the purportedly irrelevant canon have sacrificed the ideal of collective identity that constituted its most laudable feature. To settle for education as personal autobiography or identity is tacitly to accept the worst forms of political domination. (1986, 133)

American applications of poststructuralist indeterminacy exalt a "private epistemology"—or a multitude of private epistemologies—in the apparent belief that expanding cultural or cognitive "differences," thereby undermining established, hierarchical patterns of reasoning, is an effective counteragent to the white, male, capitalist power structure. These ideas are looking more and more like a second wave of the sixties countercultural faith that if people just do their own thing the political establishment will be undermined. What the counterculturists painfully learned was that Lyndon Johnson's and Richard Nixon's thing was bombing Vietnam, attempting to crush political dissent, controlling public opinion through propaganda, and selling political influence to the highest bidder. Nothing could serve the interests of the Johnsons, Nixons, Reagans, and Bushes more than a movement whose unbridled affirmation of cultural diversity reinforces, if it does not emulate, the atomization of mainstream political culture and compounds the obstacles to the electorate's gaining critical understanding of the forces that manipulate it and being able to communicate and organize, beyond the barriers of multiple subcultures, toward concerted political opposition. In the past decade or so, poststructuralist celebrations of pluralistic discourses in culture and education have often ingenuously disregarded the simultaneous, inversely proportionate, nationwide consolidation of wealth and corporate and media ownership, as well as the narrowing of access to humanistic education because of rising costs, budget cuts, and pressures toward uncritical vocationalism.

Teaching Political Conflicts

In my sophomore course in argumentative writing and the research paper, described in "Teaching the Political Conflicts" and "Teaching the Conflicts About Wealth and Poverty" (1995), I attempt to counteract the modular, politically sanitized structure of most college courses by focusing in depth for a full term on a single issue in current events, as mediated through the rhetoric of political speeches, news reporting, and journals of opinion or California ballot initiatives. In recent years, the topic studied has been the pros and cons of Reaganomics and its effects on the status of the rich, the middle class, and the poor and on public services and the quality of life in America. Many students' initial reaction is bored resistance and protest that these subjects are too difficult and only of interest to political science majors.

My students have had so little exposure to reading, hearing, or writing extended lines of reasoning that many greet incredulously the hypothesis I present at the beginning of the course that their federal student grants may have been cut, their tuition raised, and the courses they need to graduate not funded due to a state budget crisis in order for the California government to lower the taxes on Walter Annenberg's Palm Springs estate or in order for the IRS to provide Bunker Hunt with additional millions with which to try to corner the world silver market. They have simply never made any connection between income in the private sector and the funding of education or other tax-supported public services, or else they have been indoctrinated with the most simplistic version of supply-side economics telling them that increased profits and low tax rates among the wealthy automatically trickle down to benefit everyone equally and provide increased tax revenues. (Their faith in Reaganomic principles has been shaken as little as their current hero Rush Limbaugh's by the minor detail of the drastic declines in federal and local revenue in the wake of Reaganite "tax reforms.") Most do not even know the meaning of the term "progressive taxation," so they believe that flat-rate taxes and tax cuts are equitable because everyone pays or saves the same percentage and the rich pay the most in dollar amounts; they don't understand that under flat tax reductions the rich pay less relative to their after-tax savings and hence are constantly increasing the gap in wealth and power between them and those in lower income brackets. (This is how Proposition 13, the regressive 1978 California property tax-cut initiative, was sold to financially pressed middle-class homeowners by a realtors' lobby, with the consequence of immense savings for business property, landlords, and upper-bracket homeowners, while the middle class has gotten peanuts, rents have increased unabatedly—contrary to the backers' campaign promises—and both local and statewide public services, particularly education, have been drastically reduced by tax-revenue shortfalls.) A ten-week English course is scarcely adequate to develop a coherent exposition of the elementary economic principles and multiplicity of possible ideological viewpoints involved in these issues, along with application to them of rhetorical analysis and exposure to research resources. Needless to say, a marxist or other socialist perspective on such issues is almost wholly precluded because it would need to be prefaced by at least another ten-week exposition of basic socialist principles. With all the limitations on what can be covered on even this one topic throughout any such term, however, the experience at least has the value of demonstrating to students how much more complex political issues are than is recognized in campaign rhetoric, the mass media, and most other nonacademic discourse, how narrow a range of ideology mainstream American discourse permits on such issues, and how that discourse works against any coherent system of analysis. I believe that this important lesson is what justifies such a course as one in rhetoric, *not* political science, since the latter discipline typically stresses empirical approaches to particular cases to the neglect of the rhetorical principles needed for analysis of any particular case and for an understanding of the restrictions on American political discourse in general.

Avoiding Dogmatism

In conclusion, the version of cultural studies that I have sketched out here must certainly include marxism and other varieties of socialism (e.g., the recent revival of communitarianism) that have been excluded from the American cognitive agenda, along with their problematic relations to feminist, ethnic, Third World, and popular culture studies. This is not to say, though, that it should consist *exclusively* of these studies or the viewpoint of their advocates. In my own teaching and writing I have become convinced that it is both ethically untenable and pragmatically unwise to propagate left views as the one true faith. In these heady days when leftist scholarship has gained unprecedented respectability (even though it is far from having attained the stranglehold on academia claimed by conservatives), we need to beware of the tendency to take left views as givens and to assume that students and colleagues share them.

In my literature, composition, and mass media courses, I discuss these problems with students at the outset, explaining that my own publicly aired views are democratic socialist and that I will be exposing them to those views—not as "the truth" but as points of contrast with conservative, liberal, and libertarian views.

Their task is to arrive at an understanding of the areas of disagreement among these viewpoints, to locate sources expressing these disagreements, and to identify and evaluate the rhetoric distinctive to each source's viewpoint. My grading, then, is based not on whether the students' views agree with mine but on how skillfully they have located, understood, and analyzed opposing lines of argument; I have found this to be an effective rule of thumb, and although it is impossible to avoid subjectivity in grading altogether, the large majority of my students have found this policy fair in principle and in practice.

Even though I believe an integrative view is essential to cultural studies, there is no avoiding a multitude of such views. There is certainly nothing to prevent teachers with conservative viewpoints from taking the same approach in their courses, and the best of all possible courses might be team-taught by a leftist and rightist, or a liberal and a socialist, airing their disagreements in class. Conservative intellectuals have been presenting their own version of cultural studies in journals like *New Criterion, Commentary, American Spectator,* and *Chronicles: A Magazine of American Culture,* as well as books like Allan Bloom's *The Closing of the American Mind,* Roger Kimball's *Tenured Radicals: How Politics Has Corrupted Our Higher Education,* Dinesh D'Souza's *Illiberal Education,* and the books on the politics of the news and entertainment media by Robert and Linda Lichter and Stanley Rothman. I have found it effective to assign these sources against leftist ones for comparative rhetorical analysis.

To be sure, there is a major drawback in attempting to present left perspectives to students simply as a possible alternative to established, and presumably equally defensible, modes of thinking. College students immersed since birth in indoctrination to capitalism, American nationalism, and WASP male ethnocentrism have built-in defense mechanisms against left views. If they are assigned to find and evaluate the best arguments on the right versus those on the left, many simply project their prior prejudices on sources and seize on the flimsiest rationalizations to judge the rightist arguments superior. Such occasions can bring out Stalinist instincts in teachers, tempting us to forgo fair play and revert to presenting material in as one-sided a manner as rightist views have been presented to many students every day of their lives.

I believe the Stalinist temptation must be resisted, as I said earlier, on both ethical and practical grounds. In the contemporary world, where leftist constituencies—including the working class, nonwhites, feminists, Third World peoples, and left intellectuals—are relatively powerless, their most legitimate strengths must derive from moral and intellectual integrity, in opposition to conservatives' skimpily veiled rationalizations of sheer power and privilege. In practical terms, leftists simply cannot get away with unethical power plays, since any such attempts are instantly jumped on by the watchdogs of the Right, blown all out of proportion to worse abuses by the Right, and exploited to discredit the entire Left. Witness the Tawana Brawley case, or the way that a few sentences of Marcuse's foolhardy fantasies about the Left's suppressing rightist opposition in "Repressive Tolerance" have been exploited as a pretext for twenty years of ritual exorcisms by conservatives of Marcuse's complete body of work, or the way some liberties that Michael Moore took with the chronology in his documentary *Roger and Me* were used as an excuse for mainstream critics to dismiss the film and deprive it of an Academy Award nomination. So it is necessary for leftists to maintain academic integrity and equilibrium—but it is far from easy. It may be difficult, for example, to draw the line between exposing students to left views and forcing those views on them, but I believe we must observe that line scrupulously—more scrupulously than conservative faculties typically do, especially in business-oriented disciplines.

Another tribulation is the grumbling we frequently hear from both students and colleagues to the effect that "this course should be in political science, not English." Even if we are not stigmatized by students, colleagues, and conservative pressure groups as doctrinaire leftists, we are stigmatized merely for being monolithically "political" in our approach to teaching. To tell the truth, I myself get tired of always feeling compelled to emphasize political dimensions of literature, composition, and rhetoric, and I hate being labeled a monomaniac on that subject, which by nature I am not. But humanities teachers are virtually obliged to overcompensate for the depoliticization of American culture, because no one else is compensating at all. It is the kind of no-win situation that is typical of the way the dominant system perpetuates itself: at least at colleges like Cal Poly, teachers who blandly evade uncomfortable political subjects tend to be more popular with students than those who confront them, so all the social pressures work toward conservatism.

In a broader perspective, there is no sensible reason that the burden of confronting the politics of culture should be placed exclusively on the shoulders of university faculties in English and other humanistic disciplines involved in cultural studies. We need to turn our energies to a critique of the avoidance of politics, and controversy in general, in American primary and secondary education. Some of the time we spend on advanced theorizing might be better spent lobbying for the introduction of basic political concepts, as well as critical thinking about ideological issues and viewpoints and the way they permeate both high and popular culture, as a required part of elementary and secondary curricula.[6] The more such instruction eventually gets installed in those earlier levels of education—where it belongs—the less we university faculties will have to compensate for its lack by emphasizing political dimensions of literature and composition to an extent that admittedly can become tiresome for both students and scholars.

NOTES

1. On corporate funding of NAS and other conservative scholarly and journalistic enterprises, see Wiener (1988, 1990).

2. For a fuller survey of the left sources of cultural studies, see Lazere (1987, 1–26).

3. See Lazere (1986–1987) and the readings and bibliographical references in "Media, Literacy, and Political Socialization," Lazere (1987, pt. 6). Ohmann (1987, 275–293) takes issue with some aspects of Bernstein's and Mueller's positions.
4. For a comprehensive survey of Freirean pedagogy, see Shor (1987).
5. See "Camus and the American Reader" (Lazere 1973, 227–254) and Lazere (1981).
6. An advisory committee of university faculty members to which I belonged succeeded in incorporating the study of basic political terminology and ideological differences in the 1985 revision of the California Board of Education's *Model Curriculum Standards: Grades Nine Through Twelve.*

WORKS CITED

Bloom, Allan. *The Closing of the American Mind.* New York: Simon and Schuster, 1987.
California State Board of Education. *Model Curriculum Standards: Grades Nine Through Twelve.* Sacramento: California State Department of Education, 1985.
Derrida, Jacques. *Of Grammatology.* Trans. Gayatri Chakravorty Spivak. Baltimore: Johns Hopkins University Press, 1976.
_____. "Racism's Last Word" and "But, beyond. ..." In *"Race," Writing, and Difference,* ed. Henry Louis Gates (Chicago: University of Chicago Press, 1986), 329–338, 354–369.
Fox-Genovese, Elizabeth. "American Culture and New Literary Studies." *American Quarterly* 42:1 (1990):15–29.
_____. "The Claims of a Common Culture: Gender, Race, Class, and the Canon." *Salmagundi,* no. 72 (Fall 1986):131–143.
"Gayatri Spivak on the Politics of the Postcolonial Subject," interview by Howard Winant. *Socialist Review* 90:3 (1990):81–98.
Gibbs, Nancy. "How America Has Run Out of Time." *Time,* 24 April 1989, 58–67.
Hirsch, E. D., Jr. *Cultural Literacy.* Boston: Houghton Mifflin, 1987.
Kimball, Roger. *Tenured Radicals: How Politics Has Corrupted Our Higher Education.* New York: Harper and Row, 1990.
Lauter, Paul, ed. *Heath Anthology of American Literature.* Lexington, Mass.: D. C. Heath, 1990.
Lazere, Donald. *The Unique Creation of Albert Camus.* New Haven: Yale University Press, 1973.
_____. "American Criticism of the Sartre-Camus Dispute: A Chapter in the Cultural Cold War." In *The Philosophy of Jean-Paul Sartre,* ed. Paul Arthur Schilpp (Library of Living Philosophers, 1981), 108–121.
_____. "Literacy and Mass Media: The Political Implications." *New Literary History* 18 (1986–1987):237–254.
_____. *American Media and Mass Culture: Left Perspectives.* Berkeley: University of California Press, 1987.
_____. "Back to Basics: A Force for Oppression or Liberation." *College English* 54 (1992):7–21.
_____. "Teaching the Political Conflicts: A Rhetorical Schema." *College Composition and Communication* 43 (1992):194–203.
_____. "Teaching the Conflicts About Wealth and Poverty." In *Left Margins: Cultural Studies and Composition Pedagogy,* ed. Karen Fitts and Alan W. France (Albany: State University of New York Press, in press).

Marcuse, Herbert. *One-Dimensional Man.* Boston: Beacon Press, 1964.

———. "Repressive Tolerance." In *A Critique of Pure Tolerance,* ed. Robert Paul Wolff, Barrington Moore, and Herbert Marcuse (Boston: Beacon Press, 1969).

Ohmann, Richard. *Politics of Letters.* Middletown: Wesleyan University Press, 1987.

Schor, Juliet B. *The Overworked American: The Unexpected Decline of Leisure.* New York: Basic Books, 1993.

Shor, Ira, ed. *Freire for the Classroom: A Sourcebook for Liberatory Literacy.* Portsmouth, N.H.: Boynton/Cook/Heinemann, 1987.

Thoreau, Henry David. *Walden and Other Writings.* New York: Modern Library, 1950.

Twain, Mark. "Corn Pone Opinions." In *Great Short Works of Mark Twain* (New York: Harper Perennial, 1967), 188–192.

Wiener, Jon. "A Tale of Two Conclaves: Campus Voices Right and Left." *The Nation* 247:18 (12 December 1988):644–666.

———. "The Olin Money Tree: Dollars for Neocon Scholars." *The Nation* 250:1 (1 January 1990):12–14.

Wolin, Richard. Review of *The Passion of Michel Foucault,* by James Miller. *Dissent,* Spring 1993, 259–263.

21

Something Queer About the Nation-State

MICHAEL WARNER

BECAUSE THE TERM has been understood to promise so much, it's embarrassing that both the word "queer" and the concept of queerness turn out to be thoroughly embedded in modern Anglo-American culture. Having energized a subcultural style, a political movement, and a wave of rethinking among intellectuals, queerness has come to stand for a far-reaching change in sexual politics. Under its banner some have gone so far as to herald a general subversion of identity. Others have linked queer politics to a globalizing culture of postmodernism. In my view these readings of queerness have vaulted over the conditions in which queer politics has made sense. The term does not translate very far with any ease, and its potential for transformation seems mostly specific to a cultural context that has not been brought into focus in the theory of queerness. Even in cultures with well-organized gay movements and a taste for Americanisms there has been little attempt to import the politics with which the label has been associated here. In the New World Order, we should be more than usually cautious about global utopianisms that require American slang.

The historical moment of queer political culture, so understanding itself, is remarkably recent. As a politically usable term, "queer" dates not even from the Reagan years but from the Bush-Thatcher-Mulroney era. Both the political language of queerness and its subcultural style—and these two have become very closely associated—made their first appearance, as is well known, in the context of AIDS organizing.[1] First in ACT UP, then in Outrage and Queer Nation, queer rhetoric came into competition with lesbian/gay liberation rhetoric primarily in relation to the state. All of these groups were explicitly organized around a language of "direct action," meaning non–state-mediated action. ACT UP's self-definition reads: "a diverse, nonpartisan group united in anger and committed to direct action to end the AIDS crisis." Direct action here means (nonviolent) enterprises that have urban space and public-sphere mass media—not state agencies or political parties or even service organizations—as their main contexts. Equally important is a concept of "activism" as an informal mode of representation. In some ways this set of groups and the practices associated with them have implicitly carried an enormous faith in the public sphere. They have believed that political struggles were to be carried out neither through the normal state apparatus nor through revolutionary combat but through the nonstate media in which public opinion is invested with the ability to dissolve power.

Queer activism has never seemed traditional, however, because it scorns the traditional debate style that forms the self-understanding of the public sphere: patient, polite, rational-critical discussion. The officials, civil servants, and pundits who cling to that self-understanding have been consistently viewed by queer activists as mystifying their own exercise of power and as practicing a kind of media management that conflicts with their own claims about open debate. Queer politics, by contrast, has evolved around a frankly skeptical and often instrumental relation to the public sphere: its experiments in public art were from the beginning accompanied by sound-bite management, expert public relations, and what is called social marketing.[2]

At the same time, queer politics has essentially abandoned the traditional conception of civil disobedience, which values the expression of individual integrity as a moral act regardless of its effect. For many in queer politics this conception seems as naive as the ideology of open public discussion and for the same reasons. Civil disobedience and direct action count as strategic obstruction—not acts of personal morality but something to be managed through a media strategy. Public opinion, though virtually the sole medium in which politics was carried out by these groups, has been viewed as a toxic cloud of irrationality, to be steered out to sea by any means at hand.

Queer politics has been innovative because of the degree to which it cultivates self-consciousness about public-sphere-mediated society and because of the degree to which that self-consciousness has been incorporated into the self-understanding of a metropolitan sexual subculture. These are no mean feats. Nevertheless, they point out how much the entire range of queer politics has continued to be guided by institutions of the civil-society public-sphere type, even though queer rhetoric has been in many ways critical of the liberal faith that legitimates those institutions.

Now the commitment to a nonstate public-sphere context has turned out to be determining. Some of the most serious crises in the history of ACT UP had to do with the question of lobbying and other kinds of coordination between ACT UP members and representatives of state agencies such as the (U.S.) Center for Disease Control. The government seemed at times to be listening to ACT UP in productive ways, but many were upset, as one member put it, to see some activists demonstrating in the streets against Dr. Fauci by day and then calling him Tony at

a cocktail party in the evening. What became visible in these crises was a split between the style of action specific to ACT UP and queer culture, on one hand, and,
on the other hand, a style of activism involving routine interaction with the state.
Negotiation with state agencies, as a normal kind of activism, is typically organized by ideas of minority politics, community representation, and state coordination of special interests. Those who do it typically describe themselves as lesbian and gay rather than queer—even though many such activists also call
themselves queer in other contexts.

This alignment between two different identitarian rhetorics and two different
contexts of state-related politics seems to me to have remained fairly consistent for
the past few years. In contemporary Anglo-American lesbian and gay politics, an
impressive list of contested issues bears directly on the state—from AIDS policy
and health care to military personnel policy, domestic partnership legislation,
public school curricula, National Endowment for the Arts and National Endowment for the Humanities funding, immigration policy, and so on. But most of the
imaginative energies of queer culture have come to be focused on a rigorously
antiassimilationist rhetoric invoked only in nonstate public-sphere contexts such
as Modern Language Association panels. When we hold endorsement sessions for
local politicians or draft antidiscrimination laws, we invoke a more traditional
rhetoric of minority identity. There is no QMHC, for example, and for good reason. The differences between these political strategies are not simply strategic, because each posture toward the state and toward the public sphere has strong links
with a different rhetoric of identity and sexuality. (That's also the reason style and
sexual subculture have been able to carry over much of the energy of queer politics, even though ACT UP and Queer Nation and OutRage have all been perceived
lately as having lost momentum.)

Queer theory has for the most part occupied itself with only half of this history,
describing the difference between the two rhetorics of identity and sexuality,
queer and gay/lesbian.[3] It is becoming increasingly clear, however, that these rhetorics belong not to different epochs or different populations but to different contexts. Queer activists are also lesbians and gays in other contexts—for example,
where leverage can be gained through bourgeois propriety, through minority
rights discourse, or through more gender-marked language (it probably won't replace lesbian feminism). Some people are in some contexts meaningfully motivated by queer self-characterizations; others are not. This distinction is not the
same as the distinction between those who are straight and those who are gay and
lesbian. No one always adheres to queer self-characterizations. Even when some of
us do so, it may be to exploit rhetorics in ways that have relatively little to do with
our characters, identities, selves, or psyches. Rhetoric of queerness neither saturates identity nor supplants it. Queer politics, in short, has not just replaced older
modes of lesbian and gay politics; it has come to exist alongside those older
modes, opening up new possibilities and problems whose relation to more familiar problems is not always clear.

The Anglo-American world has a heavily identitarian culture. As a result, it supercharges any form of sexuality by tying it to the individual's expressive capacities. Consumer culture, to begin with, accustoms us to link choice, affect, display, and identity. American religion has also created such a culture of sincerity that even ironic parodies of identity are ultimately read as sincere gestures of self-expression. In this context, queerness reads as a public affirmation of the expressive/affective complexities that underwrite personal singularity.[4] The culture of identitarianism has also a state-related institutional dimension. Canada, Britain, and especially the United States have a very pronounced civil-society tradition of opposing voluntary association to the state. (This may be another reason queer politics works in Anglo-American nations but has not much caught on in countries with stronger conceptions of socialist democracy.) The vast infrastructure of voluntarist culture—from churches to Twelve-Step Programs—interprets itself through an identitarian discourse to which queer is rapidly becoming assimilated.

The state also contributes more directly to the intelligibility of queerness. The modern state claims to be the agency of our wills and the site of our reason; that's why it works so well with a culture of voluntarism. The feudal and monarchical states, by contrast, did not do so; they were able to support themselves by representing their own alienness, their imposition from above, as essential to their legitimacy. Constitutionalism and representational government have both undermined that element in the self-representation of the state; the state began to represent itself as an expression or outcome of its subjects' own actions, wills, interests, debates, opinions, needs, etc. But of course it could never sustain that fiction in the everyday lives of people for whom the state is an irrational limit or, worse, the arm of hostile interests. To some extent that is true for everybody. The state, in short, creates noise. It does so even in totalitarian systems, but the noise is more audible wherever a civil-society tradition has invested nonstate association with normative significance. And nowhere has that tradition been more pronounced than in the United States over the last two centuries. As Tocqueville put it, "Better use has been made of association and this powerful instrument of action has been applied to more varied aims in America than anywhere else in the world. ... The inhabitant of the United States learns from birth that he must rely on himself to combat the ills and trials of life; he is restless and defiant in his outlook toward the authority of society and appeals to its power only when he cannot do without it."[5] In the context of this normatively sustained anxiety about an overarching social authority, queerness can resonate as a general condition of political life because of the implausibility of the modern state's representational claims.

In this culture, suspicion of the state's representational claims is not only widespread but imperative. And the imperative gives a political self-understanding to the infrastructure of voluntarist culture. When Tocqueville writes of the "principle of association," he has in mind especially the mass movements of bourgeois propriety, such as temperance, but it is important to remember that temperance and other forms of early nineteenth-century voluntary association were the pre-decessors of modern identitarian movements. They articulated a space of nonstate association, investing it with supreme legitimacy. They articulated a general and public form of association based on elective affinities. They elaborated a language of the volitional individual and the public relevance of her affective/appetitive nature. And the experience of movements such as temperance could entail a rich phenomenology of negativity—with respect to the state, with respect to public sociality, and with respect to one's own body and self-characterization—even though all of these were denied at the thematic level of control, consensus, integration, and discipline.

For few groups of Anglo-American citizens did the state seem more clearly a vehicle of hostile interests and irrationality than for gay men and lesbians at the historical moment that gave rise to queer rhetoric. National governments, dominated in Anglo-American societies by conservative reaction, were more than usually opaque to rational-critical institutions. Moreover, the state institutions most needed in the AIDS crisis—the complex web of agencies relating to health care—were being systematically inhibited by Bush, Thatcher, and Mulroney in the name of "the private sector." Seldom has the needs discourse of the welfare state been so dramatically unresponsive, so unexpressive of democratic culture, so visibly encrusted with positivity. But queer politics did not arise simply in response to those conservative policies in the executive branch. The utopian appeal of queer politics from the beginning far exceeded its ability to overcome a blockage in national administrative policy. Moreover, the period of Bushite reaction was itself in some ways only a part of long-standing crises in the welfare state's peculiar blend of regulatory administration and democratic legitimation.

These contemporary crises, which I take to be the local incitement to queer politics, have been brewing for almost exactly the same period as the homosexual and gay rights movements have been on the scene. Their nature was succinctly summarized by Jürgen Habermas in a 1984 address to the Spanish Parliament:[6] "In short, a contradiction between its goal and its method is inherent in the welfare state project as such. Its goal is the establishment of forms of life that are structured in an egalitarian way and that at the same time open up arenas for individual self-realization and spontaneity. But evidently this goal cannot be reached via the direct route of putting political programs into legal and administrative form. Generating forms of life exceeds the capacities of the medium of power" (p. 59). The more the welfare state tries to democratize by administrative methods, the more it sinks into this problem. "Social welfare programs need a great deal of power to achieve the force of law financed by public budgets—and thus to be implemented within the lifeworld of their beneficiaries. Thus an ever denser net of legal norms, of governmental and para-governmental bureaucracies is spread over the daily life of its potential and actual clients" (p. 58). Habermas sketches this crisis, largely following Offe, in order to explain the exhaustion of utopian projects for refiguring relations among state, society, and labor. (One can also hear in the background his arguments for a lifeworld conceptualization of the democratic. The system-lifeworld distinction is not, I think, any more useful for queer theory than it is for feminist theory, but the sketch of the welfare state will look familiar to any queer.)

Now, in keeping with my hunch that two identitarian rhetorics—one gay and lesbian, one queer—tend to link up with two postures vis-à-vis the state, it is easy to see that queer politics takes the contradiction of the welfare state as its opportunity, its strategic environment. Queer activism, considered as politics, presupposes and exploits the impossibility of the welfare state's own project. The alienation of the administrative state has put more and more strain on the Hegelian understanding of the state as a supreme means of self-transcendence, and at the same time an ideal of sexualized nonstate association has developed as a perceptible limit on the state's representational abilities.

But does this have any consequences for the meaning of queerness in contexts less directly defined by activism, politics, and the public sphere? Certainly it is true that many different cultural pressures come to bear at once on the significance of something as complex as queer sexuality or queer self-understanding. But the most intimate forms of life in modern culture are mediated by public-sphere forms. I would suggest even that the state-society relation in voluntarist culture is definitive in, even necessary to, the opposition of queer and normal. In saying this I follow, rather improbably, Hannah Arendt. Arendt describes the social as a specifically modern phenomenon: "the emergence of the social realm, which is neither private nor public, strictly speaking, is a relatively new phenomenon whose origin coincided with the emergence of the modern age and which found its political form in the nation-state.[7] She identifies society in this sense with "conformism, the assumption that men behave and do not act with respect to each other"—an assumption embedded in economics and other knowledges of the social that "could achieve a scientific character only when men had become social beings and unanimously followed certain patterns of behavior, so that those who did not keep the rules could be considered to be asocial or abnormal" (pp. 41–42).

The social realm, in short, is a cultural form, interwoven with the political form of the administrative state and with the normalizing assumptions of modern social knowledges such as economics. The nation-state is the political form of the social in that the social is what it both represents and administers, though in our own time this relation between the state form and the cultural form of the social has become noticeably strained. Can we not hear in the resonances of queer protest an objection to the normalization of behavior in this broad sense, and thus to the cultural phenomenon of societalization? Queers, incessantly told to alter their "behavior," can be understood as protesting not just the normal behavior of the social but the *idea* of normal behavior.

Liberal society has entailed fundamental contradictions on the subject of the abnormal, on one hand producing the abnormal everywhere as the other to a liberal and system-oriented conception of the social, on the other hand valuing it as the ground of expressive individuality. Henry Thoreau, who chewed up political economy and spat it out precisely because it presupposed the regularization of persons in its conception of the social, best articulates the dilemma when he writes, with substantial irony,

> I seek rather, I may say, even an excuse for conforming to the laws of the land. I am but too ready to conform to them. Indeed I have reason to suspect myself on this head; and each year, as the tax-gatherer comes round, I find myself disposed to review the acts and position of the general and state governments, and the spirit of the people, to discover a pretext for conformity. I believe that the State will soon be able to take all my work of this sort out of my hands, and then I shall be no better a patriot than my fellow-countrymen.[8]

Here Thoreau gives expression to that "mistrust and anxiety" toward the state that struck Tocqueville as so American. "The State never intentionally confronts a man's sense, intellectual or moral, but only his body, his senses. It is not armed with superior wit or honesty, but with superior physical strength."[9]

It is equally a mistrust and anxiety toward a social field of majoritarianism. We might expect its result to be the modern, posttraditional individual, and often enough in Thoreau that is just what happens. The perception of the state's positivity yields a new affirmation of the civil-society principle of voluntary association for which he was our first and greatest spokesmodel: "Know all men by these presents, that I, Henry Thoreau, do not wish to be regarded as a member of any incorporated society which I have not joined." Thoreau in such moments seems distant indeed from queer theory. Queer theory is commonly understood as a fundamental critique of liberal individualism, wherein the latter is understood as a belief in voluntarism and the ego-integrated self, but I distrust this metanarrative. Queer politics continues regularly to invoke norms of liberal modernity such as self-determination and self-representation; it continues to invoke a civil-society politics against the state; and, most significant to my mind, it continues to value sexuality by linking it to the expressive capacities of individuals. David Halperin and others have taught us that this expressive notion of sexuality is distinctively modern, but although queer theory expresses skepticism about other elements of the modern sexual ideology, it relies absolutely on norms of expressive individualism and an understanding of sexuality in terms of those norms.

Again, Thoreau is one of the first and clearest exponents of those norms, in their queer extremity. He frequently writes from a sense that the alignment of the state and the social monopolizes the conditions of intelligibility. At such moments he regards the experience of queerness—including not only the strange but also the nonnormal and the imperfectly intelligible—as a necessary subjective dimension. "We need to witness our own limits transgressed," he writes toward the end of *Walden*. "We are cheered when we observe the vulture feeding on the carrion which disgusts and disheartens us and deriving health and strength from the repast."[10] Such a remark may seem to conflict with the austerely integrated ego of

Thoreau's liberal political theory, but in fact there has always been a close and necessary relation between the cultural form of voluntary association and the cultural
norms of expressive individualism, a dialectic between the two implied views of
individuals—volitional and appetitive, self-determining and self-transgressing.
Thus in the same year that he wrote "Civil Disobedience," making himself the theorist of "direct action," he also wrote, in "Ktaadn," "I stand in awe of my body, this
matter to which I am bound has become so strange to me." Thoreau's anxiety
toward and mistrust of social authority, including the state and the social itself, is
always especially strong at such moments, or whenever the context allows any reference to sexuality. When he is struggling to keep his body or his eroticism representable, he is least willing to imagine rapprochement with the terms of representation established in the state/society relation.

Something very like this tension seems to me to govern the self-understanding
of queer subculture in its relation to the public sphere. Indeed, I find it hard to
imagine how the notion of queerness could have much mobilizing appeal outside
of this context of societalized society, an administrative state, and public-sphere
forms. Queerness might be opposed to any number of things—righteousness or
purity or the habitual, for example—but only when it is opposed to normal society and the representative state does it acquire the sense of transformative significance that it now displays. (Even those with little manifest interest in politics, such
as Dennis Cooper, tend to infuse queerness with this sense of transformative and
significant rejection. In Cooper as much as in the most ardent demonstrator,
queerness implies that the realm of the normal, the social, and its representation
by the state has become inaccessible, lacquered over.)

Queer politics, in short, isn't always or only about sexuality. More generally, one
might even want to say that sexuality isn't always or only about sexuality, that it is
not an autonomous dimension of experience. The demands and strategies of
queer politics are burdened by—which also means motivated or energized by—
less articulate but still powerful demands that have to do with the organization of
social and public life. In a similar way, feminist and racial movements, along with
the lesbian and gay movement, are frequently animated by displaced frustrations
with atomizing conditions of market-mediated life, frustrations that find expression in the otherwise misleading and damaging ideal of "community."

But this leads me to my final point, that we are beginning to witness an aporia
between queer politics, with its antiassimilationist, nonindividualist, noncommu-
nitarian practices of public-sphere media mobilized against both the welfare state
and the normalizing ideal of the social, and lesbian and gay politics, with its
framework of individual identity, community representation, needs and rights
discourses, and state provision. Queer politics has developed little in the way of an
agenda for the state. This assertion may of course be proven wrong, but I've given
my reasons for thinking that it's true. If it is true, then the utopianism should be
radically scaled back and filled in with some new kinds of thinking that, at this
point, are difficult to predict. There may well be a queer nation, there may in fact

be no other kind, but on the other side of its hyphen we still envision a lesbian and gay state.

In my view this is a reason not for abandoning queer rhetoric but for making articulate some of its driving aspirations. From the beginning of queer politics, queer issues were linked to political struggles not centrally identified with sexuality or with the AIDS issues of queers. "Health care is a right" became one of the slogans of ACT UP. That slogan has now entered, however fitfully, the agenda of the national state. It was a deft piece of translation, even though the specifically queer resonances of protest disappeared in that translation. Perhaps one way to reanimate the promise of queer politics would be to ask how more of the specifically queer dimensions of queer political energies and strategies could be made representable.

The potential is vast, partly because any number of factors make for a pool of queer sentiment in persons otherwise distant or phobic about queerness. Anxiety and mistrust toward the state and toward public-sphere mass majoritarianism, for example, are hardly confined to metropolitan sexual culture, but their expression has so far been much more coherent and sustained in neoconservatism than in queer rhetoric. Talk-show spectacle and mass-disaster fetishism both point to the resonance of a sense of embodied queerness in almost everybody, even while those same genres contradictorily presume the normal sociality of the audience. Queer sentiment can be largely independent of queer sexual practice and therefore an opportunity for translation work.

Beyond that, however, I would hope that queer politics can put forward in a sustained way what I am arguing has been one of its central energies all along: the positivity of the state and the normal society for which it stands. There is no utopian program on the horizon, but queer politics names this environment as a problem. The instruments that are available for naming it as a problem are themselves public-sphere forms that are oriented to the civil-society tradition. It is therefore difficult to name that tradition as a problem in public-sphere media; the temptation is always to imagine a policy redress in the area of the state or an expression of popular will to reform it, and that is to lapse back into the social imaginary against which queerness defines itself. A great deal of effort will therefore be required to keep this central issue of queer politics from being trumped, in the hierarchy of discourses, by the political end of the public sphere.

The turn back to a state-oriented politics in the American gay movement, always a danger in the public-sphere discourse environment, represents a real loss of insight and action in dominant circles of lesbian and gay organizing. In the 1993 March on Washington, for example, organizers pushed the gays-in-the-military issue, rather than AIDS, into the spotlight. In a culture of patriotism wherein dying for one's country is thought to be virtuous, this shift of emphasis did not simply enlarge the queer agenda. With its vision of patriotic death, its vision of national loyalties trumping all other partisan ties, the military issue almost seems designed to produce amnesia about AIDS. What besides patriotism could smother both the antinational sensibilities of queers who have seen so many die for no country? What could more affirm the state's expression of the nation? What could more weaken the culture of resistance to a state that has added AIDS inaction to its earlier history of heteronormative policing? In the March on Washington some people were heard chanting, "We're here, we're queer, we want to serve our country." It's possible to oppose the ban on gays in the military and still believe that this sentiment costs too much.

NOTES

1. See Lisa Duggan, "Making It Perfectly Queer," *Socialist Review* 22:1 (1992):11–32; and Lauren Berlant and Elizabeth Freeman, "Queer Nationality," in *Fear of a Queer Planet,* ed. Michael Warner (Minneapolis: University of Minnesota Press, 1993), 193–229.

2. On this point Michelangelo Signorile is especially vivid; see his *Queer in America* (New York: Random House, 1993).

3. Often the implication has been that queerness supersedes lesbian and gay identity, either because of its superior sophistication or because of its putatively greater inclusiveness. The argument from inclusiveness, by the way, seems to me especially damaging because it involves the assumption that group inclusion is synonymous with democracy. Like "subversion" or "nondiscrimination" or "transgression" it's a political formalism—a formal relation that appears to guide political judgments but that holds a place for more substantive norms that remain covert. In this case those norms are suspect not only because they are so disguised but because they are so unreflectively communitarian. The argument that queer rhetoric is more inclusive has an additional flaw: there are a lot of people—visibly, actively, impressively lesbian and gay—who do not find a home in queerness. Whatever the new term does, it does not simply replace or expand the old ones. It competes with them and if taken literally will rule out many of the people whom the revaluation of the term was meant to serve.

4. This identitarian culture has left its mark on queer theory as well. Part of my point here is that the history and promise of queer politics can be captured only imperfectly in personological theory, either in its positive liberationist variant or in its negative postmodern variant. Theorizing this historical moment in the language of identity and post-identitarian subjectivity once again returns our understanding of sexuality to the frame of the psyche—just at the moment and with just the language that had opened us onto an analysis of conflicting contexts for discourse. Queer theory inherits this predisposition from psychoanalytic identification theory, from Althusserian interpellation theory, from the uneasy graft of Gramscian deconstruction, from the American reception of Foucault, from the entire program of cultural studies, in which it is imagined that "the construction of subjectivity" is the ultimate problem of the political. Given the limitations of that program, conditions were ripe for an overinvestment in the referential flexibility of queerness.

5. Alexis de Tocqueville, *Democracy in America,* trans. George Lawrence, ed. J. P. Mayer (Garden City: Doubleday Anchor, 1969), vol. 1, pt. 2, 189.

6. Jürgen Habermas, *The New Conservatism: Cultural Criticism and the Historians' Debate,* edited and translated by Shierry Weber Nicholson, introduction by Richard Wolin (Cambridge, Mass.: MIT Press, 1989).

7. *The Human Condition* (Chicago: University of Chicago Press, 1958), 28.

8. "Resistance to Civil Government," in *Reform Papers* (Princeton: Princeton University Press), 86.

9. "Resistance to Civil Government," 80.

10. *Walden* (Princeton: Princeton University Press), 318.

22

Multiculturalism in the Nineties:
Pitfalls and Possibilities

RAJESWARI MOHAN

R. K. NARAYAN's short story "A Horse and Two Goats" presents a sadly paradigmatic moment in American encounters with others in an exchange between an illiterate Tamil peasant and a coffee magnate from New York, during which the two men talk about the same object, a century-old statue of a horse, at cross-purposes, indeed in different languages. The peasant rambles on in Tamil about the cosmic symbolism of the horse and the statue's place in the village's history, lore, and ritual: "This is our guardian, it means death to our adversaries." The American sizes up the statue and begins haggling for it: "I assure you that this will have the best home in the U.S.A. ... I'm going to keep him right in the middle of the [living] room. I don't see how that can interfere with a party—we'll stand around him and have our drinks."[1] Significantly, despite the failure of communication, the American gets his way, as the peasant attributes absolute authority to him because he speaks English and wears khaki, the regalia of the colonial state. This episode cleverly weaves together two historically important strands in attempts to engage with difference or what we now call multiculturalism. The story represents the processes by which the Western subject defines, understands, explains, and captures its other with a force of will and agency rarely accorded to the other itself, and this superior mastery is clearly credited by the story to the context in which the transaction is conducted, where the currency of the exchange, both semiotic and monetary, puts the other at an insurmountable disadvantage. Also, the other, in the person of the ironic narrator, talks back and in doing so wrests a small degree of control over the meaning of the exchange.

It is against these sorts of opportunistic, narcissistic, and heavy-handed dealings with difference, and in extension of the valiant and yet pitifully small increments of resistance they provoke, that multiculturalism is directed. In the United States multiculturalism, under various names and guises, has had a long and lively

372

history of debate and contention, given both the centrality of immigration to U.S. history and the nation's steadily growing ambitions to join the imperial game as a global superpower. Common to each periodic crisis over the term is a tension between what is perceived as the centrifugal forces of nationalism, or allegiance to the state and its economic and political imperatives, and the centripetal forces of gender, ethnic, sexual, or racial identity politics. In this spirit, Allan Bloom and Arthur Schlesinger Jr. lament the effects of women's studies and ethnic studies programs on national character, while politicians indulge in public paroxysms triggered by paranoid fantasies of national security undermined by gay and lesbian rights.[2] Since the 1980s, multiculturalism has proved to be a key player in the domestic and international realignments demanded by recessionary postindustrial economies in the West and the postcommunist global system hailed as the New World Order. In this essay, I investigate the ideological workings of multiculturalism in these contexts and suggest directions in which the project of multicultural pedagogy may be pursued to realize its potential for a radical and emancipatory remapping of the semiotic field and the social imaginary. The salutary effects of these semiotic reconfigurations in scholarship, curriculum, and pedagogy are by themselves many and by no means trivial, but the compelling worldliness of all cultural questions leads me to argue for the need to move from the cultural to other realms of the social, from the local and contextual to the historical and the systemic, from the task of interpretation to the challenge of social transformation, thereby tracking the political and economic consequences of multiculturalism's ideological remappings.

The prospect of delineating the scope of such interventions becomes all the more daunting given multiculturalism's ever-increasing elasticity. A baggy term to start with, it now encompasses expert knowledge within established disciplines such as anthropology, literature, and history and emergent fields such as African American studies, queer theory, and postcolonial and subaltern studies. It has been energized by the impulse, most closely identified with cultural studies and postmodernism, to breach the divides between high, popular, and mass cultures and shift the contours of existing disciplines by recasting their objects of analysis and their methodologies. Included in this project are not only U.S. minority cultures, non-Western challengers to Euro-American hegemony, and countercultural niches within metropolitan systems of representation but also cultural productions marked by their eccentric institutional affiliations. Recent technological innovations in electronic media, computer networks, information retrieval systems, and databases have deregulated and decentered the production of video, music, and information and aided the dissemination of alternative narratives and representations in ways that have energized the multicultural repertoire. By its range, multiculturalism makes visible the mechanisms of selection and distribution that keep the dominant cultural arrangements going and moves beyond looking at alternative canons to raise foundational questions about the institutional regulation of disciplines, especially in the humanities, through the "canonical episteme."[3] Attention to these cultural sites, practices, and issues is motivated primarily by a desire to enlarge the imagination, a desire that has gained considerable political purchase from the realization that the imaginary, in unacknowledged ways, sets the priorities and guides the "gut instincts" by which economic and political decisions of global implications are often made. Recent studies of global culture point out that as diversity becomes an important feature of production and marketing, the discourse of multiculturalism begins to play an increasingly critical role in the efficient administration of the globe in the interests of multinational capitalist networks.[4] So, while multiculturalism initially sought to make space for hitherto suppressed perspectives and knowledges by displacing paradigms of assimilation or acculturation, it has recently found it necessary to keep its oppositional edge sharp by resisting the co-optation of difference itself.

In its incarnations in the 1980s, multiculturalism was a code word for "race," yoked to signifiers that included "affirmative action" and "quotas," among others. Since the 1992 controversy over New York City's rainbow curriculum, the term has become a code word for gay and lesbian issues. Despite shifts in the ideological freight carried by the term, what remains constant is its connotation of "special interests" that supposedly weigh against an implied general interest. This tension points to the more fundamental contradictions of a society committed to equal rights coming to grips with the historical karma, if one might be forgiven a contradiction in terms, of its constitution through racial and gender inequalities, as well as struggling to maintain another of its founding fictions, the separation of church and state.

However, as the dust settles after the initial blitz of the culture wars of the 1980s, it is becoming clear that both public and academic cultures seem to be making a place for multiculturalism. Despite occasional rumbles from the Right, colleges and universities are going about discreetly implementing pluralist curricula, and the makeup of the literary canon and the questions asked of texts are going through a sea change as a result of compelling intellectual and pedagogic work that challenges academic business-as-usual. Despite highly publicized incidents of racial tension on college campuses, increasing numbers of students seeking to "promote racial understanding" are attending race-relations workshops and discussing the pros and cons of institutionalizing antiracism in speech codes and minority recruitment.[5] In the workplace, as more companies are hiring women and minorities, multiculturalism and diversity seem to be the latest catchwords in management training workshops and corporate policy statements. Even national museums, those repositories of culture, custodians of history, and shapers of public taste, are overriding their in-built conservatism and initiating changes in their displays and philosophies.[6] In the realm of popular culture, multiculturalism, as ethnic chic, reigns triumphant in music videos and clothing fashions. Indeed, in this quarter multiculturalism has proven to be an especially handy marketing strategy in the post-Fordist context, when mass markets are becoming a thing of the past and yielding to "micromasses" or subcultural niches that secure their insider status and their distinctiveness from other groups through "a semiotic glut of stylized objects" made available in the ubiquitous "specialty stores."[7]

In this context, right-wing attacks on multiculturalism appear to be diversionary attacks in a war of position aimed at containing the critical energies of the liberal academy by forcing it to cover the same ground over and over again, to make the same refutations of the same allegations in sophisticated or simple terms. The virulence of the conservative attack on the so-called cultural elite sometimes seems to be motivated by nothing more than an unwillingness to admit defeat by conceding the intellectual merit, scholarly weight, and social relevance of liberal and radical claims. The carefully orchestrated backlash against political correctness and multiculturalism in the academy is a result of a decade of effort funded by ultraright philanthropists such as the Reverend Sun Myung Moon, the Olin Foundation, the Sara Scaife Foundation, and the Heritage Foundation and made possible by the political support and technological backing of conservative publications and think tanks. Institutionally organized through prominent groups such as the National Association of Scholars and the Madison Center for Educational Affairs, the Right has created opportunities such as internships for training journalists and young conservatives groomed, in the words of Benjamin Hart of the Heritage Foundation, to "remain in Washington long after the departure of Ronald Reagan, forming an administrative, intellectual, and activist establishment."[8] So it is that while supporters of multicultural education have put forth strong and detailed responses to the right-wing onslaught, their work has rarely enjoyed the extensive media coverage accorded to Allan Bloom's *Closing of the American Mind*, Roger Kimball's *Tenured Radicals*, and Dinesh D'Souza's *Illiberal Education*. The fervor and insistence of these battles, however, betray the fact that what is being fought over is not just culture itself but the political and economic interests to which culture bears a metonymic relation. It is precisely this link between culture and politics that conservatives are determined to mystify.

As a consequence of such conservative campaigns, though the Left has developed a rigorous and thick account of the intellectual and pedagogic challenges of multiculturalism, it has been unable to capture the attention of policymakers and university administrators. Judging from the public forums, conferences, and special issues of journals devoted to the topic of multiculturalism, the liberal academy, in its defensiveness, has accepted the terms of the debate as set by the Right.[9] Conservative critics charge that the Left has installed thought police on campuses and that it encourages reverse discrimination and privileges the oppressed. The response to this charge has been a pluralistic valorization of difference. That is, multiculturalism in the academy has become a counteridentifying discourse, caught in the perpetual gesture of saying no to the discourses of the Right, in the process legitimating and revitalizing those discourses.

For instance, in a special issue of *The Humanist* devoted to political correctness and multiculturalism, Tom Foster Digby provides a thoughtful critique of the antifeminist diatribe of one member of the National Association of Scholars,

Christina Hoff Sommers, whom Digby takes to exemplify the "*cultural* stupidity that Nietzsche says results when a society is deprived of the sort of radical criticism that can keep it alert."[10] Although he is right on the mark in his analysis of the various rhetorical subterfuges upon which Sommers builds her case against feminism, Digby ultimately finds himself arguing for an ongoing engagement with feminists and multiculturalists because they are "free spirits" who, according to Nietzsche, "loosen things up, and, from time to time, deliver a wound to the stable element of a community. Precisely at this wounded, weakened place, the common body is *inoculated*, so to speak, with something new."[11]

To dismiss the NAS—with its impressive array of members, many of whom serve as advisers to government agencies that make educational policy and fund research—as "stupid" does not in any way bolster the efforts of Digby's consortium of liberal "free spirits" in countering the association's formidable success in fanning public resentment against the liberal academy. And, as I have suggested above, to locate this "stupidity" at the level of culture is to miss altogether the point that the contest over culture flares up to the degree that political and economic advantage is seen to hinge on cultural capital. The metaphor of inoculation also raises questions about the interests served by liberal support for multiculturalism: To what does the inoculation make the "common body" immune? Inoculation involves injecting a little dose of a germ or allergen that shakes up the system so that it can protect itself from large and therefore threatening invasions by the same substance. Is multiculturalism such a life-threatening disease, potentially? What specifically are the dangers of multiculturalism? Unintended as they may be, these ironies are impossible to overlook. Digby himself offers some answers to these questions in his curiously ambivalent final paragraphs, where he supports multiculturalism and feminism from his conviction that they offer opportunities for "self-renewal of the Euro-American tradition." With this assertion, Digby veers toward the well-documented practice by which Euro-American tradition, whenever faced with a crisis of meaning and identity, defines itself through opportunistic and controlled encounters with its others that usually conclude with cultural identity's being reconstructed around oppressive hierarchies and boundaries' being reinstated with renewed confidence and authority.[12] But he goes on to acknowledge the multiplicity of cultures in the United States and the world and allows that the supports of "Europatriarchal culture" are being eroded by "demographic, political, and economic forces beyond our control." Faced with this development, he concedes that the "question is not whether we will accept or reject feminism or multiculturalism but, rather, just how we will use them to renew our traditions."[13] The essay ends with this uneasy and equivocating move from tradition construed in the singular to traditions as an unexamined plurality. Underlying this uneasiness is, of course, the conservative argument that multiculturalism aims at nothing short of an all-out destruction of Western culture, and Digby's essay seems constrained by an inability to move beyond the trope of contamination or, worse, annihilation structuring these arguments. The question remains whether multiculturalism and feminism—construed as evolutionary impulses common to all lively cultures and as revitalizing opportunities for Euro-American tradition—is, in the hands of liberals, a means of containing their more radical, transformative potential. The aim of multiculturalism is not simply to give voice to the silenced and the marginalized, to reflect the achievements and values of cultures hitherto excluded from the Euro-American canon; rather, the challenge is to redress the wrongs of history by reconfiguring the social imaginary, by drawing "new and better maps of reality" through the inclusion of perspectives and information overlooked until now.[14] Indeed the notion of voice has itself been radicalized by contemporary theories that revoke the idea of voice as the individuating expression of the creative and unfettered bourgeois subject far removed from social contexts of power, difference, and struggle. Instead voice is theorized as an effect of the social and political formations that serve as the ground for the discourses, histories, and narratives through which writers give meaning to their lives.[15] That is, voice is a category that demands and enforces the movement from culture to other realms of struggle and agency. Minority and subaltern groups have welcomed the attention given to marginalized cultures and histories because it puts them in touch with empowering images of survival and triumph that counter the overwhelmingly debilitating images of destitution, crime, and victimization purveyed by the media, introduces them to discursive and communitarian networks, and makes visible to them the complex social histories informing their present. The entry of newly credentialed knowledges into the cultural arena does not replace existing values and norms with new ones; nor does it simply complete the existing cultural mosaic by adding the missing pieces. Rooted in counterhegemonic, eccentric, and oppositional histories, these new knowledges clear the space for "narratives-from-below" power networks and in doing so foreground new possibilities for social change through creative modes of resistance and opposition. In seeking to bring about an equitable distribution of social resources, multiculturalism does not seek to destroy Western culture as conservatives charge, nor should its impulse be directed at revitalizing or retooling an oppressive ideological system as Digby might seem to suggest. Instead, what seems necessary is to redraw the contours of culture, to allow new texts and discourses to critique, challenge, or otherwise counter the cultural verities of the old, to facilitate the emergence of hybrid knowledges, and thereby to shift the priorities of the economic and political realm.

In the meantime, multiculturalism has been seized upon as a smart marketing strategy made for the times. It is not difficult to come up with instances of corporate America's opportunistic deployment of the discourse of racial harmony and equal opportunity, the most notorious being the series of advertisements launched by the Italian garment manufacturer Benetton. The series is based on controversial, shocking, and sometimes risqué visuals such as rows of multicolored condoms, a black Queen Elizabeth II, a study of a hospital room where a young man is dying of AIDS, a panoramic picture of brick kilns in Bolivia where child workers, stunted from years of carrying bricks on their backs, play in the dust, and, more recently, an array of male and female genitalia of varying sizes, shapes, and hues. The popular line of garments sold by the company explicitly invokes a cosmopolitan, Third Worldist, eclectic fashion in which antiapartheid colors and gender-bender styles are promoted as "cultural transvestism." Even though charges of racial insensitivity have forced the company to withdraw some of its advertisements, it has persisted with its theme of racial harmony, its happy images glossing over the exploitation, paternalism, violence, and segregation that are the history of race relations in the United States.

Maybe, to give it some credit, this style of multiculturalism brings into public circulation discourses, images, and social issues that, for far too long and with dire consequences, have been kept silent and invisible. Perhaps too, as its advocates have argued, it makes personal and visceral what often reaches us as bureaucratic abstraction. But the unvarying caption "United Colors of Benetton" that accompanies the advertisements' stunning visuals exerts a countervailing force toward formalization and commodification by directing our attention to the visual puns and estranging effects wrought by the disposition of colors and by arrogating this play of colors—and the politics it metonymically signals—to the product line being marketed. Even the immediacy and poignancy of the images are limited in their potential to politicize. For instance, the controversial image of the AIDS patient is typical of the photographic genre analyzed by Douglas Crimp in that the "privacy of the people portrayed is both brutally invaded and brutally maintained."[16] That is, AIDS is rendered a private tragedy, and in the process the politics of the epidemic is glossed over. In the last analysis, the medium of the advertising image that, in the Benetton advertisements, elicits pity, curiosity, and sympathy is unequal to the burden of political pedagogy and consciousness raising claimed on its behalf and is quite unable to move its viewers toward either solidarity with the subjects portrayed or understanding of the social and historical forces shaping their lives. Whatever the political urgency of the issues raised, the overriding impetus of these advertisements is to map the social according to the logic of consumption such that hitherto invisible and neglected social groups and cultures appear solely as untouched markets and untapped sources of novel commodities.

Benetton's successful management of multiculturalist themes reflects a pervasive interest in questions of diversity in corporations. Management consultants and administrators responding to the diversification of the workforce have turned to race-relations and sensitivity-training workshops to contain the crisis in corporate culture provoked by its sudden heterogeneity. In professional and trade journals such as the *Harvard Business Review*, experts warn that insularity may be costly for U.S. corporations in a highly competitive global market. In one such instance, Charles Hapden-Turner, a senior research fellow at the London Business School and the Centre for International Business Studies, laments, "In the end, the American penchant for universalism may turn out to be the narrowest of parochialisms. When it comes to addressing the business challenge of the current decade, this parochialism puts American managers at a distinct disadvantage compared with their Asian and European competitors. The most rigid boundaries of business may be those in our heads."[17] Similarly, in the prevailing climate of desperate economic remedies, Victor Li, the president of the East-West Center, has launched a campaign for increased awareness of Japanese culture. Claiming that a large proportion of the barriers American sellers face is cultural rather than legal or political, Li argues that learning more about Asian culture is tied to the goal of learning more about selling in Asia. In response to such assessments, educators have seized on multiculturalism as a means of enhancing students' career hopes. A recent survey at the University of California at Berkeley, where half the student body is made up of people of color, indicates that students, eager to equip themselves well and sharpen whatever will give them an edge over their competitors in a tight job market, share this increased enthusiasm for multiculturalism. In the words of Troy Duster, the sociology professor who conducted the survey, "The smartest among them also see that in a global economy, Berkeley's multiculturalism can make them better leaders."[18]

As information networks become increasingly crucial to economic well-being, universities have served as vital sites of research by collecting data, processing information, and making analyses available for decisionmakers in the military-industrial complex, international finance and aid agencies, and diplomatic networks. Here, multiculturalism has joined area and development studies to service U.S. economic and political interests through market research, information retrieval, and strategic planning. For instance, interest in the Pacific Basin and Latin America has been supported and funded by U.S. desire to control raw materials, labor pools, and markets in these areas.[19] Although the movement of technology, information, and capital between these areas and the metropole is complexly multidirectional, powerful institutions such as multinational corporations and international finance organizations do try to channel these flows to their advantage.[20] The polyethnic university thus becomes the polytechnic of the age of information. Cultural pluralism has proven to be the free enterprise of not just the academic marketplace. It articulates the world views, shores up the institutional structures, and revitalizes the commercial and political networks of modern middle-class society in the United States.

In the late 1980s, George Bush's inauguration of the New World Order based on the "just treatment of all peoples" found its domestic partner in David Dinkins's invocation of the "gorgeous mosaic" of New York. This rhetoric, revitalized in Clinton's promise to make government "look more like America," promises a new system of social values, national and global in scope, whereby old divisions and hierarchies will be torn down. In practice, what has been demolished over the last few years in developments such as NAFTA, the Gulf War alliance, and relief efforts in Somalia are barriers to global political and military as well as economic domination by the G-Seven powers and checks to the unfolding of a new international system in which U.S. preeminence is unchallenged.[21]

The aftermath of the Gulf War has seen the consolidation of U.S. hegemony over a multinational military alliance now perched in armed vigilance over Third World nation-states, and in this context information on the economic, political, and cultural life of these new adversaries assumes strategic importance. Of renewed interest are practices initiated after World War II by the Department of Defense whereby social and behavioral scientists have been recruited to compile information that would assist the military in its warfare as well as its "peacefare" activities of pacification, assistance, the "battle of ideas," and so on, the argument being that all these activities call for information on beliefs, values, motivations, and religious and cultural organizations in various parts of the world.[22] Thus, in a much publicized allocation of the peace dividend, George Bush signed the National Security Education Act of 1991 (the very title of which formalizes the link between education and the military-industrial complex), which earmarked $150 million in trust funds to encourage the study of foreign languages and cultures, particularly those of the Middle East, Africa, and Latin America. The act was a direct result of increasing worries that ignorance of world cultures and world languages represents a threat to U.S. ability to remain a world leader.

Remaining strong through all this has been the desire to make amends to all the groups whose history, culture, and achievements have been neglected in American education, which, stressing a single national language and a selective tradition, has aimed to integrate immigrants into the national culture. For a long time, reformers saw education as a means of disciplining immigrants and the poor to work under the Protestant work ethic of an articulate and influential middle class. Education served as a means of social control, a mechanism by which the tensions and contradictions stemming from ethnic or religious difference could be diffused, and a means of forming citizens and workers willing to submit to corporate ideologies of productivity and efficiency.[23] But with demographic shifts in the twentieth century, the European, middle-class, and patriarchal bias implicit in the norm of literacy is being pressured, though the productivist ideology informing education in general remains intact. As Guillermo Gomez-Peña trenchantly puts it, "The colonized cultures are sliding into the space of the colonizer, and in doing so, they are redefining its border and its culture."[24] The ferocity of the ensuing debates over PC and multiculturalism points to the political and economic pressures generated by rising numbers of groups whose exploitation and oppression, sanctioned by ideologies of racism and sexism, served as one of the enabling conditions of the rights and privileges of democracy and progress enjoyed by the more favored groups of U.S. society. It is in this sense that Hazel Carby argues that the multicultural wars are the latest instances of the return of the repressed fundamental contradictions of a democratic society structured by racial inequality.[25] Under these conditions, when multiculturalism does find its way into general education, it takes the form of what one critic calls the "museum approach to culture" and focuses on the rituals, practices, and values that inform the communal sensibilities and everyday life of various ethnic and racial groups.[26] Often a new version of compensatory historicism, this time global in scope, ranged against the ills of a commercialized culture, is offered in place of the old monocultural agenda of general education.[27] Severed from its hidden structural supports and outgrowths—social status, political leverage, economic resources—culture becomes the stand-in for the social, and critics and reformers come to believe that cultural rather than social change will end existing inequities.

This political optimism may be traced to the fact that multiculturalism is a legacy of discourses of liberation of the 1960s, when the federal government's favorable responses to political agitation through civil rights legislation, desegregation, and affirmative action in educational institutions were often attempts at crisis containment. As Paul Sweezy notes, the government's desire to preserve corporate interests and the "national ruling class" led to a concern to maintain "an environment of civic peace and stability in which to carry on their profitable economic activities."[28] Ethnic studies and women's studies departments arose out of a need to police the crisis and ensure campus order and security, and accordingly, these programs gain visibility in times of social crisis such as the Watts riots. Similarly, the sudden receptivity of today's liberal culture to questions of race and ethnicity, instead of signaling real interest or desire for social change, may simply seek to compensate for the absence of change or tepidity of reform of the material conditions that provoke civil unrest.[29] In light of this tendency, we might be persuaded by Carby's charge that in the absence of attempts to understand and promote a vision of an integrated society, the elevation of texts such as those celebrating the black female subject under the rubric of multiculturalism becomes nothing more than "the means by which many middle-class white students and faculty cleanse their souls and rid themselves of the guilt of living in a society that is still rigidly segregated."[30]

Liberal versions of multiculturalism rely on pluralism to mystify the economic and political inequities that are in large part related to racial/gender/sexual difference. Pluralism accords equal value to the experiences and perspectives of varying, divided, and often antagonistic cultures whose members have widely divergent access to employment, education, housing, and health care. The rhetoric of tolerance, mutual responsibility, open-mindedness, and flexibility that is associated with pluralism is often contradicted by an underlying humanism that posits a common set of values collapsing nonidentical subjects, experiences, and achievements into comparable and even identical ones. In this sense, pluralism may ensure that emergent knowledges do not disrupt the regulatory and authoritarian structures of education.[31] The other side of the pluralist coin is individualism, which often reduces multiculturalism to a matter of polite and well-mannered acceptance of difference. From race-relations workshops that draw upon conflict resolution strategies developed to support corporate ideals of productivity and efficiency to speech codes that justify their necessity in terms of individual rights to protection from harassment by other individuals, the emphasis is on personal development and individual education. The emphasis on open-mindedness all too often serves as a way out of having to deal with the messy and demanding philosophical and political implications of a commitment to social diversity and multiculturalism. The pedagogical and indeed epistemological challenges involved in understanding and honoring different and sometimes antagonistic cultures, values, and histories are cheerfully elided; simultaneously, the exclusive focus on culture often means that accommodating cultural difference relieves mounting pressure to examine how even open-mindedness is a privilege enabled by the economic and political hierarchies of which cultural difference is a part and stands in for collective responsibility to change those hierarchical structures.

The hysteria over the supposed tyranny of minority points of view on college campuses seems even more gratuitous at a time when cuts in health care, education, and public services and massive layoffs are literally making life impossible for minority segments of the society. So, as bell hooks and Hazel Carby have pointed out, texts by black women writers are making unprecedented, albeit embattled, headway in the academy at the same time that de facto segregation in housing and education is taking an unprecedented toll on the lives and opportunities of black people. These developments are paralleled on the international stage by ballooning debt in Third World countries as result of exorbitant interest rates and debt-servicing charges and depressed prices for their products. Under conditions that have provided Western nations with a strong bargaining position boosted even further by the opening up of markets in the erstwhile Soviet bloc and China, freedom is cheerfully defined as the freedom to do business. Sweeping changes wrought by microchip and computer technology have vastly speeded up and increased the flow of international trade and finance, and innovative business practices have made patterns of labor and production more flexible. In sum, Western nations are poised on the brink of what some analysts have called an "ideological bourgeois renaissance," which, simply put, amounts to a high level of civil rights, a low level of political rights, and an even lower level of social rights.[32] In this scenario, whose high points might include Maya Angelou's stirring contribution to the Clinton inaugural and the rousing success of the 1993 gay and lesbian pride rally in Washington, multiculturalism plays a key role.

Under these circumstances, if multiculturalism is to be recuperated as an analytical and political category it must be dislodged from its current association with pluralism. Cultural divisions rarely signify mere difference informed by an abstract principle of equality. Rather, they are organized in hierarchies tied to existing structures of domination and exploitation and serve as complex rationalizations of the status quo. As an investigation of these hierarchies, multiculturalism cannot be a "post-conflictual state."[33] Intellectuals and scholars committed to it may have to give up the expectation that the institutional sites of knowledge production—such as the classroom, the conference circuit, the scholarly journal—

will be comforting and congenial spaces of amicable exchange of ideas. Multiculturalism, by its very focus, foregrounds the fact that these sites, like any social space, are force fields of social antagonism and contradictions that severely strain the most sincere commitment to solidarity, open-mindedness, and collective enquiry. As Foucault's point that knowledge is invariably produced through contestations becomes central to the method of multiculturalism, of particular relevance are strategies of interpretation such as cognitive mapping, transcoding, and border pedagogy and hermeneutic categories such as mediation and articulation that can unravel the historical and social interests at work in these contestations.[34] As quotidian features of work and daily life are increasingly caught up in transnational fluxes and global information loops, these heuristic devices and hermeneutic strategies become indispensable for mapping the flow of power and critically apprehending patterns of disjuncture and coherence in the global system.

Multiculturalism's emphasis on difference has been helped by postmodern critiques of Enlightenment notions of rationality, progress, and universal truth, as a result of which the idea of a singular and universal reason undergirding and encompassing all human activity has yielded to relativist accounts of alterity, variety, and change. However, against ludic postmodernism, which seeks to disperse all identity and signification in a completely open and absolute play of difference, politically minded appropriations of postmodernism's potential for opposition, resistance, and subversion seek to map difference within a complex and contingent frame of sociality. The central questions of relativism are by no means trivial: How do we understand and engage with difference and alterity without reducing them to images of ourselves or incorporating them into our frames of intelligibility and thereby replicating the insularity, arrogance, and violence of Eurocentric encounters with others? How do we get off the well-worn paths and libidinally cathected patterns of dealing with otherness and learn to listen to the other articulating its desires on its own terms? In short, how do we deal with alterity without demanding that it satisfy the needs of the hegemonic self? Motivated by a respect for other selves, spaces, contexts, and histories, relativism has put on the intellectual agenda an investigation of the crucial social and political interests served by the repressions and absences in dominant frameworks of understanding the world. It also insists that we can understand elements and productions of other cultures and avoid repeating the historical tragedies sustained by ethnocentrism only if we interpret them primarily in terms of the culture's immanent criteria of coherence and value. But, as S. P. Mohanty has pointed out, despite the best intentions relativism does not go far enough in establishing protocols of genuine and responsible dialogue between different cultures and, in the last analysis, remains a philosophical position resting on political apathy that begins as pious political wish and ends up denying the need to take the other seriously.[35] In contrast to this indifference, Mohanty advocates the study of "the plurality of our heterogeneous lives, the darker and unspoken densities of past and present that are lived, fought, and imagined as various communities and peoples seek to retrace and reweave the

historical text ... the imbrication of our various pasts and presents, the inelucta-
ble relationship of shared and contested meanings, values, material resources."[36]
These are the material and historical bases of the notion of minimal rationality
Mohanty argues is the necessary philosophical ground for dialogue between culturally different positions that would leave all parties altered fundamentally.
Based on a commitment to support quotidian struggles to preserve life and dignity in varying historical and cultural contexts, the notion of minimal rationality
would make possible political agency, help multicultural encounters move beyond
relativism, and initiate the difficult and delicate task of adjudicating between
competing narratives and claims. Mohanty's intervention points to the intellectually exciting and politically promising ground opened up by the admission that in
order to engage seriously with difference and alterity it is necessary to abandon
the false universalism of Western Civilization and its exhausted ontology.

But imaginative sympathy and engagement, however hard-won, are not
enough. Because multiculturalism treats social divisions as historical constructions and not ontological categories, it is forced to deal with matters of power and
social wealth. Attention to the historical construction of these divisions is likely to
bring about a clearer sense of the operative hierarchies and urgent issues of the
moment and thereby help set strategic priorities that sidestep a pluralistic free-
for-all. As categories such as "masculine" and "feminine," "white" and "black,"
and "straight" and "queer" come to be seen equally as historically contingent inventions, the normative status accorded to some of these categories in the name of
universality, neutrality, or natural order becomes impossible to sustain. The emphasis on historical construction is likely to counteract the swing toward identity
politics and the cult of authenticity and underscore the point that "race, class, and
gender are not the *answers* in cultural studies, the bottom line explanation to
which all life may be reduced; they are precisely the *problems* posed. ... These are
the issues to be explained and understood."[37]

Such an emphasis, for instance, drives the work of Paul Gilroy, who studies race
and blackness in the context of Britain's postcolonial decline into protracted economic and cultural crisis.[38] Gilroy draws into his study developments such as the
emergence of black bureaucrats and professionals at the very juncture that urban
black unemployment is at its highest, the panic over shifting definitions of family,
and the loss of confidence in the state's ability to maintain ideals of justice. As he
draws in these details, the scope of his critique expands to include ideas of nationhood and national belonging, ideologies of productivism and the work ethic, and
the mutually reinforcing links between legal institutions and a state characterized
by militarism and exterminism. Anchored firmly to the cultures of resistance and
opposition swelling up among racial minorities in Britain, Gilroy's analysis presents compelling arguments for the illegitimacy of the state itself. His study therefore provides a far-reaching and substantive account of the ways in which English-
ness as norm and ideal depends on hierarchies of race, class, gender, and sexuality
for its appearance of coherence and desirability, to the point that the slightest

challenge to these hierarchies lays bare the internal contradictions, uncertainties, and profound disease it papers over. Gilroy's work exemplifies the gains to be made through a multiculturalism that, through its relentless historicism, challenges existing accounts of the real as natural and reasonable. More important, it demonstrates that the repressed narratives and hidden performances of minority cultures put forth new ways of reading history and the social order and provide creative strategies of reclaiming resistance and agency.

Similarly, multiculturalist pedagogy takes as its starting point a notion of culture as a terrain of conflict and struggle over representation—conflict for which resolution may not be immediate and struggle that may not cease until there is change in the social conditions that provoke it. Rather than present culture as the site where different members of the family of man coexist peacefully, it has to develop strategies to explore and understand this conflict and to encourage creative resolutions and contingent alliances that move students from interpreting cultures to intervening in political processes. Implicit in this agenda is a shift in pedagogic emphasis from transmitting to transforming knowledge, though the full analysis of this shift had a slow start because of its alarmist construction as an irresponsible abdication of intellectual standards.[39] To extend Talal Asad's vision of anthropology, multicultural education needs to produce canny and careful cultural translators who can "test the tolerance of [their] own language for assuming unaccustomed forms."[40] The desired goal here is an understanding of the ways power enters the process of translation through the relative positioning of the different cultures (colonizer versus colonized, lender versus borrower, etc.) and the operation of discursive power through norms of logic, proof, beauty, and balance.

The important question in these pedagogic deliberations is not what texts to teach but how to teach them, and in the nineties this may be the question that frames the multicultural enterprise in general. Already, multiculturalism exerts pressure on existing disciplinary configurations and their various legitimating narratives as newly authorized knowledges challenge the content as well as the methodologies of disciplinary enquiry. As it raises these and other challenges, it fuels the growth of a language of possibility that avoids invoking the Absolute Spirit, even implicitly. In this sense, multiculturalism may very well end up posing an alternative to the humanities.

NOTES

1. R. K. Narayan, "A Horse and Two Goats," in *A Horse and Two Goats* (New York: Viking Press, 1970), 19–20. Colonial history is rife with such encounters, of which Anthony Appiah provides a recent instance in his anecdote about David Rockefeller's response to an alleged Fante statue. See Kwame Anthony Appiah, "The Postcolonial and the Postmodern," in *In My Father's House* (New York: Oxford University Press, 1992), 137–157.

2. Given that one of the contexts of the debates over multiculturalism and political correctness is the end of the Cold War, it is not surprising that anticommunist rhetoric is now being recruited against these perceived threats to national security. For a provocative dis-

cussion of the transformation of the "red menace" into the "rainbow menace" in conservative discourses, see Christopher Newfield, "What Was Political Correctness? Race, the Right, and Managerial Democracy in the Humanities," *Critical Inquiry* 19 (1993):308–336.

3. For a discussion of canonicity and the pressure brought upon it by poststructuralism, see R. Radhakrishnan, "Canonicity and Theory: Toward a Post Structuralist Pedagogy," in *Theory/Pedagogy/Politics: Texts For Change*, ed. Donald Morton and Mas'ud Zavarzadeh (Urbana: University of Illinois Press, 1991), 112–135.

4. Flexibility has become one of the hallmarks of late industrial capitalism as transfer of capital, technology, and ideology has resulted not in homogenization but in tight linkages between context-sensitive variations. For a sketch of the theoretical challenges posed by global culture in the late twentieth century to models of uneven development and state formation, see Arjun Appadurai, "Difference in Global Cultural Economy," in *Global Culture: Nationalism, Globalization, and Modernity*, ed. Mike Featherstone (London: Sage, 1990), 295–310. For a discussion of the overlap between corporate responses to this flexibility and the containment of diversity in the academy, see Newfield, "What Was Political Correctness?"

5. See, for instance, reports in *Chronicle of Higher Education*, 13 January 1993, A29; 21 April 1993, A15.

6. Among many recent developments in the museum circuit to make this point is the 1993 Whitney Biennial. See also Jerry Adler's "Great Hall of Bacteria," *Newsweek* 120 (14 December 1992):84. Adler profiles Robert Sullivan, the new associate director of public programs in the Smithsonian's National Museum of Natural History, who seeks to overhaul the museum's mode of exhibition because of his sense that "the museum can no longer be a colonial institution in a postcolonial world."

7. McKenzie Wark, "From Fordism to Sonyism: Perverse Readings of the New World Order," *New Formations* 15 (1991):44.

8. Scott Henson and Tom Philpott, "The Right Declares a Culture War," *The Humanist*, March/April 1992, 14.

9. Notable exceptions to this trend are Stanley Aronowitz and Henry A. Giroux, *Postmodern Education* (Minneapolis: University of Minnesota Press, 1991) and *Radical History Review* 54 (1992). In the latter, Michael Denning's suggestive attempt in "The Academic Left and the Rise of Cultural Studies" (21–47) to rearticulate and recuperate PC as a mode of mediation between various social movements that make up the Left and as an expression of collective responsibility in the absence of unifying grand narratives demonstrates the gains to be made when the Left refuses to accept the terms set by conservative attacks on multiculturalism.

10. Tom Foster Digby, "Political Correctness and the Fear of Feminism," *The Humanist*, March/April 1992, 8.

11. Ibid., 7.

12. The most influential study of this history is still Edward Said's *Orientalism* (New York: Vintage, 1978). For an exploration of the ways in which the crisis of modernity is negotiated through encounters with contrasting others, see Marianna Torgovnick, *Gone Primitive* (Chicago: University of Chicago Press, 1990).

13. Digby, "Political Correctness," 34.

14. The phrase is Salman Rushdie's. See "Outside the Whale," *Granta* 11 (1984):125–138, where Rushdie argues that among the first casualties of this remapping is the notion of culture as the tranquil and hermetic retreat from the political world.

15. See, in particular, Aronowitz and Giroux, "The Politics and Pedagogy of Voice," in *Postmodern Education*, 100–103.

16. Douglas Crimp, "Portraits of People with AIDS," in *Cultural Studies*, ed. Lawrence Grossberg, Cary Nelson, and Paula Treichler (New York: Routledge, 1992), 120.

17. Charles Hampden-Turner, "The Boundaries of Business: The Cross-Cultural Quagmire," *Harvard Business Review*, September/October 1991, 94.

18. Troy Duster, "They're Taking Over and Other Myths about Race on Campus," *Mother Jones*, September/October 1991, 33.

19. For a detailed and trenchant critique of the role of universities as ideological supports for the late capitalist state, see Rosaura Sanchez, "Ethnicity, Ideology, and Academia," *Cultural Studies* 4:3 (1990):94–101.

20. In this connection, see Yves Dezalay, "The *Big Bang* and the Law: The Internationalization and Restructuration of the Legal Field," in Featherstone, *Global Culture*, 278–294. Dezalay's account of the processes by which international lawyers, financial advisers, and corporate tax accountants remodel the structures of international commerce and retool the laws regulating competition clearly demonstrate the point that globalization of the market favors the strongest player and all too often entails increased Americanization.

21. See Leo Panitch and Ralph Milliband, "The New World Order and the Socialist Agenda," *Socialist Register 1992*, ed. Ralph Milliband and Leo Panitch (London: Merlin Press, 1992), 6.

22. See Edward Said, "Representing the Colonized: Anthropology's Interlocutors," *Critical Inquiry* 15 (1989):205–225.

23. The move in this direction in public school curriculum and in the general-education component of higher education was by no means uncontested. For an account of the various interests contending to shape the content and thrust of public education, see Herbert Kliebard, *The Struggle for the American Curriculum, 1893–1958* (New York: Routledge, 1986).

24. Guillermo Gomez-Peña, "The Multicultural Paradigm," *High Performance*, Fall 1989, 20.

25. Hazel Carby, "The Multicultural Wars," *Radical History Review* 54 (1992):7–18.

26. Aminur Rahim, "Multiculturalism or Ethnic Hegemony: A Critique of Multicultural Education in Toronto," *Journal of Ethnic Studies* 18:3 (1990):29–46.

27. For a sustained analysis of the crisis of general education and its partial resolution by multiculturalism, see Michael Geyer, "Multiculturalism and the Politics of General Education," *Critical Inquiry* 19 (1993):499–533.

28. Paul Sweezy, "Afterword: The Implications of Community Control," in *Schools Against Children*, ed. Annette T. Rubinstein (New York: Monthly Review Press, 1970), 288.

29. For a thoughtful discussion of these and other strategies of containment, see Sanchez, "Ethnicity, Ideology, and Academia," and Chandra Talpade Mohanty, "On Race and Voice: Challenges for Liberal Education in the 1990s," *Cultural Critique* 14 (Winter 1989–1990):179–208.

30. Carby, "The Multicultural Wars," 11.

31. Radical attempts such as critical pedagogy are not free from this problem either. See Elizabeth Ellsworth, "Why Doesn't This Feel Empowering? Working Through the Repressive Myths of Critical Pedagogy," *Harvard Educational Review* 59:3 (1989):297–324.

32. Panitch and Milliband, "The New World Order," 11–13.

33. The phrase comes from the Chicago Cultural Studies Group, though, unfortunately, the group does not press on to explore the implications of identifying multiculturalism

with conflict. See Chicago Cultural Studies Group, "Critical Multiculturalism," *Critical Inquiry* 18 (1992):544.

34. Fredric Jameson's work demonstrates the centrality of marxist hermeneutics in developing these strategies. See, among others, "Postmodernism, or the Cultural Logic of Late Capitalism," *New Left Review* 146 (1984):53–92; "Cognitive Mapping," in *Marxism and the Interpretation of Culture*, ed. Lawrence Grossberg and Cary Nelson (Urbana: University of Illinois Press, 1988), 347–357. The theory of border pedagogy is developed in Aronowitz and Giroux, *Postmodern Education*.

35. S. P. Mohanty, "Us and Them: On the Philosophical Bases of Political Criticism," *Yale Journal of Criticism* 2:2 (1989):14.

36. Ibid., 13.

37. Demming, "The Academic Left and the Rise of Cultural Studies," 38.

38. Paul Gilroy, *There Ain't No Black in the Union Jack: The Cultural Politics of Race and Nation* (London: Hutchinson, 1987); see also his "One Nation Under a Groove: The Cultural Politics of 'Race' and Racism in Britain," in *Anatomy of Racism*, ed. David Theo Goldberg (Minneapolis: University of Minnesota Press, 1990), 263–282.

39. Aronowitz and Giroux offer a thoughtful if overoptimistic account of the expected results of this shift in *Postmodern Education*.

40. Talal Asad, "The Concept of Cultural Translation in British Social Anthropology," in *Writing Culture: The Poetics and Politics of Ethnography*, ed. James Clifford and George E. Marcus (Berkeley: University of California Press, 1986), 157.

23

Curriculum Mortis: A Manifesto for Structural Change

RONALD STRICKLAND

SINCE THE EARLY 1980s, in the wake of the paradigm shift from New Criticism to the politically self-conscious postmodernism and poststructuralism currently dominant in English studies, teachers of literature have been under attack from conservative academics and journalists.[1] The terms of this attack and of the countercritiques mounted by politically and theoretically oriented scholars are by now quite familiar. Conservatives and liberal humanists charged that radical English teachers were ignoring traditional canonical texts in favor of indoctrinating students in an alternative canon of "politically correct" texts espousing marxist, feminist, and multicultural agendas. Theorists and radicals responded that the traditional canon itself constitutes a "politically correct" set of values of a different sort and that the focus of English studies should be critical interrogation of cultural texts and other discursive systems rather than uncritical appreciation of "great" literature.

My sympathies in this debate lie entirely in the theorist/radical camp. In this essay, however, I want to take up a question that has not been sufficiently addressed by either side of the debate over the English curriculum: What is the role of English studies in an increasingly technical-vocational academy? In relation to this question, I think the conservatives who are concerned that theoretically self-conscious and politically oriented approaches will mean the death of literature have been barking up the wrong tree. In the current postmodern, postindustrial academy, quasi-professional and vocational courses rub shoulders with traditional arts and sciences courses; workers, not just managers, are now trained in colleges and universities. Traditional literary study—conceived in post-Romantic terms as an

Reprinted by permission from *College Literature* 21:1 (February 1994):1–14.

escape from economic and political concerns—is fast becoming an expendable
luxury in universities whose primary function is the training and credentialing of
the growing technical-professional-managerial workforce. In this climate market
pressures, not critical theory, will doom the study of literature.[2] Yet, if conservatives have, for the most part, misread the symptoms of literary study's current
"dis-ease," radical scholars and teachers have been too often distracted by the conservatives' rear-guard attacks; we have not yet developed the kinds of institutional
structures and practices necessary for engaging the challenge to democratic education posed by the technical-vocational mission of the academy.

Most of us are complicit in this technical-vocational mission. We maintain the
luxury of teaching literature or literary theory in relatively comfortable conditions
at least partly by appropriating resources generated by "service" programs attached to English departments. These programs—composition, technical writing,
English as a second language (ESL), etc.—are disproportionately staffed by graduate assistants and nontenured faculty, and they are typically marginalized within
English departments in a variety of contexts such as office space, departmental
committee representation, curricular offerings, and graduation requirements.
Within the larger professional arena, we have a scholarship publishing structure
that tends to reward those whose specialized research is most remote from the
concerns of these "service" courses. This hierarchy of privilege needs to be dis-
mantled not merely because it is unfair for our colleagues who teach technical-
vocational courses but also because it limits the critical scope and effect of literature teachers as well.

We need to meet the challenge of the growing technical-vocational hegemony in
the academy within our own departments, in our curricula. The most promising
models for curricular change currently on the horizon are the "cultural studies"
and "textual studies" models, in which both elite and popular texts are taken as
objects of study, in which the traditional canon is opened up to include more texts
by women and people of color, and in which critical literary and cultural theories
are given primary emphasis in the curriculum and in individual courses. Those
innovations are necessary and valuable, but they don't go far enough toward redressing the narrow parochialism of traditional literary studies because they don't
engage and contest the values and assumptions of the technical-vocational training courses in the university at large and, often, in English departments themselves. In the following pages, I will explore some possible models for an English
curriculum more directly engaged in a contestatory dialogue with the technical-
vocational mission of the academy in a postmodern, postindustrial society.

Theoretical Frames:
Transdisciplinarity and Cultural Studies

One of the means by which New Criticism and its narrowly aesthetics-oriented
approach to literature has continued to fend off political and theoretical chal-

lenges in the classroom (if not in the scholarly journals) is the well-entrenched field coverage model of literary study. As Gerald Graff has demonstrated in *Professing Literature* (1988), this model produced an ostensibly pluralist literary curriculum in which specialists in particular literary-historical periods were encouraged to do narrowly focused research and teaching, each in his or her own narrow specialization, blithely ignoring the larger assumptions about literature that set the boundaries of the profession. For some time now overspecialization has been recognized as counterproductive by politically engaged teachers on both the right and the left. Compare, for example, the following observations:

> Each department or great division of the university makes a pitch for itself, and each offers a course of study that will make the student an initiate. But how to choose among them? How do they relate to one another? The fact is they do not address one another. They are competing and contradictory, without being aware of it. The problem of the whole is urgently indicated by the very existence of the specialties, but it is never systematically posed. The net effect of the student's encounter with the college catalogue is bewilderment and very often demoralization. (Bloom 1987, 339)

> Unless one fudges the definition of intellectuals in terms of purely formal and statistical educational criteria, it is fairly clear that what modern society produces is an army of alienated, privatized, and uncultured experts who are knowledgeable only within very narrowly defined areas. This technical intelligentsia, rather than intellectuals in the traditional sense of thinkers concerned with the totality, is growing by leaps and bounds to run the increasingly complex bureaucratic and industrial apparatus. Its rationality, however, is only *instrumental* in character, and thus suitable mainly to perform partial tasks rather than tackling substantial questions of social organization and political direction. (Piccone 1981–1982, 116)

The first passage was written by Allan Bloom, and the second was written by Paul Piccone—two writers who hold diametrically opposed conservative and progressive views on university education but share an increasingly widespread dissatisfaction with the myopic overspecialization of most academic disciplines. Despite the wide range of disagreement between conservatives and progressives in the academy, the undesirability of overspecialization is one thing that the two sides can agree on. The university curriculum should be a site in which different perspectives—political and intellectual positions—can confront one another. One result of overspecialization is that political and intellectual conflicts among faculty and students are displaced to the level of administration. Instead of a situation in which colleagues with different political, intellectual, and institutional positions debate specific issues, the power struggles are hidden behind closed doors as administrators negotiate funding levels. The net effect of this displacement is a systemic retardation of intellectual vitality.

I came face to face with just this sort of crippling effect of overspecialization in my own institution recently when one of my English department colleagues submitted a new course proposal for a graduate-level cultural studies course—Introduction to Cultural Theory—to the university curriculum committee. The Communications department protested the proposal, and a committee of four English faculty, including myself, met with a committee of four Communications faculty in a special meeting, chaired by a member of the college curriculum committee, to see if we could amicably work out the objections to the course. At the meeting I was surprised to learn that the Communications department faculty objected to the English department's offering such a course because, they argued, "literature" was our proper area, and "media"—which they took to be the purview of cultural studies—was theirs. We should stick to "literature," they suggested, and they would teach "media." We explained to them that we see our field as somewhat wider than that of "literature," that we're not sure what "literature" is anyway, and that, in any event, we think it's necessary to read what is not "literature" in order to understand what is "literature." Furthermore, we argued, since cultural studies is by definition a field that crosses disciplinary boundaries, the courses should be taught in more than one department—we would have no general objection to cultural studies courses offered by the Communications department. They responded that this sort of intellectual quibbling was fine for the amusement of faculty arguing in coffee rooms or writing in scholarly journals but what was really at stake here was a real-world academic turf battle—and "cultural studies" was their turf. So, neither side gave any ground, and this conflict was bumped upstairs to be settled by the college curriculum committee. That committee eventually decided in our favor; nonetheless, I think it's unfortunate that our institutional structures discourage public debates on these kinds of curricular conflicts. In this particular instance, the objection rested on such flimsy intellectual grounds that it probably wouldn't have been made in a forum open to a general audience of faculty and students. This was "academic politics" with a vengeance. The flimsiness of the objection itself was merely symptomatic of a sloppy pluralistic institutional structure that discourages the political conflict of serious intellectual debate.

If a curriculum based on liberal pluralism seems inadequate to the development of critical literacy from a left perspective, it is no more attractive to the Right. The neoconservative response to the problem of overspecialization was inaugurated several years ago by William Bennett's call for limiting pluralism and establishing a coherent, traditional curriculum based on the classic texts of Western civilization—a version of the "great books" curriculum. Bennett assumes that the most important function of humanities education is to pass on a common legacy of Western civilization to all college students. He describes this canonical tradition, in terms adapted from Matthew Arnold, as "the best that has been thought, written, or otherwise expressed about the human experience" (1984, 3). Some obvious objections to this goal are that this legacy isn't, in fact, "common" to all American citizens, that it leaves out a good deal of human experience, and that to subject students from oppressed social groups to an unqualified celebration of this tradition amounts to cultural imperialism. At the same time, the classics of Western civilization represent an important body of cultural capital to which all students should be given access. The more urgent question may be not *what* should be taught but *how* it should be taught. As Gerald Graff has pointed out, "a Shakespeare text taught by Bennett would bear small resemblance to the same text taught by [Terry] Eagleton" (1987, 193). At its best, that is, critical theory requires a rigorously critical approach to whatever is taught. Similarly, cultural studies specifically attempts to promote a critical, oppositional engagement with traditional culture, often by juxtaposing texts and perspectives of non-Western and suppressed cultural traditions to those of the European canonical tradition.

The main obstacles to a unified, coherent curriculum, as the conservatives see it, are "politicized" transdisciplinary movements that often have the effect of breaking down the walls between traditional disciplines: feminism, with its primary focus on gender as a category that is more significant than any particular discipline, and multiculturalism, which seeks a curriculum more reflective of and responsive to the experiences of minorities. But women's studies and ethnic studies programs actually tend to work against overspecialization by enlarging the area of general interaction among disciplines. Here the neoconservatives have a blind spot that corresponds to their blindness to the true source of the crisis facing traditional literature. Though it is almost always unnoticed by the conservative critics, the most serious obstacle to a unified traditional curriculum is the proliferation of and increasing importance given to technical, professional, and vocational education within the university. For radical teachers, the presence of technical and vocational programs within the university and within English departments should provide opportunities and institutional contexts for challenging the corporate-sector values and practices that characterize these programs. We need to develop curricular structures within our departments in which a debate among positions representing different value systems and social and professional paradigms can be carried on.

Amid the ongoing controversy about the ways in which intellectual and political forces such as critical theory, feminism, and multiculturalism are changing the English curriculum, one of the most powerful forces for change has received the least attention—the students. In demographic and economic terms, the academy is being asked to educate different students, and for different purposes, than was the case forty or even twenty years ago. More of our students are nontraditional college students—minority students, recent immigrants, first-generation college students from working-class backgrounds, and older, returning students. English departments are being called upon to provide a wider variety of services—including training in critical thinking, writing, and rhetoric and exposure to traditional cultural values—to students whose main purpose for attending the university is to gain specific and directly applicable training for employment. Thus, in addition to the benefits in intellectual rigor and political accountability to be gained from an ongoing critical engagement between faculty teaching technical-vocational and service courses and faculty teaching traditional humanities courses, these courses offer us access to groups of students—particularly working-class students and African American students—who often shun the humanities majors in favor of majors offering more immediate and more lucrative career opportunities.

There are some formidable obstacles to a critical engagement between litera- ture faculty and faculty teaching what I have called the "technical-vocational" and "service" courses in English departments. Cross-disciplinary interaction is always difficult to achieve and maintain in the academy because of the institutional forces for specialization that I mentioned earlier. But in this situation that prob- lem is compounded by the overlay of institutional status hierarchy. There is a per- sistent assumption among literature faculty that those who teach rhetoric, com- position, technical-professional writing, or English for speakers of other languages would rather be teaching literature but don't "have what it takes" (whatever that is). This attitude is generally reinforced by the uneven distribution of institutional rewards, resources, and prestige among the different subdisci- plines of English studies. The professional environment strikes me as a close par- ody of a feudal society—the literature teachers are the "aristocrats," living off the appropriated surplus labor of the "peasants"—teaching assistants, part-time and temporary faculty, and the teachers of the marginalized courses. And "literature" performs some of the same functions for us that it performed for the feudal aris- tocracy—it confirms (for us) that our exalted professional status is the natural re- sult of our cultural superiority.

The first move toward changing this crippling status hierarchy is to begin to treat our marginalized colleagues with more respect. By this I don't mean that lit- erature faculty should accept uncritically the value or credibility of the margin- alized positions. Quasi-professional technical and vocational programs in the universities valorize themselves as academic disciplines precisely on the basis of their association with traditional academic disciplines. Too often we have allowed them to enter that arena without demanding the price of admission: an engaged participation in the ongoing intellectual debate over social and cultural values. Any course of study within the university should be held accountable for its fun- damental aims and purposes in relation to the aims and purposes of other disci- plines and programs within the university and to the general aims of education in a democratic society. Departmental and disciplinary boundaries are not easily crossed, but the multidisciplinary structures of many English departments offer viable starting points for transdisciplinary work. If literature teachers can begin to engage the too frequently ignored teachers and students of technical and voca- tionally oriented courses in our own departments, eventually, perhaps, we can de- velop ways to interact more directly with those in other departments as well.

My use of the term "transdisciplinary" instead of the more familiar term "inter- disciplinary" marks an important distinction. "Transdisciplinary" scholarship and pedagogy go beyond a common practice of "interdisciplinary" work that merely appropriates knowledge produced in one discipline for use in another dis- cipline without questioning the basic assumptions or conceptual frameworks of either. "Transdisciplinarity," as it has been described by Mas'ud Zavarzadeh and Donald Morton, "is aware of the status of knowledge as one of the modes of ideological construction of reality in any given discipline; through its self-reflexivity, it attempts not simply to accumulate knowledge but to ask what constitutes knowledge, why and how and by whose authority certain modes of understanding are certified as knowledge and others as para-knowledge or non-knowledge" (1991, 10). Transdisciplinary pedagogy is not a matter of ignoring existing disciplinary knowledge or of merely substituting some other body of knowledge for, say, an existing literary canon. Instead, it constitutes what Dominick LaCapra calls a "transformative endeavor" that requires an "intimate knowledge of the disciplines and the related canons or disciplinary practices one is criticizing and attempting to refashion, including the sometimes valid resistances to change that they may pose." The goal of such work "is not to valorize 'blurred genres' in general" but to explore connections that appear blurred only from within narrow disciplinary frameworks (1989, 5). What LaCapra terms the "transformative endeavor" identifies what I see as the theoretical challenge to open literary study up to transdisciplinary and counterdisciplinary paradigms. We need to break down disciplinary barriers that have the effect of trivializing the work of the scholar/teacher by narrowing the range of questions that can be addressed. This requires a deliberate and concerted effort to broaden one's perspective both for teachers and for students habituated to the narrow specializations of our discipline, but the rewards—political and intellectual—will be worth the effort.

Changing the Curriculum

The English department at Illinois State University, where I teach, is a large, multipurpose department. In addition to traditional literary studies, courses in literary theory, film, cultural studies, children's literature, women in literature, and African American literature, we offer a specialization in English education for secondary teachers; we offer technical and professional writing courses at both graduate and undergraduate levels; we offer linguistics courses and courses in English as a second language (ESL) at both the undergraduate and graduate levels, with an optional Master's degree emphasis in Teaching of English to Speakers of Other Languages (TESOL); and we have a large composition-rhetoric program. Yet our undergraduate curriculum remains literature-centered. Our writing courses, our linguistics courses, and our English education courses are relegated to the margins of the curriculum, while the core of traditional literature remains relatively undisturbed. All students are required to take two introductory courses in literary genres and a senior seminar designed as a "capstone" course, looking back at the courses the student has taken. Students are encouraged to take a chronologically distributed sampling of six courses in English and American literature. This leaves room for two or three electives, which could be in literary theory, rhetoric, creative writing, technical writing, or linguistics. The English education majors,

training to be high school teachers, are routinely exempted from the full complement of English and American literature in order to make room for required education courses.

In respect to this curriculum, I think the opposition of theory versus literature
is largely irrelevant—just a family squabble within a fairly narrow sector of the department. What the current curriculum suppresses are oppositions such as literature (including literary theory) versus rhetoric, literature versus composition, literature versus linguistics, literature versus technical writing, etc. My department's
curriculum and the problems that attend it are typical and symptomatic of curricula and problems found in many other English departments. The literature-centered focus of our curricula and our departmental organizational structures inhibit our theoretical self-consciousness and our ability to engage each other in
serious debate. This affects our scholarship as well as our teaching. For instance,
among all of the excellent work in postcolonial criticism and theory from literary
and cultural studies scholars in the past ten years or so, I haven't encountered any
mention of the ongoing effects of cultural imperialism reproduced in our ESL
programs. I have read many brilliant critiques of colonialist ideology focusing on
canonical works, on nonliterary documents, and on popular culture, but none of
the postcolonial critics is thinking about the issue of cultural imperialism in ESL.
The work published in *TESOL Quarterly,* meanwhile, tends to be positivistic and
apolitical, though there have been some recent efforts to bring the insights of literary theory and cultural studies to bear on TESOL issues (see, for example, Peirce
1989; Pennycook 1989, 1991; McCall 1991), and the newsletter *TESOL Matters* provides an informal forum for geopolitical issues. But teachers of literature should
be putting pressure on teachers of ESL and vice versa. If the emergence of postcolonial and subaltern criticism in literary studies has no relation to the teaching of
ESL in the academy, how can we expect such developments to have any impact beyond the academy? As long as ESL remains a marginalized and often ignored "service" function of English departments—or, worse, a service program functioning
autonomously apart from the English department—we are missing an opportunity for a productive critical engagement with these colleagues and students. Similar critiques can be—and have been—made of the relationship of composition
and technical writing to literature in English departments. The point I want to
emphasize here is that the ill effects of our traditional professional hierarchies go
beyond the widely acknowledged problem of exploitation of graduate teaching assistants and adjunct faculty. The marginalization of these subdisciplines limits the
scope of our critical and theoretical awareness as well.

To counter this intrinsic parochialism and elitism, we need curricula that will
require all students to take a representative sample of the broader field of English
studies and require students and faculty to think through the interrelations of
various functional divisions (rhetoric, literature, cultural studies, applied and theoretical linguistics, technical and professional writing, etc.) and philosophical orientations (humanism, marxism, aestheticism, logical positivism, feminism, etc.)

within our departments and the discipline at large. Such conditions aren't reflected even in the course catalogs of departments that are often hailed and reviled
as leaders in the theory revolution—Duke University, Brown University, and the
University of California at Santa Cruz, for example—because the undergraduate
English curricula at these institutions remain firmly literature-centered. In the
curricula of these progressive elite institutions, theory courses and literature
courses coexist in an unproblematized pluralistic framework that can be maintained only in an environment uncontaminated by have-nots—a classroom free
of students determined to get access to social power through the mastery of writing, technical communication, or language skills.

Some English departments have consciously restructured their curricula in attempts to limit the trivializing effects of pluralism, however. An interesting model
is that of Carnegie-Mellon University. From Carnegie-Mellon's English department students can take degrees with emphases in creative writing, literary and
cultural studies, and rhetorical studies, and the department offers separate majors
in professional writing and technical writing. All of the students in these programs are required to take a core of four courses (creative writing students take a
core of five courses). According to the university's undergraduate catalog, the core
is designed to "include work in all three disciplinary areas of the department: creative writing, literary and cultural studies, and rhetoric" (Carnegie-Mellon 1990–
1991, 192). The catalog recommends that all students take courses called "Survey of
Forms" (fiction or poetry) and "Discursive Practices, Language, Structure, Signs"
during their first semester in the major. In subsequent semesters students take
courses entitled "Discourse and Historical Change" and "Reading Twentieth-
Century Culture." Creative writing majors take both fiction and poetry courses in
the "Survey of Forms" category.

At the time the new curriculum was established Gary Waller (then head of Carnegie-Mellon's English department) described it, in a somewhat self-consciously
ironic parody of advertising hype, as "the first poststructuralist literary curriculum" (1985, 6). Waller's "packaging" of the curriculum as the latest-up-to-date-
new-model English studies prompted Zavarzadeh and Morton to characterize the
change as a "recuperative, complicit curriculum":

> As befits his technocratic audience, Waller's rhetoric is that of an efficient manager
> concerned with the "application" of ideas (produced by others) and with "dove-
> tailing" their various parts so that he can achieve a "breakthrough," producing the
> first (post)structural curriculum for (consumption in) the profession. Waller's pro-
> posed curriculum is purely and safely cognitive; the students are taught to "under-
> stand" but not to "intervene." (1991, 23)

This critique was not unwarranted, particularly in view of the way Waller was cap-
italizing on the "new and improved" image of Carnegie-Mellon's curriculum
while downplaying the potential political implications of the change. Nonetheless,
there are some significant gains here. By requiring all students to be familiar with
a variety of discursive strategies, Carnegie-Mellon's curriculum displaces literary

formalism from its center, and it seems designed to give all students some exposure to skills of ideology critique. One wonders whether the students experience
the discursive paradigms of the different required courses as discrete bodies of
knowledge or as transdisciplinary fields of discourse that often overlap and contest each other.

One way of restructuring a curriculum to foreground contestatory relations
among various discursive fields is that of the new English and Textual Studies major at Syracuse University, where I was formerly a graduate student. The department's course catalog description of the new curriculum bears quoting at length:

> The new curriculum is organized not by coverage of a literary or critical canon but by
> a focus on the problematics of reading and writing texts. Such a curriculum attempts
> to distinguish between a traditional pluralism, in which there are many separate view-
> points and each exists without locating itself in relation to opposing viewpoints, and
> a multiplicity of positions, each of which acknowledges its allied or contestatory rela-
> tion to other positions. The purpose of a curriculum based on the latter model is not
> to impose one way of knowing on everyone but to make the differences between ways
> of knowing visible and to foreground what is at stake in one way of knowing over and
> against another. The goal is to make students aware of how knowledge is produced
> and how reading takes place and thus to make them capable of playing an active and
> critical role in their society, enabling them to intervene in the dominant discourses of
> their culture. (Syracuse University 1990, 5)

The Syracuse curriculum can be schematized as a triangle with groups of courses
clustered under three particular modes of inquiry: historical, political, and theoretical. Students begin by taking two introductory courses, entitled "Reading and
Interpretation I: From Language to Discourse" and "Reading and Interpretation
II: Practices of Reading." Then they are required to take two courses each from
two groups, one course from the remaining group, and three courses of electives
that can be from any of the groups or chosen from creative writing or advanced
expository writing courses that are not in any group.

What is particularly valuable about the Syracuse curriculum, in my view, is that
it self-consciously attempts to place different intellectual positions in contestatory
relation to each other. One aspect I find disappointing, however, is that the Syracuse program remains entirely literature- and culture-focused. The composition
and rhetoric program was separated from the English department as part of the
transformation from "English" to "English and Textual Studies." The technical
writing program was always small and marginalized, and it seems to have been entirely left out of this new curriculum, as is the creative writing program. I don't
know the exact reasons for these exclusions, though I know enough of the departmental political battles at Syracuse to suspect that the story is much too long to go
into here. Instead, humbly acknowledging that it's much easier to propose a curricular change than to get one approved by an entire department, I want to sketch
out a variation of the Syracuse triangle as it might be adapted for the department I
teach in at Illinois State (Fig. 23.1).

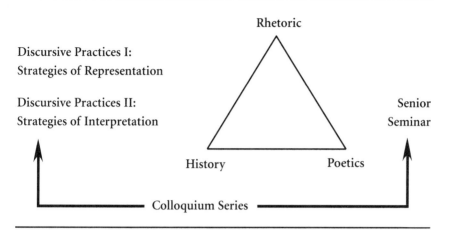

FIGURE 23.1

   Students would enter the major by taking two required introductory courses of three credit hours each: Strategies of Representation and Strategies of Interpretation. In these introductory courses attention would be given to the full range of discourses practiced in the English department—linguistics, literature, rhetoric, technical communication, etc. Then students would proceed into the triangle, here taking eighteen hours on one corner and six hours each on the other two corners. Finally, they would take the senior seminar (as is now required) for a total of forty hours. The broad categories of history, rhetoric, and poetics are intended at once to correspond to and in some ways to disrupt our current divisions. Some existing courses could be adapted to fit in these divisions. Our current genre courses and the creative writing courses might fit under poetics, while the composition, rhetoric, and technical writing courses would generally go under rhetoric. Conventional period surveys of literature might ordinarily fit under the history rubric. Literary theory courses would go under the poetics category; rhetorical theory courses would go under the rhetoric category. But a key goal of this curriculum would be to displace literature from its center in order to allow new conjunctions and juxtapositions of such fields as technical writing, cultural studies, and literature. Hence, such a curriculum would require a rethinking of the goals and assumptions of existing courses.
   All course syllabi would be self-conscious about the paradigms of knowledge and value that frame and enable their construction, and all courses would acknowledge their boundaries and boundary crossings in relation to the discursive paradigms of other courses. My hope would be for the emergence of new courses designed specifically to engage the particular problems and issues that connect two or more categories. For instance, I recently team-taught a course entitled "The Concept of Authorship and the Problems of Literary Authority" with a

member of our technical writing faculty. We investigated issues of authorship and authority in ways that foregrounded the conflicts among various historical, political, and theoretical perspectives. At least partly because of the inclusion of a technical writing perspective in the course, we gave considerable attention to changes in the material conditions of authorship arising from the transition from manuscript culture to print culture and from the uneven but steady growth of literacy over the past few centuries in England. In addition, we attracted an unusually diverse mix of literature-oriented and technical-writing-oriented students who came to the class with conflicting assumptions and expectations. This required constant adjustments of emphasis and produced a heightened sense of perspectival limits for both the students and the teachers. Again, we have a special-topics course entitled "The Rhetoric of History and the History of Rhetoric," team-taught by a member of our rhetoric faculty and a colleague from the History department. I can envision a course exploring the characteristics and consequences of English as an "international" language that would examine international uses of English in different economic, political, and cultural contexts and that could put the values and assumptions of ESL, technical writing, and postcolonial subaltern theory in productive interaction with each other. Such courses would aim to address the potential conflicts and interrelationships among different discourses within the broader field of English studies.

In the triangulated curriculum, courses specifically designed to investigate the interrelationships of different discourses would be encouraged but regulated. In these instances I would have the professor(s) develop a syllabus that demonstrably addresses the cross-sectional implications of the course and have such courses certified as counting either way for students. The department's curriculum committee (constituted so as to include faculty identifying themselves as representing the various corners of the triangle) would arbitrate the designations. My intention here would be to reward cross-sectional courses by making them more attractive to students. Finally, I would set up an ongoing colloquium series on topics of broad interest among the various subdisciplines of English studies and require students from the introductory sections and the senior seminar to attend and participate in these colloquia each semester.

In addition to the aim of requiring students to be exposed to a broader cross-section of English studies and encouraging them to consider the interrelations of various positions and orientations within the field, this curricular model might also encourage faculty to interact more directly with each other. There would still, of course, be room for professors who preferred not to interact to teach in relative isolation, on one corner of the triangle, but there would be expanded opportunities (and a sort of informal intellectual reward in the form of a heightened atmosphere of collegial discussion) for those who wished to teach in the interactive model.

This, of course, is just one of many possible patterns for the various subdisciplines within an English curriculum that could be devised for different local situations. The number of subdisciplines and their names is not as important as the need for them to be placed in productively interactive relationship to each other. The teaching of literature, rhetoric, and cultural studies should be viewed as a discursive arena in which intellectuals can develop a sustained critique of existing social values through which a critical literacy can be produced. Above all, the study of literature as the uncritical cultivation of aesthetic appreciation or the unreflective transmission of values—whether progressive or conservative—should be avoided.

I know from discussions with colleagues in my own department and other departments that the kinds of curricular changes I am calling for will encounter resistance and skepticism from those—including theorists and many radicals and progressives—who are comfortable with the current dominant hierarchy of privilege within the discipline. After viewing my plan, one of my colleagues observed that such a change would leave him, as a literature teacher, completely out of the department's mission. When I pointed out to him that the curriculum I am proposing still gives primary emphasis to literature in at least two-thirds of the curriculum (the history and poetics corners of the triangle) he was genuinely surprised though not exactly persuaded. The fact is, in his mind the department's mission is the teaching of literature, and everything else we do is just incidental— or literature is the center around which various satellites such as technical writing, composition, and linguistics orbit. Yet this model for the department marginalizes about one-third of the faculty—of approximately forty-five tenured and tenure-track members of our department, only thirty or so teach literature.

Nonetheless, I must acknowledge, the curriculum I have outlined is really only a very modest beginning toward the development of an open-ended critique of values and power relations that could resist the considerable pressures for the human sciences to serve uncritically the changing needs of the late-capitalist global labor market. Juxtaposing subdisciplinary discourses as I have suggested will not necessarily lead to a critique of what we are being asked to do. The changes I am recommending could produce a public, institutional arena for literature teachers to talk with teachers of composition, rhetoric, technical and professional writing, ESL, English education, etc., about our interrelated roles and responsibilities in the production of educated citizens. However, we would still face the difficult task of learning how to talk to each other and, yet more difficult, how to critique each other's positions.

The task at hand for English teachers of all specializations is to recognize that our work is always already highly politicized and to exploit that condition. Conflicting political demands are being made upon us in the form of the neoconservative call for us to guard the gates of traditional high culture and in the form of the corporate labor-market pressure for us to give students skills training without critical consciousness raising. Our success in resisting these pressures will be limited unless we can change our curricular and other departmental structures to allow—even to require—full participation in the intellectual life of the depart-

ment by all faculty, including those teaching the presently marginalized and devalued "service" courses. It is up to us to find new ways to engage all students and
faculty in the debate on culture and social values at as high a level of sophistication and intellectual rigor as possible.

NOTES

1. See, for example, Bennett (1984), Bloom (1987), Hirsch (1987), Kimball (1989), and
Sykes (1988). Many literary scholars have observed (and some have extensively documented) the extent to which the claim that literature transcends politics supports a conservative political agenda. See, for example, Widdowson et al. (1982), Baldick (1983), Eagleton
(1985, 1986), Stimpson (1988), Graff (1988), and Zavarzadeh and Morton (1991).

2. The neoconservative writer who has given most attention to these economic pressures
against traditional literary study is Kernan (1990). Yet, even after a detailed and informative
analysis of the social and economic forces arrayed against traditional cultural values,
Kernan returns to attack deconstruction and poststructural theory in a highly oversimplified critique at the end of his book.

WORKS CITED

Baldick, Chris. *The Social Mission of English Criticism.* Oxford: Oxford University Press
    1983.
Bennett, William. *To Reclaim a Legacy: A Report on the Humanities in Higher Education.*
    Washington, D.C.: National Endowment for the Humanities, 1984.
Bloom, Allan. *The Closing of the American Mind: How Higher Education Has Failed Democ-
    racy and Impoverished the Souls of Today's Students.* New York: Simon and Schuster, 1987.
Carnegie-Mellon University English Department. *Undergraduate Catalogue.* Pittsburgh,
    1990–1991.
Eagleton, Terry. *Literary Theory: An Introduction.* Minneapolis: University of Minnesota
    Press, 1985.
————. "The Subject of Literature." *Cultural Critique* 2 (1986):98–110.
Graff, Gerald. "What Should We Be Teaching—When There's No 'We'?" *Yale Journal of
    Criticism* 1 (1987):189–211.
————. *Professing Literature.* Chicago: University of Chicago Press, 1988.
Hirsch, E. D. Jr. *Cultural Literacy: What Every American Needs to Know.* Boston: Houghton
    Mifflin, 1987.
Kernan, Alvin. *The Death of Literature.* New Haven: Yale University Press, 1990.
Kimball, Roger. *Tenured Radicals.* New York: Simon and Schuster, 1989.
LaCapra, Dominick. "On the Line: Between History and Criticism," in *Profession 89,* ed.
    Phyllis Franklin (New York: MLA, 1989), 4–9.
McCall, Martha. "Comments on Alastair Pennycook's 'The Concept of Method, Interested
    Knowledge, and the Politics of Language Teaching': A Reader Reacts." *TESOL Quarterly*
    25 (1991):745–748.
Peirce, Bronwyn Norton. "Toward a Pedagogy of Possibility in the Teaching of English In-
    ternationally: People's English in South Africa." *TESOL Quarterly* 23 (1989):401–420.

Pennycook, Alastair. "The Concept of Method, Interested Knowledge, and the Politics of Language Teaching." *TESOL Quarterly* 23 (1989):589–618.

_____. "The Author Responds." *TESOL Quarterly* 25 (1991):749–753.

Piccone, Paul, et al. "Symposium: Intellectuals in the 1980's." *Telos* 50 (Winter 1981–1982):115–160.

Stimpson, Catherine. *Where the Meanings Are: Feminism and Cultural Spaces.* New York: Routledge, Chapman and Hall, 1988.

Sykes, Charles. *Profscam: Professors and the Demise of Higher Education.* Washington: Regnery Gateway, 1988.

Syracuse University English Department. Unpublished departmental announcement, Fall 1990.

Waller, Gary. "Working with the Paradigm Shift: Poststructuralism and the College Curriculum." *Association of Departments of English Bulletin* 81 (Fall 1985):6–12.

Widdowson, Peter. *Re-Reading English.* London: Methuen, 1982.

Zavarzadeh, Mas'ud, and Donald Morton. "Theory, Pedagogy, Politics: The Crisis of the 'Subject' in the Humanities," in *Theory, Pedagogy, Politics: Texts for Change,* ed. Donald Morton and Mas'ud Zavarzadeh (Urbana: University of Illinois Press, 1991), 1–32.

About the Book and Editors

This book resituates the political correctness debates in the humanities branch of the academy. Contending that conservatives have tainted entire academic disciplines, causing university humanists to go from irrelevant to dangerous overnight, the contributors see the PC debates as a struggle over the very purposes of higher education in the United States.

Ronald Strickland and Christopher Newfield have assembled the best and the brightest from across the academic disciplines for discourse on the future of higher education in light of PC. The essays are fresh and for the most part have not been previously published. They treat such essential issues as the attack on liberalized education, the institutional response to difference, culture wars and the profession of literature, queer nationalism, multiculturalism in the 1990s, and PC and the attack on American colleges. It is a cornucopia of voices, rich and challenging, and essential for anyone concerned about the issue of political correctness.

Christopher Newfield is assistant professor of English at the University of California–Santa Barbara. He is the author of *The Submissive Center: Emerson and the Liberal Imagination* (forthcoming) and co-editor, with Avery Gordon, of *Mapping Multiculturalism* (forthcoming). **Ronald Strickland** is associate professor of English at Illinois State University. He has written articles on pedagogy and critical theory and on the literature and culture of early modern England.

About the Contributors

Lauren Berlant teaches English at the University of Chicago and writes on the cultural/sexual politics of national identity. She is author of *The Anatomy of National Fantasy: Hawthorne, Utopia, and Everyday Life* (1991).

Evan Carton, professor of English at the University of Texas at Austin, is the author of *The Rhetoric of American Romance* (1985) and *The Marble Faun: Hawthorne's Transformations* (1992). His recent and forthcoming work includes essays on the politics of identity in American literature, pedagogy, and social practice and a section of *The Cambridge History of American Literature,* co-authored with Gerald Graff, on "Criticism Since 1940."

Sara Diamond, who holds a Ph.D. in sociology from the University of California at Berkeley, covers right-wing politics for several publications. She is the author of *Spiritual Warfare: The Politics of the Christian Right* (1989) and *Roads to Dominion: Right-Wing Movements and State Power in the United States, 1945 to the Present* (1995).

Grant Farred is a postdoctoral fellow in comparative literature at the University of Michigan.

Gerald Horne is professor of black studies at the University of California–Santa Barbara. His recent books include *Black Liberation/Red Scare: Ben Davis and the Communist Party* (1994) and *Race for the Planet: The U.S. and the New World Order.*

Jean E. Howard is professor of English and comparative literature at Columbia University. Her most recent book, *The Stage and Social Struggle in Early Modern England,* was published by Routledge in 1994.

Alice Jardine is professor of romance languages at Harvard University. She is the author of *Gynesis: Configurations of Woman and Modernity* and co-author, with Paul Smith, of *Men in Feminism.*

Gregory S. Jay teaches in the graduate program in modern studies at the University of Wisconsin–Milwaukee, where he is professor of English and Comparative Literature. His most recent book is *America the Scrivener: Deconstruction and American Literary History.* His essays on the canon controversy and on the politics of literary study have appeared in *College English*; his forthcoming essays focus on ethics and multiculturalism, recent fiction and theory, and (with Gerald Graff) the limits of critical pedagogy.

A. R. Lategola is a graduate student in sociology at the University of California–Santa Barbara. She works on urban housing issues.

Paul Lauter is Allan K. and Gwendolyn Miles Smith Professor of Literature at Trinity College. He is the author of *Canons and Contexts,* and he is on the editorial board of *Radical Teacher.*

Donald Lazere is professor of English at Cal Poly–San Luis Obispo and a member of the steering committee of Teachers for a Democratic Culture. His articles on the politics of literacy and culture have appeared in *The Chronicle of Higher Education*, the *New York Times*, and *Los Angeles Times* book reviews, *The Nation*, the *Village Voice*, *In These Times*, and *Radical Teacher*, as well as in many scholarly journals and collections.

Ellen Messer-Davidow, associate professor at the University of Minnesota, teaches in the Departments of English, Women's Studies, and Cultural Studies. She has recently co-edited, with David Shumway and David Sylvan, *Knowledges: Historical and Critical Studies in Disciplinarity* and is writing *Disciplining Feminism: Episodes in the Discursive Production of Social Change*.

Rajeswari Mohan is assistant professor of English at Haverford College. Her essays on topics in postcolonial and feminist criticism have appeared in *Genders*, *Textual Practice*, *College Literature*, and elsewhere.

Christopher Newfield is assistant professor of English at the University of California–Santa Barbara. He is the author of *The Submissive Center: Emerson and the Liberal Imagination* (forthcoming 1995) and co-editor, with Avery Gordon, of *Mapping Multiculturalism* (forthcoming 1995).

Richard Ohmann's last book was *Politics of Letters*. He teaches at Wesleyan University and is on the editorial board of *Radical Teacher*.

Vincent P. Pecora teaches in the English Department at UCLA. He is the author of *Self and Form in Modern Narrative* and essays on social theory, literature, and literary criticism.

Lisa Schubert is a graduate student in English at the University of Washington.

Joan Wallach Scott is professor of social science at the Institute for Advanced Study in Princeton, N.J. She is author most recently of *Gender and the Politics of History* and of the forthcoming *"Women Who Have Only Paradoxes to Offer": French Feminists, 1789–1944*.

Ronald Strickland is associate professor of English at Illinois State University. He writes on pedagogy and curricular reform, topics in cultural criticism, and the literature and culture of early modern England.

Richard Terdiman is professor of literature and history of consciousness at the University of California–Santa Cruz. His most recent book is *Present Past: Modernity and the Memory Crisis*.

Thomas P. Wallace, a former chemistry faculty member, is president of Illinois State University.

Michael Warner is associate professor of English at Rutgers University. He is the author of *Fear of a Queer Planet*.

Evan Watkins is professor of English at the University of Washington and the author of numerous books and essays on contemporary theory and cultural politics, most recently *Throwaways: Work Culture and Consumer Education* (1993).

George Yúdice is assistant professor of romance languages at Hunter College, City University of New York. He is a member of the editorial collective of *Social Text*.

Index